TEACHING IN THE
ELEMENTARY SCHOOL
Readings in Principles and Methods

TEACHING IN THE ELEMENTARY SCHOOL

Readings in Principles and Methods

Edited by

LESTER D. CROW, Ph.D.

Professor of Education
Brooklyn College

ALICE CROW, Ph.D.

Formerly Associate Professor of Education
Brooklyn College

and

WALTER MURRAY, Ph.D.

Assistant Professor of Education
Brooklyn College

DAVID McKAY COMPANY, INC.
New York

TEACHING IN THE ELEMENTARY SCHOOL: READINGS IN PRINCIPLES AND METHODS

LIBRARY OF CONGRESS CATALOG CARD NUMBER 61–5783

Printed in the United States of America

Preface

DURING THE PAST quarter of a century, a struggle to make teacher education more functional has been waged with some degree of success. While the larger-unit approach in dealing with elementary school subjects has emerged as a better way of procedure, relatively little has been done in teachers' colleges and departments of education in liberal arts colleges to help methods' instructors prepare their teacher trainees to guide integrated learning. Hence, in *Teaching in the Elementary School: Readings in Principles and Methods* appropriate articles from the writings of experts in each learning area in the elementary school are presented to alert college students in education to some of the currently accepted functional approaches to elementary school teaching.

The articles that have been selected for inclusion in this *Readings* contain helpful suggestions on every phase of learning in the elementary school. The organizational structure begins with a discussion of the basic principles of teaching in the elementary school, including needs and interests of children; continues with a consideration of the principles and methods of teaching in the respective learning areas, and concludes with suggestions for evaluating pupil progress and reporting to parents. The basic purpose of the selections, however, is *to focus attention on the fundamental ideas of educational leaders in the area of the elementary school in which each is especially competent.*

The selected articles have been arranged in such a way that the book can be used as a basic text. As a supplement to the many excellent books in each subject area in the elementary school, it fills a need for one compact book that contains various ideas from leading authorities in the respective fields. This *Readings,* therefore, can be used either as a text in methods in elementary school subjects, or as a supplement to methods books assigned for study in each learning area.

As the articles were selected, the editors attempted to utilize different teaching-learning approaches for each subject or learning area in order that various points of view might be presented. Consequently, both teachers-in-training as well as teachers in the classroom will find that the book contains many helpful hints to improve their teaching techniques and effectiveness.

Due to limitations of space, most of the "References" associated with these reading selections were not included. If the student wishes, however, he may readily find them by consulting the original source given for each.

The editors are especially grateful to the publishers of the articles and the authors for permission to reprint their ideas and wish to take this opportunity to thank them for their graciousness.

LESTER D. CROW
ALICE CROW
WALTER MURRAY

Contents

TEACHING IN THE
ELEMENTARY SCHOOL
Readings in Principles and Methods

Introduction

ANY ATTEMPTS to motivate children to learn with greater ease and effectiveness are worth the effort expended by those of us who are responsible for the training of young men and women to become successful teachers. During the past two decades, educators have given much thought to ways in which greater integration of learning can be made possible. Believing that the integrative process is associated closely with teacher attitudes, teacher training institutions and college departments of teacher education have been active in helping their students acquire those teaching skills that enable them to guide children in the development of thinking and behavior patterns that will serve both personal and group welfare.

The editors long have been concerned with the evolvement of teaching techniques that can help the college student become an effective teacher. Hence in *Teaching in the Elementary School: Readings in Principles and Methods,* they have brought together carefully selected excerpts from the writings of experts that deal with the principles of teaching and learning methods of the various subject areas included in the elementary school curriculum.

Although this book is concerned primarily with modern teaching methods, in many of the selected articles are included also the psychological and educational principles that underlie suggested techniques. Thereby greater appreciation of specific methods is made possible as well as better understanding of the value to the teacher of utilizing certain techniques rather than others.

In their assembling of the articles included in this *Readings,* the editors were sensitive to the fact that college instructors and students, as well as those who are teaching, need worthwhile suggestions in their search for practical and effective instructional techniques. This collection of readings, therefore, can offer anyone interested in elementary school methods some valuable source material. Moreover, the selections represent the recommendations of specialists in particular subject areas. The editors hope that the individual articles will be helpful to the teacher who seeks aid in his teaching approach in one or another subject field. We hope also that many students and teachers may be saved both time and energy in their search for teaching suggestions that can be of some benefit to them.

1. *Children Need to Be Understood* *

JOHN J. KURTZ

TOMMY fidgeted while waiting to be seen by the principal. He had been sent by his teacher for "acting up" in class. This was not a first offense. There had been a history of stubbornness, willful disobedience, and disregard for the learning tasks expected of him.

This morning after his teacher had turned down some of his written work as too messy, he had torn the paper to shreds, claiming he could not —but indicating he would not—do the work over. All this and more was included in his teacher's note to the principal.

While Tommy waited, he had time to think. He didn't like school; there was no sense to it at all. Teachers were usually unreasonable, often harsh. Nothing he did seemed to suit anyone, even at home. His life seemed a series of complaints, rebukes, and frequent rejections.

All the while, Tommy felt he was doing his best, trying honestly to do what was expected of him as well as he could. If he were only five years older, he could quit school!

After Tommy left for the office, his class combined with another for a music period. This gave his teacher, Miss Allen, time to think. Tommy wasn't really a bad boy, but he had a way of continually upsetting things in the classroom.

She thought of Tommy's family. There was an older sister who had an outstanding record in school. She wondered from something the mother had said whether this sister's record was held up to him. Such experiences might make a boy lose faith in himself and his world.

* From John J. Kurtz, "Children Need to Be Understood," *NEA Journal* (December, 1957), pp. 572–73. Reprinted by permission of the author and the *NEA Journal*.

Miss Allen wondered if she herself had, without knowing, added to this kind of feeling in the boy. Once, while Tommy was kept after school, she remembered how he had occupied himself quietly and constructively for some time. Later he had picked up some trash and put it in the waste-basket.

She had thanked him, saying, "Tommy, you have been just fine for nearly an hour. Why can't you always be like this?"

His reply stuck vividly in her mind. "I was just wondering the same thing about you, Miss Allen."

In his office, the principal was remembering previous conferences with Tommy. He knew what Tommy must be thinking out there on the bench; he had heard it all before. Yet, something must be done. He would at least extract a promise from Tommy to apologize to Miss Allen and to try to do better.

The Importance of Understanding

What help is there for Tommy's teacher, for the principal, or for Tommy? What is known about children—how they grow, learn, and develop toward maturity—that might lead to more enduring solutions to the day-by-day problems with Tommy or Mary, with Bob or Susan?

It may be difficult to believe that children are earnestly and conscientiously working at the job of growing up, and to realize how many and varied are the learning tasks that go with this job.

These tasks include the mastery of essential academic knowledge and skills. They also include learning to appreciate and participate in the sharing of human warmth and affection, learning to get along with age mates, and achieving independence or becoming a person of worth in one's own right.

Children may not always be working on these tasks in ways that we would recommend or can allow, or in ways that are likely to succeed. But children are working, nevertheless, with all their energies and with all that they know. In this sense all children are highly responsible even though their ways may be inappropriate.

In Tommy's case, both principal and teacher see the danger signals in his behavior. They need also to see in it an indication that Tommy senses that he cannot forever accept what he judges to be "pushing around" if he ever expects to become a man.

It is fortunate that children ask to be understood, for in the process of understanding, we increase our opportunity to give them the help they need.

To know that children grow at their own rate, differing one from another, helps us to understand them. To know that differing cultural backgrounds provide different ideas of what is right behavior also helps us to understand. But knowledge is not enough. To understand is to feel for, as well as to know about.

Perhaps more than knowledge, an understanding attitude will assist us most in furthering the educational achievements of children, in enhancing interpersonal relationships, and in fostering mental health for child and teacher alike.

Enhancing Interpersonal Relationships

If we see children as problems, we deal with them as problems. If we deal with them as problems, we may expect them to respond as problems. It is possible to come to see children in positive ways in spite of behavior which is seemingly obstinate or rebellious.

To see the positive is to see the dignity and worth of a child. The quality of response to be expected from individuals is in tune with the quality of approach to them. Since the child, though he may be a problem to us, is likely to be trying his best to solve a problem, he needs help rather than rebuke.

If rebuke is necessary to clarify essential standards that must be maintained, this can be done with a spirit of helpfulness—examining our own behavior as well as that of the child. Such a view of children and of teaching will not only be supportive to children in their earnest, though often fumbling, efforts to mature, but will also enrich the teacher's professional and personal life.

Furthering the Achievement of Children

Does understanding children lead to expecting nothing from them and accepting whatever they do? Quite the contrary. The furthering of their school achievement is foremost among the purposes served by the understanding of children. It is precisely because too many children are failing to realize the potential that is within them that understanding is so important.

In any school we can find children who achieve below their appraised intellectual capacity. If a child is lower in achievement than we think he should be, we should not assume that a desire on the child's part to do better is all that is necessary to change the achievement picture. Much more is involved. It is sounder to assume that the child is doing his present best, and go on from there.

We can ask, "How important is the immediate lesson, and how essential is every last detail of the course we are teaching? What significance does the lesson have for the child? Does the child have sufficient respect for and faith in his teacher to put aside his own concerns and apply himself to what is asked of him?"

Learning involves these and other matters as well as intellect. The answers we find to questions such as those above will give us truly dependable clues for helping each child achieve all he can achieve, and become all he can become.

Fostering Mental Health

It is in the area of mental health that the understanding of children makes a special contribution. If there is a highest aim in education, it would seem to be what Carl Rogers, the psychologist, has termed the development of the "fully functioning person."

In this regard, it is important to consider that the individual responds to his experiences through his orientation to the world and to himself. How he behaves is governed by how he sees the world and himself in relation to this world. To understand this about a child is to foster consciously his self picture of faith and worthiness. An old and cherished hymn has long pointed the way:

I would be true, for there are those who trust me;
I would be pure, for there are those who care. . . .

The child can behave worthily if he feels worthy, and he can feel worthy only if he is so regarded. Of course, our definition of worthiness cannot be restricted to "A"-level achievement in academic knowledge and skills. Ideas and creativity must be valued no less than the ability to remember facts and to conform to standards.

It follows from the above statement that a teacher's own self-picture is of utmost importance. Arthur Jersild, in *When Teachers Face Themselves,* reports that teachers also experience feelings of loneliness, meaninglessness, and hostility. When those moods come, it is important to remember the premise with which we began: The child is earnestly working to grow, to learn, to mature. Thus he is allied *with,* not *against,* those who teach him.

To see that children are allied with us in common growth aims is to see new meaning and challenge in our dedication as teachers. To recognize that every teacher is a constant contributor to the creation of human personality is to find high personal and professional significance.

In thinking about Tommy, Miss Allen saw she must not only deal with the immediate situation but also find ways to cope more effectively with future instances. In either case, she will be helped if guided by two basic principles:

First, a child has reasons for what he does. If we can find those reasons, we can find dependable clues for solving problems. Second, the quality of a child's response is affected by the approach made to him. Therefore, if we approach him in a favorable way, we enlist a favorable response and utilize his own inner drives to grow.

2. Adjusting the Program to the Child *

CARLETON W. WASHBURNE

MISS JULIAN has been assigned as teacher for the fourth grade. She finds in her class Ada, age 7; Bill, age 8; Carl, age 9; Dot, age 10; and Edith, age 11. There are a couple of other children of 7, like Ada; there are half a dozen eight-year-olds like Bill; there are nine or ten aged 9 like Carl; half a dozen ten-year-olds like Dot, and a couple of 11 like Edith; but we'll simplify matters by thinking of Ada, Bill, Carl, Dot and Edith whose names run conveniently in alphabetical order according to their ages. These happen to be mental ages.

Now Miss Julian had been told, rather vaguely, that she should adapt her work to individual differences. But her course of study is all planned for fourth grade; her textbooks are written for fourth grade children; and she is expected to get all the children ready for fifth grade by the end of the year. So she makes all her assignments and general explanations to fit Carl and the other nine-year-olds, and paces her work to their level. To "adapt to individual differences" she gives some special help, as far as her time

* From Carleton W. Washburne, "Adjusting the Program to the Child," *Educational Leadership* (December, 1953), pp. 138–47. Reprinted by permission of the author and *Educational Leadership*.

will permit, to Ada and Bill and the other seven- and eight-year-old young-sters, and she tries to give some "enriching" additional assignments to Dot and Edith and their ilk to keep them busy.

But by the end of the year Ada and Bill are far from having reached fifth grade standard in any subject—they and Miss Julian have become in-creasingly discouraged as the year rolled by; for all the teacher's efforts, and the children's, the seven- and eight-year-old boys and girls simply could not do the work and read the books planned for nine-year-olds. Dot, and especially Edith, on the other hand, had found the fourth grade work so easy that in spite of all the attempts to "enrich" it for them, their abilities were not challenged, they had become bored, and had developed into dis-cipline problems.

Shall Miss Julian promote all of them to fifth grade, let Ada and Bill flounder more than ever, let Dot and Edith become even more bored and unchallenged? Or shall she make Ada and Bill repeat fourth grade, for which Ada is not yet ready, and where Bill will grind through all the mate-rial he half-learned, giving both a further feeling of failure; and shall she recommend that Dot and Edith skip fifth grade, going on to sixth without any of the fifth grade learnings?

The Dilemma of Teachers

This is the dilemma of teachers everywhere. Miss Julian's room is not the exception; it is typical. In any classroom of thirty or more children an intel-ligence test will almost always show a range of at least four years in the mental ages of the children. A standardized test in arithmetic will show a range of at least four years in the arithmetic age of the children. A reading test is more likely to show a range of five years; so is a spelling test. As long as we ignore these facts and act on the false assumption that they do not exist, we shall have this dilemma, and neither universal promotion nor a regression to flunking some children and having others skip grades will resolve it.

If a man who habitually drinks too heavily in the evening tells his doctor that he has such a headache every morning that he cannot do his work effectively, and that if he stays home to sleep it off he will lose his job, the doctor will tell him that if he insists on continuing to drink to excess every evening there is no way out of his dilemma. It is equally absurd for us in the schools to insist on continuing to ignore the four-year range in maturity of the children in any grade and expect to resolve our problem by any policy of promotion or nonpromotion.

Attempts toward Solution

Our system of grading schools was developed when we assumed that all children could learn the same things at the same chronological age if they tried hard enough; failure to learn was morally reprehensible and was dealt with by the hickory stick. Those who still didn't learn, after repeated failures and repetition of grades, left school and went to work. Toward the end of the last century the hickory stick and dunce cap had been abolished in most American schools, but low marks and failures still carried with them a moral stigma that hurt as much as the switch. The large number of failures and grade-repetitions continued, and provoked discussion and a number of gestures toward reform, but almost no real solutions to the problem were discovered.

As early as 1889, however, Preston Search in Pueblo, Colorado, really faced the problem squarely and made it possible for each child to learn at his own natural rate in each subject, with no failures, grade-repetitions or grade skipping. But Search was ahead of his times. Textbooks were not so written as to make self-instruction possible; people were not convinced that any such radical departure was necessary—we had no intelligence tests or achievement tests in those days. The tremendous amount of work Search inspired his teachers to do in order to make individual progress of pupils possible, continued only as long as Search's dynamic personality aroused the necessary enthusiasm.

But by 1912, achievement tests were making people recognize that the differences in children were much greater than had been realized; and intelligence tests were coming over the horizon. It was then that Frederic Burk in the San Francisco State Normal School, following up an informal experiment by a member of his faculty, Mary Ward, started a movement to make textbooks self-instructive and enable children, systematically, to progress according to their ability. Burk's experiments, and the statistical results, caused nationwide interest. By 1919 a member of his staff was invited to become superintendent of schools in Winnetka, a suburb of Chicago, with the deliberate purpose of introducing Burk's ideas and adapting them to public-school conditions.

SELF-INSTRUCTIVE MATERIALS

Under his guidance the teachers of Winnetka worked prodigiously in preparing self-instructive text material, diagnostic tests, and administrative techniques whereby each child's work could be fitted to his maturity and readiness. The schools became world-famous, the self-instructive materials gave rise to the "workbooks" now so very common over the country, and textbooks in general became far more self-instructive than before. In the mid-twenties educators everywhere were talking about the so-called "Winnetka Plan," and along with it the quite different "Dalton Plan," developed by Helen Parkhurst after repeated conferences with Burk, and on the basis of her earlier Montessori experience. The common element between the early phases of the Dalton plan and the work in Winnetka was that both provided for individual progression. Other experiments had been begun by this time, in Chicago, in London, and many other places. The National Society for the Study of Education devoted the *Twenty-Fourth Yearbook* to a description and evaluation of such experiments. It really began to look as if schools might begin to fit their work to the children.

PROJECT METHOD

But the Project Method just then began to seize the imagination of educators and Kilpatrick said there should be no fixed curriculum. People said (with some justice) that the individual work in Winnetka and elsewhere divorced the mechanics of learning from motivating social experience. Schools heaved a sigh of relief—they didn't have to reorganize their classes, their textbooks, their administration. They sank back to their former programs, with sometimes a veneer of "projects" or "centers of interests" or "activities," as they were successively called. Most of these were about as far as they could be from what Kilpatrick had envisaged. For example, in one city, the elementary supervisor decreed that during the month of April all fourth grades should study fish. Arithmetic problems must deal with fish, reading was about fish, spelling words had to do with fish and how they were caught and marketed, geography discovered where different kinds of fish came from, and so on. This sounds fishy, but I saw it with my own eyes.

Not all efforts at activities programs were so stupidly far-fetched—I hope few were. But practically all ignored individual differences in the maturity and readiness of the children about as completely as these had been ignored before; and most continued to give the grade assignments in arithmetic, spelling, reading, etc., on a class basis, aimed at the "average" child.

"ABILITY GROUPS"

Some schools, however, threw a sop to Cerberus. They reverted to the experiments of the 1890's and organized classes in "ability groups." Some, like Detroit and Los Angeles, had whole classes of X, Y or Z students, representing, supposedly, three levels of mental ability. The "slow learners" were given watered down assignments, the "fast learners" were given "enriched curricula"; but if the children were about 9 years old chronologically, they were all given fourth grade work. The problem was not in the least solved—achievement tests given at the end of the year, in any subject, showed almost as wide a range as before, and an overlap between "ability groups" that was much greater than the differences in their median achievement. The problem of promotion or nonpromotion remained.

Then Los Angeles had a bright idea. Half the children who had failing marks at the end of certain grades were promoted in spite of their apparent failure; the other half repeated the grade. Both halves were tested at the end of the next year and it was found that the ones promoted learned more than did the repeaters. The emotional results of discouraging failure and boring repetition of assignments inhibited growth in learning, while the encouragement and stimulus of going on with their class improved the learning of the ones promoted.

UNIVERSAL PROMOTIONS

On the basis of such experience and reasoning, the schools of New York City, among many others, decreed universal promotions. Then teachers began to tear their hair. Children were further apart than ever in their ability to learn the work of the grade to which they were assigned. And they still persisted —and persist—in treating all the children in the room as if they were nearly at the same level. To be sure, teachers are usually forced into dividing a room into three groups, doing some "remedial work" with the slowest group and giving the fastest group some padding under the euphemism of "enrichment"; but the major trend of the assignments, the textbooks and the tests is on *one* grade level, not on four.

The difficulty with any attempt at grouping is that each child has his own characteristic profile of abilities and maturities. A child of second grade arithmetic ability may have fourth grade reading ability; another may have sixth grade reading ability and third grade spelling ability—and so on with all the subjects and children. And a child doesn't stay put—he may take a spurt in learning in some one phase of the curriculum and block in another.

GROUPING BY MENTAL AGE

Perhaps mental ages should be the basis of grouping? That's been tried, too, and it doesn't work, for two reasons: First, the child with a high IQ may be physically, emotionally and socially much less mature than a slower-developing child of the same mental age who is several years older chronologically. Conversely, the twelve-year-old child with a mental age of 9, doesn't fit at all in a class of nine-year-olds, interlarded with bright eight-year-olds and a few precocious seven-year-olds.

In the second place, a mental age is an average of differing functions, as a comparison of the profiles of the test results of any two children of the same mental and chronological age quickly reveals. To illustrate, in highly oversimplified form, let us look at two children of the same age (10) taking a Stanford-Binet test, and let us confine ourselves to just two test items. One item is the vocabulary test, consisting, you will remember, of a graded series of words, running from very simple, easy ones to words like "homunculus" and "limpet." A certain number of right definitions gives a child a score of eight years, a larger number gives a score of twelve years. The other item we choose to consider is the Ball and Field test. Showing the path one would take to find a lost ball in the field, if the path is not efficient but indicates that the child has grasped the idea, scores the child on the eight-year level; while a really efficient plan for covering the field, like a close spiral or concentric circles, gives him a score of twelve years. Now Robert and Helen are both chronologically 10 years old. Helen passes the vocabulary test at the twelve-year-old level, Robert at the eight-year level. On the Ball and Field test, on the other hand, Robert passes at the twelve-year level and Helen at the eight-year level. Averaging each child's score, each has passed a test at the eight-year level, each has passed one at the twelve level; so both have average scores of 10. Mental age 10; chronological age 10; IQ 100 for each: they're exactly alike! Only they aren't; there's four years' difference between them in each of the two functions measured.

Of course the scores are not worked out just like that; but the result is the same on a more complicated series of test items. *Any* child has a gap of about four years between his basal age—the level on which he passes *every* test item, and the maximum level on which he passes one test item. And the intermediate test items missed differ from child to child with the same age and IQ.

Grouping for Individual Mastery

No grouping based on an averaging of the children's mental levels and their achievement levels in various school subjects can, in the nature of things, result in real equality among the children of the group in regard to each of the various kinds of maturity.

Ability grouping is a misnomer and is no solution to our problem. Flunking some children and double promoting others is no solution. Universal promotions, by themselves, enlarge the range of differences.

There is only one solution: *Face facts.*

The facts are that children differ widely in their rate of maturing, and that each child's rate of maturing in some functions differs from that same child's rate of maturing in others. No child does good work and maintains an interest in learning unless the work challenges him to use his abilities, and unless he can achieve success somewhat proportionate to his effort.

In the light of these facts it is obvious that the school program must be adjusted to each child's maturity, recognizing a range, in regard to any one aspect of school work, of at least four years in any classroom. This adjustment must be made *insofar as we expect mastery from each child.*

That last clause is very important. Kilpatrick to the contrary notwithstanding, there *are* some fixed aspects to the curriculum—things that every literate and functioning member of our society really has to know or know how to do. Seven and 8 were 15 in Russia before the Revolution and after the Revolution, and are on this side of the Iron Curtain as well—and were even when written differently by the old Romans. And anyone in our society will be really handicapped if he thinks that the sum is 13. There have been, and always will be, for all practical purposes, six nines in 54, and it is awkward if one thinks there are seven. During the lifetime of the children now in school it is highly likely that "believe" will be spelled with the "i" in front of the "e," and the reversal, while not fatal, is liable to be embarrassing. For a long time to come, in all probability, people in our culture will end sentences with a period and begin them with a capital. And so on.

These are not the most important parts of education and need not consume an inordinate part of a child's time. They should certainly not be learned without seeing their functional usefulness. But they do need to be learned, and some of them require repetitive practice, which used to be called drill.

There are many other aspects of the curriculum which do not require common mastery. No two of us have identical knowledge of history, geography and science, for example. No two of us have read all the same books. No two of us will write identical letters or essays on the same subject, even though we may spell and punctuate alike.

In school we have many goals. We are concerned with giving every child such knowledge and habits as he needs for health and safety; we want to give every child mental health—a chance at self-expression, a feeling of security, some degree of social integration, and the adjustment to life and his fellows that these imply; there are various social attitudes of responsibility for the common welfare that we want to stimulate, and certain perspectives which we want to open up. We want to give the children, too, practice in democratic living—in respect for differences among themselves, whether of dress, customs, ancestry or ideas, and in working cooperatively with their fellows toward common goals that they really want to reach. The list is much longer. But in very few of these things are we seeking identity of response among children.

WHAT IS THE COMMON CORE?

Where we do not expect identity of response, children may be grouped in accordance with approximate social maturity, or common interests, or special needs, or even, without harm to most of them, chronological age. They can have both common and individual experiences and exposures, and each will get what he is ready for out of them. They won't be marked or graded in these things—there is no single standard of achievement. Our job is to provide a stimulating, interesting environment, a wide variety of experiences suitable to children of the range of maturity with which we are dealing. Many experiences are interesting and useful over a rather wide range, as is evident from the range of ages of children enjoying the same television show or baseball game. With wise guidance we can help each child to get as much value as *he* can from these exposures and activities.

But there is still a little hard core of subject matter (I know the word is out of style) that *every* child who is not a moron (and even a high grade moron) needs, sooner or later, to master. It is that core of skills that must be adjusted to the ability, the maturity, the readiness, of each individual child—not without real functional meaning to him, not without motivation, but at the psychological moment when he can learn, with achievement proportionate to effort.

It's not as hard as it seems. It has been done successfully over and over and under a variety of circumstances. The steps are simple:

First, identify this core, specifically. In reading, this core consists of being able to read books easily and fluently, to read aloud in such a way as to communicate easily with one's hearers, to be able to get information one is seeking from the printed word. In spelling, it is ability to spell the commonest words, to have a desire to spell all words conventionally, and to be able to look up words one is not sure about. In language and grammar it is knowing how to speak and write without violating the forms that are universally current among educated people—"We wasn't going nowhere," for example, is a form of speech which, while perfectly intelligible, excludes the user from acceptance as an educated person.

And in arithmetic there are the basic number facts, the four processes applied to numbers commonly used in problems such as everyone meets in daily living, the use of those few simple fractions that everyone uses, in the processes where they are used in almost everyone's life; simple measures in common use—and so on through a very limited number of items.

This list can be whittled down by omitting what everyone will learn without school practice—I've seen children drilled in the difference between larger and smaller, taller and shorter, heavier and lighter. But I have never seen even an illiterate who did not learn these distinctions just by living in our society. Reading the calendar, telling time, naming the months of the year—there is a whole string of topics on which we need not concentrate, because in a life of any variety of experience, children will inevitably pick them up.

And it can be whittled down at the top by omitting all things that are not really functional in the lives of most people: computing the area of a circle, the division of one fraction by another, especially if the divisor is larger than the dividend; compound interest; double discount.

I do not mean that arithmetic—or reading or spelling or language—should be confined to the small common core. An understanding of the significance and possibilities of arithmetic, far beyond this core, should be stimulated and helped wherever the response of the child warrants it; spelling should go far beyond a minimum list of words; language should be mainly creative expression of various kinds; reading should not only grow in depth of understanding, but should flower into real appreciation of literature and poetry. But these things need not be—cannot be—measured with precision; they need not be the same for all; they are outside the hard core but are the more vital part of education.

It is only the hard core—the universally needed and used skills—that must be individualized in the sense of seeing that each child achieves mastery. This mastery can only be achieved by a child when his own individual maturity in respect to any aspect of it makes it possible for his achievement to match his efforts. And we only want such ultimate mastery where uniform achievement is necessary—the same answer to 6 x 9, the same spelling of a word, the same punctuation at the end of a question.

And even these things should not, I repeat, be taught in isolation from meaning and use.

So much for the first step—the identification of the core. The second step is to see when a child is ready for any particular topic. This is not difficult. A spelling scale will indicate the level of difficulty of words that a child is ready to spell. A reading test will show the grade level on which a child can read (or, earlier, a reading readiness test will give some indication as to whether he is ready to learn to read). His own original stories will show what punctuation and capitalization he is ready to use. And in arithmetic we have pretty good evidence as to the usual mental age and the definitely needed foundations a child must have before going from one stage to the next.

WHEN IS THE CHILD READY?

The third step is to provide a little time in each day for individual work and to give each child the work for which he as an individual is ready. His many creative and social activities should have given him a background of understanding as to the functional need for what he is learning, and should give him ample opportunities for applying it. Beyond this, the inherent desire to learn, and the success in accomplishment will serve as potent motivation. When these things are insufficient, ad hoc projects can readily be devised to show a child or a small, informal group the use of what is being learned.

At this point materials have to be at hand for the individual work, especially in arithmetic. Modern textbooks and workbooks often can supply this material, if the nonfunctional and the unnecessary parts are omitted. Provision for self-correction of daily work is good for the child and saves the teacher unnecessary labor. Diagnostic tests at frequent intervals can give some indication as to whether or not real learning is taking place.

I have gone into all this in considerable detail in Part Three of my *Living Philosophy of Education,* and cannot develop the techniques here. Furthermore, many of you may devise better ones. All I want to point out is that there are techniques that make it possible to individualize these common essential skills in a classroom of the usual size, or even larger—McDade did it with fifty in a class in Chicago as did Jessie McKinder in London, not that such large classes are ever defensible.

Is it harder to individualize this part of the curriculum than to teach it the traditional way? Let me ask: Is it harder to do the possible than the impossible? It is impossible for any teacher, treating a class of children as if they were all ready for the same lesson at the same time, to get any uniformity of results. His efforts to do so frustrate both teacher and child—and at the end of the year he is faced with the unsolved problem of promotion.

A FLEXIBLE PROGRAM

But granted that this modicum of the curriculum, where we want to build a uniform base, is individualized, what happens to Miss Julian whose class we discussed at the beginning? Let us assume that Ada, Bill, Carl, Dot and Edith are of somewhere near the same chronological age, and get along reasonably well socially in spite of their spread in mental ages—not an impossible assumption. Now let Miss Julian plan her program in a way that will give these children many activities and experiences in which they can share and from which each can derive some, but not the same, benefit. Then let her know that she is expected to see just what aspect of the common core of arithmetic each of the five is ready for, and that she is not expected to get them all through fourth grade.

She gives Ada some very simple work in the meaning of the smaller numbers and what happens when they are combined. She gives Bill a reasonably self-instructive textbook and perhaps a workbook in which he learns what happens to numbers when the same ones are added together repeatedly, and how this can be shortened by multiplication; and, a little later, when he knows the meaning of the products, she lets him practice on the multiplication facts with products less than twenty until he really knows them. And so on with the rest of the children. Each is given work that fits his own arithmetic maturity. Often, for this one subject, she can group several children together temporarily, while they are mastering a topic. During the arithmetic period, she will be down among the children, helping, encouraging, showing them how to get what they are trying to learn. Each child will be progressing at his own rate. No child will feel pushed beyond his ability, or held back.

At another period, all children may be reading—but not in the same books. The room library will have books marked as to their level of difficulty and each child will know the level on which he can read with satisfaction. At spelling time, each child will be working on his own appropriate list, with a partner to dictate words to him.

But most of the day the children will be working together—doing creative work with handicrafts, colors or writing. Their discussions, their research, their committees, the teacher's talks or stories or demonstrations, the group singing, the creative dramatics, the excursions—all these will be social and stimulating opportunities to learn. Arithmetic will inevitably come in—those who can solve the harder problems that come up in connection with a discussion or a project will do so; the simpler problems will be solved by the ones on the earlier steps of the ladder. Spelling can't help coming in whenever there is anything to write; reading is equally inevitable.

The common core remains, it is true, temporarily isolated for the sake of individual mastery—just as one who plays in an orchestra gets off by himself and practices, temporarily out of context, a difficult run until he masters it. Such temporary isolation of a part of a learning process is natural, universal and necessary. The harm comes when most work is so isolated and when the isolation is neither preceded nor followed by integration in a larger whole.

But to return to Miss Julian: At the end of the year her children have all progressed, in varying degrees, toward mastery of appropriate parts of the common skills. All have had a rich year of experience in many fields. If the children have got along fairly well together and can work and play as a team, she has no hesitancy about letting them continue their group experiences together the next year, knowing that her successor will carry each child on from where he left off in that fraction of the curriculum where common mastery is necessary.

3. *Psychological Basis for Children's Interests* *

DONALD L. CLELAND

PSYCHOLOGY embraces human behavior and adjustment. Basic human behavior has changed little since primitive man, but our understanding of some of the acquired social drives has increased with each generation. One facet of these acquired social drives, *interest,* which may be defined as *an emotionalized attitude,* has received the attention of psychologists and educators for many years. Children's interests, particularly, should be the concern of every teacher in our schools.

Interests are not innate nor inherent in an individual. They are usually the result of social conditioning. Interests may be thought of as a need—a need to know, to feel or perform. A person may have an interest in certain sports, such as fishing. He, therefore, has a need to feel the thrill of a strike; the need to know the artistry of casting to a likely spot; or the actual

* From Donald L. Cleland, "Psychological Basis for Children's Interests," *Education* (April, 1959), pp. 465–69. Reprinted by permission of the author and The Bobbs-Merrill Co., Inc., Indianapolis. Ind.

need to perform, that is, to actively engage in the physical act of fishing. This need to feel, to know and to perform must be nurtured or kept alive, else the interest will wane, and if completely neglected for a long period of time, will completely die out.

Any student of child psychology knows that the maturing child, through social conditioning, has acquired certain drives or needs. Some of these may be classified as follows:

1. The need for social approval
2. The need for social security
3. The need for the realization of selfhood
4. The need for emotional release

The writer realizes that it is almost impossible to list all of the acquired social drives or needs. He, also, is aware of the fact that it is just as impossible to define and delimit these many social drives as there is so much overlapping. Neither space nor time will permit an enumeration and discussion of all of the acquired social drives. Therefore, let us turn our attention to the ones which were mentioned above.

The Need for Social Approval

The mother's or father's voice has come to represent to the child the social satisfactions he wants. The approval or disapproval which goes with these voices have a tremendous influence upon his behavior. He learns that if he behaves in an acceptable way, he receives satisfactions even though they may be in the form of words. That if he does that which is not an acceptable mode of behavior, disapproval is expressed, again, through the use of symbols. He comes to think of acts as "good" or "bad" according to standards set by the adult members of his social group—the home.

At first, these symbols of social approval or disapproval influence his behavior only when they come from the adult members of social group, his parents, his nurse, or anyone who satisfies his needs. Later this stock of symbols, words and objects grows to symbols at a higher level of abstraction, such as a flag, a motto, social amenities, philosophical ideas, political issues, etc. As he matures, he comes to seek the approval of society, or at least the social group to which he belongs.

The Need for Social Security

The desire for social approval may be the driving force which motivates him to seek security within his social group. It is natural for most children to seek a degree of security within this group. Sooner or later the child realizes, by observation, that other members of his group have acquired security by being a contributing member to the group. He realizes that they are secure because they are helping to direct the activities of the group; that they work cooperatively with the group, lending their talents and directing their energies for the welfare of the group as a whole. By contributing to the welfare of the group, not only do they win social approval, but much more important, they have also acquired a sense of belonging—a feeling of social security.

The Need for the Realization of Selfhood

As the child grows in his understanding of the different levels of abstractions of social symbols, he attains a growing concept of selfhood. As he grows he forms a broader concept of himself in terms of various traits and abilities. He becomes aware of his strengths and weaknesses, his skills, and his talents. He realizes more and more that he is a unique individual and that there are none which resemble him in all respects.

This significance in selfhood lies in the fact that his most jealously guarded possession is his own self. The self becomes an object which must be ardently defended.

This selfhood must meet with social approval and social security. In fact, this selfhood is not very different from social approval and social security. The child may read the same book the other members of his group has read. Not only does he gain social approval, and social security, he has acquired greater prestige—another step in the realization of selfhood.

The Need for Emotional Release

Emotions, unlike physiological drives, are a reaction to some external stimulus situation. They may result where there is no ready-made pattern of response. Some of the basic emotions are love, fear, anxiety, joy and excitement There are no sharp lines of demarcation between one emotion and another. Many emotional responses involve the entire human organism.

A child's fears, whether real or imagined, are as real to him as the fears a most mature person may experience. To say that a child does not experience fears, apprehensions, etc., is to classify him with some of the lower animals.

Children, as well as adults, need emotional release. If this emotional release is not realized, a lowering of the physiological functioning may result. A disease entity known as marasmus was held accountable for the death of many children during and following World War I.

A method that has been used successfully to effect emotional release is known as bibliotherapy. Understanding how others have resolved their inner conflicts and emotions has, many times, had a therapeutic effect upon a reader. Who hasn't, young or old, found solace or gotten emotional release by reading about others, real or fictional people, who had similar problems? Bibliotherapy is gaining as an established technique for affecting needed emotional release.

The need for social approval, security, selfhood, and emotional release are some of the psychological bases for children's interests in reading. The studies that have been made of children's interests are mute testimony to this fact.

Let us now turn our attention to some of the developmental patterns of growth of children. A review of these characteristics and growth patterns will aid teachers in the selection of reading materials for these children.

Kindergarten and Primary Period

1. Characteristics of the child
   a. At the beginning of the period, the child may be egocentric.
   b. Attention span is short.
   c. Is interested in the here and now of immediate environment.
   d. At the beginning of the period much imitation of adults; towards the end of the period much concerned about the opinion of peers. Becoming more and more independent at the end of the period.
   e. Becoming more and more competitive—likes to make rules.
   f. Shows some understanding of cause and effect; thinking involving use of concrete experiences to somewhat abstract symbols.
2. Implications for the reading program
   During this period a child can satisfy the acquired social needs through the use of books. The type of material contained in these books should fit the developmental growth patterns of children.

A review of the literature would indicate that children of this age group prefer stories which contain the following elements: surprise; unexpectedness; unforeseen events; happenings and outcomes; lively stories with action; animalness; things that animals do; talking animals; animals which assume some of the characteristics of people.

The Intermediate Period

1. Characteristics of the child
   a. Intellectual maturation proceeds at a rapid pace.
   b. Girls are maturing more rapidly than boys.
   c. He has a tendency to organize memory around clues.
   d. Interests are expanding beyond his immediate environment to events and activities of their peripheral environment.
   e. Individual differences are becoming clear and distinct.
   f. Gang influence becoming strong and may exercise a greater influence than the home or school.
   g. He has a strong sense of right and wrong; is perfectionistic, but loses interest quickly if discouraged.
   h. Becoming less interested in fairy tales and fantasy, but more in science, adventure and realism.
2. Implications for the reading program

At the beginning of this period, their silent reading rate equals or exceeds their oral rate, hence they will be doing more free reading. Reading interests are becoming more diversified, as is evidenced by the fact that girls will read books for boys, but boys may ignore books written for girls. They are rather responsive to the pressures of the gang, which determine to a large extent their selection of reading matter.

During this period adventure, mystery, and detective stories rank high with boys and girls. Boys are showing an increased interest in biographies, while the girls' interests in fairy stories are waning. Girls begin, during this period, to show an interest in stories centering around home and school life.

During this period it is imperative that books be selected, the content of which satisfy the acquired social needs mentioned earlier. This period is critical as attitudes and tastes develop rapidly and take on a degree of permanency.

The Advanced Period

1. Characteristics of the child
   a. This period has frequently been referred to as the awkward period.
   b. It is marked by many physical changes in both sexes.
   c. He shows concern over bodily growth, acne may present a problem, he is afraid of not being popular and is overly sensitive to the opinions of others.

    d. He usually responds better to the influence of the teacher or the gang leader than to the parents.

    e. He seems to be seeking personal independence, but frequently returns to adults for moral support. Many times he acts as if he *knew it all,* but it could be a manifestation of his own uncertainty with himself.

    f. He develops more mature performance in work-type reading, creative reading, and problem-solving situations.

    g. Language abilities are growing rapidly and he manifests increasing ability to memorize and organize.

2. Implications for the reading program

At the beginning of this period many reach a zenith in the amount of free reading. Boys continue to read mystery and adventure stories, while girls show increased interest in novels, love stories, and adult magazines. They exhibit a tendency towards identification with characters and situations about which they read. Bibliotherapy can be used effectively in solving many of their personal problems and as an aid in personality development. With increased ability to read, the teacher, through judicial guidance, can help them increase their ability to organize mentally what they read as an aid to retention; to generalize; and to gain a deeper insight into social situations. Reading critically, evaluating what they read, forming judgments, and reading as a thinking process should be stressed more and more. This age child can skim a newspaper in a few minutes or he can enjoy the deliberate, analytical reading of an editorial. He enjoys reading because he has gained a measure of success, and he is beginning to realize the truth of the convictions of the German poet, dramatist, and philosopher, Goethe, when he said, "There is no age at which no further progress in reading can be made."

Children's interests in reading are not, as stated earlier, innate or inherent. They are developed largely through social conditioning. The wise teacher can, through judicious planning and guidance, develop permanent tastes, attitudes, and interests in reading. This planning should be within the framework of the child's acquired social needs, and the developmental growth patterns that he manifests.

4 Grouping within the Elementary Classroom *

FRED T. WILHELMS

Dividing children into "teacherfuls" is the first stage in elementary-school grouping, but the real pay-off comes from what you do after your roomful is delivered to you. These youngsters are yours now, watching you, wondering what you'll be like. You're wondering about them, too, and asking yourself how you can best use subgrouping within your room to help you teach each one as he needs to be taught.

Two attitudes, neither related directly to techniques, will help you.

First, learn to expect a tremendous range of differences among the children. Learn to enjoy these differences and set your mind to making best use of them.

Only the callow think all sixth graders ought to be alike; only the mechanical teacher tries to make them so. The real educator knows that a sixth grade is primarily a group of children about 11 years old. A typical roomful of them will spread across a 6-to-10-year range on almost any variable.

This wide range creates problems. Although many educators have worked many years to narrow it down, the fact is that the total range of differences can be reduced only moderately by any device we know of.

Therefore, no matter how your group was assembled, expect it to include huge differences. Learn to think of this as normal and acceptable, and stop yearning for uniformity—you probably wouldn't like it anyway. Look for every chance to pool differences to produce added strength, and get on with your job of taking each child forward as far as you can.

Second, dedicate your grouping to the well-being of the individual. Leave it to the half-teacher to see grouping merely as a handy way of forming clusters that he can teach with ease.

If you think of grouping the wrong way, it becomes a way of flattening out individuals to fit some mold; if you think of it the right way, it helps you to take each child where he is and fit your instruction to him.

The finest thing about working with small groups is that it makes each

* From Fred T. Wilhelms, "Grouping within the Elementary Classroom," *NEA Journal* (September, 1959), pp. 19–21. Reprinted by permission of the author and the *NEA Journal*.

child highly "visible." Don't throw away that chance for clear vision by putting on the blinders of stereotypy.

Maybe the greatest hazard in this whole grouping business is that it causes some teachers to search constantly for *similarity*. Use your grouping to let each child be *more* of an individual, to help yourself think of him *more* as a person in his own right.

Now let's assume that you are going to have a good bit of grouping in your room, and go on to a few specifics.

Ability groups. It's probably a good thing to do a limited amount of grouping within your room along ability lines, perhaps especially in reading and arithmetic. Such grouping frees the ablest to proceed as only they can, while it offers the less able precisely the help they need.

This should be done field by field, so that the groupings can be as different as they need to be in, say, arithmetic and reading.

In grouping for any one field, the best index is probably some combination of the student's previous record in that field, as shown by grades and achievement-test scores, and some measure of his potential, as shown by aptitude or general-intelligence scores, or by what you know about the student.

But interest and motivation can be much more important than a few points on some test score, so reserve the right to use your own good common sense.

You may be tempted to place under-achievers in a high group to stimulate their rapid growth. In some cases this may work very well. Studies show, though, that often this only discourages the student and leaves him worse off. Your intuitive perception of the individual child will be the best guide.

You may be tempted, too, to give high status to the youngsters who are attractive, well dressed, well mannered, and from good homes. Here is a place to be stern with yourself. Use objective data to check your personal imagery. The purpose of grouping is not to grant favors to some, but to make wise arrangements for each.

When you are forming such ability groups, adapt content and methods to the needs of each group, *no matter how radical the adaptation may need to be.* Use as rich a variety of instructional materials as you can get your hands on. Ability grouping is futile if the several groups then go on with basically the same content, with no differences except small changes in pace or amounts covered.

Strength in diversity. Some grouping ought to be based on the strength that comes from diversity. Often differences are just what we need.

For example, in a broad, active social-studies unit with the work divided up among committees, a committee is lucky if it includes a variety of abilities: some bookish members, some youngsters with artistic and musical and mechanical abilities, some with ability to organize and lead, some contemplative planners, some aggressive doers, and so on. There isn't the slightest need to group by general ability levels; the group needs a range of abilities suited to a range of jobs.

In the daily life of the school—not only in the subject classes, but also on the playground and in the management of the room's affairs—many jobs demand just such pooling of peculiar strengths. Because we in the schools tend to be so oriented toward similarity, we ought deliberately to teach ourselves to value and use diversity.

Interest grouping. Interest is a much better basis for grouping than is commonly recognized. Have you ever had one of those boys who is virtually a nonreader at school, but who puts together airplane models from directions you yourself can hardly read? Sometimes a strong drive enables a child to go way beyond his apparent ability, and that's always a lovely thing to encourage.

It isn't always easy to distinguish between a real drive and a froth of interest that collapses as soon as the going gets rough. But a sensitive teacher can do it most of the time, and it pays to gamble now and then. Any child, bright or dull, is likely to produce his best when he is in a group on some job *simply because he wants to do it.*

Grouping by need. Sometimes a very specific need is the common center for a group. Thus, you find that four youngsters can't handle zero in multiplication, or you sense that a half-dozen pupils don't know how to manage the introductions when their parents visit school.

The need doesn't necessarily have anything to do with their general ability or their long-term interests. So you have one or two private sessions —whatever it takes—and then the group dissolves as quietly as it was born.

Friendship grouping. For some purposes, friendship and congeniality are the best cement. A schoolroom ought to be an easygoing, happy place where good pals can get together now and then to tackle a job.

This can be overdone, of course. Any teacher knows that if certain children were left to themselves they would tag along with certain other children into any group for any purpose. Important, long-range groups probably shouldn't generally have friendship as their focal point; though one can amiably watch it from the corner of his eye in forming any group.

But for some purposes—well, why not help boys and girls to the same enjoyments you cherish for yourself?

What we've been portraying so far is just the opposite of the set situation where youngsters are divided once and for all into three layers: poor, average, good. A lot of things are going on in different ways. There is flexibility and a fluid, open society, where the idea is simply to do the best we can for each child as each opportunity comes along.

There's a calm, easy facing of the fact that Al is a whiz at arithmetic and Jenny gets along fairly well, while Bob needs a lot of help on even simple problems. But Bob and Jenny and Al haven't ever been classified poor, average, or good *as human beings*. And because we have seen them at work in such varied situations, we aren't even much tempted to think of them that way. We merely size up each situation and take what seems like the best next step.

If we analyze this further, we can see a few general principles:

At any given time, each child is in at least a couple of different groups formed on different lines. Over a year's time he is in a number of groups, based on a great variety of criteria. In the various groups he has had opportunities to lead and to follow. Whatever his level, he has had a chance to achieve authentic successes in his own way and to contribute to the group.

Some of the groups have been long-lasting—perhaps the reading groups are a good example. They give the security of a reasonably permanent home base.

Some of the groups are of a passing nature, with a very brief life corresponding to the need that brought them forth. Certainly there should be reasonable flexibility, so that a youngster can move from one group to another—perhaps more from personal than for academic reasons. But there should never be a need for undue preoccupation with this.

The longer-lasting groups, particularly, give us a wonderful chance to teach democratic self-management—group process, if you will. Our times demand, as never before, that youngsters grow up with attitudes and skills that will enable them to move easily in group situations and help manage affairs.

Children aren't born with the ability to cooperate or to take leadership. Help them learn. Keep the situations simple at first and supervise the group activities, but build for growing independence. Teaching group process is one of the important goals of grouping within the classroom.

No youngster has been in all the desirable groups; no youngster has always been made to see himself as slow. The names of the groups have been neutral, often given just the chairman's name. The children have helped decide how some groups were formed; often they've had their own choices. Planning has been keyed to work to be done, and every single child has had more good breaks in the year than he could have had if your sensitivity in grouping hadn't put him in spots that let him do real work successfully.

Finally, let's remind ourselves of two general ideas. First, don't forget that your room as a whole is a group, too. Build it up. Don't get so pre-occupied with handling it in bits that it loses its force and unity.

Second, remember that grouping isn't a way of teaching. It is simply a technique of classroom management that helps you create an environment in which you can teach better. That total environment is what really matters. Don't sacrifice it to some pat system. Don't worry overmuch about technical refinements in your grouping.

Do your worrying on behalf of individual children. If you do what seems sensible in each case and work everlastingly for the good of every child, you can be sure that grouping will help you make your room an interesting, happy, and effective working place.

5. *Methods of Individualization in Elementary School* *

ROY PATRICK WAHLE

CHRIS IS six feet and one inch tall today in his stocking feet. He's a solid 185 pounds. He won his letter in football last fall; he's a three-sport boy because baseball is his favorite and basketball is fun. This summer he took up golf. Already, he outdrives his father and seems to outbirdie his mother whenever she has the good fortune to par. He's at the top of his class in social studies, and that's about it! No, there's something more.

* From Roy Patrick Wahle, "Methods of Individualization in Elementary School," *Educational Leadership* (November, 1959), pp. 74–79. Reprinted by permission of the author and *Educational Leadership*.

Chris should have been entering junior high school this year, but he is half-way through instead. You see, Chris is only 12 years old. But someone felt it would be better if he skipped the second grade. Somehow he didn't belong there. Chris likes the world, but there are days when he moans: "Gee! Dad, it's tough being an adult child!"

Chris is different. But so are his friends. They differ in dentition, visual maturity, language development, sexual maturity, emotional stability, character traits, chronological age, and mental ability. Everybody knows that the most startling fact about being a human being is human individuality. Individuality is, at the same time, the most charming reality. Educators speak reverently of the sacred personalities of children.

There is a doctrine of individual differences which modern teachers acknowledge but frequently ignore. It is difficult for human beings to see others except in terms of their own self-images. Teachers may attempt to convey a fact or concept to an immature mind in a way that is comfortable and comprehensible for the teacher. It may be exceedingly difficult for the teacher to accept the reality of confusion or misunderstanding on the part of the learner. Yet we must remind ourselves that thirty children may learn thirty different things in thirty different ways each time the teacher helps to develop a group experience in a classroom.

Methods of individualization in the elementary school must be feasible, applicable and appropriate. Individualization of the guidance and instructional program is more a matter of spirit and atmosphere than it is pronouncement and rule. But there are marks by which one may discern the elementary school and the school district which are more concerned about children than about things.

Marks of Individualization

Let us examine some of these marks which denote that individualization is paramount: (a) the library is the center of learning, (b) there are numerous approaches to similar learnings or conceptualizations, (c) there is flexible grouping based upon defensible criteria, (d) attention is directed to the exceptional, (e) a class is a group of separate human beings, (f) guidance nourishes curriculum and curriculum serves guidance, (g) classes or instructional groups tend to be small, (h) informed generalists direct the school's administration, (i) a respect for scientific inquiry and experimentation prevails, (j) parents and patrons help define the goals and purposes of education, but professional educators define and designate the methods and techniques.

The library is the center of learning. The printed symbol is the most efficient device ever invented by man to transmit his culture and to broaden personal experiences and understandings. Better elementary schools early establish, by symbol, facility and practice, the central importance of books and their contents. Individualization in reading and research is a basic necessity of our times. Full-time year-around library service at each elementary school is a practical goal.

But a library is more than books. It should encompass all instructional materials and devices which will enrich meanings. A librarian is the essential member of the teaching staff whose knowledge of books and instructional materials will enhance the motivational and learning quality of any lesson or individual searching which children must pursue in order to grow in understanding.

There are numerous approaches to similar concepts. Chuck is 4 years old. He recognizes the symbols of our number language. He learned them while playing cards with his sister. He can count past 23, but Chuck does not understand fully what these pleasantries are all about. If he is sent for six spoons he may bring nine.

The concepts which are symbolized by the numeral "6" must be approached in many meaningful and interesting ways. This requires creativity, ingenuity and patience. Better elementary schools use the community and its resources. Interesting people and places are anticipated and visited. Art serves music and music serves art; sharing periods, science tables, work benches and outdoor education contribute to a living structure of education. When does the picture of a horse in the reading text actually become, for the child, the real Nellie at the farm or zoo? When do the hardships and triumphs of the pioneer woman become attributes of a flesh and blood mother? Many differing experiences which may lead to a similarly important concept may help conceptualization enrich a mode of living. A concept then becomes alive through the activity it inspires.

There is flexible grouping based upon defensible criteria. Wherever children gather together there will be grouping. Good elementary schools concern themselves with the criteria used for determining the varying instructional groups which are inevitable in mass education. Old forms are consistently questioned in the light of deeper knowledge about human growth and development. There is nothing sacred about twenty-five or thirty or ten within a group. Neither chronological age nor the intelligence quotient taken alone offers a legitimate basis for grouping, yet we persist with the graded structure of the elementary school or select "gifted children" by a score on a test! Research again and again supports the negative value of retention, but we maintain a blind faith that repetition of unlearned material will guarantee its comprehension!

It appears possible that some form of ungraded program, when maturation and its manifestations of reading readiness and reading ability are major concerns, will better answer the perplexing problem of grouping in the primary school. Does it automatically follow, however, that an ungraded program necessarily provides a sound structure for grouping at the intermediate level?

We believe that when a child first learns to relate in a social circumstance we should provide him with an understandable and manageable situation. Why, then, do we continue to generalize that six-year-old boys are as ready to read and do the work that schools expect as are six-year-old girls?

Bellevue found, in a comprehensive study of its elementary children, that many of the boys who were above average in intelligence persisted in low reading groups through all six elementary grades! Surely, the grouping criteria needed to be examined. They were then examined and, consequently, the Continuous Growth Program was introduced as an experiment.

Two years have elapsed. Evidence is accumulating which indicates that if children are allowed to proceed at their own rate through the primary grades, reading problems are reduced and individual self-confidence is enhanced. No longer need children sit next to children simply because nature decreed that they would be born in the same year. Human growth is related to a calendar, but not as intimately as our elementary graded classifications might imply. There are better criteria for grouping than birthdays.

In the primary grades, a single criterion for grouping might be the level of demonstrated ability to read. The ability to read is not singular. Rather, it appears to be a reflection of complexities captured, in the primary years, at least, by the multiple phenomena of maturation and growing self-realization.

Bellevue's experimental Continuous Growth Program has substituted nine levels for the primary grades. The levels correspond roughly to the existent levels of the prepared readers beginning with the preprimer. The ninth level is especially designed for rapid learners. Theoretically, a child may require from two to four years to complete the eight or nine levels before he enters the fourth grade. The majority will require three years of effort.

We do not claim that the Continuous Growth Program is original or unique, but, for Bellevue, it is indigenous. It grew out of local inquiries and developing insights. It is a part of our search for a better individualization of instruction in the elementary school.

We believe that the Continuous Growth Program, through its simple structure, may serve to respond appreciably to the perplexing problems of retention, acceleration, exceptional children, continuous failure, repetition of materials, grouping by chronological age, flexible grouping, fixed standards of achievement within a stated time, and good mental health practices in the classroom.

Attention is directed to the exceptional. There is a thought, yet unproved, that the quality of a school's service to all its pupils is related to the quality of its efforts with the handicapped and with the gifted. Better elementary schools look forward to the day when they may offer a complete community educational service to all children in their attendance areas.

Something inhumane happens to a child who leaves home to become institutionalized in his elementary years when he need not have been sent away. Rapid learners should have the opportunity to learn rapidly; if the ungraded primary will assist, let us examine it. If the ungraded intermediate will assist, let us likewise examine it. Let us not forget, however, that all children, whether gifted or not, must have opportunities to work and plan together somewhere and sometime in their school careers. Mutual appreciation and understanding will preclude factional suspicions.

Democracy may be affected by our methods for individualization in the elementary schools.

A class is a group of human beings. Unfortunately, the exigencies of mass education have tended to equate a class to a cubicle in a building. The four walls of the classroom must become unlimited if quality instruction is desired. A class is a vital social group with important subgroups. It is a miniature society which the alert teacher quickly perceives and utilizes.

Teachers must recognize isolates, subgroups, the total group and all the internal interactions. Attitudes toward school, toward vocational choice and toward life and its purpose may be affected by these interactions. The teacher of a group of human beings must be as eager about each child individually as he is about what is being planned and learned.

Guidance nourishes curriculum and curriculum serves guidance. There is a unity between guidance and curriculum which thwarts attempts at separation. The changing nature of society and its shifting demands are consequential but surely subtle. An elementary school will study the varying degrees of knowledge acquired by pupils outside the school, the impact of TV, travel, community displays and events.

Bellevue recently shifted downward the teaching of many scientific concepts. School people recognized that environmental influences now apparently produce readiness and motivation for the learnings earlier than was believed appropriate a few years ago.

We know more than ever before about the symptoms of predelinquency, and other undesirable deviations which appear in some elementary school children. Better schools are attempting to put this knowledge to use in realistic elementary guidance programs. A psychologically oriented guidance program will translate a child's poor academic achievement or questionable discipline into helpful psychological interpretations. Teachers may then be helped to work more closely with the reality of the child's world rather than with an inaccurate opinion.

The understandings about children which enlightened guidance practices develop must affect the school's curriculum development. Otherwise, there may be danger that the school environment, which may unwittingly help produce deviations in some children, will proceed without correction.

Classes or instructional groups tend to be small. The existence of elementary classes beyond the reasonable limitation of thirty pupils displays a disregard on the part of patrons for the efforts of teachers to individualize instruction. It is widely known that research has not produced conclusive evidence concerning maximum sizes for various instructional purposes. Hence, it must be surmised that better elementary schools will continue to group for various purposes without a preconceived limitation upon size. But if due regard is to be maintained for the important personal relationships which should be established between teacher and pupil, excessive numbers in groups cannot be acceptable. The sacred personality of the child and his uniqueness are neglected if the teacher-pupil ratio enlarges beyond human endurance.

Informed generalists direct the school's administration. An administrator of an elementary school who does not perceive and help teachers design with him the entire pattern of guidance and instructional efforts in the elementary school will distort the children's learning. It is advantageous for a principal to have specialized in some scholarly pursuit in order to help establish a refined appreciation of the services of scholarship and for the sake of his self-acceptance. An administrator of an elementary school, and, equally important, the administrator of school districts, must feel and promote the meanings and values of the humanities as well as the sciences. Administrators must be generalists in order to accomplish this approach to universality!

Central to everything the educator does is the child. The educational plan for children determines the nature of the financial plan and the building program for education. Education is a community effort involving parents, ministers, teachers, youth organizations and other individuals and groups.

An administrator who merely tolerates certain segments of the elementary program should examine the reasons for his feeling. He may need to examine the nature of his preparation and do something about omissions within his preparation if he is responding in an emotional context only.

A respect for scientific inquiry and experimentation prevails. Mother traveled in her Conestoga wagon between Iowa and South Dakota no faster than Julius Caesar or George Washington would have traveled the same route. Not long ago she flew from the West Coast to New York City in an overnight, relaxing flight. Every generation today sees more technical change than all previous generations saw.

No elementary school's staff can ignore the frontiers of science or its methods of inquiry. A good school examines new possibilities even if they appear to be mere variations of older forms. Changing conditions may suggest the adaptation of older forms as well as the creation of new forms. Pilot projects are stimulating to teachers; whether they produce changes in program or not, teachers are better in instruction when they know that they are respected as professional persons.

Parents and patrons help define the goals and purposes of education but the professional educator defines and designates the methods and techniques. Educators cannot permit the erosion of their attempts at professionalization. Parents who want to tell educators how to teach are about as unwelcome in the school scene as they would be if they attempted to direct the surgeon's activities in the operating room of a respected hospital.

Parents know what they want for their children, and they must be heard and heeded. Educators are obligated to inform parents concerning the expansive panorama of society and its varying demands upon children and their schools.

Ten ways in which instruction is geared to the individual in better elementary schools today have been suggested. Will they help you determine whether your school and your school district are more concerned about children than about things?

6. Interest, Effort, and Success— Bases for Effective Reading *

PAUL WITTY

H UGH was 9 years old when we first met—a fine boy, enthusiastic and intelligent. But he had one serious shortcoming. He was unable to read and his secure world was being threatened because his parents, teachers, and friends were causing him to be increasingly disturbed by his limitation.

Standardized tests were given—unwisely it seems now. When words were dictated to find his spelling ability, Hugh wrote *something,* but in only one case in twenty did he write the word dictated. Thus he had learned to comply in his own way to the demands of an impossible situation.

Later I asked him to read aloud some very simple paragraphs. Here the situation was even more embarrassing. He stumbled through the first three paragraphs—mispronouncing, inserting and omitting words. In desperation, he tried to use some phonetic rules which he had practiced again and again. Hugh had been subjected to several phonetic "systems" and had become hopelessly confused by the variations and contradictions in these systems. Moreover, Hugh had seldom been led to appreciate differences as well as similarities in the pronunciation of words. When he met words such as *again*, he began pronouncing *ag,* then he noticed the *in,* and finally *ain.* At last he abandoned his efforts to unlock this word. Some words, such as *school,* which he had already encountered many times, were omitted and substitute terms were introduced. And when Hugh met words such as

* From Paul Witty, "Interest, Effort, and Success—Bases for Effective Reading," *Education* (April, 1959), pp. 480–86. Reprinted by permission of the author and The Bobbs-Merrill Co., Inc., Indianapolis, Ind.

enough and *through* he recognized an insurmountable difficulty and gave up. The blood rushed to his face; "stress" was apparent in every action. Finally, he remarked plaintively, "Mr. Witty, I'd like to show you a boat I built."

We examined Hugh's miniature vessel. His excellent craftsmanship enabled the boat to sail jauntily on a nearby pond. I asked him to tell me about the construction of the boat. He complied and I recorded his fine story. When I read it back to him, he asked, "Did I really say that?" We put many of the words on cards, and read each word several times; then we turned to the complete story which I read aloud to him. Soon he was able to read the story himself. At this time we examined the words on our cards again, noticing beginnings and endings as well as other phonetic characteristics. Then we compiled a list of words which began in the same ways or had other similarities. We also made a list of words in which pronunciation was unusual and irregular. Soon Hugh had acquired a secure "stock" of words which he recognized instantly and pronounced correctly. We composed stories using these words, and added a few others we were learning.

Later simple books on topics related to boats and sailing were introduced; the meaning of many new words was now derived from their context and Hugh found great satisfaction in pronouncing these words and giving their meanings. The process continued in the same way—secure accomplishment built in association with interest and success. As we proceeded with systematic instruction and application, Hugh's insecurity vanished and his reading proficiency increased.

Importance of Interest

The importance of the interest factor in effective reading instruction has been emphasized over and over again by leaders in education. However, surprisingly few comprehensive studies of children's interests are available, and practical techniques for the classroom teacher to use in studying, evaluating, and employing children's interests are also scarce.

Interest is an elusive, subtle and sometimes fleeting characteristic. Yet when captured or awakened it can provide unusual impetus for sustained effort and accomplishment as the foregoing account of Hugh reveals. In this account one sees the value of successful accomplishment in fostering and sustaining an interest in schoolwork. One may note also the importance of successful attainment *from the first* and the significance of the provision of systematic instruction.

The importance of orderly systematic instruction is insufficiently stressed in the literature on the interest factor. We will find that interest is engendered by successful accomplishment and the mastery of the skills in any subject field. Such acquisitions have special significance in remedial endeavor. It should be recognized, too, that it is intensive effort that in many cases really educates. Goals should be attainable but they should require effort as their level is gradually raised, and accomplishment is recognized. Accordingly, we should provide in the primary grades a program that is challenging and that calls forth sustained effort. It does not seem that the use of some of the conventional teaching materials actually accomplishes these objectives. Preprimers and primers sometimes utilize a far too meager vocabulary, repeatedly employed in almost meaningless situations. Thus not only the bright child but others become convinced that reading is a profitless or unrewarding pursuit. In addition, some schools give too little attention to word analysis and phonetic study—intelligently associated with meaningful acquisitions.

The importance of assuring the development of adequate skills that will engender reading for interest can not be overemphasized as a goal of primary instruction. Moreover, the acquisition of increasing proficiency so as to make possible enjoyable and successful reading of more difficult and varied materials continues to be important as the child progresses in school. Even in the junior and senior high school, it is necessary to emphasize reading skills and to provide for their mastery and successful application. It should be recognized that securely mastered skills provide an effective basis for building interest in reading. To be interested in reading, pupils at every level must be led to enjoy the act of reading as well as the results.

Let us now examine the record of another pupil and his gains, traceable in part to the judicious use of books to satisfy individual needs and interests:

Bill, age 10, was brought to the Psycho-Educational Clinic by his mother, who asserted that Bill never read anything but the comics. Moreover, Bill was said to be just like his father who "never reads." Bill's weaknesses and limitations were stressed in his presence with reiteration on the statement that Bill never read anything but the comics. At the conclusion of this recital, the examiner asked Mrs. X to name a few books that she had read recently. After considerable hesitancy and embarrassment, she recalled one title only—a book she had read at the time she had seen a movie of the same title.

Bill's health and general physical condition were excellent. Moreover, his IQ was 128, his academic achievement was slightly above his grade placement, and there was no doubt of Bill's competency insofar as reading skills were involved. However, Bill had received low average or borderline marks in every school subject. When he was questioned concerning his wishes, he replied: I want to be just like my father and do the things he does." To questions about his vocational ambitions and his favored recreational pursuits, his responses reflected his admiration for his father. Bill's father, it seemed, was a man thoroughly acquainted with airplanes, horses, and the customs of people of South America. Bill indicated also an attachment to his cousin—a former lieutenant in the Army. If Bill was unsuccessful as a representative to South America, he might, he said, enlist in the Army.

Bill's program of reading was planned in accord with his interests, and was designed to satisfy certain needs. Accordingly, he was provided with short stories about airplanes and South America. The stories presented a reading difficulty on the level of his demonstrated ability. He progressed rapidly in reading several *New World Neighbor* books about South America. He stated that two travel books illustrated by Disney contained the best stories he had ever read. Suitable books about horses were then procured. Bill enjoyed several of the stories in Fenner's *Horses, Horses, Horses.* He read Farley's *The Black Stallion,* James' *Smokey, The Cow Horse,* and *King of the Wind.*

By this time Bill was enjoying reading. To assure further mastery of habits and skills in reading he received systematic training in several books devised for use in the Army, the *Army Reader* and *Meet Private Pete.* These experiences proved particularly rewarding. Bill reported his satisfaction in discussing the contents of these books with his cousin.

In Bill's case, many factors contributed to his progress. His reading gains were attributable in part to his more successful mastery of skills as well as to the close association of his reading experience with his needs and interests. Some of his improvement was undoubtedly traceable also to improved conditions and modified attitudes at home. After several weeks, Bill's mother telephoned, stating that "everyone was now reading at home." Bill's gains were fostered, too, by discussions of books with his father and with his cousin, as well as by opportunities provided for him to contribute to class projects information he had accumulated through reading.

Most teachers will grant the worth of a program that satisfies interests and fulfills needs. Many are well acquainted already with tests and measures that will enable them to ascertain each child's reading ability and hence to begin instruction on a level at which success is assured. But they may be less confident about procedures for studying interest and may inquire: How is it possible to ascertain the interests of boys and girls in a typical classroom?

A number of practical child-study procedures have been devised which classroom teachers can utilize effectively. One of the most widely used of these approaches is the anecdotal method which has been fully described by Daniel Prescott and his associates. In its simplest form, the anecdotal method is merely a transcription or a record of behavior or conduct which the teacher believes to be significant. A combination of anecdotal with other methods is used by some teachers in attempts to understand children's behavior and needs. For example, a teacher may observe that on the playground John tends habitually to associate with younger children and strives to be the leader at all times. In the classroom, too, John repeatedly seeks attention. When he is not the center of interest, he is inclined to withdraw from each group. A notation of such observations is filed as a part of John's record. On investigating the home, the teacher may discover additional related facts of significance. In this case, she finds that eight-year-old John, the youngest of a large family, has been for several years the object of excessive attention on the part of indulgent parents and older brothers and sisters. This concern started when John was 4, following a serious and prolonged illness. Fully recovered at 6, John continued to demand attention until the life of his home came largely to revolve about his whims and desires. An appreciation of these facts caused John's teacher to plan a series of experiences in which he was led gradually to take his place as a contributing, considerate member of various groups. Discussion of John's needs with his parents brought the establishment of a more wholesome home regime and a change in attitude. Under these conditions, John's behavior as well as his accomplishment improved. Increase in the use of child-study techniques in this way by regular classroom teachers is indeed heartening.

The Interest Inventory

Another child-study technique, widely used by teachers is the "interest inventory." Guided by an inventory, the teacher and the pupil discuss informally topics such as favorite leisure activities, hobbies, play preferences, movie and reading habits, familiarity with community places of interest, and modes of transportation. The following items selected from Part I of the *Northwestern University Interest Inventory* illustrate this type of question: "When you have an hour or two that you can spend just as you please, what do you like best to do?" Are you making any collections? Of what? Do you have a hobby? What?

The *Inventory* includes questions related to the child's personal and social problems. Here is an illustrative item:

Suppose you could have three wishes which might come true. What would be your first wish? Second wish? Third wish?

Part II of this *Inventory* contains a list of eighty play activities reported as favorites in extensive investigations of school children. Study of the extent and nature of each child's play activities may yield important insights as to his interests and also as to the adequacy and maturity of his social development.

Part III of this *Inventory* is a list containing titles of popular books. Discussion with the pupil of his reading often adds to the teacher's understanding of a child's needs. Part IV is designed to help the teacher evaluate the child's responses throughout the interview. It contains a check list to be used in describing and interpreting the child's attitude, his understanding of the questions, and the reliability of his responses. Items are included to encourage the teacher to estimate the adequacy of the child's play life, his background of experience, and his association with others. Finally, the teacher selects worthy interests that can be satisfied or extended by reading. On occasion, the teacher may find so meager a pattern that she recognizes immediately a responsibility for helping the child to acquire new interests.

By associating instruction in reading with worth-while interests, the efficiency of learning is usually heightened. The study of children's interests thus has become a central concern on the part of many efficient teachers. One child expressed unwittingly the value of such an effort: "My teacher helps me most because she understands me. She always knows the right thing for me to read. And she always shows me how to get the book I need."

A Most General Interest

When one investigates the interests of children, he will discover the affection of children for TV and the seemingly disproportionate amount of time given to televiewing. Of course, children and youth also give considerable time to listening to the radio. And they spend additional time in reading the comics. Some critics assert that these activities consume so much time that little is left for outdoor activities or for reading from books of superior quality. On the other hand, some writers point out that a favored pursuit such as televiewing may be employed to engender interest in reading.

It is difficult to state just how much TV has influenced reading, either adversely or desirably. There are, of course, diverse opinions. But one writer, Arnold L. Lazarus, states:

. . . Whether because of TV or in spite of it, youngsters (both elementary and secondary) are reading more than ever, according to unanimous reports of librarians, (school and public).

Although children may, on the average, be reading somewhat more today than formerly, there are many who read poorly and others who read very little. But almost without exception, they are attracted by TV.

From the first, children followed the electronic Pied Piper with enthusiasm. "TV is the greatest thing I know," said seven-year-old Tom, whose parents had just bought a TV set. And his somewhat older sister Mary said, "I like TV better than radio or anything else. It's exciting and you learn from it too."

Children now spend upwards of twenty hours a week with television during most of the year. Throughout the summer they average about fourteen hours a week. High school students devote less time to TV—between fourteen and seventeen hours a week most of the year. From such figures one may see that television emerges as a favorite leisure "activity" of children and youth.

Even before TV came to us, writers pointed to children's increasing tendency to turn to sedentary activities such as riding in an automobile, listening to the radio, and watching other people compete in sports. "Bleacher athletes" instead of participants were being developed. Today with TV consuming so much time, many children appear to be dominated by passive pursuits and by a search for entertainment—largely effortless and often profitless. Edgar Dale writes:

Our almost compulsive search for entertainment is a malady that can both debilitate and destroy. . . .

We need entertainment just as we need sleep, but we can have far too much of it. Entertainment provides vitamins but few calories. We need the meat and potatoes of education.

In a similar vein, Marya Mannes comments on the present-day domination of a quest for recreation:

I doubt whether even among the privileged classes during the days of Pericles, Ancient Rome, the Middle Ages, or the Renaissance, entertainment was more than periodic and less than an occasion. And I know that during my own average youth, only four or five times a year did we go to a play, and to a movie never more than once a fortnight. These were excitements long anticipated and long remembered. The thought of having them constantly accessible never entered the mind. If it had it would have been rejected as preposterous or sinful. Nowadays it seems preposterous *not* to avail oneself constantly of diversion, since a flick of a knob can produce it.

I do not propose to draw any somber conclusions from this fact of our civilization except to point out that the whole man or woman does not need nor want this constant diversion. That is why, except for professionals concerned either productively or critically with the media, you will find very few people of spiritual or mental substance who turn on television or radio more than a few hours a week. When they do, it is to seek reality and not to escape from it.

The antidote to the undesirable aspects of TV, radio, movies, and the comics, lies in the provision of a constructive program of guidance for children and young people. In working together on such a program, parents and teachers should try to offer boys and girls opportunities for play and creative pursuits of many kinds that will balance their craze for passive activities. Together, they should discuss the merits and limitations of favorite TV programs, and develop criteria for the use of leisure.

There has been during the past year, a large amount of criticism of the reading ability and reading habits of boys and girls. Often TV is pointed to as an activity detrimental to the development of interest in leisure reading. Single panaceas have been proposed; for example, the teaching of phonics by parents. Such an effort would help little in meeting this complex problem. Of course many children do need to be helped to develop more effective habits and skills in reading. The ability to recognize new words and to pronounce them is one of these skills. But such children usually need to develop other skills such as critical reading and rapid silent reading. And they need to be encouraged to read widely too, and to cultivate a permanent interest in reading as a leisure pursuit. Certainly the establishment of better reading habits and skills is a necessity for many children if they are to be led to enjoy reading. This will mean the introduction of better primary instruction and the use of more meaningful teaching materials. Not only do we need a more effective introduction to reading in the primary grades, but we need also a continuous program of help and guidance in reading throughout the elementary and secondary school.

It is true that many widely used textbooks especially at the primary levels, include materials that are too repetitious, limiting and uninteresting. There are, however, some textbooks which contain a minimum of such materials. These books, less frequently used, introduce children to highly exciting stories—old and new—of unmistakable merit.

There is, in addition, the world of children's literature which should become a part of a balanced reading program. Films and film readers may also be used to advantage in such a program.

Parents and teachers should gain acquaintance with many excellent recently published books as well as with children's classics, and they should encourage children to become regular patrons of the library. In home as well as in school, they should strive to provide an atmosphere conducive to wide reading.

TV does offer a real temptation for children who read poorly to escape into a pleasant, effortless pastime. For other children, televiewing may consume too much of their time and lead to little development or progress. But interest in TV can become an asset if parents and teachers will attempt not only to help children read better, but also to encourage them to associate reading with worth-while interests engendered by presentations on TV.

In the case of other strong interests this same procedure may be used to advantage. Accordingly, strong interests should be studied and utilized as avenues for engendering stronger motivation and satisfaction in productive educational effort. Such endeavor recognizes the necessity for the cultivation of more effective habits and skills which may in themselves lead to greater interest and zeal for learning. This combined emphasis on the roles played by interest and by skill will undoubtedly result in more efficient and successful learning.

7. *Reading Readiness* *

THOMAS J. MALONEY

IT IS WELL for the teacher to come face to face with the reasons for failure in first grade reading. Frequently, despite the use of the best techniques for teaching beginning reading, the teacher's efforts are not rewarded. The truth of the matter is that many of these six-year-old children are physically, mentally, socially or emotionally immature for such a demanding task. Many youngsters also lack a proper experience background. They do not have the necessary common concepts to give meaning to the word symbols which they must use in beginning reading. Too early an attempt to teach reading to these children results in failure, discouragement and emotional involvement for the child at a time when he should taste of success. For the teacher this represents expenditure of tremendous effort with little reward.

Remember, children who seem to be remedial readers are often actually readiness problems. Children who enter first grade come from a variety of

* From Thomas J. Maloney, "Reading Readiness," *Grade Teacher,* Special Section to Help You Teach Reading (April, 1955), pp. 27, 70. Reprinted by permission of the author and *Grade Teacher.*

backgrounds. Some have had rich kindergarten experiences while others come directly from homes of limited background. Time spent on a reading readiness program at the beginning of grade one will provide a smoother shift from kindergarten or home. Failure, and its attendant emotional problems, will be reduced. Dividends will be paid as the beginning reading program develops.

An attempt is made here to summarize, very briefly, the factors which make up readiness for first grade reading and to discover how we may evaluate the child's readiness for beginning reading. Then we will consider what constitutes a good broad program of reading readiness for grade one and discover when we may introduce the beginning reading program.

What Factors Make Up Reading Readiness?

GOOD PHYSICAL HEALTH

The six-year-old must possess sufficient physical vigor to attempt the job of reading. Also, it is apparent that the child with deficiencies of sight or hearing will have difficulty with reading. If his sight is defective, he will not be able to make the fine visual discriminations necessary to distinguish one word from another. If his hearing is defective, he may mistake one spoken word for another. Poor hearing reduces the child's vocabulary and he will lack ability to sound words.

EXPERIENCE

Words are only symbols. If the child lacks sufficient breadth of experience, the common concepts which the printed words represent may be a complete blank for him. Good home and kindergarten training will provide this experience. Children lacking these experiences are not ready for first grade reading.

SOCIAL DEVELOPMENT

Some six-year-old children are infantile and overdependent. They will be hampered in their attempt to read in a group situation. Proper social development of the child is necessary for reading readiness.

EMOTIONAL DEVELOPMENT

Adjusting to school is a big job. If the six-year-old child comes to school emotionally disturbed, his reading efforts will be blocked. Furthermore, too early attempts to read will increase the child's emotional stress. Good mental hygiene is essential for reading readiness.

MENTAL AGE

Frequently the six-year-old child does not have a six-year-old mentality. Although there is no magic in the concept, it is safe to say that with the common approach to beginning reading, a mental age of 6 or 6½ is necessary for successful beginning reading.

LANGUAGE SKILLS

Fluent oral language is necessary for reading readiness. A child must have a rich oral vocabulary and be able to express ideas in sentence form if he is to attempt to read. It is also vital that the child should be able to listen attentively and remember what he has heard.

INTEREST IN BOOKS

An interest in books along with an awareness of the help and pleasure they may bring is essential to reading readiness.

When Is a Six-Year-Old Ready for First Grade Reading?

OBSERVATION

Take time during the beginning of the school year to make a systematic inventory of your pupils' readiness for reading. This is easily accomplished. Consider and remember the readiness factors listed above. Give your children a free program which permits active play, participation in group activities and games involving sight and sound discrimination. It is important to provide opportunities to develop oral language, lessons involving attentive listening to the teacher or fellow pupils, as well as activities demanding motor coordination, exercises involving interpretation, excursions and opportunities to "read" books and to listen to the telling of stories.

During this time observe the child's social and emotional adjustment. Note the child's attention span. How mature is his conversation? How adequate is his motor control? Can he follow directions? Is he overdependent, shy or aggressive? Does he participate successfully in the group situation? Is he interested in stories and books? Does he pay close attention to differences as he looks and listens?

These will be some measures of his readiness. Use the best services you have available to test his sight and hearing. A statement of health from the child's physician, when given in detail, is most helpful in determining the physical state of the child's readiness for reading.

CONFERENCES

You can discover much about the child's readiness to read if you consult with those who know him well. Confer with his parents and his kindergarten teacher. Learn about his strengths and weaknesses at home and in previous school situations.

TESTS

There are several reading readiness tests which may be administered by the classroom teacher. These frequently provide good measures of specific factors of the readiness situation such as auditory and visual discrimination, motor control, articulation and language. These tests often indicate likely rate of progress in reading throughout the year.

Intelligence tests, where wisely administered by competent persons, will provide basic information concerning readiness, including the child's mental age. Several of the publishers of standard reading series have provided excellent reading readiness booklets. These are often set up so that the teachers may use them as informal tests of various aspects of the child's reading readiness. As such they are very helpful.

8. *Reading Is a Private Affair* *

ROMA GANS

MANY TEACHERS today ask questions about grouping children in reading. On what basis to group? How to work with groups? How measure the success of groups? These are important questions, but in the quest for grouping the paramount importance of what robust Jerry or jovial Sally or silent Alice do in their own intellectualizing must be respected because that is what makes them grow as readers.

Have you ever noticed a young toddler look intently at a magazine page which he opens on the floor? What does he see? What is he thinking? We wonder, but most likely this remains his private affair. At 3 or at 4 we

* From Roma Gans, "Reading Is a Private Affair," *Grade Teacher,* Special Section to Help You Teach Reading (April, 1955), pp. 26, 66. Reprinted by permission of the author and *Grade Teacher.*

commonly observe one of these investigators fingering the print on a box or container, lost in serious study. Is he thinking, I wonder what these letters spell, or, Now what can this mean? He may by now ask, What does this say? or even report, Here's an *o*. However, just what goes on in his thinking we may not entirely discover.

So too with the six-year-old who sits and silently looks into his primer or a book from the library shelf, or the great investigator of 8 who peruses a shopper's guide, or the teen-ager lost to all activity about him as he digs into a story in a magazine, or for that matter, the adult with breakfast coffee at hand serenely working his way through the Sunday newspaper.

Our reading can be described, discussed and examined, but its most important characteristic is that it involves our innermost thinking which we may or may not reveal. Therefore it is a private affair, even when it goes on in a group.

This is "unhandy" for today's teachers, with their classrooms virtually heaped with children. For example, the first grade teacher with thirty-four sprouting readers noticed that Angela responded to all the work of the day in a responsive manner. She listened, while suggestions were given to her group; she helped a latecomer turn to the correct page; she listened as the first member started to read. When her turn came, she began, then paused before saying the word "come." What was going on in that pause? Was she trying to remember where she had seen that word before, and with the help of such memory, recall the word? Was she spelling it to herself to give her the boost to recognize it? Was she thinking, What word would make sense in this sentence?

In beginning reading these pauses would tell a teacher so much, if one could fathom what they meant. Some children tell how they figure out a word. This is an excellent practice, and wise is the teacher who encourages it. But—how find time and a calm enough classroom atmosphere in which to establish such personal relationships with one child? That is the $64 question for the most competent teachers of our time. Actually a child profits immeasurably from such guidance; parents hope for it, and the general public seems to imply that it should be going on. It does, wherever a teacher respects the personal qualities in reading, and transcends the handicaps in the teaching situation to accomplish the almost impossible.

The Family Can Help

It is heartening to see a busy mother accept an interruption as the busy teacher does, to listen to an eager reader display his progress by reading from a book, or spelling a newly acquired word or relating a discovery made while reading an advertisement or article in an encyclopedia. Older brothers and sisters play a very helpful part in listening, aiding and abetting younger sprouts. In a meeting with parents in Yonkers, New York, on the topic of Helping Youngsters Succeed in Reading, several intermediate grade teachers brought their pupils to the meeting. The assumption was that these eleven- and twelve-year-olds would listen to a lecture and the parents' discussion that followed it. Not so. Once the discussion began, parents and children entered in with equal insight, understanding and helpful suggestions.

Comprehension Is Vital

Getting the meaning out of what is read, commonly called *comprehending* is of course central to the skills of reading. Why read if it means nothing? Even to the very young listener *meanings* are important. Yet we find great personal variation in this complex power. Some read and ramble on, not thinking or half understanding, while others may almost be seen to pause and think. Which youngsters are becoming critical thinkers? Which seem unable to dig in even if they are able to pronounce and even grasp the meaning of the words? These are important questions for every teacher to answer about each youngster.

Many ways have been devised by teachers and publishers to help teachers know the progress of children as thinking readers. Standardized tests, workbooks, exercises in textbooks are frequently used. Creative teachers think up fascinating ideas of their own to add to the more common ones. For example, in one sixth grade each pupil submitted one sentence for a "balmy" test. The sentence could be a statement of fact or a "balmy" idea. "Balmy" was used by these youngsters to mean phony, or untrue. Each contributor was held responsible to know the correct answer, true or balmy, for his sentence. The test was duplicated with the thirty-two sentences, followed by the donor's name and a space for writing in "true" or "balmy." The teacher reported that the discussion which followed this test was more challenging and vigorous than any she had ever experienced. She gained information, not only from the sentences submitted but also by the responses and the subsequent discussion, about the individual quality of thinking of each one of the class. This she followed up with individual work for the noncritical and developed more penetrating work in reading for the deep thinkers.

Reading Must Be Individual

Such experiences as the foregoing reveal the waste of time for keen thinkers to do so-called regular grade work. They also indicate the waste to continue source work for youngsters who need help on methods of work basic to learning. One teacher, unsatisfied with her progress in finding time to guide pupils in such personal manner, was told by a jaded "specialist," "Oh, forget about it. This personal reading is the kind of stuff college professors dream up and talk about. It can't be done in school." To speak glibly about the ability to teach each child according to his needs is a disservice to the valiant teacher who struggles to approximate this goal. But to wave it aside as impossible is to make a hoax of teaching.

To add to the already enormous responsibility of helping each child to grow from the step by step of word recognition to critical independent reading, one more phase of reading needs mentioning, namely taste. Whether or not each youngster acquires a preference for good books or trashy ones, a newspaper of high professional quality or one of tabloid qualities, and reading content based on clean, decent interests or that catering to the lurid and the obscene, that is also the teacher's and parent's concern.

Much is involved in the development of personal preferences for printed matter. Many youngsters are educated to prefer the bad by the very absence of the good. Many, through lack of worthy interests in home and school, pick up, through chance contacts, interests of an undesirable order. Some may remain "tasteless"—reading whatever someone urges them or whatever is handiest. Therefore the importance of a program of education and a quality in family life which gives youngsters a chance to get interested in desirable things cannot be overemphasized. Nor can too much stress be placed on the need to have an unlimited supply of books, magazines, newspapers and bulletins available. And, of course, as much quiet time for reading, both in and out of school, as can be managed.

Teachers and parents discover children's interests and tastes more readily in a situation where materials are easily accessible and youngsters pick up and put down at will. Then, if there is a relaxed discussion about reading in the classroom and in family gatherings, one can discover what children like, what intrigues them, what bores them and, at times, why they are irritated by reading. One pensive boy in the third grade said, "I like to read when it's quiet and I don't have to stop right away. But here and at home there is so much noise, and just when you get started you always get told to do this, do that. That's what I don't like about reading."

From the points here presented a teacher can develop a plan of action for teaching reading on a personal basis. Let no teacher feel guilty if he only approximates these suggestions. To find time and comfortable moments for personal guidance in crowded schoolrooms and despite hectic schedules is indeed difficult. But to make plans toward doing a better job in reorganizing the personal side of each child's reading assures the teacher of progress toward this goal. Organizing groups to work together is a helpful practice for boosting reading growth because children are able to assist one another in a wholesome way under the teacher's supervision. However, the responsibility to guide each child in becoming an avid and selective reader demands that a teacher strive to know what each child is acquiring, not only in skills and general reading power, but also in his attitudes toward reading and his preferences. My hat goes off to the teachers who valiantly struggle to meet this responsibility and to the parents who also sense the possibility of helping youngsters in this important private affair—reading.

9. *An Individualized Reading Program* *

CHARLOTTE L. MILLMAN

W E STARTED with four groups in September based on the standardized reading test plus teacher judgment and informal textbook test. Six children on grade three level read from *More Streets and Roads;* a second group on fifth grade level was reading *Merry Hearts and Bold;* a third group read *More People and Progress* (grade six) and the fourth group read *Paths and Pathfinders.* (Grade seven to ten).

To initiate the IRP, I asked the class to evaluate our reading program. These were the major criticisms:

1. Some of the stories in the basic reader were boring and were read only because they had to read them.
2. Some children read faster than others and had to wait for the entire group to finish the story before it could be discussed.
3. The skills taught to the entire group were often not needed by some individual in the group.

* From Charlotte L. Millman, "An Individualized Reading Program," *Elementary English* (October, 1958), pp. 386–88. Reprinted by permission of the author and the National Council of Teachers of English.

When I suggested IR the class was most enthusiastic. They liked the idea of self-choice, self-pacing, and fluid grouping in skills they needed. They wanted to know if they might take the books home to read. This might be done, I said, if they brought the books back to school each day. Failure to do so would mean they might forfeit the privilege of reading the book at home.

What books to use? That was the first problem. Our classroom library consists of books excellent for reference in social studies, nature, and science. Since few of these books were likely to be selected I told them they might select books from our school library (which is next door to our room); they might bring books from their home libraries (which I must first approve) and books from the public library.

I had prepared a chart showing that there were books to suit every interest: Adventure, Animal Stories, Arts, Hobbies, Biography, Circus, Baseball, Cowboys, Fairy Tales, School Stories, Holidays, Funny Books, Mysteries, Myths, Nature, Science, Sports, Travel, Series Books, Poetry Books, People and Faraway Places, Magazines, etc. We discussed the advisability of reading many different types of literature. We suggested browsing and reading several pages of a book before "taking it out." I "advertised" several books by showing illustrations, (Robert Lawson's *Ben and Me,* Lawson's *They Were Strong and Good,* A. A. Milne *Now We Are Six*). I read several pages of funny parts from Herbert's *Remarkable Improvement, Homer Price* and *Rootabaga Stories.*

We discussed and initiated routines to be followed. Each day there would be two librarians who would sit at the classroom library table. We have a box of library cards on which the child enters the title of the book and date. The librarians will check. Each child would set up his reading notebook. He would record daily the following information: Date—Title of book—Pages read that day—Summary of pages read—Interesting words.

What do we do when we finish a book? That was the next problem for discussion. We decided that we could write a book review and illustrate it; write a blurb; make a book jacket; prepare a panel discussion with others who have read the book; find out something about the author; follow directions and make something after reading a "How to" book; perform an experiment suggested in a science book; write a poem; give a summary to the class; describe the characters; read funny parts or exciting parts or mysterious or poetic parts to the class. I in turn would keep a record of each child's reading with notations as to specific oral and silent reading skills he needed drill in. I explained how the reading period would be conducted.

It was now time to select a book. Several chose to continue reading their

Basic Readers; two selected *Science for Today and Tomorrow* from the classroom library; another chose *Children's Literature* from the classroom library. The rest (about thirty of the thirty-six children) chose books from the school library (*Book of Myths, Venus Boy, Miss Pickerell Series, Pippi Longstocking, Homer Price, Better Baseball, Dr. Doolittle, Prehistoric America, The Straw Ox, Wizard of Oz, Tom Edison, Boy Inventor, McWhinney's Jaunt, Mr. Twigg's Mistake, Blue Ribbons for Meg, It Happened to Hannah, Just-So Stories, Spanish Cave, Now We Are Six,* etc.).

We got down to reading. Actual reading time is about thirty-five to forty minutes. I work with three or four children one at a time at my desk to discover silent and oral reading weaknesses. I make note of common skill weaknesses and teach such skills to the groups that need such drill. The groups are fluid, not fixed. They are based solely on common weaknesses as I discover them day by day in the individual interviews. After the individual interviews, I walk around the room and note what is being done by several rows of children—asking how they like the book, is it too easy—too hard— have they read anything else by that author—asking a question about a page read—suggesting some interesting words to look up in anticipation of pages beyond what they've read.

The last ten minutes we call the "Sharing Time." I call several to read their brief summaries of pages read today; several to read any interesting words found (interesting because of pronunciation, multiple meaning, etc.); poetic figures of speech (many such in *Mio, My Son* and *Rootabaga Stories* and *Just So Stories*); humorous passages; facts learned; description of character or background. I sometimes ask for alternate titles or alternate endings.

From the individual interviews I plan my class and group lessons. I found instruction and drill needed in the following:

phonics (blending)
word attack–compound words; initial consonant sounds
lessons on varying pronunciations of vowel sounds
lessons on accent; syllabication
lessons on multiple meanings of words
recognizing and understanding sequence
transposing ideas into own words
making inferences
getting the central thought
skimming
following directions
how to use the telephone directory

how to use the *World Almanac*

how to use *Who's Who,*

Since we started the program my records show that the number of books read range from one book read by Michael Amerosa to seventy-eight read by Linda Sultan (in school and at home) with the average number of nine.

Our class chart "Books on Parade" is faithfully filled in by each child who finishes reading any one of some fifty books. They indicate by different colored circles whether they thought the book was excellent, good, fair, or poor. We have some fifty or sixty book reviews written by classmates which are eagerly read for leads to the next book the child wants to read. Our autograph collection of popular children's authors is growing by leaps and bounds and we're hoping to entice a real live author to come and visit our class. We're in the process of completing a huge mural for the school library of favorite scenes from our favorite books. We're completing our puppets of story-book characters and writing an original puppet show for auditorium presentation. We have promised to lend our puppets to the Highlawn Branch of the Brooklyn Public Library for display.

The children in my class like the Individualized Reading Program.

10. *Reading Tips for Beginning Teachers* *

RALPH C. STAIGER

AND MARY BAIRD

E ACH YEAR a group of inexperienced teachers enters the teaching profession. Some are newly graduated college men and women; others are mature women who have raised families and now are doing their part to relieve a teacher shortage; there is a sprinkling of retired servicemen who want to teach. But no matter what the background of beginning teachers, they usually have qualms about facing a classroom full of youngsters for the first time.

* From Ralph C. Staiger and Mary Baird, "Reading Tips for Beginning Teachers," *Education* (May, 1958), pp. 538–41. Reprinted by permission of the authors and The Bobbs-Merrill Co., Inc., Indianapolis, Ind.

It is to the prospective and beginning teacher that these suggestions are made. Although the tips are primarily concerned with reading instruction they must of necessity touch upon other influences which are general in nature, but which affect reading. Children do not learn to read in a vacuum. All the other activities and influences in a classroom can affect the success of your reading program. Judge for yourself how these tips can help you become a successful teacher.

Make friends. Perhaps it is unnecessary to remind a teacher that personal relationships with pupils can color their learning to read. Many a retarded reader has been helped to overcome his difficulty because his teacher, a reading clinician, or a tutor took an interest in him and gave him confidence. Learning to read is an individual matter for every child. If the learning atmosphere is a friendly, stimulating one, reading skills will more likely be absorbed. Occasionally a teacher lavishes false attention and praise on a child. Children see through this false attention quickly. It is usually a good idea to underplay the friendliness and make it genuine instead of broadcasting affection to the winds and have none of it land on fertile ground.

Make friends with parents, too, if you want to be a successful teacher. In your pupils you have excellent public relations agents. Use them. Parents are usually much interested in what their children are learning. When you have an opportunity to praise a child for a job well done, a note home will pay big dividends.

Take a positive attitude with parents instead of a negative one, and watch your parent-teacher relationships become useful and solid. Don't be two-faced with parents. They will see through your false praise, too. It will take them somewhat longer than their children to uncover your hypocrisies, but they will find you out eventually.

Open criticism by parents can do considerable damage in destroying a child's faith in your work. Avoid it by giving each child a taste of success from the first day, and showing him by your actions that you are proud of his accomplishments.

Enjoy yourself. Pity the person who hates children, but is teaching school. And pity the children in his class. Your day will go quickly, and you will be happier, if you relax and enjoy your work.

Most children enjoy learning. If they sense that you, too, are enjoying the story at hand, and enjoy leading them to full understandings they will continue their happy attitudes toward learning. Pleasure and enthusiasm are contagious.

Expect variations. Your class will contain children of many sizes and descriptions. Although they will usually have about the same chronological age, your pupils will have varying abilities and interests. Don't expect that all will profit from reading instruction at the same reader level. And don't attempt the impossible—teaching them so that they will all be reading at the same level. Research studies show that when a class has had good teaching, the pupils will vary even more at the end of the year than they varied at the beginning. Good teaching makes the good readers better, and helps the poor readers become good. Good teaching does not "bring everyone up to grade level."

Find out as soon as you can about the variations in reading ability in your class, so that you can adjust your instruction early. And try not to make permanent decisions about a child's abilities. Changes will occur during the year—spurts of growth in reading that will give you big thrills, for you will know that you are doing a good job.

Know Where You Are Going. How you fit into the total picture of your school's reading program is something you ought to find out early. Discuss the over-all program with your principal or supervisor, and plan your work so that you will not be a square cog in the machinery. The amount of guidance you will get varies in different school systems. Usually an understanding of the details of a program can be had from the local course of study and/or your teacher's manual. It will be worth your while to study these early so that you will know what the jobs ahead will be.

Organize and Plan. Once you have an overview of the program, time spent in planning, getting materials ready, reading the coming story, and otherwise establishing readiness in yourself for teaching the lesson will be time well spent. Time spent in the afternoon, or before the children arrive in the morning in getting ready will pay off in peace of mind.

Every once in a while, it will be useful to take stock of how you are doing your job. Try to be objective about yourself and your youngsters, decide what changes you must make to better meet their needs and yours.

Planning ahead does not necessarily mean planning every detail: It should mean instead making your job easier because you know where you are going and how you expect to get there. Don't overorganize to the point that when unanticipated events take place you will be left with only a blank expression on your face. Children's ideas are many and varied; they will often be ahead of you.

Use your manual. The teacher's manual which accompanies your reader is designed to lighten your load, help you plan your work, and make useful suggestions. If you do not have a manual available, ask your principal or supervisor for a manual. If none is in the building, write—

preferably on school stationery—to the publisher. He is interested in your using the readers in the most efficient way, and will usually provide a manual at little or no cost. It is wise to mention in your letter that you are using his readers in your classroom.

For a beginning teacher, there is no better friend than a manual. You will probably find, after a while, that you will want to vary from the suggestions somewhat. Since the authors of the series could not possibly anticipate every situation you will find yourself in, variations are usually a good idea. In fact, be alert for the manuals of other publishers for ideas. Remember, though, that the activities suggested in a manual are usually too much for any one lesson. You will soon see that only those parts of the manual which are useful to your pupils should be followed. Use your manual for help in preparing a lesson, teaching it, grouping your children, testing supplementary reading and individual help.

Balance skills. In deciding what you should choose from the manual, try always to keep the needs of the pupils in mind. Don't go overboard on one type of word-recognition exercise to the exclusion of other skills. If your pupils have had a great deal of practice with one type of exercise in previous classes, and you are satisfied that no more learning or useful overlearning is taking place, omit that exercise.

Reading is not the only avenue of learning, and teachers must use many approaches to help children understand concepts of various kinds. Pictures, models, recordings, motion pictures, television, and other aids should be used whenever they do a better job than reading can do. Children should use their skills of observation and listening as well as reading skills for learning.

Keep records. There is much value in keeping records of achievement in reading and in other areas. A daily notation of observations will be a big help when report card time arrives. Standardized tests will help you judge the reliability of your observations. Sometimes a teacher is surprised to find that the pupil who has been uncommunicative and apparently dull is really absorbing more than anyone realized.

Samples of children's work should be kept, along with your observations and test scores. Parent conferences are usually more constructive and pleasant when evidence is at hand. Your opinion is worth far more when it is backed up with documents, and examples of work will help a parent understand what you are doing better than any verbal explanation.

As soon as possible, you should acquaint yourself with any previous records available. The school's permanent record card might contain valuable information for helping to understand a child. But make your own judgments. Your predecessor might not have been as objective as you are, and might have passed a one-sided picture on to you.

Foster outside reading. The reading done in school is designed ultimately for the purpose of having the pupils read well in their daily activities. A reading program based on basal readers alone is anaemic, for readers should be steppingstones to many varied reading activities. Encourage, by many means, your children to read books and magazines in which they have an interest, and which they can read. Brightly colored book jackets are like magnets which draw young children to the library table. Book clubs, book programs, book games, book exhibits, talks about books, and book-exchanges among pupils will encourage an interest in reading outside of school.

A final word. Part of your pay as a teacher will be in the achievements of your pupils. While this will not buy groceries, it is certainly worth considering. Unfortunately, there will be days when you will have to look carefully to find evidence of achievement. Everything you have planned falls through, your pupils seem to miss the point, and you feel that all your work is for nothing. It is perfectly normal for this to happen occasionally—"The best laid plans of mice and men gang aft agley." Don't feel too let down if this happens once in a while. If it becomes a regular occurrence, and your days never seem to go right, it is time to take stock of yourself, your students, your plans, and your work. Try not to let yourself get in this position. The chances are you won't.

11. *Looking Ahead in Teaching Reading* *

NILA BANTON SMITH

WE ARE on the brink of a new epoch in reading instruction. Our imperatives are clearly outlined. We have but to observe the onrush of social forces about us, to feel the impact of the new psychologies and philosophies, to examine recent research in order to know that reading instruction must change in many ways.

* From Nila Banton Smith, "Looking Ahead in Teaching Reading," *NEA Journal* (October, 1955), pp. 416–17. Reprinted by permission of the author and the *NEA Journal*.

In the future, reading instruction must concern itself with much more than pedagogy. It must mesh more directly into the gears of vital social problems and needs. It must make its contribution to American life and ideals. This necessity can be illustrated by a brief review of the history of reading instruction in our country.

Reading in the Past

During our first historical period of reading instruction, both method and materials served the religious motive, which was the all-controlling force in the out-of-school life of early Americans. During the period following the Revolutionary War, both reading methods and materials took upon themselves the obligation of building good citizens for young America.

As years passed, security for the new nation became assured. Then followed a tranquil period in which there were no urgent social problems. Education settled down to the pedagogy of reading, and reading materials were selected in terms of the particular pedagogy which was popular at the moment.

During this period of complacency, extending to the present, we have hidden our heads in the sand of pedagogy and concerned ourselves largely with such things as methods and vocabulary and readability. We have grown mightily in our knowledge of these things and are teaching reading less painfully and more effectually because of this knowledge.

But now the situation has changed. Again we find America thrust into a period of insecurity. Is it not time for us to take stock of our urgent social problems and to examine the contribution which reading instruction might make to the exigencies of American life? If the answer is "Yes," then certain musts are in order.

Carry-Over Interests

We must strive, as we have never striven before, to develop wide, permanent, carry-over interests in reading. Social change is striding across the reading habits of America with a heavy tread. Reading is now faced with many competing agencies. Radio, television, movies, and picture magazines afford the average person about all the entertainment and information that he desires.

Rather than accept a brief summary of news items from a commentator, together with his particular interpretation, Americans need to read widely for themselves, to sift personally the wheat from the chaff, and to draw their own conclusions. All this means that we must exert ourselves as never before in developing vigorous, permanent interests in reading.

To develop more abiding interests, instruction in reading must be made increasingly attractive to children. Teachers must put to work all their enthusiasm, energy, and ingenuity, not only in making the most of every reading situation, but also in causing every reading activity to be fascinating.

More challenging materials are needed. Children of today are sophisticated; much of the material they are supposed to read in school is below their level of intelligence and understanding. They must be surrounded with quantities of books of appropriate difficulty dealing with an almost endless variety of subjects.

The present-day child is far beyond the naïveté of the child of a generation ago. We must meet him on his own ground and in his own world if we expect to deepen and hold his interest in reading.

Thoughtful Reading

Not only must we develop a keener interest in reading, but we must also develop the ability and desire to abstract deeper meanings from what we read. If future America is to meet its pressing problems, it must be an informed America. An informed American must understand fully what he is reading. Passive acceptance of surface meanings is not enough. We need to *think* as we read.

All too often experiences which children receive in working with reading in the classroom are those in which not much thinking is done. It is the type in which they simply give back some statement from the text: "What was Mary playing with?" and the text says, "Mary was playing with her doll."

The teacher of today must stimulate children to react in many different ways to the meanings which reading conveys. Children must be taught to question, reason, compare, draw inferences, generalize, interject ideas of their own, seek interaction of these ideas with others, and draw independent conclusions. Thinking in connection with reading must be cultivated vigorously so that the real significance of statements may be completely understood.

Critical Evaluation

Important as this matter of grasping deeper meanings is, we must go still further. In this age of high-pressure salesmanship and wide dispersal of propaganda we must place much more emphasis upon *critical* reading.

Critical reading calls for additional steps in thinking. It involves getting the facts and interpreting deeper meanings, as discussed above. It also makes use of the personal judgment of the reader in deciding upon the validity of content. In critical reading, the reader evaluates and passes judgment upon the purpose, the fair-mindedness, the bias, or the truthfulness of statements made in text.

Speed of Reading

Another must which present-day civilization exacts from us is that of developing a new streamlined type of reading ability. Adults the country over are flocking to reading laboratories to learn how to read faster. Of the basic three R's, reading is the only one which has failed to develop greatly in speed during the past fifty years. We have both shorthand and typewriting to speed up the writing process. We have many kinds of machines, including the electric computer, to speed our arithmetic. But we still read at the same old pace!

People everywhere complain that they do not have time to read. Lack of time is not the basic problem. It is lack of skill. They need the skill to read more in the time they have. While streamlining technics are more appropriate at the higher levels, much could be done in the upper elementary grades to establish reading habits which will gear into the tempo of modern living. This must be done if reading is to make cultural advances commensurate with our technological and living-standard advances.

Part of Total Growth

One of the most profound truths about reading which has been discovered in recent times is that the development of this skill is a function of total growth. The maturing child grows in many ways—reading is just one of these ways. In other words, growth in reading is "part and parcel" of total child development, and as such can be evaluated only in conjunction with all the growth factors which influence achievement of this complex skill.

The era of considering reading as a mental act in itself is rapidly passing. New relationships among reading growth and other aspects of child growth are being discovered daily. Investigation has shown that there is a relationship between reading ability and physical maturation, health defects, diet, emotional disturbance, social adjustments, experiential background, and growth in the other language arts. Teachers and parents alike must become more keenly aware of the dependence of reading success upon these other factors.

Patterns of Growth

Another important must emerges from the longitudinal studies which are being made of children's growth over a period of years. The idea of the need to recognize the *whole child,* which budded and flowered in recent years, is now being replaced by the conviction that we must recognize the *child's whole life.*

The continuity-of-growth concept is manifesting itself in instruction in several ways. Teachers are becoming more open-minded about and skilled in accepting each child at his particular level of development and fostering his growth from that point on instead of fretting because many of their pupils are not up to their grade expectancy. Many high schools are adding courses in developmental reading in order to assure continued reading growth at the higher levels. We must continue these beginnings and expand them.

Research tells us that there are different cycles of growth in individual children. We must learn more about these cycles and respect each child's growth status at any one time in gauging the intensity of reading instruction which it is safe to provide. The long-time vision of child life and the careful study of individuals in terms of continued growth patterns will help us in removing many anxieties about those who are slow in undertaking reading and those who are not making regular year-by-year increments of reading growth.

Many other and lesser musts could be mentioned as next steps. Those discussed above, however, would seem to be imperative if the kind of reading instruction we offer is to contribute most adequately to the development of the individual as well as to the best interests of American life.

The Challenge

Reading is so fundamentally embedded in American life and American schools that mirror-like it reflects changes both in education and in social life. For this reason, reading in 1955 flings out a strong challenge to all of us. It has a scope and a sequence, a breadth and depth never before envisioned. If this vision is skilfully and enthusiastically implemented, then we should have much better readers in 1956 and 1957 and in all decades ahead—and America should profit accordingly.

12. Developing Basic Reading Skills through Effective Class Organization *

EMMETT ALBERT BETTS

How can basic reading skills be more effectively developed through class organization? This question is an old one, beginning with the introduction of the concept of mass education. The history of education is, in fact, the story of the rise of regimentation and subsequent attempts to break the lock step created in our classrooms.

Of professional literature on this topic there is no shortage! Administrators have devised plans to *regiment* a whole school system into *differentiating* instruction. Other educationists have experimented with grouping and individualized instruction in the classroom. Today ardent protagonists of some plans cause many teachers to approach the problem with mixed emotions. And someone has defined mixed emotions as the feeling the young man has when he watches his mother-in-law drive over a cliff in his brand new Thunderbird convertible.

Sincere and dedicated teachers of America are raising these questions:

Should language readiness and reading readiness books be used for *all* beginners?

What is to be said for five-year-olds having a need for reading?

How do we know when a child is ready for reading?

How much reading should a child achieve before promotion?

What can we do for children who omit and substitute words, use lip movement, and finger point?

How can we group children to help slow readers? Average readers? Fast readers?

How many groups should I have in my class?

How can we take care of individual differences in reading abilities in a social studies class?

What is the best and most reliable reading test?

How do you find the reading level of a child with a serious reading difficulty? Of an average child? Of a gifted or talented child?

Where can we get materials of a low reading vocabulary with high interest level?

Is individualized reading the best way to take care of individual differences?

* From Emmett Albert Betts, "Developing Basic Reading Skills . . . through Effective Class Organization," *Education* (May, 1958), pp. 561–72. Reprinted by permission of the author and The Bobbs-Merrill Co., Inc., Indianapolis, Ind.

Can individualized reading be substituted for group reading of a basic reader? If so, how can I organize the class? How can I be sure each pupil is learning phonic and thinking skills?

These questions and variations of them reflect concern about the improvement of reading instruction through class organization, appropriate materials, and effective methods. It is quite evident that the organization of the class is directed toward the goal of providing for individual differences in the maturity of pupil skills and interests. It is equally clear that the use made of instructional materials depends upon class organization as well as the teacher's concept of the goals of directed reading-study activities. Then, too, procedures and methods are tailored to fit different types of situations. Class organization, therefore, is of necessity discussed in terms of (1) goals of instruction, (2) appropriate materials, and (3) effective methods.

Levels of Professional Competence

The key to the problem of class organization is the professional competence of the teacher. At the lowest level are those teachers who operate at a zero level of competence—the regimenters who give all pupils in the class the same textbook and evaluate growth in terms of A-B-C-D or S-U report cards. At the top of the list are the "tenth-level" teachers who challenge all pupils in the class by means of teacher-pupil planned class, group, and individual activities. Between these two extremes are the teachers at different levels of competence—ranging from those who group primarily to help the *low achievers* to those who administer efficiently group and individualized reading programs for *all* pupils. How to help teachers at different levels of competence to improve their teaching requires differentiated supervision, in terms of individual levels of professional achievement.

Regimentation

In early American elementary schools, instruction was largely individual. Following the Revolutionary War a great experiment in mass education was undertaken. As the American free-school system was taking its first faltering steps, graded schools were introduced followed by graded textbooks. While the avowed purpose of these schools was to equalize educational opportunity, they fell into a lock step and the narrow, calendar-dictated curriculum was organized on the basis of adult interests and needs. Regimentation, therefore, became—and still is!—a serious peril in education.

Administrative Plans

About one hundred years ago, William T. Harris, Preston W. Search, John Kennedy, and other stalwarts in education began to wage a vigorous, ceaseless campaign against the lock step in education. Their plans, however, were administrative procedures for a whole school system, including (1) the frequent reclassification of children during the school year, (2) individualized activities preceding group recitations, and (3) coaching laggards by an assistant teacher in the classroom.

Later—in 1913—Frederic Burk introduced an individualized plan of instruction, which is now better known as the Winnetka Plan. By 1920, the Dalton, or contract, plan of providing for individualized instruction was favorably received.

Following the introduction of the intelligence scale by Binet and Simon in 1905, special classes were organized for the mentally handicapped. Over the years, special classes have been expanded to include the physically handicapped (including the brain-injured) and the gifted. More recently, clinical services have been developed to help emotionally disturbed children and the educationally retarded.

With the exception of plans for special classes, administrative plans for providing for individual differences had serious weaknesses. They tended to regiment classroom administration and promotion policies. They perpetuated a one-ladder curriculum for all children to climb. In general, they fell into disfavor because differentiated instruction is, in reality, put into operation by different teachers in different classrooms in different communities.

Classroom Plans

During the 1920's, standardized tests and informal inventories for evaluating reading achievement were developed and favorably received. While the standardized tests did not reveal the *wide* range of differences in the classroom, they did call attention to the *fact* that the same educational prescription could not be given to all children in the same grade.

In 1921, Fernald and Keller published their tracing technique for teaching word perception skills to certain types of nonreaders. Their use of this technique heightened interest in both remedial and corrective reading. Equally important, it called attention to the *fact* that the same methods could not be used for all children in the same class.

In the early 1930's, many challenging data were reported on retarded readers and nonreaders: (1) Eighty per cent had normal or superior intelligence. (2) Eighty per cent were boys. At this time, 25 to 40 per cent were failed in the first grade because they had not achieved some adult standard set for them in reading. Furthermore, there was more retardation among the pupils in the upper 50 per cent of the class than in the lower 50 per cent.

The above and other events appear to have stimulated experimentation on how to develop basic reading skills through effective classroom organization. Between 1921 and 1938, three basic plans were reported: (1) grouping on the basis of achievement, (2) grouping on the basis of pupil interests, and (3) individualized reading. Most of these plans also provided for the occasional, informal grouping of children who need special help on blending in phonics, outlining, or some other specific skill. All of them emphasized the role of the teacher in providing for individual differences. Variations of these three basic plans have been reported recently in a spate of articles.

Grouping: Reading Levels

Since basic textbooks in reading are used in most schools, grouping children by reading levels is a generally accepted practice. In the beginning, this plan was used primarily to do something for low achievers, and slow readers. Gradually, however, the concept of helping *all* the children in the class has emerged.

There have been variations of the plan for grouping by reading levels. First, children in the primary grades and in the intermediate grades have been grouped by reading levels for departmentalized reading instruction one period a day. While this plan may be better than regimentation, it increases the chronological age range within a group, regiments the school schedule, introduces problems of the child's integrating his school experiences, and tends to divorce reading from the language arts and the rest of the curriculum, and often underemphasizes the role of interests and motivation in learning. In reality, this plan regiments differentiated instruction in the classroom, defeating accepted goals of reading instruction.

In most schools today, however, children are grouped for reading instruction within the classroom. Three or more groups are organized to provide for the slow, average, and fast readers. How many groups are organized depends upon the professional competence of the teacher, the range of pupil abilities, and other factors.

Effective grouping by reading levels embraces several important concepts: (1) independent reading level, (2) teaching, or instructional level, (3) listening, or hearing, comprehension level, (4) interest level, (5) directed reading-study activities, (6) etc. It is essential to the success of this plan, for example, that the teacher knows (1) how to estimate reading levels and (2) how to guide the group from their teaching to their independent reading levels in each directed reading activity. While the sequential skill program is built into the teaching plans for *different* basic textbooks, this plan is effective to the degree that the teacher understands these concepts.

Most teachers who group by reading levels also plan for (1) class projects, (2) free, or independent, reading, (3) small informal groups to help individuals with specific skill needs, and (4) grouping in science, social studies, and other learning areas on the basis of interests.

Some teachers have experimented with pupil leaders—monitors or helpers—of groups. Others have depended more on self-aids for groups working on study-book and other independent activities. Teacher-pupil planning is one of the keys to the successful working of other groups and individuals while the teacher is directing the reading activity of a group.

Grouping by reading levels, like all other plans, has its limitations. In the first place, there is a wide range of reading abilities and interests within a reading group. The twelve-year range in a typical sixth grade, for example, poses some very real problems regarding (1) the number of groups and (2) the availability of appropriate materials. Some teachers report they can manage no more than three groups, which, of course, does not meet the needs of all pupils in the class; other teachers can administer several groups. In addition, teachers are always searching for books, magazines, and other materials of interest to different individuals in the class. A basic reader, for example, is written for a given age level, but some retarded readers may have mature interests and a very low level of reading ability.

Grouping: Interests

It is a fairly common practice to organize groups of children to pursue different interests. This is done in preparing a play, a dramatization, or a puppet show; in performing science experiments and preparing reports; in pursuing a unit of the social studies; and so on. This type of group activity extends reading into the heart of the curriculum, promotes the dynamic relationships between pupils, develops the ability to select and evaluate relevant materials and to draw conclusions, and motivates learning. Effective grouping in terms of interests usually requires considerable *class* planning and evaluation as well as *group* and *individual* activities.

When interest groups are organized, materials are made available in terms of the independent reading levels of the pupils. This requirement makes it necessary for the teacher to know the reading level of each pupil and the readability of a generous supply of books and other materials.

Pupil selection of relevant topics of interests and readable materials—of books they want to read and can read—is basic to interest grouping. For self-selection of reading materials to operate effectively, the pupil needs (1) to have a firm grasp on the reality of his own reading abilities and (2) to have clearly in mind the purposes of his contribution to the group undertaking. In other words, the group needs guidance; self-selection does not mean a laissez-faire, or "hands-off," policy is followed by the teacher.

Interest grouping, too, has its limitations:

1. Teachers need to achieve a high level of competence to administer effectively the diverse activities of groups.
2. More time is required for the teacher to plan when and how reading skills are developed and there is the ever-present possibility that skill development is haphazard rather than sequential.

Individualized Reading

The major goals of reading instruction are to help the child (1) mature in his interests, (2) make automatic his use of phonic and other word-learning skills, and (3) develop thinking and related abilities required for *independence in* reading and study activities. The acceptance of these goals —and they appear to be reasonable!—requires systematic planning (1) for the sequential development of interests and skills and (2) for self-selection when the child has achieved to the point where readable materials are available to him.

In the 1930's a number of plans for individualizing reading was reported in grades one to six. These plans made use of "single copies of a large number of books" on the assumption that "learning to read is an individual job." These plans provided for (1) informal estimation of reading levels, (2) records of daily or weekly progress, (3) "simple checkups" with emphasis on reading to an audience, (4) a wide range of references, fiction, and other materials, and (5) individual guidance, combined with group and class instruction.

These early plans were reported as "individualized reading," "individual guidance," "reading for enjoyment," "informal reading," and so on. The authors of these plans were not deluded into thinking that the goals of reading instruction could be achieved by a *plan* or *the* plan of individualized reading. Instead, they were deeply and justifiably concerned that individualized reading should be encouraged by definite planning. At the same time, they organized for class and group instruction to insure interest and skill development. That is, they recognized the values and limitations of individualized reading in an effective reading program.

Individualized reading is receiving increasingly popular approval. In fact, a relatively large amount of literature is now available, although the great bulk of it is an expression of opinion rather than validated facts. Probably no scholars in the psychology of pedagogy of reading, however, would recommend individualized reading as the sole basis for reading instruction. For that matter, very few teachers would go that far.

Self-selection. One of the outstanding merits of individualized reading is the emphasis on self-selection of independent reading. This emphasis can place a high value on pupil and peer motivation when appropriate group and class activities are planned around independent reading. The value is defaulted, however, when the child has merely to read to the teacher for five to fifteen minutes each week.

Recently, a cartoonist showed a frustrated master sergeant drilling recruits and yelling: "How are you going to learn to think for yourselves, if you don't do what I tell you to do!" Unlike the frustrated sergeant, master teachers do give children opportunities "to think for themselves" in setting up their purposes for reading, in selecting appropriate materials, and in evaluating what they read in terms of their purposes. But these master teachers do not confuse self-selection with aimless, unguided, and unfruitful activities of their pupils. They know that self-selection operates effectively when they give competent guidance.

Individual development. Another significant merit of individualized reading is the opportunity for the child to proceed at his own pace. This opportunity, too, is of high value when he is maturing in interests and acquiring the skills needed to meet those interests. But this opportunity is denied pupils when they fail to get systematic guidance in the myriad of interests and skills they need for growth in reading. The extent to which individualized reading is developmental depends upon how expert the teacher is in providing for specific learnings, either through the use of a well-planned basic reader or some other equally well-planned sequence.

Indivdual attention. A third merit of individualized reading is the attention given to each child in the class. Of course, the value here depends upon the professional competence of the teacher. However, there are very real limits to the amount of time a teacher has for twenty-five to forty pupils in a class. There is also a limit to the amount of time a teacher can give to reading instruction. There is always a need to help individuals in all curriculum areas, but can reading instruction be effective when the child receives only seven to fifteen minutes of help a week?

A highly individualized plan of reading instruction requires special administrative skills on the part of the teacher. If administering three or more groups in reading has taxed her skills, she may find the record keeping and other administrative details of a highly individualized plan overwhelming. Since small group activities are necessary to most individualized plans, this type of teacher might well perfect her skills in handling small groups before organizing her class into one-member "groups."

Leaders in education long ago emphasized the fact that *learning is an individual matter.* They also realized that teaching is concerned with a social *group,* ranging in size from the total class to one member of the group. The goal of differentiated instruction, therefore, is to help each individual realize his potential, without penalizing any other pupil in the group.

Learner needs. A fourth merit of individualized reading is the attention given to the specific needs of each pupil. In most plans these needs in word learning, thinking, and interests are identified in individual conferences and small group activities. Help is given to the child, who is motivated by an awareness of his needs, in both individual conferences and small groups of pupils having common needs. For this purpose, basic readers and study books, special workbooks, and informal activities are used.

How effectively individual needs are identified and provided for depends upon the professional insight of the teacher, the adequacy and systematic use of informal inventories, the sequential introduction of new learnings in the instructional material, and many other factors. Since *individualized* instruction is the goal of all plans for classroom organization, this problem of meeting individual needs is not peculiar to any one plan.

Library facilities. A fifth merit of individualized reading is the attention given to the need for a wide range of reference books, fiction, magazines, and newspapers. This wide range covers both interests and reading abilities. Since children, like adults, can read only that material which is available to them, the teacher uses all of her initiative in keeping a flow of books through the classroom from the school library, community library, homes, and other sources.

Here again, library facilities are essential for individualized reading regardless of which basic plan of organization is used. Basic readers used in grouping by reading levels, for example, serve as springboards to worthwhile independent reading.

Individual and Group Activities

Fortunately, there are few teachers willing to depend upon individualized instruction alone. All master teachers provide for individualized reading. But they also use class activities to plan and evaluate projects. They plan for grouping by reading levels and interest areas. They know that having a child read to them only every fourth or fifth day would not make sense to an educational psychologist, a competent business man, or a parent.

Opinions and Facts

For developing basic skills in reading, class organization goes hand in hand with the use of effective methods and of appropriate materials. One of the major problems in class management is the study of and provision for individual needs in motivation, achievement, interests, word-learning skills, and thinking abilities. How this problem is handled depends upon (1) teacher competence, (2) size and composition of the class, (3) library and textbook facilities, and (4) other factors.

In recent publications on the teaching of reading a wide variety of *opinions* are expressed. There are those who sincerely believe, for example, that individualized reading, or grouping by reading levels, or grouping by interest areas or some other single plan of differentiating instruction is the *one* way for *all* teachers to teach *all* pupils in *all* classrooms. Then, too, there are those who believe that a two-book plan for the intermediate grades is an adequate solution. Though the road of progress in reading is strewn with ill-conceived, one-shot plans of improving reading instruction through classroom organization, each generation seems to breed its own variety of cultism.

Experimentation by classroom teachers needs to be encouraged, but generalizations cannot be based on one teacher's experience in one classroom in one school system. It is a well-known fact that teachers vary widely in their levels of professional competence. For this reason, supervision is differentiated to help individual teachers mature in their professional competence. For this reason, too, plans evolved in classrooms must be tested and evaluated over a period of years by scholars in the psychology and pedagogy of reading with the help of experts in statistics and experimental design.

Differences

In a typical fourth grade class, the children range in reading abilities from those who can barely struggle along in a preprimer to those who enjoy the *Reader's Digest,* encyclopedias, and other materials which would challenge the best efforts of the average eighth or ninth grader. There are those, too, with anxieties and other emotional problems which interfere with their learning. Then occasionally there is a child with a subtle brain injury which blocks his attempts at learning. Overlaying these differences are wide variations in maturity of interests, word-learning skills, and thinking abilities.

Since education increases differences, this range of achievement in attitudes, skills, and abilities is increased as the children progress (or regress!) through the fifth and sixth grades. In a typical sixth grade, for example, there are the Johnnies who have never read a book on their own—even a preprimer—to those who read avidly high school and even college books on meteorology, satellites, radio communication, and other areas of interest.

Yes, educating all the children of all the people has been attempted in few places on this planet. But we are committed to this task because we are firm in our belief that all citizens are born free and equal—that we must, therefore, provide equal learning opportunities for all individuals. It is to this end that a century of progress has been made. The history of this century is the story of many leaders' attempts to break the lockstep in education created by the post Revolutionary War plan for mass education.

Reading Levels

Basic to any plan for differentiating instruction is the achievement of each individual in the class. In a fifth grade class, for example, Johnny is unable to remember *here, the, my,* and other common words in a preprimer. For him, self-selection of reading materials exists only in fantasy rather than in reality; he needs special help. If he has normal or superior intelligence, he may require the help of a clinical psychologist who understands language disturbances.

In the same fifth grade class, Tommy can read a second reader on his own—without lip movement, finger pointing, substituting words, and other signs of difficulty. In a third reader, Tommy shows no signs of difficulty but he occasionally comes to a word he cannot identify or an idea he doesn't understand. He needs help from his teacher who knows how to teach him the necessary skills so that the next time he recognizes the word and can apply that skill to similar words. He also needs help from his teacher who knows how to identify and to help him with specific comprehension needs. His independent reading level, therefore, is second-reader; his teaching, or instructional, level, is third-reader.

But Tommy is not interested in reading second readers written for seven-year-olds. His fairly high intelligence, his curiosity about science and history, and his opportunities to listen in on reports and conversations have helped him to mature in his interests. He, therefore, needs books with a high interest level but a low readability level.

Mary, another fifth grader, can read a fourth reader on her own and a fifth reader under teacher supervision. When seeking books and magazines for independent reading, she selects those at or below fourth-reader level. She has an adequate concept of her own skills in a reading situation.

Mary, along with eleven other pupils, is having an enjoyable experience in a fifth-reader story book and the accompanying study book. In each selection of the story book, Mary finds the need for new word-learning and thinking skills. At the beginning of a directed reading-study activity, the selection is at her teaching, or instructional, level. After the teacher has (1) prepared the group for reading the selection, (2) guided the silent reading, and (3) given specific help on word perception and comprehension, Mary can read the selection—silently or orally—on her own. Also, on her own, she can complete the study book activities which improves her use of reading skills. In each directed reading-study activity, therefore, Mary and the rest of her group is taken from their teaching level to their independent reading level.

Goals of Instruction

Over the years a substantial amount of respectable research has been accumulated on three major goals of reading instruction:

1. The development of worth-while *interests* which take the child to reading and which are satisfied through his increasingly effective reading-study skills.
2. The acquisition of *phonic* and other word-learning skills to the point where they are used automatically.
3. The maturing of *thinking* and related comprehension abilities needed to solve problems and to get genuine satisfaction from reading-study activities.

A comprehensive plan for the teaching of basic skills through class organization is effective to the degree that it embraces the above three goals. When any one of these goals is underemphasized or overemphasized, pupil progress is impeded.

Highly competent teachers know the interests of their pupils, understand how interests change and develop, and are alert to the need for helping children mature in them. For these reasons, they systematically use informal inventories of interests to estimate levels of maturity and to evaluate growth. They confirm these estimates by systematic observation of pupil interests in different types of situations and by encouraging the self-selection of books and other materials for independent reading and study.

Master teachers, too, are keenly aware of the phonic and other word-learning skills of the different pupils in their classes. They systematically use informal inventories of phonic skills, for example, to estimate achievement and specific need. They know that when a word, or telling, method is used, their pupils resort to saying the letters of words and to using other inappropriate skills.

To offer positive guidance, a master teacher takes these necessary steps:

1. *Readability of material.* Provides appropriate materials which each child can read without signs of difficulty.
2. *Need.* Gives the child—in an individual or group situation—help on word learning when he has a need for it. The kind of help given depends upon (1) the part of the word causing the difficulty, (2) previously learned skills, and (3) the need for learning a new skill.
3. *Meaning.* Insures pupil understanding of the use of the word in its context.
4. *Listening.* Helps the child to hear the undistorted sounds of letters and syllables in the word. This help on listening gives the child a learning set to see the letter and syllable phonograms in the word.
5. *Seeing phonograms.* Guides the pupil in relating the sounds heard in the spoken word to the phonograms representing those sounds in the written word.

This guidance requires the systematic teaching of phonic skills, beginning with the first words the child learns. It includes the sequential development of skills to deal with initial consonants, final consonants, and vowels of one-syllable words. It also includes the application of these skills to the syllables of words—without setting up for the child an artificial dichotomy between phonics and syllabication. It includes, too, the extension of phonic skills to the interpretation of pronunciation symbols in the dictionary. For the best interests of the learner there need be no trichotomy of phonics, syllabication, and pronunciation symbols; instead, his learning is facilitated by well-planned sequences of learning.

6. *Blending.* Takes the pupils a step further by blending the parts of two whole words to make a new one.

This includes, for example, blending the *b* of *bill* and the *l* of *left* to make the *bl* of *black*. It also includes blending the first part of one word with the rhyming part of another; for example, the blending of the *sk* of *sky* with the *ate* of *late* to make *skate*.

7. *Checking meaning.* Helping the child to form the habit of making sure the word he identified by means of phonic skills fits the context in which it is used.

8. *Making rules.* Helping the pupils to make generalizations about consonants, vowels, and syllables.

9. *Applying skills.* Giving the pupil opportunity to apply his newly learned phonic skills to unknown words.

In addition to being keenly aware of each child's interests and phonic needs, master teachers are very much concerned with teaching children how to think. With pupil interest to motivate the reading and with the pupil's automatic use of phonic skills, the teacher is prepared to deal with the major concern of reading instruction: *thinking.*

Here again the teacher is as much concerned with specifics of comprehension as he is with specific interests and specific word-learning skills. These needs in learning how to think embrace six major concerns:

1. Purposes—felt needs—which motivate the child to read.
2. Personal experiences out of which the child makes his concepts.
3. Attitudes which influence the child's (1) inclination to read on a topic, (2) accuracy of interpretation, (3) recall of ideas, and (4) tendency to rationalize.
4. Use of language to deal effectively with ideas (language ability includes interpretation of definite and indefinite terms, classifying, indexing, awareness of shifts of meaning, use of context clues, differentiating between language used to report facts and to influence attitudes, etc.).
5. Ability to discriminate between fact and opinion, to evaluate relevance of ideas, and to draw conclusions.
6. Versatility in adjusting rate and depth of comprehension to purpose.

These three goals of reading instruction—interests, word-learning skills, and thinking abilities—are inseparable essentials. These goals are ever kept clearly in mind by master teachers and conscientious authors of textbooks. To understand these goals requires a reasonable degree of scholarship in phonetics, phonics, perception, semantics, language structure, psychology of thinking, child development, differential psychology, and children's literature as well as in the pedagogy of reading. How a typical class of children with a possible twelve-year range of reading abilities is to be organized to achieve these goals has been a formidable challenge to thinking educators for more than a century.

Summary

To find one plan of class organization to be executed effectively by all teachers with all children is as difficult as finding a word to rhyme with *orange*. The purpose of class organization is to provide *equal learning opportunities for all children* in the classroom—to promote better learning conditions in all curriculum areas. This *is* a worthy goal of reading instruction, but the fact remains that a few children need special services; for example the mentally limited, the brain-injured, the emotionally disabled.

Challenging differences. In the first place, there is no such thing as a homogeneous group. When children are grouped by reading levels, for example, the best readers need to meet at least one new idea or word in about eighty running words in order to be challenged by new learnings. The less able children in the group may meet as many as one new word in twenty-five or thirty without showing signs of difficulty. Furthermore, differences in mental ability, verbal aptitudes, motivation, experience, etc. make occasional regrouping necessary.

Nor is there such a thing as a homogeneous group so far as interests are concerned. While master teachers can help a class or a group to develop a community of interests, nevertheless, individuals vary in the strength of their interests in a given topic.

Moreover, grouping in reading does not dictate the membership in an arithmetic or science group. Differences in the educational profile of each individual explain this fact. A given pupil, for example, may be a poor speller but a whiz in arithmetic and even in reading. This fact is both a blessing and a challenging problem in education. It is a blessing for a child to excel in art or arithmetic computation when he is a poor reader. It is an interesting challenge in a classroom to deal with the *different* needs of children and to depend upon the special contributions of different children.

Emotional climate. Some teachers complain that poor readers have weak defenses for their egos because they stand out in contrast to their age mates. They may go to absurd extremes to conceal the reading levels of books. This is done on the false belief that children cannot and do not evaluate themselves and others.

Yet, some of these same teachers will appoint group leaders to *tell* other children words they want to know. This practice is bad for at least two reasons: (1) A word, or telling-method is notoriously ineffective for developing phonic and other word-learnings skills. (2) Many poor readers are not aware of their perceptual inaccuracies. Furthermore, very bad human relationships can be developed unless both leader and pupils are prepared, in attitudes, for the undertaking.

How a child feels about his low status in reading does not depend upon the class organization but upon the emotional climate in the classroom. Awareness of real achievement, the attitude of the teacher toward the pupils, and the attitude of the pupils toward each other—all these attitudes contribute to the child's self-concept. These attitudes can be developed in classroom situations where instruction is differentiated by some practical means. Of course, frustration is compounded in a regimented classroom.

High achievers. Most teachers know that a child who either can't read or is a very poor reader is like a soldier without a gun or a baseball player without a bat. Probably for this reason the history of differentiated instruction highlights concern with mentally, physically, emotionally, and educationally handicapped children. For the same reason, low achievers tend to have higher achievement quotients than high achievers. One of the chief dangers in group or in completely individualized instruction is the tendency of the teacher to give the lion's share of her time to the low achievers.

A lay person can identify a nonreader or crippled reader, especially one who cannot remember words. But it takes a highly competent teacher to identify the child who has not learned to organize information, to draw conclusions from related facts, and do other types of thinking.

Many teachers, for example, are lulled into neglecting high achievers by the cliché: "If children enjoy books, the more they read and the better they read." While there may be a grain of truth in this platitude, there is real evidence that high achievers need as much, or more, guidance in reading as the low achievers. Nevertheless, these high achievers too often are turned loose in their classrooms or the library, without benefit of competent guidance.

Differentiated instruction. Discussions of interests, phonics, thinking, group dynamics, and other crucial elements in education are so much prattle when the child is frustrated in a regimented classroom. Therefore, the purpose of any plan for differentiating instruction is to reach the individual in the group, where he is in attitudes and skills.

How to provide for individual differences is a problem of mutual concern to children, parents, and teachers. In no successful plan, for example, can the active participation of parents be side-stepped. The dreams of educators must face the test of reality because, in a democracy, the citizens will have the kinds of schools they want.

When the last word is written on the topic, it will be seen that differentiated instruction reflects an attitude toward the individual. In our democracy, individuals have equal opportunities to participate in government. It has long been the responsibility of teachers—dedicated to the concept of democracy—to provide equal learning opportunities for all children in the classroom.

13. Relation of Basic Instruction in Reading to the Total Reading Program *

WILLIAM S. GRAY

GROWING concern has been expressed recently because many pupils are unable to interpret easily and effectively the reading materials assigned in the various curriculum fields. Three possible explanations have been offered for this situation. The first is that pupils on the average are not taught to read as well today as formerly. A recent survey of related evidence fails to support this contention.

A second explanation is that the training given during reading periods, while very valuable within limits, fails to develop the specific reading skills needed in many study activities. A third is that whereas a broad foundation of basic reading attitudes and skills is developed in reading classes, they are not further developed and refined in the various curriculum fields, nor extended to meet the distinctive needs faced in many study activities. Such assertions have led to challenging questions concerning the relation of basic instruction in reading to the total reading program. The issues involved are so important that attention will be focussed upon some of them in the discussion that follows.

* From William S. Gray, "Relation of Basic Instruction in Reading to the Total Reading Program," *Education* (May, 1954), pp. 535–43. Reprinted by permission of the author and The Bobbs-Merrill Co., Inc., Indianapolis, Ind.

Background Facts

In approaching this problem it will be helpful to review briefly a series of notable changes in teaching reading which have occurred during the last half century. Of major importance is the fact that the concept of reading that has influenced school practice has been a dynamic one. It has changed from decade to decade as the role of reading has expanded both in and out of school. It has changed also as scientific studies have made clearer the nature of the reading act and the basic processes involved.

A detailed study by Smith of both the theory and practice of teaching reading showed that at the beginning of this century the effort to develop good oral readers was still the "order of the day," that the development of "an appreciation for and permanent interest in literature" was a prominent aim, and that "getting the thought from the printed page" was beginning to receive attention. The view also prevailed that reading was a highly specialized skill and sole responsibility for its development should be assumed during so-called reading periods. As a result, little or no guidance in reading was provided in the content fields. It was further assumed that by the time pupils had completed the elementary grades, they had satisfactorily mastered the art of reading. High school teachers therefore gave little attention to the reading attainments of their pupils and felt no responsibility for increasing their ability to read. The arts of *learning to read* and of *reading to learn* were thus sharply differentiated in practice.

But notable changes soon occurred. As a result of significant social developments between 1900 and 1920, the use of reading in adult life increased rapidly. For similar reasons school curriculums were greatly modified and enriched. Furthermore, comparative studies of oral and silent reading supplied striking evidence of the greater economy and efficiency of the latter. By 1925 emphasis in teaching reading centered more and more largely on the development of the attitudes and skills involved in the comprehension of what is read and in speed of reading. Vigorous effort was also made to cultivate keen interest in independent reading. As the amount and variety of the materials read in the various curriculum fields increased, evidence accumulated that the effectiveness of the use of reading in various learning activities was greatly improved through appropriate guidance in reading. The chief purposes of such guidance were to aid pupils in understanding the materials read and to increase their efficiency in reading for different purposes.

By 1937, the concept of reading had undergone further expansion. Because of its great value in enriching the experiences of children, reading was conceived as a form of experience, as are seeing and hearing. Furthermore, as its use in various curriculum fields increased, reading was recognized as a vital aid to learning. The fact was recognized, therefore, that a good reader not only perceives words and grasps the meaning of passages, but also reflects on the significance of the ideas apprehended, discovers relationships among them, and clarifies his understanding of them. Further analysis showed that efficient readers react in various ways to what they read and combine the new ideas acquired with previous experience. The latter step is essential if wrong ideas are to be corrected, new understandings and rational attitudes developed, and improved habits of thinking and behaving acquired.

This expansion of the concept of reading brought a clearer recognition of the challenging responsibilities involved in developing efficient readers. It also gave definite support to two convictions that had been developing rapidly during the twenties and thirties. The first was that instruction in reading must be continued throughout the elementary- and high school period, and the second that basic instruction in reading must be supplemented at each level by carefully planned guidance in reading in every curriculum field. Accordingly, vigorous effort has been made during recent years to develop carefully coordinated school-wide reading programs extending from the kindergarten to the university.

One of the challenging problems faced in developing such programs relates to the division of responsibilities among the various areas of the curriculum for training and guidance in reading. Definite help in solving this problem has been secured through detailed studies of the attitudes and skills involved in efficient reading. The findings showed that they belonged to two general types. The first includes those that are common to most reading activities in which children engage. The second includes those that function more or less largely in specific curriculum areas. In harmony with these findings, vigorous effort is being made today through basic instruction in reading to introduce and establish insofar as time permits the attitudes and skills belonging to the first group. Building upon this foundation carefully planned guidance is being given in the respective curriculum areas to maintain and refine the basic attitudes and skills and to promote the development of others that are needed for efficient reading in each area.

The validity of this plan is supported by the results of research. Following a review of related studies, Traxler and Townsend concluded that there is "a great deal in common between reading in a single field and reading in general and that improvement in general reading ability should have a favorable effect upon ability to read in a specific field." The additional fact was pointed out by other investigators that the extent of this relationship varies among the respective curriculum fields. All the evidence available, however, supports the contention that vigorous effort should be made at every level to develop a high degree of competence in the attitudes and skills common to all reading activities.

But such training is not enough. Numerous studies show conclusively that carefully planned guidance in reading in specific curriculum fields is greatly needed and results in increased competence in reading assigned materials. As a result pupils are able to achieve the purposes of study more fully. These findings justify the conclusion that "schools face the responsibility not only of developing basic competencies in reading but also of promoting specialized abilities and adjustments essential in reading effectively in the various content fields."

Major Purposes of Basic Instruction in Reading

While basic instruction in reading gives large emphasis to the development of the attitudes and skills common to most reading activities, it is by no means limited to that aim. A survey of recent recommendations shows that there is wide agreement on the following aims of a well-conceived basic reading program.

1. To promote along with other school activities increased readiness for beginning instruction in reading and for later stages of progress.

2. To expand and enrich the experience of pupils through guided reading of material relating to the major areas of interest of the respective age groups taught. Experience shows clearly that vital content and challenging purposes for reading are essential to rapid progress in becoming efficient readers.

3. To promote continuous sequential development of the attitudes and skills and language understandings that are common to the various reading activities, both silent and oral, in which pupils engage. Several distinct advantages attach to this plan. It insures the systematic and orderly introduction of basic attitudes and skills, provides vigorous emphasis on them at the time it is needed, and makes use of special materials and techniques of teaching to facilitate maximum progress on the part of groups and individuals.

4. To acquaint pupils with a portion of their literary heritage and to develop any special reading attitudes and skills essential to an understanding and appreciation of the various kinds of literature appropriate to the age group taught. The importance of this aim is emphasized by the increas-

ing need for an enriched cultural background on the part of all American youth.

5. To provide stimulation and guidance in establishing the habit of wide personal reading on the part of each child. A significant measure of the vitality of a reading program is the extent to which children engage in self-initiated reading activities.

Whereas each of these aims merits detailed discussion, we are especially concerned here with the nature of the common reading attitudes and skills that should be emphasized in basic instruction in reading. Continuous study of this problem during recent years has shown that they can be organized under four headings. In presenting the outline that follows the fact is recognized that in the actual process of reading they function as a unit and more or less simultaneously.

1. *Perceiving words and nonverbal symbols.* This involves: recognizing the identity of words and other symbols and of recalling or finding out their pronunciation and meaning.

2. *Securing a clear grasp of meaning,* which involves:
   a. Recognizing the meanings that are directly stated, which includes at least four steps:
      1) Identifying meanings of words and groups of words that are appropriate to the context.
      2) Fusing separate meanings into ideas.
      3) Recognizing the sequence and interrelatedness of ideas and the author's pattern of organization.
      4) Identifying specific aspects of meaning, such as the central or key idea; important points and supporting details; vivid descriptions, characterizations, examples; the chief proposals, propositions, conclusions.
   b. Recognizing meanings inherent in the passages but which are not directly stated, for example: sensing implied meanings, drawing inferences, making generalizations on the basis of the facts presented, identifying assumptions underlying statements, arguments or conclusions.
   c. Enriching one's understanding of passages by recalling all one knows, or can find out, that illuminates or makes clear their meaning.

3. *Reacting to what is read.* This includes:
   a. Considering thoughtfully, in the light of known facts, principles or valid standards of judgment, the general worth, significance, accuracy or quality of what is read.

    b. Responding emotionally to such items as the value of the ideas
expressed, the choice of words used, the rhythm of expression.

4. *Integrating the ideas acquired through reading with previous experience*
so that understandings are clarified and extended, rational attitudes
developed, interests broadened, and improved patterns of thinking and
behaving acquired.

The development of the various attitudes and skills implied in the foregoing outline is one of the most challenging tasks that schools face today.
Experience has taught that they cannot be developed in full at any one level
of educational advancement. They are the product of continuous guidance
throughout the entire period of elementary and secondary education, and
even later. The most that can be done at any given level of school advancement is to promote their development to the extent that they serve the
immediate needs of pupils and prepare for oncoming stages of development. Those schools which provide a carefully coordinated continuous program of basic instruction in reading will go far, as a rule, in laying a broad
foundation for efficient reading in all school activities. Those which do not
provide such instruction often fail to achieve other important aims of the
reading period and to provide the background needed for further progress
in and through reading in other curriculum areas.

A Content Suited to Its Functions

If basic instruction is to achieve its major purposes the materials read
must be carefully selected. Of primary importance is the fact that they must
be of genuine interest to the children taught. This is essential if boys and
girls are to be attracted to reading as a desirable form of activity and to
apply themselves eagerly to assigned tasks. In the second place, the materials relating to the respective interest themes should be organized and
studied as units to insure vivid and lasting impressions. Experience shows
that the themes which usually make a more or less universal appeal relate
to everyday activities of children, the social world in which they live, interesting people, times past, distant places, scenes and events, the world of
nature, the fanciful and the make-believe.

Obviously, the content of many of the units used in basic instruction in
reading will be similar in many respects to that used in other areas of the
curriculum. There is a fundamental difference, however. The selections
used do not consist of samples of the content in specific fields which have
been taken out of their broader contexts. They consist rather of self-contained units that are directly related to the immediate interests of pupils and

can be interpreted in the light of their previous experiences or those that can be readily developed. The use of such materials is essential not only in enriching the experiences of the reader but in laying a foundation of the attitudes and skills common to the various curriculum fields.

A third characteristic of basic reading materials is that they include an abundance of fine stories with challenging themes, lively plots, memorable characters, and distinguished style. Repeated studies show that such materials are universally liked by children. When properly selected they introduce pupils to the world's finest literature for the respective age groups taught. They provide a growing acquaintance with a part of our cultural heritage. And by their very nature they cultivate increasing preference for reading materials that are artistically written.

The supplementary reading materials provided through classroom and school libraries should be as broad in scope as the varied interests and themes suggested in the preceding paragraphs. They should also vary in difficulty in harmony with the range in reading ability of the group served. Through the use of appropriate stimulation and guidance rapid progress can be made among most pupils in developing keen interest in reading and in cultivating well-balanced reading preferences.

Guidance in Reading in Other Curriculum Areas

As soon as pupils have learned to read very simple material with reasonable ease and understanding, more or less use is made of reading as an aid to learning in various areas of the curriculum. At first the reading activities are very informal and the materials used are often prepared by teachers. Very soon, however, it is necessary to rely more or less largely on printed materials. In preparing such materials, authors and publishers endeavor to limit the vocabulary and forms of expression used to those already mastered during basic reading periods. Some new words are needed, of course, in discussing specific topics. In the course of time, however, the materials used begin to take on distinctive characteristics. This is due to the fact that each field has its own content and vocabulary and makes use of special patterns in organizing and presenting ideas.

As children attempt to use such materials, difficulties arise. It is not an easy task, for example, to interpret the language of arithmetic, science and geography, to translate the new verbal and nonverbal symbols into clearly apprehended meanings, to see the implications of the ideas secured and to judge their relevance and value. In fact, genuine difficulties are faced on every page. As pointed out earlier, experience and the results of research show clearly that basic instruction in reading, even at its best, is inadequate to meet these varied needs. In addition much carefully planned guidance in reading is essential in each school activity in which reading is used as a vital aid to learning. Some of the purposes and types of guidance that are most needed will now be considered.

1. *To maintain and strengthen basic reading attitudes and skills.* Of large importance is the responsibility of teachers in all curriculum areas to maintain and strengthen the reading attitudes and skills introduced during basic reading periods. As is true in the case of the skills needed in the other language arts, efficiency is attained as a result of continuous guidance in all school activities in which they function. This involves in the case of reading certain preliminary steps of which the following are typical: helping pupils to identify problems for study that are significant and worth while; building an adequate background to insure an effective start in attacking the selected problem; and directing attention to a few key words in a fashion that will associate meanings with them appropriate to their contextual setting.

A first reading of assigned material should be directed by specific aims, such as a clear grasp of the major ideas presented and their contribution to the solution of the problem studied. This step should often be taken during a supervised study period in which the teacher endeavors to identify the difficulties which pupils are encountering and to supply needed help to individuals or to the group as a whole. In this connection use should be made of the methods used during basic reading periods insofar as they apply. It is confusing and ineffective, for example, to suggest methods of word attack which are radically different from those developed in the reading class.

Following the first reading and discussion of findings, it is desirable, as a rule, to extend interpretation through rereading and discussion that is guided by more penetrating questions. Individual responses should be clarified, and at times radically modified through cooperative thinking and the pooling of judgments. In making these proposals, the fact is recognized that the specific procedures adopted will differ radically from day to day in terms of the problems studied, the types of materials available, and other conditioning factors. In various ways, however, teachers should endeavor to maintain and further develop the basic reading attitudes and skills, as pupils make efforts to apply them in various learning activities.

2. *To develop the new understandings and skills needed.* As the foregoing steps are taken, special attention should be given to the development of the new understandings and skills in reading needed to achieve the learning goal sought. A comparison, for example, of an arithmetic, a social

studies book, a geography or a science text shows that they are organized differently and make use of varied aids to understanding. An important responsibility of each teacher is to aid pupils in becoming acquainted with the ways in which different textbooks are organized and the nature and purpose of their various parts. The training given should be highly functional in the sense that children acquire a growing understanding of textbooks and other reading materials and skill in using them as aids to learning.

A second problem relates to the pupil's need for help in attaching appropriate meanings to the verbal and nonverbal symbols used in each field. The child may learn in a reading class to respond correctly to the word "fifth" as used in the sentence, "John is the *fifth* boy from the end of the seat." This is no guarantee, however, that he understands the word "fifth" as a fractional part of a whole. Building readiness for and developing this concept is a specific responsibility of the teacher of arithmetic. Similar statements could be made concerning scores of words whose forms, pronunciations and common meanings are well known but which are used to represent radically different concepts in various fields. Likewise the teacher of each subject is responsible for helping pupils acquire a mastery of essential technical words and to attach appropriate meanings to the nonverbal symbols used.

A third problem relates to the development of the habits of thinking while reading that are essential in achieving the goals of study in specific fields. Geography, for example, aims to train pupils to explain many of man's activities in terms of his natural environment. Science aims to promote growth in making generalizations about nature and her laws based on known facts. Arithmetic aims to develop ability to perceive quantitative and spatial relationships and to engage in clear thinking that involves them. Progress is achieved not only through class discussions but through careful reading and study. Experience shows, however, that pupils need specific help in each field in grasping the relationships implied in the materials read, in following the line of reasoning adopted by the author, and in recognizing the validity of the conclusions reached.

A fourth problem is very closely related to the third. It is not sufficient for pupils to recognize the relationships and patterns of thinking that characterize specific fields. They should also learn to apply them in interpreting other materials read. This means that as pupils read descriptions in geography of human activities, attitudes, conditions of life, and man-made features, they should seek to explain them in terms of factors in the natural environment of the region involved. This is what is known as geographic interpretation. It is an art that is acquired by far too few pupils. It results from carefully planned guidance over a long period of time as pupils read descriptions that should be so interpreted. Ability to interpret geographically is not only essential in the study of geography but also in much of the general reading which individuals do throughout life. What has been said concerning geographic interpretation could be said with equal emphasis concerning the need for training in effective interpretation of materials read in all other fields.

3. *To develop a high level of efficiency in reading for different purposes.* As indicated earlier, the major aims of teaching differ to a greater or less extent in the respective curriculum fields. Similarly the reading done serves different purposes. In a carefully planned laboratory study, Judd and Buswell secured striking evidence that the mental processes involved in reading vary widely with the reader's purpose. This conclusion was further supported by the findings of Gans who compared the steps involved in reading when taking a general reading test and when engaging in critical reference reading to solve a problem. She found that whereas there are many steps or processes common to the two situations, there are also significant differences between them. Reference reading, as a rule, requires a far broader conceptual setting, a grasp of more complex interrelationships, and constant reformulation of the problem as the study proceeds.

Even a brief survey of the purposes served by reading in different curriculum fields reveals a challenging array: to identify the important conditions of an arithmetic problem and to decide on the steps to take in solving it; to identify the facts that justify a generalization in a science text; to gather and weigh the evidence needed to solve a social studies problem; and so one might continue indefinitely. But one may ask, will not the training given in reading for one purpose aid in developing competence in reading for other purposes? As a result of an intensive study of this issue, Gates and Van Alstyne reached the conclusion that there is some transfer from one situation to another. However, "it is so small that it cannot be depended upon to develop desired abilities. They must be developed specifically. We may accept with gratitude the increments from transfer, but never be willing to accept them as a substitute for direct training."

Concluding Statements

The foregoing discussion should be greatly extended but space will not permit. The evidence that has been presented, however, supports the following conclusions: (1) The developments of competent readers is a function of the total school program. (2) Needed training begins as soon as pupils enter school and continues to expand as their interests broaden and as they face increasing challenging and difficult reading tasks at successive levels of advancement. (3) Many of the foundations for efficient reading are established through basic instruction in reading as it seeks to develop at successive levels the attitudes and skills common to the various reading activities in which the pupils taught engage. (4) Through guidance in reading in the various curriculum fields these basic attitudes and skills are maintained and further developed. Furthermore, the specialized understandings, attitudes and skills needed to achieve the purposes of study are cultivated vigorously in the respective fields. The fact cannot be overemphasized that competence in reading develops most effectively as a result of a carefully coordinated school-wide program in reading extending from the nursery to the university.

14. Parents and Teachers Want to Know about Reading *

EMMETT ALBERT BETTS

"WHY ARE THERE so many more reading difficulties in this generation?" This question is uppermost in the minds of many parents today. In fact, some parents have become alarmed over the situation.

Teachers Face the Question

This same question was raised by many teachers during the 1930's. Before that time very little research on reading had been put to use in the classrooms. Certainly, very few teachers were informed about child development, retardation in reading, phonics and other word perception skills, reading readiness, thinking, reading difficulty of materials, and other ideas which are common knowledge today. In fact, not much was known about individual differences in learning to read.

As the facts about learning to read, teaching methods, and instructional

* From Emmett Albert Betts, "Parents and Teachers Want to Know about Reading," *Education* (January, 1958), pp. 289–99. Reprinted by permission of the author and The Bobbs-Merrill Co., Indianapolis, Ind.

materials became generally known, teachers gradually revised their notions about teaching children to read. As late as the 1930's it was common practice to try to teach all first graders to read—whether they were admitted at 4, 5, or 6 years of age. Children who reached some arbitrary standard of reading achievement were promoted to second grade and the others were failed. At each grade level, every child was given the same textbooks regardless of his capacity to learn or his achievement.

The result of this practice was compounded frustration for many children. Some children who could have made faster progress were discouraged because they had to use the same books as all other pupils in the class. Many children were held in the same grade for one, two, or more years— creating a serious overage problem. In fact, twelve- and fourteen-year-old children could be found in first grade classes—humiliated and irritated, of course! As soon as the law allowed, they did a sane thing; namely, dropped out of school. This foolish practice of solving pedagogical problems by eliminating the pupil could not survive.

Retardation: Facts

Studies of children during the 1930's revealed many facts which at that time were startling. First, about 25 per cent of the children were reading below their mental capacities. These children became known as retarded readers and nonreaders.

Second, more of the children in the upper half of the class were retarded in reading than in the lower half of the class. That is, they were reading at levels far below their general mental abilities. This fact clearly indicated the need for a wide range of reading materials in a classroom to challenge the superior readers as well as the poor readers.

Third, about 80 per cent of the retarded readers were found to have normal or superior intelligence. This fact was a shock to teachers who had entertained the false belief that a poor reader had to be dumb! Now there was a new ray of hope for many nonreaders and retarded readers.

Fourth, about 80 per cent of the retarded readers were found to be boys.

These facts led to intensive study of the cause of reading difficulties. It soon was clear that there was not one cause, but many causes:

1. Premature teaching, that is, attempting to teach a child to read before he was qualified, or ready, to do so.
2. Frustrating the pupil with books that were not suitable to his reading level, rather than challenging him with materials at his reading ability level.

3. Faulty visual skills which caused or contributed to the child's difficulties in reading.
4. Impaired hearing which contributed to his inability to hear all the sounds of the words and to his inattention in class.
5. Anxieties and other emotional disabilities which caused or contributed to deficiencies in attention and/or concentration and, therefore, in reading.
6. Brain injuries—recognized or undetected—which caused an inability to learn to read by usual methods.
7. Mental or emotional immaturity.

Prevention and Correction

These and other factors in reading difficulties soon became common knowledge among teachers, psychologists, and doctors. Long before the parents became fully aware of the retarded reader problem, several steps were taken to help him:

First, teachers began to group children within the classroom so that each child had an equal opportunity to learn at his own level of achievement. This practice calls for parent-teacher cooperation, based on an understanding of the wide range of individual differences in a classroom and of what to do about them. When this mutual understanding is lacking, parents often misinterpret what is being done in the best interests of their children.

Reading: Now and Then

Second, special consultants, supervisors, and corrective reading teachers have been added to school staffs. In the long run, school officials probably will conclude that there is a need for a reading clinic for the nonreader and severely retarded reader and for demonstration teachers who can help classroom teachers with problems of grouping children within the classroom.

Third, reading clinics to deal with extreme reading disabilities have been set up as separate units or as one unit of a psycho-educational clinic.

Why are there more reading difficulties now than in grandfather's day? When grandfather was of school age anyone who could not read or who had difficulty in learning to read was believed to be just plain stupid. This opinion gave the teachers an excuse; of course, they could not teach a child the complex process of reading if he were mentally below par. In short, most of the facts recited above were not even discovered in grandfather's day.

The facts seem to indicate that Johnny reads as well as his father, grand-father, or great-grandfather. But Johnny's father and grandparents didn't read very well, either! So there is considerable room for improvement.

The fact, then, is that there probably are no more reading difficulties in this generation of children than in previous generations. Instead, teachers and psychologists today know more about individual differences. Equally important, they are doing something about them. And this doing brings in the parents.

Each year new facts are being discovered about why Johnny can't read and why Jimmy can, about the reading difficulty (readability) of books, and so on. After each new fact has been discovered and tested, then the problem is how to put it to use.

Doing something about new facts is exactly what has been going on in some schools. Different plans have been and are being tried out in good schools. It is the making of these changes to square with the facts that has caused parents to ask questions. In schools where the parents have been in on the facts and the proposed changes, things have gone smoothly. These parents see that Jimmy is getting a better deal than his father or grand-father.

Psychologists have learned that people are suspicious of scientists—until they get some glimmer of understanding of what scientists are doing. Since parents are people, they want to know why Johnny is in this group and Mary is in another group in the classroom. And it is important that parents do understand what is going on, because Johnny and Mary need the peace of mind that comes with intelligent guidance from their parents and teachers.

Parents Face the Question

For some years, parents have become increasingly aware of the reading needs of their children. Special attention has been given to their children at all school levels. They have read newspaper and magazine articles and books concerning the teaching of reading written by responsible journalists and teachers. They have also read books and articles by uninformed and irresponsible journalists! They have been given antidotes and cure-alls that seem simple but are based on few, if any, facts. And they have been given sensible over-all views based on scientific evidence. It is little wonder that many parents are confused.

In many communities, through citizen's committees, parents are taking positive, constructive steps to study the situation. They are studying methods, materials, and, best of all, they are studying children. From the reports made to date, it appears that these committees have been effective: more citizens see the reading problem in complex relationship to the problems of education in general. Parents as partners of teachers are beginning to see that times have changed, progress has been made. Then, too, teachers are learning to cement closer relationships with parents. Perhaps the long recognized gap between research and classroom practice will be lessened.

Patience and persistence will be required to get at one of the major issues: adequate support for teachers' colleges and graduate schools of education. At present the overworked and poorly paid teachers of teachers must be considered. Perhaps the time is coming when citizens will use the ballot box to support institutions for teacher education as well as they now support medical, dental, engineering, and other professional schools.

Differences Are Important

Children learn to crawl, stand, walk, and talk at different ages. By the same token, they also learn to read at different ages. A few children, for example, learn to read at age 3 or 4 but most children do not catch on to reading until they have passed their sixth birthday. In short, they may be admitted to grade one when they have attained the calendar age of 6 but this does not mean that any teacher in the world can teach all of them to read at that age!

The child who learns to talk at 2 years certainly has a far better chance of learning to read at age 6 than the child who doesn't learn to talk until age 3 or 4. This statement is obvious to parents and teachers. There are big differences among children in readiness for reading and in the rates at which they progress.

When the first grade teacher meets her class on the first day, she finds they present a variety of needs. One or two may read, know the names of the letters, can write legibly, and use all speech sounds accurately. A few children are still learning the sounds of speech, the difference between *tomorrow* and *yesterday,* the days of the week, and color names. The rest of the class falls between these two extremes. Since the modern teacher knows it would be absurd to put all of them in the same book, she groups them according to their needs.

As the children go through the school year, they become even less alike. Differences in reading and other abilities are increased. Training and schooling increase individual differences rather than decrease them. By the end of the first year, one or two or three pupils may still need more preparation for beginning reading. And a few may be able to read third readers with as much satisfaction as the average third grade child.

Should the teacher recommend that all children who cannot read a first reader—at least 30 per cent or 40 per cent of the class—be retained in first grade? Should she recommend that the best readers be sent to the third grade? The answer, of course, is a quite clear-cut "No": in the first place, children excel in different activities; some have more aptitudes in reading while others have more aptitude in numbers or science or art or music. In general, the gifted excel in many things and the mentally retarded are poor in many things.

This does not mean, however, that the same level of achievement will be found for a child in each subject. No matter how they are grouped for classes, individual differences in both capacities and abilities will be there, and the differences will be more apparent as time goes on. Secondly, children tend to make better emotional and social adjustments when they are kept with children of their own age. For these and other reasons, nearly all of the children are sent to a second grade teacher.

Each year the range of differences is lengthened. By the time the average class is in the third grade, for example, there are one or two children in the beginning reading stage and there are one or two who can compete on even terms with the average seventh grader. When this class is in the fifth grade, the range is likely to be from the preprimer or primer level of reading ability to as high as the twelfth grade level. In the junior and senior high schools, this range in reading abilities is increased, not decreased. These are the facts with which teachers must deal. These are the facts which parents must understand in order to guide the development of their children to effective adult citizenship—with peace of mind.

Aids to Learning

Over the years, reading programs have been built around one or more of a half-dozen widely used series of basic readers. These readers are graded in reading difficulty (readability!), all beginning with one to three paperbound preprimers for beginners and a clothbound primer and first reader. Until fairly recently one book was offered for each of grades two and three, inclusive. Now the practice is to offer two books graded in difficulty for these grades. Gradually, these reading series are being extended for use through the junior and senior high school levels. It is also common practice to provide a study book or workbook for the preprimer program and one for each book above that level.

The selections in the basic readers provide the materials of reading and the study books provide for the systematic development of (1) interests, (2) phonic and related word-learning skills, and (3) thinking and related aspects of comprehension. The basic readers and study books make up a team of teaching materials for a reading-study program.

In addition to the basic readers and study books for the pupils, a teacher's guidebook is provided for each book in the series. These guidebooks describe how to group children, how to direct reading activities in the basic reader, and how to use the study books for skill development. Equally important, they offer many suggestions for independent (individual) and group reading of both fiction and factual material. In this way the basic reading program is used as a springboard into the world of reading for fun and for information.

When a child has reached third-reader level, he usually begins to use a simple dictionary. He also begins to expand his reading interest to real life stories. Soon he takes a lively interest in informative selections. By the time he has attained fourth-reader level ability, he has been initiated in the independent use of authoritative encyclopedias, atlases, and other reference books.

Dictionaries help the child with the pronunciation and some of the important uses of a word. But his endeavors to get him understanding takes him beyond dictionary definitions. He needs to know where a place is, who made a discovery, who did something big and dramatic, how things are made and operated, and a host of related ideas. He needs something into which he can put his intellectual teeth. Many of these needs are met in the authoritative, readable, and extensive entries of an encyclopedia. Skillful use of an encyclopedia improves basic skills, enriches the school program, and provides needed information.

A basic reading program is designed to develop a competence and a readiness for reading in the larger sense. A well-taught lesson in a basic reader leads into books of fiction and of fact to satisfy the needs of the growing child. Supplementary readers and other textbooks, fiction, reference books, atlases, maps, globes, models—all these are aids to learning. All are needed for the satisfying and well rounded living of child and adult.

Three Essentials for Reading

Sally, a kindergarten child, comes to the teacher with a wild flower she has picked on the way to school. She wants to know what it is called. Or, Jimmy brings in a tattered cardboard box containing a little green frog and wants to know more about it. Maybe the teacher does or doesn't know all the answers to these questions. But she does know that these are good healthy *interests* which lead to ideas, concepts, and attitudes. So she turns to an authoritative encyclopedia—yes, even for kindergarten children. Here she finds for Sally not only faithful reproductions (in color!) of flowers but also authentic information about rules for picking wild flowers and where and how they grow. In the same volume, the teacher finds answers to Jimmy's questions about frogs.

Before this little informal session is over, several things have happened. All the children who took part in this discussion were more interested in flowers, frogs, and tadpoles because they knew more about them. One question led to another and interest was heightened. Moreover, they had discovered how wonderful and interesting a good book can be. Many of them asked to look at the pictures in the other volumes! Thus other interests were fostered and learning was improved.

Interest. Parents often ask what they can do to get their children ready for school. Should they teach them the A B C's? How to read? The answer, of course, is to teach them how to get along with other children, how much fun it is to hear good stories read or told, how interesting everything is. In other words, parents can and should encourage their children to develop interests which take them into reading. Interest is a starting point.

At age 2 or 3, Jimmy asked many "what" questions: what is this Mama? By age 4 he is asking "why," "how," and "when" questions. By age 5, he adds, "where" questions. These questions need to be answered—sincerely and authoritatively. One good source is an authoritative home and school encyclopedia, recommended by competent authorities.

Why make such a big point of children's questions? Simply because they need answers in order to mature in their interests—to grow up in their questions and in their abilities to think with facts.

One of the first essentials in being ready for beginning reading is *interest* which takes the child to reading. As these interests are nurtured by parents and teachers, the child's comprehension is improved. He gets the feel for language, spoken and written. And he learns to think. (After all, reading is one form of thinking.)

By the time the child can read a fourth reader, he not only has learned where he can get answers to his questions, but also he has made a start on the road to independence in using references himself. He is interested.

From kindergarten age and on, children are interested in facts and show that they can reason. At age 6, they enjoy hearing animal tales and realistic stories about children. They show a marked increase in the ability to tell the difference between fact and fancy.

By age 7, they begin to read on their own, but are usually eager to take time out to hear a good story or some verse. They like to classify things; for example, to make scrapbooks about something. They begin to expect cause-effect explanations of their "why" questions, to move from adult-centered to child-centered groups.

At age 7, children enjoy fairy tales and this stage reaches its peak at 8. At 8 they begin to show interest in real life stories. By age 9 there is an interest shift from the fanciful to the factual. If they have grown up in homes and schools where adults have consulted reference books, they will turn quite naturally to an encyclopedia. They crave information about dinosaurs, Indians, powered flight, horses, and a variety of other interests. And they like to get this information on their own, using a table of contents, index, and other ways to locate it.

By age 10, boys are looking up how-to-do subjects on inventions, mechanics, model airplanes, radio, etc.; girls, on cooking, sewing, etc. Boys go in a big way for stories about legendary heroes; girls, for biographies of women.

These interests expand, calling for ever wider sources of information. By age 12 the reading interest is at its peak. All the years of nurturing interests of children now pay big dividends.

Between the ages of 12 and 16, interests become intensified, specialized, and stabilized. Up to about the age of 9, children depend a lot upon adults for attitudes and ideas. Their experiences with books vary from rich to poor, depending upon the attitudes and guidance given first by parents and later by parents and teachers. After age 9, children begin to break these bonds of dependency because they want to do things on their own. How well they do after age 9 depends upon how well parents and teachers have done their job before that time.

The first golden age, then, for developing permanent and worthwhile *interests* in reading is that period before 9 years. If the parents read widely and enjoy discussing what they read, it is easy for children to take a similar interest. Of course, the materials suitable for children must be available in the home as well as in the school and the public library.

The second golden age is that period from 9 years and on. Children begin to take longer and longer flights back into time. These flights take them farther away from home—to other communities, states, countries and even into outer space. As interests mature, the adolescent delves deeper into science, history, economics, etc. Interest in reading is established as a permanent and worth-while activity.

Phonics and related word-learning skills. "What about phonics?" This is a question of considerable concern to many parents. And to teachers, too!

Interest is the starting point for learning anything, but especially for learning to read. It is only one of the first essentials, however. A beginner must learn to tell one word from another—if he ever learns to read. The ability to associate the sounds of words with letters and groups of letters, as in syllables, is one good way to tell one little group of wiggley lines from another. So phonics and all the other skills that help to identify words quickly and accurately make up another first essential in reading.

Good readers don't guess at words. Even though *house* and *home,* for example, look a little bit alike, they mean two different things to people who are raised in homes where there is love and faith and compassion. And so a child who feels this difference can make better and faster use of his phonics skills. He is taught to use meaning clues with the phonic clues to the bare word form.

Phonic skills help the child—or adult—to pronounce words but they do not give him the idea the word represents. If all a child can do is pronounce words he sees in print, he, of course, cannot read. It is fairly easy to learn how to pronounce words in Latin, German, Spanish, or French, but learning to read one of these foreign languages calls for understanding the ideas.

Interest is something that is brought to reading. Parents and teachers don't give separate lessons on interest alone. Interest is developed in tadpoles, jet engines, or Einstein's theory of relativity. Interest is ongoing, a part of a satisfying activity.

Phonic skills are an inseparable part of the reading act. They help the beginner and the experienced reader to get at the idea when he associates the letters of whole words with the sounds of whole words that he understands when he listens to them or uses them in his speech. If the child is to use his phonic skills to get through to the idea, he must be able to use them automatically so that he can keep his one mind on the idea. For this reason, he learns his phonic skills in an actual reading situation rather than by studying a list of isolated, meaningless words before he reads.

Sincere parents often ask, "What about phonics?" with one eyebrow raised. Then they may inquire, "Why don't they teach phonics today?"

Cold, recorded facts show that the authors of teacher's manuals for widely used basic readers have never dropped phonics. Before any responsible author can drop phonics he must substitute a better way to analyze words for identification purposes. So far, that better way has not been discovered.

Thinking and related aspects of comprehension. Today, more and more parents ask, "What can we do to help our children increase their reading speed and comprehension?" These often are the parents who are satisfied with the help their children are getting on phonics.

Comprehension is a topic which should be first-order concern to more parents and to more teachers. Researches have indicated that much more attention needs to be given to this aspect of reading.

The process of making a concept and of drawing a conclusion is called thinking. The product is called comprehension or understanding.

Parents and teachers need to follow up on children's interests. They also need to guide children in extending and deepening those interests. This is one of the first essentials in improving comprehension.

Of course, the child who has difficulty in identifying words because he lacks phonic skills has a slim chance of comprehending. He is so busy attending to the word form with his one mind that he must give up understanding the idea.

So interest, phonic skills, and thinking go hand in hand. They are three essentials for learning to read and for being a competent reader.

Learning how to think in a reading situation has its hazards, too. In the first place, thinking is done only in terms of the experience of the reader. If, for example, an eight-year-old has never seen a *sieve* and doesn't know its general purpose, it is difficult, if not impossible, to get the idea across with words alone. If his parents, teachers, or playmates have influenced his attitudes one way or another on a topic, his comprehension of what he reads on that topic is increased or decreased, depending on whether his attitudes are favorable or unfavorable toward the topic.

Then, too, thinking can get bogged down in language. The word *range* or *foot* has different uses or meanings which the child must understand in order to think straight. These shifts in the uses of words are language hazards for inexperienced readers.

Colorful expressions such as "Looking down your nose at someone," "Spring is just around the corner," and "Steam is king" are quite meaningless to children in the primary grades. Likewise, some children in the sixth grade may have difficulty in understanding, "Half a loaf is better than no bread." In order to understand these highly imaginative expressions children need to do a lot of growing up and to have help.

In the use of reference books, such as an authoritative encyclopedia, the child can learn a lot about systematic thinking. First, he can learn to state his problem clearly. The very young child simply wants to know about ducks, alligators, clouds, or where rubber comes from or other things which are easy to keep in mind. The older child and adolescent is concerned with more abstract concepts, ranging from woodlore to atoms. Unless the older pupils learn to state their problems clearly, their reading may take them on interesting but unrewarding bypaths, unrelated to their needs.

A second step in thinking calls for a knowledge of authentic sources of information. Both the reputation of authors and the ratings of encyclopedias, dictionaries, textbooks, and other reference materials are to be considered. Many children, for example, have a healthy respect for Roy Chapman Andrews and Wilfred Bronson in science.

Learning to judge whether a statement is a fact or an opinion is a third essential in learning to think. For example here are two statements in an authoritative home and school encyclopedia about flowers:

"the color, perfume, the dainty forms of flowers delight everyone."

"Many beautiful American wild flowers are becoming rare."

The first statement is quite clearly an expression of the author's attitude, an opinion; the second, a statement of fact because it can be verified.

Many arguments in both classrooms and living rooms arise because the participants have not learned to think clearly about facts and opinions. Most scientific reports and entries in encyclopedias present opinions as well as facts. But able writers give their readers many clues as to which are being presented. To get his thinking straight, the child needs learning experiences that will teach him when he is dealing with facts and when he is dealing with opinions.

A fourth step calls for the evaluation of the material selected for reading. When children are in the kindergarten and primary grades they learn easily to tell whether a statement is related to their topic or totally unrelated. As they become more mature in their attitudes and skills they learn to tell how closely related a statement is to their need. In short, they learn to judge the degree of relatedness of information to their purposes.

Organization of facts and opinions is a fifth essential in learning how to think. Outlining, for example, is a skill that requires long-time nurture. Kindergarten children take the first step when they learn to list housekeeping duties, what they want to find out on a field trip, the steps in a simple experiment with the germination of seeds, etc. Children in the intermediate grades, however, begin to deal with much more complex concepts. For this reason they are concerned not only with the coordinate main ideas but also with the coordinate subideas that are related to each main idea. Outlining is one way for children to learn how to think clearly by organizing their ideas.

Summaries, charts, graphs, written reports, and other ways of organizing information are all ways of teaching the child how to think—how to comprehend. Heads-up teaching and authentic, well-written reference materials are necessary for the healthy emotional and intellectual growth of the child. Moreover, this is a job for both parents and teachers.

Setting up a problem, sifting out facts from opinions, testing the relevance of information to a need, organization of information—all these are steps in getting ready to use it. The big dividend comes when conclusions, or generalizations, are made.

By experimentation and hearing the teacher read from an authentic reference, the primary-school child draws a conclusion about what kinds of metal a magnet will attract. By experimenting with models and consulting an appropriate reference, the older boy learns how an airplane flies. By collecting and organizing information about himself and possible vocations, the senior high school youth makes a choice of vocations. All of these are conclusions, mighty important at each age level. When training in how to think clearly and straight has been started in the home and has been nurtured in terms of the growing child's needs, he becomes a thinking adult.

When the child puts a cardboard box over a growing plant and finds, after a few days, that it has turned white, he learns to draw a conclusion between the effect (white color) and the cause (absence of light). When the older child learns the relationship between mosquitoes and disease he learns about cause and effect. Therefore, learning to think calls for learning to draw conclusions from cause-effect relationships.

To solve a mystery, a person collects relevant facts and draws a conclusion. By collecting related facts about the improvement of transportation and communication, the older student draws a conclusion about how fast the world is "shrinking." His problem is to collect enough relevant facts and to reorganize them so that he can draw a reasonable conclusion.

When the "Kentucky Fact Summary" on page 28, Volume K-L, of one encyclopedia is consulted, verifiable information is found. But the population figures are for a given date. Therefore, the child needs to learn to date his facts before drawing a conclusion.

Drawing conclusions from analogies is fraught by many dangers for children. For this reason authors of authentic materials very carefully select their analogies. For example, here are some samples of readily understood analogies in one encyclopedia:

The charges which make it [lightning] are built up by churning air inside a thundercloud.

Liquids can dissolve solid materials or capture and hold gases in solution (See Solutions). Thus they serve as a kind of transportation system for dissolved materials.

In Summary

Teaching the child how to read is a mutual undertaking for parents and teachers. To do this job, they need to keep three aspects of the reading process in mind:

1. The development of *interests* which take the child to reading materials within his ability and which contribute to permanent and worthwhile reading habits.
2. The development of *phonic* and related word perception skills to a point where they are used automatically.
3. The development of the ability to *think* in reading situations.

Teachers assume all three of these responsibilities when they join the teaching profession. But by no means can parents rightfully shirk the first and third responsibilities. Reading parents tend to produce reading children.

15. Comprehension in Reading *

E. W. DOLCH

THE PROBLEM of comprehension is best understood if we begin by asking ourselves why it is that primary children so easily comprehend their basic reading books. After all, any successful reader is just seeing familiar words in new arrangements. So the primary children are usually seeing words which are familiar to them. The writers of primary readers are careful to use only such words. Then the new arrangements of these familiar words tell stories about familiar things—the loss of a bicycle, the visit of a relative, a trip to some recreation place, and so on. The new arrangements give the children pictures that they easily "see" in their imagination. Or the new arrangements of familiar words give the children new ideas, but ideas close

*From E. W. Dolch, "Comprehension in Reading," *Education* (May, 1956), pp. 536–40. Reprinted by permission of the author and The Bobbs-Merrill Co., Inc., Indianapolis, Ind.

to their daily experience, such as the need of carefulness, the generosity to a new neighbor, the banding together of a group to give an amateur circus, and so on. So the problem of comprehension is not great in the primary grades, since the familiar words give new pictures that are not too far from experience or new ideas that are not too far from the children's thinking.

Beginning with the middle grades, however, comprehension becomes a major problem, and it remains so all the way through high school and college. It is not so great a problem, of course, in the voluntary reading of the children. Most of that voluntary reading is fiction which tells stories that are not too hard for the children to imagine. Much of that voluntary reading is about hobbies, such as science or trains, or photography, or the like, and here again, the reader knows a lot about the subject and the words tend to be familiar and the pictures or ideas not too far from previous knowledge. Incidentally, we must remember too that when the child does his own selecting in this voluntary reading, he almost always chooses books that are easy *for him,* that is, a grade or two below the one in which he is reading (not necessarily below the one in which he is sitting). We all choose easy books for voluntary reading, no matter how experienced adults we may be; and again, this means easy *for us.*

The problem of comprehension comes up, however, in the assigned reading of the school. This is chosen by the curriculum committee so as to be somewhat hard for the children. Not too hard, it is hoped, but "hard enough for them to have to work at it." We might well question this philosophy. There is good reason to believe that most people learn more from easy reading than from hard reading. It is usually the case that the one who boasts of his hard reading is really doing reading that is easy for him at the time. But let us put this dispute aside and admit that the assigned reading of the middle grades and on through high school is "hard" for most or at least for many children.

This "hardness" is easily explained. There are at least three reasons. First, there are many words of unknown meaning or of unusual meaning. Second, the new arrangements are in long sentences, with many modifiers, and often with inverted order. Third, the pictures or ideas these new arrangements are planned to give are far from the child's experience, and so hard to understand.

That the assigned material naturally grows harder is easily understood. If the primary grades deal with the child's own ideas and local environment, the reading of later grades starts to go away from this familiar core. In space, the reading matter deals with all parts of the globe. In time, the reading matter goes back to ancient times and even to the cave man. In maturity, the reading matter deals with the occupations and interests of adults, and of very specialized adults at that. If the primary reading dealt with the grocer, the middle grade reading may deal with the steelworker, and the upper grade material may deal with the concerns of the financier or the congressman.

Again, there is argument that the assigned reading matter should not go so rapidly away from the background of children, that the change should be more gradual. The trouble seems to be that in the upper grades at least, the material is prepared by specialists who have no idea how hard their mental pictures and ideas are. The geography is doubtless written by a geographer who has spent thirty years in the study of the subject. The civics is written by a specialist who knows government as well as the child knows the backyards of his own block. In the senior high school there is the same trouble or worse. No one seems to have thought that for one to understand, the words must be familiar and the new arrangements must not give pictures or ideas that are very far from the background of the reader. So grade by grade the reading matter gets farther and farther over the heads of the average child of the grade. He may cease to try to understand and begin just "to read his lesson," which often becomes "saying the words with little or no understanding."

Of course, much of this difficulty could be solved by the committees selecting textbooks for the children. They might follow one rule: "The child attacking this subject for the first time must have what is actually a *primer* in the subject. It must sound like a primer to us." Instead, the usual committee chooses a book that sounds all right *to them*. That usually means it sounds something like the college textbook they had in the subject. To them, the words are familiar, and the mental pictures and ideas are not too far from their background. But they have had four years of college, years of general reading, years of travel, and so on. The child knows his own home town, a few years of school, and little else. How can the book that "sounds right" to the teacher be at all right for him?

Granted, however, that we have a textbook chosen by a committee as "containing the best of the subject" and we have children who are expected to comprehend it. Let us go back to our basic principles. The words must be familiar and the new arrangements of those words must make pictures or ideas not too far from the reader's background. How can we reach this situation?

Obviously, the first and best thing we can do is to concentrate on the new words. If these are blanks or are misunderstood, there can be no meaning to the sentences or any sense to the paragraphs. Here the average adult just has no idea of the child's limitations, and children will never admit those limitations for fear of being laughed at by those adults. One rule to follow is to remember, "Children will understand only in terms of their own experience." That is, no matter what the books say, the comprehension is in terms of the reader's past. For instance, the history book dealing with the Revolution constantly speaks of "guns" of all kinds, from pistols to muskets, cannon, and so on. But to the child this means the guns he sees now. It means repeating weapons, magazine loaders, and even smokeless powder. The child is astonished when we explain that in a battle, after the first volley, the men often could not find each other in the smoke. Children do not realize why men had bayonets and swords. After one shot, a man was through with shooting, for he had no time to load his gun down the barrel as he had to.

Similarly, when we say the men of India "plant" a crop, the children think of the plows, harrows, drills, and so on that they know. They never heard of scratching the ground with a pointed log. If we say savages "cooked their food," the children give those savages frying pans and stew pots, and so on. Children always understand in terms of what they know.

Knowing this fact, a good teacher or parent will be on the lookout for such "miscomprehension." He will see at once where a child will think the wrong thing, and will set him straight. With the average school textbook, that is a real job. But we must follow the rule, "A little really understood is better than a lot of mere words soon forgotten." Teachers have to select the essentials, see that they are really understood, and let a great deal of the rest go for lack of time.

For this purpose of understanding there is nothing like an enormous file of pictures clipped from magazines and picture sections of papers. The children can make such a file. Let some of the pictures be arranged geographically by country, city, and building. Let other files be by occupations, such as "India, farming," and "Switzerland, cheesemaking," and so on. In making such a file there is enormous learning. In using it, there is much understanding of new words and mental pictures, and ideas.

If time is taken to make sure the words are understood, then we must ask about the new arrangements of words that give new pictures and new ideas. Now, making new mental pictures takes time. If the text describes a medieval city, we must all go slow in order to build that city in our minds. We must see what the houses are made of, what kinds of windows and roofs there are, if there is a court or backyard to a house, and the like. Then we need to see the width of the street, how it is paved, and where the drainage runs. Then we need to see what a store looks like, and what is in the store.

How many stores? What does a market look like? How big is the city? How is it walled, and so on? Then we have to ask about drinking water and sewage. How did they wash their clothes? Was there soap? What did the people eat, and how did they get it and cook it? Was there coal or wood? What kind of stoves? As we have said, all this takes time, as the building of any city in the mind would. So, beyond the meaning of the words, we have the problem of making mental pictures.

It is to help at this point that the reading books have pictures. They do not have enough pictures, though, or often the right pictures. But the pictures need to be studied too. Otherwise, the children do not see what is in them. For instance, the child will see the holes in the buildings as windows, but he will assume that the windows have sashes which go up and down as do those in his own house. He has to be led to see the casements. And he will not note the small panes unless he is asked why they are so small. In fact, it is often found that the most useful comprehension in a book is got by studying the pictures with the class. After they have noticed all that is in the pictures, they will have understood most of the subject, and they will understand the reading matter much better.

We have said the books go quickly away from the child's experience in the directions of space and time. But still harder to cope with are the new concepts that are far away from the child in the direction of maturity. For instance, no child will ever understand the troubles Lincoln had with his cabinet. The adult considerations have never entered his experience or comprehension. Then children just will never understand violent differences in feeling between sections of their own country, for they have lived in only one section and assume that all other sections are like their own. The westward movement of people, with its strange changes in living conditions, its social problems in a raw country populated by men only, its confusion of law and lawlessness, and so on, will always be outside the comprehension of children of the present day. Of course they can understand details of it, but the whole drama is too complicated, too much a confusion of adult drives and prejudices, and so on. Full comprehension here demands a maturity beyond that of the grade child.

We have said, "Children will understand only in terms of their own experience," and we have then gone on to include in that experience pictures from books and magazines. We must not forget too the moving pictures children see. Many of them teach more geography and history and social science than many books. Children who have never even seen the sea can get some understanding of the problems of adventure and exploration and seafaring life if they see some of the powerful moving pictures based upon the sea. The Chinese adage, "A picture is worth ten thousand words" may be a slight exaggeration at times, but at other times it is literally true.

"Comic style" books presenting the stories of novels may also be a great help. After a child has seen the pictures of people and places which one of these illustrated stories presents, he can go to the book itself and this time will find many more words to have familiar meaning and will find the new arrangements of words giving more easily new mental pictures and ideas. If these "comic style" books were better done, they would be much more helpful.

The teacher who is widely read and greatly traveled can be of much help to children in comprehension of their textbooks. Such a teacher has seen much for herself, and she is on her guard against "miscomprehension." If she has been to Southern California she can guard against misunderstanding of irrigation of orange orchards and the like. If she has been to New York city, she can look out for misunderstanding of the underground system by children who live in places that have nothing like it. The way this teacher guards against misunderstandings is by reminding the children of things they know but about which they do not think at the moment. Most towns pump their water from underground as they do in Southern California, and the teacher can remind them of this. Most children know that water runs downhill, and so the teacher explains how the orange grove is tilted slightly so that the water spreads through the ditches. In many ways the teacher every day reminds the children of things in their own experience which will help in comprehension of their textbooks. Only the teacher can do this, because only she knows the local situation and knows what experience her children really do have.

Finally, we must suggest the difference between spontaneous comprehension and "determined" comprehension. The primary child comprehends without half trying. His comprehension is spontaneous. The child with much experience may be comprehending spontaneously most of the time. But for a great many children a large part of the time, there must be "determined" comprehension. For without determination to comprehend, the child will go over the material once, shrug his shoulders and say, "I don't get it," and that will be all.

The teacher gets determined comprehension in two ways. One way is by "selling" the lesson beforehand. She can tell about some interesting experiences of her own or that she has read which are directly related to the lesson. Then many children will think, "Say, I want to see what the book says about that," and so they have the determination to comprehend. Many teachers do this selling job before every assignment, and it is a wonderful device. Another way is for a teacher to bring up some question which will appeal to the children and arouse some question in their minds. Then the lesson is assigned, with the promise that it will have the answer or bear upon that answer. For instance, "Does an afternoon siesta prove that people who take it are lazy?" Well, read the description of the countries which have that custom and see what you think.

Both these methods require imagination and take time and thought. Instead, a teacher may resort to the old policy of force and say, "Find the answers to these questions or else." Such a plan will get a "going over the lesson." But the children will be looking for a word pattern that fits the word pattern of the questions. There is little guarantee of comprehension. If they get the "right answer" and the teacher asks what it means, they may say, "I don't know, but that is what the books says." This attitude is one of our greatest blocks to real comprehension in school.

To summarize, a child will comprehend if he meets familiar words which, in new arrangements, give him new mental images and new ideas. But he will always comprehend in terms of his own past experience. If the material is hard, the teacher will help by bringing him pictures which make new words have familiar meaning. She will help by telling of her own experiences in words which he can understand. She will help by reminding him of his own experiences which he does not think of but which will help him get the new word meanings and the new mental pictures and ideas.

16. *The Challenge Faced in Promoting Desirable Reading Interests* *

WILLIAM S. GRAY

THE FACT has long been recognized that one of the best measures of the vitality of the reading programs in our schools is the extent and quality of the personal reading of children and youth. During recent decades increasing effort has been made by teachers to promote wide reading interests

* From William S. Gray, "The Challenge Faced in Promoting Desirable Reading Interests," *Education* (May, 1959), pp. 551–56. Reprinted by permission of the author and The Bobbs-Merrill Co., Inc., Indianapolis, Ind.

and to cultivate preference for reading materials of superior quality. That much remains to be achieved is evidenced both by surveys of reading interests and by the deep concern of many parents concerning the small amount and the unsatisfactory quality of the personal reading in which their children engage.

In the hope of throwing light on the nature and extent of the problems faced in promoting desirable reading interests and habits, the discussion that follows does three things: it reviews briefly major trends during recent decades in the personal reading of elementary- and high school students; it reports pertinent findings of two studies made recently among youth and adults; and it discusses certain implications of the facts presented which merit careful consideration by both teachers and parents.

Trends in Personal Reading

In a summary of relevant studies made prior to 1925 the following significant conclusions were reached: (1) The percentage of pupils who read independently increases rapidly during the middle and upper grades and is relatively high during the high school period. (2) The average number of books read independently averages (for the pupils reporting) from ten to twenty a year in the sixth, seventh and eighth grades. Two distinct trends were identified during the high school period: "to decrease the average number of books read" (in certain high schools); and "to maintain a high average throughout the period" (in other high schools). (3) The habit of reading magazines and newspapers is almost universal above the fifth grade. In interpreting the foregoing conclusions two facts should be kept clearly in mind: first, the relatively small number of schools in which studies had been made; and, second, the highly selective character of the high school population during the first quarter of the current century.

More recent studies at the elementary-school level confirm the view that an increasing percentage of pupils throughout the grades engage in more or less personal reading. At least three factors have contributed to an increase in the percentage of pupils in the lower grades who read books and in a larger number of books read by pupils at all levels. They are greater emphasis on extension, supplementary and library reading in most schools, the production during recent years of a wealth of simple attractive trade books adapted to the interests and maturity levels of pupils in the respective grades, and the provision of time for free reading during school time. The foregoing findings are based on all the personal reading both in and out of school in which pupils engage. A recent study by McCullough reports that only 25 to 48 per cent of the fifth grade pupils in three school systems reported any out-of-school personal reading. This finding gives cause for real concern to the extent that it is representative.

Reports on newspaper and magazine reading reveal equal if not greater participation than formerly among pupils in the middle and upper grades. When the use in school of weekly newspapers especially prepared for children is considered the percentage of pupils who read news regularly has greatly increased at all grade levels. According to the findings of McCullough, the fifth grade pupils in her study do little out-of-school newspaper or magazine reading. An encouraging fact is the increasing interest during recent years in informational as contrasted with fictional material. On the other hand, mass media have provided serious competition for the leisure time of pupils in many homes. Furthermore, recent studies of the quality of the materials read shows clearly that much remains to be desired, particularly when comic books and comic strips are considered.

Surveys made recently among high school students show that newspaper and magazine reading is practically universal and greater in amount than formerly. However, the extent of book reading is disappointingly small on the average. Reports from abroad reveal the fact that this is true also of the reading of adolescents in most countries where pertinent surveys have been made. The explanations usually offered for decreased personal reading among high school adolescents are the increasing proportion of youth from the lower socio-economic and cultural groups who now continue in school, the emergence of strong social interests, the heavy demands made on the students' time by assigned study activities, and vigorous competition for their free time by mass media, particularly television. The fact that the extent of book reading is much greater in some schools than in others of similar type gives rise to the hope that significant improvement is possible.

Results of Studies among Youth and Adults

During the last few years, the writer has carried on two extensive studies the findings of which are pertinent and illuminating. One aim of the first (thus far unpublished) was to find out the extent of the newspaper, the magazine and the unassigned book reading among high school and junior college students. Data were secured from groups of students in six large high schools and five junior colleges.

An analysis of the questionnaire returns showed that newspaper reading was an almost universal activity among the high school students reporting.

The percentages by grades were 97 in the ninth, 96 in the tenth, 99 in the eleventh, and 92 in the twelfth. The corresponding percentages for magazine reading was 67, 61, 64 and 52 and for unassigned book reading was 43, 32, 20 and 29. Of special significance is the range in the percentages of students in the different schools who reported book reading. In the ninth grade they varied from 17 to 77, in the tenth from 8 to 65, in the eleventh from 4 to 39 and in the twelfth from 21 to 45. The ranges in the number of books read were narrower in the case of the last two grades than they should have been because pertinent data were not supplied by one school which ranked high at the freshman and sophomore levels.

Corresponding data for the junior college students who participated were as follows: 88 per cent reported newspaper reading, the range being from 77 to 100; 48 per cent reported the reading of magazines, the range being from 38 to 61; and 32 per cent reported unassigned book reading, the range being from 13 to 41. A comparison of the averages for the high school and college students is very revealing. It shows that the junior college students ranked lower in newspaper, magazine, and unassigned book reading than the high school students, with the possible exception of book reading at the junior and senior high school level. The chief reasons given by the college students for the limited amount of book reading reported were: the heavy demands made on their time by assigned study activities; and the urgent need to engage in part-time remunerative activities in order to pay college expenses. The decreasing extent of personal reading among those of wider education is unfortunate and presents a very challenging problem to schools and colleges.

Let us look next at the extent of personal reading among adults. For pertinent data reference is made to findings in a recent intensive study by Gray and Rogers. This study aimed among other things to find out the extent and nature of the reading done by three groups of adults; nine having an eighth grade education or less; twenty-one having from nine to twelve years of schooling; and eight having more than a high school education. The limited number of adults who were studied is due to the fact that they were subjected to intensive interviews and to reading tests based on current events, editorials and feature articles. Those who cooperated held various types of positions, ranging from that of janitor to divisional executive, in a large mercantile establishment of a Midwestern city.

On the basis of the evidence secured each adult was rated on five-step scales of maturity in eighteen aspects of reading. They related to interest in reading, purposes for reading, nature of the materials read, the recognition and construing of meaning, and thoughtful reaction to and use of the ideas acquired. An analysis of all the information secured revealed a number of significant facts concerning the extent, patterns and relationships of the personal reading of adults.

The most impressive fact identified was the low ranks received in general by the 38 cases on the various maturity scales. Whereas most of them expressed keen interest in reading, the amount of time devoted to personal reading was disappointingly small. As was to be expected, the college group ranked highest. On the average, however, they did not surpass the mid-point in the total range from gross immaturity to the high level attained by nine additional adults who were reputedly well-read, superior readers. Two selective factors doubtless operated in the case of these college graduates. Adults having a college education who find employment in a mercantile establishment apparently lack the interests which lead to wide reading of superior quality. It appears also that the nature of the work and recreational activities in which most of them engage is not such as to stimulate interest in extensive, high-quality personal reading.

The ranks on the maturity scales of the adults who had received elementary-school training only and who had gone to high school for from one to four years averaged about a half rank below those who had gone to college. They were very similar for the two groups with respect to "interest in reading," "purposes for reading," and "materials read." Those who had gone to high school, however, averaged slightly above the elementary-school group in reading competence. The amount of personal reading reported by members of each group was distinctly limited. It consisted largely in most cases of some newspaper and magazine reading but very little book reading. These findings harmonize in general with the results of other studies of adult reading interests.

As the facts revealed through the interviews and tests were studied in greater detail certain relationships stood out impressively: (1) Interest and purposes for reading are less closely related to amount of school training than in competence in reading. (2) The maturity of reading interests and purposes appear to be more closely related to the extent to which an individual's activities extend beyond the range of his immediate needs. Whereas this conclusion is based on negative findings, it will be supported shortly by the results of other studies. (3) Low competence in reading seriously limits the amount of reading in which an adult engages. Because of strong motivation a few individuals may use reading in more mature ways than their competence in reading would suggest. On the other hand, the fact that an adult possesses the skills involved in efficient reading is no guarantee that he will engage widely in personal reading. To do so he must have acquired in school or later compelling motives that lead him to read for pleasure or other rewards that have meaning and significance to him.

Characteristics of Highly Mature Readers

Attention is directed next to certain facts revealed through interviews and tests given to twenty-one reputedly well-read adults. The purpose of this study was to determine more fully the characteristics of maturity in reading and the factors that influence their development. Of this number nine ranked at the highest level in all of the criteria of maturity in reading for which scales were developed. Each of the others scored very high on most of them, but ranked below the highest level on one or more of the criteria.

The facts secured from these twenty-one mature readers revealed many common characteristics. However, they appeared in varying forms and combinations in harmony with the distinctive characteristics of each adult and the conditions that impelled him to read. Each adult possessed a center or focus of interest to which much of his reading related and which served both as a motivating force and as a vital factor in interpreting what was read. Each displayed keen interest in people, things, events and problems outside his sphere of daily living. The specific items varied widely in character, but in every case there was a vital interest that extended far beyond the individual's everyday survival needs.

Each was keenly aware of his responsibility as a group member and of a social role that involved opinion leadership and constructive social participation. Whereas this recognition influenced the amount and kind of reading of most mature readers, some read widely and interpreted deeply for purely personal reasons. Each was characterized by an ever-expanding range of reading interests that lead to broader reading and deeper interpretation and to continued growth in and through reading. Finally, every mature reader possessed a high level of competence in reading which enabled him to focus his attention on the meaning and interpretation of what he read, to react thoughtfully to the ideas acquired and to integrate them effectively with previous experiences in the same or related fields.

A study of the factors that seemed to be most vital in influencing the development of maturity in reading among these adults was very revealing. It showed first that whereas there is substantial correlation between the amount of education and personal reading, it is by no means the sole factor. For example, the twenty-one highly mature readers varied all the way from little more than an eighth grade education to completion of a Ph.D.

degree. The study showed also that the cultural influence of the home was a vital factor. Each of the mature readers had the advantage of some cultural stimulation at home which varied widely in amount and kind. However, their reports revealed clear evidence of a favorable attitude in the home toward reading and its inherent values, as well as toward other forms of cultural contacts.

Of major importance is the fact that each of the mature readers reported that at some point in his formative years he had had rewarding contacts with good literature. He had also received carefully planned instruction which aided him in discovering the various values inherent in good literature and in acquiring a growing appreciation of it. These constructive influences often began to operate during early school years. But in some cases they were delayed until high school or college years. But in the case of each reader there were such contacts and guidance and a keen awareness of their value.

Concluding Statements

The facts secured through the studies referred to above justify a series of conclusions and pointed questions. Because of the limitations of space little more can be done here than identify some of the problems faced.

1. Definite progress has been made during recent decades in stimulating interest in reading among elementary-school pupils. This has been due largely to the increasing effort made by teachers to promote desirable reading interests, to the increasing number of carefully prepared, attractive books that are published yearly, and to the provision in school of time for personal reading. Since the extent of the personal reading of books by elementary-school graduates decreases materially as they leave school or continue their education, certain challenging questions arise: What error or deficiency occurs in our efforts to stimulate permanent habits of personal reading that results in disappointing results after pupils leave the elementary school? Is it enough merely to provide opportunity for pupils to engage in unassigned reading of their own choice? Since students in high schools and colleges vary widely in the amount of personal reading in which they engage, what are the factors or conditions that lead to much personal reading among students in some cases and very little in others?

2. Since inability to read was found to be a limiting factor in respect to amount of personal reading in which children and young people engage, two pointed questions arise: Does instruction in reading in the grades carry pupils to a level of competence that enables them to read the materials that

are of most interest to them as they mature? Can we justify any longer the failure to continue developmental reading instruction in high schools?

3. The reports from the more mature readers indicated that the home is a vital influence in stimulating interests in cultural pursuits, including reading. This suggests three challenging questions: Are teachers thoroughly familiar with the extent and nature of such influences in the homes of their respective pupils? Does the school surround pupils with sufficient cultural influences to make up in part for the deficiencies of some homes and to reinforce those in others? Is there sufficiently close cooperation between teachers and parents to insure maximum progress in promoting desirable reading interests and tastes?

4. The information secured showed clearly that mature readers have acquired compelling motives for reading and centers of interest that lead to wide reading. In our efforts to develop wide personal reading are we concentrating too largely on the stimulation of reading as an end in itself? Are we giving sufficient time to the stimulation of interests and curiosities in all school activities that serve as motivating centers for personal reading? Do content teachers assume their full responsibility for stimulating in their respective fields challenging interests that lead to self-impelled avocational reading? In some way or other we must establish interests in things, events, people and activities that will lead to ongoing personal reading.

5. The reports indicated that each mature reader had at some time in his school experience come in contact with a teacher who helped him to identify the values inherent in good reading. Are we providing in our schools today the guidance needed to help pupils discover the rewards and values inherent in good literature in addition to those that the pupils are prepared to acquire on their own? These and other related questions merit serious study if we are to develop a generation of young people and adults who turn to reading regularly as a source of pleasure, inspiration and guidance.

17. Phonics: Syllables *

EMMETT ALBERT BETTS

MASTER teachers and practicing specialists in reading have long recognized that efficient reading requires the *automatic* use of phonic and other word-learning skills. When these skills are not taught, the child, left to shift for himself, develops his own system. Unhappily, these haphazard, pupil-developed systems too often are clumsy and ineffective. Hence, there is a need for the systematic teaching of these skills, according to the child's needs.

Systematic Preparation

One of the first steps in the systematic development of phonic skills is taken before the child is introduced to reading—whether he is in the kindergarten or the first grade. At this time, there are two considerations:

First, there is a need to develop oral language (listening and speaking) skills as preparation for reading readiness activities. For example, the child is taught how to listen to a simple story and how to tell a story in sequence; how to discriminate between simple shapes of pictured things and between sounds in general; how to think in sentences; how to interpret pictures, etc.

Second, there is a need to develop a readiness for reading, which takes the child into the beginning steps. For example, the child is taught how to discriminate between letters and between word forms; how to discriminate between the rhyming parts of words; how to read from left to right; how to associate names with characters in a book; how to read one-line texts of a picture story; etc.

So far as the school is concerned, systematic, informal, and differentiated preparation for reading begins when the child enters school in the kindergarten or the first grade. This preparation develops (1) interests which take the child to reading, (2) awareness of the sounds of spoken words and of the angles, curves, and vertical lines of written words, and (3) ability to think in his language.

Beginning Reading

At this point the teacher makes a decision regarding how she will teach the child to tell one word from another. She may decide to use the word, or

* From Emmett Albert Betts, "Phonics: Syllables," *Education* (May, 1959), pp. 557–63. Reprinted by permission of the author and The Bobbs-Merrill Co., Inc., Indianapolis, Ind.

telling, "method" to develop what has been called a sight vocabulary. This telling approach—dignified by the pedagogical term *word method*—is a memory test for the pupil. A child with the necessary attention span may survive this method by working out his own system.

This word "method" has one advantage: the teacher needs no preparation in either phonetics (the science of speech sounds) or phonics (the relating of speech sounds to their letter representatives). Moreover, she can be indifferent to *need, meaning, auditory set, feedback, generalizations, applications,* and other factors in the perception (i.e., knowing) of words.

The chief disadvantage of the word, or telling, "method" is that too many children become confused by having to memorize a large number of sight words (i.e., words they can recognize at sight) before they are helped with the relationships between sounds and phonograms representing them.

On the other hand, the teacher may decide to use a phonic method with beginners. In this instance, she helps them to:

1. Associate the first sounds of spoken words with the first letter or letters; e.g., the sound of *m* in the spoken word *me* with the letter *m* in the written word *me;* the sound (blend) of *st* in *stop* with the letters *st.*

2. Associate the rhyming part of a spoken word with the letters (vowel or vowel-consonant) representing those sounds; e.g., the sound *ook* in the spoken word *look* with the *ook* in the printed word *look;* the sound of *ay* in *play* with the letters *ay.*

3. Blend first consonants of words; e.g., the *b* of the spoken word *big* with the *l* of the spoken word *look* to make the sound of *bl* in the spoken word *blue.* (The next step is the identification of the letters *bl* in the written word *blue,* representing the blend.)

4. Blend the first consonant sound of a known word with the rhyming part (vowel or vowel-consonant) of another known word to make a new word; e.g., the first consonant of (*m*)y with the rhyming part of *c* (*an*) to make *man.* (The next step is the identification of the phonograms *m* and *an,* representing the blend.)

5. Check the use (meaning) of the word in its sentence setting.

When the teacher elects to teach phonics to beginners, she assumes that they need as much (or more) systematic help in telling one word from another as they will later. She also takes for granted that learning to know a word calls for a study of (1) the word form as well as (2) its meaning.

Systematic Sequences

The foundation for building phonic skills is laid in the language readiness and reading readiness stages of learning. An awareness of the relationship between the sounds of spoken words and the letters representing them in written words is taught as the child meets each new word in a reading situation. In beginning reading, as well as during the latter part of the readiness stage, this phonic learning is reinforced by teaching the child how to use picture clues (e.g., to names or action), configuration clues (e.g., comparing or contrasting lengths and shapes of words), and context clues (e.g., *and* to connect two ideas) to word identification or recognition.

In general, the following sequence appears to have merit:
1. Letter phonics
   a. First consonant sounds of words
   b. Rhyming parts of words
   c. Vowels and final consonants
      1) Analysis of the rhyming parts.
      2) Generalization regarding the sounds of vowels and consonants in syllables; e.g., one vowel in a one-syllable word usually has the short sound.

   (Note: The child first learns the sounds of letters in words. Later, he studies the different phonograms that represent a sound; e.g., short *e* may be represented by *e* in *red* or *ea* in *bread.*)
2. Phonics of syllables
   a. Syllables
      1) Hearing number of syllables in spoken words.
      2) Identifying syllables in written words.
   b. Inflectional endings; e.g., *ing* as in *working* and *er* in *brighter*
   c. Suffixes; e.g., *ly* in *kindly*
   d. Roots
   e. Prefixes; e.g., *un* in *unhappy*
   f. Accent (stress)
3. Respellings in dictionary

The above sequence takes the child gradually from letter phonics to syllable phonics to dictionary respellings. There is no need to break this sequence into three different, unrelated parts (i.e., to trichotomize). For example, the child applies his letter phonics to the syllables of words. He applies his letter and syllable phonics to the interpretation of respellings in the dictionary. Therefore, the child's learning sequence is continuous.

Generalizations: Vowels

It is a truism that rote memorization of phonic rules contributes nothing to the child's automatic use of phonic skills. In fact, some pupils are confused because they do not understand how or when to apply a rule. Therefore, the memorizing of rules is a far cry from the making of generalizations (rules) based on personal observations of words.

The problem, then, is to help the child make generalizations based on his own experiences with groups of words. For example, common words include *man, and, at, can, has, hat, ran,* etc. having a short *a* vowel sound. Before the child concentrates on this vowel sound and the letter representing it, he has learned:

1. The sounds of *c* in *can, h* in *hat,* etc.
2. The sounds of the rhyming parts (vowel-consonant) in *m(an)*, *h(at)*, etc.
3. The sounds of the last consonant in *ca(n), ha(s),* etc.

The next step, then, is to help the child tune his hearing to the short sound of *a*. To take this step, it is necessary for him to contrast the short *a* sound with some other sound. Since common words include *big, did, this,* etc., he may be taught to hear the differences between the vowel sounds in *his—has, big—at,* etc. If he has no emotional or hearing handicap to block his learning, he soon learns to hear (to contrast) the sounds of short *a* and short *i*.

After the child learns to hear a given vowel sound, he is taught the letter representing that sound. For example, he generalizes that the letter *a* in *has, hat, back,* etc. represents the same vowel sound. He also generalizes that the letter *i* in *him, his, this,* etc. stands for the same vowel sound.

While words with the short *a* sound are being met daily in the child's reading, words with other sounds of *a* are met. For example, he frequently sees *came, late, make, name,* and other words with the long *a* vowel. Therefore, he is guided in the examination of *man, and, at,* etc. so that he obtains enough related facts to decide that when only one letter *a* is seen in a word, this *a* is usually short.

This same procedure is followed to help the child generalize on short *i* (e.g., *did, big*), short *e* (e.g., *get, yes*), short *o* (e.g., *not, got*), and short *u* (schwa as in *nut, brush*). After he has generalized on three more short vowel situations (e.g., short *a, e, i*), he is prepared to make a broader generalization: one letter in a word may have its short vowel sound. This rule applies to the words *black, best, big, box, but.*

Up to this point the child has been guided through a sequence of generalizations regarding (1) each short vowel sound, (2) the letter usually representing each sound, (3) the sound of a specific vowel letter in word with only one vowel letter, and (4) the short sound of different vowel letters in words. This same procedure is used for long vowel sounds and other vowel situations.

The final step in the teaching of generalizations (rules) regarding vowel letters and their sounds is their application to new words. In first and second readers, the pupil is guided into applying the short vowel rule, for example, to *fun, fish,* and many other one-syllable words. However, he is also meeting more and more two-syllable and larger words (e.g., *little, kitten*) to which he can apply the short vowel rule. But first he must be able to hear syllables in spoken words and to see these syllables in written words. Later he learns to hear accented syllables and to decide which syllables of a written word may be accented.

Generalizations, or rules, regarding the sounds of phonograms is somewhat hazardous. For example, there are about 68 chances in 100 that words ending in a final *e* have a long vowel sound as in *take, five, rode,* and *use.* There are 32 chances in 100 that this type of word will have some other vowel sound as in *done, come, some.* Some rules have even fewer applications while others—such as the long *e* sound of *y* in *windy* and *many*—may have more applications. For this and other reasons, the child is taught (1) exceptions to rule and (2) habit of checking the meaning of the word in its sentence or paragraph setting.

Three vowel rules appear to be acceptable:

1. One vowel letter in a word usually is short as in *hat, egg, hid, got,* and *but.* This also holds true for accented syllables as in *att(a)ck* and *att(e)ntion.*

2. A vowel is usually long in a word ending with *e* and the *e* is silent as in *safe* and *ice.* This applies to accented syllables as in *repl(a)ce.*

3. When two vowel letters are side by side, the first is usually long and the second is silent as in *g(oa)t* and *s(ea)t.* This also holds true in accented syllables as in *l(ea)dership.*

Generalizations: Consonants

One of the first steps in teaching consonant sounds is to help the child tune his hearing to them. He is taught, for example, to hear the simple sound of *m* in *my* and the blend of *st* in *stop.* Then he is taught to hear, for example, the simple sound of *l* in *tail* and the blend of *lt* in *felt.* In teaching both first and last consonants, the child first learns to hear the undistorted consonant sounds in words before he identifies the letters which stand for those sounds.

It is easy for the child to say the sound of long *a*, the sound of *er*, and other vowel sounds in isolation without distorting them. On the other hand, he cannot say the isolated sounds of *b, p, st*, and other consonants without distorting them. Therefore, it is necessary for him to hear and say consonant sounds in combination with vowel sounds; that is, in syllables and words.

Confusion results when the child is taught that *buh-erd*, for example, is *bird*. *Bird* is a one-syllable word, but the distortion of the consonant sound produces a two-syllable word. This confusion is compounded when an attempt is made to teach him to hear the syllables in *singing, kindly,* and *happen,* and other two-syllable words.

Here are some examples of the types of generalizations regarding consonants that are taught:

1. Consonant letters before the vowel may be blended to make a sound, as in (*st*)*op,* (*tr*)*ain,* and (*pr*)*etty.*
2. Consonant sounds after a vowel may be blended to make a sound, as in *ju*(*mp*), *sta*(*nd*), and *re*(*st*)*less.*
3. The *wh* in *when, what,* etc. stands for the *hw* sound.
4. The *qu* in (*qu*)*ick, s*(*qu*)*irrel,* etc., stands for the *kw* sound.
5. The *ck* at the end of a syllable, as in *ba*(*ck*), *qui*(*ck*)*er,* stands for the *k* sound.
6. The *nk* in *drink* and *bunk* stands for the *ngk* sound.
7. The *c* before *e, i,* and *y,* as in (*c*)*ent,* (*c*)*ircus,* and (*c*)*ycle,* stands for the *s* sound.
8. The sound of *g* before *e,* as in (*g*)*em* and (*g*)*eography,* often stands for the *j* sound (soft *g*).

Generalizations: Syllables

The number of syllables in words tends to increase at successive reader levels. For example, the beginner meets *a, and, the,* and many other common one-syllable words more often than he meets *airplane, something, experiments,* and other words of more than one syllable. This situation makes it possible for the child to make automatic the application of his phonic skills to one-syllable words and to gradually apply these skills to the syllables of longer words.

As the child learns his letter (or phonogram) phonics, he begins to apply his skills to the syllables of words. This application of phonics to the syllables, or pronunciation units, of words is done in four steps:

1. Hearing the number of syllables in common spoken words, as in *singing, farmer, many.*

2. Identifying the syllables in written words, as the *sing* and the *ing* in *singing.*

3. Deciding which syllable is accented, as *cross* in *across* and *gard* in *garden.*

4. Applying phonic skills to the syllables of new words, as the *ar* or *er* in *f(ar)m(er).* (This activity is usually introduced in Step 2.)

The above four steps are used to introduce the child to syllable phonics. They take the child from *hearing* the syllables to *seeing* the syllables. Finally, they help him apply what he already knows about letter phonograms to syllables. This procedure makes the learning of syllable phonics very easy because there is no break in the sequence of learning.

In reading situations, however, the child begins with the unknown written word and applies his phonic skills. Using the learning skills listed above, he can be taken through these steps:

1. In how many places do you see a vowel or a group of vowel letters that has one sound?

   In the word *f(a)th(er)*, he would see vowel letters in two places: *a* and *er*. In *explode*, he would see vowel letters in three places. But he knows that the final *e* is usually silent, leaving "sounded" vowel letters in two places.

2. Then how many syllables does the word have?

   He soon learns that a word has as many syllables as it has vowel situations. For example, he sees the *e* and the *or* in *r(e)p(or)t* and decides it has two syllables. Or, he notes the two *e*'s and the *o* in *d(e)v(e)l(o)p* to decide that it has three syllables. He also learns syllabic *l, m, n, r,* and *y,* as in *nick(el)*, *freed(om)*, *butt(on)*, *rubb(er),* and *carr(y).*

   When deciding how many syllables an unknown word may have, the child also looks for the *ed* ending. He has been taught to observe that *ed* adds an extra syllable when the root word ends in *d* or *t,* as in *banded* and *hunted.* In other words—such as *begged, cooked, sailed*—the *ed* does not add an extra syllable.

3. Which syllable is accented?

   This step is omitted until the child has (1) mastered the first two steps and (2) learned to identify common root words, inflectional endings, prefixes, and suffixes.

First, the pupil learns that many two- and three-syllable words are accented on the first syllable, as in *(fath)er, (happ)en, (gent)le, (luck)y, (fish)ing, (sick)ness, (poss)ible, (med)ium.* His previous experience with syllabic *r, l, m, n, r, y;* with inflectional endings (e.g., *ing*); and with suffixes (e.g., *en* in *golden* and *less* in *restless*) gives him a feeling for the unaccented second syllables.

Second, the pupil learns to identify common unaccented first syllables, as in *(a)bout, (de)scribe, (ex)cuse, (in)tend, (re)port.* He generalizes that the accent is on the first syllable of a word unless it begins with a common unaccented syllable.

4. What vowel rule will help you with the first syllable?

In accented first syllables of unknown words, a vowel rule may be applied. For example, the single vowel (short) rule may be applied to *(sadd)le, (emp)eror, (blizz)ard, (cott)on, (num)ber.* The rule for two vowels side by side (long) may be applied to *(paint)ed, (dream) ing, (moan)ing.*

Vowel rules may be applied to other accented syllables, as in the second syllable of *in(vent), ex(plain), be(side).*

Because pupils have already established the habit of left-to-right-word attack, they are taught to quickly identify common unaccented last syllables (e.g., the *er* of *butter*) as well as common unaccented first syllables (e.g., *in* in *invent*). Or, they may rule out the first and and last syllables, as in *(com)press(or).* Developing this type of versatility in the use of phonic skills helps pupils to quickly strip a word down to one unknown syllable which may be quickly analyzed into consonant and vowel phonograms for identification.

5. What is the usual sound of a given phonogram?

To increase the pupil's versatility, he is taught the usual sounds of common phonograms. For example, he learns very early that the usual sound of the last syllable *y* in *many, happy,* etc. is long *e.* The usual sound of *ar* in *farther, charging,* etc. is the sound of the name of the letter *r;* of *oi* and *oy,* as in *app(oi)nt* and *ann(oy),* is *oi;* of *ir* and *ur,* as in *bird* and *curtain,* is the *ur* of *hurt;* of *or,* as in *corn,* is the sound of the word *or;* etc.

6. What is the word? What does it mean in the sentence or paragraph?

When the child meets an unknown word in a sentence, he may use the context to identify it. However, when he uses phonic skills to identify the word, he is taught to always check the word in its setting to see if it fits. This attention to meaning develops the automatic use of phonic skills so that the pupil can keep his mind on the thought of the context. Developing phonic skills in isolation from reading situations (1) develops word callers, (2) overemphasizes phonic and other perceptual skills in the reading process, and (3) lowers comprehension. Phonic skills are developed in purposeful reading situations so that they are used automatically in all reading activities —leaving the reader's mind free to think about what he is reading. After all, the materials of reading are concepts rather than word forms.

Summary

For the beginner as well as the more advanced pupil, learning (or knowing) a word requires (1) facility in applying phonic skills to phonograms, including syllables, of written word forms for pronunciation purposes and (2) ability to identify the specific use (or meaning) of the word. In other words, perceptual skills and thinking abilities are inseparable; each is indispensable.

Foundations for word perception are laid in the language readiness and reading readiness programs. On these foundations, the beginner immediately builds his use of letter (phonogram) phonics. These letter phonic skills are gradually and easily applied automatically to the syllables of words. In turn, these letter and syllable phonic skills (including the identification of roots and affixes) are raised to higher levels when the pupil applies them to the interpretation of pronunciation symbols in the respelling of dictionary entries. Hence, the development of word perception skills is continuous from the readiness level through the mastery of dictionary skills.

18. *A Directed Reading-Thinking Plan* *

RUSSELL G. STAUFFER

MUCH HAS BEEN SAID in recent years about practices and procedures for the individualization of instruction—particularly reading instruction. With the publication of the *Twenty-fourth Yearbook of the National Society for the Study of Education,* copyright 1923, a solid foundation was laid for

* From Russell G. Stauffer, "A Directed Reading-Thinking Plan," *Education* (May, 1959), pp. 527–32. Reprinted by permission of the author and The Bobbs-Merrill Co., Inc., Indianapolis, Ind.

this kind of thinking about instruction and at a time when the problems of mass education were beginning to increase rapidly. Part I of this yearbook was "A Report of the National Committee on Reading" and Part II was a report on methods for "Adapting the Schools to Individual Differences." Guy Whipple, editor of Part II, stated the issue well. He wondered whether or not it would be desirable and practical to carry differentiation to the complete individualization of instruction. In Part I of this yearbook the phrase "differentiated reading instruction" occurred with such frequency that it might well have served as a title for that part. The natural affinity of these two ideas is evident in the statement found in Part I to the effect that to provide appropriate instruction, pupils must be taught either individually or in groups which are more or less homogeneous. Thus the abridgement of the basic ideas was to be accomplished by the use of ways that combined group and individual work.

In 1959, while we are again hearing much about individualizing reading instruction, the procedure that continues to be the most widely practiced is to teach reading through groups. And the traditional way to accomplish this is through the use of basal readers. Generally speaking it is safe to say that teachers have broken away from some of the practices that handicapped them in their attempts at differentiating by and through group instruction. More and more, children are being grouped according to their independent and instructional reading levels. Membership in the groups is not rigid and children are grouped and regrouped according to their needs and interests as well as their abilities. As a result, the basal reading book approach is being viewed more and more as only one way to teach children how to read.

Reading as Thinking

In recent years, too, much has been said about thinking and about reading as thinking. As early as 1917 Thorndike published a series of articles on reading as a thinking-reasoning process. He showed how pupil answers to clearly stated questions about the meaning of a passage were so irrelevant and wrong as to baffle analysis. Then he concluded, among other things, that reading was much like problem solving and that a major need was for the pupil to have the right mental set or purpose or demand. Other studies followed which also viewed reading as a thought-getting, interpretive process.

In 1930 John Dewey had this to say about reading, "He who has learned as we call it to read without having learned to judge, discriminate, and choose has given hostages of independence to powers beyond his control. He has prepared for himself a readiness to undergo new modes of intellectual servitude." Later, David Russell defined thinking as a process which involves a sequence of ideas that move from a beginning, through a pattern of relationships of one sort or another, to some conclusion. Then he added that if children are to be sheep following blindly the ideas of the printed page they must develop into thinking individuals, critical of sources, definitions, assumptions, and techniques. Apparently then, the pupil who does not learn to deal with reading as a thinking process undergoes an intellectual servitude that deceives and deludes and sets at naught that which reading for meaning aims to accomplish.

Russell goes on to say that whether or not the pupil develops into a blind reader or a thinking reader is primarily the decision of the teacher. "The decision seems to rest largely in the hands of their teachers at both elementary and secondary levels." This is the same conclusion reached by John DeBoer after reviewing some of the views of different writers on critical reading and by Durrell and Chambers. The latter two also say that it seems as if teachers are about to realize that effective reading-thinking is better done in discussion groups of various sizes than in either whole-class or individual activities.

The Verbalism Curtain

To differentiate reading instruction so as to involve each pupil in a reading-thinking process is unquestionably the goal to be achieved. This means that reading must be more than the pronunciation of words, the reciting of phonetic or grammar rules, the verbatim parroting or rote memory of passages, and the accomplishing of a reading activity stimulated largely by teacher questions.

For some time now the outcry against the insidious "lock step" has been repeated, and to some degree the pattern has been broken. For some time, too, the outcry against the insidious "round-the-robin-oral-reading" practice has been heard and the practice has been largely eliminated.

However, in many ways, classroom practices used to direct a reading activity have saddled the learner with an even more corrupting procedure —the practice of "round-the-robin comprehension." This is the procedure whereby the teacher asks almost all the questions and the pupils play back answers from a text, usually verbatim. There is no examining of clues available and declaring of purposes in terms of a pupil's or a group's background of experience, intellect, language facility, interests and needs.

There is no adjusting of rate to purposes and materials; no reflection; no weighing of facts and inferences; no reading and rereading to make judgments; and no generalization. This is the procedure whereby the teacher tries to anticipate all word recognition needs in advance of the reading so that the mechanics of reading can be accomplished without any word mishaps. So called "new" words or hard words are analyzed on the chalkboard prior to the reading, thus denying the pupil the opportunity to use his word attack skills to recognize a word that fits a context and should help him complete his search for meaning.

These are the procedures that have dropped the verbalism curtain in education, thus dooming the would-be learner to new modes of intellectual servitude. These are the procedures that led Betts to say in his article on "Reading is Thinking" that what our pupils need is more help on *how to think* in a reading situation.

A Directed Reading-Thinking Activity Plan

As stated earlier, it seems that authorities are in agreement that (1) children can be taught to read and think, and that (2) the decision to do so seems to rest largely in the hands of their teachers.

This being the case, then, it would follow that a first step toward the differentiation of reading instruction on a reading-thinking level would be the fostering of proper attitudes on the part of the teacher. If teachers are to accomplish plans for the teaching of reading as a thinking process, their attitudes toward what and how this can be done must be favorable. Their attitudes must reflect the following:

1. Children can think. They can assess a situation and draw inferences about what is happening and about what may follow. They do this in terms of their own interests, attitudes, and concepts.
2. The recall and use of ideas is enhanced by the increased interest and attention that results from clear-cut specific or general pupils' purposes for reading.
3. Pupils are more apt to be active in the total reading-thinking act in a situation which forces them to confirm or deny their own convictions in a "what do I know" and "what do I want to find out" approach.
4. The attitudes of a pupil are much more apt to be modified in a situation where he is encouraged to think, read, and reflect and then discuss with his peers who too have thought, read, and reflected.

A skilled reader differs from others because of what he does in order to read. As a result how and what he reads is different. He examines all clues available, reflects over them in terms of his experience and knowledge, and then sets purposes according to his informed judgments.

As the reading is done, the reader checks what he finds against his purposes. Then he either (1) sets new purposes, (2) reads on in the same material or seeks other material, or (3) stops reading because his purposes have been accomplished.

A second step toward the differentiation of reading instruction on a reading-thinking level is the grasping of certain basic principles and assumptions which underlie the effective development of a group-directed reading activity. The plan may be mapped as follows:

I.   Identifying purposes for reading
   A. Examine clues available in the
     1. Title and subtitles
     2. Pictures, maps, graphs, and charts
     3. Material: adjusting to information as it is read and to readability
   B. Declaring purposes in terms of the
     1. Reader's background of experience, intellect, language facility, interests and needs
     2. Experience, abilities, interests and needs of the group
     3. Content of the material: concepts of time, place, people, number, science, aesthetics, and humor
II. Guiding the adjustment of rate to purposes and material
   A. Skimming: to read swiftly and lightly
   B. Scanning: to read carefully from point to point
   C. Studying: to read and reread so as to pass judgment
III. Observing the reading
   A. Noting abilities to adjust rate to purposes and materials
   B. Recognizing comprehension needs and providing help by clarifying
     1. Purposes
     2. Concepts
     3. Need for rereading (silent or oral)
   C. Acknowledging requests for help with word recognition needs by providing immediate help in the use of
     1. Context clues: meaning clues
     2. Phonetic clues: sound clues
     3. Structural clues: sight clues
     4. Glossary clues: meaning, sound, and sight clues
IV. Developing comprehension
   A. Checking on individual and group purposes
   B. Staying with or redefining purposes

   C. Recognizing the need for other source material
   D. Developing concepts
V. Fundamental skill training activities: discussion, further reading, additional study, writing
   A. Increasing powers of observation (directed attention)
   B. Increasing powers of reflection by:
      1. Abstraction: reorganizing old ideas, conceiving new ideas, distinguishing between ideas, generalizing about ideas, and making inductions and analyses
      2. Judgment: formulating propositions and asserting them
      3. Reasoning: inferring and demonstrating, and systematizing knowledge deductively
   C. Mastering the skills of word recognition: picture and language context analysis, phonetic and structural analysis, and dictionary usage
   D. Developing adeptness in the use of semantic analysis: levels of abstraction, shifts of meaning, referential and emotive language, definite and indefinite terms, and concept development.

It is evident at once that this reading-thinking plan is not a process standing alone to be used only in directing the reading of material in a basal reader. Its doctrines are fundamental to problem solving, abstracting, and propaganda analysis and similar frequently occurring activities of children and adults. The attitude of straight thinking required to draw inferences, to evaluate relevances, to grasp sequences, to draw tentative conclusions and suspend judgment can be used and can be taught through suitable classroom procedures in most curricular areas.

It is evident, too, that critical reading and thinking are not learned in isolation. The process of examining materials, both verbal and concrete—in the perspective of related objective evidence, comparing the evidence with some norm or standard, and making judgments—requires a content.

Also apparent should be the fact that children can think and read critically about matters related to their experiences. A six-year-old may not be motivated or intellectually able to comment on the validity of a historical doctrine, but he may, as one boy did, think critically about a story when he questioned the fact that three ducks in a line was "a *long* parade of ducks."

The six-year-old girl who said, "I found the answer to my question and can read the line that proves it," was taking a major step toward judging the relevance of a statement to a purpose. She wanted to know if Susan, the girl in the story, had found the penny she had lost or had found another penny. The statement the six-year-old used for proof was, "Susan found the penny." To know that the answer found does or does not fit the question asked is truly a chief step on the royal road to critical reading.

Early in life children manifest ability to think critically, to size up a situation and almost intuitively put together the two and two of a social setting and sense what is happening. From playing peekaboo to dealing with mysteries is not too big a jump. From a sensing of the meaning behind pet names and nicknames to appreciating the humor of a "moron tiptoeing past the medicine cabinet" is not too difficult a semantic hurdle.

Furthermore, it should be evident that the give and take of a group situation provides the intellectual milieu needed to stimulate purposeful thinking, reflective reading, and informed judgments. One idea leads to another—one pupil's ideas rouse another's—as a story situation is studied. And the result is that even six-year-olds discuss a situation with astonishing objectivity rather than argue pointlessly.

It is during the meeting of minds which occurs when purposes are set, confirmed, or revised that true individual differences are to be observed. At the same time the strength of convictions soundly established can meet the test of a minority position in an atmosphere charged with integrity and forthrightness. The nine-year-old who refused to change his mind about the story being a true story in the face of overwhelming odds (he was the only one of ten to think so) and was shown to be correct as the story progressed learned a lesson essential to being a thinking citizen in a democracy.

To get children started on the road to reading-thinking, the controlled selections of a basal reader provide excellent material. Children can be more nearly grouped so that all the members of the group are reading at their instructional level. The stories or selections are about events or ideas within the scope of their experiences—socially, historically, numerically, geographically, aesthetically, scientifically, and humorously. The length of the selections permit easy reading within the time limitations imposed on a school day directed reading session by a varied curriculum. At the same time the stories are so structured as to provide the challenge of something new. So the objectives of a directed reading-thinking activity plan can be accomplished by challenging the pupils but not frustrating them.

Soon enough both the pupils and the teacher learn that (1) the reading-thinking technique is applicable in most curricular areas, and (2) that many questions raised cannot be answered in basal readers and that reading elsewhere must be done. This is especially so as the reading ability and interpersonal contacts of pupils extend the range of materials about which they may read and think critically. In one directed reading activity a group of nine-year-olds had four unanswered questions requiring additional reading: Could airplanes fly over the North Pole in 1940? Are snow-capped mountains covered the year round? Can a panda be housed in a zoo in a warm country? How do panda mothers take care of their babies?

In Summary

Reading instruction can be directed in such a way that the total act becomes a reading-thinking act. Children can be taught how to think and read critically within the limits of their experiences and intellectual maturation. Training should begin when children start to school and should continue through high school and college. Reading, like thinking, is a mental process that is probably not accomplished by a unitary ability so much as a collection of related abilities. Also, like thinking, reading involves a sequence of ideas that move from a beginning, through a pattern of relationships, to a conclusion.

The teacher's attitude is crucial. She must recognize the importance of directing reading as a thinking process. She must understand and plan so thoroughly that the dynamics of a directed reading situation allow her to take full advantage of ideas evoked. She must not stress conformity but freedom of thought. She must encourage an intellectual boldness and straightforwardness that will not tolerate mental servitude to anything but the truth.

19. *Teaching the Slow Reader* *

EDWARD W. DOLCH

THE SLOW LEARNER in the regular classroom is in either of two situations. In one case, the child is promoted every year on the theory behind what is called "social promotion." In the other case, the child is retained until his mental age is about the same as the mental age of the group. That is, he will be physically older than the others but mentally at about the same level. At times, these two conditions both appear in part; that is, a child

* From Edward W. Dolch, "Teaching the Slow Learner," *Grade Teacher* (April, 1955), pp. 29, 73, 74. Reprinted by permission of the author and *Grade Teacher*.

may be retained somewhat because of his slowness but, because of his physical growth, he may not be retained enough to make his mental level equal to that of his grade. Since, after all, social grouping tends to be on mental age, a combination of retention and social promotion is perhaps the wisest plan. The result is that most slow-learning children are a little older than their grade, but still a little behind it mentally.

Before talking about definite methods, we should present a principle that must dominate all the plans for teaching reading to the slow learner. For these children, the teacher must definitely and finally abandon the belief that "getting children through books means the teaching of reading." Such a philosophy may work for many children, but it will not work at all for the slow learner. Of course, the teacher may, by hook or crook, get the slow learners through books, but they will not have learned how to read.

Four Goals

Instead, the teacher must think always that the child must follow the path of learning to read, regardless of the methods or materials used. If she keeps this path in mind, she will adapt all methods to her purposes. The path to learning how to read has four requirements:

1. Continual desire to learn how to read
2. Steady acquiring of confident sight vocabulary
3. Very gradual beginning of the use of sounding attack
4. Ever-present interest in "finding out what it says"

All the machinery of classroom management must take these four requirements into account. For instance, the slow learners will always be in what the teacher calls the slow group. But we find that in nearly every classroom, this grouping definitely kills the very first step, the *continual desire to learn how to read*. Instead, the typical attitude of the slow group is "don't care." So the teacher must take some steps to keep the desire to learn to read or she may as well give up at the start. One method is to have the slow children sit in with the average group and be interested in the stories, learn the word meanings, and so on, and then to have them meet again in an "extra group" for easier work. Another method is to get the slow group new books of great interest, and not let the other children spoil these books by reading them first. Still another method is to get the whole room to be proud of the progress of the slow group and to applaud and encourage them. Let each slow learner choose a "helper" to sit beside him and to tell him words when he asks for them. In fact, very drastic methods must be taken to stop the common practice of having a group of slow learners herded off by themselves, cut off from the rest and looked down upon by all present. This is the basic emotional problem of teaching the slow learner, and it is more important than all the other problems.

The second step, the *steady acquiring of a sight vocabulary,* is not helped much by standard readers. All of them have too many new words per page or per story. The slow learner just does not acquire words so fast. Typically, he is given a book in which he has to be told a dozen words every time he tries to read. Not even the brightest child can learn words when he is told so many at one time. If the slow learner gets three new words a day, he is doing fine. Many can learn only one new word a day, if we are to count the words that stick and not those learned for a short time only.

So sight vocabulary is not learned unless a limited number of words is chosen, and that limited number is continually repeated *with interest.* Uninteresting repetition is useless. Of course the plan is to select from the reading those words which will be naturally repeated, and not any which have to be artificially introduced. The most common words, therefore, are the common verbs, adjectives, prepositions, and so on. So the teacher must choose a selected, limited vocabulary for the slow. All other words should simply be told to them as they are met with in reading. But the selected vocabulary must be practiced continually *with interest,* and there is no way to do this but by playing word games. Such games are part of the equipment of every classroom that works with slow learners.

The next step, the developing of sounding attack with slow learners is a real problem. Sounding ability grows, in most children, with maturity. For instance, it has been found that 7 years mental age seems to be required for the using of sounding. But the slow learner may not reach 7 years mental age until he is 8 or 9 years old. With regular chronological promotion, this means third or fourth grade. Before that time, we should try only ear training with the slow children, and not harass them and confuse them with standard phonic lessons. Use of sounding requires analysis and synthesis, which demand rather keen use of the ear and mind. Sounding may, at some time, be a fine avenue for helping in reading for the slow learners, if they have not been taught to dislike the subject and if they develop their powers slowly. Sounding games will help in that development.

Interest Must Be Caught

The fourth requirement, an *ever-present interest in "finding out what it says,"* is hard to maintain in slow-learning children. Most of our reading materials in school depend on imagination. That is, a story is told which the child has to imagine, and thus he is eager to find out the outcome of the story. This eagerness is present in the slow-learning child if we are sure to "get him into the story," as we say, and then if we do not "lose him." If the child loses interest, either because of strangeness of the story, because of slowness of getting it, or because of vexation about words, the eagerness to "find out what it says" will disappear, and the child will become just a "sitter."

Finally, we must follow the principle that "reading should never stand in the way of anyone's education." Those who are poor readers, and even those who cannot read, can be educated. They can do arithmetic and understand and like it merely if someone will read to them the verbal problems. They can love geography simply by studying pictures and having someone tell them what the book says about them. They can learn of health, of civics, of science, and in fact of anything just by audio-visual methods, without letting poor reading stand in their way. In other words, we must abandon the old rule that "those who are good readers shall be educated; all others will be given up as hopeless." Since this country is a democracy, and since every individual is of great worth to himself and to his country, each must be developed to his utmost. Let us teach a child, even a slow learner, as much reading as we can; beyond that, let us see that he learns all he can anyway.

20. *What Research Says about*
Teaching Reading *

ARTHUR I. GATES

R EADING can no longer be regarded as a number of simple skills which can be taught once and for all purposes in a few formal reading lessons. On the contrary, reading is a complex array of learning procedures which must be developed for, and in the process of, effective learning in all daily activities in and out of school.

* From Arthur I. Gates, "What Research Says about Teaching Reading," *NEA Journal* (October, 1953), pp. 402–3. Reprinted by permission of the author and the *NEA Journal*.

Reading and the Other Language Arts

What a child learns in one language art affects his abilities in others. Reading, listening to spoken language, speaking, carrying on discussions, writing, and spelling are all closely related. The way a child learns to listen to the spoken word before he enters school affects his approach to reading.

The classroom teacher's management of oral reading in the classroom may have a permanent effect upon the way the child talks to other individuals or to groups. The methods a child develops to work out the recognition and pronunciation of printed words will affect his techniques in spelling. Reading must, therefore, be taught in the course of developing a complete language arts program.

Reading and the Total Program

Each subject-matter area requires certain specialized patterns of reading abilities. In the schoolroom, reading should, therefore, be taught in connection with or as a part of all school activities.

It is also true that the kind of reading abilities learned in a school depends greatly on the objectives set up for various subjects and upon the materials and procedures employed in them. Many schools, for example, provide instruction in the types of reading important in out-of-school life, such as the reading of newspapers and business reports.

What the pupil does in all areas of learning depends in great measure on how the development of his reading abilities is guided in all his daily activities. Hence the dictum: "Every teacher, a teacher of reading."

Reading Is a Complex Process

It is often incorrectly assumed that the skills involved in reading are rather simple, obvious things. They are not. When a child tries to learn to recognize a word, he may pursue any one or more of a score of different procedures, some of them excellent, some fair, others poor. In any event, no one method is adequate for all words; the child needs to learn a number of different techniques and how and when to use them.

Techniques Must Be Taught

In learning to read, as in learning all other complex skills, a learner is not at all sure to hit upon good techniques "naturally." It is a rare person

—child or adult—who, left to his own devices, will naturally learn anything but a poor hunt-and-hit method of running a typewriter, or a slap-and-swat method of playing tennis, or the wild swing in striking a golf ball. Unguided trial-and-error learning in all these areas rarely produces good techniques, even though it often yields superficially satisfying quick results.

Instruction Must Continue for Years

Even the superior learners profit by continued guidance in reading throughout the elementary school and into higher levels. The techniques of word recognition, such as simple visual observation combined with simple phonetic analysis, may be quite adequate for the short words in grade one, but wholly inadequate to deal with complex, nonphonetic, and polysyllabic words in the intermediate grades.

There is a tendency for teachers in the intermediate and upper grades to become so much interested in the products of reading, that is, the facts and ideas learned in the various subjects, that they forget to note the process. They may sometimes mistakenly assume that a child who learns the material and reports it well is necessarily a good reader and will become an even better reader. Sometimes pupils rated as best in the content subjects are deficient in their reading skills.

Children Must Want to Help

Children can, from an early stage, learn to identify many important techniques and become interested and able to guide their own learning.

As long as schools have as much to teach and as many pupils to handle as they have today, it is not only advisable but necessary for the teacher to make the most of the possibilities of helping the pupils learn how to learn by themselves. Teachers sometimes fail to realize that teaching a child certain techniques of reading is not the same as teaching him the technique of learning to read. We need to teach the pupils as much as possible of the techniques of learning to read by themselves.

Skills Develop Both Continuously and by Stages

Reading abilities tend to move forward from one level to a higher one, and certain types of performance must evolve from a simpler or lower stage. It may be futile and sometimes disorganizing to a learner to force him to acquire an ability far in advance of present performance.

Some of the older teaching programs embodied the fault of assuming that many important abilities followed a series of sharply defined steps when in fact they developed rather in a continuous, or nearly continuous, line of increasing complexity. For example, it used to be thought that children's comprehension at the beginning was at best a low level of mere recognition of what the passage said, that little selection or thinking was possible. Actually children can, and should, be induced to engage from the beginning in many forms of thinking during and after reading.

In early stages they can read for the purpose of "summarizing" or "outlining" or "judging" or "applying" what they read. These are not skills to be put off until the third or fourth grade, but are to be encouraged from the start. Beginners will not read in these respects as intelligently and subtly as they will later, but the differences are in terms of degree, not of kind.

The classroom teacher will watch both the total performance and its component processes. If the pupil shows failure to gain in all-round ability, the teacher will seek to determine what components have gotten out of balance.

A component skill may move forward either too rapidly or too slowly for the good of the whole. Thus a pupil may push his skill in working out the recognition of words by letter phonetics to a point where it blocks the growth of ability to use larger wordparts. A pupil may push his speed of reading so far as to result in inadequate comprehension, or so slowly as to result in unnecessarily thorough attention to details.

Reading Abilities Come from Many Experiences

One of the objectives of education is the development of those abilities needed to read efficiently and intelligently a great variety of materials.

The best methods of reading differ according to the nature of the content, the form of organization, and the reader's purpose. The most effective way of attacking a reading assignment in geometry, for example, is usually different from the best procedure to employ in canvassing a file of newspapers to find items bearing on a particular topic.

Reading Ability Must Include Good Taste

The program in reading not only teaches children effective reading techniques, but develops an interest in the superior types of content. The most obvious illustration is developing a taste for better literature. The term "literature" is usually employed to mean works of fiction, popular science, essays, poetry, and the like. It is also important to develop an interest in reading on vital topics in newspapers and magazines.

These various types of literature are not best handled under some general formula such as the teacher might employ in analyzing the good choice of a typical adventure story. Each type requires on the part of the teacher a certain background of understanding of the problems themselves as well as the shrewd understanding of how best to guide the child in using the material to solve his problems.

Basic Techniques Are Essential

Teachers may be bewildered by the statement that the pupil should develop the techniques for reading a very large number of kinds of material and purposes. He may wonder whether this means that there is an unlimited number of quite distinctive basal techniques.

There are many, but a definitely limited number of techniques or groups of techniques represent the foundation upon which many combinations or patterns of reading skills depend. The following list may suggest, even though it does not describe, such a group of basal techniques: skill in word recognition, skill in getting meaning, skill in adapting reading rate, skill in adapting understanding to purpose, and skill in reading for temporary or permanent use.

These are basal techniques or groups of techniques of great importance. Most of the diversified forms of reading represent merely new combinations or patterns of these basal techniques. Few types of reading can be done well unless these techniques are quite well in hand. Indeed, the most important skills of all—the abilities to think, reason, evaluate, relate, and organize ideas during reading—depend upon ability to skip and skim at different rates, to vary the degree and kind of comprehension, to combine and shift from reading to recall.

21. An Inductive Approach to Word Analysis *

CONSTANCE M. MCCULLOUGH

WHEN I was on the threshold of my teens, I went to visit some friends on a farm. City-bred, I thought that horses that were white were older than horses that were gray. There was a lot for me to learn in those two weeks.

One experience of that visit impressed me more than any other. I helped to bring in the cows one night, and the next night asked for the privilege of bringing them in all by myself. Not realizing the density of the ignoramus with whom he was dealing, my host consented.

I went out alone, down to the pasture along the strip of woods, rounded up the cows, and got them started up the lane toward the barn. My bosom swelled with pride in my accomplishment and with affection toward the beasts that were cooperating so well. Full of confidence, I began to stride ahead of the herd. But when I reached the barn and looked back down the lane, I could see the swinging tails of cows headed for the pasture again.

I never think of the teaching of word analysis without remembering those cows, for they told me more in a short time about the relationship between a teacher and a group of learners than a good deal of the research in reading. With all due apology to proud parents and fond teachers, I must report that children are much like cows. You never can tell where they are in their thinking if you get ahead of them. You have to prod with questions and let them take the lead. Otherwise, chances are good that you will lose them and arrive at the barn—the end of the lesson or the end of the book —without them.

The essence of an inductive approach to teaching word analysis is just that. The teacher fences off the desired area and the children go up the lane; the children are the first to discover; the teacher encourages from the rear until everyone gets to the barn.

Auditory Exercise

Take the problem of teaching the sound of the initial consonant *b*. First, the teacher has to make sure that the children can discriminate between the

* From Constance M. McCullough, "An Inductive Approach to Word Analysis," *Education* (May, 1955), pp. 583–87. Reprinted by permission of the author and The Bobbs-Merrill Co., Inc., Indianapolis, Ind.

sound of *b* and the sound of other letters. She says, "I am thinking of the name of a person in this room. It begins like *Billy* and *Bobby*. What do you suppose it is?" She hopes that someone will say *Betty* or *Bernard* or *Bonita*. But perhaps little Milly will say, "Peter". The teacher will say, "Let's listen. Do these words begin alike: *Billy, Bobby, Peter?*" Milly, reading the teacher's face better than the sound of the initial consonant *b*, says, "No," but she's really not sure.

The teacher must spend a good many little game periods with Milly and her kind until Milly's batting average is championship level. It won't help if the teacher says, "Look, Chum: *Billy* and *Bobby* begin with the same sound as *Betty, Bernard,* and *Bonita*. Now, remember this." Milly will be memorizing instead of listening to initial sounds. No, the teacher must stay behind the cows. "I'm thinking of something that begins like *ball* and *bat* and it's a game." "I'm thinking of something that begins like *box* and *bag* and it is on the table." Something to eat, something to wear, whatever it is, the teacher must keep after the group until the children catch on. Perhaps the teacher can work this into a game that reinforces some other learning—reminds the children of facts they are learning in other subject areas.

As seatwork, the children may draw pictures of words that begin with that sound. A chart may be made of such pictures. In meaning for the children, such a chart is superior to a chart the teacher makes of commercial pictures.

If the initial sound is *s* and a child says that *circus* begins like *see* and *say,* the teacher should accept this offering in the ear training exercise, for these words do, indeed, begin alike in sound.

Visual Exercise

When the children can hear the initial sound of *b*, they are ready to look at words containing that initial sound, and to determine the letter which makes it. Notice that the *ear* training *precedes* the *visual* lesson. Now that the children have proved that they can distinguish the initial consonant sound *b* from other sounds, the teacher takes them on to the visual exercise.

Since children learn a new task better if that task involves known facts, it is better to use in the visual exercise, words the children have in their reading vocabulary—sight words familiar to them. This implies three things: (1) The visual exercise will not be undertaken unless and until the children have mastered by sight two, but preferably three or four or five words that start with *b*. (More words are preferable to fewer words because the more examples the children have of the principle they are trying to discover, the easier it will be to observe.) (2) Even though, on occasion, children who are invited to engage in the visual exercise are operating at different vocabulary levels, there will be an attempt on the part of the teacher to keep the vocabulary at the sight vocabulary level of the poorest reader in the group. Otherwise, the poorest reader will be not only the poorest reader but the one for whom the exercise is made deliberately more difficult by the use of words he does not know. Perhaps this suggests that, ordinarily, the first visual lesson should be administered to a relatively homogeneous group—a group reading at the same level of sight vocabulary —and that only later visual exercises should involve mixed groups. (3) Obviously, the children will have been reading for some time before such a visual exercise is undertaken, since the limited vocabulary of the beginning reading books does not start with a cluster of *b* words, such as: "Billy bumped his buttons on the back bench." When parents complain that their children are not learning phonics, this is the teacher's answer. The ingredients for the lesson are not yet assembled. One might just as well say, "Why haven't you baked that three-egg cake today?" Answer: "Not enough eggs yet."

Since children forget something they do not use, two other precautions should be taken in the use of the visual exercise: (1) The visual exercise should be introduced when it will be useful in the solution of new words. If the next story the children are to read will contain a *b* word, it is a good time to introduce the visual exercise. Then, (2) in introducing the next story the teacher will not tell the children the word. She will, rather, present it with a picture or put it into a revealing context: "The *baker* makes bread and cake," and let the children guess from the picture or verbal context, and from the initial consonant, what the word must be. By her encouragement of the use of the new learning, the teacher does not let it rust out.

The visual exercise goes something like this: The teacher says, "I am thinking of some words you have been reading. They begin like *ball* and *boy*. What are they?" As she says *ball,* she writes *ball* (in manuscript if the children are accustomed to manuscript) and stands so that all can see the word as she writes it. As she says *boy,* she writes *boy* under *ball,* so that the *b*'s are in a column, directly under one another:

ball
boy

This means that, as the teacher writes the *b* in each word, the children hear that sound in the teacher's pronunciation of *ball, boy,* or whatever word it is; the sight and sound of the letter occur simultaneously.

Jimmy volunteers, *"Box."* The teacher says and writes *box,* immediately under *boy.* "Now, let's all say these words and listen to hear whether Jimmy is right." The group says, *"Ball, boy, box."* "Does *box* begin with the same sound as *boy* and *ball?"* They agree that is does. Bobby offers, *"Baby,"* and the teacher goes through the same procedure as with *box.*

When four or five words are in a column on the blackboard, the teacher decides to see whether or not the children are arriving at the barn. "Let's say the words over together and listen to the beginning of each word again." The children look and listen. "Does anyone notice anything alike about the way the words *look?"* Algernon will say that they are all short words. He is still in the pasture. But, if the teacher is lucky and the children are ready, Joe will say, "They all begin with the same letter." The teacher looks at him as at a diamond stickpin on the floor of the supermarket. "Say that again!" Joe sticks out his chest two more inches and says it again. "How many of you think you see what Joe sees in these words?" Those who see and those who are good politicians indicate that they do. Algernon tries hard to come out of the pasture, but he may not make it that day.

"Who would like to come up to the blackboard and draw a line under the letter in the first word?" Joe had better have the honor. "Who would like to draw a line under the letter in the second word?" Some children who have not caught on up to this time may be helped by this stress. Meanwhile, the opportunity to go up and find the right letter gives Joe and his like a great deal of satisfaction. (A variation of this which emphasizes form is to overlay the initial *b* in each word with colored chalk, different children doing this.)

Generalization and Application

Now to close the barn door: "Who can tell me what he knows from this? When a word begins with this letter, what do we know about its sound?" John, the philosopher, may come through: "When a word begins like that, I know it begins like *ball* and *boy* and *box* and *baby.*" Perhaps, to dramatize the statement, the teacher will write a *b* above the words in the column on the blackboard. She may, in addition, engage the children for a few minutes in proving their point by finding other words beginning with *b,* on charts and signs about the room. Young children enjoy the physical relief of this field trip off the chairs.

But, before she dismisses the group, she says, "Let's see whether we can use what we know. I shall write a sentence on the blackboard. Read it to yourselves and see whether you can recognize the new word." She writes a sentence in which all the words are known to the children by sight except the new *b* word: "Pony's home is in the barn." After time for silent reading, Martha is selected to read the sentence. "How did you know, Martha?" Martha says, "I knew because Pony's home *is* in a barn and because *barn* begins with the same letter as *ball*."

The follow-up can be one of several tasks. The teacher may have other such sentences, which the children are to read, in which they are to underline the *b* in the strange word, and for which they are to draw a picture representing the new word. She may have sentences with the *b*'s left out, for the children to insert. She may have them find sentences in their readers containing *b* words. She may have them make up their own sentences containing *b* words. She may have them make a list of all the words they know that begin with *b*. She may have them trace over the *b*'s that begin certain words, using a bright color. Some of these exercises are better than others, in that they stress meaning as well as form. The exercises in which the children write or trace over the *b*'s are good because of the tactile experience with the shapes of the letters.

The next day the teacher may appear with a chart, which the children may call their *ball* chart:

b-   *ball*
        boy
        box
        baby

As the children learn new *b* words, they will add them to the chart.

Special Problems

If, in the course of the visual lesson, a child offers a word that does not begin with the consonant under discussion (say, *circus* for the *s* sound in *see* and *say*), the teacher will write the word to one side, not in the column with the other words. After the generalization has been made that words beginning with that sound begin with that letter (*s*), she will point out that *circus* begins with the same sound also, and that there are other words which begin with the same letter as *circus* and begin with the sound in *see* and *say*.

Notice that, in all this discussion, it has not been necessary to name the letter or to attempt to sound it alone—"buh". The reason the name of the letter has been avoided is that it is easy for the children to confuse the name of the letter with the sound the letter makes, and they may try to sound out a word by spelling it out. The reason the consonant sound has not been given in isolation is that it is impossible to sound the consonant without some sort of vowel accompaniment. This makes the blending more difficult. (This is not true in the case of vowel sounds. One may say, "The *a* sound in *cake* and *say*," without confusing the listener.)

Syllabication

The inductive approach may be applied to all phases of word analysis. In syllabication, for instance, the first job is ear training, the child's own discovery of the number of syllables in different words. "Let's tap out these words as I say them. How many taps can you give to beat out the word *return?*" Ultimately, the teacher says, "These beats are called *syllables.*" She writes *syllables* as she says, "Syl-la-bles. Let's all say it." One fine day, she puts several words of different lengths but of one syllable on the blackboard, directly under each other:

> catch
> go
> mitt
> bat

She asks how many syllables are in the first word, and so on, and after each word she has a child indicate the number of syllables. Then she asks how many vowel sounds they hear in each word. The blackboard record becomes:

Word	Syl.	Vowel
catch	1	1
go	1	1
mitt	1	1
bat	1	1

"Can you tell the number of syllables in a word by something else besides tapping out the words?" "Yes," someone says, "there is a syllable for every vowel." The teacher wants, "There is a syllable for every *sounded* vowel," but the exercise does not warrant that conclusion. Another day can be devoted to words like *came, strange,* and *toe;* another day to words like *tail* and *fear,* and still another to words like *boil* and *mouth.* In *came,* the *e* is silent; in *tail,* only the *a* is sounded; and in *boil* and *mouth,* the two vowels form a single, new sound. As children mature, the generalizations which they make about word analysis may well be expressed on the charts they make recording their knowledge of word parts.

Materials in Keeping with the Inductive Approach

Teachers who appreciate the soundness of the inductive approach to the teaching of word analysis use the children's sight vocabulary to construct exercise materials. They use suggestions from the manual and workbook of the basal reader. While they may gather ideas from other books, they always translate them into the sight vocabulary of the children. They are careful, too, to avoid materials which make the discoveries for the children, taking the initiative for learning out of their hands. If the printer has already shown which parts of the words are alike, by use of colored inks or bold type, the child is a willing follower in practice but a doubtful follower in thought, and there is no telling how many cows are headed back toward the pasture. (Is he thinking, "Color all the see-aitches," or is he really associating sight and sound?) The efficient teacher of word analysis is one who keeps clearly in mind the processes through which children must go in the accomplishment of the tasks she sets, and one who lets neither improperly constructed commercial materials nor pied pipers lure her away from her position of encouragement from the rear.

22. The Classroom Teacher and Speech Improvement *

LUCILLE MAY

IT IS an unusual teacher who is not desirous of teaching speech improvement to the children in her classroom. And not only does she want speech improvement techniques, she is asking for them. The first words the speech correctionist hears are, "What may I do to help this child with his speech problem?"

We live in a talking world. Without speech, or with poor usage of speech, a child in our present-day world will be severely handicapped when seeking a position later in life. A 1937 survey found there were approximately four million school-age children in the United States with defective speech; more than there were crippled, deaf, and blind combined.

The question now arises: How is the teacher who is not a speech therapist to proceed with the problem of speech defects in the classroom? Probably the first step is for the teacher to see if she herself has a speech defect. A tape recording may point out that her voice is not pleasing or has a defect. Children are imitators and will try to speak exactly as she does. Therefore, a teacher must be certain she has no problem before attempting corrective work with children.

A teacher doesn't necessarily have to be an expert to teach correct sounds to children. Neither does she have to spend extra time teaching particular sounds. Stress on certain sounds may be done during the reading, spelling, social studies, or arithmetic class.

If one or more children in the classroom do not pronounce a certain sound, it is more practical to practice on this one sound until it is mastered

* From Lucille May, "The Classroom Teacher and Speech Improvement," *The Instructor* (May, 1956), p. 87. Reprinted from *The Instructor* by permission of the publishers.

before starting to work on a new sound. Suppose one or two children are using the *th* sound for the *s*. Let the children hear the correct sound over and over. Show words that start with *s* and then let children write them. Hearing the correct usage will do much to improve the sound.

Do not become discouraged if it takes several days or even weeks before the child is capable of producing the sound. Notice the conversation used by the child, especially the words in which he uses the sound incorrectly. Calmly correct the child in a few of these words. If he has been able at times to make the correct sound, insist that at a certain period each day he use the sound correctly, if only for five or ten minutes. Do not correct constantly when he makes a mistake.

It may be of some help to the child if he can see how the sound is made. Show him how to place his lips, teeth, and tongue and then have the child watch his own mouth in a mirror.

Children often remember a sound by giving it a name, such as Sammy Snake for *s*.

A teacher will be surprised to find how many times the sound can be put in a reading conversation or other subject. She may read a story to the class adding words, with the mispronounced sound, to the story. A flannelgraph story may be told using the sound. In arithmetic, soap, seats, saws, and so on, may be added, subtracted, or divided.

Music is one of the best and easiest methods to teach a speech sound. Most children are very fond of music or like rhythm. They thoroughly enjoy musical games. Music is more deliberate than conversation or reading and many words are repeated over and over again. Many of the newer songbooks have all the desired sounds in songs. Often it is possible to use the sound in physical education periods.

The teacher should attempt to schedule a conference with the parents. Try to suggest in a diplomatic way that the child is missing certain sounds and ask to have cooperation from the home.

Many speech problems are emotional problems. In our modern age, often both parents are out of the home working all day. By evening they are tired and tense, not realizing that the strain is affecting their children.

Sometimes the parents may be striving for the child to reach a goal beyond his ability. They may be trying to make the child equal the accomplishments of older siblings. The teacher should suggest to the parent that a great deal of rest and a calm attitude on the part of the family will help.

Praising a child for things he does well is another suggestion for the parent to follow, and should also be practiced in the classroom. Give the child opportunities to help both in the home and in school with duties that will develop his talents and confidence in his own abilities. Encourage a child to speak through hobbies or games. Never, never call a child a speech defective or allow others to do so. Above all, allow the child to live a normal life and do not single him out from other children.

23. *Improving the Young Child's Speech* *

BARBARA K. THOMPSON

THERE IS frequently confusion between the concept of speech therapy and speech improvement.

Speech therapy refers to the diagnosis and treatment of consistent deviations from the norm, as, for example, when a child always has his "wabbits wunning up the woad."

Speech improvement refers to the treatment of deviations *within* the range of the normal. These deviations generally are inconsistent. The speech may have a slovenly or immature sound.

Many teachers will consider the kindergartner or beginning first grader who is having trouble pronouncing the *l, r,* or *s* sounds still within the norm for his age and level of maturity. This is the child whose needs may be met by additional experiences in listening, discriminating between sounds, and identifying sounds—a program within the framework of the classroom situation.

But if this difficulty with the sounds has not been alleviated by second or third grade, most teachers will consider this child in need of remedial training and will refer him for speech therapy—a program carried out in smaller group units, possibly on an individual basis, by the speech therapist, apart from the regular classroom.

The classroom teacher can be very effective in carrying out a speech improvement program, particularly if she possesses the inspiration, energy, and education necessary to devise a program which has clear-cut objectives, interesting techniques, and an appeal for young children.

* From Barbara K. Thompson, "Improving the Child's Speech," *NEA Journal* (December, 1959), pp. 13–14. Reprinted by permission of the author and the *NEA Journal*.

The first step is an analysis of the speech needs of the group. Many children simply have poor speech habits such as rapid or breathy speech or a voice that is too loud, too weak, nasal, husky, or offensively whiny.

Others demonstrate slight or inconsistent defects in articulation, chronic mispronunciation of words, or unusual behavior that may indicate a hearing loss.

Below are listed some objectives of speech improvement, together with some suggested techniques that may be helpful in reaching the objectives. Kindergarten, first grade and second grade teachers may choose those which are best adapted to the grade level or needs of their pupils.

Developing the ability to speak so that all may hear and enjoy. A simple technique to use, particularly with the youngest children, is to have them call out their names so that others may hear.

"About me" activities are also helpful early in the school year. The child may stand at his seat or come to the front of the room to tell something interesting about himself, his family, or his pets.

Exciting poems or chanting games may be used to increase the voice intensity of the quiet child.

Developing the ability to discriminate between sounds. Kindergarten children can be introduced to listening techniques by having them see how many sounds they can identify while their eyes are closed: mechanical sounds, human sounds, animal sounds, and musical sounds.

A phonics program teaches children to discriminate between sounds. Rhyming games are both fun and helpful for first graders. The teacher gives the initial stimulus, and children try to find words that rhyme. She says, "Man"; they answer, "Can, fan, ran."

As children progress still further in the speech improvement program, they will practice applying their skills with particular emphasis on initial sounds. Poems are often good practice material, and the teacher can choose those which emphasize difficult sounds.

Eliminating minor speech problems. Such problems as lisping, indistinct speech, careless use of words, or too soft or loud a voice usually respond to the practice a classroom teacher can provide her pupils.

Creative play is useful with the very young child as it affords practice on isolated sounds as well as the opportunity to improve gross muscle coordination.

One example is the "fairy queen game." One child, using a ruler as a wand, moves about the room touching the children and turning them into clocks, crows, or tops. At her touch, the crows fly through the air crying "k, k, k"; the clocks swing their pendulums saying, "t, t, t"; and the tops spin around humming "m, m, m." When the children are turned into something else, they immediately take on a new sound.

First graders often enjoy the tire game. One child is the tire going flat, saying "s, s, s," as he slowly sinks to the floor. The class pumps him up saying, "s, s, s," as they pump, and the "tire" slowly rises.

Some children need help to develop skill in the use of their tongue, lips, or breath stream. The teacher may have the children construct pin wheels to be used in an exercise practicing breath control. First the children hold the pin wheels close to their faces, blowing gently. As they hold them further away, they must blow harder to make the pin wheels turn. All blowing is quiet blowing.

To develop tongue control, children can practice making the watch sound, *t,* using the tip of the tongue, then make the coughing sound, *k,* and use the back of the tongue. Or they make the tongue move both ways, *t-k* and *k-t.* The teacher can use a visual aid such as a clown with an open mouth and a tongue depressor painted red for a tongue. The children are encouraged to imitate the movements of the "tongue" as the teacher manipulates it.

Developing the ability to participate in class discussions and storytelling. Show-and-tell time in kindergarten is a good way to encourage the child to speak in a group situation. Young children also enjoy making up stories to tell about pictures they draw.

Later, pupils may be asked to tell one- or two-sentence stories about familiar experiences: going shopping with mother, bathing the dog, or operating an electric train.

Developing self-expression and encouraging dramatization. Young children become more expressive when they have learned to observe and imitate. Learning to follow changes in pitch, rate, expression, volume, rhythm—one of the basic objectives in music education at the kindergarten level—is also basic to speech and can be an effective technique in teaching children to imitate.

Older children may study the way in which our voices reflect our feelings. The teacher may ask them to imitate her when she says, "Good morning," "Don't do that!" or "Watch out!" Or the teacher may suggest an emotion or describe a situation of happiness, sadness, excitement, fear, and let the children give their own spontaneous reactions, selecting their own words and inflections.

Creative dramatics is a highly useful tool to the teacher of the speech improvement program. It coordinates the use of fine and gross muscles and is good for ear training and socialization. It is additionally useful because it allows the child emotional release.

Dramatic play is an excellent opportunity for the teacher to note carry-over; that is, whether the children are using the better speech which they would use in a formal, highly structured lesson, in a less formal, less structured situation.

Playing a role gives a child additional opportunities to practice "new voices": He varies his rate, pitch, and inflection of speech as he would seldom do in ordinary situations.

The activities listed serve only as suggestions for carrying out the objectives which have been outlined. The detailed planning is left to the imagination and skill of the teacher using them. One of the objectives at all grade levels is to make speech improvement pleasant and fun for the students. Let's make it pleasant and fun for the teacher, too! Through this sharing of enjoyable experiences it is hoped that the teacher will come to a more satisfying concept of speech improvement and that the quality of oral communication of her students truly will be improved.

24. *Practices to Develop Voice* *

ASSUMING THAT THERE IS no physical anomaly, it is safe to say that every voice is capable of being improved. Basic considerations in the improvement of voice are (1) a willingness to cooperate in the training of the physical mechanism and (2) a recognition of the relationship between voice and psychological reactions to situations.

The training of the vocal mechanism is not a complex process, but it does require consistent and conscientious practice of relaxation, breathing, and phonation exercises. Regular practice of this type should result in a gradual, habitual functioning of the physical mechanism in the correct production of voice.

A recognition of the relationship between voice and psychological re-

* From "Toward Better Speech," Curriculum Bulletin, No. 5, 1952–53 Series (New York: The Board of Education of the City of New York, 1953), pp. 25–35. Reprinted by permission.

actions to situations is vitally important in the development of good voice because it is emotion which gives color to voice. In short, "your voice is you." Attitudes and moods are reflected in the voice of the speaker and, in the same way, the voice of the speaker affects the attitudes and moods of the audience. For example, when one is happy the voice is lively and bright, and the audience response is usually favorable; when one is depressed the voice is tired and dull, and audience response is usually a passive rejection of the speaker and his ideas; when one is angry the voice is harsh and strident, and antagonism develops in one's audience.

The following suggestions which employ psychic imagery and muscular coordination will help materially in securing desirable development of quality and audibility.

RELAXATION

Attention may be directed toward extremes in the degree of tension and relaxation (indicated in parenthesis) through the dramatization of the following every day experiences:

1. Dropping into a chair after playing a vigorous game of volleyball (*completely relaxed*)
2. Listening to a radio presentation or viewing the screening of a tense mystery (*very tense*)
3. Walking away from a group in an angry frame of mind (*extremely tense*)
4. Walking into the doctor's office feeling very ill (*conflict of tension and relaxation*)
5. (a) High dignitary at a state function (*poised, confident*)
   (b) Actress walking on to the stage to make an appeal for Red Cross, etc. (*poised, graceful*)
   (c) Mother sitting in a chair singing a lullaby to the baby (*poised, controlled in relaxation*)
   (d) The president of the student council addressing the students in the assembly (*poised, comfortable, assured*)

Rhymes to be "acted" by children.

Can You? [1]

Can you hop like a rabbit?
Can you jump like a frog?
Can you walk like a duck?
Can you run like a dog?

[1] Lucille Schoolfield, *Better Speech and Better Reading* (Magnolia, Mass.: Expression Co., 1937), p. 194.

Can you fly like a bird?
Can you swim like a fish?
And be still like a good child,
as still as you wish?

MILDRED EVANS

Trees in the Wind [2]
I'm a tree in the woods;
I sway in the wind,
My hands are the leaves;
They fall from the tree.
How softly they float
From the top of the tree.

Pleasant, audible voice is impossible if there is undue strain on the vocal mechanism. The chief strain is apt to be in the region of the larynx and the lower jaw. The exercises, indicated in the following directions to children, will help relieve muscular tension:

1. Drop the head forward on the chest. Let it hang until it seems to pull the body down with its own weight. Dangle the arms loosely. Without bending the knees, allow the head to descend toward the floor. When your relaxed fingers touch the floor without the slightest stretching, resume an upright position. Repeat this relaxation several times. Be sure you are slumping, not stretching to the floor. Children may pretend to be "rag dolls."
2. Swing arms rhythmically forward and back from the shoulders. Be sure that the joints of fingers, wrists and elbows are relaxed.
3. Close hands tightly. Then open and shake the muscles of hands and wrists. Repeat 3 times.
4. Let the head fall forward on the chest, allowing it to pull itself down by its own weight, rather than by effort. Rotate it, as if it were a "rolling cannon ball on a thread," dropping it over the right shoulder, then backwards, over the left shoulder, and front. After several silent rollings, say sleepily, as you rotate your head, "Easy— ah, lazy—ah," dropping (not pulling) the jaw on each "ah" sound.
5. Mimetic (imitative) exercises. These should be within the experience of the children:

Throwing a basketball
Pitching a baseball

[2] Sarah T. Barrows and Katharine Hall, *Games and Jingles for Speech Development* (Magnolia, Mass.: Expression Co., 1936), p. 40.

Rowing a boat
Turning like a windmill
Imitating a seesaw
Raising an anchor
Skipping rope

BREATHING

All voice is made by allowing the exhaled breath to press against the vocal bands and causing them to vibrate. Therefore, a steady, sustained breath stream under control is necessary for audibility and good tone quality. The following exercises are suggested for learning the proper habits of breathing and for increasing power and control of the exhaled breath.

1. Stand easily with feet well apart. Place the hands flat on the waistline with the finger tips of one hand just touching the finger tips of the other; place the thumbs with the rest of the fingers. If the little fingers are placed at the natural waistline, the great muscle which must expand and contract lies under the hands. The slowly inhaled breath should cause the entire torso to expand. The greatest expansion should take place through the center of the body. This expansion should cause the finger tips to part. (The pupil may thus measure the amount of expansion.) It is well to accompany the pressing out of the exhaled breath with the use of voice as soon as possible.

2. Take a quiet breath through the nose and mouth to a count of four. Ready, inhale, 1-2-3-4; exhale, 1-2-3-4.

3. Increase the count by ones to eight. Place the hands first on the front of the body; then on the ribs at the side, then on the back with the thumbs forward. Make sure that there is steady expansion in all directions as the breath is inhaled and a steady contraction as it is expelled.

4. Take in a quick breath and let it out with a hiss as slowly and steadily as possible. Avoid tension.

5. Take in a quick breath and count out slowly, 1-2-3-4-5-6-7-8. Increase by ones to fifteen.

   The foregoing exercise may be modified with the teacher counting during these exhalations and encouraging the children to better their own records for slow exhalation.

6. Inhale quietly (no command) and recite the alphabet rhythmically, a-b-c-d (breath) e-f-g-h (breath) i-j-k-l, etc. Increase the letters until thirteen may be said easily on one breath.

Rhymes that appeal to the imagination are very helpful in working with young children, for example:

> My puppy likes to sleep awhile,[3]
> Beside the dinner pan.
> He sleeps and breathes so gently there
> Sh! Listen if you can.
> *Breathe—2-3, out 2-3, etc. slow—deep.*
> My puppy likes to chase a cat
> Around or up a tree!
> He runs so fast he huffs and pants
> When back he runs to me.
> *Pant 2-3-4-5. Rest—Pant 2-3-4-5.*

Giving appropriate responses in the following situations may serve as breathing exercises which stress exhalation:

ah (ɑ:)

a. Smelling the fragrance of a lovely flower
b. Showing delighted surprise at seeing a birthday cake
c. Saying "ah" for the doctor
d. Watching baby kittens playing

oh (oᴛŭ)

a. Showing disappointment because you must rake up the leaves (or do some other chore) instead of going to a ball game
b. Showing surprise at the explanation of a trick
c. Displaying sadness because a puppy has been injured

oo (u:)

a. Reacting when a bottle of ink has spilled on the desk
b. Imitating the soft blowing of the wind; the harsh, fierce winter wind howling; the eerie, ghostly sound heard on Halloween night

Cautions:

1. The teacher should not give any command which will result in rigid posture or any tension of muscles around the waistline.
   > Useful suggestions to pupils for posture include:
   > Stand at ease.
   > Keep your weight on the balls of your feet.
   > Carry your head as though you wore a crown.
2. Stress should not be placed on the amount of breath. *Control* should be emphasized.

---

[3] *Ibid.*, p. 28.

3. Quick breathing should not be encouraged at first. Quiet expansion should be stressed.
4. Exhalation rather than inhalation should be stressed.

Following are criteria of effective breathing for voice production:
a. Inconspicuous, effortless inhalation
b. Exhalation controlled by coordinated action of muscles around the center of the torso
c. Absence of up-and-down movements of the shoulders or upper chest
d. Breath not wasted during phonation

PHONATION

As soon as the basic concept of control of exhalation has been established, the teacher should link breathing exercises to phonation. Pupils should avoid forcing the tone and should work, not for extraordinary volume, but for clear, pleasant, well-modulated voice quality. Pupils should not force the mouth open by pulling the jaw down; they should allow the jaw to drop. Pupils should begin by producing the vowel sounds and should assume a standing position while practicing them.

Following are lists of the two types of vowel sounds:

LONG

ah	(ɑː)	*a*rm
ay	(eɪĭ)	*ai*d
ee	(iː)	b*ead*
aw	(ɔː)	b*orn*
oh	(oʊŭ)	*ow*n
oo	(uː)	z*oo*

SHORT

a	(æ)	*a*pple
e	(eɪ)	*e*nd
i	(ɪ)	*it*
o	(ɒ)	*o*ffice
u	(ʌ)	*u*p

Pupils should practice making each sound until it can be made accurately and easily. The sounds should then be combined into groups of two, three, four, five, and six. The exercises may be varied by having the vowels given with rising, falling, and level intonation.

Additional practice can be given by having pupils employ the sounds in words: (1) nouns, (2) phrases, and (3) rhymes:

(1) ah-Arthur; ay-Amy; ee-Edith; aw-horse; oh-boat; oo-shoe.

(2) ah-in a car; ay-by the day; ee-up a tree.

(3) ah-ah-ah-Do you see the star?

Rhyme material:

> I'm a funny little clown [4]
> AH-OO-EE-OO
> My mouth is open wide when I say
> AH-AH-AH

> I'm a jolly little clown [4]
> Yah, Yaw, Yah
> I can smile and I can frown
> Yah, Yaw, Yah

EXERCISES FOR DEVELOPING RESONANCE

1. Hum the following: (to be hummed first *down* each of the three columns; then *across* each line).

mmmah	nnnah	hungah
mmmay	nnnay	hungay
mmmee	nnnee	hungee
mmmaw	nnnaw	hungaw
mmmoh	nnnoh	hungoh
mmmoo	nnnoo	hungoo

2. Say:
   "When it's foggy in the bay [4]
   Then the fog horn blows this way
   N-N-N-N
   When it's foggy late at night,
   Fog horns blow till it is light,
   N-N-N-N"

3. Make the *ng* sounds ring in your nose in the following:

sing, sang, song	ding, dang, dong
ring, rang, rong	bing, bang, bong
ling, lang, long	kling, klang, klong

4. Imitate the sounds made by familiar objects:

plane	zoom	small bells	ting-a-ling
drum	bm-bm-bm	large bells	ding-dong
tom-tom	boom-boom	gong	bong-bong

[4] *Ibid.*, pp. 14–15, 21, 39.

5. The creative abilities of the children may be stimulated by encouraging them to weave stories around the sounds, i.e., "The Story of the Bells," "Singing Toys" and "The Toy Shop." Singing the words of the verse and humming the chorus of familiar songs—school songs, popular songs, Barber Shop Quartet idea, or singing rounds. The following songs may be used effectively: "Flow Gently Sweet Afton," "Bonnie Banks of Loch Lomond," "America The Beautiful," "Jingle Bells," "The Stars and Stripes Forever," "Anchors Aweigh," "Rock-a-Bye Baby," "Blue Danube."

Selected passages, rhymes and poems containing nasal sounds: "The Bells" by Poe, "The Cataract of Lodore" by Southey, "Old King Cole," (nursery rhyme).

6. Composing rhyming jingles provides practice material as well as amusement.

7. Building ladders of rhyming words is a similar device:

song	sum	done
dong	thumb	none
bong	rum	gun
bing	gum	sun
ting	dumb	fun
ding	some	dun
sing	come	run
ring	hum	bun
bring	drum	ton

Cautions:

1. The teacher should not encourage humming exercises unless she is sure that there is no tension in the pupil's jaw or larynx. The pupil should hum with his lips slightly apart. He should roll his head about on his neck while holding a sustained hum.

2. Loudness should not be stressed at first. Volume should be increased gradually.

3. Sustained tones should be alternated with explosive ones to establish control.

Criteria for good resonance:

1. Round, centered tone
2. Pleasant modulation and flexibility
3. Audibility without effort
4. Clear tones

AUDIBILITY

Audibility, a primary factor in developing good voice, is that characteristic which makes the speaker heard by his audience. There must be recognition of the need to vary the amount of voice according to the size of the room and to the size of the audience.

Power and ability to project voice may be developed through:

1. "Tossing" words, as one tosses a ball, from one person to another.

   Children standing at the front of the room toss the word ball to children standing at the rear of the room. This may be varied in many ways such as having children face one another at varying distances— center of room, rear of room, far corner, etc.

   Children not facing one another tossing word ball over their heads.

2. "Echoes":

   The teacher may say a word or phrase and have either one child, a small group, or the entire class be her echo.

Teacher says:	One Child or Small Group or Entire Class:
a. "Come back"	a. Echoes repeat phrases
b. "Go away"	b. Echoes repeat phrases

3. A listening committee of pupils may be trained to function at all times during class sessions. The committee's responsibility would be to acquaint the speaker with the fact that he cannot be heard. A quiet signal such as raising the hand, may be used. This will eliminate interrupting the speaker and thus distracting both him and his audience.

4. Further devices include: paging, train announcing, using a megaphone or microphone.

Voice Faults

Broadly defined a voice fault may be regarded as any condition of voice that attracts undue and unpleasant attention. More specifically a voice fault is any anomaly of pitch, quality, or volume. These faults may be due to a great variety of causes: physical, mental, emotional, or functional.

Whenever the class teacher discovers that a child's voice attracts continued unpleasant attention or is habitually different, to a marked degree, from the normal voice she should recommend that the child be examined by a throat specialist. If, after examination, it has been determined that a physical condition is the cause of the voice problem the advice of the physician should be followed most carefully in all corrective procedures. A trained speech teacher should work very closely with the class teacher in carrying forward the rehabilitation program for these serious voice cases.

There are, however, many minor voice faults which are the result of habitual misuse. These voice faults will respond readily to a systematic program of voice training. The commonest voice problems found among school children are inaudibility, hoarseness, stridency, nasality, and excessively high pitch. The following suggestions provide the basis for a simple routine of voice hygiene which will improve or correct nonorganic voice faults. The essentials of this routine include habits of physical and mental health, relaxation, and breathing. This is important as these exercises condition the body for the work to follow.

Suggestions for Treatment of Voice Faults

Improvement or correction of the nonorganic voice faults listed in this section is within easy reach of anyone who is willing to follow a simple routine of voice hygiene. At least one relaxation and one breathing exercise should be part of every voice lesson.

NASALITY

The following exercises are designed to correct nasality:
1. Develop flexibility and control of soft palate through:
   a. Panting
   b. Alternating nasal and oral production of vowels
2. Relax the throat muscles by:
   a. Yawning
   b. Rolling head on neck while chanting vowels
3. Concentrate attention on exhalation through the mouth by exercises involving blowing: blowing out a candle, blowing a pin wheel, blowing feathers. Use the same technique for "blowing out the vowel sounds" preceded by the aspirate *h*—such as *hoo, hah, hee*. Hold the sound until all breath is expelled.
4. Combine the front vowels produced with the lip and tongue tip consonants to pull the tone forward—*bee, bay, bear, tee, time.*
5. Give the pupil exercises in ear training to enable him to discriminate between the correct and incorrect sound. For example, the teacher may say the word "man" producing the vowel sound nasally and then repeat the word producing the sound correctly.

INAUDIBILITY

The following are steps which should be taken to help pupils project their voices.

1. Create an atmosphere of *audience interest* when the pupil is to speak.
2. Make sure that the student is *prepared* to speak.
3. Give the pupil a *specific* speaking assignment, avoid blanket assignments. Stimulate enthusiasm and original thinking on the part of the pupil.
4. Build up self-reliance and self-confidence through praise and encouragement.
5. Help the pupil to increase volume through the proper use of diaphragmatic breathing plus the active use of lips, tongue, and lower jaw.
6. Direct the attention of the speaker to listeners who are farthest away.
7. Set up listening committees to check on the audibility of the speaker's voice.

STRIDENCY

To help the pupil whose voice is strident:

1. Develop a more positive social attitude on the part of the pupil and cooperation on the part of the class.
2. Improve the general tone of imagination and sympathy of both the pupil and the class.
3. Give the pupil opportunities to serve as leader and member of the group.
4. Keep the volume and pitch of voices of the class as a whole at conversational level.
5. Give the pupil exercises to develop a recognition of the most economical use of voice in various speech situations. He should become aware that the space to be covered and the size of the audience are determining factors.
6. Have the pupil dramatize characters which would require deep, measured tones.

HIGH PITCH

For pupils with high pitch the teacher should:

1. Use general relaxation exercises.
2. Initiate efforts to remove, if possible, the causes for inferiority and insecurity.

3. Check on the pupil's sleeping and playing habits. Try to remove the causes of overstimulation. Check with the school nurse on endocrinological balance.
4. Give ear training exercises using the piano or pitch pipe, if possible.
5. Encourage pupil reading and recitation of legato selections (smooth and connected with no breaks between successive tones) with deep, measured voice.

CHRONIC LOW PITCH

In cases of chronic low pitch, the teacher should:
1. Make certain there is no pathological condition of the vocal bands by referring the pupil to competent medical authority.
2. Where chronic fatigue or disease is present the teacher should follow the advice of the physician who usually will prescribe rest, no vocal practice, and no use of voice.
3. Give practice in articulation for nicety and precision. Use phrases or sentences in which the consonants *l-t-d-n* are repeated frequently.
4. Teach the technique of the audible whisper. (The classroom teacher should consult the teacher of speech for assistance in this technique.)
5. Where no physical cause is revealed, give exercises in light rapid articulation and nonsense verse. For example: "tip-tap-toe"; pitter-patter"; "bubble-bubble-bubble."

25. *A Remedial and Developmental Speech Program* *

EDNA LUE FURNESS

Mend your speech a little,
Lest you may mar your fortunes.

—SHAKESPEARE, *King Lear*

OF THE THREE communication tools, speaking, reading, and writing, speech stands apart as the principal instrument with which man controls his social environment. Most teachers would agree that, socially, oral language is "a very important source of intellectual stimulation and a very significant human response."

* From Edna Lue Furness, "A Remedial and Developmental Speech Program," *Elementary English* (May, 1955), pp. 289–95. Reprinted by permission of the author and the National Council of Teachers of English.

The social success acquired through speech is not that which is sought by men and women of high society; it is not contingent upon a person's affluence or upon his friends' influence. It is that social success which is shown by one's ability to handle himself well in ordinary speaking situations, and to mingle easily and freely with other people in any walk of life in which the social relation is a requirement.

Relationship of Speech and Reading

Authorities seem to agree that there is an intimate relation between speech and reading, anatomically, physiologically, and psychologically. However, they do not seem to be in agreement about the relation between speech deviation and reading disabilities. On the basis of the relatively few studies made concerning the relationship of speech defects and reading disability, Thomas H. Eames has drawn certain broad generalizations: (1) Neurological lesions in the language centers or their interconnections may impair both speech and reading. (2) Failure or inadequacy of auditory association and discrimination may predispose to either speech or reading difficulty. (3) Speech defects occur in a certain proportion of reading failures and *vice versa*. (4) Emotional reactions to speech difficulties may impair reading. (5) Oral reading is more difficult for a person with a speech defect.

Relationship of Speech and Writing

As is pointed out in the *English Language Arts,* published by the National Council of Teachers of English, there is reason to consider written and spoken expression as closely related, and as affected by each other. Preliminary to make a statement, a speaker often finds it advantageous to write out his proposed remarks, or at least to make an outline. Conversely, attempting to discuss a question is frequently efficacious in clarifying thought before writing. Basic sentence structures are the same for speaking and writing, although there are several distinctions which might be made. To cite an example, usage is affected by the face-to-face situation, and hence often varies with respect to speech and writing. The sentence fragment is frequently accepted in oral speech, e.g., conversation; but, as the authors of the *English Language Arts* note, is less acceptable in writing. Both speech and writing are useful in "identifying confusion, and in clarifying thinking" that is in process.

Another observation may be made. In the process of living together, school children talk and write. The quality of their talking and writing depends on the quality of their living. If their living is natural, wholesome, and creative, their speaking and writing will be also.

Objectives of Speech Instruction

Speech education purposes to locate and diagnose speech defects and to make the speech deviate (and every other student) an effective speaker. According to a statement made in the *Thirty-Fourth Yearbook* of the National Society for the Study of Education, the aims and objectives of speech training are:

1. To establish correct attitudes on the part of the student toward the speaking situation.
2. To make the student conscious of his own speech patterns and the speech patterns of others, to the extent that he is aware of how he and his fellows speak.
3. To discover the student's speech handicaps and inadequacies, and by efficient re-education to redirect the use of his speech mechanism.
4. To allow students with special abilities in speech to achieve creatively and artistically.
5. To contribute to the development and stabilization of the personality of the student through the application of the principles of mental hygiene as they relate to performances in verbal communication.
6. To develop the speech of a child in such a way as to contribute to the growth of the whole child in school and society.

Translated into terms of pupil purposes, these objectives will mean the acquisition of good speech habits for use in the home, school, and community, for the purposes of conversing, interviewing, telephoning, giving or seeking information, making social introductions, reading aloud, storytelling or acting, participating more fully in club activities, and developing personal and social competency. Thus modern speech education is defined in terms of functional importance of speech skills in a democracy.

When an individual, child or adult, speaks without drawing adverse attention to his manner of speaking, he is said to have "good" or "normal" speech. If, however, his speech (i.e., articulation, phonation, voice quality) is unusually conspicuous because of some deviation from an accepted norm, it is said to be defective or disordered. According to Travis, speech is considered to be defective not only when it is conspicuously different from an accepted norm, but also when it is unintelligible or inaudible, when it is unpleasant to hear or "see," when it is characterized by repetitions and blocks, when it is deficient in symbolic formulation (e.g., high-frequency deafness) and expression, or when it causes the user to become anxious or maladjusted. Thus, while actual faults in the rate, the force, the quality or distinctness of speech may be due to the misuse of the physical mechanism, in almost every case these physical phenomena are outward symptoms of a type of personality, an attitude toward life, or an emotional imbalance.

Speech defects vary in degree or seriousness. Some are the result of physical or mental disorders so grave and far-reaching that the speech teacher does well not to attempt to treat them. Others, organic or psychological in cause, require the services of the physician or the psychiatrist in addition to the speech specialist. Such defects are severe stuttering, cleft palate, spastic speech, aphoria, persistent hoarseness, and mutism, as well as the speech accompanying hearing defects.

The more common speech handicaps are merely functional. They are the result of habits that may be changed by retraining. They can be recognized by the teacher, and most of them can be safely handled at the classroom level: lisping, indistinct speech, foreign accent, cluttering, vocal difficulties (nasal and denasal), the monotonous and high-pitched voice, and particularly speech problems involving simple substitutions of sounds, additions, omissions, and distortions on the part of children who have deep-seated personality or physical handicaps. With proper assistance by the professional speech therapist, classroom teachers with some training in speech correction can contribute a valuable service that cannot be rendered by the therapist alone.

In the following pages an attempt is made to present in outline form information concerning possible causes and teaching procedures for speech handicaps. Elaboration of the information presented may be found in the writings of educators such as Backus, Barber, Betts, Dawson, Fernald, Hildreth, Rasmussen, Raubicheck, West, Kennedy, and Carr. It is conceivable that this information may be of service to the teacher in setting up a program of speech development suited to the needs of all members of a class: a program in which the superior child has the opportunity to perfect his speech abilities, and the immature or defective child receives some of the specific retraining he needs.

Disabilities	Possible Causes	Suggested Teaching Procedures
A. *Physiological Articulation* Neglect of final consonants, vowels, consonant blends	Carelessness. Illiterate home.	Set an example by enunciating distinctly. Give phonetic training exercises. Practice sentences for *ng:* "He sang, 'Spring is coming.'" Practice sentences for *nk:* "The ink was pink." Have pupils compare their recorded speech patterns with those of precise speakers.
Omissions, substitutions, distortions, additions of sounds	Faulty tooth structure, palate. Nasal obstruction. Hearing loss. Malocculusion. Mental impairment. Faulty learning. Persistence of infantile speech habits. Emotional maladjustments. Anxiety. Frustration in speech situations. Discouragement. Poor sound discrimination. Short auditory span. Parental baby talk. Improper speech standards in home.	Show pupil the distinction between correct and incorrect sound. Teach correct production of the sound. Practice on production of the sound. Eliminate or minimize the effect of factors causing the defect. Use the correct sound in nonsense syllables, words, or running speech. Compliment child on successful pronunciation. Motivate younger children by attractive materials, games. Motivate older children by desire to improve speech and classroom standing.
Lingual protrusion lisp	Loss of front teeth. Faulty occlusion between the upper and lower teeth. Hearing impairment. Excessive timidity. Over-docility. Prolonged infantilism.	Ask child to close teeth tight, keep tongue inside, blow his breath out between the center front teeth. Ask pupil to imitate the teacher's example, aided by the mirror. Combine ear training and explanation of the production of the correct sounds. Recite words, phrases, and sentences containing the *s* sound in all positions.
Lateral emission lisp	Malformation of teeth or jaws.	Help pupil acquire feeling of proper breath placement. Request subject to pretend to blow out a candle or to blow soap bubbles.

Disabilities	Possible Causes	Suggested Teaching Procedures
Voice Monotonous voice	Paralysis. Disease. Fatigue. Poor coordination. Vocal mechanism unfitted to respond to demands of the mind. Absence of thought and emotion. Unvaried intellectual life.	Listen to storytelling records in which voices are flexible. Dramatize stories in which a variety of emotions are depicted. Dramatize stories like *The Three Bears.* Imitate different kinds of bells: alarm clock, telephone, doorbell. Have pupil record voice and listen to the results. Read aloud for meaning. Try to express ideas in various ways.
Breathiness	Improper coordination of breath supply with degree of closure and tension of vocal folds. Failure of the vocal processes to come together because of overstrain in childhood. Improper use of diaphragm.	Put subject at ease. Have pupil hold feather in front of mouth, and keep feather stirring as long as possible while sounding *s, sh, z, zh, v, f, w, wh* (voiced and unvoiced). Have pupil pretend to be St. Nick, as he chants, "Ho, ho, ho, ho."
Hypernasality	Cleft palate. Deviate septum. Lazy tongue, lips, soft palate. Lack of precise closure of the velopharyngeal port. Paralysis of the velum muscles. Abnormal growths in nasal passages caused by accident, tumor, overgrowth of normal tissue. Faulty oral habits. Poor breathing. Faulty articulation.	If the cause is organic, refer case to a physician. Help pupil eliminate bad habits of speech persisting after removal of nasal obstruction. Dramatize situations in which characters have cause to yawn, whistle, or pant. Have pupil say "Ah" loudly, then repeat it softly. Have subject imitate sounds of farm animals.
Insufficient volume	General health factors. Lack of confidence. Personality and adjustment difficulties.	Check on pupil's general health. Encourage development of self-confidence. Correct academic difficulties.
Rhythm Cluttering	Prolonged illness. Anemia. Physical or emotional shocks. Insecurity. Use of nonpreferred hand for writing. Speech conflicts (fear of interruption, speech competition). Failure to coordinate thought and articulation.	Insist that pupil slow speech down. Encourage articulation of consonants and prolongation of vowels.

Disabilities	Possible Causes	Suggested Teaching Procedures
Stuttering	Striking deviations in size, length, shape of palate or tongue. Dental irregularities. Overshot or undershot jaw. Paralysis. Pathological tissue. Chorea. Myxedema. Lesions in the central nervous system. Family history of stuttering. Birth injuries. High fevers during development of speech. Retardation in motor coordination. Prolonged emotional strain. Confused laterality.	Avoid ridicule. Provide proper rest and hygiene. Create genial atmosphere in home and school. Help pupil to face problem frankly; build his confidence in ability to handle speaking situations. Train learner to eliminate unnecessary and undesirable speech mechanisms. Have subject write on various topics. Have him read aloud what he has written. Assign pupil a part in marionettes or puppet shows.
B. *Psychological* Emotional maladjustments	Self-consciousness. Feeling of inferiority. Aggressiveness.	Know pupil's home conditions. Establish a feeling of belonging to group. Give pupil sense of security. Discover pupil's particular interest. Lead learner to center attention upon other persons' thoughts. Have pupil relate short personal experiences. Provide sympathetic atmosphere where subject may have freedom of expression in rhythm, art, dramatization. Provide situations calling for cooperative effort. Have group discussions on routine matters such as fire drill, using drinking fountains, behavior in school library. Give individual work.
Delayed speech	Lesions in the dominant hemisphere. Deafness. Poor coordination due to disease or paralysis, prolonged illness. Low mentality. Lack of necessity or motivation for speech. Shift of handedness or confused hand preference. Shock during act of speaking. Emotional conflicts. Improper teaching methods used by parents. Necessity for learning two or more languages simultaneously. Failure of parents to utter individual words, small words, or name things to the baby.	Use easy, interesting, familiar, and frequently repeated vocabulary. Relate reading, speech, and writing to familiar concepts: home, pets, store, toys, etc. Have short periods of work. Provide for informal conversation.

Disabilities	Possible Causes	Suggested Teaching Procedures
Baby talk	Defective hearing. Severe illness. Low mentality. Jealousy of another child. Feeling of rejection by parents. Immaturity, mental or emotional. Attempt to gain old status of security. Parental pampering. Parental encouragement of immature speech. Bad example of parents. Bilingualism. Difficulty in discriminating accurately between sounds heard in speech of others and sounds being enunciated.	Set correct pattern. Visit the home. Encourage parents to set correct pattern. Promote a wholesome classroom atmosphere. Use pictures related to familiar home and community activities. Help pupil to hear and enunciate discriminatingly.
Neurotic hoarseness	Feeling of inferiority. Tension. Insecurity. Emotional imbalance. Persecution psychosis.	Help pupil find poise, security, and emotional reserve.
Stammering	Laryngeal cramp. Inferiority complex. Transitory amnesia. Weakness in visual imagery. Lack of cerebral dominance. Insecurity.	Regulate rest, diet, and exercise. Maintain sound emotional and mental attitudes at home and in school. Provide opportunities for group activity. Have corrective program aim at readjustment of person to speech situations in life. Help pupil gain self-confidence. Have language and guessing games, and games in which physical action accompanies word.
C. *Pedagogical* Inability to answer questions	Inattention. Day-dreaming. Lack of concentration. Interest outside the topic.	Help pupil attend to problem at hand. Plan a lesson on questions: "What is your name? Where do you live? Name the members of your family?" Show approval of definite, clear answers.
Slovenly speech	Malnutrition. Inactivity of the jaw. Logy tongue. Mental states of dejection, weariness, submission. Lack of mental guidance. Carelessness in following articulation models. Imitation of older members of the family. Parental encouragement.	Instil self-respect and desire for respect of others. Instil ideas of moral, civil and social equality. Say words and phrases carefully after a good model. Take part in dramatizations.

Disabilities	Possible Causes	Suggested Teaching Procedures
Foreignisms	Foreign language in home. Tendency to use a patois. Limited vocabulary. Poor reading comprehension.	Provide informal, everyday contacts with English-speaking children. Give systematic training in English phonetics. Furnish the pupil exercises in ear training. Encourage the pupil's conscious imitation of teacher. Foster simple choral reading.
Usage errors	Low level of language development. Indifference. Lack of pride in language usage. Imitation of speech patterns of family and friends. Unwillingness to change to normative language usage.	Emphasize content. Praise the better speech of some children. Note errors made. End the period by repetition of correct form. Use phonograph recordings of readings, stories, and dramas.
Poor sentence structure	Lack of familiarity with grammatical construction. Poor language habits. Imitation of family and friends. Impoverished home life.	Use words in sentences from first grade on. Give exercises to distinguish between a complete sentence and a sentence fragment. Have pupil learn to speak and write in sentences. Develop sentence consciousness by building of an incidental reading lesson based on vital group experience, such as an excursion, a rainy day. Secure variety and style in sentences by transposing the order of sentence parts. Have pupil put phrases and dependent clauses at the beginning of sentences.
Disorganized thought	Lack of purpose. Inability to see logical relationships: cause and effect, sequence, subordination. Deficiency in ability to do abstract thinking.	Insist that pupil make himself understood. Make certain he understands what others say. Suggest topics for discussion which have a definite sequence of ideas such as "What I did." Have storytelling based on pictures. Have pupil think through what he has to say, while keeping standards in mind. Teach older students the meaning of purpose, plan, main idea, proper partitions and transitions, subordination of details, adaptation of thought and material to the purpose, audience, and occasion.

26. Speech Disorders Found in School Children *

JACK W. BIRCH, JACK MATTHEWS,
AND ERNEST BURGI

Articulatory Disorders Are Most Common

Articulation disorders are those disorders of speech in which the person has some abnormality associated with the way he produces or uses the sounds that make up speech.

Disorders in articulation are by far the most common kinds of speech problems found in children of school age. They are also the problems about which teachers can probably do most. For these reasons we have dealt with articulation problems in detail. Defects of articulation usually involve either (1) substitution of one sound for another, (2) distortion of sounds, (3) omission of sounds, or (4) some combination of these disorders. In the majority of the cases, there is no organic defect which is causing the disorder. In some instances, however, severely deformed mouth, lip, or tongue structure, or some abnormal teeth structure might contribute to the problem.

In general, the classroom procedures for improvement in articulation involve the teaching of correct ways to produce the speech sounds. The specific procedures may vary depending upon the age of the class.

Delayed Speech Has Various Causes

Delayed speech is a term which indicates that the level of speech ability is retarded in comparison to the child's age. It usually means the continual use of infantile speech beyond the age when most children have developed better speech. The child's speech development may have been interrupted by prolonged illness or injury, or for some other reason. In some instances of delayed speech, the child may not speak at all because he has never learned to talk.

In school, delayed speech problems are most likely to be seen by the kindergarten and early elementary teacher. If the child has numerous problems involving sounds that the average child of his age produces accurately,

* Reprinted from *Improving Children's Speech,* by Jack W. Birch, Jack Matthews, and Ernest Burgi, (c) 1958, Public School Publishing Company, Test Division of The Bobbs-Merrill Co., Inc., pp. 37–43.

if his speech is babyish or incomplete, a diagnosis of delayed speech may be indicated. The speech improvement procedures suggested for the kindergarten and early elementary grades will frequently prove beneficial for the child with delayed speech. If the speech is delayed because of some lack of maturation or because of mental retardation, it may be necessary to wait for a certain amount of general development before speech therapy will be successful. When speech seems unusually delayed, parents should be advised to have the child examined by a speech therapist, a pediatrician, and a psychologist. The results of these examinations should provide clues to what to do about the child's speech.

Stuttering Is Very Complex Behavior

Repetitions and hesitations in speaking are part of the normal process of the child's learning to use language. Stuttering involves much more than the simple repetitions, prolongations, and hesitations heard in the speech of most kindergarten and first grade children. All of us engaged in such repetitions and hesitations as children, though we may not recall it now because it was a natural part of our development. These repetitions and hesitations did not mean we were stuttering. Even as adults many of us are less fluent than we realize, but we do not consider ourselves stutterers. The nonfluencies we notice in children should not be classified as stuttering. We seldom find stutterers under 9 or 10 years of age.

Stuttering occurs when children persist with nonfluent speech until they develop marked fears and blocks in their speaking. If the young child's parents, relatives, and teachers evaluate his developing speech as stuttering and attempt to eliminate his normal repetitions, the child develops fear and apprehension of speaking situations. There is reason to believe that the *evaluation* of the speech as abnormal and the *fear associated with speaking* constitute the abnormality in young children who "stutter". *Unless fear and apprehension are present, the child's repetitions and hesitations are, in all likelihood, normal.*

When fears become associated with speech and continue for some time, the child develops ways of disguising or avoiding his repetitions and hesitations. He may avoid feared words or speaking situations. He may develop various devices which, for a limited time, help him to initiate speech and "get started." If this type of activity persists until the child reaches high school, he usually has developed several secondary *symptoms* of stuttering. He may hold his breath, clasp his hands tightly while speaking, whistle to get started, close his eyes, or do similar things. His speech no longer has simple repetitions, but instead shows severe *blocks* during which he may be contorted or seem almost paralyzed. He may or may not make any audible sounds. Most stutterers have marked fears about speaking and are able to predict those situations in which they will have the most difficulty. In some speaking situations they will have no trouble at all—in others they may be practically speechless. Stuttering seems to be variable, not only from time to time in the same person, but it varies a great deal between individuals.

Teachers Can Help in the Treatment of Stuttering

The treatment of the nonfluencies we see in children in the early grades is primarily a job for the family and teachers. It is difficult, because it requires that the child be given no indication that there is any concern about his speech. If the child does not appear concerned about his speech, if the nonfluencies are easy and effortless, he should not be made to feel any concern over it.

Do not call the child a stutterer. Do nothing which will make the child feel there is something wrong with his speech. Above all, parents and teachers should develop the ability to listen to the child comfortably without criticism or tension. Do not call his attention to his speech with such requests as, "Stop and start over," "Slow down," or "Take a deep breath." The kindergarten and elementary-school teacher can help the child most of all by accepting his speech as it is, learning to listen to the child comfortably and providing as many relaxed speaking situations for him as possible. Group speaking activities, such as choral reading programs and other group activities where all the children recite in unison, will help the child to develop normal speech rhythms.

Conferences with the parents to help them develop these same attitudes toward hesitant speech are beneficial. This type of treatment is obviously *preventative*. It is an attempt to create an accepting environment for the child and lessens the risk of having his speech evaluated as abnormal, since such an evaluation may lead to the child's developing marked fears and apprehensions about speaking.

Children Who Are Known Stutterers Can Be Aided

What can the teacher do to help the child who really stutters? First of all, a speech therapist should be consulted if at all possible. But even without the aid of a speech correctionist the classroom teacher can be of help in a number of ways.

1. The teacher should help the child develop any special interests and abilities that he has. Any increase in healthy personality development and sense of accomplishment will do much to help speech.

2. Help the child talk frankly about his speech problem. This tends to reduce some of the anxiety centering around speech. It helps him face the problem more objectively.

3. Help him to stutter more easily; do not encourage him to *stop* stuttering. The person who stutters cannot tolerate the nonfluencies that occur in his speech. He is constantly trying to be fluent. That seems to be one of his problems. The harder he tries to stop stuttering, the more difficulty he is likely to have. It is best even to avoid praising him when he does occasionally speak without stuttering. Accept whatever kind of speech he has. Any of the group activities suggested in this booklet which involve a number of individuals speaking in unison may be used. Do not give him drills, exercises, or oral recitations to help him stop stuttering. Instead encourage him to stutter in different ways without being concerned or worried about it.

4. Let him know that you are sincerely interested in him. His parents and teachers must learn how to listen to him comfortably if they want to help him. Let him talk. Do not interrupt or "feed" him the words.

5. Do not force him to recite orally in situations which he fears a great deal. Only the teacher and the student together can decide what to do about oral recitations. Some situations may bother him a great deal. It will usually hinder rather than help his speech to force him to recite in these situations. Sometimes an agreement to substitute other work for some oral recitations seems to be the best answer.

6. Try to help him find some extra-curricular activities in which he can participate successfully. He will usually have no difficulty in choral reading situations or singing.

These are only a few suggestions to help the classroom teacher in her approach to the problem of stuttering. There are other suggestions in the following sources:

Stuttering, prepared for the American Speech and Hearing Association by Charles Van Riper, under the editorship of Wendell Johnson. (Published and distributed by the National Society for Crippled Children & Adults, Inc., 11 S. LaSalle Street, Chicago, Illinois.) 1948.

8 Keys to Normal Speech and Child Adjustment, by Leon Lassers. (Speech Aid Series, Leon Lassers, San Francisco State College, San Francisco 2, California.) 1945 and 1949.

Speech Problems of Children, Wendell Johnson, editor. (Grune & Stratton, New York.) 1950. Chapter 9.

Voice Disorders Are Rare, but Important

Children's voices vary a great deal in quality, pitch, and flexibility. Many voices are not as pleasant or as flexible as they should be, and yet they are not really considered defective. In order to decide whether or not a voice can be considered defective, we must return to our criteria for a speech disorder which were presented in chapter I. The child's voice should be loud enough to be heard under ordinary conditions; the quality of the voice should not be unduly harsh, husky, breathy, or nasal; the pitch level should be suitable for the age and sex of the child; and the rhythm and melody of the voice should be adequate.

Voice disorders among school-age children are relatively rare. However, they can constitute severe problems. Voice disorders sometimes result from organic disorders such as hearing loss, disease, or injury affecting the vocal folds or some other part of the speech mechanism. Sometimes disorders of voice result from severe emotional problems. Physical growth itself sometimes contributes to problems of voice. The size and shape of the larynx and the vocal folds in adults is quite different from that of the child. The voice of the adult differs from the child's voice. The difference between the voices of childhood and adulthood are more obvious in the case of the male. Occasionally the voice changes from childhood to adulthood cause problems for the adolescent. Although the average boy may see the beginnings of voice changes around 12 or 13 years of age, he will not usually experience the major discomforts associated with unpredictability and roughness of voice until around 16 to 18 years of age. Thus voice problems of that kind will confront the secondary teacher. Girls are less likely to experience difficulties with voice change. Occasionally the adolescent girl will develop excessive breathiness or huskiness which may need help.

It is important for the teacher to let the child know that a voice problem is not a laughing matter. Make every effort to understand the feeling that such a problem may create in an individual. Acceptance and understanding by the teacher will help a great deal to overcome the acute embarrassment and discomfort that some adolescents experience at this time.

A child with such a voice problem should always be referred to a physician for an examination. The teacher may be called upon to cooperate or help with whatever therapy procedures are advised.

The voice is one of the most accurate indicators of emotional state and level of adjustment. Anything we can do to improve the voices of school children will be of value. Group activities, such as choral reading selections, can be used to advantage in promoting pleasing voice quality, pitch, and loudness.

Foreign Dialect Can Handicap Children

In some sections of the country foreign dialect is a common speech problem of school children. Foreign dialect results from the influence of some other language upon American English. The extent and severity of the problem is decided by the particular foreign language involved, the age at which English was learned, and whether or not the child's parents speak English. The child's specific problems will depend upon the differences between the foreign language and American English. Differences show up in (1) individual sound production (an articulation problem), (2) melody pattern (a voice problem), (3) use of idioms, and (4) grammatical structure.

Approach the problems of articulation in foreign dialect in the same way as has been suggested in previous chapters for each grade level. Melody pattern differences are essentially a problem of voice. The group activities previously recommended will help. Grammatical structure and use of idioms calls for teaching the correct English grammar and English idioms. The English teacher knows best how to do that.

Be aware that the child with foreign dialect may have difficulty in obtaining acceptance and understanding from his classmates, particularly if he belongs to a racial minority group. Encourage his participation in extracurricular activities. Encourage the development of special interests which will win him recognition. Further the understanding of his problems by the other children by setting a good example. Remember that children enjoy teasing and ridiculing the youngster who is different. Forestall their behavior.

The correction of foreign dialect should take place in kindergarten and the early grades, since the child is still rapidly assimilating the speech characteristics of his environment at these levels. One of the most essential items for the early grade teacher to keep in mind is that of providing these children with examples of good American English through her own speech.

Hearing Losses Can Cause Speech Defects

Hearing loss affects the child's speech. Among the common symptoms of hearing loss in children are defects of voice and articulation. If a child is born deaf or extremely hard of hearing, he will not learn how to talk at all unless he receives a great deal of special help. If he cannot hear the sounds of speech, he will not learn to make them on his own.

The regular classroom teacher is seldom confronted with a hearing problem this severe. The classroom teacher should, however, be aware that hearing problems do affect children's speech and that a child's hearing is frequently impaired to an extent which affects his speech and his school progress without anyone having knowledge of it.

Hearing loss can occur any time. The child who hears normally in first grade may have defective hearing when he returns from summer vacation to start second. Look for these signs or clues which mean there is the possibility of a hearing loss. Disorders of voice or articulation, inattention, behavioral problems, frequent mistakes in carrying out instructions, cocking of the head, apathy, and similar behavior should lead the teacher to recommend hearing tests.

In addition to the use of such speech improvement activities as have been outlined in preceding chapters, the teacher can do many things to help the hard-of-hearing child in her class to get the most out of his classwork. The following suggestions will help.

1. If he wears a hearing aid, learn how to help him with it. Become familiar with how to replace batteries and cords and how to take it on and off.

2. Help his classmates to understand the nature of his problems.

3. Select extracurricular and class activities in which he can participate successfully.

4. Seat him to his advantage for both *sight* and *hearing*. Do not put yourself between the child and the source of light. Be sure he can see your face full front. Seat him near you but not so close he must crane his neck to see you. The *first row* is often not the best place, particularly if it is very close to the front blackboard.

5. Be sure he understands the topic of conversation at all times and understands all new material and assignments. Most hard-of-hearing children become discouraged if required to ask for repetitions day after day. Write new assignments on the board and then turn and face the class when making the assignment orally.

These ideas will suggest the general concepts the classroom teacher might employ in handling the hard-of-hearing child. Thoughtfulness and consideration of his special problems will pay big dividends in terms of his school progress and social adjustment. Further suggestions which may help the teacher in handling hard-of-hearing children are found in the following source:

Keaster, Jacqueline, "Children with Impaired Hearing," in *Speech Problems of Children*, Wendell Johnson, editor. (Grune & Stratton, New York.) 1950.

27. The Relationship between Reading and Spelling *

RUSSELL G. STAUFFER

THIS IS an article for parents and teachers. It is about spelling and reading and about how these two facets of language are related. All parents want their children to read and write—which usually means to spell. They want them to succeed.

In the United States, where all the children of all the people must be served, we try to equalize the educational opportunities for all. This is well-nigh impossible and especially so because we place a high premium on each individual's achieving his optimum.

Today's world is a reading and writing world. Ability to read is needed at every turn. Similarly, ability to write is required—at home, at school, at work, and at play. The day of writing an X rather than signing a name has long been passed. Anyone who cannot read and write is truly out of step. This, then, is why parents are so genuinely concerned.

What Is Reading?

When reading is defined as getting meaning, it goes well beyond the recognition of words. It becomes synonymous with thinking on the one hand, and with entertainment and fun on the other. Therefore, even during the initial stages of learning, reading is used as a means to learning and enjoyment.

* From Russell G. Stauffer, "The Relationship between Reading and Spelling," *Education* (December, 1958), pp. 206–10. Reprinted by permission of the author and The Bobbs-Merrill Co., Inc., Indianapolis, Ind.

Reading for meaning goes well beyond rote learning. It is far more than a simple mechanical skill, a series of rhythmic eye movements, or a process of accurate word recognition. It is a complex organization of patterns of the higher mental processes. As Dr. Gates says: "It can and should embrace all types of thinking, evaluating, judging, imagining, reasoning, and problem-solving."

This broad conception of reading does not mean that word attack skills and accurate word perception are of no consequence. Rather, it implies that the emphasis is not upon skills of this nature but upon purposeful reading.

Techniques of word recognition are important. Command of phonetic and structural analysis skills is essential. These skills can help the reader attack new material in order to get it to yield its meaning. The steps for attacking the structure of words are numerous. Even so, authorities are agreed that the skills should be taught. When the pupils have a need for word attack skills and are ready to use them in functional activities—activities in which they are engaged in a search for meaning—then the skills should be taught.

What Is Spelling?

To name or to write or to print in their proper order the letters of, as a word—this is spelling. Spelling is concerned with the form of the word, either its spoken form or its written form, or both. Spelling requires accurate reproduction or recall of the letters in their proper order.

The accurate speller must be a producer. To do this, impression must precede expression; intake must precede outflow. To produce by writing usually goes well beyond spelling to the production of ideas. This implies that spelling skill should be so efficient that the writer can write words quickly and correctly and, in most instances, without pausing to think about the spelling.

Research shows that the best spelling intake is through visual presentation. In other words, knowledge of the written form of the word to be spelled is most advantageous. Stated another way, spelling is predominantly a visual perception skill.

The foregoing is not to imply that careful pronunciation with a focus on syllables does not help recall. What is meant is that emphasis during learning should be on visual presentation or "seeing" the word. Yet, at the same time, it is known that "saying" the word as well as "writing" the word does increase the effectiveness of learning.

Relationships between Reading and Spelling

Reading and writing are facets of language. Both facets utilize visual imagery. Both use the written form.

Listening and speaking are also facets of language. Both of these facets utilize auditory imagery. Both use sound.

It seems almost too evident to state, therefore, that a close relationship exists between reading and spelling because both facets of language use visual form. Research shows that this is true. Similarly, close relationships exist between listening and speaking.

The correlations between reading and spelling are relatively high. Studies show that children spell words they can read with much greater accuracy than those they cannot read. This is true at all levels.

At the primary level where reading instruction and spelling instruction are initiated, the relationship between the two skills seems to be most apparent. This is the level at which teachers seem to grasp more clearly than at any other the relationship between spoken language facility and the acquiring of facility with written language. This is true because circumstances force the recognition of the relationship.

Children starting to school come equipped with varying amounts of oral language facility. They can talk and listen. They know how to communicate orally, even though they do not know about the complexities of language— its syntax and grammar.

Research shows that the best single yardstick of a child's readiness for reading is how well he talks, or the extent of his oral language facility. As a matter of fact, this verbal facility is a good measure of the child's intelligence. Ability to use words is significant probably because it indicates a wide experience with things and people, and as such is a symptom of both intelligence and maturity. While word training may encourage the growth of a child toward "intellectual maturity," it cannot create such growth. This is something that can be created only by more experience, along with the correct use of words to communicate the experience.

Beginning reading instruction. Primary level teachers usually initiate reading instruction by following one of two plans or by combining the two. Many first grade teachers start reading instruction by using a so-called experience approach. What they do is utilize as fully as possible children's experiences and oral language facility as a source for a reading vocabulary.

The procedure is as follows: The child dictates to the teacher stories, reports, or just ideas, preferably about things he has experienced. Imaginative stories may also be used. The teacher records what the child dictates.

After accumulating many dictated charts, particularly individual charts, the child begins to recognize frequently recurring words or unusual, vivid words. This is the first step toward learning to read. Once the child sees that he can read the printed words and can do so in different places, then he begins to look for word recognition clues he can use to read more words.

At first, the words the pupil knows are recognized entirely by their form. He becomes amazingly sharp at recognizing small differences both in and among words and remembering them. All this is done largely by form clues or by the word's configuration. Teachers call these sight words because the pupils recognize them at sight without needing to use phonetic or structural analysis clues.

By the time the pupil has accumulated a sizeable sight vocabulary and is turning to books, he has also picked up the spelling of a few words. The writing activities of a first-year program alert him to the need for reproducing words in writing. As a result of these activities he discovers that he can reproduce (spell) some of the words he can read. In other words, the *recognition* (reading) of the words by their meaning and form has also facilitated the *reproduction* (spelling) of the words.

This process of word recognition utilizes a series of interrelated language factors and does so in logical sequences. The process starts with the child's own experiences and the vocabulary he chooses for telling about them; to the seeing that reading is only talk written down; to the recognition of his own words because he is the author as well as the reader; to the distinguishing between words by their form; and finally, to the spelling reproduction of the words he can read because he used meaning clues, visual form clues, and auditory (sound) clues.

Some teachers use only a basal reader approach. They follow the word introduction plan set up in the preprimers. The authors of whatever basal reader program is used have tried to introduce words on a carefully structured word-by-word plan. The words they choose to introduce first, second, third, and so on, are usually selected from studies of children's spoken vocabularies. This is the way the authors try to select a reading vocabulary that will contain words that are common, frequently used, and meaningful. It is an attempt at identifying an average situation. Even though the so-called stories built on a few words represent an awkward use of language, the controlled repetition helps the pupils to recognize and remember the words introduced. In turn, these are the words the children pick up and spell first.

In other instances teachers combine the two approaches—an experience story approach and a basal reader approach. This is a good compromise, in many ways. But again, the result is the same insofar as reading and spelling are concerned. The recognition of the printed form (reading) facilitates the reproduction of the printed form (writing).

Test-study. Thus far the discussion should lead one to conclude that reading and spelling are closely related because of the visual form of words. The more efficient one is in reading, the more the recognition of words becomes so facile that almost all words are read as sight words. This, in turn, means increased spelling ability, even at higher levels.

One might conclude that words to be spelled should be presented visually. Ability to spell words that can be read, but have not been studied, implies that both spelling and reading are predominantly dependent upon visual imagery.

This dependence upon visual imagery is substantiated when the test-study method is used. By this approach, words to be learned for spelling purposes are first tested. The results show that pupils have already learned—incidentally, through reading—many of the words being tested. Furthermore, the results of the pretest show each pupil which words or which word parts he needs to study. In addition, research shows that if the pretests are immediately corrected by the pupils, learning is much more efficient.

Similarly, if a pupil learns to use word attack skills on words he doesn't recognize while reading, he becomes a more efficient reader. This is especially true if he is given help while reading in a content area such as science or arithmetic. Meeting the troublesome word in a context permits the reader to take full advantage of all meaning clues available, and then, if necessary, concentrate on the hard spots by using phonetic and structure clues. When skills are taught in practical, firsthand, need situations the learner is much more apt to remember the skill and, better yet, to apply it in new situations. Some teachers persist, however, in teaching phonetics using isolated words, removed from a meaningful setting, and remote from a felt need. In these situations phonetic skills are usually quickly forgotten and are nonfunctional.

Teaching word attack skills in response to a real need as described above is as functional an approach to the skill as teaching spelling by the self-correction method. The learner sees the spelling error he has made in a spelling context (a word) and as a result is much more apt to remember the skill learned and apply it to other words. As in reading, the case is the same in spelling, when the teacher tries to teach "hard spots" and looks for transfer to real situations, the pupils usually don't make the transfer.

A rule frequently stated in reading is: Never teach phonetics in isolation. A similar statement might be made about spelling rules.

In addition, words selected for spelling study are chosen on the basis of frequency of use. For instance, the most commonly occurring 2,000 words with their repetitions make up 95.05 per cent of the running words in adult writing. Since most high-frequency words in writing are also high-frequency words in reading, it is to be expected that the frequent reading of common words contributes to spelling success.

Even so, among the words repeatedly met in reading there are some that are spelling demons. These spelling demons do show up in the test-study method and then can be studied carefully.

Other Curriculum Areas and Spelling

The conditions reported about the relationships between spelling and reading are true in a large sense about spelling and the other curriculum areas. Easy, frequently encountered words in other areas are usually spelled correctly even though unstudied.

Results vary if the vocabulary of a particular curriculum area is very technical, less frequent in occurrence, and more uncommon. Here, as is true when a learner deals with any new area, acquisition of concepts is of first importance. The concepts must be learned if reading in an area is to be successful. So then, the teacher in a special area of the curriculum has as a first task the teaching of concepts essential to understanding that area. As this is accomplished, not only is efficient reading made more possible, but spelling is enhanced.

As the pupils make progress in using the dictionary, in proofreading, and in associating sounds with letters, they also show progress in the number of words they can spell at the first presentation. Pupils who constantly discover that they can spell many words they have not studied are motivated to try to spell and write more. As a result they learn even more words and concepts from other subjects in their curriculum.

All this implies that, when spelling instruction is coordinated with instruction in the different curriculum areas, greater skill will result. It also suggests that if, in turn, attention is directed to the study of the words not yet learned, both spelling ability and motivation will be increased.

Summary

It is evident that, because reading and spelling utilize visual form, the relationship between the two is relatively close. Because correct pronunciation is important to both reading and spelling, auditory imagery, as well as the kinesthetic imagery of writing, contribute to success in both areas. Frequent recontact with words as in reading and writing and distributed learning for spelling seem to yield best results.

Checking spelling ability by the test-study method is a functional approach to spelling in that it shows the learner that he can spell many words he has not "studied." And, as in reading where word attack skills are required to unlock a word while reading, so in spelling by the test-study method, hard parts are identified and the self-correction yields excellent results. A rule of thumb that might be declared is: Always avoid asking a child to spell a word he cannot read, regardless of the curriculum area in which it occurs.

28. Experiences Which Develop Spelling Ability *

ERNEST HORN

IN THE great majority of schools, spelling texts or workbooks are utilized in the teaching of spelling. However, the development of spelling ability is not limited to what is done in periods specifically devoted to teaching spelling. It is essential that the work of the spelling period be efficiently coordinated with what is done in other curriculum areas to develop spelling ability.

Learning to Spell through Reading

Spelling and reading abilities are closely related. Correlations reported between spelling and reading are nearly as high as those reported between intelligence and reading. Few persons who are excellent readers are poor spellers and few, if any, poor readers are good spellers. However, some students in the middle ranges of ability in reading are excellent at spelling, while others spell very poorly.

That pupils learn to spell many words through reading them has repeat-

* From Ernest Horn, "Experiences Which Develop Spelling," *NEA Journal* (April, 1954), pp. 210–11. Reprinted by permission of the author and the *NEA Journal*.

edly been demonstrated. It seems reasonable to expect that the more often a word is seen in reading, the more probable it is that pupils will learn to spell it. Yet among the words repeatedly met in reading are many spelling demons. If abbreviations, proper names, and derived forms not reported by Thorndike are omitted, all but nine of the 100 words which, according to Fitzgerald, are most frequently misspelled in grades two to six are among the 1000 words of highest frequency in reading. It is possible that, because these words are so familiar, little or no attention is called to their spelling in the process of reading.

It has been suggested that when new words are met in reading, the pupils take time to learn to spell them. While a good many words could undoubtedly be learned in this way, many would be words not likely to be used by children in their present and future writing. Most of the spelling errors in writing are made on familiar rather than on strange words. This suggestion seems objectionable, moreover, because it is likely to be unfavorable to development of good reading habits.

The pupil's attention will be directed to spelling, of course, in looking up unknown words in the dictionary and in differentiating such words as *quiet* and *quite, except* and *accept,* which have similar configurations and sounds but different meanings.

The contributions of reading to spelling, however, are not limited to the words children learn to spell. Many auxiliary abilities are developed, such as use of the dictionary, improvement of pronunciation through oral reading, and ability to associate letters with sounds. There is some evidence that instruction in phonics is more beneficial to spelling than to reading even though given in connection with the reading program. In reading, however, the emphasis is upon letter-to-sound relationships, and identification of words is further assisted by configuration and context. In contrast, spelling requires the pupil to decide what letters to use to spell sounds, and, except in the case of purely phonetic words, this is a difficult decision to make.

The potential contributions of reading to spelling, then, are substantial. As reading abilities are developed, spelling is improved. On the other hand, deficiencies in reading are serious handicaps in learning to spell.

Learning to Spell through Writing

The potential contributions of composition to spelling are great indeed. Such creative writing as letters, bulletins, items for the school newssheet, and reports on special problems constitute important motives for learning to spell and aid in the maintenance of words which the child has learned in his spelling lessons. The more the occasions for writing in school resemble the occasions in which writing is done out of school, the more likely it is that learning of the most important words will be facilitated.

The statement is sometimes made that the words children need in their written work are the words in the spelling list for their grade. This, of course, is partly true, because the number of words in the spelling list is restricted. The lists for each grade presumably include the words most commonly written in that grade, and these words, according to the evidence, are likely to be written with great frequency.

Of course, other words will be needed. Many of them, however, will have only transient value. Moreover, which additional words are needed will vary from pupil to pupil.

In schools which have regular or occasional spelling lessons but do not use a text, words for the spelling lessons may include words misspelled in written work. And even in schools which base spelling instruction primarily upon a text, words misspelled in written work are sometimes taught either in separate lessons or as a supplement to the regular lessons in the book. When this is done, the chief emphasis should be put on words most important in present and future writing. It seems undesirable, moreover, to take the time of the entire class to study words misspelled by only a few.

Policies differ as to how rigorously spelling errors in written work should be corrected. Too much emphasis on correct spelling, especially in lower grades, may discourage children from writing. Correct spelling is a factor in acceptable written compositions and there should be increasing emphasis upon it in intermediate grades and beyond.

This implies that there be a definite plan for correcting spelling errors. The evidence indicates that the mere checking of spelling errors does little good unless accompanied by an effective plan for learning the words which have been misspelled. The more pupils accept responsibility for detecting spelling errors and eliminating them, the better.

Contributions of Speech and Handwriting

Shortcomings in speech, such as mispronunciations and articulatory defects, have been found to be related to disabilities in spelling. It is to be expected that removal of these shortcomings will be reflected in better spelling. In many words, such as *athletic, government, probably,* and *experiment,* mispronunciations are a major cause of misspelling. Most modern methods of teaching spelling include correct pronunciation as an essential step in learning. An interesting problem is created by regional differences in pronunciations. It seems desirable that teachers, in pronouncing words in spelling lessons, use the pronunciations characteristic of cultivated speech in the locality in which the school exists. Abundant opportunities for speaking help develop fluency in expression, which is likely to be carried over into written work, with potential benefits to spelling.

Pupils who write legibly and with reasonable speed have an advantage in taking tests in spelling because they can write the words in the time allowed, are not penalized because of illegible letters, and can give their entire attention to spelling without being distracted by handwriting difficulties. Furthermore, poor handwriting is frequently cited among the factors that cause difficulty in spelling. Handwriting is a special problem in teaching spelling in the primary grades. Manuscript writing is taught in grades one and two in the great majority of schools and, although the evidence is somewhat conflicting, it is generally believed to have beneficial results on both reading and spelling.

Contributions of Other Curriculum Areas

Some pertinent evidence is provided by the results of experiments on the ability of children to spell words not studied in spelling lessons as compared with *studied* words of equal difficulty, according to spelling scales. In brief, easy *unstudied* words are spelled about as well as easy studied words, but as the difficulty of the words increases, the *studied* words are spelled with much higher accuracy. At all levels of difficulty, however, there is clear evidence that considerable learning does take place outside the spelling period.

Much more significant for planning instruction in spelling is the evidence from tests given before words were studied. These are of two types: (1) tests given at the beginning of a term on words to be studied during that term and (2) tests given before the study of the weekly lesson. In some schools a test consisting of words sampled from the words to be taught during the term is given at the beginning of the term. The median per cents of accuracy that have been reported range in most instances from about 25 per cent to more than 60 per cent and are much higher in schools where pupils have developed superior abilities in reading and written composition. It seems reasonable to assume that this range in the per cent of accuracy is accounted for chiefly by differences in the effectiveness with which reading, written composition, and other language arts aside from spelling have been taught in these schools.

Additional evidence is furnished by the results of tests given before the study of weekly lessons, which show that many of the words have already been learned. Some children spell all or most of the words correctly before study, but very poor spellers may misspell all or nearly all.

It is evident that children learn to spell many words in activities outside the spelling class. They also make progress outside the spelling class in using the dictionary, in proofreading, and in associating sounds with letters. There is some evidence which suggests that, when spelling lessons are highly motivated and efficient, pupils develop an interest and conscientiousness in spelling in other curriculum areas, with the result that the contributions to spelling from these areas are increased.

The fact that children learn to spell so many words outside the spelling class points to the need of coordinating instruction in spelling periods with the development of spelling ability in other activities. It suggests that motivation will be increased and much time saved if the pupil's efforts are directed to study of words he has not yet learned.

Whether it is practicable to teach spelling only in connection with the other language arts is a debated question. The evidence indicates, however, that what is done with spelling in connection with other language arts needs to be supplemented by direct, systematic instruction in spelling periods, especially in the case of pupils of below-average spelling ability, and for all pupils in the learning of difficult words.

29. *Two Key Factors in Spelling Success* *

ELEANOR M. JOHNSON

MANY COMPLEX factors affect the learning of any skill. In spelling, proficiency in the various areas of the language arts, handwriting skills, methods of teaching, and other items influence the ability to spell. Because of space limitations, this paper is concerned with two key factors which influence spelling, namely; meanings and word structure patterns. These two factors are common to several of the language arts areas.

* From Eleanor M. Johnson, "Two Key Factors in Spelling Success," *Education* (January, 1956), pp. 271–74. Reprinted by permission of the author and The Bobbs-Merrill Co., Inc., Indianapolis, Ind.

Interrelationships of the Language Arts

Language is a means to good living. The effective use of language is essential to child development and social adjustment.

Normal language development is a necessary part of child growth. Adequate social adjustment calls for language facility. The child who doesn't know when and how to speak is a social misfit. The child whose reading ability lags seriously is frustrated in and out of school. The child who does not learn to write and spell is handicapped in his school and vocational adjustment. An adequate language arts program fits the child for useful living in a world of language. Language development is facilitated by systematic concurrent instruction in the various language skills.

All the language arts—listening, speaking, reading, writing and spelling—are related processes in language development. Listening and speaking are inseparable parts of oral language. Reading, writing, and spelling are facets of written language.

Research workers have found a high degree of relationships between the several language arts areas. These interrelated language abilities give us a multiple approach to language development and tend to reinforce each other. For example, all the language arts areas are related through vocabulary.

Meaningful Vocabularies

To use these inherent relationships effectively, we need to see more clearly the role each media can play in the growth of meaningful vocabularies.

Listening. The infant learns to listen to language. Speech noises made by his family begin to take on meaning when the words are related to his personal experiences. As the child grows he continues to listen to stories and conversation with increasing understanding. He becomes accustomed to hearing stock expressions which he will later meet in print. Listening enlarges the child's stock of word meanings. Depending upon home environment and opportunities for listening, the child will enter school with a broad background of vocabulary meanings or a very limited one.

Speaking. The ability to comprehend and use language orally indicates the child's potentiality for progress in reading, writing, and spelling. Ordinarily, the child advances no faster in reading, writing, and spelling than his oral language development permits. Printed and written words most easily learned are those in the child's everyday conversation.

Schools must provide many opportunities for oral language based on the child's interests and experiences. Speech work (choral reading) that emphasizes accuracy in pronunciation, oral language practice (dramatizations, conversation, reports) that contributes to correct usage of words, and discussion that clarifies word meanings are types of oral language which develop meaningful vocabularies.

Reading. Reading enriches vocabulary in several ways. Through reading, the child extends his spoken vocabulary by coming in contact with meanings of words which are new to him. Again, the reading context gives practice and familiarity in using language correctly. Reading often stimulates a desire to write, creates occasions for writing, and furnishes ideas for creative writing.

Writing and spelling. The urge to communicate with others in writing involves spelling, facility in handwriting skills, and a meaningful vocabulary. Since spelling and writing are used together, they should be taught together. Experience in written expression is essential to learning to spell. If a child uses in written expression the words he is learning to spell, he will master spelling more quickly. The more opportunities the child has for writing items of interest to him, the more readily he learns to spell.

Implications for spelling. To develop meanings then, children need to be given rich experiences in all areas of the language arts—listening, speaking, reading, writing and spelling. A rich language program which utilizes children's interests will use all the language skills and keep all phases of language advancing together. Thus, growth in meaningful vocabulary will take place on all language fronts.

"Studies show clearly the effect of experience, environment, and stimulus upon the use of language and the development of vocabulary in particular."

Meaning and Spelling

In a summary of 140 studies with implications for possible causes of spelling disabilities, Spache concludes, "Vocabulary knowledge is a more significant determinant of spelling success than intelligence, particularly in the first five grades . . . a low meaning vocabulary is more likely to be a cause of spelling difficulty than is low reading ability."

Learning to be effective must have meaning. When applied to spelling this means that a word whose meaning (or meanings) is unknown is not going to be used by the child in either spoken or written language. Not only the commonest meaning of a word but common multiple meanings should be developed. Thus, we must build vocabulary by extending and enriching meanings. The child's experiences with extended meanings have implications for use in his reading, speaking, listening, and writing vocabularies. Increased familiarity with words gives him a sense of word power and many spelling failures are eliminated. The child should not be tested on spelling the new words until he becomes familiar with them from the meaning angle.

Word Analysis Skills

The purpose of spelling is to help each child to develop an effective method of learning to spell the words he needs to write. Spelling is effectively taught to the extent that the learner becomes independent in this respect.

To achieve success and independence in spelling (and reading), the pupil must learn and *use* phonics and a variety of word analysis skills. A soundly planned program of word recognition is not limited to phonics. It is a broad program which utilizes phonics as only one part of the total approach.

Individual needs. Since children vary in their needs for instruction in phonics and the various word analysis skills, careful diagnosis of individual needs should precede the introduction of word analysis on all levels. Diagnosis should be made several times a year on all grade levels.

The child feels a consciousness of great power as he learns the internal patterns of words. Interest is self-propelled as he realizes the mastery he is getting over words.

There have been many studies in word recognition. Research indicates that a carefully organized program of word analysis involves several major types of training which each child should have if he is to achieve independence in word attack whenever he has occasion to spell and write a strange word.

Phonics and spelling. Controversy about phonics continues today as it has in the past. Phonetic study should begin with visual-auditory discrimination. Considerable research is now available to indicate that training in both auditory and visual perception is essential for success in spelling and reading. We need to place greater emphasis on this type of training than we have in the past. As a foundation for all work in spelling and reading, the child must be able to recognize the sounds that he hears in a word and to associate those sounds with the appropriate letter symbols.

This training can be made interesting to the child by using games, puzzles, picture dictionaries, and other functional procedures.

Training in word analysis. After a child learns to recognize the sounds and symbols for initial and final consonants (visual-auditory perception), he is ready to note familiar parts of words—endings, base or root words, suffixes, prefixes, syllables, forming plurals. He learns that many longer words are made up of roots and added elements. By putting these parts together, the pupil can work out words for himself as he needs to spell them. He has a key by which he can write words he has never had occasion to spell before.

Training in the dictionary. Learning to use a dictionary is an essential part of learning to spell. A strong dictionary program starts with dictionary readiness in grades two and three. Picture dictionaries are used in grades two and three to introduce children to alphabetizing as well as to give training in visual-auditory perception.

In grades four to eight, children need training in order to use a dictionary effectively. Comprehensive and thorough dictionary training helps the pupil with his spelling and broadens his understanding of words and their usage. Dictionary training includes these skills and elements—alphabet, alphabetical order, division of dictionary into parts, guide words, key words, diacritical marks, pronunciation (respelling), meanings (more than one meaning, shades of meaning), syllabication and accents, synonyms, homonyms, antonyms, abbreviations, designations for verb, adjective, adverb.

Spelling rules. The number of rules for teaching spelling has been materially reduced in recent years. Some rules have as many exceptions as applications. Children should be referred to rules as such only when they are at the point of needing to do more generalization for independent spelling and are mature enough to understand the application.

Conclusion

Helping the child to learn meanings and word analysis skills enables him to learn to spell with enthusiasm, confidence and economy of effort.

Pupils can acquire rich meaningful vocabularies in a functional way through a rich integrated language arts program which stems from vital everyday experiences.

Through a systematic, well-organized spelling program, children can learn and use a group of phonic and word analysis skills which are necessary for success in reading and spelling. If these skills are not acquired, there is evidence that failures and maladjustments are sure to result.

If we want better spelling, we need to place greater emphasis on meanings and word analysis skills.

30. Some Issues in Learning to Spell *

THOMAS D. HORN

R ECENT evidence indicates that spelling achievement in the United States is lower now than it was thirty or forty years ago. There are a number of reasons for this. For one thing, there is certainly decreased emphasis on spelling in comparison with other curricular areas. The breadth of education very rightly has been greatly expanded in more recent years.

Unfortunately, along with the decreased emphasis on spelling has come a lowering of the prestige value of spelling insofar as pupils are concerned. Although no one is likely to suggest we go back to the "spelling school" days, children must develop both a consciousness of spelling and a conscience for spelling. The lack of these two things results in poor spelling accuracy.

Considerable misunderstanding of the nature of incidental learning has apparently been a major cause of the growing opposition to systematic teaching. This is coupled with a lack of systematic appraisal, largely because of a mistaken opposition to spelling lists and tests. The end results of unsystematic teaching and appraisal are fatal to spelling achievement.

While the number and kinds of words taught have decreased, the benefits of integrated spelling instruction have not generally been used effectively. As a matter of fact, there now exists widespread acceptance and use of teaching methods which have been shown to be *inferior*. It is over some of these issues that subsequent discussion takes place.

1. To learn to spell effectively, you study first, then test over what has been studied.

Ever since the Gates study over twenty-five years ago, we have known that the test-study method of teaching spelling, when properly used, is superior to the study-test. Gates suggested that study-test might be used in grade two. Subsequent studies done recently clearly show that, using the test-study method with an immediate correction of the test, the test-study method is superior to the study-test method even in grade two.

In order to determine the extent of incidental learning relative to spelling words, the first step must be to find out which words are already known. This is done by testing. Children need have no fear of tests if they under-

* From Thomas D. Horn, "Some Issues in Learning to Spell," *Education* (December, 1958), pp. 229–32. Reprinted by permission of the author and The Bobbs-Merrill Co., Inc., Indianapolis, Ind.

stand that tests serve an important instructional function in addition to the function of measurement.

Anyone concerned with individualized instruction in spelling desires immediate knowledge of which words which students need to study. From the standpoint of interest and efficient study, each child should concern himself only with those words he does not know how to spell. By testing before study, attention is focussed immediately upon the job at hand, misspelled words.

In spite of all the evidence showing the superiority of testing before study, current instructional materials and methods typically use the study-test method. This lag between what is *known* and what is *done* in spelling instruction is discouraging.

2. Because of incidental learning, a special time need not be set aside for the study of spelling.

This issue is related to the previous one, but extends the utilization of incidental learning to the erroneous conclusion that little or no systematic study is necessary for developing spelling ability. In classes where "spelling is taught all day," rather than in a systematic fashion, spelling results are rarely anything but inferior.

Lack of systematic instruction and systematic use of inferior methods undoubtedly constitute the major causes of low spelling achievement. When children can be shown which words they need to study and the results of efficient study, there is little need for concern over meaningful hard work. It is time to put a premium on a job well done.

3. Words can be learned more readily if they are presented in context.

The important relationship of reading context to meaning is well known to most teachers and parents. Likewise, many (but not all) good teachers are good spellers. The oversimplification and misapplication of these two factors has resulted in widespread presentation of spelling words in contextural form. We have known for thirty-five years that the contextural presentation of spelling words is inferior to the list presentation, yet many teachers and authors of spelling materials persist in using the inferior method.

There is no argument about the value of context to identifying word meanings in reading. There is considerable argument about the value of context to correct spelling. The issue of teaching the meaning of every word before learning to spell it will be discussed as the fourth issue.

It is more than a little surprising that so few persons have noticed the spuriousness of the context method of presentation. True, context clues are quite necessary to efficient reading. *BUT,* the context of spelling is in writing. The spelling needs of each individual differ according to what he is trying to write. To have each pupil *read* a concocted paragraph containing some spelling words not only negates the principles of individual instruction, but directs attention away from the real business of spelling and writing.

The combined effects of the study-test method and contextual presentation of words have been shown to be consistently inferior to the test-study and list presentation of words. Why then must we continue to use such methods?

4. In order to learn to spell, the meaning of each word must be taught.

This is another example of the attempts to make use of the correlations between reading and spelling and the erroneous extension of context clues in reading to the area of spelling. When a child reads a word, he does so to the extent the symbol has meaning for him. When a child is expressing himself in writing, he is trying to communicate his meaning through written symbols.

In teaching spelling, we are trying to enable the child to write the symbols correctly. His context is the writing of ideas. For the person attempting to read the child's writing, the context is whatever has been written. Of course, handwriting needs can hardly be separated from spelling needs.

Most courses of study in spelling consist of the two to three thousand high-frequency words in terms of child and adult use. Almost every child has had these words in his speaking and listening vocabularies for a number of years before he learns to read. Meaning is rarely a problem with these high-frequency words. Why then, when learning to spell, should each child have to listen to the development of meanings he already knows? To do so is a wasteful procedure.

When children do not know the meaning of a word, the word usually is not in the central core of high-frequency words. Obviously, individual pupils many times go far beyond this central core, even as early as grade three. This is where meanings and the use of such references as the dictionary should be taught.

5. Each child should have his own list of words to study rather than any general course of study.

This kind of statement generally grows out of the concern for individualized instruction. It is too bad that so little attention is paid to the fact that the words of greatest frequency of use for both children and adults are pretty much the same. Although it is quite true that writing vocabularies are individualized, the two to three thousand words of highest frequency are pretty much the same for everyone.

It is at the point where pupils need to depart from the central core of words that individual vocabularies needed for writing begin to show wide differences in scope. Indeed, it is the qualitative differences in vocabulary that set the fine writer apart from the mediocre ones. As more and more opportunities for composition are provided, wider differences in vocabulary needs becomes apparent. It is in the opportunities and needs for writing that the benefits of integrated approaches have great promise.

However, for the central core of two to three thousand words (sometimes called the "security segment"), it is a waste of time to set up "individual" spelling lists for children. The same words appear time and time again. When children need words beyond the central core, this is where the individual list becomes valid.

Related to this problem is the logical but incorrect notion that so many new words of high frequency are coming into the language that any list is out of date the day it is printed. Evidence concerning "new" words is discussed more at length in a later article (See: "What's New in Words These Days?").

6. Just spell the word the way it sounds.

Thiss staytmeant iz enuff too mayk won shreak (sic). Despite some very interesting evidence on similar phonetic elements in spelling words, the perfidious nature of the English language makes most attempts to teach spelling by phonetic generalizations questionable. Nevertheless, many well-meaning parents and teachers advise children to spell words the way they sound. The difficulty is that so many words, particularly polysyllabic words, just are not spelled the way they sound.

One of the most common types of misspellings is the phonetic misspelling. Thus we get *shur* for *sure; lettrs* for *letters; trie* for *try; fue* for *few; coll* for *call; uv* for *of; pensl* for *pencil; therd* for *third; forth* for *fourth; theese* for *these; past* for *passed* (and vice versa); *red* for *read; arithmatic* for *arithmetic;* and *mayks* for *makes.* One can see from this that a child making these mistakes could well be following the direction to spell the words the way they "sound."

It is unfortunate for would-be spellers that for all the sounds we need to spell, our English alphabet has but twenty-six letters. In addition to this limitation, there are three relatively useless letters included in the twenty-six: c (spells *k* or *s* sounds), q (spells *k* sound), and *x* (spells *eks, k,* and *z* sounds).

Like many worth-while things, there does not seem to be any short cut to learning to spell. Although some phonetic generalizations hold true consistently, e.g., initial consonant sounds like *b,* time is better spent in learning to spell needed words rather than learning generalizations. This is true for most spelling rules.

7. Spelling tests may be considered of minor importance in modern spelling methods.

Education is still trying to recover from overconcern about the effect of tests upon the whole child. Certainly the atmosphere of fear that sometimes accompanies testing is not desirable, but the solution is to remove the undesirable atmosphere rather than to forego all testing. In fact, one reason for the current attitudes toward tests is the failure to understand the instructional functions of tests in addition to the function of measurement.

Like many things, tests are not inherently bad, but they can be misused with unfortunate results. When used as part of the test-study method with the corrected test technique, spelling tests have been found to be the most effective single method of learning to spell.

Pretesting a group of children using a sample of the words to be studied during the year shows which children need considerable systematic study of spelling and which might well be excused from study. Testing at the beginning of each unit of work is the only way the individual child knows for sure which words he needs to study.

With such obvious desirable uses of spelling tests, one wonders why some consider them subversive, undemocratic, and bases for undesirable competition. Each of us is "tested" every day in some way. How else do we and others evaluate our effectiveness in order to improve the quality of our contributions to society? It is this testing or "proof of the pudding" that shows the way to better things.

31. *What about Spelling?* *

EMMETT ALBERT BETTS

IN PARENT-TEACHER meetings on spelling, there is much concern over these questions:

Why aren't children learning to spell today?

Why does my child spell the words correctly on a Friday test and do poorly on the same words the next week?

* From Emmett Albert Betts, "What about Spelling?" *Education* (January, 1956), pp. 310–25. Reprinted by permission of the author and The Bobbs-Merrill Co., Inc., Indianapolis, Ind.

Why isn't my child taught phonics in spelling?
What can I do to help my child learn how to spell?

Spelling—Now and Then

"Children don't spell as well today as they did when I went to school," insisted Mrs. Morgan, an irate parent. "Something must be done about spelling."

Mrs. Morgan, of course, was expressing an opinion—one shared by many parents and businessmen. Her dissatisfaction with the status quo (defined by Amos and Andy as "de mess we're in") can be a healthy attitude if she gets the facts and does something helpful about the situation.

Educators and psychologists have been very much concerned about the improvement of spelling abilities. In school attics and storage vaults they have found tests given to children from 1845 to the present. When the children of 1919 were given the tests used in 1845, they proved to be better spellers. Comparisons between the spelling test scores in 1928 and 1938 showed no differences. Similar comparisons between test results in 1929 and 1947 gave the 1947 children an edge. In short, today's children can hold their own or do better than their parents, grandparents, or great-grandparents.

Many citizens—including a great many high school and college teachers—believe that children cannot spell as well today as their ancestors. This belief is not supported by the facts.

Yet there are too many teachers in schools and colleges who throw up their hands in despair. They try to talk themselves out of their responsibilities by blaming teachers at the next lower level.

The fact that children can spell as well or slightly better than their ancestors is not a comforting one. Harris, for example, found that the average child in seventh or eighth grade can spell the words in third grade spellers. This fact means that a few cannot spell the words in a second grade speller while a few can spell all the words in an eighth grade speller. The irate Mrs. Morgan was right: "Something must be done about spelling."

Poor Spellers

There are many causes of poor spelling which need to be considered by parents and teachers:

1. *Limited mental ability*. High intelligence is no guarantee of spell-

ing ability. On the other hand, considerable mental maturity is essential for learning to talk, read, and write. The mental maturity of poor readers and spellers, of course, cannot be assessed by either group or individual tests of intelligence which require reading and writing. It is too easy and morally wrong to label a retarded speller or a nonspeller as a dullard on the basis of most tests of intelligence in common use.

2. *Limited reading ability.* Nonreaders and poor readers cannot be expected to be good spellers. No one expects a child to learn to talk until he has a substantial listening vocabulary. Likewise, he usually learns to spell words from his reading vocabulary. If, for example, he cannot identify *man, will,* and *look* in his reading, he is likely to have difficulty in learning to spell and to remember them.

It is as silly to try to teach a child to spell before he can read as it is to teach him phonics before he can read.

3. *Hearing impairments.* Certain types of hearing impairments can cause faulty pronunciation, monotonous pitch, inattention, and other behavior which contributes to poor spelling.

4. *Visual defects.* Some children cannot see clearly what is written on the blackboard; some cannot see clearly print held at book-reading distance; and a few cannot see clearly at either distance. Furthermore, a few children find that the print blurs or doubles. These and other evidences of visual defects can contribute to poor spelling.

5. *Faulty listening skills.* Some children spell *month* for *months, witch* for *which, pronounciation* for *pronunciation* because they neither hear nor say the words correctly. Occasionally, a child cannot give other words that rhyme with a simple word like cat. Some have difficulty in matching the beginning sounds of words, as (*st*)*ore* and (*st*)*art.* Many have not learned to hear the syllables in *happy, wishes, discover, advantages* when they are said in a normal conversational tone.

Listening to the groups of sounds in a spoken word and pronouncing a word correctly gets the child *set* to see the groups of letters representing those sounds. If the child is brain-injured, has a hearing impairment, or has not been taught to listen to the sounds of words, he is handicapped in learning to spell.

6. *Poor handwriting.* Among other things, learning to spell calls for considerable eye-hand coordination. Occasionally, a child may have a tremor in his handwriting, possibly indicating a neurological

problem. Some children grasp a pencil awkwardly or give other evidence of a lack of motor coordination. Usually, however, eye-hand coordination develops as the child grows and as he gets intelligent help on his handwriting problems.

Sometimes awkward handwriting and reversals of letters are evidence of slow maturity or of the use of a nonpreferred hand. Neither parent nor teacher should force the child into the use of either the right or the left hand for writing, eating, or other one-handed activities.

7. *Overemphasis on phonics.* The child who spells *tid* for *tide, thred* for *thread, hight* for *height, coler* for *color, curnel* for *colonel,* or *manyoufacture* for *manufacture* is thrown for a loss because he tries to spell the word the way it sounds. Of course, the child who spells words the way they sound is working against big odds.

8. *Poor study habits.* Some children are poor spellers because they try to spell words the way they sound. Others are miserable spellers because they try to spell each word letter by letter. Of course, letter-by-letter spelling of all words a child needs for writing is an impossible feat because it places an impossible burden on his memory.

Pupils often do not make progress in spelling because they merely write the correct spelling of a word while looking at the printed or written form of it. Copying a word, of course, is a far cry from writing the word from memory and, then, checking the spelling against the correct form.

9. *Inability to judge spelling accuracy.* Because of indifference or carelessness, poor spellers often are not aware of incorrect spellings. Until they have learned to proofread for misspellings, they are not likely to look up correct spellings.

10. *Inability to visualize words.* Because of defects of attention, concentration, and other problems, some children cannot recall the visual image of a word. These children may need to reinforce the visual image by hearing the word, by saying correctly its syllables, by tracing it, and by writing it from memory.

Informal Spelling Inventories

Before a parent or a teacher can help a child with his spelling, she must know his level of spelling achievement. One of the most direct ways to get this information is to give him an informal spelling inventory.

The following is an informal spelling inventory. It was made by taking a random sample from the words introduced at each grade level in a number of widely used spellers.

Level II

1. will	11. walk
2. some	12. happy
3. at	13. off
4. good	14. live
5. but	15. four
6. man	16. boat
7. look	17. five
8. store	18. as
9. morning	19. grow
10. take	20. next

Level III

1. laughing	14. face
2. oh	15. lost
3. could	16. seeds
4. know	17. dry
5. letter	18. few
6. yellow	19. dark
7. don't	20. safe
8. yard	21. flying
9. grass	22. among
10. rained	23. gold
11. stand	24. stopped
12. which	25. I'll
13. songs	

Level IV

1. food	10. won't
2. pins	11. wear
3. trade	12. burn
4. race	13. thick
5. honey	14. wishes
6. choose	15. sounds
7. color	16. mouse
8. family	17. tomorrow
9. build	18. less

19. cost	23. breakfast
20. pages	24. mailed
21. broken	25. Sept.
22. voice	

Level V

1. born	14. capture
2. biggest	15. blood
3. ought	16. coffee
4. gallon	17. railroad
5. writing	18. promise
6. Wednesday	19. newspaper
7. test	20. earn
8. badly	21. fact
9. discover	22. record
10. sort	23. simple
11. quiet	24. valley
12. shade	25. bow
13. tin	

Level VI

1. rapidly	14. trial
2. against	15. accept
3. all right	16. sailor
4. general	17. conductor
5. common	18. reduce
6. usual	19. explore
7. choice	20. sense
8. success	21. diamond
9. lock	22. faint
10. defeat	23. object
11. carefully	24. fright
12. complete	25. limb
13. doubt	

Level VII

1. ability	5. generally
2. expense	6. envelope
3. liquid	7. affect
4. replace	8. improvement

9. present
10. steer
11. split
12. namely
13. decrease
14. extremely
15. noble
16. corrected
17. mystery

18. securing
19. cocoa
20. deposit
21. introduce
22. explaining
23. aware
24. advertising
25. mayor

Level VIII

1. advantages
2. extreme
3. science
4. reaction
5. disagreeable
6. experience
7. continually
8. enable
9. organization
10. conference
11. undoubtedly
12. hence
13. subway

14. declare
15. banquet
16. concern
17. magnificent
18. definite
19. efficiently
20. transportation
21. capitol
22. fraternity
23. evidently
24. resolution
25. esteem

ADMINISTRATION

The following is an outline of how to administer an informal inventory:
1. Explanation of purpose: to find spelling levels
2. Explanation of "rules"
   a. Give examples of words to be spelled orally [e.g., *see* (sea), *I'll* (aisle, isle)].
   b. Explain that the word will be pronounced, used in sentence, and pronounced again before it is to be written.
3. Procedure
   a. Pronounce each word distinctly.
      1) Use a conversational tone.
      2) Say each word without distorting sounds of phonetic elements or syllables.
   b. Use the word in a sentence to bring out one meaning very clearly.

    c. Pronounce the word again, without distorting its sounds.

    d. Have the students write it in a column on ruled paper.

4. Test levels

    a. Give tests at each speller level to determine each student's achievement.

    b. Determine the *achievement* level, finding the highest level at which a score of 92 to 100 per cent is obtained.

    c. Determine the *instructional,* or teaching, level by finding the highest level at which a score of 74 to 88 per cent is obtained.

CRITERIA FOR SCORING

Correct spellings are checked ($\checkmark$); misspelled words may be indicated by the Cross of St. George (X). Errors include:

1. Improper sequence of letters
2. Failure to capitalize a word (e.g. *wednesday* for *Wednesday*)
3. Failure to place a period after an abbreviation (e.g. *Sept* for *Sept.*)
4. Omission of an apostrophe in a word (e.g. *isnt* for *isn't*)
5. Omission of a hyphen in a compound word (e.g. *cureall* for *cure-all*)
6. Omission of an inflectional ending or a suffix (e.g. *page* for *pages; farm* for *farmer*)
7. Failure to space between the two words of a two-word compound (e.g. *allright* for *all right*)
8. Illegible handwriting, including the placement of the dot for the *i* (as in *believe*)
9. Misspellings caused by failure to attend to the use or meaning of the word (e.g. *I'll* for *isle* or *aisle*)

INTERPRETATION OF MISSPELLINGS

The following questions are considered in the interpretation of misspellings:

1. Does the student know how to use the word correctly?
2. Does he hear the correct pronunciation?
    a. Can he identify the number of syllables in it?
    b. Does he pronounce it correctly?
3. What is his "level" of reading achievement? (That is, is the word within his listening, speaking, and reading vocabularies?)
4. Does he need to use a tracing or a kinesthetic technique for learning to spell?

SPELLING LEVELS

Here is an illustration of how to estimate spelling levels, using the scores of two pupils:

Level	John		Susan	
II	100%		100%	
III	96%	(Achievement Level)	100%	
IV	84%	(Instructional Level)	96%	
V	60%		92%	(Achievement Level)
VI	24%		80%	(Instructional Level)
VII	4%		64%	
VIII	0%		28%	

John needs to be with a group at Level IV; Susan, at Level VI. John may review the study list words for Level III; Susan, for Levels IV and V.

A twenty-five-word sample of the words at each speller level is adequate for estimating instructional levels. In fact, a twenty-word sample at the second grade level is adequate.

Usually these informal spelling tests will show gradually decreasing scores at succeeding speller levels.

SURVEY TESTS

When the time for studying a new class is limited, the teacher may use an abbreviated spelling scale as a timesaving device. For this reason, the following scale is given:

my
get
gave
black
pony
_____Grade II ends here

cows
stick
park
rose
gray
_____Grade III ends here

bite
feast
getting
hurry
ours
_____Grade IV ends here

quite
known
offer
holiday
bridge
_____Grade V ends here

grind
cleaner
foolish
scarce
willow
_____Grade VI ends here

cliff
returning
advice
scattered
heaven
_____Grade VII ends here

celebrating
aircraft
angle
advantage
appreciated
_____Grade VIII ends here

The above scale is administered in the same way as all other tests given herein. That is, each word is (1) pronounced, (2) used in a sentence, and (3) pronounced again before the pupils write it.

The abbreviated scale is a handy device for screening out pupils, especially in high school and college, who deviate from most of the group.

Grouping

One of the primary purposes of a basic spelling program is to help pupils learn to spell the words they need in their writing but do not know how to spell. Since pupils in any grade do vary in their needs, a plan for grouping is used.

All pupils in a class have spelling needs. The few pupils who can spell 92 per cent or more of all the words at their grade level should concentrate on those words they need for their curriculum activities. The remainder of the pupils may be grouped in terms of their instructional levels in spelling. Occasionally, small groups may be organized for help on auditory perception, adding suffixes, spelling demons, or other specific needs.

The results of informal spelling inventories are discussed with the pupils, individually or in groups. In this way, pupils become articulate regarding their spelling needs. They take an interest in learning to spell the most commonly used words first. They learn how to identify their own groupings of spelling needs. In short, their interest and motivation are based on personal needs.

There is no need for a pupil to be kept in the same spelling group all semester or all year. Two, three, or four pupils may work in teams to clean up their spelling records at lower levels. They can do this and continue work with a group at their basic instructional level. For these reasons, grouping is flexible.

When some type of grouping plan is used, the pupils are happier because they are successful. Furthermore, many of them—both high and low achievers—will make two or more years' growth in spelling. An effective grouping plan provides the most favorable learning conditions for *all* pupils in a class.

HOW TO HELP CHILDREN

Here is a quick run-down on how to help children improve their spelling:

1. *Readiness.* A child can copy a square or a triangle at a younger age than he can reproduce them from memory. Word forms offer more curved and straight lines than a simple drawing of a square or a triangle. Furthermore, the child has to put more into the identification or reproduction of a word than he does in copying or reproducing a line drawing of a simple geometric form.

Before a child can be taught to spell a word, these minimum conditions must be met:

a. The word must be in his reading vocabulary. That is, he must be able to identify its form and meaning before he can reproduce (spell) it.

b. He must be able to hear the sounds and to say the word correctly.

c. He must know the names of the letters he is to use in spelling the word.

d. He must learn eye-hand coordination, a difficult task for many beginners.

e. When he begins to spell, he must be taught how to form the letters of each word—both capital and small letters.

f. He must settle on the use of either the right or left hand for writing.

Premature teaching, especially when the child is put under pressure to learn, confuses and frustrates the beginner. On the other hand, delayed teaching—unwarranted by the facts—can retard the child's development.

There is a best time to teach children how to spell. Parents and teachers can help children to a good start by getting and understanding facts on each child's readiness, or development.

2. *Individual differences.* Most parents know that children do not learn to walk, talk, or button their clothes at the same age. They soon catch on to the fact that their children differ widely in the ages at which they learn to read and write. For example, a few exceptional children can read and write at 3½ years; other exceptional children may not learn these same skills until they are 9 years or older. This wide range in the language development of different children must be understood by both parents and teachers in order to help the child make the right start in spelling.

For most children, learning to spell follows a sequence. First, they learn to listen and to talk. After they have learned to say the sounds and to use the words in sentences, they are interested in street signs, billboards, and other uses of written language. That is, they are ready for reading. By the time they have mastered their preprimers and primers, they have picked up the spelling of a few words and are ready to reproduce (spell) words from their reading vocabularies in their writing.

Of course, children arrive at the first-reader level at different ages. However, when they do arrive, other types of differences will have been noted. One of these differences is in the ability to recall words learned in reading and the ability to recall the correct spellings of words. In short, a few children will need special help in order to remember words in reading and writing.

This special help in spelling is not necessarily more time and effort, using the same ways that other children use. For example, at least one child in six hundred may need to learn by tracing words, known as a *tactile* technique. Others in this special group may get off to a good start by another method, known as a *kinesthetic* technique. Unfortunately, these techniques have been developed in clinics and very few teachers are qualified to use them.

Parents and teachers who try to treat every child alike are missing the point made by researchers of child development and of learning. No two teachers, husbands, wives, or children are alike. Often there are big differences in the calendar ages at which children are ready for help on spelling and in the ways they learn to spell. The calendar age or the school grade cannot be used as a basis for deciding *when* or *how* a child is to learn to spell.

In summary, parents and teachers can help children by:

a. Finding out what help the child needs in hearing the sounds of words and in saying the words

b. Making sure the words he is trying to spell are in his reading vocabulary

c. Finding out how he can learn to spell words

3. *Common words.* A few words are used often by both children and adults. For example, Ernest Horn reported that three words (*a, I, the*) make up 10 per cent of the total running words used by adults.

Godfrey Dewey reported that the six commonest words (*a, and, in, of, the, to*) in his study made up more than 20 per cent of all words used. These six plus three more monosyllables (*is, it, that*) made up more than 25 per cent of all running words.

In general, ten of the commonest words (monosyllables) make up about 25 per cent of all the running words:

Leonard Ayres: *a, and, for, I, in, of, that, the, to, you*

Godfrey Dewey: *a, and, I, in, is, it, of, that, the, to*

Ernest Horn: *a, and, be, for, I, in, of, the, to, you, we*

Henry Rinsland (after Sigmund Folger): *a, and, I, in, it, of, the, to, you, we*

Fifty of the commonest words make up nearly 50 per cent of the running words used in writing. One hundred of the commonest words make up slightly more than 50 per cent.

Five hundred of the commonest words make up more than 80 per cent of the running words used in writing; 1000, about 90 per cent; 2000, about 95 per cent; 3000, more than 97 per cent.

To help beginners learn to spell and to help poor spellers, it is reasonable to start with the most commonly used words. Certainly a child should learn to spell *to, and, we,* and *have* before trying to spell *today, ancient,* or *disappear.*

Commonly used words (e.g., *with, this, get*) tend to have fewer syllables than less commonly used words (e.g., *television, various, semester*). This is another reason for learning to spell the commonest words first.

Less commonly used words often are made from commonly used words. Hence, it seems reasonable that a child should learn to spell *what* and *ever* before *whatever, with* and *in* before *within, ship* before *shipment,* and *dark* before *darkness.*

Commonly used words tend to be less abstract than the less commonly used words. *Mother, home, we, and, friend,* and *down* represent fairly simple concepts as contrasted to *ancient, amateur, administration, chemical, constitution,* and *proportion.*

The commonest words are found in the first books of a series of spellers. At higher levels, the words tend to be less commonly used, longer, and more difficult to understand and to learn how to spell. For these reasons, parents and teachers can help children by starting with the commonest words. In learning to spell these commonly used words, they are preparing themselves to spell the tens of thousands of other words needed in science reports, letters, and other writing activities.

4. *Attitudes.* One of the first steps in the improvement of spelling ability is the development of the right attitudes. This step includes:

    a.   Using writing situations—e.g., letter writing and reports on special projects—in which the pupils engage with enthusiasm

    b.   Developing an awareness of the value of correct spelling in business

    c.   Developing an awareness of the value of correct spelling in social situations, such as letter writing

    d.   Developing an awareness of improvement by commending accurate work and by showing gains on frequent informal tests

    e.   Helping the child to diagnose his own needs in handwriting, spelling, word usage, etc.

Real improvement begins with the development of a spelling conscience, of good attitudes toward correct spelling.

5. *Needs.* Another first step is the development of an awareness of correct and incorrect spelling. This step includes:

    a.   Proofreading for spelling errors

    b.   Keeping lists of misspelled words that have been respelled correctly

    c.   Forming the habit of looking up doubtful words

    d.   Checking weekly tests against the basic speller list to detect errors

e. Studying only those words misspelled on a pretest in a basic speller
f. Mastering the spelling of words used in writing activities, beginning with the most commonly used ones
g. Learning to use an appropriate dictionary for checking the doubtful spellings of words

To insure a spelling consciousness—an awareness of correct and incorrect spelling—is one of the major goals of instruction.

6. *Meaning.* The very first step in helping a child to learn to spell a given word is to make sure he knows how it is used—its meaning! In the first place, he is not going to use a word in his spontaneous writing until he knows its meaning. There is no point in forcing a child to learn to spell a word which he cannot use. In fact, learning to spell meaningless words is a sure way of teaching a child—especially a highly intelligent one—to hate spelling.

Second, the meanings of *I'll, aisle, isle,* and other words of this type (homonyms) govern their spellings.

Third, meaning is a key factor in learning a word and in remembering it. When a word is in a child's listening, speaking, and reading vocabularies, he has a running start on its use in his spontaneous writing.

The words *to, for, because, he,* and others of this class get their meanings from relationships with other words in a sentence or a paragraph. The meanings of *cat, bird,* and *ball* come from direct experience with things in each class. However, the meanings of *democracy* and *faith* are higher level abstractions. These and other relationships must be considered in helping the child to understand the use or uses of a word.

At all times the teacher must take the pupils into her confidence. She needs to explain why meanings are keys to spelling. Moreover, she must encourage her pupils to ask help on words when the meanings are hazy or unknown.

7. *Syllabication.* The syllable is one of the keys to good spelling. Hearing the syllables in a word gives a set for seeing and writing the letters representing them. Writing a word by syllables directs attention to pronunciation units, thereby strengthening the visual image of a word with auditory and motor images.

Before a child tries to learn to spell a word, he needs to know (1) its meaning and (2) its syllables. Training in listening to both phonetic elements and syllables is started during or before the reading readiness stage and continued through beginning and advanced stages of reading.

In his first basic spelling book, the child learns to listen for one- and two-syllable words: *go, going; home, mother; boy, children; at, away; in, around;*

pig, rabbit; etc. As he climbs the spelling ladder, he listens for syllables in longer words: *anywhere, arithmetic, examinations, representative.*

When the child listens for the number of syllables in a word spoken by his parent or teacher, he should hear an undistorted pronunciation of it. He hears *away* not *a-way; vacation* not *va-ca-tion.* When the syllables of an isolated word are overemphasized, he hears distorted sounds. Furthermore, the normal pronunciation of isolated words is not the same as the pronunciation of these same words in connected speech. For example, the word *seven* is often pronounced *seb-m* rather than *sev-n* in general American speech.

The child who hears and says *witch* for *which, supprise* for *surprise, liberry* for *library,* and *goverment* for *government* is likely to misspell them. Therefore, he needs to (1) listen for the syllables and (2) say the word correctly.

In order to get transfer from the spoken to the written word, the parent or teacher says each syllable as she writes it. For example, she says *sur* and writes the syllable; then *prise* and writes it. The word, of course, is written as a whole. The child then examines the whole word for each of its syllables before writing it from memory.

Both beginners and poor spellers can be helped by learning to write the word by syllables. That is, he says *serv* and writes it. Then he says the syllable *ice* and writes it. The whole word is written without a pause between the two syllables. Furthermore, each syllable is said with the same sounds as when the whole word is said.

After the child has accumulated a number of words of a certain type, he may generalize regarding syllable breaks. For example, he may see that the consonant before *le* at the end of a word goes with it: *a ble, ta ble, cir cle.*

Skills in hearing, saying, and writing syllables are learned by good spellers. Learning these skills prevents letter-by-letter spelling used so often by crippled spellers.

8. *Visual imagery.* In order to match the letters to the sounds of the syllable, the child learns to visualize a word. Hearing the word sets up the auditory imagery to strengthen the visual image. The visual examination of the word for its syllables coupled with saying and writing the syllables further strengthens the visual imagery through kinesthetic imagery. In order to prevent phonetic spelling and/or letter-by-letter spelling, the child is taught to visualize the word by syllables.

One of the secrets of recalling the visual image of a word is (1) writing it from memory and (2) checking the spelling against a correct one. This point is missed when the child merely copies the word. It is highly important for the child to hear, see, and write each syllable correctly on his first contact with it.

9. *Whole words.* When a child reads, he sees the word as a whole. When he writes, he writes the whole word. A reader or writer sees the whole word—unmutilated by syllable, accent, or diacritical marks.

Listening to syllables or examining a written word for syllables is done with whole words. That is, the child is taught to hear, to see, and to "feel" the parts of whole words.

10. *Rules.* There is no justification for a blind faith in spelling rules. Certainly, any sensible parent or teacher knows that rules learned by rote (by heart) are soon forgotten. In spite of popular opinion, there is no magic in a spelling rule.

Rules are generalizations based on related facts. For example, after a child has learned to spell *come-coming, give-giving, move-moving, write-writing* he may see that the "final *e* is dropped before adding ing." The ability to make this generalization depends upon his mental maturity as well as on his need for learning to spell these words.

Most rules have limited usefulness because of their exceptions. For example, "most plurals are made by adding *s* to the singular" as in *eye-eyes.* However, the plural of *address* is *addresses,* of *calf* is *calves,* of *man* is *men.*

Another example of exceptions is the rule of "*i* before *e* except after *c* or when sounded as *a* in *neighbor* and *weigh.*" The rule fits *belief* and *friend.* It also fits *ceiling* and *receive, weight* and *eight,* but it does not fit *ancient, either, science,* or *seeing.*

Three important decisions are made regarding rules to be considered: First, to how many words can the rule be applied? Second, how many exceptions to the rule must be made? Third, when is the child ready, or mature enough, to make the generalization and apply it?

Most children will make their own generalizations about spelling. For this reason, it appears to be necessary to guide them in making useful generalizations:

a. Guide the child in making a generalization only when he has a need. For example, when he has several plurals, suffixes, or *qu* words.

b. Before considering a rule, make sure the child has enough words of one type to be able to make a generalization (e.g., boy-boys, egg-eggs, etc.) from his own experience.

c. Help the pupil make his own generalization (rule) by examining a group of words which fit the rule.

d. Help the pupil to understand why a rule fits some words. For example, let him try to pronounce the plural of a word ending in *s* without adding *es* as in *dresses*.

e. Help the pupil to apply the rule to words which are new to him so that he learns to use it.

f. Guide the child in finding exceptions to the rule so that he will learn to avoid pitfalls. (This may lead to another rule.)

g. Teach the child to use simple rules first. For example, forming plurals by adding *s* or *es* is more easily understood than doubling the final consonant when adding a suffix.

h. Prepare the child for a generalization by having him consider specific elements beforehand. For example, he deals with silent *e* in *make* long before he must write *making*. And he deals with each of these situations long before he generalizes about "dropping silent *e* before adding *ing*."

i. Consider only one rule at a time so that the child can gradually develop a feeling of security.

j. Keep the number of rules to a minimum in order to aid learning and avoid confusion.

k. Provide many opportunities for review through application of a rule.

Here is a list of spelling situations meriting consideration:

a. Forming plurals of nouns by adding *s* to the singular
   boy, boys
   egg, eggs

b. Forming plurals by adding *es* to words ending in *s, x, sh, ch*
   dress, dresses
   box, boxes
   wish, wishes
   porch, porches
   witch, witches

c. Forming plurals by changing *y* to *i* and adding *es*
   baby, babies
   berry, berries

d. Forming plurals by changing the singular form
   foot, feet
   tooth, teeth
   mouse, mice
   man, men
   woman, women

c. Using an apostrophe in a contraction
    aren't, are not
    I'll, I will or *I shall*
    won't, will not

f. Using a period after abbreviations *A.M., Dec., doz., Mr., P.S.*

g. Forming singular possessives by adding *'s*
    John's
    father's

h. Forming plural possessives by adding *s'*
    boys'
    girls'

i. Dropping final *e* when adding a suffix beginning with a vowel
    make, making
    bathe, bathing
    use, usable
    cure, curable

j. Keeping the final *e* when adding a suffix beginning with a consonant
    hope, hopeful
    nine, ninety
    sure, surely
    advance, advancement

k. Changing *y* to *i* before adding a suffix that does not begin with an *i*
    apply, appliance
    copy, copied
    marry, marries
    try, tried

l. Doubling the final consonant of a one-syllable word before adding a suffix beginning with a vowel
    big, bigger, biggest
    spot, spotted
    run, runner, running

m. Doubling final consonants of words in which the last syllable is accented and has a short vowel before adding a suffix beginning with a vowel
    admit, admitted
    begin, beginner, beginning
    refer, referred

n. Noting the *kw* sound of *qu*
    quick, quiet, liquid

How to Confuse Children

There are many children who are confused and disturbed about how to spell words. Here are some examples of practices that contribute to their dilemma:

1. *Spelling before reading.* Begin to teach him to spell words before he has learned to read. The fact that he cannot tell one word from another adds to his confusion in learning to spell—but insist that he memorize how to make the letters and the order of the letters in each word. This practice not only confuses him but also teaches him to hate spelling. Furthermore, he gets the idea that the only way to learn how to spell a word is to memorize it.

2. *Difficult before easy words.* If he is having trouble with spelling, always drill him on words at his grade level. For example, if he is in the fifth grade, drill him on words in the fifth grade speller. The fact that he doesn't know how to spell words in the second grade, or third grade, or fourth grade speller should not be considered. Assume that he doesn't need to know how to spell the common words used by children and adults; he only needs to know the words at his grade level.

This practice is based on the idea that he can learn to spell *biggest, don't, gallon, Wednesday,* or *promise* before he learns to spell *big, do, at, look,* or *take.* Of course, this won't make sense to him, but this is a part of the plot to confuse him. By the way, this common malpractice is very successful in making poor spellers.

3. *Distorting sounds of the word.* When you dictate a word for the child to spell, exaggerate the sound of each part so that he hears only weird distortions. For example, say *five* as *fuh-eye-vuh.* Or, say *grass* as *guh, r-rr, a-a-a, suh.*

Better still, accent unaccented syllables. For example, have him hear and say *be* in *began, con* in *conductor, ent* in *patent, a* in *about* and *aboard.*

These practices can be trumped by having him listen for silent letters. Make him hear the *b* in *climb, k* in *knife, w* in *write.*

The distortion of sounds in words helps to confuse the child in what he *hears* and how he *says* the word. This confusion, in turn, causes him to spell words the way he has been taught to hear and say them—distortions and all. Moreover, he can carry these bad habits over to his oral reading and practice stilted word calling, without attending to the ideas.

4. *Phonetic spelling.* Teach the child to spell words by isolated sounds. For example, drill him on the consonant sound *dge* in *edge* so that he will

write what he hears in *a(ge)*, *(j)u(dge)*, *sol(d)ier*. Or, drill him on the sound of *a* in *gate* so that he will misspell *br(ea)k, n(ei)gh, pl(ay), st(ai)n, and th(ey)*.

One of the most common errors made by poor spellers is spelling the word the way it sounds. The fact that Dr. Ernest Horn reported the word *circumference* can be spelled phonetically more than one billion different ways should not cause a loss of faith. After all, the plan is to confuse children. Don't give up; it's being done by parents and, sometimes, by teachers every school day.

5. *Letter-by-letter spelling.* Teach the child to spell each word laboriously letter by letter. For example, teach him to spell *geography* by saying or whispering the letters *g e o g r a p h y.* Never let him hear the syllables *ge og ra phy* before he spells it because that would get him set to spell the word correctly.

Letter-by-letter spelling rules out any sensible aid for him. It divorces the written word from the spoken word, putting the child entirely on his own without an effective way to learn to spell. In short, it will cause him to bog down and to give up the job of learning to spell before he gets very far.

6. *Isolating parts of words.* Not to be overlooked is the practice of spelling words by separate parts. In order to clutter the child's mind, for example, have him write *separate* as *sep a rate*. This, of course, is not the way the word looks in reading and it is not the way it will look when he uses it in a letter or report. Moreover, it is not the way he will write it in a composition. In other words, to make sure that the child cannot spell the word automatically when he has his mind on the ideas he is trying to express, have him write in separated syllables at the time he first learns to spell it.

A milder variation of this practice is to write one or more of the syllables in a different color of pencil, chalk, or print. This distorts the visual picture which the child gets of the word so that he will be stopped short when he tries to identify or write the word in a normal situation.

This practice of isolating written syllables in order to call attention to them may not produce as much confusion as distorting the sounds of the word. It, however, will add to the confusion.

7. *Word forms before meaning.* In order to cut down the child's chances to recall the spelling of a word, rule out attention to its meaning. This emphasis on the naked word form is given in some schools by offering each class a printed list of spelling words which is to be memorized at the rate of five to twenty words each week. It is done in some homes by having the child practice long hours on the tedious oral spelling or writing of words pronounced.

When attention is given only to the empty word form, the child may learn to spell *to, too,* and *two* but he won't know how to use them in his writing. He may learn to spell *gown, privilege,* and *substance* on a test but he is tripped up when he needs to use them in his writing. More important, he may not recall the spellings at all because they were not learned in a thinking situation.

8. *Memorizing rules.* One of the best ways to cause a child to labor over his spelling when he wants to write is to have him memorize a set of rules. There is, of course, a big difference between the required memorization of a rule and the active process of making a generalization from experience. The first is rote memorization (memorizing by heart!); the second, thinking through how a group of words are related until a conclusion is made and tested. But forget the fact that you can't give a child a concept or an attitude—that he must make his own concepts and attitudes out of his personal experience. After all, our concern is with confusing him.

To give the child a mind-breaking burden, set him up so he must sort out the right rule from a whole pack of rules every time he wants to spell a word. For example, make him memorize the rule that the plural of words ending in *s* (*dress*), *x* (*box*), *sh* (*wish*), and *ch* (*porch*) is formed by adding *es*. This should be done before he has a chance to "feel" how to say the singular and plural forms and before he has seen a group of these words. To clutter his mind, put your faith in the memorization of rules that are meaningless to him. He may forget them readily and, if he doesn't, he may bog down in despair.

9. *Repetition.* A very effective way to stifle interest and to insure poor spelling is to make the child write 100 times. There must be something attractive and magical about this practice because it is used so often. The child knows exactly what he has to do: write the word aimlessly a definite number of times. His task is clean cut; he can turn to something worth while and interesting just as soon as he has done it. Since he is giving his attention neither to the meaning nor the spelling of the word, he can misspell it as badly as he did before.

10. *Oral spelling.* Most people learn to spell on the ends of their pencils because they need to spell when they write. That is, they learn to write so automatically they can give their attention to ideas.

To upset the word basket for the child, have him practice spelling the words orally. In this way, writing the word and seeing the written word will, indeed, be a *new* experience for him.

Learning to spell words orally may help him to win spelling contests but it is not likely to help him to write. This practice may not confuse him but it does keep him from learning to spell written words.

11. *Sticking to lists.* To keep the child from spelling correctly in his writing, let him spend all of his precious time and energy on learning to spell special lists of words.

In the first place, the authors of these lists tell you that learning to spell about 3500 words will insure the correct spelling of about 96 per cent of all running words used by children and adults. They sometimes fail to explain that they are talking about *running* words rather than the thousands of *different* words needed. Furthermore, they often fail to explain that it is necessary to learn *how to spell* these 3500 words rather than to memorize them if thousands of other words are to be spelled correctly.

Secondly, compilers of spelling words often fail to explain why basic spelling textbooks are insurance policies or springboards to better spelling.

One way to keep the child from becoming a good everyday speller is to limit his spelling instruction to basic textbooks in spelling. Never encourage him to proofread his letters, reports, and other writings because that would make him aware of his needs. And never teach him to correct his errors by applying what he learned in his spellers, because he may learn to spell thousands of additional words.

12. *Spelling crimes and punishment.* To get the child to take an interest in correct spelling, make his punishment fit his crime. Deny him recess periods, force him to stay after school, make him drill on words at home— punish! punish! punish! Build a strong dislike for spelling and maybe he can be made into a chronically poor speller.

Many well-intentioned parents—and some teachers—have ways to keep children from learning to spell or from becoming better spellers. The dozen ways discussed above are only a few samples. If children have become emotionally involved with spelling errors, they are hopelessly frustrated by these practices. If they have undetected brain injuries which handicap them in learning to spell, they flee from the very thought of writing. On the other hand, if they are blessed with superior intelligence and emotional stability, they may survive mistreatment and become good spellers.

32. Teaching Spelling by Teaching Syllables and Root Words *

WORTH J. OSBURN

THE ABILITY to syllabicate is undoubtedly an important factor in learning to read and spell, but our techniques for teaching syllabication are woefully inadequate. In order to formulate a basis for such techniques, it is necessary to know which syllables are of most importance. It is assumed that the importance of a syllable can be gauged in terms of the frequency of occurrence of the syllable in materials which children read and write.

In the technique reported in this paper, the Rinsland word list [1] was used as source material. An inventory was made of the initial, medial, and final syllables of all polysyllabic words in that list.[2] A summary of the frequencies of occurrence of all syllables that occur ten times or more is given later.

As a first approach to teaching syllabication in reading and spelling, we use the words shown in Table 1 as a diagnostic test. The key syllables are underlined, and the frequencies of occurrence are shown. For diagnosis in reading, these tests are given individually. The child is asked to pronounce the words. If we find, for example, that the pupil cannot sound the last syllable in *going,* we believe that he will have similar trouble with the 880 additional words in his reading which have the same syllable. This holds true for each of the other syllables with which he has trouble.

For spelling diagnosis, the tests are given to groups. In looking over the child's completed paper, we are concerned only with key syllables which are misspelled. The first task is to get the pupil to spell correctly the syllables which he will need most often in his writing. When a syllable is missed either in word recognition or in spelling, the inventory is used to find other words which contain the troublesome syllable.

The polysyllabic words in the Rinsland list contain approximately 23,000 syllables. At first sight, the task of teaching recognition or spelling of this number of syllables seems utterly hopeless. Fortunately, the truth is quite

* From Worth J. Osburn, "Teaching Spelling by Teaching Syllables and Root Words," *Elementary School Journal* (September, 1954), pp. 32–41. Reprinted by permission of the University of Chicago Press.

[1] Henry D. Rinsland, *A Basic Vocabulary of Elementary School Children* (New York: Macmillan Co., 1945).

[2] W. J. Osburn and Mrs. C. J. Sheldon, "A Syllabic Inventory" (available in mimeographed form from the University of Washington Book Store in Seattle, Washington).

to the contrary. Marvelous as it may seem, we find that, when we have taught carefully the fifty key syllables in the Diagnostic Test, the pupils need little further help because they learn to profit from transfer.

Table 1

A DIAGNOSTIC TEST IN SYLLABICATION FOR READING AND SPELLING BASED ON FREQUENCY OF OCCURRENCE OF SYLLABLES IN WORDS IN RINSLAND WORD LIST

Initial Syllable	Frequency	Medial Syllable	Frequency	Final Syllable	Frequency
1. *re*-ceived	209	1. an-*i*-mals	277	1. go-*ing*	881
2. *in-to*	203	2. Jan-u-*a*-ry ...	161	2. start-*ed*	338
3. *a*-round	149	3. sev-*er*-al	131	3. moth-*er*	323
4. *de*-cid-ed	146	4. dec-*o*-rat-ed ..	107	4. on-*ly*	290
5. *con*-tains	145	5. af-*ter*-noon ..	81	5. hous-*es*	212
6. *ex*-cept	141	6. el-*e*-phant ...	79	6. va-ca-*tion* ...	210
7. *un*-til	99	7. pe-*ri*-od	75	7. ver-*y*	193
8. *com*-mon	95	8. reg-*u*-lar	72	8. pret-*ty*	95
9. *dis*-cov-ered ..	82	9. In-*di*-an	56	9. re-*al*	84
10. *en*-joy	81	10. won-*der*-ful ..	44	10. ta-*ble*	82
11. *an*-oth-er	68	11. car-*ni*-val	40	11. af-*ter*	75
12. *o*-pen	65	12. gym-na-*si*-um.	40	12. base-*ment* ...	73
13. *e*-ven	63	13. ar-*ti*-cle	40	13. sto-*ry*	69
14. *pro*-gram	58	14. ear-*li*-est	35	14. larg-*est*	65
15. *ac*-ci-dent	56	15. o-*ver*-alls	34	15. sev-*en*	48
Total	1,660	Total	1,272	Total	3,038

The Slow-Learning Child and Transfer

We are told that the amount of transfer that takes place in learning is due, in a large measure, to the learner's ability to perceive identical elements in separate activities. Since this is true, one very useful approach to the teaching of the slow learner is to make him conscious of identical elements.

Our study of the syllables in the Rinsland word list has served to emphasize the possibilities in the pupil's recognition of the identical elements in that list. The Rinsland word list contains 14,571 words, of which approximately 9,000 are words of more than one syllable. The total number of syllables in these polysyllabic words is around 23,000. In round numbers, the distribution of syllables is as follows: 9,000 initial, 9,000 final, and 5,000 medial. If a child could not be taught to recognize identical elements in different words, he would have to learn each of the 23,000 syllables separately. This, of course, is utterly impossible. Our only hope lies in transfer and in our ability to teach the recognition of identical elements. These elements are to be found in the syllables that recur in the list.

The syllable that recurs most frequently is final *-ing,* which is found in 881 of the 9,000 words. With perfect transfer, a child who has learned the *-ing* syllable in, say, *going,* will know that syllable in 880 more words. This is transfer at its best so far as the Rinsland word list is concerned. Unfortunately, when there are final syllables which occur but once, such as *-brance* in *remembrance,* there is no profit from transfer, at least in relation to identity of syllable elements. This is true also of initial and medial syllables under similar conditions. Nevertheless, there is a substantial amount of transfer to be obtained by teaching the recognition of identical syllables. For the list as a whole, the amounts are as follows: initial syllables, 76 per cent; medial syllables, 91 per cent; final syllables, 75 per cent.

Implications for Spelling

Syllabication is important in reading and even more important in spelling. We can hardly expect pupils to recognize or to spell words of more than one syllable until they are conscious of the syllables that are involved. In spelling, the problem is much more difficult because we cannot expect pupils to spell correctly syllables which they cannot hear. It is for this reason that unaccented syllables give so much trouble in spelling. It is necessary, therefore, to give particular attention to unaccented syllables that sound alike but are spelled differently. Some of those in the Rinsland word list are described below.

Initial Syllables

The figures after each syllable indicate the number of words in which each syllable occurs.

1. *ac-* (56).

Difficulty is encountered in three groups: (1) before a second syllable beginning with *ci* or *ce;* (2) before other syllables beginning with *c;* and (3) before a second syllable beginning with *q.* There are eleven words (for example, *ac-cent, ac-cept*) in the first group. The tendency here is to use *x.* Warn the children that there are only two words which begin with the initial syllable *ax-.* They are *ax-is* and *ax-le.* There are twenty words in the second group. In these there is a tendency to omit one of the *c*'s (for example, *a-count* for *ac-count*). Remind the pupils to use two *c*'s in all words of this sort except:

a-cad-e-my
a-cross
a-cute

In the third group, we find six words (*ac-quainted, ac-quire,* etc.). See that the *c* is not left out. Only one word, *a-qua-ri-um,* is spelled without the *c*.

2. *de-* (146), *di-* (43), *dis-* (82).

When in doubt, begin with *de-*. Sixteen of the *di-* words are accented on the first syllable and so give little trouble. The words which the pupil will miss by using *de-* are, in the main:

di-gest   di-rect   di-vide
di-lap-i-dat-ed   di-van   di-vine
di-men-sions   di-ver-sion   di-vorce
di-plo-ma

The *dis-* words that are likely to be heard and spelled with *des-* are:

dis-patch   dis-pute
dis-place   dis-solve
dis-play

3. *em-* (21), *im-* (42).

Words in these categories are real problems. Practice in discriminating short *i* and short *e*. Clear pronunciation by the teacher is essential.

4. *en-* (81), *in-* (203) (see section 3 above).

5. *ser-* (1), *sur-* (23).

When in doubt use *sur-*. The *ser-* word is *ser-mon*.

6. *ter-* (12), *tur-* (9).

The *ter-* syllable has two sounds. If pronounced correctly, such words as *ter-ror* and *ter-race* are not likely to be begun with *tur-*. The only troublesome words are *ter-mi-nal* and *ter-mite*. Use *tur-* when in doubt.

Medial Syllables

1. A single vowel (24).

When the pupil is given a word like *animal* to spell, he seems to have a choice among the spellings *an-a-mal, an-e-mal, an-i-mal, an-o-mal, an-u-mal,* and *an-y-mal*. Which shall he use? Similar uncertainty seems to arise in connection with all the 724 words which have a single vowel forming the middle syllable. What shall we do about it? It has been suggested that we ask the pupils to write each word with the troublesome middle syllable written in a color different from the rest of the word. It should help, also, to present these words with the middle syllable missing and ask the pupils to learn how to fill in the blanks correctly. This would require lists containing words like:

mag–zine	vi–lin
an–mal	an–thing
vin–gar	reg–lar

Use the inventory. Get clearly in mind the words that the pupils in the grade which you teach are supposed to learn. This includes all the words that the pupils should have learned in the grades preceding yours.

2. Vowels preceded by a consonant (899).

There are 899 words which contain medial syllables formed by the vowels preceded by a consonant. Fortunately, many of these can be pronounced clearly enough for the differences in sound to be heard. But pupils still have trouble with syllables containing *i* and *e*. For example, how is the child to spell the second syllable of the words *Indian* and *independent?* Other examples of confusing sounds are found in *ap-pe-tite* and *hos-pi-tal, ce-re-al* and *pe-ri-od, an-te-lope* and *beau-ti-ful*. Watch for these words in your word list.

3. *-al-* (21), *-el-* (14), *-il-* (3), *-ol-* (3), *-ul-* (0), *-yl-* (0), *-le-* (4).

Of these, only *-al-* and *-el-* occur with any frequency. Among the twenty-one *-al-* words, five have accents on the *-al-* syllable and so are not troublesome. These words are:

mor-al-i-ty	re-al-i-ty
met-al-lic	in-di-vid-u-al-i-ty
na-tion-al-i-ty	

The remaining sixteen -*al*- words and all the -*el*- words will need special attention.

The -*il*- words are:

> aux-il-ia-ry
> civ-il-ized
> ster-il-ized

The -*il*- in *aux-il-iary* is accented, so that only two words are troublesome. The three -*ol*- words are:

> phys-i-ol-o-gy
> car-ol-ers
> car-ol-ing

The first is accented on the -*ol*- syllable and the other two are derivatives from *car-ol*.

The -*le*- words are:

> huck-le-ber-ry   pe-tro-le-um
> o-le-o-mar-ga-rine   u-ku-le-le

4. A single consonant in front of -*al*-, -*el*-, -*il*-, -*ol*-, -*yl*-, and -*le*- (109).

There are 109 of these words. Fortunately, seventy-six of these words are accented on the middle syllable. Some of the others which will need special attention are:

> e-qual-ly   fer-til-ize   gen-tle-man
> quar-rel-ing   bat-tle-field   ri-val-ry
> ac-ci-den-tal-ly   cut-tle-bone   mar-vel-ous
> cap-i-tal-ist

5. -*an*- (10), -*en*- (21), -*in*- (20), -*on*- (7), -*un*- (7), -*yn*- (0).

Most of the -*an*-, -*en*-, and -*in*- syllables are unaccented and therefore troublesome. The -*on*- words are:

> cham-pi-on-ship   im-pris-on-ment
> dem-on-strate   lem-on-ade
> eb-on-y

All are worth watching since none has the accent on the middle syllable. The -*un*- words are unaccented expect *re-un-ion,* but it should be possible to make the unaccented syllables clear as they are given out.

6. Single consonants in front of -*an*-, -*en*-, -*in*-, -*on*-, and -*un*- (149).

Most of these syllables are either accented or are easy to hear. The following words will need additional attention:

car-bon-ate	cit-i-zen-ship
con-cen-tra-tion	sud-den-ly
com-mon-ly	gar-den-er
cur-ren-cy	o-pen-ing
en-vi-ron-ment	car-pen-ter
i-ron-ing	ri-pen-ing
mes-sen-ger	tur-pen-tine
i-sin-glass	lis-ten-ing
per-son-al	fat-ten-ing
poi-son-ing	but-ton-hole
rea-son-a-ble	cot-ton-seed

7. -ar- (7), -er- (131), -ir- (0), -or- (12), -ur- (9), -yr- (0).

Outside of the -er- words and all the -or- words, the troublesome words are:

schol-ar-ship	res-ur-rec-tion
sug-ar-cane	Sat-ur-day
pol-ar bear	

Advise pupils to use -er- as a medial syllable when they are in doubt.

8. Single consonants in front of -ar- (15), -er- (256), -ir- (8), -or- (29), -ur- (21).

Many of the words thus formed have accented medial syllables. There are, however, some which need special attention. They are:

neigh-bor-hood	cut-ler-y
o-dor-less	gal-ler-y
dan-ger-ous	hol-ler-ing
ea-ger-ly	can-ner-y
fin-ger-print	part-ner-ship
gin-ger-bread	mas-quer-ade
tan-ger-ine	o-ral-ly
hand-ker-chief	spon-sor-ing
pop-u-lar-ly	gut-tur-al
reg-u-lar-ly	fa-vor-ite
ar-til-ler-y	

9. *-ced-* (5), *-ceed-* (6).

The *-ced-* words are:

an-te-ced-ent	se-ced-ing
pre-ced-ing	se-ced-ed
pro-ced-ure	

The *-ceed-* words are:

ex-ceed-ed	pro-ceed-ing
ex-ceed-ing-ly	suc-ceed-ed
pro-ceed-ed	suc-ceed-ing

Note that one of the *e*'s drops out in *pro-ced-ure*.

10. *-sion-* (4), *-tion-* (23).

The four *-sion-* words are:

com-mis-sion-er	oc-ca-sion-al
con-gres-sion-al	oc-ca-sion-al-ly

Use *-tion-* in all other words.

Final Syllables

1. *-al* (84), *-el* (17), *-il* (2), *-ol* (1), *-ul* (0), *-yl* (0), *-le* (13).

In most of the *-al* words, the *-al* is a suffix. That is, it is preceded by a word root that the pupil should know, such as *addition-al* and *agricultur-al*. In some cases, however, the preceding roots are rather obscure or not root words at all. These cases are:

a-e-ri-al	in-di-vid-u-al	ped-al
an-nu-al	loy-al	pet-al
cen-ten-ni-al	man-u-al	punc-tu-al
cor-al	ma-te-ri-al	re-al
fed-er-al	med-al	roy-al
gen-er-al	met-al	sev-er-al
i-den-tic-al	per-en-ni-al	

The syllable *-el* is never a suffix. If the pupil does not recognize a word root in front of the final syllable, it is safer to use *-el*. The two *-il* words are *civ-il* and *dev-il*. The *-ol* word is *car-ol*. With three exceptions, the *-le* syllable follows only after previous syllables ending with *-ck*. The exceptions are:

> pi-noc-le
> tab-er-nac-le
> u-ku-le-le

2. Single consonants before *-al, -el, -il, -ol, -le* (302).

The following words will need attention:

al-pha-bet-i-cal	in-ter-val	man-tel
chem-i-cal	lar-val	pu-pil
com-i-cal	la-bel	an-vil
e-co-nom-i-cal	can-cel	wee-vil
e-lec-tri-cal	an-gel	sym-bol
lo-cal	chan-nel	i-dol
ras-cal	colo-nel	par-a-sol
ver-ti-cal	flan-nel	cap-i-tol
le-gal	fun-nel	pis-tol
for-mal	ken-nel	raf-fle
nor-mal	tun-nel	ri-fle
jour-nal	quar-rel	ruf-fle
prin-ci-pal	sor-rel	scuf-fle
mu-nic-i-pal	squir-rel	peo-ple
e-qual	dam-sel	an-kle
u-ni-ver-sal	tas-sel	muz-zle
car-ni-val	tin-sel	puz-zle
fes-ti-val	ves-sel	

Words ending in *-tal, -ful, -ble, -cle, -dle, -gle, -ple,* and *-tle* may be found by consulting the complete inventory. The *-ful* words are the only ones containing *-ul*. There are no words which end in *-il*.

3. *-ance* (13), *-ence* (16).

Pronounce the words as clearly as possible.

4. *-ant* (14), *-ent* (15).

Pronounce the words as clearly as possible.

5. Single consonants in front of *-ance* (9), *-ence* (10), *-ense* (8).

The words ending in *-ance* are:

sig-ni-fi-cance	coun-te-nance	nui-sance
a-bun-dance	or-di-nance	dis-tance
am-bu-lance	ig-no-rance	im-por-tance

The words with final *-ence* and *-ense* are:

con-fi-dence	in-tel-li-gence	vi-o-lence
ev-i-dence	per-ti-nence	oc-cur-rence
prov-i-dence	si-lence	sen-tence
res-i-dence		

frank-in-cense	de-fense	ex-pense
li-cense	of-fense	in-tense
con-dense	im-mense	

6. Single consonants before *-ant* (14), before *-ent* (101).

The fourteen words which have their final syllables formed by single consonants before *-ant* are:

ap-pli-cant	con-so-nant	ig-no-rant
va-cant	pen-nant	res-tau-rant
a-bun-dant	rem-nant	dis-tant
in-fant	oc-cu-pant	im-por-tant
gal-lant	cor-mo-rant	

One hundred and one words form their final syllables by a consonant in front of *-ent*. Seventy-three of these end in *-ment* (see syllable inventory). The others, not including a few more which have accents on the *-ent* syllable, are:

ac-cent	pres-i-dent	con-ti-nent
cres-cent	res-i-dent	op-po-nent
de-cent	stu-dent	per-ma-nent
in-no-cent	a-gent	prom-i-nent
mag-nif-i-cent	in-tel-li-gent	fre-quent
re-cent	re-gent	cur-rent
ac-ci-dent	be-nev-o-lent	con-tent
con-fi-dent	ex-cel-lent	ex-tent
in-ci-dent	si-lent	

7. *-ar* (11), *-er* (323), *-ir* (0), *-or* (14), *-ur* (0).

Advise the pupils to use *-er* when in doubt. Give special attention to the *-ar* and *-or* words which are given in the complete inventory.

8. A single consonant in front of *-ar, -er, -or,* and *-ur* (282).

Consult the syllable inventory under *-lar, -ber, -der, -ger, -ner, -per, -ter,* and *-tor.* Additional words are:

cal-en-dar	for-mer	bach-e-lor
ce-dar	ham-mer	par-lor
beg-gar	con-quer	tai-lor
cou-gar	lac-quer	ar-mor
vin-e-gar	gey-ser	hu-mor
vul-gar	mi-ser	ru-mor
gram-mar	bea-ver	gov-er-nor
can-cer	fe-ver	mi-nor
gro-cer	o-ver	va-por
of-fi-cer	sil-ver	er-ror
sau-cer	fer-ti-liz-er	hor-ror
soc-cer	blaz-er	mir-ror
dif-fer	har-bor	ter-ror
of-fer	la-bor	pro-fes-sor
suf-fer	neigh-bor	spon-sor
trans-fer	am-bas-sa-dor	sup-er-vi-sor
but-ler	cor-ri-dor	fa-vor
hol-ler	o-dor	fla-vor
pro-pel-ler	splen-dor	sur-vi-vor
as-tron-o-mer	ma-jor	ra-zor
drum-mer		

9. *-est* (65), *-ist* (8).

All the *-est* words are superlatives, except *for-est, hon-est,* and *in-ter-est.* The *-ist* words are:

art-ist	ex-ist	typ-ist
cap-i-tal-ist	or-gan-ist	vi-o-lin-ist
chem-ist	tour-ist	

All represent occupations except *exist,* which is accented on the last syllable, and *tourist.*

10. *-cian* (5), *-sion* (24), *-tion* (210).

Obviously, it is best to use *-tion* when in doubt. The *-cian* words are given below:

mag-i-cian	mu-si-cian	pol-i-ti-cian
math-e-ma-ti-cian	phys-i-cian	

Roots of all these words end with *c,* and all the words represent occupations.

The final syllable *-sion* follows no other root words but those ending with *-t, -de, -ss, -rt, -rs,* and *-nd.* The syllable *-tion* follows none of these except *-nd.* The only troublesome words are:

at-ten-tion	ex-pan-sion
in-ten-tion	ex-ten-sion

Latin Word Roots in the Rinsland Word List

Of the 14,571 words in the Rinsland word list, 4,382 come from Latin roots directly or, in the case of 209 words, from Greek by way of Latin. This means that approximately 30 per cent of the words have Latin roots. There are also 289 words, or about 2 per cent, which come directly from the Greek. Among the Latin word roots, eighty-two occur ten or more times, thus accounting for 1,631 of the 4,382 Latin word roots in the entire list. Among the Greek word roots, six occur ten or more times, thus accounting for seventy-nine of the 289 Greek word roots in the list.

These data show that knowledge of Latin and Greek word roots can play a substantial role in the building of vocabulary in the elementary school. It should be worth while to acquaint our pupils with the eighty-two Latin words and six Greek words which contribute most to our elementary-school vocabulary.

Three Spelling By-products

1. *Apostrophes.* Apostrophes are small in size and are easily overlooked by the pupil. But teachers seem to love those little marks! As a result, mistakes in placement or omission of apostrophes constitute by far the most frequent error in written English. But the apostrophe is not very important, after all. If we consider the Rinsland word list as a fair representation of the words which a child should know and use at the end of his first eight years of school, we find that only 221 of the 14,571 words in the list involve apostrophes. There are 176 words in which the apostrophe is used to denote possession. Of these, only sixteen are the possessive forms of plural nouns. These words are:

babies'	horses'	rabbits'
boys'	ladies'	soldiers'
folks'	mothers'	teachers'
friends'	parrots'	uncles'
girls'	peoples'	
grandmothers'	pygmies'	

Table 2

SYLLABLE INVENTORY SUMMARY SHOWING FREQUENCY OF SYLLABLES OCCURRING
TEN TIMES OR MORE IN 5,944 WORDS IN RINSLAND WORD LIST

Initial Syllable

SYLLABLE	FRE-QUENCY	SYLLABLE	FRE-QUENCY	SYLLABLE	FRE-QUENCY	SYLLABLE	FRE-QUENCY	SYLLABLE	FRE-QUENCY	SYLLABLE	FRE-QUENCY
re-	209	man-	33	fire-	18	gen-	14	su-	12	bur-	10
in-	203	or-	33	af-	17	ab-	14	ter-	12	cel-	10
a-	149	at-	29	es-	17	pol-	14	to-	12	char-	10
de-	146	col-	29	ev-	17	post-	14	vol-	12	cir-	10
con-	145	par-	29	har-	17	rec-	14	am-	11	cop-	10
ex-	141	se-	29	min-	17	reg-	14	bal-	11	cross-	10
un-	99	i-	28	mo-	17	cap-	13	bar-	11	dan-	10
com-	95	pa-	28	oc-	17	hon-	13	cour-	11	ef-	10
dis-	82	ma-	26	sun-	17	li-	13	dec-	11	el-	10
en-	81	can-	25	vi-	17	pan-	13	fif-	11	fu-	10
an-	68	mis-	24	wa-	17	sand-	13	fin-	11	gar-	10
o-	65	po-	24	but-	16	so-	13	hard-	11	grad-	10
e-	63	res-	23	mar-	16	sup-	13	high-	11	hap-	10
pro-	58	sur-	23	out-	16	va-	13	mod-	11	house-	10
ac-	56	op-	22	pen-	16	win-	13	mu-	11	mag-	10
ad-	53	cor-	21	pi-	16	wood-	13	play-	11	mas-	10
ap-	47	em-	21	pur-	16	ab-	12	pos-	11	mer-	10
be-	45	grand-	20	snow-	16	air-	12	quar-	11	mus-	10
for-	44	mon-	20	fa-	15	bat-	12	sat-	11	pop-	10
di-	43	sub-	20	of-	15	hand-	12	set-	11	rat-	10
car-	42	ca-	19	sea-	15	hol-	12	sev-	11	sen-	10
im-	42	la-	19	up-	15	me-	12	some-	11	sta-	10
al-	40	no-	19	ba-	14	mi-	12	thir-	11	suf-	10
ar-	39	twen-	19	black-	14	na-	12	trans-	11	sug-	10
as-	37	u-	19	cot-	14	sol-	12	back-	10	ta-	10
pre-	35	au-	18								

Medial Syllable

Syllable	No.	Syllable	No.	Syllable	No.	Syllable	No.	Syllable	No.	Syllable	No.
-i-	277	-ci-	32	-al-	21	-tu-	15	-ap-	11	-ful-	10
-a-	161	-ra-	31	-en-	21	-at-	14	-cov-	11	-low-	10
-er-	131	-to-	30	-fi-	21	-el-	14	-duc-	11	-par-	10
-o-	107	-ing-	28	-in-	20	-it-	14	-es-	11	-pect-	10
-ter-	81	-ta-	28	-pa-	20	-lec-	14	-gan-	11	-sa-	10
-e-	79	-y-	28	-ten-	19	-pi-	14	-mu-	11	-sid-	10
-ri-	75	-per-	26	-ven-	19	-com-	13	-no-	11	-so-	10
-u-	72	-ra-	26	-ma-	18	-fer-	13	-pe-	11	-te-	10
-di-	56	-ber-	25	-ra-	18	-port-	13	-pen-	11	-tin-	10
-der-	44	-la-	25	-ag-	17	-pos-	13	-pli-	10	-am-	10
-ni-	40	-is-	23	-mi-	16	-tur-	13	-an-	10	-ble-	10
-si-	40	-tion-	23	-po-	16	-de-	12	-co-	10	-cat-	10
-ti-	40	-ty-	23	-ish-	15	-den-	12	-et-	10	-ger-	10
-li-	35	-ca-	22	-ry-	15	-mer-	12	-fac-	10	-lu-	10
-ver-	34	-cu-	22	-ton-	15	-or-	12	-fec-	10	-ro-	10

Table 2 *(cont.)*

Final Syllable

Syllable	Frequency	Syllable	Frequency	Syllable	Frequency	Syllable	Frequency	Syllable	Frequency	Syllable	Frequency
-ing	881	-tor	38	-dy	21	-ence	16	-days	13	-bling	11
-ed	338	-ness	36	-ship	21	-ward	16	-dles	13	-cy	11
-er	323	-ic	34	-tered	21	-cles	15	-ens	13	-gled	11
-ly	290	-ters	34	-ber	20	-ent	15	-ened	13	-n't	11
-es	212	-ous	34	-dle	20	-ger	15	-gle	13	-ons	11
-tion	210	-der	32	-ple	20	-lar	15	-le	13	-ther	11
-y	193	-ings	32	-ting	20	-pers	15	-ples	13	-to	11
-ers	135	-ties	31	-um	19	-ant	14	-ted	13	-tures	11
-ty	95	-less	30	-house	19	-bled	14	-ten	13	-ding	10
-al	84	-ries	30	-let	19	-bles	14	-tles	13	-ern	10
-ble	82	-ies	29	-on	19	-cle	14	-board	12	-fied	10
-ter	75	-ping	29	-a	18	-ders	14	-it	12	-its	10
-ment	73	-tle	27	-ate	18	-els	14	-near	12	-lets	10
-ry	69	-et	25	-ered	18	-ets	14	-ning	12	-sions	10
-est	65	-per	25	-ish	18	-land	14	-son	12	-sy	10
-tions	56	-ny	24	-low	18	-or	14	-tain	12	-tains	10
-en	48	-sion	24	-way	17	-side	14	-tal	12	-time	10
-full	44	-tive	24	-el	16	-tic	13	-tals	12	-tled	10
-man	43	-men	23	-als	16	-ance	13	-ar	11	-try	10
-ments	42	-age	21	-day	16	-by	13			-ure	10

There are thirteen words consisting of a verb and *not,* like *hadn't,* which require an apostrophe. Apostrophes are needed also in thirty-two other contractions:

all's	jack-o'-lantern	'twas
four o'clock	jack-o'-lanterns	we'd
he'd	ma'am	we're
he'll	o'clock	we've
he's	she'd	what's
here's	she'll	where's
I'd	she's	you'd
I'll	they'd	you'll
I'm	they'll	you're
I've	they're	you've
it'll	they've	

The emphasis which many teachers place upon the apostrophe in these 221 words seems out of all bounds. These words represent less than 2 per cent of what the child needs to learn. Furthermore, this overemphasis results in harmful transfer. When we ask pupils to spell plurals and we get *can's* for *cans,* we usually reward them with a zero.

2. *Abbreviations.* There are sixty-four abbreviations in the Rinsland word list. After each of these, in order to spell it correctly, the pupil must put a period. The abbreviations represent less than one-half of 1 per cent of the total words.

3. *Hyphenated words.* The Rinsland word list contains ninety-five hyphenated words, such as *ill-bred.* Forty-eight of these represent numbers, like *forty-eight.* Among the rest, four seem worthy of special attention. They are:

co-operate	co-operative
co-operation	pre-existing

It is to be hoped that teachers will not fall in love with hyphens.

Syllable Inventory Summary

Table 2 presents syllables occurring ten times or more in 5,944 words in the Rinsland list. For example, *re-* occurs in 209 of the words. Syllables that occur less than five times are found in 3,046 of the words. Monosyllabic words are not included.

33. *Spelling Games That Teach* *

PAUL S. ANDERSON

M UCH in the same way that interesting books are kept in a library corner, various word games might be put in a place in the classroom where students can go when free time is available.

Self-challenging, the games described below can be enjoyed by one pupil or by several. Thus, the slow learner need not be discouraged by unequal class competition. Soon the children will be devising their own spelling games.

The children should be taught to use the dictionary to check the spelling of unfamiliar words.

Word Pyramids

Start at the top of the pyramid with one letter. The player then adds one letter, rearranging previously used letters if necessary, to make a new word. He continues to see how high a pyramid can be formed. Examples:

a	i	a
at	in	am
eat	tin	mat
meat	thin	team
steam	hints	mates
stream	things	master

Spelling Golf

Open a book at random and place a sheet of paper on the page so that it covers up all but the first three letters that appear next to the left-hand margin. Write down the three-letter groups that appear in the first nine lines. An example:

som	exa	tha
the	fol	and
lif	spe	oft

---

* From Paul S. Anderson, "Spelling Games That Teach," *NEA Journal* (September, 1957), p. 398. Reprinted by permission of the author and the *NEA Journal.*

Each player has a copy of the list. The object of the game is to keep the score low by making words with the addition of the fewest letters. If the three letters already form a word, enough letters must be added to change it.

Using the above list as a nine-hole golf course, one player might have a score sheet like this:

some (1 stroke)	spend (2 strokes)
them (1 stroke)	that (1 stroke)
life (1 stroke)	andiron (4 strokes)
exact (2 strokes)	often (2 strokes)
fold (1 stroke)	*Total: 15 strokes*

A variation might be to see how many letters can be added.

Dictionary Challenges

This game consists of answering the following types of challenges:

1. How many synonyms for the word "funny" can you find?
2. How many meanings can you find for the word "run"?
3. How many adjectives can you find that would describe food?
4. How many words can you find for a group of people, such as a class?

Descriptive Crosswords

The student selects any noun and writes it vertically. The object is to write horizontally an adjective that could describe the noun for each of the letters in the vertical word. Here's an example, using "girl":

Gracious
Ignorant
Regal
Languid

Humpty Dumpty

Write any word vertically on the left side of the page. (Avoid words with j, i, q, c, x, y, and z.) Leave a wide space and write the letters of the word in reverse order on the right margin. The space between is to be filled with letters that will make words. Each letter counts one point, and the object is to see how many points can be earned. A deduction of two points is made for each incompletion or error:

b	laste	d	(5 points)
o	unc	e	(3 points)
m		b	(minus 2 points)
b	otto	m	(4 points)
e	ch	o	(2 points)
d	um	b	(2 points)

Score: 14 points

34. A Comparison of a Typical and an Intensive Method of Teaching Spelling *

ROBERT T. CALHOUN

AN EXTENSIVE STUDY of the effectiveness of various methods of spelling instruction has been conducted for a number of years at Chestnut Hill Academy, where the writer formerly taught. Different teachers and class groups have attacked the problem from varied points of view.[1] The phase of the study with which this article deals compared a routine workbook method with an intensive method of teaching spelling. A fifth grade group consisting of nineteen boys was used for the study. All the teaching involved in the experiment was done by the author, and the population of the group remained constant.

The typical approach followed a series of activities based largely on a workbook. This method was used for seven months, and then the pupils' achievement was measured during the spring testing program. Following this, the method of spelling instruction was changed, and, although only

* From Robert T. Calhoun, "A Comparison of a Typical and an Intensive Method of Teaching Spelling," *The Elementary School Journal* (November, 1954), pp. 154–57. Reprinted by permission of the author and the University of Chicago Press.

[1] Carl H. Delacato, "A Comparison of Two Methods of Teaching Spelling," *Elementary English,* XXIX (January, 1952), 26.

two months remained in the school year, the spelling program was expanded and intensified.

The basic differences in the two approaches used are shown in Table 1.

Table 1

BASIC DIFFERENCES BETWEEN TWO SPELLING APPROACHES COMPARED IN ONE SCHOOL

	Typical Approach	*Intensive Approach*
Length of time in operation	7 months	2 months
Time spent per week......	100 minutes	100 minutes
Activities pursued	Workbook activities (5 days)	Workbook activities (3 days)
	Original sentences or story (weekly)	No sentences (conditional upon satisfactory achievement)
	Word list	No word list
	Infrequent spelling bees (once or twice a week)	Regular spelling bees (four times a week)
		Discussion of spelling goals

The Typical Approach

From September until March the instruction in spelling consisted of what may be called a typical approach. It was based on a workbook, with daily activities to provide repetition in learning the week's eighteen or nineteen words. The year's work included 555 "new words." The boys completed the activities in the regular sequence described below.

FIRST DAY

The week's words were introduced in a relevant story. Recognition of the words was checked by having the story and then the word list read aloud. The words were then underlined in the story and placed in blanks beside matching pictures.

SECOND DAY

Practice in using the words was given by means of different exercises. These exercises consisted of work with meanings, phonics, and correct usage. Use of a small dictionary in the workbook provided an opportunity to become familiar with this aid to language development.

THIRD DAY

Each boy wrote the week's words in sentences or in a story to check comprehension and to afford an opportunity for meaningful repetition. A practice test was then given so that each boy could ascertain his proficiency in spelling the words.

FOURTH DAY

Review and practice were accomplished by means of a word game. The members of the class were expected to spend time learning those words not yet mastered.

FIFTH DAY

A final test on the week's words was given. The words missed were written and then spelled orally.

These daily activities were augmented by two others. First, each boy was expected to keep a list of the words that he misspelled in his daily written work. Compositions, reading workbooks, and assignments in other subjects were the sources of these words. The words were to be studied, and periodic tests were given on each boy's accumulated list. Infrequent spelling bees constituted the other activity. Easy word lists were used for a beginning, and then various textbooks from grades three to five were used as sources of words.

Intensive Approach

The first step in the intensive approach, which was used in April and May, was the abandonment of the lists of missed words. These lists had become a burden to the slower pupils who missed many words, and they had little real value for the better spellers.

The problem of how to improve spelling was discussed with the boys. The group felt that the week's work was stretched out over too long a period. It was decided, therefore, to combine the five activities into a three-day program. This plan allowed a longer work period on each of the three days spent on the week's words. The drill work was done the first day; the practice test and review work were done the second day; and the final test was given on the third day.

The value of writing the week's words in sentences or in a story was questioned. It was assumed that boys who could learn the week's words without writing them in sentences were being asked to engage in meaningless repetition. Therefore, as a means of motivating more effective study, it was proposed to the class that boys who had perfect scores on three consecutive weekly tests would be excused from writing the following week's words in sentences. When a boy did not write the words in sentences and failed to attain a perfect score on the final test for that week, it was felt that he needed the repetition provided by the sentences, and he was therefore required to begin again in his efforts to reach the "spelling list." This plan elicited a good response. Those pupils who were on the spelling list had an envied status, and those not eligible for membership worked hard to attain or regain this privileged position.

Another phase of the intensive method was the emphasis on spelling bees, making use of supplementary word lists. Because of the wide range of achievement, the members of the class were divided by the teacher into two groups. Fifth, sixth, and seventh grade word lists were used for the upper group; and third, fourth, and fifth grade words for the lower group. As each boy was spelled down, his name was placed on the figure of a ladder in the order in which he went out. The boy who stayed up longest and was rated Number 1 in his group was given the first word the following day and risked being the first to go down. This system afforded each boy an opportunity to compete with pupils of nearly equal ability on words at his own level. It also afforded him an opportunity to watch the changes in his daily standing and tended to foster alertness toward the words spelled by others.

For variety, a baseball spelling game was used. In this game the players "reached base" or advanced other players by successfully spelling the words "pitched" to them.

In addition, the teacher often discussed with the class the desirability of acquiring "both a spelling consciousness and a spelling conscience." The members of the group were encouraged to be more conscious of their spelling needs and to exercise a greater conscience in remedying their needs. The implications of such a goal were gradually developed, and the phrase began to take on real meaning to the members of the group. This theme was thereafter mentioned repeatedly as a reminder of the ultimate objective of the spelling program.

Results

1. The median growth during the typical instruction was one year, while the intensive method produced progress of one year and four months (see Table 2).

Table 2

PROGRESS IN SPELLING MEASURED BY STANFORD ACHIEVEMENT TEST OF 19 FIFTH-
GRADE PUPILS DURING INSTRUCTION UNDER TRADITIONAL AND INTENSIVE METHODS

Date of Test	Grade Level				
	FIRST QUAR-TILE	MEDIAN	MEAN	THIRD QUAR-TILE	RANGE
September	3.9	4.6	5.1	5.9	3.8– 7.4
March	4.4	5.6	5.9	7.2	3.9–10.1
June	5.0	7.0	6.7	8.3	4.5–11.3
Growth from September to March (traditional method)	0.5	1.0	0.8	1.3	.....
Growth from March to June (intensive method)	0.6	1.4	0.8	1.1	.....

2. The growth at the first quartile was five months under the typical method and six months during the intensive instruction.

3. The progress shown at the third quartile was one year and three months during the typical period of instruction and one year and one month as a result of the intensive approach.

4. Eight months was the average growth made in seven months under the typical method, and the intensive method produced the same amount of progress in two months.

Summary and Conclusions

Judged by the test results and the time factor involved, the intensive method of spelling instruction was productive of much greater growth for the majority of the class than was the typical approach. The discussions during the two months of intensive spelling instruction seemed to develop both a spelling consciousness and a spelling conscience. The author is of the opinion that this activity helped the boys to become more aware of their spelling needs than they had previously been and more willing to work toward improvement in this area. The results indicate that an intensive approach to spelling, stressing understanding and appreciation of the goals and techniques of spelling instruction, will greatly aid pupils in increasing the effectiveness of their study of spelling.

35. Important Features of the Handwriting Movement *

FRANK N. FREEMAN

BOTH THE scientific and the widespread practical concern for the hand-writing movement are comparatively modern. It is only about fifty years since physiologists and psychologists started to analyze and record the movement made in writing, and it is only a little longer since classroom teachers paid any attention to the kind of movements their pupils made in writing letters and words.

Handwriting Movement Is Complicated

Scientific studies have sought to describe the handwriting movement rather than to advocate one over another. They have, however, thrown some light on the characteristics of efficient movement. They have shown, for one thing, that the movement is not the simple thing we are wont to think it is. For example, when we write a letter or a word, the pressure of the fingers on the penholder and of the pen point on the paper is continually changing. Two facts stand out which are important. One is that these changes are very delicate and complicated. The other is that they correspond closely with the forms that are being produced. If the pressures are wrong in force or timing, the movement goes astray and the form is

* From Frank N. Freeman, *Teaching Handwriting* (Washington, D.C.: National Education Association, 1954), pp. 14–18. Reprinted by permission of the author and the Department of Classroom Teachers and the American Educational Research Association of the National Education Association.

distorted. The pupil has to learn to make this complicated series of pressure changes in order to produce the correct forms. The pressure changes come to him through the feeling of the movement—the kinesthetic sensation. These have to be built up to connect with the form through a long course of trial and error. This is one reason why much systematic practice is necessary. The same thing is true of the changes in the speed of the writing movement that take place during the writing of a letter or a word. If the average person were asked about the speed of movement of the pen as it traces the forms of the letter, he at first would not understand what the question meant. Then, if he were asked whether the pen moves at an even speed or speeds up and then slows down many times during the writing of a word, he would reply that it moves at an even speed. Similarly, he would likely say that the eye moves at an even speed across the line of print in reading. Actually, the pen continually speeds up, slows down, or pauses as it makes the gentler or sharper turns. As in the case of pressure, the speed changes correspond closely with the forms of the letters. It takes long, long practice to learn to make these delicate changes so as to form the letters accurately. Also, the writer feels the changes in his muscles and joints even though he doesn't think about them.

Rhythm is a special case of speed changes. It is the feeling of the movement—or the sight or sound—accompanied by the sense of time. In writing, it is not simple like the waltz or two-step, but complicated like modern music.

Composition of Handwriting Movement

The other big feature of the writing movement we may call the make-up or the composition of the movement. Does it consist of movements of the fingers, of the arm, or of both the fingers and the arm? Since these parts of the body have received varying degrees of emphasis, we must pass judgment upon rival claims and procedures. Some have advocated the arm movement, some the combined movement (in which we may perhaps include the European "traction" movement), and some would do nothing about movement, thus letting the pupil fall into the finger movement.

Here we get help from observation, backed by experimental studies. The first observation is that very few people, even after training throughout the elementary-school years, attain an *exclusive* arm movement. As we go up the grades, a larger proportion come somewhere near it, but many do not. A second observation is that the exclusive arm movement is difficult to make except under ideal conditions, such as a good-sized desk on which both arms may rest and with the paper in front of the body. A third observation is that, with the average writer, as good results are had with the *combined* movement as with the exclusive arm movement.

Now let us turn to the finger movement, in which the hand is turned far over on the side, is planted on a given spot and remains there, perhaps rolling over to the right, while the fingers, unaided, make the letters. This habit is almost sure to be established if no instruction about movement is given. The result of the finger type of movement is open for all to see, and it has been demonstrated by scientific study. The writing is uneven, the letters are poorly formed, and the strokes are heavy. The hand and fingers, moreover, become cramped.

Because of the impracticability of the exclusive arm movement and the inadequacy of the finger movement, leaders in the teaching of handwriting turned thirty or more years ago to the combined movement. In this movement the hand is not turned over on the side but only about halfway over. It rests on the third and fourth fingers, not on the side. It is not planted in one place, but slides across the page while the letters are being formed. The arm and hand may have a share in the formation of the letters. The fingers, relaxed, grasp the pen lightly in completing the letters. This movement is comfortable and practical; it has the advantages of the arm movement without suffering its rigors. It avoids the quite unnecessary discipline which is necessary in order to keep the fingers from the very natural tendency to take a share in forming the details of the letters, and at the same time it keeps the arm moving, jointly with the fingers, to help in making the longer strokes and to carry the hand along the line. The combined movement avoids the cramping of the muscles which is likely to occur when the extreme finger movement is used.

Relaxation and Movement

The principle just referred to, stated positively, is the principle of relaxation. It appears in all acts of skill. Just what is relaxation? Obviously it is not absence of contraction of the muscles, either in making a movement or maintaining bodily position. In any performance a few muscles must contract, others relax, and still others maintain a suitable state of partial contraction (called tonus). Efficient performance requires that the muscles producing a movement contract with the proper force, at the proper time, and that the opposing muscles relax at the same time. This ideal condition, then, is not complete relaxation but only enough to prevent undue tensions in the muscles concerned in the act, or in the other muscles of the body.

Automatization

In the early stages of learning to write, the child's attention is absorbed in thinking of the forms he is producing and of the movements by which he produces them. During this early stage it is difficult for him to think about the meaning of what he is writing because he is so occupied with the mechanics. As the child gets more and more skill he needs to pay less and less attention to the *how* of writing and can think more and more of *what* he is writing. We call this automatization. It is a necessary process if he is ever to use writing as a fluent mode of expression.

The classroom teacher does not need to do much about automatization except to understand and recognize it. There are some points, however, that should be kept in mind. One is that, since the child cannot keep equally in mind what he is writing and how he is writing it, there should be periods in which one is emphasized, and other periods in which the other is stressed. A second point is that the writing may become automatic too soon or too late. If too soon, the learner freezes serious faults into his writing habit instead of keeping it flexible long enough to overcome the chief faults. On the other hand, keeping the writing habit from becoming automatic too long makes the writer permanently self-conscious about his writing; he can never use it as a free and easy means of expressing thought, as he does, for example, with speaking. Both extremes should be avoided.

Kinesthetic Control

When any movement has become automatic it is very largely relegated to what is called "kinesthetic control." This means control by the sensations of movement in the hand and arm, instead of a careful inspection of the forms of the letters by the eye. The eye then has to watch the writing only enough to guide the general features such as the size or the alignment. This natural development should not be interfered with. In fact, in some cases where the child has unusual difficulty and his muscles become cramped, relief can be had by giving emphasis to the sensations of movement, that is, for the time being, giving them *special* emphasis.

36. *Teaching Handwriting* *

FRANK N. FREEMAN

HANDWRITING is more than a skill. It is also a means of communication and a way of expressing meaning. This fact gives it a special importance among skills, and governs the methods by which it is acquired. If the proper methods are used, handwriting becomes a smoothly working and efficient means of expressing thought.

Standards of Speed

Standards in speed have to be set largely on the basis of comparative performance. We cannot conveniently study (at least we have not) the various situations in which handwriting is used and the speed demanded in each. We have simply recorded the variations in speed among individuals, or among groups who had been taught in different classes or schools, and have struck an average.

So far as different schools or classes are concerned, this may be used as a goal for those below the average. We cannot use the average as a standard for individual children except as a mild incentive for those below that point.

The speed of writing is flexible. Without special training, the pressures that come from the requirements of school life or of office work will cause the typical individual to increase his writing speed until it reaches about one hundred letters per minute. An adult who does a good deal of writing may easily reach 130 letters per minute.

Standards of Quality

Before the modern era of measurement in education, the only standard in quality of handwriting recognized was perfection. As soon as the question of standards came to be viewed realistically, it was clear that perfection was totally unattainable and therefore not an effective aim.

Attempts have been made to assess the quality of the writing of adults in various occupations and the quality demanded by these occupations. The most serious study of this kind revealed that on the Ayres Scale the average

* From Frank N. Freeman, "Teaching Handwriting," *NEA Journal* (November, 1954), pp. 482–83. Reprinted by permission of the author and the *NEA Journal*.

quality of the writing of occupational groups varied from 48 for college professors to 81 for employes in the account-sales department. Ten of the twenty-four occupational groups wrote better than 60 and one better than 70. The conclusion was that 60 is good enough for social correspondence and for most occupations; 70, for teachers in the elementary schools and most commercial workers.

What Is a Standard?

To some of us a standard means a quality of performance to be required of all pupils without which they shall not be permitted to advance to the next grade. Others, rejecting this obviously severe requirement, would abolish standards altogether.

Cannot standards be useful without doing violence to the facts of individual differences? Yes, if we recognize the standard for just what it is, an *average* performance and a desirable *minimum* goal, but not a hard and fast requirement.

Natural and Artificial Motives

Motives may be classified as *natural* or *artificial* (some prefer the terms *intrinsic* and *extrinsic*). Natural motives grow out of the situation in which one lives; artificial motives are concocted by the classroom teacher or parents for the special purpose of inducing the child to do something that he would not do if left to himself.

Natural motives, other things being equal, are better, because the child feels that it is well to do the thing he is prompted to do; it fits in with the situation. Artificial motives are usually less effective because the child recognizes that they arise from the wishes of a particular person; they have force because of the child's desire to please this person. Natural motives are likely to be more permanent, and less influenced by the child's desire or lack of desire to please the person who set up the incentive.

Competition as a Motive

Competition probably is neither so bad as its critics would have us believe, nor so benign as its proponents make it out to be. Used in moderation, it does not harm a child, nor does it rule out other, and perhaps worthier, motives. Some children, unresponsive to other motives, may be incited to learn by competition.

It is wise, however, to stress as of first importance the value of doing something well because it is useful and because it enables us to play our part in our society. Competition, used in moderation, supplements the other more social motives.

The Role of Meaning

The ultimate purpose of handwriting is to express and communicate meaning. No one writes, ordinarily, to make forms so that they may be admired chiefly as forms.

This intimate connection between writing and meaning affects profoundly the nature of the act of writing. The meaning and the physical movement do not just happen to go together. Their union makes writing fundamentally a different thing from the movements by themselves or the meaning by itself.

Natural and effective writing is developed when the child writes with meaning from the beginning, or at least after a few preliminary exercises. He starts by writing words, not isolated letters or meaningless exercises. Very soon he is writing simple sentences and is composing his own "story." In order to make this possible he uses simplified letters (manuscript) and easy tools (the chalkboard and crayon or large pencils). His forms are crude at first, and only gradually become more accurate. He will, of course, need help in writing specific letters. But his strong desire to write is kept, and serves as a motive to the steady improvement of form and of efficiency of movement.

Incidental Learning

The belief that sufficient skill in arithmetic, spelling, and handwriting can be gained without special practice has been advanced for a long time. The application of this belief goes under different names at different periods, but the basic idea is the same.

In school activities, technique must be mastered by a certain amount of systematic practice. This argument for the need of systematic practice does not imply that all the child's writing should consist of such practice, or that practice should be given without proper introduction.

We have already said that writing should have meaning for the child from the outset. It is never "just on the paper." Even when he is singling out a word or a letter for special practice, he should realize that this is a part of a complete piece of writing that conveys a message.

Effect of Growth

Parents and classroom teachers are not always aware of the fact, but a little careful observation will show that the young child is awkward in his movements in comparison with an older child, or an adult. If we always remembered this, we would be more patient with the young child and more tolerant of his early efforts. We would not so often think that he is stubborn or lazy when he fails to do the things that seem so easy to us.

The other lesson to be drawn from the child's poor control of movement is that the task should be easy at first and only slowly increased in difficulty. This fact is now generally recognized. There was a time, not so long ago, when first graders were forced to write with ink and a fine steel pen, to make letters the same size as those used by adults, and to drill in long exercises, using the difficult extreme arm movement. That time, we hope, is gone forever.

Styles of Writing

The questions regarding the best style of writing to teach have come under two main issues: that concerning vertical versus slanting writing; and that concerning manuscript versus cursive.

The issue concerning vertical writing has been pretty well settled in favor of writing with a moderate slant as the most widely approved style, both in the opinion of those who have done research on the subject and of supervisors and textbook writers.

As to manuscript writing, opinion and practice are not so nearly unanimous. Theorists are divided into three camps: those who would use cursive writing exclusively, those who would use manuscript writing exclusively, and those who would use manuscript writing in the first two or three grades and then change over to cursive. About 85 per cent of the larger cities now follow the third practice.

The objection is sometimes made that switching over from manuscript to cursive writing violates the law of habit and introduces an added serious difficulty. Those who raise this objection do so on the basis of theory rather than experience. Experience based on careful experiment shows that the child can learn cursive writing in the third grade after two years of manuscript writing more easily than he can learn it in the first grade, and the quality of his writing in later grades is equal or superior to that of pupils who started cursive in the first grade.

How Taught?

Handwriting used to be treated as a skill that was not affected by the subject matter which was being expressed. The contrary view, now generally accepted, is that handwriting is affected greatly by the purpose and type of subject matter and that an adequate program of learning to write seriously considers other parts of the curriculum.

This conclusion makes it necessary to include in the practice exercises materials from other parts of the curriculum and to give attention to the quality of the writing that the child does during the entire school day. Thus, in part, we bridge the gap between the tangible and the intangible outcomes of achievement. We can do both, and the sooner we get to the task the better.

37. Readiness to Change from Manuscript to Cursive *

LUCY NULTON

WHEN SHALL WE help a child change from manuscript to cursive writing?" is a question which has bedeviled teachers some few decades—almost since the introduction of manuscript writing to this country, when its strongest advocates answered, "Never! Abandon cursive writing. It is archaic, impossibly difficult for children, and too standardized."

However, cursive writing continues to be used in our culture, it remains personally distinctive to each individual, and children do learn it (albeit not always well or happily) and the problem has become: When is the most effective time to begin cursive writing? When can children make the transfer with clearest imagery and smoothest execution, with the least frustration and waste of time for both children and teacher?

In relation to most things which we attempt to teach to human beings

* From Lucy Nulton, "Readiness to Change from Manuscript to Cursive," *Elementary English* (October, 1955), pp. 382–83. Reprinted by permission of the author and the National Council of Teachers of English.

we have almost come to accept as fact that the learner must be *ready* to learn this thing. Readiness is basic to learning. It would seem only common sense to be guided by the same idea when we attempt to decide at what point we should teach children cursive writing.

Certainly, we can't say every child should begin cursive writing at the age of 10, or 6, or 8. We know such a statement to be unsound in respect to beginning reading. Writing is equally individual. While most of the children of a given grade group may be able to start, there will be some who are not able, some who are distinctly unready. Though we may say, "By and large, most children are ready to change to cursive writing when they are about _____ years of age, we must still watch each child closely and ask ourselves, "Is *this person* ready?"

But as we ask, how shall we recognize a child's readiness to begin cursive writing? What do we look for? The following statements may help us to define readiness as we observe each particular child.

This particular, individual child should show sufficient control of fine muscles to:

> direct a pencil, chalk, or crayon in forming recognizable lines other than simple circle and straight line (this may be in drawing as well as in writing);
>
> control the pencil, chalk, or crayon in a flowing movement from form to form with some evidence of rhythm, rather than in jerks and stops;
>
> be able to do some of such coordinated movement without extreme tensing of muscles and without evidences of emotional disturbance (watch muscles of arm, fingers, mouth and tongue);
>
> show exhilaration or some other evidence of satisfaction with the accomplishment of such control;
>
> be able and willing to make large letters, rather than tight, cramped, very small ones.

The child should voluntarily and repeatedly make connecting lines between letters, try slanting letters, and experiment with elaborating forms of letters. These are evidences of awareness of differences in forms, of muscular control, and of desire to try out other ways of writing. Such experimentation usually occurs preceding and during the times when he is persistently asking, "When can we learn to write like grownups?" "When can we write *real* writing?" These questions, too, are usually, though not always, evidences of readiness.

The child should have a fairly clear idea of relative sizes of letters and parts of letters in manuscript, so that he does not confuse sizes and parts.

He should be able to write all letters, small and capitals, in manuscript, without too much deliberation or uncertainty as to form. (Perhaps confusion of *b* and *d, p* and *q* should be exceptions to this point.)

The child should show evidences of enjoying the process of putting ideas on paper through manuscript writing. He should be able to write a simple story or letter of three or four short sentences without having to ask for help on every sentence and without becoming tired.

The child should show awareness of cursive writing, repeatedly expressed interest in attempting it, and some ability in being able to recognize a few words written in cursive writing.

The child should be emotionally mature enough that he can experience a few failures or repeated partial successes without becoming upset.

He should be able to listen attentively, to watch another's movements closely, for the length of time necessary to write slowly a three- or four-letter word, without "fits and starts" of attention and without becoming tired and upset.

He should be able to follow simple directions.

His eye movements should be fairly well habituated to the left-to-right direction in manuscript writing.

If the child enters cursive writing experiences with enthusiasm, but later goes back to manuscript or mixes the two, this is not necessarily evidence of unreadiness for cursive writing. It is more probably indication of the facts that (1) ideas come faster than writing skill and (2) he is still uncertain of how to form certain letters in cursive writing. However, if he persistently reverts to manuscript unless encouraged toward cursive, or if he shows distaste for cursive, impatience with it, or an unusual decrease in the amount of writing he does, he is indicating that he is not ready for further experiences in cursive writing. He should not be pushed or coaxed into practicing cursive forms.

Writing, in any form, is a means to an end—the end of communicating to others our ideas, fancies, feelings. Whether one writes manuscript or cursive, is, after all, not so important as that he shall *have* ideas, fancies, feelings and be able to share them with other humans.

When making the change from manuscript to cursive writing we don't want our children to be plagued with Sam Weller's attitude toward learning the alphabet, "As to vether it's vorthvwhile to vork so hard to learn so little is a matter of opinion."

38. The Transition from Manuscript to Cursive Writing *

FRANK N. FREEMAN

THE PRACTICE of beginning instruction in handwriting with manuscript and changing to cursive before the end of the primary period has become almost universal in the schools of the United States. The exact time of making the transition, however, still varies and no uniform practice exists. It is therefore desirable to find out what the trend on this matter is, and whether the factors can be discovered which indicate what is the best time to make the change.

The variation in practice on this point, as well as a cursory examination of the reasons assigned for changing at one time or another, indicate the question is a complex one, involving many factors. It is therefore one of those issues which is difficult to determine with exact scientific certainty, because so many factors would have to be measured against each other. Also, because some factors favor one time and others another time, it is a matter of judgment which are the more important, and the final balance in favor of one time or the other may not be very great. However, it is important to review all the relevant facts and considerations and to make the best judgment we can on the best time of making the change.

In order to supplement previous knowledge on this matter, and to gather fresh data, the writer recently sent a questionnaire to 1,294 school systems in all the states of the Union. This questionnaire was sent to all the cities of 10,000 population and over, with no selection except that by size. The number of copies sent out was 1,294, and the number returned 861 or 66 per cent. This gives a sufficient basis for conclusions concerning current practice.

The main purpose of the questionnaire was twofold, first, to ascertain at what time the change is most commonly made, and second, to discover, so far as possible, the reasons for the choice of time. The first is a simple point of fact, while the second involves a large element of judgment, self-analysis, and interpretation. In addition to these two main points, answers were sought on three supplementary matters.

* From Frank N. Freeman, "The Transition from Manuscript to Cursive Writing," *Elementary English* (October, 1958), pp. 366–72. Reprinted by permission of the author and the National Council of Teachers of English.

The full questionnaire follows:

1. At what grade level do you begin instruction in cursive writing? _____
   Which semester? _____
2. What considerations led you to choose the grade in which to change over?
   a. The opinion of authorities (If so, which authorities do you follow?) _____
   b. Your own experience (Have you tried more than one grade? Yes _____ No _____) _____
   c. Theoretical considerations (Effect on ease of written expression, difficulty of changing, degree of establishment of the habit of manuscript writing before changing, etc.) _____
3. Do you carry manuscript writing into the upper grades as a supplementary style of writing? Yes _____ No _____ Comments: _____
   _____
4. At what grade level do you begin ink writing? _____ Which semester? _____
5. What tools do your children use for ink writing? Steel Pen? Ball Point? Fountain Pen?

The answers to question 1 are tabulated in Table 1. In sixty-six cities the change is made in either one of two grades. The returns from these cities are entered at the bottom of the table. Each grade is entered in the main part of the table so that the total number of entries is sixty-six greater than the number of cities.

It will be seen that the greatest number of cities make the change in grade 2-2 or grade 3-1, with the preponderance in grade 3-1. A considerable number choose grade 3-2. If we combine all the cities into two groups with the dividing line at the end of grade 2 we find that the change is made in grade 2 or below in 355 cities and in grade 3 or above in 570 cities. We may summarize current practice, then, by saying that it is almost universally in favor of making the change in either grade 2 or grade 3 but that the trend is strongly in favor of grade 3.

We have seen that the trend of practice is in favor of making the change in grade 3. However, a great many school systems make it in grade 2. It will help us in coming to a decision on the relative merits of these two times if we can find out why this diversity exists. Some light may be thrown on this question if we classify the replies by states. It will not be necessary to include all the states, but only those from which a fairly large number of replies were received. Since the purpose is to get a clue as to why one grade

Table 1

ANSWERS TO QUESTION #1

	Size of City			
Grade in which change is made	10,000 to 20,000	20,000 to 50,000	50,000 to 100,000	100,000 and over	Total
1-1	3	3	3	1	10
1-2	2	3	0	0	5
2-1	10	3	0	2	15
2-2	159	104	39	23	325
3-1	202	140	43	47	432
3-2	55	35	15	11	116
4-1	5	1	7	1	14
4-2	0	2	0	0	2
5-1	2	0	1	0	3
5-2	0	0	0	0	0
6-1	1	0	0	0	1
6-2					
7-1					
No cursive		1	1		2
No answers	439	292	109	85	925 2
				Total	927

Grade in which change is made	10,000 to 20,000	20,000 to 50,000	50,000 to 100,000	100,000 and over	Total
2-1 or 2-2		1			
2-2 or 3-1		35			
3-1 or 3-2		29			
3-2 or 4-1		1			66
					859

rather than the other was chosen, furthermore, those states have been selected in which there is a fairly large preponderance in favor of one grade or the other. These replies are summarized in Table 12.

It will be seen that the choice is in favor of changing in grade 3 in the states of California, Illinois, Iowa, Kansas, Massachusetts, New York,

Table 2

SUMMARY OF REPLIES FROM STATES FROM WHICH A CONSIDERABLE NUMBER OF REPLIES
WAS RECEIVED, AND IN WHICH THERE WAS A CONSIDERABLE PREPONDERANCE IN FAVOR
OF GRADE 2 OR GRADE 3

State	Grade 2	Grade 3-1	Grade 3-2
California	22	47	18
Illinois	17	24	8
Indiana	20	3	
Iowa	8	16	3
Kansas	1	14	3
Massachusetts	6	14	8
New York	18	26	8
Ohio	47	6	
Pennsylvania	54	11	3
Texas	18	27	3
Wisconsin	6	19	3

Texas and Wisconsin, while it is in favor of grade 2 in Indiana, Ohio and
Pennsylvania. This difference cannot be due to any difference in the children, or of the laws of learning that govern teaching procedure. It must be
due to the opinions that prevail in the different states. These opinions may
be embodied in the writing systems which are most commonly used in the
various states, or in the authorities who are followed in making up the
courses of study for states or for individual school systems. Our next step
in trying to run down the reasons for choosing one or the other grade, therefore, is to examine the authorities that are cited for the choice.

Question 2a asks whether the choice of the grade in which the change is
made is based on the opinions of authorities. This question is interpreted
somewhat broadly to include general authorities and research, committees
of teachers, the directives of the system used, etc. The replies are summarized in Table 3.

Not all the respondents gave opinions of authorities as the reason for
their choice of the time of changing over, but the breakdown of those who
did is given in this table. The majority of those who did give this as their

Table 3

THE "OPINIONS OF AUTHORITIES" CITED AS REASONS FOR THE TIME OF CHANGING OVER

Reasons Cited	Time of Changing			
	2-2	3-1 or 3-2	2-2	3-1 or 3-2
General authorities and research	26	58		
Tradition and practice	13	12		
Area policy and surveys	7	25		
Teacher committees, opinion, experience and experiment	70	70		
To suit spelling programs	2	3		
Subtotal			118	168

Reasons Cited	Time of Changing			
	2-2	3-1 or 3-2	2-2	3-1 or 3-2
To conform to System A			104	47
To conform to 13 other systems			59	94
To conform to state adoptions			12	33
Total			293	342

reason favor the transition in the third grade, either 3-1 or 3-2, by 342 to 293. All those who cite particular reasons under this general head, with one exception, either favor changing in the third grade, or, in three instances, choose the two grades in equal number. The one marked exception is the group which cites the practice of one widely used system as making the change in grade 2. This system is set up to provide change in this grade. Of the schools which give systems as their authority, however, forty-seven actually make the change in grade 3. If we subtract the votes for those who cite this system as their authority from the totals we get 189 who prefer grade 2 as against 295 who prefer grade 3.

In summary, on the references to the "opinions of authorities," those who cite tradition and practice, teacher committees, etc., are evenly divided between grade 2 and grade 3, while those who cite general authorities and research, or area policy and surveys, prefer grade 3 by two or three to one. Among those who cite handwriting systems as their authority, the adherents of one system prefer grade 2, while the adherents of the other systems prefer grade 3. In general, the view of the majority who base their choice on the opinions of authorities favors the change in grade 3.

The opinions of authorities give us a greater preponderance in favor of grade 3, but still there is a considerable diversity among them. There is room for doubt as to which authorities are right. If we have to choose among authorities without going behind them we would probably side with the greater number, but this is not an entirely satisfactory basis of choice. It is desirable to go beyond a census of votes and probe into the reasons underlying them. This we will try to do by examining the theoretical considerations cited in favor of one grade or the other.

The theoretical considerations that led to the choice of the grade in which to make the change are summarized in Table 4. In the first part of the table are listed the reasons which are given by those who in the majority of cases favor grade 3, though some give the same reason for changing in grade 2. Thus, eighty-nine thought that it was desirable to master manuscript before changing to cursive, and that this could not be done satisfactorily until grade 3-1 or 3-2. Twenty thought it could be done in grade 2. It was thought by sixty-six that the maturity and muscular coordination necessary to learn cursive was attained only in grade 3, while twenty were of the opinion that this was obtained in grade 2-2. Forty-one thought that manuscript should be continued throughout grade 3 in order to take advantage of the ease of written expression which ensued from its use, while only two dissented. Twenty-four against three felt that children did not seem ready to change until grade 3, and fifty-three against thirty thought it was easier to make the change in grade 3. Finally, thirty-five against seven believed that the change in grade 3 was better suited to the development of reading. They phrased this in various ways. Some said that reading skills were not sufficiently developed until grade 3, others that the preliminary reading period is not over until this grade. If we total all these opinions we find that eighty-two are given in favor of changing in grade 2 and 308 in favor of grade 3.

On one consideration, namely the readiness to change, the vote was nearly equal, viz. fifty-five to sixty-one. This may reflect in part the fact that some children are ready to change before others, a point we shall consider more fully in a moment.

On a few considerations, the vote was in favor of changing in grade 2.

Table 4

THEORETICAL CONSIDERATIONS LEADING TO THE CHOICE OF THE GRADE
FOR CHANGING OVER

Considerations Favoring Grade 3	Choice of Grade			
	2-2	3-1	3-2	3-1 & 3-2
Mastery of manuscript before changing	20	73	16	89
Maturity, muscular co-ordination and child development	20	50	16	66
Written expression helped by better developed manuscript	2	30	11	41
Majority seem ready	3	19	5	24
Easier to make	30	43	10	53
Better suited to reading development	7	29	6	35
Subtotal	82	244	64	308
Considerations nearly equal				
Recognition of readiness	55	55	6	61
Considerations favoring Grade 2				
Heavy curriculum load in Grade 3	10			
Teacher who taught manuscript makes the change	5			
Prevents children starting on their own	8			
Prevents manuscript being too firmly fixed	8			
More time for handwriting in Grade 2	2			
Miscellaneous	4	3		
Subtotal	37	3		
Total	174	302	70	369

These are listed in the lower part of the table. Since the total mention on
these points is only thirty-seven it is perhaps not worth while to go into
them in detail.

Altogether, the theoretical considerations, according to the respondents,
favor the choice of grade 3 as a time to change from manuscript to cursive

even more strongly than do the authorities. In 372 cases, the votes are in favor of grade 3, while less than half as many, or 174, favor grade 2.

These opinions are based on observations of children, and so should be carefully weighed and given a great deal of credence. While they are not as objective as are the results of scientific measurement, they are vastly more reliable than is offhand opinion unsupported by specific reasons. On the other hand, it is to be noted that the same reason is sometimes given for different conclusions, and we must recognize that even these opinions are not infallible. They are, however, the best we can get short of scientific experimentation.

We may now endeavor to interpret these findings. It is reasonable to conclude that the difference in practice and opinion on the question of when the change from manuscript to cursive should be made is due partly to two underlying facts. The first is that some factors actually favor the change in grade 2 and others the change in grade 3, so that those who believe the change should be made in either grade can cite good substantial reasons for their view. For example, in favor of grade 2 are the heavy curriculum load in grade 3, the advantage of having the change made by the teacher who teaches manuscript, the prevention of children making the change on their own and the prevention of the manuscript habit becoming too fixed. To these may be added the eagerness of some children and parents to write in cursive. On the other hand, certain, even more important, factors seem to favor grade 3, viz., the desirability of mastering manuscript before making the change, the attainment of sufficient maturity and muscular coordination before tackling cursive, the advantage of retaining manuscript as a ready instrument of written expression through grade 3, the postponement of the change until the majority seem ready, the making of the change when it is the easier, and the postponement of the date to avoid interference with the development of reading. A large majority of the respondents think that these factors favor the change in grade 3.

On one point the opinion seems evenly divided; this is the time at which the readiness to change may be recognized. (This seems at variance with the vote on the time when the majority are ready. No explanation for this variance suggests itself.) It may be that this even division is due partly to the fact that some children are actually ready before others. This is the second of the underlying facts mentioned above. The significance of this fact is that any method that is used should be flexible enough to permit some children to begin the change earlier than others, or for some to postpone the change after the majority have begun it.

A few hints may be given as to how we may judge whether a child is ready to change from manuscript to cursive. First, he should have a fairly good mastery of manuscript before changing to the more complex form of writing, as indicated by a good recognition of the forms of the letters and a satisfactory control of the movements of writing them. This will warrant us in expecting that he will be able to form a clear idea of the form of the letters and the words in the cursive form, and will be able to acquire the continuous and more complex movements involved in forming the letters and connected strokes of cursive. These, along with the child's desire to change and ability to apply himself, will indicate that he is ready.[1]

Summary

This survey of practice and opinion on the question of the best time to change from manuscript to cursive leads to the following findings and conclusions.

1. The prevailing practice in the cities of the U. S. of 10,000 and above is to make the change in grade 3. The number in which the change is made in grade 3, of those who reported, is 570 as against 355 which make it in grade 2.

2. There is considerable variation in practice among the states, which may be attributed largely to a difference in practice among the systems used.

3. The citation of authorities for the time of making the change indicates a good deal of diversity, though the majority favor the change in grade 3.

4. The theoretical considerations cited as reasons for making the change in one or the other grade strongly favor grade 3 by a vote of 372 against 174.

5. Pending more objective scientific investigation, which would be difficult, the weight of evidence seems to be in favor of changing from manuscript to cursive in grade 3.

6. Any program should probably be flexible enough to allow for some individual variation in making the change.

[1] A helpful discussion of this matter appears in an article by Lucy Nulton, in *Elementary English,* official organ of the National Council of Teachers of English, for October, 1955.

39. Teaching Penmanship in the Fourth Grade *

SISTER M. LAURENTIA, D.D.R.

N̲O ONE will doubt the importance of teaching the first grader to write manuscript, nor the value of teaching the second or third grader cursive writing. But how much importance is given to the teaching of handwriting in the fourth and fifth grades—the levels at which the child can begin efficiently to make use of his skill as a tool? True, most daily schedules make provision for a penmanship period of ten to fifteen minutes, but it is probably safe to assume that many teachers of the fourth and fifth grades frequently succumb to the temptation to use the penmanship period for "more important work." The children know how to write, we feel; why not spend our time more profitably in new learnings? Such reasoning is fallacious, for, although the child has already devoted some three years to learning letter formations, now he must be taught to evaluate with a critical eye what he has been doing more or less blindly during the first few years.

The results of a recent experiment indicate that an organized program of handwriting instruction in the fourth grade yields adequate and far-reaching returns. The experiment is a forceful argument to all fourth grade teachers to be as conscientious and meticulous in preparing for the handwriting lesson as in preparing for any of the so-called "important" subjects.

Sizing Up the Situation

Enthusiasm is a fair barometer of success. A part of every teacher's job is to "sell" the subject matter to her pupils, and once the children become sufficiently enthusiastic, success certainly will follow. Throughout my years of teaching, I have found that penmanship practice seemed to evoke the least enthusiasm from my pupils. My enthusiasm too, consequently, remained at a low ebb, which in time passed over to the children, generating a vicious circle of poor teaching, lack of enthusiasm, and pitiful results. Handwriting seemed the "step child" in the curriculum.

Remembering the words of my psychologist friend, "As we think, so we are," and enlarging upon them with "As we read, so we think," I began an

* From Sister M. Laurentia, "Teaching Penmanship in the Fourth Grade," *Catholic School Journal* (March, 1959), pp. 27–29. Reprinted by permission of the author and the publisher.

ambitious reading program devoted to handwriting. I soon discovered that most of the available reading material on teaching handwriting dated back to the 1920's or early -30's and some, even farther back. The few articles written in the past two decades were confined mostly to pleas in one form or another, for reinstating handwriting in the curriculum. Several methods books contained a paragraph, or a chapter at most, on methodology in handwriting, but generally, the material was meager. That others were experiencing the same attitudes that I had found in my classes was apparent. Some excellent material written more than a quarter of a century ago gave me the impetus for an experiment with my fourth graders. I decided to build my year's program in handwriting on a tripod of (1) diagnostic procedures, (2) remedial work, and (3) motivation.

Establishing the Need

It is now generally conceded that handwriting should be taught instrumentally; that is, the child should write with a purpose. His handwriting is merely the means, or the instrument, to attain a particular end. However, in the fourth grade there is still need for practice on the skills involved, the end being the perfecting of that skill.

Accordingly, when the fourth graders' faces register distaste for drills, for penmanship simply for practice sake, the teacher's work is to show the child the *need* for perfecting that skill. One of the best ways to do this is to set before the child attainable goals—slightly above their present achievement. If the fourth grader has tangible evidence that he is writing at the rate of forty-four letters per minute when he should be writing seventy-five letters per minute, he will have a definite aim. Better yet, if by progressive ratings, by the keeping of progress charts, and by sustained drills, he is able to follow his progress toward that goal, the child's distaste will rapidly change to enthusiasm. My first task was to point out to the children the need for rapid and accurate writing.

The realization by the pupils of this need was but the initial step in motivation. It provided "penmanship readiness" in the minds of the children; it provided the first surge of ambition and an effective impetus to the desire to achieve. Other motivating devices such as charts and graphs, repeated ratings, and success of achievement itself, provided the wherewithal to keep the children keeping on; but fundamentally, it was this initial motivation—this realization of the need—which provided the most effective drive to success.

Preliminary Preparation

In order to know specifically, and numerically, the intelligence and achievement ratings of my class, the Otis Beta and the Stanford Achievement tests were administered. Results of the Otis Beta showed that, of the fifty children who took the test, three had IQ's above 120, which might properly classify them as mentally superior. One child had a score below 90; several were in the low 90's. These might be classified as slow learners. The mean score of the class was 105.58. The mental ages of the group ranged from a high of 13 years 4 months to a low of 7 years 10 months. These variations, though wide, were considered sufficiently normal to retain all fifty children in the experimental group.

The results of the Stanford Achievement test, elementary battery, also showed the range commonly found in a normal classroom. Of the fifty children taking the test, three were two or more full years above their grade placement level in achievement. Three were almost two years below their level. Almost 50 per cent of the children were at their grade level or a half year above or below that level. As in mental ability, the achievement record showed that the class was normal in achievement and might be used for the purposes of the experiment without fear that great variations in achievement would invalidate the results.

Rate and Quality Scales

Teaching handwriting to fourth graders is more than teaching handwriting. It involves analyzing specifically their difficulties, and then applying remedial techniques. According to my plan, the first step in this analysis would be the administration to the group of rate and quality scales. I planned further to record the results of the scale, to follow the analysis with remedial measures for a period of three or four months, and then to administer the rate and quality scale a second time, noting the possible increase in either factor. Such increase, I considered, might reasonably be attributed to the methods of instruction.

At the beginning of this experiment, I administered the Gettysburg edition of the Ayres Scale as well as Paul West's American Handwriting Scale to the children. Both scales, in my estimation, provide with a relatively high degree of accuracy. Directions for scoring quality were followed very precisely, since the scoring of handwriting quality is somewhat subjective in nature. To offset this factor, the scoring of the children's handwriting specimens was done three times. After the first scoring, a numerical value was assigned to a particular specimen on the back of the paper. The papers were then placed in groups according to the ratings given on this first scoring. To determine whether all the papers merited the same rating in any particular group, the papers were critically examined and compared, and any changes deemed necessary were made. Then all papers were shuffled and put aside until the next day. A similar procedure was followed on the second marking, but this time the ratings were put on the front. After all the papers had been scored, differences between the first and the second scorings were settled by a third rating the following day.

The result of this first writing showed that the quality ratings of the children ranged from 20 to 80 on the Ayres Handwriting Scale, and the speed of writing ranged from 31.5 to 92.5 letters per minute. In order to make such figures meaningful, it is well to state at this point that the norm for fourth graders on the Ayres quality scale is 46, whereas the speed norm is fifty-five letters per minute.

The American Handwriting Scale was also administered to the group. Results of this showed that scores on the quality scale ranged from a low of 63 to a high of 93. The scores on the rate scale ranged from a low of 29 to a high of 85. Norms on the American Handwriting Scale for fourth graders are as follows: 75 for quality, and 59.5 for rate. A comparison of the mean score of the class (79.2 in quality; 50.3 in rate) indicated that the class as a whole was above the norm in quality and below the norm in rate. It was obvious that the remedial work for a while at least, must aim at increasing the rate of the majority of the children, while still retaining, or improving their quality standings.

Determining Types of Defects

The samples of the children's handwriting which were taken for determining their rate and quality according to West's Scale were used again in determining those elements of their handwriting which called for special remedial treatment. Each sample was studied to determine characteristics such as letter form, slant, motor control, coordination, and spacing. The defects were listed in appropriate columns as slight, serious, or most serious. This chart, with a list of each child's defects was solely for my use in remedial work.

A second analysis of specific defects was made according to Freeman's Chart for Diagnosing Faults in Handwriting. This chart is concerned with the elements of uniformity of slant, uniformity of alignment, quality of line, letter formation, and spacing. The children were graded on a 1 to 5 point scale, and specific defects were pointed out to them to be used as the basis for the remedial work which was to follow.

Determining Causes of Defects

Statistically, it was relatively simple to determine what each child achieved, both in quality and speed. However, such an interpretation did not tell *why* the child was slow; or *why* his quality was below the norm; or *why* his writing was exaggerated, eccentric, or irregular. Yet such a knowledge was even more necessary than mere statistics, for the purpose of the experiment was to diagnose the difficulties and to follow up the diagnosis by remedial measures. To this end, each child was observed more or less rigidly. In general, writing disabilities seemed to be traceable to three general causes: physical, psychological, or pedagogical.

1. *Physical causes.* Physical causes were not to any great extent responsible for poor or slow writing. To a degree, however, fatigue, poor eyesight, lack of motor coordination were underlying causes in some instances, and needed steps to overcome such difficulties were taken. Also in this category may be mentioned the left-handed writers. To some such writers handwriting presented a distinct problem until they were assured that they did not have to slant their writing with a right-handed slant. Nor were they expected to adjust their writing to the models on the board. Instead, each child was given a model alphabet in accord with the slant he preferred— vertical, backhand, or slightly backhand. These children, too, were permitted to turn their desks so that the light came over the right shoulder. Understanding such physical causes as the reason for poor writing was helpful in overcoming some of the defects in writing.

2. *Psychological causes.* In the teaching of handwriting as in the teaching of any other subject, some children present special problems. Some of their difficulties were due to causes which might be classed as psychological: lack of interest and attention; a desire to imitate eccentric writing; reversal errors; emotional factors. Children with such difficulties required special attention.

Primarily, the problems of interest and attention were matters of motivation. By using certain external motivating devices, such as graphs and charts, the attention and consequent interest of many children materially improved. Emotional factors were treated as individual cases required. Here the problem seemed one of instilling proper confidence into the child.

Generally, such psychological difficulties yield to rapport between teacher and pupil.

3. *Pedagogical causes.* By far the greatest number of defects were due to what may be called pedagogical causes; that is, the failure of the teacher to recognize the real problem that writing presents to the child. Writing has become automatic for adults; it is not that for most children of the fourth grade. Unless the teacher thoughtfully considers every angle that the problem of handwriting presents to the child, her teaching is apt to be inadequate, and difficulties and defects will multiply. With this thought in mind, every effort was made to provide instruction that would be both adequate and meaningful.

Organization for Remedial Work

Diagnosis and remedial instruction immediately suggest, if they do not demand, the need of individual attention. The first requisite at this point, therefore, was an organization which would permit and encourage individual attention. The wide range in rate and quality, the varying types of handwriting defects, the varying abilities found among the children—all these demand an organization conducive to individual instruction. Exclusive mass instruction would be neither adequate nor advisable. However, no teacher is naïve enough to believe that she can give individual instruction to fifty children during a fifteen-minute penmanship period. For economy and utility there was need for group instruction as well.

After a careful analysis of the results of the rate and quality scales, and after a study of the various types of errors made by the individuals, a method of organization was planned which would include provision for the following: (1) general class drills; (2) individual instruction for the group that was above the norm in both rate and quality; (3) individual instruction for those who were below the norm in rate, but above in quality; (4) individual instruction for those who were below the norm in rate and in quality. This divided the class into three groups, which would still insure a certain amount of individual attention without attempting the impossible of providing individually for each child.

The Program of Remedial Work

Remedial work throughout the course of this study for the improvement in rate consisted of frequent comparison of pupil writing rates with the norm for the grade. One of the most effective speed builders was the reduction of the size of writing. Other exercises consisted in the writing of alphabetic sentences under time pressure; or the writing of the letter *a,* for example, in groups of fives every five seconds. The children also took dictation exercises at the rate of one letter per second, which was slightly above the grade norm.

Counting for letters and words was also found to aid the children in the acquisition of speed. In writing letters in groups of fives, I counted "One, two, three, four, five," for each group. In writing three-letter words, the count was "one" for each word, the counts being given every three seconds. In writing sentences, the children were merely urged to make an effort to keep up with each word as it was dictated. The children kept records of these timed writings to determine whether or not they were progressing toward their goal of fifty-nine letters per minute.

Improvement in quality followed Freeman's Chart for Diagnosing Elements in Handwriting. This chart diagnoses elements of five types: slant, alignment, quality of line, letter formation, and spacing. On specific days we worked on each of these elements. Transparent sheets having the correct slant upon them were used to help the children discover their incorrect habits in slant. Also, it was found helpful to have them draw slanting pencil lines on a page in various places, each a space in height, before the writing lesson commenced. After these lines were inspected and approved, the child used them as a guide for practice in his writing.

Problems of alignment are closely allied to slant. Incorrect paper position was often the cause of incorrect alignment, and the pupils were given specific instructions on how to slant their paper, to hold their pens, and to sit relative to the paper as a means of correcting defects of alignment.

Many children received low quality ratings because the quality of their line was not consistent. Some of the group needed teaching in the correct manner of holding the pen. They were taught to hold it sufficiently near the point, slanted toward the right shoulder, and used with a medium pressure. Too great pressure caused the lines to be thick, and the letters to run together. Those children who showed this tendency were cautioned to release their grip on the pen and to hold it somewhat back from the point. Frequent reference to the quality of the line throughout the course of this experiment alerted the children to be conscious of such matters as pressure, method of holding the pen, and lack of rhythm in writing.

Letter formation, of course, received the greatest amount of remedial treatment. In many cases, here, it was a matter of insight. Children had to be shown that certain letters have to be closed; that some are tall, some half space, and some, like *t* slightly more than half. We practiced on under-curves such as are found in the end of *e* and *a* and *r;* on overcurves common to *a* and *c* and *h*. In other words, each letter was analyzed—but now to a child who has acquired the ability to make certain distinctions of which he was incapable in the lower grades.

All penmanship, properly so called, was remedial in the sense that any deviations from the models were analyzed, and a definite attempt was made to have the child look with critical eye to his work. Thus, problems of improving rate and quality were considered in the remedial work.

Four Elements in Motivation

The first important element both in instruction and in remedial teaching is the arousal or renewal of the interest of pupils in good penmanship. From the very outset of this experiment, provision was made for motivating the children toward good handwriting. Generally, this motivation included four elements: (1) emphasis on the value of legible and rapid writing; (2) means for making the handwriting program functional; (3) comparison of handwriting with penmanship scales; (4) class and individual progress charts.

1. *Emphasis on the value of legible and rapid writing.* As the child advances into the intermediate grades, writing becomes more and more an integral part of the day's work. He is beginning to see that the way he writes is a help or a hindrance in his daily tasks. He is beginning to appreciate the value of legibility and ease in writing, and these factors serve as motivating devices for him.

Throughout the course of this study, the importance of handwriting as a means to an end was pointed out to the children. An effort was made to remind the class of the importance of handwriting at times other than the formal penmanship period. For example, when the children were told to copy a selection from the board and study it for homework, the more rapid writers had a few minutes to spare in which they could begin learning the selection. The advantage of an early start was pointed out to them as being a direct result of good writing. If a problem was incorrect because it had been copied incorrectly, the class was reminded again that the blame could be laid to handwriting, and the occasion was used to stress the value of accurate writing.

The value of good penmanship was further impressed upon the children by special privileges accorded to good writers. These children were permitted to write invitations to other classes when special assemblies were held; they made name cards for the Christmas party; occasionally they were permitted to take the teacher's place in writing on the board. In other words, while the children were being taught the specific elements of writing —spacing, slant, alignment, etc.—they were also being educated in the worth of legible handwriting.

2. *Making the handwriting program functional.* Meaning is an integral part of the act of writing. According to Freeman, one of the foremost authorities in handwriting today, "The ultimate purpose of handwriting is to express and communicate meaning." [1] To this end, writing during this experimental study was considered not as an isolated element, but as a skill to be used in many of the classes. The children were required to apply the methods learned during the writing period to all written work. Thus, during the time that the children were doing arithmetic exercises, they were reminded to observe proper posture, or to make their figures carefully, to write on the line, etc. Such correlation served to make the handwriting course more functional. Specific writing activities were also planned to make the writing instruction more functional, such as the writing of cards, sending invitations, get well cards, illustrated compositions, etc.

3. *Comparison of handwriting with penmanship scales.* A motivating device very popular with many children was the opportunity they had to compare their writing periodically (about once in six weeks) with the West's American Handwriting Scale. After the first rating, each child knew his own quality rating and was encouraged through practice to better his score. The children graded their own work on subsequent writings, and though their ratings may not have been too accurate, the mere fact that they were making comparisons with these printed models served as a motivating device.

4. *Charts and graphs denoting progress.* Both individual and class charts showing the progress of the children served as motivating devices. Class charts recorded both rate and quality of the writing, and indicated the progress of the class as a whole after each six weeks' rating. Individual charts were even more interesting to the children. On these were plotted their rate and quality standings. To make the chart more meaningful, the norm for the fourth grade was also indicated.

Final Rating—Results of the Experiment

After the twenty-four-week experiment, I planned to make a comparison with the group's first writing rates with that which was administered at the

[1] Frank N. Freeman, *Teaching Handwriting* (Washington, D. C.: American Educational Research Association of the National Education Association, 1954), p. 9.

end of the experimental study. Only one scale—the American Handwriting Scale—was administered for the final rating. Though I was rather certain that there would be definite improvement, the amount of improvement in certain individuals was surprising as well as encouraging. The chief point of interest at this point was the amount of gain made possible through an organized system of remedial work. According to the table comparing the initial and final rate of the children, all but seven of the group increased the quality of their writing during the twenty-four-week period. The increase of each child ranged from 3 to 9 quality points. Although this increase in individual ratings does not appear great, it is well to remember that the majority of the class was almost up to the grade norm in quality on the first rating. Hence, a very great increase could not be expected. No one's quality rating decreased, despite the emphasis that had been placed on speed throughout the course of the work.

In rate, there was a wide range of increases evident between the first and the final ratings. No student's rate of speed remained exactly the same. All but three increased their rate of writing by from .5 to 24.5 letters per minute. Twenty-eight of the children increased their speed by more than 10 letters per minute, while five of these increased more than 20 letters per minute. The final test of three children was written at a lower rate of speed than the initial test. However, all three showed an increase of 6 points in quality, and two of the three were above the grade norm in rate despite the decrease of their first rating. As a whole, the class mean rose from 79.2 to 84.8 in quality, and from 50.3 to 60.6 letters per minute in speed.

In making these comparisons, it is well to remember one factor: although it would be satisfying to consider that all gains in speed and quality were due to the remedial work which was done, it is perhaps more correct to attribute at least part of the gain to such factors as maturation and growth. Practice in taking the test may also be considered a conditioning influence. Nevertheless, barring these two elements, it is apparent that significant gains in speed and quality were due, to a large extent, to the methods of instruction used throughout the course of this experiment.

40. Proposed Plan for the Development of Basic Habits * [for Left-handed Children]

LUELLA COLE

A. *Grades 1–3.* The teachers in the three earliest years are the ones who determine a child's fundamental habits of school work. It is essential that they should start the sinistral on the right path by emphasizing three vital points. For purposes of clarity and emphasis, the subsequent suggestions will be turned into specific directions to the teacher.

1. **Be sure** that left-handed children turn their paper so that it is at right angles to their arms. Until they reach a level of self-direction that permits them to be "different" from other children without being acutely uncomfortable, they will need constant checking on this point, because they imitate their right-handed neighbors and turn their sheets to the wrong position, even after the teacher has just reversed the angle for them. One has to explain to them, not once but many times, that the important thing is the angle of arm and paper, and that in this respect they are just like everyone else, once their paper is reversed. It makes a good demonstration for a teacher to gather her sinistrals together at her desk, grasp a pencil in each hand and show the similarity of the two positions. In any case, whether by sweet reasonableness or by an exercise of adult authority, the paper must be kept at a reversed angle, or all is lost. All that most children need is to be reminded, by a glance or a gesture, to adjust their papers; but it is the teacher's responsibility to give the necessary instructions and signals. If there is more than one sinistral in a room, they might well sit together in a group and imitate each other.

2. **Be sure** that left-handed children hold their pencils at least an inch from the point, and an inch and a half is better. The reason for this adjustment can best be explained to a small child as being the simplest way to keep his hand from blocking his vision. The teacher needs to check each sinistral often, until the grip on the pencil has become automatic.

3. **Be sure** to provide each sinistral with a card that contains an alphabet written either vertically or with a slant to the left. Whenever the children are writing anything, the left-handed pupils should prop their little cards

* Reprinted by permission from *Handwriting for Left-handed Children,* Grades 1–6, by Luella Cole, (c) 1955 Public School Publishing Company, Test Division of The Bobbs-Merrill Co., Inc., pp. 14–18.

up in front of them and copy from the cards, rather than from the board or from an alphabet printed for dextrals.

It is absolutely essential that the teachers in the beginning grades instill the two fundamental habits of placing the paper and gripping the pencil; they should also begin instruction in the proper slant. If the primary teachers of a school wish to make such an arrangement, it is suggested that the teachers of grade one be responsible for the correct position of the paper, those in grade two for the correct grip on the pencil, and those of grade three for introducing the correct slant. However, each teacher should be prepared, upon a favorable opportunity, to give additional training and explanations, provided these agree with those of other teachers in the school.

B. *Grades 4–6.* The first thing is to check each sinistral for the possession of the three fundamental habits he should already have.

1) Does he reverse his paper?
2) Does he have a correct grip on his pencil?
3) Does he write with a vertical or "backhand" slant?

Since some new pupils have entered the school from systems in which sinistrals receive no special instruction, and since some of those who have been through the work of the lower grades have not profited greatly by it, a teacher in these intermediate grades needs first to determine each child's progress to date and to train or retrain any who have not yet acquired the first three habits. Since the children are now older, they are more able to guide themselves and to understand explanations; they therefore learn faster than pupils in the primary grades. It is of little use to proceed with further instruction until each sinistral has been brought up to the level he should have reached at the beginning of grade four.

1. **Be sure** each sinistral uses a slant that is comfortable for him and is somewhere between perpendicular and a considerable slant to the left. This insistence on slant is primarily a preparation for the use of ink. A teacher should stand behind each sinistral in turn as he writes with a pencil and try to substitute mentally a pen for the pencil. Does his hand pass immediately over each lower loop before ink would have had time to dry? An extreme slant to either right or left will produce this result.

2. **Be sure,** when the pupils begin to write with ink, that all sinistrals use fountain pens with fairly blunt points, but *not* ball points.[1] If a child's

---

[1] In the writer's opinion, children should not use ball points, because the ink does not flow easily enough and the user has to push. Children's besetting sin in penmanship is their tendency to lean too hard on the pen. The ball point accentuates this tendency.

slant is within proper limits, if his pencil grip is an inch or more from the point, and if his paper is correctly placed, he needs only a proper pen to write as easily with ink as any other child. The pen point must be blunt enough to be pushed vertically up the paper without going through it. It would be best, if at all feasible, to have the school provide fountain pens with appropriate points for use by the sinistrals during school hours, until they can acquire similar pens of their own.

3. **Re-educate** any sinistrals who have already acquired bad habits. It is not too late, but the relearning will take time. You first explain to the child that you want to show him how to write easily, and you demonstrate to him the proper position, grip, and slant. You then reverse his paper (if necessary) and insist upon a grip an inch and a half from the pen point, so that his hand will be well below the line of writing. Give him some small cards, each with a single word written at two or three possible slants, and let him experiment with slants until he finds one that feels right to him. While the re-education is going on, he should be excused from written work; if he is not, he will go on practicing his maladjustments because, at the moment, his old habits produce faster results than his new ones. For some weeks the burden of writing should be kept commensurate with his acquisition of new skills, so that he will not be tempted to revert to his bad habits.

1. Shirley's writing before remedial work.
2. Shirley's writing six weeks later.
3. Robert's writing before remedial work.
4. Robert's writing six weeks later.

The results of re-education in six weeks' time, with ten to fifteen minutes of practice a day are shown in the preceding illustration. One child had recovered exactly the same speed she had had at the beginning, and the other had already increased his speed about ten per cent. The boy had had an extremely bad hook, while the girl wrote from a cramped position. At the end of the first two weeks they were able to write their spelling lessons with their new method, and by the end of the first month to do more written work than they had turned out before the re-education began, partly because they wrote so comfortably that they did not mind writing for longer periods.

During his period of re-education a child is breaking one set of habits and learning another. He is therefore under a temporary strain. The practice periods should be short (ten minutes at first) but frequent (at least one a day); and the pupil should do no other writing for at least two weeks and perhaps three, until he is so comfortable in his new adjustment that he uses it spontaneously.

Conclusion

Left-handed children should write just as easily and naturally as right-handed children. The reason they do not is to be found in the methods of instruction, which force them into distortions in order to meet the requirements. For successful teaching of sinistrals, teachers must first grasp firmly the idea that no feature of handwriting is of enough importance to be worth distorting even one child in order to produce it. There are only three criteria for judging handwriting: (1) Is the script legible? (2) Can it be produced fast enough to meet practical requirements? (3) Is the writer comfortable and relaxed? The approach just outlined will produce left-handed writers who write as rapidly, as comfortably, and as legibly as anyone else. There have already been millions of victims to the insistence upon a Spencerian slant. In the field of handwriting it is more than time to pursue to its conclusion the doctrine of natural development by teaching sinistrals how to write comfortably and naturally. See the two models on the next page. Either style is acceptable.

a b c d e f g h i j k l m n o p q r s t u v w x y z A B C D E F G H I J K L M N O P Q R S T U V W X Y Z This writing is vertical. Write this way if it is easy for you. 0 1 2 3 4 5 6 7 8 9

a b c d e f g h i j k l m n o p q r s t u v w x y z A B C D E F G H I J K L M N O P Q R S T U V W X Y Z This writing slants to the left. Write this way if it is easy for you. 0 1 2 3 4 5 6 7 8 9

The models on this page, somewhat enlarged and on stiff paper, may be purchased separately for desk use by pupils.

41. A Remedial and Developmental Program in Listening *

EDNA LUE FURNESS

> All languages are easier to learn by practice than from rules. That is to say, by hearing, re-reading, copying, imitating with hand and tongue, and doing all these as frequently as is possible.
> —JOHN AMOS COMENIUS, The Great Didactic

GLANCING into the history of mankind's cultural development, we realize that listening is an art of learning as old as the human species, antedating speaking and writing in both the phylogenesis of the race and the ontogenesis of the individual. Long before man expressed his thoughts in writing, ideogram, or alphabet, he communicated orally. So that for centuries listening was the principal procedure by which a man acquired an education and enlarged his experiences vicariously. The cultural traditions and moral precepts were handed down from "a speaking father to listening son, from a talking teacher to listening student." Some of our greatest teachers—Homer, Socrates, Christ, and Mohammed—used speech and listening more extensively and more effectively in their teaching than they used writing and reading, as George Murphy reminds us.

But with the introduction of the printing press nearly four centuries ago, listening slowly gave precedence to reading and the printed page. The art of

* From Edna Lue Furness, "A Remedial and Developmental Program in Listening," Elementary English (December, 1955), pp. 525–31. Reprinted by permission of the author and the National Council of Teachers of English.

listening and the culture of oral tradition were largely replaced by a concern for print and the practice of measuring literacy in terms of reading ability. Indeed, in the early days of printing it was generally believed that a populace able to read the printed page could develop into a more civilized cultural group. Hence, for more than three centuries, Anderson notes, the Western world became increasingly conscious of print, and the major responsibility of securing information was placed on the eye.

Importance of Listening

Now, in less than twenty-five years, those ubiquitous agencies, i.e., the radio, sound motion picture, and television, which epitomize the impact of the spoken word, which so largely mold the popular mind today, and which place an increasing premium on listening, have returned to the ear its former pre-eminence. These innovations, together with the ease with which we assemble today, have greatly increased the amount of listening.

An important study of the frequency of adult language activities further confirms the importance of the aural phase. Some years ago Paul T. Rankin conducted a survey to determine the relative proportion of time spent by adults in various types of communication. He found that the average adult spends 70 per cent of the total waking time in some form of communication. Of that time, 11 per cent is spent in writing activities, 15 per cent in reading activities, 32 per cent in speaking activities, and 42 per cent in listening activities. Obviously, the receptive forms, listening and reading, occur more frequently than the expressive forms, talking and writing. And as Rankin points out, the emphasis on the four language arts in the school, measured by the relative time allotment, is inversely proportional to the frequency of their use in life.

When we observe how much of our time is devoted to listening for the purpose of learning and social communication, we are properly astonished at the lack of any adequate consideration of this skill by education. We consciously teach children to read, to write, and to speak, but we do not devote an equal amount of time in teaching them to listen intelligently. However, education is awakening to the importance of listening comprehension, and for several years authorities in the language arts have insisted that teachers assume responsibility for the development of critical listening. When the National Council of Teachers of English created a National Commission on the English Curriculum, it appointed a Committee on Listening, charged with the responsibility of studying the problem of listening at all educational levels, from kindergarten through college.

Objectives in Listening

According to a statement by Althea Beery, who is one of the pioneers in this phase of communication, the objectives of listening are:

1. To show courtesy in disagreeing with the speaker.
2. To watch for transitional phrases.
3. To hold the thread of the discussion in mind.
4. To discount bias in a speaker.
5. To listen to content that does not affect the listener directly.
6. To take notes during a speech or report.
7. To write a brief summary of an oral report.
8. To show by remarks that the listener has been considering what has been said.
9. To reserve judgment in listening to different viewpoints in discussion.

Relationship between Listening and Reading

Speaking and listening, writing and reading, are reciprocal processes of communication. Why speak if no one is to listen? Why write if no one is to read? An analysis reveals that listening and reading are similar processes psychologically. Both are impressive skills, and involve the perceiving of ideas from others. On the other hand, listening and reading are not identical, and the two need to be developed consciously and separately. Each demands more than passive reception; and as W. Wilbur Hatfield notes, each has an active aspect. The listener must attend (give his mind) to what he is hearing. He must hear the words distinctly enough to recognize them, and the mere recognition involves some sort of recall of previous experience. The meaning of the words heard, like those of words read, depends entirely upon past association—the physical, social, and language contexts in which they have been met before.

Just as we have gradually become resigned to the realization that from 15 to 20 per cent of our students in secondary schools are retarded in reading and need a program of remedial and developmental reading, so we are beginning to realize that a considerable percentage of our students have not listened for comprehension and that an even larger percentage cannot listen discriminatively," so Mersand writes. The following analysis is an attempt to present in outline form an over-all picture of listening disabilities which may be present at any level, from elementary school through college. Noted in the chart are possible causes for specific listening deficiencies; noted too are teaching procedures which may be a boon to the teacher who is saying not only "listen" but also "listen and you will learn." An elaboration of this information as presented in outline form may be found in the writing of Harlen Adams, Harold Anderson, Althea Beery, James I. Brown, John Caffrey, Mildred Dawson, J. J. DeBoer, Clyde Dow, Edyth Hadley, W. W. Hatfield, J. N. Hook, S. B. Kegler, Elizabeth McDowell, Eva Moore, Ralph G. Nichols, and Miriam Wilt.

AN ANALYSIS OF LISTENING DISABILITIES, CAUSES, AND TEACHING PROCEDURES

Disabilities	*Possible Causes*	*Suggested Teaching Procedures*
Physiological Faulty auditory discrimination	Unable to hear sounds. Unable to distinguish between two sounds of differing frequencies (tones). Does not recognize similarities and differences in the sounds of words and word elements. Hears a certain range of pitches (vowels or consonants—low or high tones). Has such disabilities as: partial deafness, middle ear infection, partial blocking of eustachian tube, diseased or enlarged tonsils and adenoid tissue, nerve involvement, improper development of auditory nerve relative to acuity at the time speech is learned. Poor auditory memory. Social factors: mispronunciations heard in home, foreign accent, sectional speech, tension.	1. Give individual tests with a pure tone audiometer. 2. If an audiometer is not available, use a watch, or observe child's reactions to words spoken in a normal tone. 3. Urge delinquent listeners to improve over-all personal health, to regulate diet and bodily comfort. 4. Place child in front of room with better ear toward teacher. 5. Encourage child to watch faces of those talking. 6. Train ear to hear differences in vowel sounds as well as similarities of voiced and voiceless consonant sounds. 7. Have pupils listen to low tones and high tones on piano. 8. Sing two tones and ask pupils to tell whether tones are same or different open up high or low. 9. Have pupils speak their names and addresses on an RCA microphone record and then play back. 10. Have pupils listen to passing vehicles, trucks, automobiles, streetcars and airplanes, and identify sound with source. 11. Train pupil to recognize

AN ANALYSIS OF LISTENING DISABILITIES, CAUSES, AND TEACHING PROCEDURES *(Cont'd)*

Disabilities	Possible Causes	Suggested Teaching Procedures
Physiological (Cont'd)		likenesses and differences in speech sounds in complete sentences or thought groups. 12. Use songs and poems for dictating and repeating. 13. Pronounce words which have same beginning sound: *cake, come.*
Poor motor coordination	Unevenness of growth. Result of hereditary factors.	1. Engage in rhythmic activities and games.
Speech problems (faulty enunciation, articulation, pronunciation, speech defects)	Lowered power of auditory discrimination. Substitution of one sound for another: *dough* for *go.* Poor speech habits. Inflexibility of tongue. Enlargement of tongue. Foreign language spoken in home.	1. Teach correct placement of tongue and lips. 2. Train pupil to hear distinctions between *where* and *wear, witch* and *which.* 3. Hear rhyming words. 4. Identify rhyming similarities. 5. Tell original stories, tall stories, fables. 6. Give oral reports, choral readings, dramatizations, debates. 7. Repeat tongue twisters. 8. Have child listen to a playback of his speech. 9. Listen to speech of associates. 10. Teacher should use a conversational tone in oral reading. 11. Refer child to a clinic or speech correctionist.
Fatigue	Poor physical condition. Inadequate diet. Poor eating habits. Inadequate rest or poor habits of sleep. Too much close work. A too heavy schedule. Too many outside activities. Excessive homework or home duties.	1. Check child's general physical condition. 2. Confer with parents about physical diagnosis, in carrying out remedial treatments, in giving child adequate rest and relief from tensions or distracting outside duties and disturbances.

AN ANALYSIS OF LISTENING DISABILITIES, CAUSES, AND TEACHING PROCEDURES *(Cont'd)*

Disabilities	Possible Causes	Suggested Teaching Procedures
Physiological (Cont'd) Fatigue		3. Recognize signs of fatigue or boredom as a signal for closing the listening period.
Physical discomfort	Room is too warm, humid, or chilly. Noises distract. Speaker uses ungainly gestures, speaks in guttural or loud voice, looks over the heads of his audience.	1. Provide classroom conditions and environment conducive to easy and uninterrupted listening: proper temperature, comfortable seats, proper lights. 2. Adjust acoustic conditions of classrooms. 3. Avoid strong draft, a hot, sticky atmosphere, a cramped position, loud talking. 4. Avoid unseemly gestures, lack of poise, a grating or shrill voice. 5. Help pupil acquire a pleasing manner of presentation.
Psychological Lack of listening readiness	Poor health. Poor hearing. Muscular incoordination. Low mentality. Lack of general language facility. Deficiency in oral language. Mental and physical immaturity. Lack of experiences which provide a meaningful background and earlier learning activities. Lack of an adequate and pertinent listening vocabulary. Lack of good speaking and comprehension vocabularies. Lack of purpose for listening. Failure to see relationship between listening and his other activities. Lack of independence and desire to learn.	1. Increase child's background of experience. 2. Present concrete materials. 3. Give special oral directions. 4. Give pupils meaningful activity along with opportunity to execute specific directions. 5. Arouse pupil's interest, by relating subject matter to interests and past experiences. 6. Have child envision the actions, feel the emotions, admire characters portrayed in graphic oral reading. 7. Have younger children sense time sequence. 8. Have older children determine main points in

AN ANALYSIS OF LISTENING DISABILITIES, CAUSES, AND TEACHING PROCEDURES *(Cont'd)*

Disabilities	Possible Causes	Suggested Teaching Procedures
Psychological (Cont'd) Lack of listening readiness		a discourse, and make a mental outline of what they hear. 9. Provide speech activities as conversation, discussion, story telling, and dramatizations. 10. Have child listen in order to answer specific questions. 11. Teacher must have speech free from defect and should be sensitive to speech sounds.
Emotional maladjustments	Emotional imbalance caused by: auditory impairment, conductive deafness, self-consciousness, oversensitiveness, speech defect, nervous tensions and frustrations, inferiority feeling toward listening, resulting from child's inability to master listening. Lack of parental interest in child's school life. Tension in school or home. Confusion in classroom. Poor social adjustment to school or to associates. Too much competition. Change of schools and teachers during the year.	1. Discover hearing defect in early stages. 2. Discover as far as possible child's personal anxieties. 3. Confer with parents. 4. Teacher must be a good listener. 5. Teacher should listen attentively and courteously. 6. Avoid sarcasm, ridicule, and disparagement. 7. Give child a sense of security, self-reliance, self-respect, and importance. 8. Provide opportunities for child to establish a feeling of successful accomplishment in listening tasks. 9. Encourage competition with self. 10. Be generous with praise and recognition for child's efforts and progress.
Personality traits	Prejudice. Egocentricity. Narrow-mindedness. Improper attitude toward school, teachers, subjects, speaker, or cause. Antagonism. Resentment of unsympathetic or sarcastic teacher. Boredom. Lack of interest in subject. Nervousness.	1. Cultivate fairmindedness. 2. Provide interest-provoking background.

AN ANALYSIS OF LISTENING DISABILITIES, CAUSES, AND TEACHING PROCEDURES *(Cont'd)*

Disabilities	Possible Causes	Suggested Teaching Procedures
Psychological (Cont'd) Retarded mental development	Lack of meaning vocabulary. Inability to get meaning from verbal stimuli.	1. Develop child's speaking, writing, and hearing vocabularies in so far as is possible.
Pedagogical Lack of interest	Meager experience or none at all in listening experience. Unhappy experiences. Material for listening below child's interest level. Material too mature for child's interest level. Failure to recognize purpose for listening.	1. Use material related to child's personal experiences and concerns. 2. Furnish child with materials within his interest level. 3. Have children play listening games, the object of which is to remember proper sequence, to pronounce distinctly, and to listen accurately. 4. Provide audience situations such as plays, charades, programs.
Lack of purpose	Failure to distinguish between listening for pleasure and listening for information.	1. Listen for news. 2. Listen for directions which one expects to follow. 3. Have pupils listen for the answer to a definite question. 4. Have pupils listen to a question, with the intention to answer. 5. Listen to an argument in order to answer it. 6. Listen to form an opinion on a controversial issue.
Half listening	Poor listening habits. Listening without purpose. Expectation of entertainment.	1. Establish good listening habits in classes, clubs, pupil activities. 2. Be interested in materials that interest the child. 3. Have pupils understand purpose of listening activity. 4. Have children use more than a word or sentence in response to a question.

AN ANALYSIS OF LISTENING DISABILITIES, CAUSES, AND TEACHING PROCEDURES (*Cont'd*)

Disabilities	Possible Causes	Suggested Teaching Procedures
Pedagogical (Cont'd) Half listening		5. Evaluate quality of listening by observing changes in pupil behavior, habits, attitudes, and ideals.
Failure to listen discriminatively	Does not grasp organization of materials. Fails to grasp significant points. Unable to relate content with purpose. Fails to discriminate between fact and principle, ideal and example, evidence and argument, essential and less important.	1. Discuss personal experiences. 2. Listen to story read by teacher. 3. Have pupil read a story. 4. Have a panel discussion. 5. Provide opportunity for purposeful listening, definite note taking, discriminating judgment in selecting a theme topic, and in using illustrations.
Failure to listen critically	Has inadequate listening vocabulary. Listens to refute arguments with which he disagrees. Listens to support ideas he holds. Does not recognize significance of statements. Does not evaluate worth of statements. Does not discover relationship between ideas.	1. Reserve judgment. 2. Discount bias of speaker. 3. Ask for source of information. 4. Require evidence for statements made. 5. Watch for indefinite emotionalized terms. 6. Distinguish fact from principle, argument from evidence. 7. Detect false inferences and unsupported generalizations. 8. Distinguish relevant from irrelevant material. 9. Detect hidden purposes.

42. Learning to Listen—Listening to Learn in the Elementary School *

DORA V. SMITH

LISTENING can never be taught as a thing apart. Underlying all listening is the basic speech assumption that words should have consequences.

If so, the words should be heard by everyone in the room. They should be clear and interesting to the listeners, whose reactions should be observed by the speaker. Children should feel, as they talk before a group, signs of quickening life in their audience. If they do not, something is wrong with the speaking.

As broader units of instruction become more common in the schools, children learn more and more from each other. When each child is responsible for one aspect of a larger topic which the children are studying in common, listening becomes a major element in learning, a means of obtaining more information that any one child could possibly find for himself.

Teaching listening, then, becomes a matter of helping children analyze and use the skills appropriate to each kind of classroom activity.

What is a speaker in the classroom aiming to do, and what does his audience hope to learn from him? If he gives a good talk, he will tell his listeners early what his purpose is, and he will summarize his major points at the end. In between, he will enumerate points, present examples, or develop his ideas in a variety of interesting ways.

He will also furnish the group with certain clues to the organization of his talk. Perhaps he will use sequential words, such as *first, second, third*. Perhaps he will use such words as *next* or *before this* or *after this*.

If the children are good listeners, they will discover his purpose, watch for his summary, and follow his clues to the organization of his thought. In evaluation afterward, if there is confusion concerning what has been said, members of the group will ask themselves whether the speaker failed to make his clues clear.

Time out to test the results of both the speaking and the listening or to let the speaker himself test the results of his speaking will pay large dividends.

* From Dora V. Smith, "Learning to Listen—Listening to Learn in the Elementary School," *NEA Journal* (February, 1958), pp. 100–101. Reprinted by permission of the author and the *NEA Journal*.

Following the speaker's thought is the first essential. After that, examining it critically becomes necessary.

If the listening situation comes in "show and tell" periods, the sequence may be one of events rather than ideas. "Tell them in the order they happened," is the usual advice of the children.

Interest may also be aroused in picture-making words. The painter uses color and line to transfer his image to an audience. "How good are words for doing the same thing?" asks the teacher. Paints can show the swerve of a car narrowly averting a collision. Words can add the screech of the brakes.

Children learn to listen for words that make them see, hear, smell, feel, and taste.

An approach to learning through problem-solving requires another type of listening which has been much less carefully analyzed thus far—listening in order to participate in discussion and planning.

The process which children must use in their morning planning, in the development of various activities and units, and in their evaluations at the end of the day is one of selective and reflective listening. They seek to create, not to follow, a line of reasoning.

Each pupil must assume his share in contributing ideas. Each must speak so that everyone may hear, avoid duplicating suggestions, and help to select and evaluate ideas presented. "Is this suggestion a good one for our purpose?" a pupil asks himself. "Is it better than others that have been made? If so, how can I say so without hurting someone else's feelings?"

In addition, what is said must be fitted into a total plan being outlined on the chalkboard. "Where does this idea fit in?" asks the teacher. "What do we need to do next? What have we agreed on?"

In short, the process is totally different from that developed in listening to reports. Children must realize this. They must set up standards for dealing with this situation and develop means of checking their performance against the standards set.

Here again, teaching listening becomes a process of expediting learning in the carrying on of the normal activities of the school day. It is not something to be added to the curriculum.

A much less intricate but equally important process is listening for a series of details—to follow directions, for example. Teachers complain that much time is wasted in the classroom by needless repetition of instructions.

Perhaps teachers should be careful to announce that directions are to be given and then pause to see that everyone is ready to begin to listen. Instructions given slowly, in simple language, and in orderly sequence should be followed carefully by every child. The listener should be encouraged to ask questions and to jot down instructions in his notebook.

Listening for understanding is not the only important listening activity. Listening for enjoyment and appreciation also plays a significant part.

Constance McCullough, in her *Language Arts in the Elementary School,* emphasizes the importance in early speech and reading instruction of helping children listen for the sound for which each letter stands: "*s,* the tea-kettle sound," for example. "The teakettle sits on the stove, sss-sss-sss," and so on.

In *Helping Children Write,* Mauree Applegate tells how she took her children on a "sound tour," beginning with listening to the ticking of the clock: "It's like fairies softly marching," said one child. "Like the tapping of a woodpecker on a telegraph pole," said another. "Like the snipping of the barber's shears," said a third.

This process of matching sounds with words stimulates imaginative perception which enriches life for children and opens the way to creative expression.

Another experience in which boys and girls delight is listening to story-telling. There is a pleasure in hearing a story told that cannot be had from reading it to oneself—that is, if one is as good at listening as at reading.

The storyteller who would succeed must live with images in the story until they become his own. So also the children must learn to make the story come to life through exercising their own imagination.

Yielding to the cadence of the sentences helps children feel the mood of the story. When the adventures of the hero or heroine involve the emotions, boys and girls enter into the experience as if it were their own. Words which appeal to the senses stimulate such a reaction.

Children can learn to listen in order to visualize the scenes, to become acquainted with the characters, to follow clues to the outcome of the plot. A story well told keeps the listener guessing to the end, but once the end is reached, he should be able to go back over the plot, saying to himself, "I should have guessed *there,* and *there.*"

Ability to retell the story, keeping events and clues in sequence, is a sure test of good listening. Emelyn E. Gardner and Eloise Ramsey in *A Handbook of Children's Literature* say that another test of good listening is the silent response of the listener who "craves the pleasure of living intimately with his own reactions."

Successful choral speaking of verse depends on intelligent listening—critical listening to appropriate sound effects—the slow, lingering tones of "Long, Long Ago," the sudden jumps and twists of the squirrel in "Whisky,

Frisky," the bumps and jumps and thumps of "The Goblin." Such effects are helpfully discussed in Mardel Ogilvie's *Speech in the Elementary School.*

Winifred Ward in her *Playmaking with Children* reveals how listening to their own performance of a play not only improves the children's acting, but leads to an appreciation of drama in general. Character portrayal is at the heart of the discussions: "Did the actor live the character? Did the story tell smoothly? Was it always clear?" By means of questions like these, children grow in interpretive power and enjoyment of drama.

Listening to radio and television makes two kinds of demands on children—listening for sheer pleasure and listening for information. The two require different mind sets, which children must learn to differentiate. Much of the listening—though not all of it—which boys and girls do for enjoyment is done outside of school. Helping them search for better programs is the chief function of the teacher in this phase of learning to listen.

Ruth Harshaw's "Carnival of Books," available to local stations on tapes, is a program that may well be discussed in class. Older children may be urged to listen to it.

Most large communities have local stations which, with the cooperation of school or library or women's clubs, have storytelling hours. In these periods, the best of books, old and new, are presented. Nature programs are also common. Films such as Walt Disney's *Bear Country* and *Vanishing Prairie* are now edited for school use.

Acquainting children with such programs and giving time for discussion of them in school will do much to help pupils make use of the riches now available on radio and television.

Listening, then, is a means of learning in every activity of the school day. Careful analysis of the skills required in each situation pays dividends in both improved listening and improved learning.

43. Let's Take the Straightjacket Out of Writing *

ARTHUR S. GREEN

"G-d created man in his own image; therefore, man should create and bring forth like G-d."

—FROEBEL, *Education of Man*

IF SOMEONE were to ask, "What is one of the greatest needs in the language arts program in the schools of today?" the answer would undoubtedly be, "The creative, expressive approach."

One of the most satisfying of all human experiences for children and adults is to make something. Yet today when standardization and automation bring about conformity and uniformity, where mass education is barely realized through mass communication, the creative potentialities of our children are often crushed early in life. If education is to be taken in the assumption of its literal classic meaning, which is *educere*, "to draw out," then every child ought to have an opportunity to develop his creative capacities of human experience.

Educators of the not too distant past have failed to recognize one thing about writing; the development of creativity and expressiveness. Instead, the writers of textbooks for children have regimented writing directives by dismissing the perceptual powers of childhood. Theirs was characterized by step-by-step commands, questions whose answers were brief and objective, and the copying and writing of sentences from memory. Children were expected to write certain ideas, someone else's, alike as imposed by the autocratic teachers whose ideas in turn came from autocratic directives in teaching materials. Such a philosophy made no allowances for the development of thinking, much less expression, in children.

How different is the creative, expressive approach to writing! By its very nature it functions best in the present-day democratic environment of the schools of the land. Take any concept that describes democratic teaching or learning—"change," "individual differences," "self-realization," "interest," "revision"—and you have the essential common denominators of a sound creative, expressive writing program.

* From Arthur S. Green, "Let's Take the Straightjacket Out of Writing," *Education* (April, 1956), pp. 494–97. Reprinted by permission of the author and The Bobbs-Merrill Co., Inc., Indianapolis, Ind. Arthur S. Green is also the author of *Creative Arts and Crafts Activities* (Minneapolis, Minn.: T. S. Denison and Co., 1960).

"I heartily believe in this approach for my children," many teachers say, "but *how* do I do it?" The answer to the question of *how* to promote creative expressive writing that is as free from formularization and regimentation as possible, yet without being haphazard with "the chips falling as they may," is not easy. In fact there are as many different explanations as there are children times their compositions. What's more, there are no books to which teachers can turn to with, "Here are all the answers in one place!" primarily because the self-expression of children comes from children as individuals—not from books. What's more, many teachers attempt this approach with the proper attitude but are so overcome with problems that they often revert to the stereotyped methods of the past, closing the doors on creativity and expression forever.

Perplexing as the problem may be, teachers can save themselves from turning to lock-step directives by considering two vital aspects of any creative, expressive writing program. These are (1) the role of the teacher, and (2) the subject matter.

The Role of the Teacher

The role of the teacher is that of resource person. First, in initiating new topics for consideration the teacher guides class discussion by encouraging children to speak for themselves in voices that are clear, original, and unafraid, by throwing out leading questions, pitting one child's idea against another's, helping children organize their thoughts, and by recapitulating and summarizing. Through class discussion she opens new doors or, better yet, helps children open the doors of discovery for themselves. By discussion she motivates each child to shine in some way and gives all children an opportunity to learn from others by sharing ideas. Briefly stated, the discussion period preceding the writing experience should be a conversation, an interchange of ideas among students by discussion itself and other interaction.

In order to promote responsive participation in discussions on the part of the child, the authoritarian kind of leadership which stifles democratic activity must be abandoned for an atmosphere where permissiveness and encouragement are the foremost common denominators. Otherwise the teacher's role is still little more than that of taskmaster; the writing that follows is still little more than penmanship, the creativity is forced imitation, and any expressive or creative writing that follows would be in spite of the teacher.

After the initial discussion which usually ends with the writing of a list

of ideas or suggestions or a general outline on the board or an oral sum-
marization, the teacher continues as a resource person throughout the
writing period. When a child asks questions like "How do you spell 'ham-
mock'?" or "In what part of the atlas will I find the subject of Eskimo?,"
answers such as "Use your dictionary" or "Don't you know that yet?" are
not unlike the traditional army type dismissal. Rather than close the doors
of discovery and self-inquiry the resourceful teacher might spell out the
first two or three letters of the word for the child, referring his first question
to the guide in the use of the dictionary, his second to the use of the atlas
or encyclopedia index in the library.

The resourcefulness of the teacher is not limited to discussion leadership
and the finding and spelling of words, however. The teacher should acquaint
the child with as many perceptual aids to learning as possible in order to
give the child more "meat" and more choices about which to write. If a
child needs help in finding information about a chosen career of engineering,
for example, referral to the "E" volume in the encyclopedia set on the shelf
is not enough. The child should be referred to the pamphlet section in the
school or community library. The teacher might even suggest that he send
a letter to the engineering department of a university, requesting a brochure.

The Subject Matter

The subject matter of creative expressive writing is not isolated. There is
an infinite variety of topics which children can choose from that take their
cues from a great diversity of school and out-of-school sources. They may
follow from a textbook or workbook, language arts and otherwise. They
may arise from a class project or unit on any subject. They may be the outcome of expression of student interests or experiences. They may integrate
with the broad fields or subjects of learning such as language arts, social
sciences, practical and fine arts, science and mathematics, and health,
recreation, and physical education. Finally, children are moved by the spirit
of reading stimulating literature itself. A library book, for example, may
encourage a child to write a reflective paper review of his impressions about
the book. Similarly, a poem may inspire a child to describe his personal
reactions to it. Better yet, he may write original poetry about the subject
elicited in the poem he read.

Though the above suggestions fall into the pattern of the more formal
philosophies of individual school systems and the methodologies accompanying them, I have found that regardless of the method or philosophy of
education, the following organization of topics children most readily write

about results when allowing as great a freedom of choice on the part of the child as possible:

1. *Let's Be Ourselves.*

   This area might well be entitled "Me, Myself, and I." It is centered about those personal experiences of children in which they are most interested themselves. Here they write more directly about all their perceptual experiences in the world, their pets, their likes and dislikes, their aspirations, events in their lives, and what certain things mean to them. Sample titles are "My Summer Vacation," "What I Like about My Community," or "I Express My Chosen Career."

2. *Use Your Imagination.*

   Here the child expresses his fantasies in a world of make-believe by writing about such topics as "Tall Tales," or "The World of the Future."

3. *On Being Artistic.*

   Here children integrate their writing with creative, expressive art by writing about their drawings, or drawing about their writings, with such topics as "What This Picture Means to Me," or "Imaginary Pictures to Imaginary Stories."

4. *What Did I Learn?*

   Based on integration with subject matter, children enjoy writing about such topics as "Safety First," or "My Biography of ———."

5. *Forms of Writing.*

   Here children explore and experience forms of writing other than the essay or story type. These include dialogues, letters, skits, diaries, reporting, poetry, and television and radio scripts.

Regardless of what the approach to varying topics, the object should be always to make available to each child a maximum of choices and material to suggest to him the best possible creative, expressive writing.

Conclusion

The resourcefulness of the teacher and the subject matter of creative, expressive writing go hand in hand. Together they help the child succeed in making the most of the world he perceives through his writing experience.

44. Democratic Processes Foster Creativity *

LUCILE LINDBERG

FROM A beautifully designed stage, the puppets dramatically spoke their lines. The effect was bizarre, unusual, wonderful. Never had the audience seen anything like it. As the curtains closed, people clapped enthusiastically. The puppeteer took his bows. Then he stepped back into place and once more picked up his dolls. *He* had created them and *he* could manipulate them in any way he wished. The glory of a creative performance was all his to be shared with a responsive audience.

Many teachers engage in this same kind of manipulation in their classrooms. They prepare settings with clever games, intriguing seat work, attractive bulletin boards, unusual classroom presentations. Then they create their play. Boys and girls are moved through a series of carefully organized units or projects. The year is completed and there are those who shout "Bravo! How do these teachers do it? Where do they get all their marvellous ideas?"

However, there are others who sense a superficiality. Yes, these have been striking performances and, if the characters had been puppets, applause could be given unstintingly. But they were not puppets; they were living, breathing, human beings, and no matter how artistically a teacher maneuvers, so long as it is *his* purposing, *his* planning, *his* experimenting, children can achieve no more than a pseudo creativeness.

Clever Teaching

From time to time we hear teachers say, "I'm not creative. Other teachers think of clever things to do and I have only humdrum ideas. I am not artistic. I'd like to do creative teaching, but I fear for me this is impossible."

Are they confusing creative teaching and clever teaching? Creative teaching is not something which can be switched on and off in rapid succession. It is not a performance. It does not consist of taking human beings and moving them like puppets to secure an artistic effect. It is not a phenomenon to

* From Lucile Lindberg, "Democratic Processes Foster Creativity," *Education* (October, 1958), pp. 76–83. Reprinted by permission of the author and The Bobbs-Merrill Co., Inc., Indianapolis, Ind. Dr. Lindberg writes from her own experiences in a democratic classroom with children, her doctoral study of several such classrooms, and her present experiences in teaching adults at Queens College, Flushing, New York.

be achieved only by those teachers who have been especially trained in music, art, and drama.

Creative Teaching

We are *all* capable of creative teaching for we are *all* creative persons. The human organism is creative in every respect. There are many illustrations of this in the way in which our bodies are capable of adapting themselves to a variety of conditions. Our diets vary from day to day, yet the body can digest this food and convert it into fluids which are easily absorbed. Each cell is able to select from a stream of food those elements which are especially needed for its functioning. This adaptability is possible because of creative processes which are in operation in our bodies. To the extent that these processes are effective, we are able to maintain a state of vigorous physical health.

In our social living, too, creativity in any group is possible as appropriate processes develop. In this country we are committed to democratic processes as being the ones which most effectively foster creativity. To the extent that we live democracy in our classrooms, and to that extent only, can we help children release their energies and develop their values. If we would be creative teachers, helping boys and girls learn to use democratic processes should be our chief concern.

As boys and girls develop an awareness of the nature of the world about them and of their own place in it, they stretch out to express themselves. They have much to say and they say it through many media—music, painting, drama, poetry, behavior. They say it through every part of their living. Democracy stimulates an unfolding of each individual.

All of us, at some time, have felt the thrill of creative teaching. It may have been fleeting, but even a touch of it is enough to stimulate us to desire more. We haven't always known what it was or what made possible the experiences that meant so much to us, but we have responded to the spirit of creativity.

All of us are creative persons and have the potential for developing into creative teachers, but this will not happen by magic. It takes hard work on our part—hard work mixed with feelings of both exultation and depression. It takes a democratic insight into the importance and value of each individual person.

Some of us will start with a tiny part of our program. Others will wade into many parts at once. As we become more aware of democratic processes we will begin to note both our own creative behavior and that of the children. What can we do to get these processes operating with our children? What are these democratic processes which can give such an impetus to creative teaching?

Interest Areas

Democratic processes are means through which a group is able to make intelligent decisions concerning the solutions to its own problems—decisions which give each individual fullest opportunity to grow and develop. There are many things we can do to start these processes operating in our classrooms.

1. We can help boys and girls *discover* the many *materials available* and *learn to use them.* Books are an important resource. In the past five years publishers have made available hundreds, yes, thousands, of fine books for children. What a shame, at a time of such abundance, to have thirty books all alike in a classroom. Each child then has an opportunity to read only one book, whereas when we have thirty different books each child has before him thirty titles from which he can select several.

It is true that there are areas of interest where we still are not able to secure as many books as we need, but teachers are becoming increasingly resourceful in filling in these gaps. One evening, after spending two hours in the library doing careful research, one third grade teacher carefully printed in neat manuscript four small books which she took to school with her the next morning. Each of them contained some information which at least one child in her class had been trying to find. They were entitled: *The Assistant Superintendent, What He Does; Indians in Brooklyn; Nylon—Its Origins; Planting Tulip Bulbs.* The pages had been sewed neatly into cardboard covers. There were no pictures, but since she had left spaces for them, she knew that the children would soon draw or paint appropriate illustrations.

Eleven children had brought in newspaper clippings that same morning. Each was given a piece of folded paper so that his clipping could be mounted and an appropriate title printed on the outside. Three children brought in books which had been given to them. Each one told in a few words what kind of a story it was. Then arrangements were made to put them temporarily into the classroom library so that other children could read them. Two children had brought bright-colored pictures for the picture file. After mounting these pictures, each child went to the primer typewriter and typed labels.

What a richness of reading material was brought into this classroom in one day! And this was not an unusual day! The children were becoming acquainted with many materials as day after day they were continually introduced to a wide assortment of new ones.

The materials were read because the teacher made certain that each day the children had plenty of time for reading anything they wished. She had arranged seven low dividers in a zig-zag fashion over by the windows in such a way that nooks were provided, so that the children could sit and read, feeling that needed privacy apart from others, yet of them, while they were in full view of the teacher.

This classroom was filled with books, but there was a wealth of other materials as well. There were yards and yards of parachute cloth. It was badly damaged, but served very well as both boys and girls cut and sometimes sewed to make costumes for a series of quick dramatizations. In the course of one day, butterfly wings, a king's cape, a bride's veil, a rich lady's dress were fashioned from it. The custodian had brought turkey feathers back from the country and several Indian headbands were soon in evidence.

Two huge corrugated boxes contained wood scraps. They hadn't been easy to secure, but teacher and children hunted persistently and finally found the builder of a large apartment house who was willing to let them have the pieces. Two paper bags of sawdust from the same source were providing a new experience in modeling.

An electric plate was pulled out of the cupboard when it was found that the supply of finger paint was low. From the files came a well-fingered recipe and a new supply was soon available.

Both teacher and children were growing in the creative use of materials. When children receive adequate opportunity each material introduced into a classroom provides opportunity for experimentation, and each bit of experimentation sends the children out into the community for more materials. They begin to see the world about them as a storehouse of unlimited supplies. They are not hemmed in by four walls. They develop confidence in what can be accomplished, a broad vision, and resulting flexibility in ideas.

2. We can help boys and girls *discover and appreciate* the many exciting *people* around them. In one fifth grade, they found that they had important resource-people connected with their own class group for a study of Europe. Among them, they could claim parents or grandparents from England, France, Greece, Italy, Poland, Portugal, and Russia. Three grandmothers came at their request. Each of them, with a large map set up beside her, told of the things she remembered. Other parents and grandparents

worked and could not come to school, but at home they told the children stories of the countries of their birth. The teacher helped each child type his story and they were flashed on a screen for the whole class to read and enjoy together.

Jenny's father, who was an architect, came and demonstrated the principles involved in making a roof stay in place. He also brought samples of new building materials and a magazine which showed how these materials are used. When the fire inspector came he took the children on a tour of the building to show them the kinds of infractions for which he was looking.

Quite by accident, the boys and girls discovered that the reading specialist was a baseball enthusiast who remembered the days when all the big players were just getting started.

Roy's father played in a dance band, and he kept Roy instructed in the latest steps. Roy, in turn, passed this information along to the class.

Harriet's mother belonged to the League of Women Voters, and Harriet made all the League material on world trade available. She was also able to keep the class informed as to when there would be good television programs on this topic.

As children's concepts of people expand they have more to say and more ways of saying it. Those about them have something important to offer and so do they. Children develop confidence in themselves. They do not hesitate to express feelings and ideas both verbally and in writing. As they become increasingly aware of the importance they have as persons they reach out for a wider variety of media. All their living becomes more creative. Classroom organization reflects this, and teachers find themselves growing and developing with the children.

3. We can help boys and girls *develop a desire to explore*. Children need to feel free to explore ideas as well as materials. They must feel free to express themselves naturally and spontaneously. Sometimes children are hesitant to voice their questions because they are made to feel that what they ask does not have enough significance. A teacher doesn't have to say this in words. A tone, a glance, an overemphasis on the value of one child's contributions are all that is needed to put a damper on further questions from the whole group. If children are made to feel that they should already know something, they hesitate to ask for help or to wonder aloud.

If we want to give children a real opportunity to explore they must feel that questions can be of many kinds. If, as in some classrooms, the only questions which are acceptable are those concerning subject matter and textbooks, not many questions are likely to occur.

There are some questions to which answers cannot be given, but if children are wondering they need to ask these. Some children's questions are embarrassing to adults, but if we expect to get a genuine searching on the part of children, they must be encouraged to ask whatever they need to ask.

Children's questions will take us far beyond the four walls of the classroom. The four-year-olds left their sandbox and went across the cement yard to look at a puddle one of them had spotted. When they arrived they couldn't find the water. They went back and again they saw it gleaming across the play yard. They scampered over once again, and again it was gone.

Finally, tired out and discouraged, John said, "It's the sun. The sun plays tricks on us."

"We call it a mirage," said the teacher. "Why don't we all watch to see if we find them anywhere else?"

In one kindergarten room, the upper part of the windows were of green glass. Joe looked across the room. "The blocks are green," he said. Then he added, grinning from ear to ear, "They aren't really green; it's the light. It's colored light because the window is green. If I stood there would I be green too?"

"Why don't you find out?" the teacher asked him.

Not only do we encourage them to ask questions, but we encourage them to seek answers to their questions, helping them feel resourceful in doing so.

Some sixth grade boys wanted to make a missile. The teacher knew nothing about missiles. She really had no idea whether such a thing was possible or not. But she respected this desire on their part. They might never make a missile, but they could at least explore. They could find out what was involved and if they didn't do it they would know why not.

In a third grade the children asked, "What makes mountains?"

"What could make them?" their teacher responded.

They compiled a long list of possibilities and for days they contrived experiments to check their hunches.

In an atmosphere where it is safe to explore, wondering increases and children think deep, deep thoughts and express ideas of rare vision and insight. They become increasingly aware of their own uniqueness as individuals and learn to cherish their creative quickening.

4. We can help boys and girls *develop skill in making* intelligent *decisions*. Decision-making is central to all democratic processes. As children develop a sense of achievement in ability to make decisions they develop confidence in forging ahead with their own ideas. They come to sense that they have the power to create new ideas and that the ideas are worth sharing with others.

Children learn to make decisions by dealing with those choices which affect their own day-by-day living. They can play an important part in determining what they will study and what they will undertake in their own classrooms.

These decisions cannot be arrived at quickly by asking simple teacher-formulated questions. The teacher must develop skill in helping boys and girls become aware of their interests and needs. He must have skill in helping them discriminate as to which of these will be most worth their time. Since they cannot work on all their interests, decisions must be made as to what are their purposes, what is valuable, and where to focus attention.

We can help them work out criteria for deciding. If we permit them to decide according to the whim of a moment they can chain themselves to tasks which they do not really want to be doing and which lack values. On the other hand, if we tell them exactly what to do they are tied to our decisions and cannot develop the skills which they need.

By raising questions a teacher can help children consider what will be involved with each venture they will undertake and whether or not this is the kind of thing they need to do. A group of seven-year-olds was deciding what story would be dramatized for its Mother's Day program. One story was highly dramatic and the children were enthusiastic about it.

"Let's think through very carefully how we would work on this before we make our decision," the teacher said. "What would we do first?"

They began to list on the board, step by step, what they would do. Finally they came to selecting the characters.

"But there are only four characters," someone said.

"Let's not do that story," several immediately suggested. "We want more characters than that."

"Let's not, let's not," the rest of the children cried.

"We don't need to use that story. There are many others from which to choose," the teacher said, "but should we think again about what is involved before we suddenly decide?"

So the children were encouraged to think things through carefully, every step of the way according to their own abilities and in their own way. In the end they arrived at a plan which hadn't occurred to either teacher or children in the beginning, but which gave every child an opportunity to participate and involved every child in decision-making.

By helping children develop questioning attitudes and techniques in decision-making the teacher was helping them recognize the potentials they had. As groups and individuals become aware of this power they are able to use it creatively. Then activities undertaken in the classroom become increasingly creative—unique to that group. The teacher doesn't need to search for clever ideas. It becomes, instead, a matter of helping children decide which idea is of true value.

5. We can help boys and girls *learn to plan* effectively. Further power is developed when children find out that not only are they growing in decision-making, but they have within their beings, both as individuals and as group members, the capacity to plan. There is nothing ordinary about what they do because every step of the way they create their own procedures.

One sixth grade was having difficulty with fractions. They examined their plans for the next week and decided where they could best place practice periods and what could be deleted from present plans. Then they tackled the problem of how they would work on the fractions. Could they help each other? How?

At the end of their planning, Ruth said, "I felt so helpless this morning. Now I feel sure I'll be able to improve my work in fractions."

The principal announced to one second grade that the painters would be coming next week and that the class would be meeting in the lunchroom for several days. They set about to plan how they would manage. What should they take with them? How would their supplies be stored in the lunchroom? Would they need to change plans so as to carry on projects more appropriate to that room? Other classes began coming to the lunchroom at 11:30. What would they do at that time? And so it went, with question after question. Then came the planning for what they would need to do to get their room ready for the painters. How would they store and protest their things?

When a class has many things to do they need to plan their organizations carefully. They learn to divide into smaller groups so that each task can be accomplished efficiently.

Said Sara one morning: "We have more to do than we can do, but if we plan carefully we'll get it done. Committees are wonderful. Everyone works so hard and it all fits in together."

Yes. Children feel power and freedom when they are learning to plan. Their energies are released to move in many areas and yet they move with direction and purpose. At first creative effort may be slow but, as children feel its thrill, creativity bursts into being in the whole scene.

6. We can help boys and girls *develop skill in evaluating* their *own efforts*. When children have carefully thought through their purposes, they are able to assess their success in attaining these goals. Here, too, a teacher is needed to help them recognize the values they are using as they decide whether or not a venture has worth.

"Wonderful," the fifth graders said about their trip to the waterfront. "What was so wonderful about it?" the teacher wanted to know. With great interest the group began to tell her. She listed on the board the values they had found.

"If you were going to place them in order of importance which would you put first?" she asked them.

This brought forth a lively discussion and ended with a careful weighing of values. They decided that they wouldn't all place the items in the same order, but that some did rank above others.

In a nursery school, a three-year-old told his teacher: "I like having the frogs here."

"I'm glad," she said. "What's so special about having the frogs in this big dishpan?"

The talk that followed was simple, but even at age 3 the child was able to get a clearer idea of what makes a good learning experience.

A first grade was making plans to plant a garden. A parent across the street had plowed several long furrows across a vacant lot for them. They knew just what they would plant. They had sketched out the area for each kind of seed. Now, how were they going to manage so that all of them could help?

The teacher asked if they had learned anything from their trip to the library which would help here. They found many applications. Then they thought about how they took turns going to the cloakroom. They were able to evaluate past experience in order to clarify plans for the present.

When boys and girls begin to see clearly what they are doing and to analyze how they have done it, their potential for a higher quality of activities increases. They become more creative in what they say and do. The discipline which arises from self-analysis gives children a feeling of freedom through understanding. It lays a strong groundwork for creative living.

7. We can help boys and girls *develop an awareness of* the *values derived from using democratic processes.*

We are concerned that children not only use democratic processes, but that they become aware of the part these processes are playing in making their living satisfying: that they not only enjoy life, but that they retain this joy and that they know its origin. We want them to understand that past experiences cannot be recreated, but that continually more valuable experiences can be developed. Because they understand democratic processes they are able to create many kinds of experiences and life may always have meaning.

If children are aware of the part these processes have played in making possible the way of life they value, they may in the future be less apt to allow those who use dictatorial processes to change their way of working and living, and more apt to recognize the danger of losing an atmosphere wherein it is possible to develop ideas.

We are teaching creatively when we have democratic processes in operation and children are developing an awareness of these processes. We are teaching creatively when boys and girls are becoming increasingly aware of what is happening within them and about them. We are teaching creatively when the children feel a power over the tools of learning and power to discipline themselves in their use.

As children become aware of the potential they have, they are able to use it. When they realize that deep within themselves they have a never-ending source of energy and ideas they begin to draw upon it more and more.

When we work out interesting devices to "motivate" them to be creative we fetter children and hold them back. Creativeness in teaching consists of helping develop the processes which make inner self-motivation grow. The skill of creative teaching is the ability to help others recognize and develop that creativity which they, as human beings, already possess.

45. Creative Living in the Kindergarten *

DOROTHY PETERSON

K INDERGARTEN is especially significant, for the child's whole philosophy of life has its roots in these formative years of his existence. Since a five-year-old is utterly uninhibited, his natural reactions are a constant joy to observe. At this time, he acquires the ability to accept correction constructively and to use it happily as a step toward a well-integrated adult life.

Children of this age are enthusiastic for every type of work. What better policy, then, than for the kindergarten teacher to follow a program so constructed that the lives and minds of the children will be directed into activities that lead to their growth and articulate expression?

* From Dorothy Peterson, "Creative Living in the Kindergarten," *Education* (October, 1959), pp. 109–11. Reprinted by permission of the author and The Bobbs-Merrill Co., Indianapolis, Ind.

A Post Office Project

In our school, we recently completed a post office unit of study. A father of one of our kindergartners acted as our guide. Upon leaving the building, the class noted the Michigan state flag and the United States flag flying over the new building. Twenty-eight five-year-olds gathered beneath the flag pole at a suggestion from one of the group, and gave the pledge to the flag as passers-by stood at serious attention.

On another occasion, our school postman visited us in his uniform and carried his brown leather bag. All gathered around to touch the arm insignia on his uniform, the cap badge, and the brown leather bag.

After describing his work, the postman asked if anyone had a question. One little girl volunteered, "I don't know any questions, but I just love you!" The post office booklet the class later made revealed on paper their impressions and thoughts from the experience.

Healthy Mental Attitude Fostered

A healthy mental attitude is as important as a healthy body. To watch the children in their make-believe world and to listen to their conversation in the playhouse, bring continuing delight. Personality is developed through these simple spontaneous dramatizations.

A mother called to her little girl, "Dear, will you go to the orchard and get Mother some apples? I want to make an apple pie." When the daughter returned with the apples, Mother said, "Oh! You got beautiful ones! Now run out and play while I bake!"

In songs and rhythms the children express themselves with grace and poise. A tambourine or castanet dance can transform a shy, plain little girl into an unself-conscious, flashing Spanish dancer, as the rhythm of the music sends her twirling about the room. Self-consciousness and timidity are then replaced by satisfaction and joy of accomplishment.

Gym a Real Source of Pleasure

Days on which we are scheduled to use the gymnasium for various physical activities are anticipated with great enthusiasm. One child recently sighed sadly, "This is a Nothing Day!"

"What do you mean?"

"No gym, no movies, no nothing."

A challenge such as that stirs one anew to a different "Something Day." That something, at present, is Mary Ann Moreno's mother, who comes twice each week to teach our group some Spanish. We started with *Buenas dias, adios, gracias, niño, niña,* and of course that means doing the Mexican Hat Dance with more zest than ever.

Gym-time brings creative activities galore. Last week a girl asked, "Can't we be fish and go out for a swim?" Lying on stomachs, propelled by head and feet the fish wiggled across the floor. It indeed was easy to see a school of minnows flashing by.

Another day, eight boys had arms around each other in a football huddle. I wondered what would come from the plans they were discussing. When the music started, the activity was good and worthy of praise.

Dramatization Favored

Early habits of school life are established now. A child is taught respect and reverence for the school and its program. Working in groups to build impressive structures is sure to bring dramatic play into action.

Several girls constructed a large castle, beside which was a trap to catch the wicked witch; but to offset that unhappy prospect a pleasant courtyard offered opportunities for the princesses to laugh and play. That day was special; the princesses had graham crackers and milk in their courtyard.

And then came a day when the boys built a castle and made a counting house in which the king could count his money. The school librarian, Miss Pomeroy, provided pennies from book fines, so that, if this particular story is ever repeated, real money can be used.

Enthusiasm Always Uppermost

All the holidays are of tremendous importance. The teacher readily uses the children's enthusiasm to help heighten oral expression. It is then that self-expression and originality abound.

Stories read and reread, told and retold, are never boring. After listening to the story of Rumpelstiltskin, how he got several pieces of jewelry for his work, and finally his dramatic departure, one of the smallest called out, "Did the queen ever get her jewelry back?"

The much loved story of Peter Rabbit inspired Susan to make a clay model of Mr. MacGregor, and one of Peter sitting in his high chair, his mouth opened wide to take the dose of camomile tea.

Some of the expressions are cause for a hidden smile, such as "Are we going to do any scissoring today?" One little girl confided she had to leave school in a hurry to get to church for her "kitty-chasm" class.

Children are kept alert and interested by thinking of new things to do, by sharing, planning, and manipulating. Margie, who loves to paint, recently brought forth two lovely houses. "This one," she pointed out proudly, "is named 'Holiday House,' and this one is 'Fancy House.' "

Appreciation Stressed

The gift of appreciation for the beauties of nature is evidenced at this early age. Martha, a child thus endowed, recently described a scene she witnessed as she stood on the stair landing in pajamas and housecoat. The sky, all aglow with brilliant colors on a winter morning, filled her with wonder and awe. She brought to the class the vivid description of a thrilling experience.

The park near the school is observed closely for the many changes that result from a variety of nature's moods. After a newly fallen snow we can trace the tiny tracks of the squirrel and follow him to his hiding place.

These experiences help the five-year-olds to become more articulate and to encourage talk that makes their language development effective. New words, as *compass, magnifying,* and *magnetic* are added to their vocabularies.

A train trip the class enjoyed brought imaginative perceptions that were enlarged upon by the moment, resulting in a variety of stories that ranged from seeing monkeys in the trees to a cowboy on a horse. These stories poured forth so freely and with so little effort that the train-ride experience proved a very valuable one for fluency of speech. Thus communion grows.

Need for Understanding

A personal triumph comes to the teacher when a shy or less fortunate child, no longer withdrawn, takes his place in the group, speaking with ease and confidence. Then it is the teacher smiles gratefully. The divine help she had sought to guide this very young child has been given to her!

Truly she is filled with the reverence that inspires her daily prayer: "God, be in my heart and help me to understand."

46. *Classroom Climate Can Promote Creativeness* *

L. THOMAS HOPKINS

For the past fifty years peoples all over the world have become increasingly aware of their creative origin and self-development. This new insight has to some degree affected all cultures; the schools to a greater extent than other institutions. It has been more favorably received and encouraged by educators in this country than abroad. Yet there are strong differences of opinion as to its validity, meaning, and use. The questions raised are: Do all persons or only a few create? Should all persons or only a few be allowed to create? In what areas should this permissiveness be granted? What will be the effect upon the culture if more persons do create?

All Persons Are Creative

Fortunately, some of these questions can be eliminated upon the evidence. All persons do create; all persons will create whether or not those who control the culture accept it. Thus the attitude of the educators should be:

1. To recognize that all persons create at all times whether they be teachers or pupils, educators or laymen.
2. To furnish the classroom climate in which such creativeness can be released, accepted, respected, and guided.
3. To help each person, child or adult, understand his own creative process and accept the results of his behavior upon himself and others.

These three aspects of the education problem will now be considered.

1. *Why are all persons creative at all times?*

Most dictionaries define the word *create* as "to bring into being." If this be true, every baby at birth has created himself for he has brought himself into being from the fertilized egg. He has accomplished this in interaction with a sympathetic external environment which has released, accepted, and

* From L. Thomas Hopkins, "Classroom Climate Can Promote Creativeness," *Educational Leadership* (February, 1956), pp. 279–82. Reprinted by permission of the author and *Educational Leadership*.

respected his ability to do so. He has guided his growth by the internal inter-action of his genes to fulfill the promise of his conception. At birth he knows, on the autonomic or visceral level, the process of his own growth. The energy or life is in him. It is outgoing, intaking, converting, accepting, and eliminating. It is a mutual cooperative relationship between him and his external world. His great purpose after birth is so to live in his new world as to raise his process to the level of conceptual action, since this is necessary for his highest self-maturity. And every baby at birth ap-parently wishes to achieve this for it is his life-fulfillment. He struggles con-tinuously against oppressing external conditions to realize it.

Some authorities state that to create means to evolve new thoughts or meanings or values from one's own experience thus remaking it into a more functional or useful organization. No person ever sums his experiences. Rather, he develops among them personal relationships called meanings or value judgments around which he unites what he accepts to meet his needs while he rejects what he believes to be of little present or future use. These personal meanings and values constitute who he is to himself and are his selectors of his external behavior toward others. As he remakes his experi-ences through these evolving meanings he transcends his old or existing self to higher behavior levels. To do this he must find in the existing external culture the same cooperative support for his creative process as he received in his intra-uterine life. This support is difficult for him to find. The adults who control the culture allow him "to bring himself into being" and to con-tinue after birth to evolve his own physical structure by his normal process. But they try to deny him his birthright to create himself through his own evolving meanings within his own experiences. They want him to accept their controls, their patterns of experience, their directions of behavior. They believe that he is born with two processes of growth—one for his physical development, and another called "learning" through which to acquire those aspects of his existing external environment that they select for him. Such a dualism denies him the integrative unity which he must preserve. While adults cannot prevent him from using his normal biological process in homes and schools, they set an environment lacking the sym-pathy, encouragement, and leadership which he must have to conceptualize his process on the higher levels of meaning necessary for his maturity. Thus he creates himself out of vague, unclarified meanings and values with un-satisfactory results to himself and others. He never really understands who he is or why others treat him as they do. Thus he is forced by an unsym-pathetic environment to arrest his development at some appropriate level of self-preservation.

2. *How can classroom environment help the child create himself?*

There are many necessary things which constitute a classroom environment. Some are visible, such as physical equipment, books and supplies, children and teacher. Many are invisible. They are inside each person and are not open to inspection or public examination. Yet these internal responses to the external world are the stuff out of which the self is made. Most classrooms are organized on the dual or traditional theory of learning, which blocks or suppresses these internal meanings. The outside pressure is for the child to take in and pass back in form acceptable to the teacher the materials she has taught. His internal responses to these demands are rarely known to him or to her. To help the child create himself, the classroom has to be changed from an authoritarian to a cooperative field. The teacher and pupils must work together to set the psychological conditions within which each child will release his inner responses so that he may receive help in clarifying them.

Building a Creative Climate

Since a cooperative psychological field cannot be patterned, I will discuss it under building the atmosphere, the ways of working, the process, the results.

AS TO ATMOSPHERE:

Every classroom has a feeling tone which each person receives by direct empathy. If he is to release his inner meanings he must emotionally believe that he is wanted as a member, that he has qualities which the others recognize, believe in and accept, that he is and can be different from others yet work with them mutually and cooperatively, that he has a right to grow up as his unique self, that every person is helping him develop all of his emergent possibilities as he is helping all others do the same. This feeling tone has been described in such words as belongingness, wantedness, security, status. These qualities are difficult to define verbally but they are as present as the people, they are as active as the life of the group, they are as certain to affect members as the air they breathe, they are a minimum essential for any normal self-development, they are the basis for the relaxed control of the internal environment, so necessary for each person to create intelligently the new meanings by which he transcends his existing self. At the outset and in process this atmosphere is affected more by the teacher than by the children since she knows how to develop it while they have to learn. She never knowingly injects conditions that destroy it, she helps children verify their contributions to it. She accepts, respects, and helps them clarify their feelings as the internal motivation of their external behavior.

AS TO WAYS OF WORKING:

Such a feeling tone is rarely present in classrooms in schools and colleges. To create it the group must evolve new rules of the game or what children call ways of working. These revolve around the kinds of activities in which they engage, the way they manage them, and the center of emphasis in the learning. Here there are certain basic conditions.

First, the teacher must help the group remove all fears, threats, external demands from authoritarian experiences which keep the emotional tension too high for mutual interactive responses. These fears are inside the teachers and children as value judgments from past experience and are tendencies to action in present situations. They must be brought out in the open and reinterpreted on a more thoughtful basis. Once understood the tensions which surround them can be relieved while internal strength is being developed.

Second, the group must locate *new areas of need* or interest on which they can work together to reduce the hurts from old activities and to develop the new rules of the game in the more human atmosphere. Since all behavior is an attempt to satisfy need, improvement in behavior comes through selecting and clarifying *in process* the need which lies back of the action. Children must study their own needs in their own groups by their own creative process, better to understand themselves and thereby to improve their behavior. They improve very slightly when trying to work on adult needs which they cannot feel and study as belonging to them.

Third, each child must be free to create the new meanings necessary to release and emerge himself. In the new atmosphere and with his energy released to study his need his whole experience undergoes a reorganization. The center shifts openly from some outside adult to him. For the first time he feels what it means to face himself in his own life situations realistically. His whole field is more fluid, or less regimented. He perceives differently the released past experiences and evolves new arrangements in present situations. These original insights or meanings bring new needs and give new purpose to his behavior, so that he selects and creatively assimilates an increasing quantity and variety of the surrounding culture. And the teacher helps everyone promote a group quality which respects his normal right to create these new meanings which become his better self.

Fourth, the group members must understand through use or through personal empirical examination the process of their own creativeness which is their own life fulfillment. Since all children are born with this process and have it in common with all others, they are quick to feel its positive value. But this feeling of well being is not high enough for growth throughout life. They must know the process conceptually so that they can recognize how it works in them, can describe it to others, and can lead groups in releasing and developing it. Such a level of meaning is reached over a period of years. It can be learned by any person with normal ability. It should be accomplished by all high school graduates. And it must be achieved by parents and teachers who have major responsibility for helping children become mature adults.

AS TO RESULT:

There is always a feeling tone in every classroom. Within it each child locates and works on his needs and creates his meanings or value judgments which become himself. Within it he tries creatively to assimilate his environment so as to become a mature person. But the whole experience is difficult for him to manage *alone,* for others are less interested in his world than they are in imposing their world on him. Thus neither he nor they understand the process of their own growth.

The educational problem is whether to continue such traditional classroom conditions or whether to reorganize them around the modern evidence on growth, learning and self-development. Since the child will create himself in whatever environment he may be located, it seems reasonable that classrooms should furnish the emotional tone, the basic experiences, and the emergent intelligence through which each person, including the teacher, can continue his development. With his higher level of maturity he will have greater willingness and ability to create with others a better life for all.

47. The Meaning of FLES *

NELSON BROOKS

THESE FOUR LETTERS—sometimes pronounced as a word, rhyming with *chess*—stand for the term *Foreign Languages in the Elementary Schools* and refer to a post-war phenomenon of country-wide proportions, whose existence was officially recognized in 1952 by the Office of Education in Washington, D. C., and by the Modern Language Association in New York.

FLES is essentially an adaptation of the supreme psychological fact of the learning of the mother tongue: that any child can learn any language with nothing to go on save what he was born with and the "language in action" of those about him. We recognize of course that circumstances are not the same as in the learning of the mother tongue. The learner already knows one language well. Rather than learning at home he is in school, and instead of being within the limits of the culture in which the target language is in current use, he is in another country. If so, how certain can we be that the child will learn the new language as he did the mother tongue? It turns out that the degree of certainty is surprisingly high, provided that right conditions are created and the right things done. From a study of many programs that vary considerably with regard to starting point, time schedule, course content, and continuity, there emerges a pattern that appears to typify the best both in what may be observed and may be recommended.

There are many considerations that suggest the third grade as an optimum starting point. On the one hand, the child of 8 has already become

* From Nelson Brooks, "The Meaning of FLES," *Teacher Education Quarterly* (Fall, 1958), pp. 27–29. Reprinted by permission of the author and the *Teacher Education Quarterly*.

familiar with the school world in which he is to spend so much of his time. He has already become literate in his mother tongue—an intellectual achievement of immense significance—and has by now a sharpened sense of awareness of the business of learning. On the other hand, he is still young enough to enjoy talk for its own sake, to imitate new sounds with an almost mirrorlike accuracy, and to accept and use new expressions without feeling a strong urge to take them apart or to compare them word for word with the mother tongue. Time will bring about changes in these factors that will make the beginning of a second language markedly more difficult if he postpones his start until later years.

There is general agreement that the best time schedule is a fifteen- to twenty-minute class daily, occurring in regular school hours and as early in the day as possible. Language achievement at this level is necessarily limited in extent but is of a special quality not attainable later, and will be enhanced or negated according to the learnings that follow in subsequent years. The chief concerns with regard to continuity are that the skills of hearing and speaking must not be permitted at any point to become dormant, that the learner be given full credit for accomplishment in these skills (traditional measurement in terms of grammar and translation are wholly inadequate for this) and that these acquired skills be fully integrated with those of reading, writing, and structure control that will of course be encountered as learning proceeds. The learner's participation in the new language experience will be in terms of his involvement in the threefold interplay of hearer, speaker, and situation. By choosing situations with which he is already familiar and presenting them first in linguistic terms and eventually in cultural terms that are authentic in the area where the new language is spoken, the learner is gradually made bilingual within the limits of possibility. This is done by making only the slightest use of the mother tongue, by resolutely avoiding all conscious analysis of grammar and all translations from the target language into English, and by requiring that the skills of reading and writing be made to wait until the learner is sufficiently secure in hearing and speaking the new language; this usually means in the elementary school about two years' experience before reading and writing are begun, and then the material read and written must consist of what is thoroughly familiar to ear and tongue.

The preparation of materials to be used in FLES classes is a serious and difficult matter of great complexity. It requires the collaboration of experienced and expert teachers whose efforts must be modified and reinforced by constant references to three adjacent disciplines: descriptive linguistics (with regard to language), psychology (with regard to learning), and cultural anthropology (with regard to meaning). Of materials currently in print, only those prepared by the Modern Language Association—and these are modest enough—can presume to meet these requirements.

To qualify as a FLES teacher, an individual must of course understand and like children, and should have a sufficient degree of performance competency to "model" the learnings that are desired. He or she must also have made a special study of the discipline of second language learning and must have an acquaintance with the American school world at the elementary-school level. FLES teachers now in service are usually either specialists who have trained for teaching positions of this kind, or are high school (occasionally, college) teachers, who can readily accept the protean transformation required by the change in level. Some are classroom teachers at the elementary level who have acquired the necessary language competency and have received training in the teaching of a second language to children.

The outcomes of FLES are of at least three kinds: language achievement, attitude shifts (toward those who speak the new language), and individual growth. The first of these is readily apparent and accessible to measurement. The second and third are no less apparent, but when we wish to measure and express changes in attitude and in personality we lack the devices and the neat symbols that seem adequate when we are dealing with language achievement. As far as attitudes and improvement of self are concerned, evaluations of FLES will for the time being probably have to be content with anecdotal records.

Important as it is for its own sake, FLES is no less so for having shed much light upon the nature of language learning at the secondary level and in college. The basic elements found in FLES coincide with those of any language course—at whatever level—that is founded upon an understanding of second language learning in formal education. The most important of these may be briefly stated as follows:

Language is first of all something you say.

Reading and writing must wait until hearing and speaking are well established.

The learner must be involved in the threefold interplay of hearer, speaker, and situation.

Nobody talks in single words: the memorization of word lists is a waste of time.

Language learning is not problem-solving but habit formation.

Language functions not by analysis but by analogy; grammar as usually presented does more harm than good.

At the start, the learning of structures must be maximized while vocabulary is minimized.

Until the learner is well along in his mastery of the new language, translation into English is not only pointless but detrimental.

No skill once developed may be allowed to fall into disuse.

Anyone with an intimate knowledge of the possibilities and achievements of the FLES programs soon realizes how thoroughly the language courses at the upper levels must be revised, not only if justice is to be done to the products of FLES, but also if these advanced courses are ever to accomplish even a modest share of what is claimed for them in every syllabus and catalog. A wholly new understanding of the language skills and the order in which they may be mastered, of the harmful effects of the book, of grammar, and of translation when ineptly used, of the radical difference between the learning of Latin and of a contemporary language, of the importance of a model to go by, a person to talk with, and a suitable situation to talk about, of the relationship of talk to writing and of language to culture—all this is apparent or implied, vigorously, in FLES.

48. [Foreign] Languages in the Primary Grades: Principles and Techniques *

THEODORE ANDERSSON

THE EARLIER a language is taught in the grades the more natural can be the method. The speaker of a foreign language *behaves* differently from us, and this characteristic behavior is absorbed by primary-school children through the eyes, through the ears, "through the pores." The training of auditory and vocal organs, of gestures and facial expression, which to grownups is a highly complex and elusive process, is to our young pupils literally child's play. And let us remember that children, who are born with an almost unlimited language-learning potential, have not at the age when

* From Theodore Andersson, *The Teaching of Foreign Languages in the Elementary School* (Boston: D. C. Heath and Co., 1953), pp. 49–53. Reprinted by permission of D. C. Heath and Co.

they begin school developed those great differences in language aptitude which plague adolescents and their teachers.

What then are the principles governing the natural learning of a foreign language? The first—after the proper rapport has been established between teacher and pupils—is the creation of suitable visual impressions. I have suggested that to learn a foreign language is to learn to behave as the foreigner behaves. The eye plays an important part in the language-learning process. The children's eyes are glued on the teacher as he speaks the new language, watching his mouth, his face, his gestures, in short, his whole behavior. The teacher plays a new role before the fascinated eyes of the children, who can't wait to try out in the same role themselves.

If, as in the case of Carlos Rivera in El Paso, the teacher is a native speaker of the language being taught or, let us rather say in this connection, a native actor of it, there is of course no problem; the children merely imitate his total behavior. However, if the teacher is not a native speaker or actor, he must, in order to achieve a similar effect, resort to someone who is. Native speakers can sometimes be invited into the classroom to help enact a scene. It may also be possible to take the class into an environment where the language is spoken natively and where the whole behavior conforms to the language pattern. But there are many communities in which neither of these techniques is feasible. In that case, a third possibility remains: that of showing a motion picture in which the behavior of the foreign people is depicted and their natural speech is heard. It is of course not sufficient merely to run off such a film once or twice. The children must be allowed to observe all the essential patterns and must be given ample opportunity to re-enact them. It goes without saying that such films as we have are still far from adequate. Instructional films tend to be unnatural and other types of films have not as yet been adapted to instructional use. We may, however, confidently look forward to the development of satisfactory language-teaching films, for this need is very apparent.

The eye is useful too in associating sounds with objects, without reference to the written word. The classroom objects lie immediately at hand and can be supplemented by others brought into the classroom by the teacher or by the children. Miniature houses complete with furniture, barnyards filled with animals, and fruit stands are regular classroom props. Still other visual aids are large pictures, preferably in color; charts; maps; and filmstrips or other projections. Lacking other means, the teacher can, however unskillfully, draw on the board or have the children draw on the board pictures of objects or scenes which have been mentioned.

We should not fail to consider in passing the usefulness of the sense of touch and, to a lesser degree, of the senses of smell and taste. To be able to touch or handle the objects that one talks about or to smell flowers or to taste foods on occasion is to give them a full-bodied reality.

The second principle governing the natural learning of a foreign language is the creation of what may be called a "climate of sound." If one is dropped into a foreign environment, one is immediately surrounded by a new and strange climate of sound. Grownups who do not know the language are confused and frustrated by this and often fall back on the hope that someone will come to their assistance by speaking English. Children, on the contrary, are intrigued and begin immediately to absorb the foreign sounds. They arrange them almost intuitively in sense patterns and within a few weeks have adapted themselves to the new situation and are beginning to speak the language.

Ideally, the best way to create the new climate of sound is for a teacher who speaks the second language natively to speak nothing but this language. We have noted with what ease a child in a multilingual environment moves from one language to another with speakers of different languages. It is ideal if a child can associate a language with an individual. Carlos Rivera, who describes vividly the techniques that he uses in the first grade,[1] adheres to this principle by speaking only Spanish to the children. In fact, he is presented to the classes as a gentleman "who understands a little English but does not speak it."

Not every school system will be able to create these conditions. If the teacher is not a native speaker of the second language or a close imitator of a native speaker, he should seek the aid of one. In these days of technological advancement this is easy. If a native speaker cannot be present in person, he can be introduced by means of tape, wire, or disc recordings or by means of the sound film. Radio and television are also beginning to be used more widely. In Sweden, English is being taught simultaneously by radio in seven hundred schools. And in Washington, D. C., French and Spanish are being taught on a city-wide basis by means of television. Language lessons by television, intended for adult audiences or children, are already offered in many places. For example, Professor Manuel H. Guerra, of the State University of New York, College for Teachers at Buffalo, began a weekly fifteen-minute program on December 4, 1952, called "Fun to Learn about Latin America," in which he salutes a different country each

---

[1] See "The Teaching of Spanish in the First Grades of the El Paso Public Schools," *Hispania,* Vol. 35, No. 4 (November, 1952), 452–57, and *A Manual of Materials, Aids, and Techniques for the Teaching of Spanish to English-Speaking Children. First Grade.* (School Board, El Paso Public Schools, August, 1952), 75 cents.

week, displays its flag, features its local customs and songs, and discusses its history, geography, economy, and population.[2] While there is room for much greater use of these technical aids, to the teacher himself falls most of the task of providing constant examples of how the foreign language is spoken.

There is a third basic principle of successful language teaching in the elementary school and especially in the primary grades. This is the principle of translating as much as possible of the new language into action. Love of action seems to be universal with children. Every action and every situation can be dramatized. Greetings and presentations are actions which can be exploited in various ways. Carlos Rivera tells of the children's delight in presenting their parents when they visited the Spanish classes during National Education Week. All the classroom activities should be both verbalized and acted out, but an imaginative teacher who knows the imitative and creative powers of children will not stop here but will elaborate games and dramatic skits based on ordinary everyday activities, extracting from them their full interest. Children delight in playing the role of teacher or leader and can be called on frequently for this purpose. When the family unit is introduced they play the role of each member of the family, in the living room entertaining company, in the dining room at the table, in the kitchen preparing a meal, in the bathroom getting cleaned up, leaving for work or school, and so on.

Certainly the use of familiar experiences and everyday activities is the most natural way to introduce a foreign language, but another source of interest is the culture of the people whose language is being studied. How do the foreign children live? What do they do? What are their schools like? Their homes? What are their holidays and how do they celebrate them? What games do they play? What songs do they sing? All this fascinating material can be introduced by the teacher through stories or by means of pictures or movies. The games, songs, and dances can be learned and whole scenes dramatized. In connection with social studies, children in some Spanish classes make pottery and weave baskets and textiles. In this way a beginning is made in the important field of international understanding.

The possibilities for action are numberless. Let me mention a few. Young children like to color pictures, to cut out colored pictures from magazines and paste them in notebooks, to make and dress paper dolls, to draw pictures on the blackboard or in their notebooks, to make puppets

---

[2] For a description of this and seven other TV language programs see *FL Bulletin,* No. 5 (The Modern Language Association of America, 6 Washington Square North, New York 3. N. Y., May, 1953).

and put on puppet shows, to make valentines and other holiday cards, to repeat rhymes and nonsense verse, to play lotto and guessing games of various kinds, and to go on tours to points of interest.

Language programs in the elementary school are now so numerous as to have become somewhat standardized in their content as well as in their techniques. Several curricular guides have been written [3] and they all agree on the kind of material which is suitable for treatment in the early grades.[4] Most first grade reading texts in English deal with the family, the home, pets, clothing, the farm, health habits, and the like. It is therefore natural that these same subjects should be treated in the foreign language. Numbers, the days of the week, the months, dates, colors, and telling time are also usually introduced early, though not necessarily all in the first grade.

In such a program as that of El Paso the printed word is not seen until the third grade, when a beginning is made in associating printed words with objects and sound patterns. The theory that the ear and the tongue should be thoroughly trained before written symbols are introduced is unquestionably sound.

As Carlos Rivera suggests in his article, the second year should build on the first and add to it units which are common at this level, such as community helpers—the policeman, postman, and fireman. He also considers a good picture book for coloring useful in the second grade. Other units which have been mentioned in connection with grade two are fruits, vegetables, foods, numbers, parts of the body, school, pets, the garden, health, and safety. The overlapping which is apparent from grade to grade is indeed desirable since it serves to correlate progress and review. Thus, for example, the classroom, which forms a natural unit for grade one, can be followed by corresponding units on the school in grades two and above.

In grade three the language units again naturally follow the expanding horizon of the child's world. If the language arts and social studies are focused on the community, the foreign language should emphasize the same theme. Units already introduced in grades one and two may be reintroduced and elaborated. Numbers, which appear in almost any language class from the beginning, lead naturally to arithmetical operations of greater and greater complexity. Other units which in some school systems are associated particularly with the third grade are the calendar, age, telling time, the flag, and community services.

[3] Carlsbad, Cleveland, El Paso, Los Angeles, Louisiana, Somerville, N.J., Tucson, Washington, D.C.

[4] A most logical and natural sequence of units for the first grade is offered by Carlos Rivera in the article and in the *Manual* already cited. He has also carried his planning through grade two and has published lesson plans.

The opportunity to relate foreign languages to the language arts, to the social studies, and to number work is apparent. The relationship between languages, music, and art is equally natural. If nature study is begun in the primary grades, this adds a further possible dimension to language study.

49. Teaching Foreign Language in the Elementary Schools *

ELIZABETH E. THOMPSON
AND ARTHUR E. HAMALAINEN

Some Organizational Issues

In this section four organizational issues will be discussed. These issues are of great importance to many persons involved in or contemplating the addition of foreign language to the elementary curriculum.

1. WHEN SHOULD FOREIGN LANGUAGE TEACHING BE STARTED?

A growing number of school systems start foreign language teaching in kindergarten or in first grade. Some justify the introduction of foreign language at this early age in the light of statements by Theodore Andersson and others, and by the research of linguists and neurologists which indicates that children learn foreign languages best when they are very young. Recently there have been some statements and research refuting this point of view. Many language programs start in the third grade after the children have acquired skills in primary reading in order that there will be no added difficulty during the earlier years of a child's adjustment to school. The decision to begin the language program at third grade or at a higher level in some school systems is sometimes due to expediency, for it is frequently possible to provide teachers or specialists for this level and in some cases also for fourth grade, but not enough teachers to extend the program to lower grades. Some teachers believe that children tend to remember better in third grade than they do at a younger age.

In other places the program is instituted first in the upper grades, i.e.,

* From Elizabeth E. Thompson and Arthur E. Hamalainen, *Foreign Language Teaching in Elementary Schools* (Washington, D. C.: Association for Supervision and Curriculum Development, 1958), pp. 27–32. Reprinted by permission.

fifth and sixth. One reason for this upper grade placement might be the fact that often the only language teachers available are high school teachers who possibly can adjust more easily to children in the upper grades than they can to primary children. Another reason might be the fact that the effect of the experimental elementary foreign language teaching on the high school language program can be more quickly ascertained since the fifth and sixth graders involved would enter high school in only two years. In many such places where the program has started in upper grades it tends to be extended to a preceding grade or grades each year as teachers are available. Thus in some schools the programs are being extended gradually upward in the grades from the first, as in El Paso and Carlsbad; and in others downward to the primary grades, as in Fairfield and Brighton.

Some schools have initiated the entire program at once in all grades, but this plan is used chiefly when workshops and manuals are available for in-service education of teachers. An example of such a plan is in the Los Angeles schools where a program was started in all grades by the direction of the superintendent of schools with workshops provided for in-service preparation. Although participation at these workshops contributes to teachers' receiving added increments on the salary schedule, not all of them are able or interested in attending such meetings. Thus in Los Angeles even though the excellent manual and the recordings and teacher materials have been available for a program in all grades, teaching of Spanish is not practiced in every classroom. The Cleveland plan includes all grades, first through sixth, but foreign language instruction there is not available to all elementary children; it is restricted to children of high IQ. Thus only a small proportion of the entire school population receives this foreign language instruction.

2. HOW CAN CONTINUITY IN FOREIGN LANGUAGE TEACHING BE ACHIEVED?

When concern is felt for the development of language skills, continuity in the program becomes very important. In the visits to the various schools it was observed that one effort toward continuity of this kind was the employment and use of special teachers to teach the language. Such situations were observed in Atlantic City, Brighton, Cleveland, Fairfield, and Lake Forest. Generally, these special teachers present language to a class for periods of fifteen or twenty minutes daily, or three times a week. One exception to this is Cleveland where the time devoted to French was one-half hour to forty minutes daily. In a majority of cases, the special teachers traveled to the classrooms in the various schools, except in Cleveland where the classes go to rooms designated for French instruction.

When the specialist is used in this manner the language teaching is frequently unrelated to the classroom experiences of the children. It may be observed that the classroom teachers frequently have no direct responsibility for the program. Often the classroom teacher leaves the room during the language period. Furthermore, because of the language deficiencies of most of the classroom teachers the actual experience which the children have with the language tends to be limited to the relatively short period of time each week given by the specialists.

In addition, the "specialist" programs tend to be largely teacher-directed and subject centered rather than pupil-teacher-planned and experience centered. This situation often occurs because time is not available for the specialist to plan the work with the individual teacher in terms of the interests, needs and experiences of the particular class. One such specialist reported teaching over one hundred classes per week for fifteen or twenty minutes in a number of different schools. Thus, this individual had contact with about 3500 children. Other specialists teach in both the elementary and high schools or in nearby colleges. Obviously, there is little opportunity for them to know the children, or to plan and teach in the light of knowledge of individual children or of class interests and experiences.

Continuity in the program is also attempted in situations where the specialist tries to teach the language with the assistance of the classroom teacher. The teacher endeavors to learn the language by observing and listening to the special language teacher. A few interested teachers in these systems are making the effort to learn the language through adult education courses and other available opportunities. This lends itself to a somewhat more integrated approach to the teaching process, although it was observed that these programs suffer many of the shortcomings of that conducted by the specialist alone.

Another attempt to provide continuity is found in those school systems which have workshops in the teaching of foreign languages. In such places as San Diego, Jamestown, and Carlsbad, special teachers or supervisors not only teach children, but also carry on an in-service training program for teachers. At these workshops the teachers usually learn the language through the aural-oral method. Through grade level committees, they also frequently prepare cooperatively some unit materials for each elementary grade level. Thus the teachers are active participants in building their course of study through their in-service education program. At the initial stage, a special teacher or supervisor teaches the language classes and illustrates with children the techniques discussed in the workshop. As the teachers grow in competence and adequacy they take over their own foreign language teaching, using the materials which they have developed in their workshops. In general, it might be said that in the workshop programs the special teacher's or supervisor's responsibilities decrease as the number of classroom teachers become prepared and as their interest in teaching their own language classes increases. In Los Angeles, where the program has been in operation over 10 years, there are no special teachers but workshops continue to be conducted for the benefit of interested teachers who care to utilize the materials which have been developed by others.

The extent and quality of the foreign language program in the cities with a workshop plan depend largely upon the interest, efforts and language abilities of the classroom teachers, whose attendance at workshops is generally voluntary. Under this plan when a teacher is uninterested in teaching a foreign language or has a language disability the special teachers try to arrange their schedules to teach such groups. When this is impossible, a consistent development of the language skills is lost since the next teacher does not continue the program. Too frequently, the next teacher the child will have knows, from his participation in the workshop program, only the same vocabulary, phrases and activities as did the teacher of the previous grade. Thus, the child's experiences in language may not be deepened or extended to any marked degree during his next school year.

A plan with neither the specialist teaching the classes nor a workshop is found where a classroom teacher, competent in speaking a foreign language, makes foreign language instruction a part of his teaching. Such situations have been observed when a teacher makes language instruction an integral part of his classroom work, related to art, music and social science. The language experiences of his class thus can become a part of the living of the entire school. For example, in one school, at a "French table" during lunch time only French is spoken by any child, teacher or parent in the school who cares to participate. Through this means a sensitivity to a foreign language, as well as a rich experience in a real situation for communication, is provided not only for this class, but is also shared by others in the school and community. Although this is a desirable practice, it may not be justifiable if we accept the criterion that the program should grow out of real needs of children rather than emerging from contrived situations.

3. WHAT METHODS AND TECHNIQUES ARE EFFECTIVE IN FOREIGN
   LANGUAGE TEACHING?

The validity of any teaching technique should depend upon the need it serves and the purposes it achieves. The methods and techniques observed in presenting a foreign language tend in most instances to elicit children's interest, but this is achieved most frequently through the use of manipulated artificial situations. The aural-oral method, i.e., only hearing and speaking the language, is generally practiced. In fact, in current programs children seldom, if ever, hear the language teacher speak English. In most cases children have two or three years of this aural-oral teaching before they are introduced to reading the foreign words. This principle of developing facility in oral expression as a readiness for reading the foreign material is consistent with modern practice in primary reading. After the children have considerable experience in speaking and reading, the writing of the foreign language is then introduced and encouraged through stimulating experiences and activities. The methods observed in most elementary foreign language teaching today are different from the former grammatical-analytical approach, and much more consistent with accepted current curriculum trends. Such procedures apply principles basic to language development— first one hears the language, then he speaks it, following this he reads it, and later on he writes the language. However effective the methods, they do not justify the existence of any program. Method and purpose, practice and goals must always be interrelated so that they will contribute to the fulfillment of children's basic social and emotional needs.

There is a similarity of activities and materials in many classrooms throughout the country. For example the language teacher most generally knocks at the door creating a situation through which children learn the conversation pertaining to greetings. This in some cases becomes a pattern and is repeated needlessly long after it has any significance for the children. The vocabulary, taught largely through the use of pictures, is practically the same in most communities. This vocabulary consists of words and phrases pertaining to pets, the home, things in the room, names, time, nature, colors, arithmetic and social studies. The vocabulary tends to be static partly due to the fact that frequently the teacher knows only these words. There is un-due emphasis on memory and oral repetition—learning by rote this set vocabulary with the use of concrete materials, pictures, articles and other media to stimulate interest and convey meaning. There does not seem to be any emphasis upon the building of an individual class vocabulary or conversation related to the unique and actual daily classroom interests or experiences of the children such as their grocery trip, a new turtle, the class bakery, their garden. Language should grow out of the spontaneous expressions of children.

In large classes of thirty-five or forty, the children usually answer the teacher's many questions in chorus. With this procedure, which is apparently deemed necessary so that all children have an opportunity to vocalize, it is difficult to determine whether individual children are pronouncing words correctly. There is little opportunity, because of class size and limitation of time and the subject centered orientation in the teaching, to make adequate provision for individual response or conversation. This might be more easily possible in a class organization which provides for small group work based on children's interests and abilities. In Lake Forest and Cleveland most language groups include only half of the regular class, from fourteen to sixteen children. Here, with ample opportunity for each to respond individually, the children develop a greater fluency and more accurate pronunciation of the foreign language taught.

A lack of self-consciousness, an interest and enjoyment of the program are generally evident on the part of the children in such situations. On the whole they seem to derive considerable pleasure from repeating the many unusual sounds, but in many instances the children do not seem to regard the learning primarily as a means of communication. It might be well to note in this regard that new strange meaningless sounds seem to appeal generally to many elementary children, as evidenced from their frequent fascination with "Pig Latin" and the "secret" languages which children sometimes create. In many situations the teacher's enthusiasm and the use of concrete materials contribute to the children's undivided attention. Frequently when they participate in using foreign vocabulary in dramatics, puppetry activities, singing foreign songs, and in the jingles and games such as "Simon Says," the interest may be due to the fact that these language activities provide a diversion from the regular class work. It might be questioned whether children will sustain a real interest in a foreign language over a long period of time especially if they begin to see little or no use for it in their out of school experiences.

In some classes in mixed population areas, the children who speak other languages but who know little English are separated from the rest of the class during foreign language teaching. The classroom teacher often uses this period to teach these children English. This practice tends to emphasize language differences in such a way that children are isolated one from the other rather than using their language abilities and differences as a contribution toward the growth of the group. In other schools foreign speaking children participate with the language teacher in the teaching of their own language to their classmates. Such children of foreign backgrounds through the insight of their teachers seem to gain status and a sense of adequacy in the group because of their language contributions. Most foreign speaking children in our schools need such recognition.

Various audio-visual aids are being utilized to a limited extent in a number of programs. Recordings of lessons by the supervisors are used by some classroom teachers. The radio programs by the supervisors tend to result in more interest when children, while listening in their classrooms, participate by responding to the activities suggested by the radio speaker. These aids have a place in the program but should never be used as a substitute for personal contact. Children benefit most from a face-to-face relationship.

CHAPTER **VIII** TEACHING
SOCIAL
STUDIES

50. [Social] Objectives for the Lower Elementary School *

I. JAMES QUILLEN

SCHOOLS ARE the instruments through which cultures are perpetuated. The people who form a cultural group establish and maintain schools in order to make sure that children and youth learn the behavior necessary to continue and improve their way of life. The major functions of American schools are to conserve, transmit, and improve our cultural heritage and to develop wholesome and effective personalities commensurate with the potentialities of each child. The objectives of the school are to develop in children and youth the behaviors necessary to achieve these ends.

In considering objectives for each grade level, it is important to keep constantly in mind the objectives for the total elementary program and for the school as a whole. In fact, teachers in the lower grades should point their work toward the achievement of objectives that extend through the range of general education.

The personality of the individual is not developed segmentally. One does not develop an understanding of the community during one year and an understanding of the world during the next. On the contrary, understanding of broader social relationships is an extension of personal-social relationships that take place in the immediate environment. Thus a teacher who is directing young children in home, school, and community experiences needs to be cognizant of their effects on the development of an understanding of social relationships that encompass state, nation, and interdependent

* From I. James Quillen, "Objectives for the Lower Elementary School," in M. Willcockson (ed.), *Social Education of Young Children* (2nd ed.; Washington, D.C.: National Council for the Social Studies, NEA, 1956), pp. 24–28.

world. The same principle applies to attitudes, skills, and abilities. Developing effectiveness in cooperation, for example, is a process that covers the experiences of many years, perhaps a lifetime.

Enough has been said to indicate that objectives for the lower elementary school should be stated as a part of a broader statement of objectives for the school as a whole—at least from kindergarten through high school. In stating objectives for the school, as a whole, it is necessary to take into consideration the nature of our changing industrial-urban culture, the ideals and values we seek to realize, and the nature of the individual needs, growth, and development of children and youth. Broadly speaking, the objectives of the school are a description of behavior characteristics essential to the realization of democratic values within the realities of our changing culture.

After objectives for the school as a whole have been stated, the behaviors which need to be stressed in each major division of the school—primary and intermediate, junior and senior high school—need to be defined. Finally, the objectives for each grade, class, and unit of study should be stated. In this process, the description of behavior becomes more and more specific, and the behaviors designated as objectives for particular units of study contribute directly to the development of the broader patterns of behavior designated for the school as a whole.

Objectives as Behavior

Until recently objectives for teaching the social studies were usually stated in terms of broad principles such as developing good citizenship, or in terms of subject matter such as knowing the world distribution of natural resources. Both have limitations. Statements in terms of broad principles are often too general while statements in terms of subject matter are sometimes so extensive that it is almost impossible to remember and use them effectively.

For this reason, teachers and curriculum workers have turned more and more to the definition of objectives in terms of the behavior the school seeks to develop. For example, a cooperative student:

1. Works well with a group or committee
2. Respects constituted authority
3. Recognizes and carries out his share of responsibility
4. Supports group and school activities
5. Volunteers to bring in additional data or help in school projects
6. Meets his obligations promptly and to the best of his ability

7. Adjusts his interests to the best interests of the group
8. Treats others and their ideas with respect and courtesy.[1]

Behavioral statements of objectives include covert as well as overt behavior, knowledge and attitudes as well as skills and abilities. The advantage of behavioral objectives is that they direct the attention of the teacher to the actions of the children and give direction and meaning to classroom experiences. At the same time they provide a definite basis for effective evaluation which becomes the process of observing, recording, interpreting, and reporting the behavior of students.

Objectives Are Interrelated

Lists of behavioral objectives can become as lengthy as those of subject matter unless they are organized in patterns which reveal their interrelationships and focus upon the total personality of the child. Objectives can be divided into: (1) knowledge and understanding; (2) values and ideals, including attitudes, appreciations, interests, and loyalties; and (3) skills, abilities, and habits.

It is helpful to use these three basic divisions, but each category should also be stated in terms of a theme interrelating with the other two. Thus the general objectives for teaching the social studies become (1) the development of an understanding of our changing world; (2) the development of high standards of value and ideals—a conception of the world as it ought to be; and (3) the development of individual competence necessary to participate in the world as it is, yet in a manner conducive to the achievement of desired values and ideals.

These objectives can easily be remembered by the teacher; they focus upon the development of the total personality of the child and provide a framework within which to define specific objectives. The behavioral statement of cooperation, for example, would be placed under the second objective—values and ideals. Following are suggested behaviors for the kindergarten and primary grades.[2]

Knowledge and Understanding

Knowledge about and understanding of the changing world may be further divided into basic information; concepts (geographic, personality,

[1] James Quillen and Lavone A. Hanna, *Education for Social Competence* (Chicago: Scott, Foresman and Co., 1948), pp. 55–56.
[2] Some of the suggestions in this section were developed in the Los Angeles County program where the author of this chapter was a consultant in social studies.

and abstract); and broad understandings and generalizations.[3] In connection with the suggestions that follow, it is assumed that the home, school, and neighborhood will be the centers of interest in the kindergarten and first grade, the neighborhood and immediate community in the second grade, and the expanding community in the third.

KINDERGARTEN

Social education in kindergarten is somewhat informal. Objectives in knowledge and understanding relate to objects, persons, and information in the immediate environment. For example, children can begin to gain understanding and knowledge about the family and the school; how members of the family travel from place to place; the different ways in which fathers earn a living; how food is prepared and homes are kept clean; how members of the family play together on holidays, birthdays, and vacations; and how the school helps children to have fun with others and to keep healthy and happy. A beginning can be made by recognizing the dependence of the family on other people and places in the neighborhood—the store for food and clothing, the post office for mail, and public transportation for travel. The teacher can note elementary concepts of time, place, and distance.

FIRST GRADE

In the first grade where the same general area is emphasized, children can begin to recognize that the family meets certain basic needs; it provides affection, food, shelter, clothing, and a place to rest, play, learn, and be with others. First graders can understand why children go to school; the general layout of their schoolroom, building, and grounds; the materials available for their use; and the persons in the school who can help them to meet their needs. This knowledge can be extended to the neighborhood to include contributions of the grocer, postman, and others.

Basic geographic concepts and understandings will include direction, distance, and location in relation to the home, school, and neighborhood. Such natural features in the immediate environment as rivers, valleys, hills,

---

[3] By a concept is meant a word which has significant meaning; for example, *democracy, environment,* and *America.* Concepts can be divided into: (1) personality—the name of a significant person; (2) geographic—the name of a significant place; and (3) abstract—a word like *democracy* which stands for an idea or a group of ideas. A social understanding is a generalization which gives meaning to a number of related concepts and facts—for example: "The American people are becoming increasingly interdependent among themselves and with other peoples of the world."

and mountains can be recognized and named. Man-made roads, bridges and buildings can also be recognized, named, and their uses discussed.

A beginning can be made in civics by helping children to understand the regulations in the school and neighborhood for their safety and health, the rules that govern proper conduct in the school and home, and the way family and school groups are organized to get things done. The role of the policeman, postman, and fireman in local life can be observed, experienced through dramatic play, and discussed. The historical tradition can be utilized in developing understandings of holidays, birthdays, grand-parents, and the like.

SECOND GRADE

In the second grade, experiences in social learning can be focused somewhat more sharply than in the kindergarten and first grade. More attention can be given to social functions and social living in the neighborhood and immediate community. Perhaps one of the best ways to begin is to focus on some one function, such as the production and distribution of food, which lies directly within the child's experience and which offers rich possibilities for observation, construction, dramatic play, and other activities. Following is a list of possible understandings:

1. Food is a basic need of all people and all animals.
2. There are many people who earn their living and assist us in satisfying our needs by producing and distributing food.
3. Soil, topography, and climate affect the raising of foods.
4. Foods are grown, preserved, stored, packaged, distributed, and prepared for eating.
5. Tools, machines, and improved techniques help man to grow more food with less work.
6. More food can be grown through the cooperation of many people.
7. Growing food requires constant and careful work.
8. There are rules concerning weights and measures, sanitation, and quality which growers and distributors of food must follow. These rules are made and enforced by the government to protect the buyers of food from disease, dishonesty, and fraud.
9. Ways of growing, preserving, distributing, and preparing foods have changed as a result of new inventions and ways of living.

All of these understandings grow out of experiences with the dairyman, poultry grower, wholesale and retail grocer, and inspectors; with produce markets, soil, orchards, erosion, fertility, tractors, spray guns, weights, measures, laws, and rules. Here also is an opportunity for elementary concepts of interdependence and changing ways of living. Children can begin to appreciate their dependence on the work of others, the contributions of tools and techniques to human well-being, and the need of social organization and cooperation in the satisfaction of needs.

THIRD GRADE

In the third grade the emphasis is generally on the expanding community. The child's own or another in the local area is selected for study. Often the local community is compared and contrasted with historical and contemporary communities using handicraft tools and techniques, for example, pioneer communities, a Pueblo Indian community, a Mexican or Samoan community.

Social understandings that can be developed in the third grade include:

1. Communities are made up of many people, doing many different kinds of work.
2. People living in communities carry on many social functions to satisfy their needs.
3. People living in communities depend on each other and on other communities.
4. Communities contain many different kinds of buildings which serve many different needs.
5. Communities use many different ways of communication and transportation.
6. The work of the community is made easier by the use of tools, machines, and many kinds of techniques.
7. Social organization makes it possible for many people to cooperate in the satisfaction of needs.
8. The government of the community assists in protection, sanitation, recreation, education, and many other ways.
9. The geographic environment affects community living in many ways: location, recreation, ways of earning a living, transportation, clothing, housing, fuel, food, and the like.
10. Communities using handicraft tools and techniques are more affected by the geographic environment than those using machines.
11. All communities have histories which help to explain their ways of living.
12. We can understand our own communities better by comparing and contrasting them with other communities.
13. All communities are changing.
14. Changes in tools and techniques affect ways of living.

15. Everyone has a responsibility for making the community a desirable place in which to live.
16. We should become acquainted with community workers and officials and cooperate with them in the improvement of community life.

Study of the community on the third grade level also introduces basic concepts such as: business, maps, rent, taxes, rural, urban, advertisement, inspector, state, vote, traffic, policeman, wholesale, retail, church, theatre, recreation, sanitation, factories, company, foreman, manager, weights, measurements, contractor, museums, exhibits, assemblies, mayor, city council, health department, housing, parks, schools, libraries, hospitals, laws and regulations, city hall, courts, and so on. Names of community leaders are learned. Certain geographic concepts can be stressed: the natural and man-made features of the local environment; characteristics of the local climate; location of the community in relation to the surrounding area; directions to key places; flora and fauna.

Values and Ideals

Objectives within the general category of values and ideals may be further divided into attitudes, appreciations, interests, and loyalties. Since all of these are even more developmental in character than understandings, information, and concepts, no attempts will be made to break them down into grade-level divisions. In the kindergarten and first grade the major problem is to modify the egocentrism of the child and develop in him the desire and ability to work effectively in group situations. The emphasis upon experiences in the home and school provide excellent opportunities for developing these behaviors. In the second and third grades attitudes toward others, loyalty to broader groups, appreciations of varied aspects of the environment, and the broadening of interests may be extended into the neighborhood and immediate and expanding community.

The program of social education in the kindergarten and primary grades should assist each child to:
1. Recognize and respect the rights of others
2. Recognize and respect individual differences
3. Take pride in and care for property used in common, personal property, and property that belongs to others
4. Listen attentively while others speak
5. Share responsibility with others
6. Assume responsibilities and carry them out to the best of individual ability

7. Develop and seek to achieve individual and group standards of performance
8. Respect and adhere to group regulations
9. Use reason rather than prejudice and force in attempting to solve individual and group problems
10. Be concerned about the effects of one's actions on others
11. Seek to work cooperatively and harmoniously in group situations, using democratic procedures and techniques
12. Be loyal to home, school, community, and nation
13. Begin to recognize one's responsibilities as a citizen in an interdependent world
14. Appreciate the contributions of others and the finer things in one's environment
15. Develop interest in and appreciation of art, music, literature, wholesome recreational activities, attractive personal appearance, and community beautification and improvement

Skills, Abilities, and Habits

The development of effectiveness in basic social skills is one of the major tasks of elementary education. It is obvious that no extensive analysis of this area can be made here. However, it is important to point out that social education is concerned with the development of fundamental skills, and that one of the best ways to accomplish this is through experiences in social situations. Hence, in developing understanding, knowledge, values, and ideals, the teacher should be concerned about such basic social skills as reading, writing, speaking, listening, observing, and using numbers. In the light of the present school program and the emergence of mass communication special emphasis should be given to listening and observing; in the modern world the individual gains more information through these skills than through reading.

Experiences for developing reflective thinking and problem-solving, both major objectives in social education, can begin in kindergarten and the primary grades. To encourage reflective thinking the teacher can utilize common childhood problems—getting safely to school, keeping clean, protecting and preserving property, and getting along with others.

Problem-solving (also called the unit method of teaching and learning) involves behaviors like those outlined in the four categories below:

1. Recognizing, analyzing and defining a problem situation. What is

going to be studied? What are its important aspects? What questions need to be answered?

2. Setting standards as to what is right and desirable in the solution of the problem being considered. What is desirable in this problem situation? What is it we want to achieve?

3. Collecting, verifying, organizing and interpreting information. What information is needed? Where can it be secured? Who can secure it? How can it be put together? What does it mean?

4. Forming, verifying, and applying conclusions to the problem situation. What can we learn from the information collected? How do we know it is true? How can it be used? How effective is our solution of the problem?

These behaviors can be used in a modified form in the study of any area or in planning and carrying out a project, but in the latter the question becomes: "What is to be done? How is it to be done? Who is going to do it? How well has it been done?"

Planning and evaluation periods also offer opportunity for practice in reflective thinking and problem-solving.

Effectiveness in leadership and followership is important in social education. The behaviors involved can be developed through participation in group activities in the classroom and elsewhere.

Habits that can be practiced constantly as they apply to social education are punctuality, accuracy, courtesy, alertness, cleanliness, neatness, and industry.

51. *Social Studies in the Middle Grades* *

LORETTA E. KLEE

MANY TEACHERS believe that cooperative planning with students can sharpen social studies learning experiences. But, of course, these teachers recognize the need for a balance between cooperative planning and preplanning by the teacher.

* From Loretta E. Klee, "Social Studies in the Middle Grades," *NEA Journal* (December, 1952), pp. 583–84. Reprinted by permission of the *NEA Journal*.

Two important factors should be considered in seeking this balance:

The first is existence of individual differences among teachers in creative ability, flexibility in meeting unexpected situations, cultural backgrounds and training, skill in relating learning experiences to the needs of children, and acquaintance with resources which may be needed in the social learning experiences.

The second is the experience of children in grades four, five, and six in group planning. To what extent are the boys and girls skilful in the processes of cooperative planning? To what extent may they be expected to attain the purposes which they have formulated and at the same time be learning the skills of group purposing, planning, executing, and evaluating?

The Workshop Approach

Some schools are experimenting with a workshop approach in social living in the middle grades. The teacher does only a broad type of planning, in terms of needs of the pupils. He anticipates learning experiences which may arise, considers possible procedures to meet them, and looks ahead to the kinds of resources which may be needed.

The workshop approach means learning activities continuously and cooperatively planned day by day to meet specific and long-range problems and needs. Thus children learn how to plan and think through their problems. Because children see greater meaning in their cooperatively planned activities, it is hoped that they will work harder and that more functional learnings will result.

Proponents of this approach say that even when cooperative planning fails to produce the desired results, students analyze the reasons for the failure and learn by the experience. Thus, failures of cooperatively planned activities, followed by careful evaluation, are more effective in teaching pupils to think critically than more smoothly run experiences preplanned by the teacher.

Opponents of cooperative pupil-teacher planning workshops for children in the middle grades have asked these questions:

How can needless repetition and wasteful duplication be avoided when pupils do so much of their own planning? Are there not serious gaps in learnings? Do not pupils become so entangled with the process and mechanics of cooperative planning that they find it difficult to follow through efficiently on the problems under consideration? How can a teacher plan ahead to meet the needs of his class as to materials and learning experiences when so much of the situation is unstructured in advance? Are pupil effort, interest, and resultant learnings in direct proportion to the amount of participation the pupils have had in planning?

The Middle Way

In an effort to realize the values of pupil-teacher planning and to avoid the difficulties, some schools have tried a system of restricted choices. Learning activities and goals are largely teacher-planned, pupil planning is largely in terms of specifics. The teacher must be able to justify the learning experiences in terms of the over-all program and the philosophy of the school system.

Somewhere between the formally organized unit and an unstructured workshop approach probably lies the answer for most children in the middle grades. The issue must be resolved in each community in terms of the place of the social studies, the purposes of the total school program, and the abilities of teachers to guide the learning experiences of boys and girls at their maturity level.

Grade Sequence vs. Free Planning

Another problem is what the relationship should be between basic framework and freely planned learning experiences. Is there value for teachers and pupils in drawing an outer circle of functional knowledge, understandings and appreciations, positive social attitudes, and skills toward which teachers should guide all children in the middle grades?

If so, in daily classroom learning experiences teachers and pupils might plan their points of departure and work together in ever-widening inner circles of learning as they are guided toward the more comprehensive outer circle.

Some children would never completely reach it, nor would they be under any compulsion to do so. Other children would attain much more as they reached out in accordance with their abilities to increasingly larger circles of their own.

Some teachers of nine-, ten, and eleven-year-old children feel the need of guidance in planning social studies learning activities. At the same time, they recognize the dangers of a basic framework which becomes a body of content to be covered or mastered by all boys and girls within the middle grades. In terms of the many differences within the learning environment, no able teacher would view such a basic framework as either helpful or psychologically sound.

In schools where the faculties are composed of master teachers who work closely together and where there is a wealth of human and material learning resources, it is possible to develop really effective learning experiences without a guiding framework. In such a situation teachers are able to acquaint themselves with all aspects of the learning environment of the boys and girls, and a high degree of interrelationship among learnings can be attained.

Having an abundance of material as well as human resources, teachers are able to get the appropriate movie, recording, or reference book at the time of need. These schools, in brief, have the conditions which are requisite for the effective functioning of freely planned learning experiences in a laboratory or workshop organization.

Guidance Needed

In less favorable educational environments it may be desirable to have a basic framework of goals and suggestive learning activities. What are some of the advantages which are seen in a guiding basic framework?

There would be an opportunity for teachers to plan ahead for effective use of materials. Teachers in many schools must order multisensory aids well in advance of use. In some communities a thorough evaluation or screening of all printed materials must be made before they are put into the hands of pupils.

How to develop interests, abilities, and skills poses a problem for many teachers as they work with no basic framework to guide them. Sometimes a teacher has difficulty determining the kinds of learning experiences his pupils have previously had. Because some school systems do not have adequate inter- and intra-school communication, what might be rich, sequential, unified learnings are more accurately described as "shreds and patches." The complexity of modern society is another reason we need guidance and a basic framework, say some teachers.

The implication for the balance between the amount of guidance given in the form of basic framework and the responsibility which must be assumed by teachers for the development of freely planned learning experiences is clear. What teachers seek is a *guiding* framework in terms of goals and resources and opportunities to use a variety of methods in working toward the outer circle—unity and harmony within the whole through diversity!

52. The Individual Counts in Effective Group Relations *

LELAND P. BRADFORD
AND GORDON L. LIPPITT

IN THE PAST twenty years, the social scientist has devoted a good deal of attention to the study of group behavior and problems of human relations. Some people have expressed concern lest this research and emphasis detract from the importance of the individual.

No more serious question could be raised in this age when individual freedom and growth throughout the world is threatened by the ravages of Communism and other forms of totalitarianism. The submergence of the individual into blind and abject subservience faces us unless the democratic ideal of individual freedom and opportunity to develop according to individual potentialities can be maintained and strengthened.

As a matter of fact, our *basic* question today is how to help in the development of strong and wise individuals who can, alone and with others, reach good decisions about their problems.

Rather than submerging individuals, recent experimental efforts in group behavior and human relations have at the very core of their purpose the maximizing of the contribution of the individual and his personal worth in his relations with others and the developing of his ability to make further contributions. To substantiate this point of view, let us set down some principles and then elaborate upon them.

1. *Leaders, supervisors, and administrators trained in effective human relations are more sensitive to the needs of individuals than untrained ones.* Inept and untrained leaders are too intent upon applying rules and maintaining their own leadership position to be aware of the many individual resources within the group or to be sensitive to individual feelings and needs. With the increased knowledge of the social sciences, more insight has been gained into the effect of various patterns of leadership, supervision, and administration.

The frustration coming from the thwarting of individual needs under autocratic leadership is well-known through the numerous studies made of both youth groups and industrial organizations. Even when the leader has no intention of being autocratic, rigid adherence to procedural rules and

* From Leland P. Bradford and Gordon L. Lippitt, "The Individual Counts in Effective Group Relations," *NEA Journal* (November, 1954), pp. 485–87. Reprinted by permission of the *NEA Journal*.

lack of sensitivity to the needs and interests of individual members can block participation and create apathy in the group.

On the other hand, when a leader is aware of the individual needs and differences that exist in group situations, he recognizes the potentialities that lie within these individual differences and helps each individual make his peculiar contribution to the decision-making process. Studies have shown that leaders who are sensitive to the needs and feelings of individuals as well as conscious of the task to be done, accomplish more than leaders merely concerned with the group task.

2. *In effective group relations, the group becomes sensitive to the needs of its individual members.* In building effective group relations, individual members become more aware of the potential contribution of each member of the group. It is only when the group members become sensitive to one another that they become aware of their responsibilities to one another.

A group can become a resource to an individual in helping him know how he can develop his own initiative, express his opinions and ideas, and then translate them into effective action. Sound group relations help the individual to realize that he has a unique contribution to make to the group, and—most important—that the group encourages him to make such contributions.

Furthermore, groups that are helped to grow in maturity and understanding of their own problems and process in turn help their members to improve as independent individuals.

An effective group recognizes that it needs different contributions and so encourages individual differences. An ineffective group or leader punishes differences among members and tries to enforce a rigid conformity.

3. *In effective group relationships, the individual shares in the setting of group goals which affect his own situation and in determining the methods used in reaching the goals.* In autocratic and manipulated situations, the individual has little if anything to say about the goals, purposes, or methods of his own activities and work. In effective group relationships, the individual is asked to share in the setting of the goal and in making suggestions relative to how it can be reached. It is only in such a social climate that the individual can become important to the determination of that for which he is striving.

Conversely, it is only through the individual's being permitted to participate in the setting of group goals that such goals have value for him.

4. *Expression of individual differences of opinion and frankness of feelings are more easily possible in a permissive situation than in*

an autocratic, manipulated one. In group problem-solving of a demo-cratic nature, there is the encouragement of a permissive, informal atmos-phere. Such an atmosphere is important in determining whether an indi-vidual feels free to speak honestly and frankly. It not only encourages him to participate when he is ready to do so, but actually makes it seem natural and easy for him to express his ideas.

In many rigid and formal situations, feelings and differences remain un-spoken throughout the meeting, but serve to disrupt and delay the problem-solving process at a later point. In a democratic group situation, differences of opinion are encouraged and brought into the open where the group can find the common factors within those differences and thus build to a solid and accepted solution. Unspoken or unexplored differences encourage widely varying interpretations and perceptions of individual members.

However, it should be clearly understood that resolving differences to reach a decision is *not* merely an attempt to get people to like one another and, through a false sense of morale, come to quick or "happy" decisions.

5. *The utilization of the consensus method of decision-making makes the individual important.* In some groups—say, a legislative ses-sion or an official board meeting—it is practicable to use Robert's Rules of Order to expedite the records of such a meeting. However, out of the re-search in the field of human relations has come a practice employed in many group situations of emphasizing the use of consensus rather than the vote.

In many of the problem-solving groups in which people work it is feasible and desirable to use the consensus method of reaching a decision: The issues with their various facets are discussed until the group reaches agreement among all its members as to the next steps for action, and individual differ-ences are aired, examined, and considered. Sometimes a group will need to withhold the decision until further facts are collected to determine which individual within the group has best understood and reported a situation.

A group that seeks consensus before rushing to a vote protects the indi-vidual from being overridden by the majority and finding himself in the "minority" and, as a result, rejected. The individual's difference of opinion is respected and given full consideration by such a group. The group seeks decision not by lining up sides, by coercion, or by emotional appeals, but by bringing out different contributions, weighing them, and endeavoring to find solutions that contain the best of the contributions made.

6. *In effective group relations, the individual is encouraged to feel independent, is delegated responsibility and authority as the group members develop trust in one another, and is encouraged to grow and*

improve. As a group grows in effectiveness—whether a committee, staff, or community group—a common trust among the members is developed, and group standards allowing for individual differences are established. Such a group is not only able to delegate responsibility and authority to various individuals to act for the good of the larger group, but is better able to assess the resources among the members, to use them more wisely, and to stimulate improvement among members. In this way the individual is encouraged to act on his own initiative and given freedom of action.

The ideal group life develops the individual's security in his interpersonal relationships and helps him to understand his own and others' functions and contributions to the group. Thus, an individual gains the respect of the group for his individual contribution, with the result that the group is more ready to sanction his individual action when it is brought before the larger group.

7. Group relations research indicates a wide range of needed individual contributions. A group requires at different times many different kinds of contributions. Ideas need to be presented, differing opinions need bridging, suggestions need reality testing, procedures need to be recommended, support to hesitant members needs to be given, group direction needs to be checked, and tension reduced.

These roles have been defined in three large categories: task centered, group centered, and individual centered functions. At different times the group needs contributions from its members in each of these categories. Unless they are made at the appropriate time, the group suffers and its task is less effectively completed.

The important concept gained from this research is that we need to understand the wide variety of needed member contributions for effective group operation and the opportunity presented for great differences among individuals in their contributions.

Effective groups are those in which individual versatility is developed by encouraging each member to express his own thoughts and needs, to help other individuals, and to contribute both to the group task and to group maintenance.

Ineffective groups are those in which the leader plays a variety of roles—moderator, summarizer, arbitrator, policeman, supporter, suggestor of ideas—while members are supposed to confine their contributions to a limited pattern. Anyone breaking through this rigid mold is seen as a disrupter.

An effective group permits individuals to behave in accordance with their own personality and needs, as well as in regard to the wide range of group needs. By the individual's becoming aware of his role and of the group's sensitivity to the needs of the situation, effective human relations can take place.

8. *Individual action and responsibility are more likely to result from shared decision-making than from autocratic decision-making.* In the democratic group process, in which all members of the group share in making decisions, the individual cannot but feel responsibility and involvement in those decisions. As a consequence, he is involved in assuming responsibility for the actions that follow the decisions.

In many situations it has been shown that autocratic leadership frequently brings quicker decisions but longer periods for implementation of those decisions. If the individual feels his opinion does not count and he is not invited to share in the decision-making process, he cannot feel there is any responsibility on his part for what happens after the decision is made. It is really not his decision; it is someone else's.

In the democratic decision-making process it may require more time to reach a decision, because of the shared process of decision-making, but the implementation of that decision requires less time because of the involvement and the understanding of the individuals concerned. Here the effect of good group relations is such as to increase the individual's feeling of responsibility and contribution toward carrying out the decisions in which he is involved. Thus the over-all elapsed time in the democratic administration of the decision-making process is briefer.

As individuals are involved in both making and carrying out decisions, more aspects of their abilities are uncovered and more opportunities for personal growth are presented.

9. *Leadership is a skill which is acquired, not inherited.* In the past, it was thought that certain individuals, because of their personalities, were limited in their ability to achieve leadership. In addition, it was felt that certain persons inherited the personality traits necessary to leadership.

The studies of the social scientists in the last fifteen years invariably indicate that leadership grows out of the situation, and is not merely a sum of personality traits. Studies in social psychology have shown that persons with vastly differing personalities may be effective leaders by acquiring the skills of problem-solving leadership. It was further shown that such skills are not inherited. As someone so aptly stated, "Leaders are made, not born."

Frequently these skills are communicated and learned from parents, teachers, business associates, and others. In addition, experience in leadership training by numbers of colleges, schools, and organizations proves that leadership skills can be "taught as well as caught."

Such a concept of leadership gives the individual hope that he can be a leader. This is an additional contribution of the study of group relations to the benefit of the individual in our society.

These nine points have attempted to show some of the ways in which the emphasis and concern of the social scientist with the study of group relations have at their core the importance of the individual.

Social science, by discovering what happens in group situations and what causes different individual behavior, and by contributing to the recent growing movement of leadership and membership training has aided materially in freeing and developing the individual, rather than submerging him in the group.

All educators know the importance of the basic social drives of an individual. Three of these basic drives are a sense of belongingness, a sense of achievement, and a sense of recognition. In the complexity of today's world, with our industrialized society, the individual frequently does not develop the security that comes from the satisfaction of these three basic needs.

Groups can serve these basic drives. When a group has learned how to become sensitive to the individual needs of all its members, each individual is helped to feel that he belongs to the group and that the group wants him as a member. Such a group affords him success experiences and recognizes him for them.

The work of the last twenty years in the social sciences needs no apology for its recognition of the importance of the individual. The individual and his relationships with others are, and will continue to be, the prime concerns of those who add to the knowledge of how people work, learn, and play.

53. *Geographical Understandings* *

FRANK E. SORENSON

IT WILL NOT surprise most elementary supervisors and teachers to read that the foundation on which formal geography teaching rests is often weak and crumbly, that it lacks mortar and even essential bricks. The problem is clearly one of providing a firm foundation for the more formal

* From Frank E. Sorenson, "Geographical Understandings," in M. Willcockson (ed.), *Social Education of Young Children* (2nd ed.; Washington, D. C.: National Council for the Social Studies, NEA, 1956), pp. 56–59.

geography teaching which usually begins in grade four. The foundation effort may well be termed: "A Beginning Program of Geography Readiness."

Geography readiness is that phase of the teaching and learning process that contributes directly to children's desire and ability to acquire the concepts and understandings essential to an appreciation of the association of the earth's lands and peoples. This concept implies an informal but carefully planned series of readiness experiences for grades one through three; also a more formal group of developmental readiness activities for the middle and upper grades.

In planning geography readiness programs for young children, it seems appropriate for each contributor to start with a list of basic assumptions. The following are submitted for the reader's consideration:

1. All elementary teachers need to develop and maintain an instructional environment which stimulates learning.

2. Lower grade teachers (K-3) should not teach geography as a formal discipline but should provide the essential foundation instruction in a well-organized, systematic program of geography readiness; this program should be centered first in the local community and later in type communities spread over the United States.

3. Geography readiness programs at lower, intermediate, and upper grade levels should be flexible and provide a wide variety of learning activities appropriate for both group and individual development.

4. The chief objectives of a geography readiness program should be:

    a. To help children acquire in their early years at school an inquisitive attitude toward those elements in the environment that provide early essentials such as food, clothing, shelter, communication, and transportation.

    b. To give children elementary experiences in community study so they will discover how families use what is available for daily needs and how some things must come from other communities. For example, guided trips to a master farm, mill, creamery, store, factory, or newspaper office can be good learning activity as well as suitable background experience for instruction to follow.

    c. To acquaint children with the customary learning aids that are to be used increasingly as they advance in geography study, such as maps and globes.

    d. To help children acquire progressively a determination to know lands and peoples everywhere through books, radio, television, and travel.

The following principles may serve as program guidelines as the teacher plans and implements programs of geography readiness. Others can be added.

1. In the primary grades geography readiness activities are usually associated with the language arts and social studies instruction.
2. The pattern of geography readiness is to be one of graded learning experiences and opportunities that elevate the children almost unconsciously. Familiar concepts are to be the doorways to many expanded understandings of their community.
3. Effectiveness of the geography readiness instruction can be evaluated in part by noting the extent to which the children derive emotional satisfaction from each act and their degree of pride in learning. This implies that children like to do things that have meaning and interest for them.

Pattern of Instruction

A random survey of courses of study suggests the following pattern of lower grade instruction in social studies:

Grade 1—Area: Home and School
General Objective: To help children gain an understanding and appreciation of the nature and function of home and school in our democracy.
Geography Readiness Objective: To introduce children to the sources of their food, clothing, shelter, forms of communication, and transportation.
Readiness Suggestions:
1. Guided Conversation—Encourage each child to talk about:
   a. the kinds of food he likes
   b. the places that raise this food
   c. the steps his parents must take to secure it
   d. the best ways to store food
   e. the need to earn money to buy food
   f. the kind of clothing needed by a family
   g. the steps necessary to make this clothing
   h. the places where the clothing comes from
   i. the need to earn money to buy it
   j. the different kinds of houses in the community and reasons why they differ
   k. the materials needed to build a house

    l. the source of those materials

    m. the things that go with a house such as a furnace or heating stove, kitchen and bathroom items, furniture, shrubs and grass for the yard.

2. Guided Reading

Arrange for the children to read interesting stories that tell about home and school; use a carefully graded text of words and concepts; and lead toward the achievement of the geography readiness objectives. The alert first grade teacher will arrange the reading table with many general readers easy in content, and others that tell about food, clothing and shelter. The children will also read stories in their social studies text. Selection of these books is an important step in the development of a guided reading activity leading to geography readiness.

3. Picture Study

In the highly visual magazines of today there are wonderful pictures to use in teaching about food, clothing, shelter, communication, and transportation. For example, a collection of airplane pictures displayed carefully on the floor or on a low bulletin board could start a series of geography readiness activities such as: (a) writing together a story entitled "Children Also Fly," (b) a trip with mother to the local airport, (c) an oral reading lesson on the Weather Man, (d) a vocabulary lesson on words like pilot, co-pilot, radio, weather, airplane, airport, airmail, fighter, bomber.

4. Playing Store

Another activity that contributes to geography readiness is the building and operation of a "play store." This can be followed by a trip to a real store where the man in charge will show the children that their food comes from many places.

Grade 2—Area: The Local Community

General Objective: To help children gain an understanding and appreciation of the nature and function of the local community.

Geography Readiness Objective: To help children discover the ways in which their day-to-day activities are affected by (a) the location of the community, (b) the ever-changing weather, (c) the riches and limitations of surrounding land and water.

Readiness Suggestions:

1. Guided Conversation—As a part of a series of reading or social studies lessons encourage children to answer such questions as the following:

a. Where do we live? Can we find our community on a map? Is our community large or small? Why? Is our community close to or far away from other communities? Which of the neighboring communities have you visited? How did you make the trip? Why did you make the trip?

b. What is the weather like today? Do we have both cold and warm weather each year? Do you think cold or warm weather is best? Why? What kind of clothing do people wear in warm weather? Cold weather? When is the farmer busy in his fields —in cold weather or in warm weather? How do animals prepare for cold weather? Warm weather?

c. In what ways is our community rich? Poor? Does our community have farms? Ranches? Forests? Fish? Animals? Factories? Can you tell all about a hill? A valley? A mountain? Is our community near an iron mine? A coal mine? A copper mine? Is there a river or lake nearby? If so, how is each used? What do we use each day that comes from other communities? How do we tell people in other communities what we need? Does our community have a railroad? An airport? Good roads?

d. Many workers help to make our town a good place to live. Who are they? How do each of these workers help us?

2. Guided Reading

There are many wonderful reading and social studies books for grade 2 which contribute to geography readiness. They include *The House by the Railroad Track, Getting Ready for Winter, Summer Time, The Useful Forest, Beautiful New Houses, The County Fair,* and others. Children can use them for:

a. Leisure reading at the reading table or at their seats

b. Factual reading to discover the answers to questions by the teacher

c. Comparative reading to discover more about other places

d. Vocabulary study to learn new words and their meaning

3. Picture and Map Study—The community is often rich in picture and map resources. Here are a few suggestions for their use:

a. Unit bulletin board displays on subjects such as: Our Land, Our Weather, Our Workers, Our Products, How Products Travel

b. Daily lesson materials when they contain information pertinent to the topic under consideration

c. Scrap books on topics of pupil interest and need

d. Vocabulary and concepts study for the development of geography readiness. The nearby filling station has maps that should prove useful, and airline officers are very generous about supplying them. In addition the teacher and the children should have daily contacts with a simplified globe. It is wrong to assume that the children's community is only as large as the area they cover from day to day. If they have brothers or fathers overseas their community includes faraway places. The second grade teacher must plan her geography readiness program accordingly.

4. Community Study

A wide-awake teacher plans five or six yearly excursions into the community. Mothers will often provide cars and supervision. The purpose of the field trips is to help children understand the institutions and services which provide their daily needs such as food, clothing, shelter, communication, and transportation. Suggested places to visit are: a dairy farm or mill; a clothing factory or store; a lumberyard or furniture factory; the telephone or telegraph office; the local newspaper office; the truck or railroad terminal; the airport.

5. Motion Pictures

When it is not practical to take children into the community, community agencies and services often can be brought into the school through the use of motion pictures. Any standard university or school motion picture catalog will suggest appropriate titles. The teacher should however preview all films.

Grade 3—Area: Type Communities in the United States

General Objective: To help children gain an understanding and appreciation of the chief kinds of communities found in the United States, thus teaching the lesson of community responses to the local physical environment.

Geography Readiness Objective: To help children discover how families live and make a living throughout one year in the well-characterized type communities such as lumbering, mining, manufacturing, and trading; also how several communities work together for the good of all.

Readiness Suggestions:

1. Guided Conversation

Guiding learners from the known to the unknown through conversation is a basic procedure of good teaching. In this way children's experiences become the doorways to new learning situations. In conducting reading or social studies lessons the third grade teacher may find helpful the following lead questions or statements:

a. Where in the United States is our community located? Can we find it on a map of the United States? On the globe? What large cities are near our community? How far must we travel to reach the mountains? The oceans? The State Capital? The National Capital?

b. This week we want to have several pupils in the class tell about interesting journeys they have taken to other places in the United States. We will find these places on the map. Who would like to be the first to tell about an interesting trip?

c. Today Mr. X is here to tell us of his visit to a community that is different from ours. When he is finished you may ask questions. (This activity suggests a procedure for using parents and other adults as resource persons when type communities are being introduced.)

d. Let us make a list of some of the different kinds of communities in the United States. We can add to this list as we discover new ones. (The list should include ranching, general farming, dairy farming, lumbering, fishing, manufacturing, trading, suburb, metropolis, seaport, county seat.) Let us locate one of each of these communities on the map of the United States.

2. Guided Reading

Many teachers prefer to emphasize factual reading in a program of geography readiness for third grade children. To assist with this effort a number of social studies texts have been prepared. Some of the leisure books on the reading table may tell about individual communities while others include stories of six or more differing communities.

3. Picture and Map Study

Miss Y, a third grade teacher in a small community school near Lincoln, has assembled a wonderful collection of pictures and maps to use in teaching about type communities in the United States. When asked how she collected them she offered these suggestions:

a. Pictures can be found almost daily in current publications and from other requested sources.

b. The children help to collect them. For example, when studying Joe's *Many Goats and His Sheep* they look for pictures of grazing in the arid Southwest.

    c. For filing, pictures are labeled and mounted on heavy sheets of paper of the same size. This also makes it easier to use them on the bulletin board or with the opaque projector.

    d. Pictures are classified according to type communities and are kept ready for immediate use.

    e. Pictures are reviewed from time to time to eliminate poorer ones and continue the search for better ones. Miss Y collects, files, and uses maps as she does pictures. The fact that finding simplified maps is not easy only makes the effort more challenging. "Pictures and maps can be used successfully in a dozen ways," says Miss Y. "These include (1) overview material for unit introduction, (2) highlight material for teaching concepts, (3) visual material for testing, (4) development material for teaching new geography words and concepts, and (5) atmosphere material to stimulate thought and questions.

4. Community Study—The following topics may suggest appropriate activities:

    a. How many automobiles are there in our community? How are they used? Where did they come from?

    b. How many airplanes are there in our community? How are they used? Where did they come from?

    c. What foods are produced in our community? What foods are sent to us by other communities? What foods do we sell to other communities?

    d. Where are the communities that produce the clothing that we wear? What, if anything, do we send in return for clothing? How are these products shipped?

    e. Where does our community get its building materials? Why do all the people in the United States want to protect the forests?

Miss Y has also found that children and their parents will take a great interest in their community if they are asked to help prepare a community museum. The collections may be permanent or temporary.

5. Motion Pictures

There are many motion pictures useful in carrying out the Geography Readiness program in grade 3. Selections should be carefully made so that each will tell the story of what life in one type of community is like.

54. Efficient Use of Geography Texts*

ANNICE DAVIS ELKINS

TEACHERS highly successful in teaching reading often face difficulties training children to use geography textbooks efficiently. Pointing up the problem are several contributing factors.

First, there is a shift in procedure from *extensive* to *intensive* reading. Concern is not on *learning to read* but rather on *reading to learn*.

Second, many reading skills are needed in reading geography textbooks. Not only is the material of the work or study type, but there are pictures, maps, graphs, the index, and statistics, which must be read if complete understanding of the text is to be achieved.

Third, in a normal classroom there may be a spread of as much as five years in reading ability. Modern texts are usually written on an easy reading level for a given grade. However, in a class of varied reading ability not all pupils can be expected to read the text fluently.

Furthermore, a child with high rating in reading basic readers is not necessarily able to read correct meaning into geographic materials. Many specific geographic skills and abilities are needed for understanding geography textbooks.

Thus the problem resolves into two parts. On the one hand, pupils must be trained to use work or study materials. On the other hand, they must be trained in geographic thinking.

Such skills and abilities fall into three categories: (1) securing information, (2) organizing and interpreting information, and (3) sharing and using information.

Securing Information

Simply stated, the purpose for reading geography textbooks is to find information about the kinds of people, the kinds of work, and the kinds of lands on the earth, and to find some reasons why people live and work as they do in different parts of the world. Good instruction in geography lies in the ability of textbooks and teacher to make both the people and the land on which they live *real* to the child. Every boy and girl should be given

* From Annice Davis Elkins, "Efficient Use of Geography Texts," *NEA Journal* (February, 1952), pp. 81–82. Reprinted by permission of the author and the *NEA Journal*.

some understanding of the problems people face in establishing ways of life.

The purpose for reading must not only be clear to the child, but his desire to read must be aroused. Planning the assignment with the help of the class helps to create this desire to read. Picture reading also whets the pupil's interest.

Let's consider the matter of pictures for a moment. Everybody knows that pictures play an important role in modern textbooks. Pictures often serve as a springboard for the introduction of a unit. They are valuable in establishing correct imagery with proper geographic terms. They furnish vicarious experiences so needed by readers when actual experience is lacking.

Both teacher and pupil should be able to: (1) observe what is seen in the landscape either firsthand or from pictures, (2) classify what is seen (man-made or natural features), and (3) interpret what is seen (give reasons which help explain man-made in relation to natural features). Such training begins with field trips about the community.

Through these trips relationships between man's activities and his natural environment become gradually a part of the child's thinking. For example, a picture showing cattle grazing on the pampas of South America has *real* meaning if the child has seen cattle grazing in his own environs.

Maps and globes are also valuable in this prereading venture. The language of maps must be understood before they can become effective tools of learning.

First, a child must read meaning *into* maps. He must *see* oceans where the maps are blue. Pictures are invaluable in teaching map symbols.

After having acquired the ability to read meaning *into* maps, the next step is to read meaning *out of* maps. This interpretation of what map symbols mean enables the child to visualize new areas. For example, if he can compare the latitude, nearness of mountains to the sea, and the warm ocean current of Alaska with similar conditions in Norway, he can anticipate Norway's climate, its forests, and its fishing.

Observation from both pictures and maps should be recorded on the board in tentative statements to be checked for accuracy by reading textual materials. Often there are questions which arise from the pictures or maps. New ideas are discovered which cannot be answered from previous study. Such questions give purpose for further investigation by the child.

After gathering all the information possible from pictures and maps, teacher and pupils can then select observations and questions to be checked by reading. The teacher should guide pupils into organizing these in outline form.

An appraisal of the ability of the class to locate information in the textbook is helpful. For example, suggestions from the class can be made as to key words to be looked up in the index of the textbooks in order to find answers to class questions. A star might be placed by questions to be answered from statistics. These are only two of many ways such checks can be made.

Organizing and Interpreting Information

Pupils must acquire skills in geographic thinking in order to read a text intelligently. This involves the ability to see the relationship between geographic conditions in a certain area and the established pattern of living there. Pupils must learn to see the relationship between climate, landforms, location, soil, and such natural resources as forests and minerals and the nature of the people, their political and social ideas, their experience in industries, their opportunities for contact with people of other lands. These understandings are built slowly by means of daily guidance.

In the fourth grade such understandings begin with seeing the relationship between the types of food, clothing, and shelter a people use and the temperatures, amount of rainfall, and the ability of the soil to produce crops.

In the sixth grade the child sees that not only natural features but cultural features involving political and social traditions and pressure of population help explain the way of life of a people. Life in India and China, for example, would be difficult to understand without some knowledge of the heritage of the people.

One difficulty a child has in reading geographic meaning into verbal materials is his lack of training in seeing the relationship between man's activities and the natural environment. *This* is the essence of reading ability in geography. A wise teacher selects paragraphs showing such relationships and works through them with the class. This is done over and over from grade to grade before the pupils use this technique independently. It is most important for geographic understandings.

The teacher puts two columns on the board. He makes one "Man's Activities" (cultural features); the other, "Natural Features." As the class finds facts about a particular area, he lists them in the proper column. For example, the following classification was made by a class after reading several paragraphs describing life in early New England:

Man's Activities	*Natural Features*
Few farms	Poor soils
	Sand dunes
Poor roads	Marshes
	Hilly
People live near the sea	Heavily wooded
	Rivers, short, with falls and rapids

Often new geographic concepts appear which must be clarified. Words met for the first time or used in a new context need explanation. Pronunciation of foreign names presents a problem to young readers. New ideas, new geographic concepts, new words—all should be anticipated by the teacher and clarified before the child begins to read.

Remembering the wide spread of reading ability in a given classroom, provision for these individual differences in reading ability must be taken into account in a reading assignment. For example, a child who reads independently may prepare an extra report from supplementary materials. On the other hand, a slow reader needs individual help in working through the exercises in the textbook. The teacher should make sure this child understands the directions given in the exercises. Often lack of understanding of these directions stymies slow readers.

Sharing and Using Information

There is a variety of ways in which information learned by pupils may be shared with the class. Many of these ways also teach the child to assimilate his information and use it in a constructive manner. At the same time a check of the reading or verbal materials can be made. Oral reports using pictures, maps, and information from the text are effective. Imaginary trips are fun.

Most texts provide exercises to be written for formal check on reading. Another form of written reports liked by children is letters describing a trip through the country. There are many constructive sharing devices that give the teacher a chance to evaluate the geographic reading and understanding of the pupil.

Three Requisites

To summarize my belief concerning reading effectiveness in the field of geography, I might say that three factors are involved in using geography textbooks efficiently:

1. Specific skills needed for geographic understandings.

2. Specific reading skills and abilities needed for reading informational materials.

3. The reading skills and abilities already at the child's command.

Weakness in any one of these must be strengthened before there can be unity of purpose. It is only through such unity that the desired effectiveness is attained.

55. *Imaginative Teaching of Geography* *

FLOYD F. CUNNINGHAM

W HAT ARE the requirements of good geography teaching? They are twofold: Geography worthy of the name cannot be taught without a vivid and lively acquaintance with detailed facts. And good geography teaching requires creative teachers.

Actually, these two requirements overlap. Thorough knowledge of the subject matter is the first prerequisite for creative teaching. The geography teacher who is not fully acquainted with his subject is likely to find himself limited to the textbook method.

Creative teaching requires a solid understanding of material beyond that contained in the text. Travel, for example, is of enormous value to those who are to be good geography teachers, but travel without a purpose is of little value. What a person gets out of visiting an area depends largely on what he takes there with him.

Creative teachers are enthusiastic about youth, about the subject, and about teaching. They use a flexible approach and vary the means of teaching to suit the ends being sought.

Some perceptive teachers use problems sensed in a classroom situation as the point of departure for discussion of problems involving geographic analysis.

Others use a laboratory-seminar approach: Pupils engage in different types of exploratory studies and firsthand laboratory experimentation. In-

* From Floyd F. Cunningham, "Imaginative Teaching of Geography," *NEA Journal* (April, 1959), pp. 40–41. Reprinted by permission of the author and the *NEA Journal*.

dividuals or small groups of pupils conduct background studies of various concepts and make experimental studies of problems and principles. Some teachers concentrate on issues and have panel discussions and resource leaders.

This list is by no means exhaustive. Alert, creative teachers are always on the lookout for new methods.

Of great help to geography teachers and to administrators is an understanding of what the study of geography has become today. Geography has moved forward from its beginnings as mere observation and cataloging of the natural features of the earth. As one well-known geographer, Preston E. James, has said:

> But geographers do much more than observe and catalog. They also analyze the significance of differences which are observed from place to place. . . . The present nature and arrangement of things on the earth have meaning with respect to the operation of physical and cultural processes in the past.
>
> To understand the significance of what is observed on the earth today it is necessary to go back to origins and trace developments. But it is also necessary to forecast the consequences. Only when the present nature and arrangement of things on the earth have been projected both into the past and into the future, has the significance of the differences from place to place on the earth been fully analyzed.

Thus, geography and geography teaching have greatly expanded. For example, today teachers emphasize the close relationship existing between geography and national policy.

Similarly, today's teachers present geography and international relations and tensions as closely related. The actions of a "have not" state in its attempts to provide itself with buffers and satellites are shown to be phenomena of political geography.

When students are helped to make more precise geographic evaluations of states and areas, they can make better interpretations of these states and areas. Such interpretations in turn can be examined for their effects upon policy decisions that may have important military and political significance.

Thus, area evaluations help students to understand better what is taking place in the world. Therefore, we are trying today to teach geography in such a way that the subject becomes functional in the understanding of current affairs. Students are encouraged to examine contemporary world problems in terms of geographic concepts.

For example, a geography teacher could use contemporary French-Algerian problems as a starting point for a study of the Mediterranean and

African areas. Students would be encouraged to do current reading about the situation in order to get a background for understanding. Maps, geography textbooks, newspaper stories, films, and slides about North Africa and France would help to begin this study.

After reading about and observing the Algerian situation, students can debate the various sides of the issue. A study of climate, resources in that part of the world, and many other factors are legitimate accompaniments to these debates. Student interest will be high because the work at hand is contemporary and alive.

Similar projects can be built around domestic political and economic issues. Offshore-oil bills which are presented to Congress could, for example, serve as a fine steppingstone to the study of American geography.

Projects such as these are valuable because they make students aware of the problems of our statesmen, and because they show students that seemingly simple questions sometimes have complex answers. At the same time, projects of this sort demonstrate the importance of geography in the understanding and solution of many contemporary problems.

Another effective way of teaching geography is by use of the unit method. This method, because it has clear objectives, is a strong tool for the geography teacher.

A well-planned and well-developed unit involves the use of significant content and a variety of enriching activities. It provides opportunities for developing problem-solving skills and helps children to achieve geographic understanding and concepts related to the topic around which the unit is built.

It cannot be too firmly stressed that a successful unit program must be built around solid objectives. The teacher must, in advance, plan the objectives in terms of what he wants the students to understand and in terms of the abilities he wants them to develop.

We are making progress in proving the worth of geographical study in appraising and interpreting the problems that face the world today. However, we must do more than we are doing to convince others of this geographical need. Perhaps the best way is by example: We must demonstrate the dynamic characteristics of geography in our own teaching and in its application to the solution of local, national, and world problems.

During the last few years, a noticeable attempt has been made to bring geographic material into the lower grades. The study of weather and climate has been introduced in some primary grades, as well as certain concepts of conservation. Map companies are now grading maps and globes, the essential tools of geographic instruction. There is also a determined effort on the part of many geography teachers to make a careful evaluation of the great amount of free material now available.

Geography is one of the most neglected subjects in the American schools, particularly in the secondary schools. We must educate our youth so that they will know how to participate in world affairs. A knowledge of other peoples—their resources and their problems of survival—is necessary if we are to learn to live together in a peaceful world.

56. *Studying Other Countries* *

LEONARD S. KENWORTHY

SOME PEOPLE say that the world is growing smaller, and in a sense that is true. But in another sense the world is constantly growing larger. At the close of World War II there were approximately seventy-five countries on our globe. Since that time twenty-five new nations have been formed, bringing the number of nations in the world today to around one hundred.

This means that the effective social studies teacher must be able to move quickly and competently from Chile to Ceylon to the Central African Federation, or from Guatemala to Germany to Ghana, or from Mexico to Morocco to Malaya.

With so many countries to study now and with the expectation that there will be more within a few years, it is more important than ever before for teachers to consider effective ways of studying other countries, to start or to enlarge their small libraries of books and their files of current materials on the various nations of the world, and to reflect on the criteria by which countries should be selected for study.

This article singles out the problem of how to study the many nations of the world, leaving the reader to explore other writings on the materials available for the study of other lands and peoples, and the criteria by which countries should be selected for study.[1]

* From Leonard S. Kenworthy, "Studying Other Countries," *Social Education* (April, 1959), pp. 159–62. Reprinted by permission of the author and *Social Education*.

[1] For material on the other two topics not treated here, see the writer's volume on *Introducing Children to the World in Elementary and Junior High Schools* (New York: Harper, 1956) and his two chapters in Ralph C. Preston's *Teaching World Understanding* (Englewood, N. J.: Prentice-Hall, 1955).

Some Pitfalls to Avoid

Unconsciously and without malice towards other lands and peoples, most of us have fallen into ways of studying other countries which do a great injustice to their citizens and give a distorted view of them to our students. It might be well for all of us to examine our current practices to see if we have fallen into such traps.

One pitfall is to present other countries as they existed yesterday, but not as they exist today. For example, we still picture the Mexican, with his serape, sleeping in the sun, with his sombrero at his side or tilted over his eyes. Or we portray Africans as naked, drum-beating savages living in mud huts in hot, wet lands. We forget or we fail to stress the fact that all Mexicans never fitted that stereotype or that all Africans did not live as we have said. Furthermore, we tend to forget the vast changes which have taken place in these and other parts of the world, with the industrialization of so many nations and the development of large metropolitan areas like Mexico City, Casablanca, Leopoldville, Johannesburg, and other urban centers.

Or we devote two or three days to a country, treating it hurriedly and superficially, content that we have "covered" that part of the syllabus, little realizing that the residue of our study will be a few unrelated and probably unimportant facts. Like the men in the fable of the blind men and the elephant, our students will have discovered the trunk or the ears or the tail and not the whole animal—or country.

In our desire to arouse interest on the part of pupils, we often fall into the pitfall of stressing the bizarre and the colorful rather than the realistic, especially at the elementary-school level. Hence we teach about the igloos of Alaska and the windmills of The Netherlands, leaving lasting misimpressions about these and other parts of the world.

Or we teach about a country as if all the people in it dressed alike, thought alike, and acted alike. We talk about *The French, The Japanese,* or *The Brazilians,* failing to stress the infinite variety within countries as well as between them. How can one gain a complete and accurate picture today, for instance, of Malaya without taking into account the large numbers of Chinese, Indians, and Pakistani as well as the larger group of Malays? Or how can one study Guatemala without stressing the large percentage of Indians as well as the Spanish and mestizos?

Then again, we may like a country very much and present only the best aspects of it—or conversely, dislike it and present only the worst phases of it.

As historians and social scientists we need to have a single rather than a double standard for studying countries. This is especially true of countries like Russia and China. One result of presenting only their weaknesses has been the tailspin into which the American public has been thrown by its recent realization that Russians, like the peoples of other countries, do some things uncommonly well.

Another pitfall into which we often fall is that of judging others by our standards. Thus we condemn India, Burma, Ceylon, and other nations for being "independent" in their foreign policies, rather than trying to understand why they have taken such a stand. Or we ridicule the French because their plumbing is not as good as ours, often overlooking or minimizing the areas of life in which the people of France may equal or surpass us.

Finally, we often tend to equate knowledge about a nation with respect for it or an understanding of it. We amass an enormous number of facts, hoping thereby to promote an understanding of that country. As a result we produce, or try to produce, little walking World Almanacs or National Geographics rather than competent, well-informed, understanding world-minded Americans.

The Many Ways of Studying Countries

There are scores of ways of studying other countries, from which competent teachers can select the ones most appropriate to their classes or the ones which they are able to handle. The combined use of many of these approaches in the study of any nation can enrich the understanding of it and provide a variety of methods for building and maintaining interest on the part of pupils.

On a recent nine-months trip to the new nations of Africa, the Middle East, and Asia, the author of this article tried out several of these approaches and found them exciting and revealing. For example, one can enter a village or city and listen for all the sounds that he hears, tape recording them for future use. In this way the dimension of sound is added to that of sight to develop a well-rounded view of a country.

Or one can stand on the side of a major highway and learn much about a nation. In Pakistan, for example, the writer saw twelve different modes of transportation on one street corner, ranging from rubber-tired camel carts carrying cotton bales to the modern limousine of the Pakistan Airways.

A view of the hats of a country can help one to understand it, for they represent history, position, religion, rank, economics, and politics. A count, for example, of the number of old men wearing the fez in Morocco as opposed to the number of young men wearing them reveals the tremendous cleavage between generations in their acceptance of innovations, for the fez is still a symbol there of the old regime.

For those competent in music, the songs of a country can tell much about its philosophy and history. In a student group at Penn State University recently a highly qualified musician was playing a piece of Indian music. When she stopped playing, one of the students asked her if she had completed the song for it sounded unfinished to him. To this question she replied, "Does life always complete itself? Does one always return to *do?*" The group stopped and thought, and through the incident gained a much deeper insight into India and Indian philosophy than lectures and books had previously revealed.

Similarly, the study of literature, of language, of movies and plays, of holidays, of children's drawings, and of a host of other subjects and activities can help us as teachers and through us our students to get inside other countries and cultures.[2]

Taken alone, these methods may give a distorted view of a country; taken together they should give as broad and deep a view as is possible without close contact with the people themselves.

What is needed today in the study of any country or culture is a multi-dimensional, interdisciplinary approach, drawing upon the insights of history, geography, sociology, social psychology, economics, anthropology, government, psychology, psychiatry, literature and language, religion and philosophy, and the arts. As social studies teachers or social scientists, we should draw upon the many disciplines in our own broad field as well as upon many related disciplines.

A Possible Pattern for Studying Countries

There are always dangers in suggesting "patterns," for they may be meaningful to the person who has developed them and not prove useful to others. Or they may become merely "patterns" rather than teaching devices for better understanding. Over a period of several years the writer has experimented with the chart or pattern for studying communities, countries, and cultures which appears below. It is hoped that this pattern will suggest

[2] For a provocative study of many of these techniques, see Margaret Mead and Rhoda Metraux, *The Study of Culture at a Distance* (Chicago: University of Chicago Press, 1953).

to both teachers and students a logical way of looking at any country. Even after much of the mass of detailed information has been forgotten they may still have a method by which they can re-examine countries which they once studied in school or new nations which they have never studied. Or they can use this pattern to look at a new community or state into which they have moved in this period of high mobility in the United States.

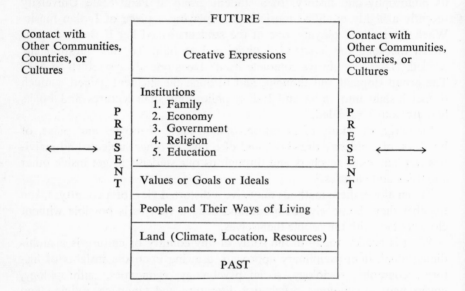

The best point for starting any study of a country is usually with its geographic base. This is the stage on which the drama of human history takes place and it is of vital importance to any nation.

A look at the geographic base of Norway should reveal the mountainous terrain of that country and explain quickly why the Norwegians have settled largely in small communities along the fjords; have taken their livestock up into the cleared patches in the mountains; have gone to sea; or have emigrated to other parts of the world. Or an examination of Libya or Jordan's geographic bases will soon show why their economies are not viable. The use of polar projection maps will explain to students why Russia feels surrounded by the various pacts of the Western world or why Cambodia and Laos and other Southeast Asia nations are cautious in their relations with China and Russia.

Then come the people—the actors on the stage which has just been examined. They cannot be portrayed in one simple tableau, for there is always an infinite variety within any given country, whether it be Kenya in East Africa, with its large African population, its small but economically and politically dominant white group, and its large number of Indians and Pakistani; or Brazil, a melting pot of Italians, Spaniards, Portuguese, Germans, Russians, Japanese, and others.

There is almost always an infinite variety in ways of living, too, within countries. This is far more true of the economically underdeveloped nations than it is of the countries of the Western world. But there is variety even in a country like France, with vast differences between the lives of the French farmers and the residents of Paris, Lyons, or Marseilles, making it ridiculous to study France by concentrating on Paris, as is so often done. How much greater are the differences in a nation like India, with the range of human activities covering the span from the most primitive life in an isolated village to the highly sophisticated existence of upper-middle-class citizens in a city like New Delhi.

In moving from the geographic base to the people, it is important in every country to see the relationships between these two factors, and to understand how the land has affected the people and in turn how the people have affected the land.

The values or beliefs of the people of any country are not easily understood by an outsider, but they are central to the study of every nation. How can one understand the institutions which have been created in any part of the world without knowing why these institutions developed? How can one understand the actions of any group of people without some knowledge of their values? Lacking such knowledge, the student will judge others by his own standards—a grievous mistake in the study of any country.

Thus any study of Southeast Asia must include at least an elementary knowledge of Buddhism, or any study of the Middle East a passing acquaintance at least with Islam. Students should also understand the belief in the importance of the larger family in most parts of the world today and of the values of tribalism in large parts of Africa. Any understanding of the Union of South Africa today must be predicated on at least some stress on the rigid, orthodox interpretation of Christianity on the part of most whites in that country, and any understanding of Russia must be based on at least an elementary knowledge of dialectic materialism, even if that phrase must be interpreted in the most elementary ways.

In every country in the world today there are deep rifts and conflicts between value systems which must be understood in order to appreciate current events in any country. Thus, in Ghana, one can only appreciate the political struggle if it is set within the frame of a titanic struggle between the tribal chiefs and the representatives of modernization and westernization, or between the various economic forces within the country. Similarly, one must appreciate the views of the zamindars in West Pakistan and of the mullahs as representing the power of Islam in order to probe below the surface of unrest in that part of the world.

In the chart on page 360, the section on values or beliefs precedes that on institutions because it is the beliefs of any group of people which have largely effected the institutions which they have created.

In all or almost all societies there are five basic institutions which people have developed. These are the family, the economy, the religion, the government, and the educational system—whether it is formally or informally organized. Some attention needs to be given to each of these major forms of human organization, even at the elementary or junior high school level of instruction.

In the future it may be necessary to add other institutions, such as the mass media, but the five we have mentioned here are central today in all societies.

In studying each of these human institutions it is important for students to know that there are problems connected with them in each country. These range from the problem of internal security in Burma, Malaya, and Vietnam to that of governmental organization in France and Italy.

As an integral part of the study of any country, students should learn about the creative expressions of that part of the world. Students need to learn that people everywhere have created in the past and are still creating. And students need to understand that the future vitality of any nation or people is dependent in large part upon its creativity.

Such creativity may yield simple and beautiful products such as the kente cloth togas for the men in Ghana or the simple wooden stools in the homes of Kenya Africans, with colored beads attractively embedded in patterns in the soft wood. Or creativity may mean the development of new ideas such as the growth of parliamentary democracy in England or the public-school system in the United States.

The emphasis in most studies of other lands and peoples should be upon the present, but the present cannot be understood without reference to the past. And no study of a country will be adequate without a look at its future. People everywhere are proud of their history; people in many parts of the world are pulled today by their hopes for the future. This pull of the future is especially apparent in the new and emerging nations of the world.

Finally, it is important to see that no country today is isolated. Each has its contacts with other parts of the world and affects and in turn is affected by other nations.

To include all these aspects of life in our studies of other countries means that we will need to study fewer countries, but to examine those few nations with far greater depth and with far greater breadth than we have usually done in the past.

57. *Community Resources* *

AMO DE BERNARDIS

R ARE IS the modern teacher who does not complain about the lack of adequate materials to carry on his teaching. Most teachers call for more books, more maps, more of this and that. But films, slides, radio, models, dioramas, and the like cost money and many schools are on economy budgets. Consequently many worth-while aids are not in sufficient quantity to meet the needs of the teachers. But they should not despair. There is a very rich laboratory for learning—the community—which is available for educational use whenever a teacher chooses to make the simple arrangements necessary. Within any community, be it large or small, there are opportunities for learning which can be used to the advantage of children and teachers, some of them more valuable than the contents of books or the images on screens.

Some school people have a tendency to withdraw from the life stream of the community and are satisfied if children merely read and talk about what goes on in the world about them, preferably in a world that is distant and strange. Some people may feel that elementary-school children are too young to be concerned with the local environment. Yet the children live each day in this environment and they are very alert to its existence, even if they do not understand it very well.

The fire station, wrecking yard, millpond, creek, garage, corner store, gravel pit—all are familiar haunts for children. The school should realize

* From Amo De Bernardis, "Community Resources," in M. Willcockson (ed.), *Social Education of Young Children* (2nd ed.; Washington, D.C.: National Council for the Social Studies, NEA, 1956), pp. 130–33.

that these and other resources in the community are effective means of teaching and learning a great many facts of the most practical nature. Besides, these experiences become a frame of reference for understanding and interpreting the life of other communities which the child may read about but never see. Field trips to these places in the community can be a most valuable aid to the child's growth and development.

Sometimes there is a tendency to look upon a field trip or a classroom visitor merely as a treat or something to be done when all the work is completed. This is a mistake. If properly planned, these outside contacts will make children aware of the relationship between school and community and at the same time heighten their appreciation of what the community contributes to their daily life. These contacts will develop the powers of concentration of the individual and improve his skill in reading, listening, writing, expressing ideas, and evaluating opinions. The class as a whole will profit by building up a common background of experiences for future activities.

The use of the community as a laboratory for teaching also offers the school an excellent opportunity to build better relationships with the public. As teachers and parents work together to locate materials and opportunities for field trips, both groups will develop better appreciation of each other's problems.

Resource Material in Abundance

Today practically every business or industry produces booklets, pamphlets, charts and films which can be used by the school. If it is located in a large city, the school has access to an unlimited number of privately produced teaching aids. In fact, many teachers complain that they are being flooded with sponsored materials, and even the teacher in a small town has access to them. Many of them contain valuable information. It remains for the school to locate, evaluate and use them.

Not to be overlooked as sources for printed and audio-visual aids are the patrons of the school. Practically every home has magazines, photographs, relics, and even some equipment which can be used by the school. People are usually very happy to loan them to schools; sometimes they are even willing to donate them to a collection of instructional materials. Properly planned and directed, the seeking out and collecting of these teaching aids can be a most valuable experience for elementary-school children, especially if the effort is tied in closely with the ongoing work of the particular class.

The selection of teaching materials is an important step in the learning process and the children should share the responsibility of choosing and using them. Ability to select and use materials from all sources is an important skill for children to develop, and at primary age they are not too young to begin. Once the materials are collected, it becomes the responsibility of teacher and class to organize and take care of them.

FAMILIAR PLACES SEEN ANEW

A field trip need not be an elaborate affair involving transportation, chaperonage, and expense. Walks into the nearby community are an accepted part of the modern elementary-school program. Worth-while places within walking distance of most schools are numerous and varied. The new house under construction, the garage, the corner store, the junk yard, the farmer's new pigs, and many others are excellent sources of new experiences for children. Even if they are already familiar to the pupils, there are many features in each case that only an adult can point out.

It is not difficult for the teacher to help her children make an extensive list of trip possibilities in the community. Too often there is a tendency to list only the unusual or the dramatic, and in small communities the idea may develop that there aren't many opportunities for field trips. This is not so. Here, for example, are a few that may be found in whole or in part in many communities:

House being built	Irrigation dam
Vegetable garden	Pumping station
Garage	Home workshop
Post office	Photography labs
Hardware store	Movie theatre
Grocery store	Department store
Dairy farm	Shoe shop
Chicken hatchery	Radio station
Cabinet shop	TV station
Bank	Newspaper
Special local industry	Grain elevator
Telephone exchange	Museum
Library	Lumberyard and mill
Fire station	Zoo
Park	Police station
Church	Bakery
Courthouse	Creamery

If teachers are to make effective use of field trips they must have a program for locating and cataloging available places in the community. The complete catalog will be an inducement for teachers to use field trips sufficiently often. If the program is properly organized, parents, children, and teachers can work cooperatively to prepare the list. Also, in this way parents are helped to understand how field trips fit into the educational program.

Some schools have found it advantageous to develop a form on which to record information about places to visit. Questions like the following will elicit important facts about them and the responsibilities which face the school:

1. How large a class can be accommodated?
2. Are guides provided?
3. What hours will classes be welcomed?
4. For what age level is the trip best suited?
5. Person to contact? (Address and phone number)
6. Nature of place to be visited?

This information can either be placed in a card file for ready reference or be compiled into a community resource handbook, but to be effective it must be kept up to date. New places must be added and others which are found to be unsuitable should be deleted.

PUPILS SHOULD HELP PLAN

A great deal of the success of a field trip depends on the planning, but not all of the arrangements should fall to the teacher. The experience of helping plan a trip to the dairy, the farm, or the post office is very worth while for students. It gives the class an opportunity to use their skills of writing, arithmetic, planning, leadership, and the like. The teacher, however, will need to keep certain points in mind to help children conduct a successful trip.

A few suggestions are:

1. Obtain the assistance of parents. They are especially helpful with younger children.
2. Be sure to obtain permission of parents for the trip.
3. Let the children cooperate in making the plans. This is an important learning experience.
4. Develop a definite plan for the trip—transportation, clothing, safety precautions, time, responsibilities.
5. Establish definite objectives for the trip. Why are we going? What do we want to learn?

6. Make plans to evaluate the trip. Did we achieve our purpose? What did we like about the trip? How could we have improved it?
7. Write thank-you letters.

Field trips and the use of the community as a living textbook will educate the teacher as well as his students. The teacher is not expected to be an expert in every subject which a class might discuss. The teacher today is a specialist in children. He knows how to plan effective learning experiences for them and how to use modern teaching materials and methods to best advantage. Thus the good teacher knows that in any community there are many people who have skills and talents he does not possess. Photographers, stamp collectors, travelers, farmers, mechanics, doctors, clerks, craftsmen, and a host of others can make valuable contributions to education in the classroom. It only remains for the school to let them know that they are needed and to inform them how they can be of assistance.

Again the teacher will profit by keeping a list, in this instance, of persons who can help to enrich the classroom discussion. The suggestions which follow for developing a list have proved effective in schools where human resources are used consistently.

1. Stimulate the interest of teachers and of laymen in the utilization of human resources in classroom situations.
2. Let the school take the lead in expanding a program of citizen participation in educational activities (although the initiative may come from any source).
3. Use laymen on a committee with teachers to plan and carry on the program.
4. Use the personal-interview method in gathering information about prospective participants whenever possible.
5. Remember that any session at which a layman is invited to contribute to a school program should be carefully planned. The layman should be given a clear and thorough explanation of the contribution he is expected to give and the class should be adequately prepared for his contribution.
6. File data of available lay personnel in such a way that the right persons may be procured for needs as they arise.
7. Keep the file active and up to date.
8. Evaluate each contribution objectively for future reference.[1]

Questionnaires to lay people in the community have been used to gather data regarding their talents. Questions usually cover such items as collec-

[1] Metropolitan School Study Council, *Fifty Teachers to a Classroom*. Committee on Human Resources (New York: The Macmillan Company, 1950), p. 34.

tions, travel, occupation, hobbies, and special skills. Once this information is collected it has to be condensed and classified so as to make it convenient for teachers, either on a card file or in a pamphlet. No matter what system is used, the following information should be given: name of person, address, occupation, field of interest, best adapted to what age, dates available, hours available.

KEEP THE VISITOR HAPPY

When people from the community come into the classroom they not only help to make teaching more worth while, but they also get a closer look at the school. For this reason it is important that the resource visitor's experience be a pleasant and profitable one. How well the planning is done and carried out will determine in a large measure how the visitor feels about the experience and how willing he is to repeat it. Many lay people are self-conscious about talking to students. A great deal can be done to ease the situation if formal talks and lectures are kept to a minimum and the emphasis placed on informal discussion and demonstration.

Although a few teachers have through the years used community resources in their teaching, there are still many who do not, perhaps in many cases because a list of people and field trip possibilities are not readily available. Some of this reluctance may also arise because the teacher lacks the necessary experience or skill to use community resources. Many schools have found it advantageous to conduct in-service programs to help teachers learn at first hand the many resources available in their community.

The most successful of these have involved not only the teachers, the administrators, but the people of the community as well. In one case where the program took the form of a workshop, a local industry made funds available for scholarships, travel, and materials. A nearby university supplied the staff and facilities. For five weeks teachers, administrators, businessmen, and others studied how to locate and use the resources of the community. The experiment was so successful that the local school people and the community agreed to make it a continuing program. Any community can plan training of this type for teachers and lay people. It has the advantage of bringing educators and the people of the community together to work on a mutual project and it helps to develop better understanding of the uses of these resources in the educational program.

58. Teaching Social Studies to Poor Readers *

FRANCES HAUSER PARK

PUPILS HAVE little interest in social studies when they cannot understand the concepts and ideas presented by the printed word. Teaching social studies and English to a group of these disinterested poor readers is my assigned duty and my pleasure. All seventh grade pupils at Washington Junior High School are grouped homogeneously by standard reading test scores which are administered during the latter part of the sixth grade. Our class consists of thirty-two seventh graders whose reading test scores ranged from the first grade through the fifth grade. Seventh grade textbooks and materials are too advanced for these slow learners, indifferent learners, and rebellious learners, so we learn social studies concepts through three other channels: (1) vision, (2) imagination, and (3) current events.

Success in our three-part program does not require much reading skill. Yet, the program is designed to let each pupil experience success by learning for himself some new and understandable concept. However, it should be emphasized that reading is not neglected in our learning. Words from our social studies are frequently used in sound and spelling drills, and stories on low reading levels are often employed. But, the learning of social studies concepts would be lost if we attempted all of it through the laborious channel of reading; therefore, we have developed the program which is the subject of this writing. The three divisions of the program are made arbitrarily in order clearly to discuss the function of each one. In practice the divisions overlap continually and smoothly.

The visual part of our program includes maps, films, and filmstrips. As we progress through the year, we build an atlas of commercial maps of each of the areas we study: Mediterranean area; Central and Northern Europe; Russia; Middle East; Far East; South and Central Africa. We also draw a freehand map of each country studied. Most of the students enjoy art work, so they embellish the covers of their atlases with original designs.

As we study each area of the Old World we color a map of that area and place a legend on it to help us read the map. To prevent mistakes and confusion, each map is enlarged on the board and colored by one of the better

* From Frances Hauser Park, "Teaching Social Studies to Poor Readers," *Social Education* (November, 1956), pp. 327–29. Reprinted by permission of the author and *Social Education*.

students. It serves as a guide for coloring individual maps. For each new country we study we add a new page to our atlas. On this page we draw the country, beginning with some geometric figure, such as a square for Egypt, a triangle for Iraq, a trapezoid for Spain, or a cone for India. Then the figure is modified into a reasonable facsimile of the country. Emphasis is on space relationship as we locate and show on the map the important physical and political features of the country. The flag and historical facts in time-line sequence complete the page.

Very carefully we establish the position of the country on the world map and on the globe. We note the directions from Fresno we would follow to reach the country, the best routes by air and ship, and the probable traveling time necessary. This discussion usually develops into imagining a trip to the country and writing about it.

A second division of the visual program is the frequent and planned use of films and filmstrips. These are preordered from the central film library to fit into the course of study. We see the physical features, the vegetation and animal life, the food, clothing, and shelter of the people and the customary life. After anticipatory discussion we follow up the viewing with more discussion. From this study of films and filmstrips comes a large portion of the imaginative part of the social studies program. With each film or filmstrip we organize our talk around the challenge, "Let us imagine we are there!"

The imaginative part of our program is developed by three means: (a) the films and filmstrips; (b) the discussions based on maps; and (c) the use of many flat pictures as the basis for teacher-directed thinking and discussion. There is a wealth of sources for obtaining excellent flat pictures: old and new textbooks; story books; encyclopedias; airline offices and advertising departments; foreign embassies and tourist bureaus; [1] and picture magazines such as *Life, Look, National Geographic,* and *Holiday.*

Discussions take place after each selected picture has been studied silently by the class. Each student is directed in this manner: "Look at the picture; notice the main things and also the background. Think of several ways in which this picture shows how the people in the country live." Thinking is also directed toward the writing of imaginative stories. The teacher reads a story and asks the class to illustrate it with proper attention to dress and background. Or, the beginning of a story may be read and the students asked to write down their thoughts for a continuation and end-

---

[1] Many of the addresses with material available are listed in Educators' Progress *Guide to Free Curriculum Materials* and in Field Enterprises' *Sources of Free and Inexpensive Educational Materials.*

ing to the story. The students are helped with spelling and sentence structure, of course, for this area of our work becomes an English lesson.

The current events part of our program is developed through a brief, daily discussion of the current happenings in the countries we are studying, have studied, and shall study. We discuss possible reasons for fortunate and unfortunate happenings, the cold war, the part of the United States in influencing opinions of the world, the effects of the fast-moving world upon life in the countries in question. We especially emphasize the vital need for bringing all study of other countries to the present in order that we may understand the country today. We emphasize how much more important it is to think about, to know, and to understand other countries today than in any past time.

A description of our study of Egypt will show how this program actually functions in the classroom. In practice no divisions exist; the visual, imaginative, and current event parts of the program function simultaneously.

After having discussed the ancient civilizations in general, our route to Egypt is shown on a world physical-political map. We travel east from Fresno, either flying by way of New York and Lisbon, or sailing from San Francisco by way of the Panama Canal and the Strait of Gibraltar; we may possibly travel west but the route would be longer and the nations might not be so friendly. Next, facts of location and climate and physical features are noted: Egypt is bordered on two sides by water and has a large river flowing through it; the Nile River is introduced as the center of both ancient and modern Egypt, since it has enabled life to flourish in spite of the desert condition—a fact we note on a rainfall map.

Many historical and geographic facts are developed through use of the materials listed below.

FILMS

Egypt and the Nile. (Encyclopaedia Britannica; color; 16 minutes.)
Desert Nomads. (Coronet; black-and-white; 30 minutes.)

FILMSTRIPS

A Day in Ancient Egypt. (Popular Science; black-and-white.)
Growing Up in Ancient Egypt. (Popular Science; black-and-white.)

PICTURES

Egyptian Embassy, Press Department, Washington 8, D.C.

BOOKS

Raymond Fawcett. *How Did They Live—Egypt.* (Purnell and Sons, 1953.)
Ruth Jones. *Boy of the Pyramids.* (Random House, 1952.)

Eloise McGraw. *Mara, Daughter of the Nile.* (Coward McCann, 1953.)

Enid Meadowcroft. *Gift of the River.* (Crowell, 1937.)

Dorothy Mills. *Book of the Ancient World for Young Readers.* (Putnam, 1923.)

Vernon Quinn. *Picture Map Geography of Africa.* (Lippincott, 1952.)

L. A. Stinetorf. *Children of North Africa.* (Lippincott, 1943.)

Alice Taylor. *Egypt.* (Holiday House, 1953.)

S. W. Wilbur. *Egypt and the Suez Canal.* (Wheeler, 1940.)

The films, filmstrips, and pictures help in imagining life in ancient and modern Egypt and serve as factual basis for our writing about life there. The books provide pictures, information, reading material, and oral reports for selected students, and stories to be read to the class. Throughout our study we note the slow penetration of modern ways of life into this ancient land. In spite of this, the inevitable influence of our rapidly shrinking world leaves its mark here. Its strategic position and role in the cold war have catapulted Egypt into the limelight. The influence of modern ideas has promulgated revolt and expulsion of monarchy.

For each country the three-part program of vision, imagination, and current events follows a plan similar to that for Egypt. We evaluate the program favorably for several reasons. We are learning spatial, directional, and topographical concepts presented by maps. We are able to grasp chronological sequence by using the time line. We are discovering that countries are real people and events, not remote and intangible places. We are gaining skill in making logical inferences from the facts seen about each country. We are gathering and retaining many facts about the countries being studied. The skills and knowledge we are gaining are valuable now and will be even more valuable later.

59. A Philosophy of Arithmetic Instruction *

HOWARD F. FEHR

Needs

The concept of *need* pervades all modern theory with regard to learning. Parents and teachers are asked to discover and help the child satisfy his needs. The child's needs are to be at the center of all educational programs. However, there has been little or no suggestion that the child must also sense the need of understanding his parents and teachers, and of their guidance and counsel. The school has as its primary task not only to serve the child to satisfy his immediate needs, but also to equip him for service to society in his later life. Hence the child has need for that elementary mathematics which is demanded of all people in our free democratic society. Children will recognize some of these needs in their own daily experience, but other needs must be shown the pupils through experience supplied by the teacher.

In this connection it is well to note that in his experience alone a child will never meet all number situations called for in later life. Nor can he, from a large number of isolated arithmetic situations, ever come to have a basic knowledge for use in later life. Accordingly, we must teach the pupils a structure of arithmetic and sufficient applications of the structure, so that in new situations, in life problems, he can use the structure for the necessary solution of problems.

* From Howard F. Fehr, "A Philosophy of Arithmetic Instruction," *The Arithmetic Teacher* (April, 1955), pp. 27–32. Reprinted by permission of the author and the National Council of Teachers of Mathematics.

A need is a feeling for something which is absent, which if present, will *tend* to give satisfaction. These needs are biogenic, such as the need for food, shelter, survival, and so on. They are also social, such as status, power intellectual satisfaction, acceptance into society, and so on. It is these latter needs with which arithmetic learning is mostly concerned. The teacher can find these needs in a number of places. They are in our everyday cultural environment as indicated in the check list of the National Council of Teachers of Mathematics. The needs for intellectual, aesthetic, and social activities may frequently arise simply and naturally from the nervous system and its interrelation with its environment. Not all children lack curiosity and not all children dislike arithmetic. The teacher is also well aware of the needs in the many, many social problems which the child will not encounter until he is much older, such as saving and spending the income, investment, insurance, loans, statistical interpretation, and so on. However, a beginning can be made by creating a make-believe adult situation for the child. (Playing store is one make-believe adult situation.)

Planning

In planning a program the teacher must at all times recall that arithmetic is a logical structure as well as a social instrument. Unless these two concepts are continually interrelated, we shall not succeed in reaching our objective of an adult who *knows, recognizes,* and *uses* arithmetic in his daily life problems. While different parts of arithmetic can be learned in various orders, the logical order cannot be violated. We must learn some addition of whole numbers before we learn some meaningful multiplication. We must know the operations with whole numbers before we can learn to operate reasonably with fractions. But we can learn some of all the operations, one after the other, in some logical order, rather than learn all of one operation before we proceed to the next. To see the structure of arithmetic as a whole, rather than as separate parts, appears to give better success in its study.

Pupils sense needs for arithmetic in the world about them, at home, on the radio, in the papers, in their games, and so on. They seldom sense a need for a complete understanding and mastery of a number system. Real problems, and problems to which reality can be given, may be used to show the pupils the need of knowing arithmetic. The experiences, however, must not produce emotional reactions which detract from the learning of arithmetic; the experience must create within the pupil a drive which makes the learning of the arithmetic obligatory to him.

All of this suggests that we plan our program of instruction with our classes. Of course it is impossible for a group of children in grades three to five to plan its own program. Children are totally incapable of reproducing what great minds operating through centuries of time have created. We can, however, from time to time, discuss with the children what we are going to do, what they think they need, and how they can best learn what thus becomes their objective as well as the teacher's objectives. We can seize on all aspects of children's interest to motivate their learning. Instead of allowing outside interests to distract attention from arithmetic, a wise teacher uses them in promoting the study. Radio, television, the movies, the newspapers, even the comics are filled with arithmetic and a little search will reveal profitable examples. The resourceful teacher will adapt all these experiences to the level of maturity of his pupils. He will also look for causes of fear, defeat, and rejection among a few pupils and find ways to reassure and help them through their interests. However, in motivating the learning through interest in experience, we must take care that eventually it is the mastery and understanding of arithmetic that is achieved, as well as a fine personality.

Meaning

Granted the child sees the need for knowing how to multiply, how shall he learn it? Shall we show him how and drill, and expect that he will know? Shall we expect him to understand (have some meaning of) every particular algorism we use? The basic philosophy of meaning as a necessary concomitant of learning is now generally accepted. The degree to which meaning is necessary, how to obtain it, and what this does to drill, are still debated issues in arithmetic teaching.

A fact, concept, or operation is meaningful to a child when he relates it to his previous learning in such a manner that it becomes a working aspect of his behavior. How well it works depends upon the child's intelligence and the degree of practice he has in using the arithmetic. Drill (or practice) is the continued repetition of an act within limits of human variation. We should note that meanings may be correct or incorrect, and repetition of incorrect meanings or operations can interfere greatly with further learning. Suppose to a child a fraction has come to have the incorrect concept "2 out of 3 for $\frac{2}{3}$," "3 out of 5 for $\frac{3}{5}$," etc. Then if he is asked to add $\frac{2}{3} + \frac{3}{5}$, he says 5 out of 8 or $\frac{5}{8}$. Thus the whole thing has meaning to him, but not the meaning we desire. The more this child practices the more he is in trouble. In this case practice makes not perfect, but a perfect mess.

So we must be very careful that the meaning the child puts into his arithmetic is the correct meaning.

Once a child has put meaning into an operation or a relationship, there must be practice or drill to secure facility and accuracy thereafter. This drill can be of a number of different types. The most common usage of drill is the repetition of the same isolated facts until it can be quickly recalled. This procedure usually depends on pure rote learning. An almost similar type of drill is the repetition of various isolated facts, such as 6×3, 8×7, 2×5, $7 + 8$, etc. This process of securing retention of concepts is also one closely related to rote learning. The more modern concept of drill is the repetition of varied facts in varied situations. This process follows the field psychology point of view; the seeing of the relations of the parts to the whole structure of arithmetic in as many aspects as possible. We believe that it will give a more permanent and more useful learning. When a new operation has been related to some past experience or concrete situation so as to be of use in new situations, it has become meaningful. Depending on how it is learned the multiplication table can become a mere rote mechanism soon to be forgotten, or it can become a long-remembered meaningful relation of numbers in an arithmetic operation.

Practice

Once children have sensed the mathematical operation, have put meaning into it, and see where it is of value, they are ready to drill. Then and then only will drill be effective. Buckingham [1] has pointed out that drill is effective only when to the child it has *purpose,* he senses its *value,* he has *confidence* in his ability to perform because of some familiarity with the operation, so that he can *direct* himself toward the deepening and broadening of his understanding.

John Dewey has expressed the place of drill in arithmetic by two excellent statements. "Practice skills can be intelligently, nonmechanistically *used,* only when intelligence (meaning) has played a part in their learning" and "An erroneous conception widely held is that since traditional education rested upon a concept of organization of knowledge that was almost completely contemptuous of living (present experiences), therefore education based upon living experiences should be contemptuous of the organization of knowledge."

[1] Burdette R. Buckingham, "What Becomes of Drill," *Arithmetic in General Education.* Sixteenth Yearbook of the National Council of Teachers of Mathematics (1941), pp. 196–225.

What then is the place of drill? It is present and must be present in our learning. The arithmetic used for solving quantitative problems demands *facility in computation which is obtained only through practice*. The learning of division and per cent, and other applications in later grades, demands facility in the use of the more elementary operations, so that the mind can give its attention to the newer concepts and relations. This faculty is gained only through practice. However, the practice comes after meaning; it comes in varied situations and problems, and because of meaning the learning is faster, more permanent, and less practice is needed than is necessary for rote learning.

Learning

The teacher may now well ask, how do we get the child to put meaning into his arithmetic? We can seek an answer to this question in asking ourselves how *we* do it. A newspaper article said the U.N. forces advanced 6 miles all along a 60 mile front. What meaning do you see in this? Do you see a soldier walking forward 6 miles, and others to his left and right doing this also? Do you see $6 \times 60 = 360$ square miles of territory has been covered? However or whatever you do, you usually go back to concrete experience and that is where learning of all type begins. So multiplication, division, fractions and so on, always have the initial learning phases embedded in concrete situations. All learning begins in a concrete experiential problematic situation in which the organism is motivated to find a solution.

Motivation is goal-directed behavior. The motivation is entirely within the child, but it is brought about partly by the environment acting on the child, and partly by the child's own internal structure. These factors cause nervous tension of the energies within the body, and the release of these tensions in physical and mental activity is the drive that sends the pupil toward a solution, that is, to learn. Without this motivation and drive, no real learning takes place. So we try to develop the type of environment, the type of stimuli that help the child to motivate his learning. When this motivation is present, then self-instruction (and all real learning is ultimately self-instruction) takes place. This motivation has its first seeds in experience, concrete sensual experience. Here is where meaning begins. But it does not and should not end at this point. However, the uses of visual and mechanical aids for learning and relearning through experimentation is a first step toward developing meaning.

The teacher must next encourage the child to abstract certain recurring properties in his experimentation and to generalize these relations into arithmetic rules and principles. These general principles must also be related to previous generalizations. Thus, the proper placement of partial products in multiplication must be related to previously learned generalizations regarding multiplying by 1, 10, 100, etc. The adding of these partial products to get the total product must also be related to the general principle of distribution.[2] It is such generalizations that the meaning of multiplication deepens and the relationship of one operation to another takes on the aspect of a structure. This is not explicitly recognized by pupils in the beginning, but the implications will later develop into a broader understanding of the subject. It is quite evident that such learning demands more, and more carefully planned, instruction on the part of the teacher. The learning may proceed more slowly, but in the end we shall get a better educational product.

Under such learning, there is a need for continuous evaluation of the patterns of thinking going on in the child's mind. Computation tests with pencil and paper are not sufficient for this. Frequent oral explanations by the pupil form a better testing device for evaluating understandings. But more important, from a point of view of learning, the children must by their own planning and teacher guidance, constantly measure their own progress, come to recognize their own weaknesses, as well as strength, and by the use of teacher-prepared tests discover where they stand, what they need, and seek advice on how to get it. We must have children more and more take on *responsibility* for their own progress in learning. This is a long-neglected aim in all school instruction.

Problem-solving

Along with this generalization and structuring of the knowledge of arithmetic, we must plan for socializing our instruction, that is for the use of arithmetic in problem-solving. In good instruction, problem-solving is always present for problem-solving is learning and learning is problem-solving. To develop the ability to solve new problems by the use of arithmetic is the greatest objective of our instruction. It is in problem situations that arithmetic can best be seen as a whole—as a completed body of knowledge. At this point, many teachers will no doubt ask: "How do you teach problem-solving?"

This is in large measure an unanswered question, but many valid suggestions to aid the developing of problem-solving ability are at hand. Per-

---

[2] The distributive law is fundamental to all mathematics and is given symbolically by $a(b + c) = ab + ac$. Hence, 256×68 is $256 (60 + 8)$ or $60 \times 256 + 8 \times 256$.

haps most significant are (1) always look at the whole problem, the whole situation; (2) seek the relationship of the parts to the whole, and the whole to the part; (3) analyze, organize and reorganize the relationships until what is known is directly related to what is wanted, then insight will occur. Thus problem-solving demands *"ceaseless attention to the building of clear, well-interrelated arithmetic concepts in all the areas of common experience."*

Preliminary to the solution of word problems are three characteristics of arithmetic instruction that have received all-too-little attention in the past. They all rely on active thinking as a mode to learning rather than on passive listening to instructions. The first is *estimation*. Of course, to make intelligent estimates one must have rather clear-cut concepts of number, the number system, and the operations. To find the cost of three articles each priced at 48 cents, the second grade child (since he knows the number system) says this price is a little less than 3 half dollars or $1.50. As he advances through the grades he continues this estimation in far more difficult situations. The second characteristic is *mental solutions* to both computations and problems. Using the knowledge he has of the structure of arithmetic, here the child reasons without the aid of pencil or paper. He does not do mental gymnastics or visualized computations, but he does secure the accurate answer. In the preceding problem he reasons each article is 2 cents less than a half dollar—3 times 2 is 6—the price is 6 cents less than $1.50 or $1.45 minus 1 cent or $1.44. This type of mental solution is to be practiced from grade one on up into high school, the problems increasing in complexity each year. Estimation and mental solutions are the great practices that businessmen use every day.

The third characteristic is the association of language with an *operation*. As subtraction is taught, such language as—*take away—how much more —what is the difference—what is left—how much less—minus—less than —lost*—and so on is used in connection with concrete objects, so that the child associates a manner of speaking with the operation of subtraction. In this way, he is able to recognize a phrase or sentence in a word problem as indicating the separating of a group from a larger group to the size of the remaining group, or the comparing of two groups of unequal sizes to find their difference. Language and concepts are highly interdependent in arithmetic.

The foregoing philosophy of instruction can and should lead to an educational product that has a healthy attitude toward arithmetic. It should result in a person who has self-assurance in the field of arithmetic because of a genuine understanding of the mathematical implications as well as the ability and compunction to recognize and use arithmetic in all life's quantitative situations. What psychology of learning is this philosophy based upon? Upon all those principles which have been common and supported by research findings in the several psychologies. The psychology largely used is that of the gestalt school, but it is supported by connectionism under its modern interpretation. To go further here into any of these psychological theories would be of no great help to interpret the point of view expressed.

60. The Content and Organization of Arithmetic *

G. T. BUSWELL

THE CONTENT of this paper will be organized into three parts: first, two matters which are basic to any improvements in the arithmetic program, namely, the relation of content to individual differences and the effects of the deferred or stretched-out curriculum; second, some proposed changes at the primary and at the seventh-eighth grade levels; and third, some comments on materials of instruction and preparation of teachers. The issues to be covered are controversial and the reader will undoubtedly supply pros and cons to supplement the discussion given here.

Adjusting to Individual Differences

Teachers of arithmetic are aware of the stepped-up volume of criticism of the schools. This criticism is not spread equally over the entire school program but rather is focused sharply on the alleged failure of the schools to provide an adequate education for that segment of the school population that is going on to college and that will necessarily supply the intellectual and technical competence that our society requires. Certainly, the problem of individual differences is not new; the volume of published data on the

*From G. T. Buswell, "The Content and Organization of Arithmetic," *The Arithmetic Teacher* (March, 1959), pp. 77–82. Reprinted by permission of the author and the National Council of Teachers of Mathematics.

subject during the last fifty years is impressive. Yet there is something different about the current criticism at least as it relates to the subject of arithmetic. It is no longer true that the arithmetic of everyday life is sufficient. The world of mathematics has moved swiftly in the last two decades. The work of a bookkeeper of a generation ago has little in common with his counterpart at present. The use of business machines and mathematical computers requires a different level of arithmetical understanding than was necessary when all computation was done by hand. The result is that the everyday arithmetic has been made simpler, as for example, when the modern market sums the total of purchases on a cash register tape which saves both the customer and the clerk the trouble of adding. On the other hand, there has developed a set of needs for a small portion of the population that are decidedly not "everyday"' in character but are highly specialized. The present program in arithmetic has been reasonably successful in meeting the everyday needs of average pupils. But for the approximate third of the pupils who are headed for higher education and for work in technology and the sciences, both physical and social, it is quite a different matter. For these pupils arithmetic needs drastic revisions and additions. To be sure, the schools have done something about this, but it has been a feeble effort. It has been blocked on the one hand by the objection that in a democracy all pupils should be treated alike and on the other by the lack of administrative effort to make provisions for a real differentiation according to needs and abilities.

In a comparative study of arithmetic achievement of eleven-year-olds in England and California, published in the February 1958 *Arithmetic Teacher,* it was found that the 1077 pupils who constituted the upper third of the English sample made scores of 38 or above on the 70-item test. Only thirteen California pupils from a sample of equal size made scores this high. It is this failure to produce superior achievement that is the chief cause for concern. That this difference is not limited to England and California is indicated in a recent letter from Dr. Herbert Spitzer saying that a doctoral candidate at the State University of Iowa had made a comparison of arithmetic achievement in Iowa and Holland. He found that the Iowa eighth grade was just about equivalent in arithmetic achievement to the Dutch sixth grade. He also reported that in Holland pupils have put in as much time on arithmetic by the end of the sixth grade as Iowa pupils have by the end of the eighth grade.

In view of the current pleas for strengthening the mathematics program, it is clear that the attempts to up-grade the arithmetic program for those pupils who expect to go to college must be pushed more vigorously. This will mean that they be put into special classes or sections where an intensive program in arithmetic can be carried on such as would be neither desirable nor possible with average and below average pupils. Obviously, there would need to be flexibility in the selection of pupils and in correcting errors in placement. These are matters of detail and are certainly no more difficult than selecting members of a first team for basketball or football. Until the principle of grouping pupils for learning in terms of interests and abilities in respect to what is to be learned is accepted, it is practically impossible to experiment with desirable modifications in the arithmetic program. But if rate of progress and content to be learned could be fitted to the abilities of the upper third of pupils, it might also be found that for such pupils the program in arithmetic could be completed in six years as is the case in many countries of the world. This would then make possible a program in high school mathematics that would really prepare students for the serious study that college students are presumed to undertake.

The Stretched-out Program

Another matter which affects the present situation is the internal organization and spacing of the arithmetic program. During the 1930's there was a good deal of discussion of what was called "deferred arithmetic." The controversy was set off by a series of three articles in the *NEA Journal* in which it was proposed that the whole subject of arithmetic be postponed until the seventh year of school. Although few schools actually postponed teaching the subject to that degree, the discussion did result in a spreading or stretching-out of subject matter over longer periods of time. One result was that arithmetic was spread down into grades one and two where, up to that time, little systematic effort had been made to introduce the subject. This earlier beginning has now become quite general. There are probably some substantial advantages for average and below average pupils in this stretched-out program, but for more rapid learners it has only aggravated an already bad situation. For them it has resulted in padding topics already understood simply to fill time while the slower pupils catch up. Many of the topics and processes covered in arithmetic are introduced in other countries from one to two years earlier than is the practice here. It is especially difficult to justify much of the work in the seventh and eighth grades for the upper third of the pupils. It would be much to their advantage to cover all the topics of arithmetic by the end of the sixth grade and then go directly into a program of secondary mathematics appropriate for bright pupils of that age. The concept of a stretched-out program needs to be restudied. It was devised for average and slow learners. For the upper third of the pupils it constitutes a serious obstacle to interest and effort, and produces both boredom and dislike. For bright pupils, the routine topics of arithmetic can be covered more quickly than is now the case and the time saved can be used to extend the program to new kinds of content that are interesting and challenging. For the upper third of the pupils, the arithmetic program can be both enriched and completed earlier than is now done.

Changes in the Primary Grades

If the current criticisms of education result in a change in public opinion that will permit a genuine effort to develop a program for bright pupils, and if schools can be persuaded to adopt, for this group, a systematically organized program covering six years, the needed changes would affect particularly the beginning grades and the seventh and eighth grades. Attention will be given first to the program for the kindergarten and grades one and two, especially for the upper third of the children in respect to intellectual and academic maturity.

The last twenty-five years have witnessed great gains in the primary arithmetic program. If one were to compare the present arithmetic material for first grade pupils with what was available in 1930, the gains would be strikingly clear. Certainly the substitution of a concrete approach to number facts as contrasted with the earlier abstract drills will be approved by all. However, even now the systematic and coherent treatment of arithmetic usually begins at grade three and textbook publishers still designate as book one, the book for the third grade. What goes on in the kindergarten and in grades one and two is somehow thought of as outside of or preliminary to a really serious effort to deal with numbers. This should not be the case. What is needed is not a *formal* program of arithmetic at this level, but rather some serious thinking about a coherent total program beginning with the kindergarten. Formality and coherence are not synonymous terms. Specifically, it is now time to gather, and give careful study to, the many miscellaneous ways that have been proposed for introducing ideas of number. While the children who learn would of course not be aware of or concerned about the coherent development of arithmetic, the teachers certainly should be aware of it and should understand what is expected at each grade level. As a psychologist, I am aware of the position that the kindergarten should be preserved for social development. But experiences with numbers are a part of the child's world, and I know of no evidence whatever that an appropriate amount of effort to develop the child's interest in numbers will in any way harm his social development. The facts simply give no support to the position that learning basic concepts of numbers are out of place in the kindergarten. In many schools such practices have been carried on for years, greatly to the advantage of the children. If anyone is skeptical, he could not do better than to refer to the chapter by Olga Adams in the monograph *Arithmetic 1947,*[1] where she describes in detail the many practices followed in her kindergarten at the University of Chicago Laboratory Schools dealing with counting, fundamental processes, measuring, using fractions, telling time, and working with circles, squares, and triangles. There was nothing formal about Miss Adams' practices, but they were certainly purposeful, seriously planned, and coherently developed. As a result, her pupils went on to the first grade with a rich background of number experiences that gave meaning and interest to their arithmetic.

Experiences with arithmetic in the beginning grades can be roughly classified into three groups. The first, and oldest, of these presented arithmetic as a set of facts to be learned with little appeal to understanding or to social uses. Abstract drills on number facts and number tables gave rise to the designation "formal" arithmetic. While some schools still follow these practices, it is hard to find anyone to defend them. A second group of practices uses concrete experiences as the proper way to introduce numbers to children. This is the most widely used method at the present time in the United States. It relies strongly on social arithmetic as a carrier of mathematical meanings. However, its aim is to lead pupils ultimately to these mathematical meanings. Much use is made of pictures, and usually in expendable workbook materials. A third way of presenting number experiences exemplified by the systems of Catherine Stern in this country and of Cruisenaire in Europe, pays less attention to socially concrete experiences and deals more directly with numbers and number relations. Although more evidence from controlled experiments on these methods is needed, they undoubtedly deserve careful study. Their use of manipulative materials is to be noted, as contrasted to the workbook type of exercises.

The weakness of the kindergarten-primary treatment of arithmetic is that it is too often looked upon as a readiness program rather than as an integral and important section of the total program of the elementary school. Primary arithmetic should be coherently related to the work that follows in grades three to six in such a way that number relations would be better understood and that many processes and topics could be introduced earlier. Much of the later aversion to the subject might be dispelled by a more carefully thought-out beginning.

[1] University of Chicago Press.

Changes in the Upper Grades

The treatment of arithmetic in the seventh and eighth grades is a product of our eight-year elementary school and it affects the brighter pupils in a particularly adverse way. In this country it is customary for pupils who are headed toward higher education to cover the same program in arithmetic and to follow the same time schedule as do average and below average pupils. Whereas in European schools, students who plan to go to college begin their secondary school mathematics at age 12, we defer it until age 14. This results in a great deal of marking time in grades seven and eight. Practically all of the topics of arithmetic have been introduced by the end of grade six. What is left for grades seven and eight is then a review of processes already taught plus applications to different social situations. To fill the time that remains, most schools introduce some materials from algebra and intuitive geometry. The suggestion made here is that, at least for the brighter third of the pupils, the arithmetic program be terminated at the end of grade six and a suitable program of secondary mathematics be begun in grade seven. While some junior high schools now attempt to do this, their work is handicapped by the fact that their pupils come through elementary schools where arithmetic is conceived as an eight-year program. If arithmetic is to be changed to a six-year program, then some of the topics will have to be introduced sufficiently earlier to allow time for thorough learning and consolidation by the end of the sixth grade. That this is entirely possible is indicated by the evidence that at least in England and in Holland this is done, not only for the top third but for the entire group of elementary pupils. Academic achievement seems to depend considerably on how society values it. Obviously, if such changes in seventh and eighth grade arithmetic were made, it would necessitate a higher level of mathematical preparation for the teachers in those grades.

The basic content of the arithmetic program is rather definitely fixed by the character of the number system and number relations. Even the sequence of topics is somewhat controlled. Essentially, arithmetic requires the mastery of the operation of a subjective number system invented by human intelligence. The possible number relations within this system are determined by the nature of the system. In our decimal system the sum of 15 and 5 must be 20; in a duo-decimal system the sum would be different. Children must learn to count, to carry on the four fundamental operations with whole numbers, fractions, and the special kinds of fractions called decimals. They must understand per cents, ratios, proportions, and the functional relations represented by the facts that if $6 = 2 \times 3$, then $\frac{6}{2} = 3$ and $\frac{6}{3} = 2$. They will then need to learn certain tables of denominate numbers with which the number of operations and processes may be used. The number operations and processes are quite independent of the societal conditions under which they are used and applied. Eventually, to be of any value, they must be applied to the practical and intellectual problems of society.

The main job of the arithmetic program is to enable children to understand the number system and to become skillful in carrying on the various operations and processes that are involved. Competent application is possible only if such understanding and skill is acquired. While learning and applying are mingled in the school program, it must be understood that the essence of arithmetic is its fund of mathematical facts and relations. One cannot apply until he has something to apply. The critical lack with both pupils and teachers is in mathematical understanding. I have experimented with college classes repeatedly in learning a number system *not based on ten,* and invariably they react with confusion. Students in educational psychology who can find an IQ from the formula $MA/CA = IQ$, are confused if asked to find MA when IQ and CA are given. In more cases than not their difficulty is arithmetical rather than psychological. Recently I asked a group of graduate students to give a quick response to the question $4 \div 2 = $ what? All responded 2. To the next question, $4 \div 1$, they all responded 4. But to the question $4 \div 0$, fifteen students out of a group of twenty-eight responded zero. To make matters worse, half of them wanted to argue that zero was correct. There must be some way to teach arithmetic to bright students so that arithmetical meanings will be clear.

Improving Teaching Materials

If improvements are made in the program of arithmetic, better teaching materials and better teacher training are necessary. While outstanding teachers can, and do, use textbooks with flexibility, for many teachers the arithmetic that is taught is the arithmetic of the textbook. Obviously, it is easier to say that teaching materials should be improved than it is to deliver pages of actually improved manuscript.

First, one must recognize the limitations of what may be done in any one textbook when applied to an entire class. For the weak pupils the book is too difficult; for the strong it is too easy. Applied exercises cannot possibly be of equal interest to all pupils. Sufficient explanation to make a concept clear to a slow learner bores the rapid learner. One might study with profit the way teachers of reading have turned to a basic book plus multiple supplementary books. This idea might be of use in arithmetic. If a basic book could be built for average pupils it could include all the facts and understandings essential to the subject. This might then be supplemented by booklets which, for the slow learner, would provide the additional explanations and practice materials that would be needed. For the brighter pupils, supplementary booklets of quite a different nature would be necessary. Rather than more explanation and practice, they would need enriching new topics and processes. For example, a booklet on nondecimal number systems might be prepared in attractive and interesting style. It would be for the intellectually curious pupil and it could afford many opportunities for mathematical imagination. Significant applications could be found, such as the use of different bases in computing machines, the use of modified number systems for automobile licenses in some states, the use of indexing systems in libraries, and many others. With travel becoming common, many bright children could be interested in a booklet on foreign money systems and the processes of computing with them. The advantages of a decimal money system might be appreciated better after such a study. A booklet might show the variety of ways in which multiplying and dividing could be done or how answers could be checked. There would be room for a booklet of number puzzles and tricks which would, in turn, contribute to a better understanding of number relations. These illustrations may not be well chosen, but the intent is to find some way to escape from the straight-jacket of uniform textbooks for all types of pupils. Rather than make longer and longer books in an attempt to satisfy all users, there might be advantages in shorter basic books with supplementary booklets for special needs. This would permit more flexible programs, especially for the many small schools where sectioning into special classes is impractical.

Improving Teaching Education

Finally, an improved program in arithmetic requires a higher level of teacher training in the content of arithmetic. This is not a criticism of teachers but of the higher institutions that train them. College departments of mathematics and departments of education must in some way find a means to provide advanced work in the subject matter of arithmetic. In most cases little content is provided that goes beyond that received in the eighth grade. Teachers of science, social studies, English, art, and music all are able to take a college major in their special fields. But arithmetic is not represented in the college program of mathematics, and in most teacher training institutions more attention is given to methods than to content. Earlier this year I gave to a group of 102 university students, who are planning to be elementary-school teachers, the same 70-item test that was given previously to a large sample of eleven-year-old pupils in England and in California. The mean score for the university students was 44 compared with means of 29.1 for English eleven-year-olds and 12.1 for California pupils. However, 34 per cent of the prospective teachers made scores below the top third of the English eleven-year-olds, and 10 per cent made scores below the mean of the California pupils. These university students are not dull. Their mean score on the American Council Psychological Examination was more than one standard deviation above the national norm for college freshmen. They simply lacked competence in arithmetic. In a few colleges, substantial and scholarly courses in arithmetic are provided, and such courses must become more common.

In the 1951 Yearbook of the National Society for the Study of Education, entitled *The Teaching of Arithmetic,* Grossnickle reported the findings from a nationwide survey of the training of teachers of arithmetic. His data revealed an amazing lack of arithmetical content in courses offered for teachers. In the following chapter of the same yearbook, Professor Newsom outlined what mathematicians think teachers of arithmetic should know. The gap between the training now provided and the training proposed is startling.

This paper has *first* emphasized the need for a better program in arithmetic for those pupils who plan to go on to college, and has urged that the concept of a stretched-out curriculum be reappraised, especially as it applies to the upper third of elementary pupils. *Second,* it proposed that the arithmetic of the kindergarten-primary grades be strengthened and integrated into the total arithmetic program, and also that the arithmetic curriculum for the brighter pupils might be completed by the end of the sixth grade, leaving the seventh and eighth grades for the serious development of high school mathematics. *Finally,* some suggestions were given about supplementary materials of instruction and about strengthening the program for the preparation of arithmetic teachers.

The main contention of the current critics of the schools is that arithmetic is failing to provide the solid basis of competence that is needed for high school and college programs in mathematics and science. We should give serious consideration to what the critics are saying. However, arithmetic is not taught for the sole purpose of training scientists. It must be organized so that all segments of the school population will be served in the ways that best fit individual needs. Most of what has been written here could have been written with equal emphasis before the first sputnik was launched. Nonscientists also need arithmetic, and, still further, arithmetic is only part of the total enterprise of education. Schools are concerned with the good life to which arithmetic is only one of the contributors. While arithmetic teachers work to improve their own subjects, they must also maintain a sense of balance in respect to the total program of education.

61. Developing Meanings Pays Big Dividends *

ROBERT L. MORTON

HERE IS SOMETHING that every teacher should frame and place where it may be seen each morning before the school day begins: WHAT CHILDREN LEARN MEANINGFULLY STAYS WITH THEM BETTER AND IS APPLIED MORE SUCCESSFULLY THAN WHAT THEY "LEARN" BY MERE DRILL.

Understanding Fractions

In recent years, we have been giving much lip service to the meaning theory. However, some of the teaching in most schools and most of the teaching in some schools is not meaningful at all. Recently, a student asked the writer how he would teach a pupil to change the fraction $\frac{2}{3}$ to $\frac{4}{6}$. When asked how he had learned it, the student replied: "I was taught to think, '3 into 6, 2; 2 times 2 is 4.' " Passing up the temptation to comment on the fact that such an expression as "3 into 6" has no meaning, we may observe that there are still many schoolrooms in which rules about changing the terms of a fraction are *delivered* to the pupil by the textbook or the teacher, are not *discovered* by the pupil, and are not meaningful. The use of concrete materials, followed by diagrams illustrating the equi-

* From Robert L. Morton, *Teaching Arithmetic* (Washington, D. C.: National Education Association, 1953), pp. 8–12. Reprinted by permission of the author and the Department of Classroom Teachers and the American Educational Research Association of the National Education Association.

valence of certain fractions, if skillfully used, leads pupils to discover the
necessary rules about changing the terms of a fraction. Out of these discoveries come such observations as the following: *If the pieces are only
half as large, there are twice as many of them; if there are only half as many
pieces, they are twice as large.* Such learning is more permanent, is more
readily applied to new situations, and is a lot more fun.

Eventually, every pupil should arrive at the conclusion that if both terms
of a fraction are multiplied by the same number, the value of the fraction is
unchanged. To change ⅔ to sixths, then, he must multiply both the 2 and
the 3 by 2. He obtains the multiplier 2 by thinking, "By what do I multiply
3 to get 6?" Of course, he divides 6 by 3 to find the answer to his question.
This conclusion leads to a useful working rule but the rule is arrived at
gradually as the result of much concrete and semiconcrete experience with
fractions. It should not be delivered, ready-made, by the classroom teacher
or the textbook.

Understanding Mixed Numbers

Getting back to our promise to tramp on many toes, let us consider as
another illustration the trick of changing a mixed number to an improper
fraction. The widespread custom seems to favor rushing speedily to the
rule: *Multiply the whole number by the denominator of the fraction and
add the numerator to the product; write the result over the original denominator.* To change 2¼ to an improper fraction, for example,
multiply 2 by 4, add 1 to the product, and write the result as $\frac{9}{4}$. Thus
$$2\frac{1}{4} = \frac{4 \times 2 + 1}{4} = \frac{9}{4}.$$

Unfortunately, the rule is the reverse of what it should be. We should
multiply 4 by 2, not 2 by 4. The reason is easily seen from the diagram.
In 1 whole there are 4 fourths. Then in 2 wholes
there are 2 times 4 fourths, or 8 fourths. To find the
number of fourths in 2, then, we multiply 4, the
number of fourths in 1, by 2. We would multiply 2 by 4 to find the number
of halves in 4, not the number of fourths in 2.

Of course, the pupils should know by this time that the product of two
numbers is the same, regardless of which is used as the multiplier. But this
is a poor excuse for reversing the direction of the multiplication in changing
an improper fraction to a mixed number. Meaningful learning is improbable
if the pupils are taught to think, "There are 4 fourths in 1 whole and
4 times 2 fourths in 2 wholes."

Understanding Formulas

Perhaps one reason for the confusion here is the fact that some teachers are confused as to which is the multiplier when an example is written in equation form. The expression $4 \times 2 = 8$ shows 2 multiplied by 4, not 4 multiplied by 2. It is standard mathematical practice to write the multiplier at the left of the multiplicand, not at the right of it, if the equation form is used. The expression $4x = 8$ means that four x's are equal to 8, not that x fours are equal to 8, although the latter statement is true if $x = 2$. We should be consistent about writing multipliers at the left of multiplicands. To be meaningful, furthermore, we should read such an expression as $4 \times 2 = 8$, "Four two's are eight," especially when providing early experiences with multiplication. When the pupil learns to read $4 \times 2 = 8$ as "Four times two equals eight," he should understand that "Four times two" means that the number 2 is taken 4 times, not that the number 4 is taken 2 times.

Understanding Division

The modern emphasis on teaching meanings should not be interpreted as a demand that every phase of every process be completely meaningful to pupils who are learning those processes. We want the pupils to understand the significance of what they do, of course, but there are *degrees of understanding.* As an illustration, consider the pupil's experiences as he learns division of whole numbers. Passing over examples having one-figure divisors, for which a similar story can be told, consider examples having two-figure divisors. The pupil's task in the example shown is to discover how many 43's there are in 26,837. He sees that 43 is larger than 2 or 26, and proceeds to estimate the number of 43's in 268. Such an approach is considered by most persons to be meaningful enough at this stage. Actually, however, this is only a fragment of the whole story. A complete understanding of this example involves:

$$\begin{array}{r} 624 \\ 43\overline{)26837} \\ 258 \\ \hline 103 \\ 86 \\ \hline 177 \\ 172 \\ \hline 5 \end{array}$$

1. The 2 represents ten-thousands. There are not enough ten-thousands to yield a ten-thousands' figure in the quotient, since the divisor is 43.
2. The 26 represents thousands. There are not enough thousands to yield a thousands' figure in the quotient.
3. The 268 represents hundreds. There *are* enough hundreds 'o yield a

hundreds' figure in the quotient. Because 268 can be divided by 43, the 6 as a part of the quotient means that we have so far found 600 43's in 26,837. Thinking, "How many 43's are there in 268?" should be a case of thinking, "How many hundreds of 43's are there in 268 hundreds?"

4. The remainder is 1037, although it is conventional to focus attention next on 103 only, neglecting the 7. This 103 means 103 tens. There are 2 tens of 43's (20) in 103 tens.

5. Finally, there are four 43's in the remaining 177 and there is a remainder of 5.

Very little understanding of the process of division would develop in elementary-school pupils' minds if such "meaningful teaching" were undertaken. Nevertheless, one occasionally finds an ambitious soul who ventures to try to put across such a pretentious development as the foregoing or a good part of it. If there is any place at all for such a complete development, it seems that it might be used as enrichment material for the most able pupils in junior high school grades.

Understanding Decimals

If the reader is not yet fully persuaded, let him insert decimal points in the divisor and the dividend as shown and undertake a fully "meaningful" development of the division process. This time the 6 shows that there are 60 4.3's in 268. If the caret device or some similar device were used, the 6 would show that there are 60 43's in 2683, which is not what we are trying to discover at all. By all means, let us teach meanings, but let us be sensible about it.

$$4.3 \overline{)268.37} \quad 62.4$$

Reteaching Is Necessary

The fact that there are degrees of understanding means that a pupil's grasp of an arithmetic process should become more and more secure at successive grade levels. Carrying in addition, for example, although introduced in grade three, should be better understood in grade four than in grade three, and still better in grade five than in grade four. For many pupils it will not be satisfactorily understood until later than grade five. Teachers should not expect all pupils to understand this process well in grade three.

All of this means that at each grade level after the first there should be a carefully planned reteaching program covering what has previously been taught. The term "reteaching" means more than a mere review. It means teaching again, at a higher and more mature level, and more rapidly, what has been taught before. It is sometimes called "telescoped reteaching." Many children who are tested at the beginning of a school year and found deficient need another chance to learn and a chance to learn more fully what has already been partially learned.

62. Good Teachers of Arithmetic Teach for Meaning *

CHARLOTTE W. JUNGE

THE TEACHING of arithmetic to young children has been a subject of research ever since the report of the NEA Committee of Fifteen at the turn of the century, which indicated that "something radical needs to be done about the teaching of arithmetic."

Early research in arithmetic was largely concerned with a determination of the content to be taught, the grade placement of the content, and the analysis of the content into its constituent skills. In recent years, in response to the changes in our philosophy of education, research has been more concerned with the nature of the learning process in arithmetic, with the nature and the place of meaning in arithmetic, and with the methods and materials used.

Recent writings have stressed the need of teaching for meaning. They indicate that arithmetic should be made intelligible and useful to the learner and that the primary purpose of instruction in arithmetic is to help children grow in the ability to think quantitatively.

Numerous studies have been made evaluating the meaning approach to teaching. They show that children taught meaningfully retain the learning longer, are able to transfer this learning more effectively to solving new problem situations, and develop the ability to think quantitatively better

* From Charlotte W. Junge, "Good Teachers of Arithmetic Teach for Meaning," *NEA Journal* (March, 1953), pp. 167–68. Reprinted by permission of the author and the *NEA Journal*.

than do those taught under a drill method. Furthermore, a method of teaching which emphasizes rational procedures appears to be the most economical route to speedy and accurate computation.

Readiness

The subject of readiness has received considerable attention in recent years. Studies tend to confirm the growing conviction that readiness for learning is based on mental maturity and inner growth in combination with previous experiences, methods of learning, interests, attitudes, and purposes.

A readiness program in arithmetic should probably be regarded as covering that period when the child's background for learning a new concept is appraised, foundational experiences are provided, and a purpose for learning the new concept is established in the child's mind.

One of the chief tasks of the teacher during this readiness period is to create a problem situation which will arouse the child's interest and provide the felt need basic to discovery and experimentation. Research in readiness indicates there is a great need for readiness testing, remedial instruction, and greater individualization of instruction.

Problem-solving and Evaluation

Research on problem-solving has produced the following conclusions: Pupils tend to score higher in problem-solving in the tests which *do not* require response to the analytic steps, and pupils who have been taught these steps do not use them except under compulsion.

Reliance on a formal system of problem-solving robs pupils of self-confidence. It in effect makes them slaves to the system. The research indicates that the teacher should supply a sufficient number of genuine problems which the pupil has a good chance of solving successfully by his own thinking, together with enough challenging problems to stimulate interest.

Many children experience difficulty in solving verbal problems because of inability to sense relationships within the problem. Improvement of reading skills in arithmetic results in better work in problem-solving.

Teaching materials should include more factual information which would help children gain number understandings through experience. Practical experience is a potent factor in success in problem-solving—particularly for below-average children.

Research places increasing emphasis upon outcomes beyond mere rote learning of facts and principles. It also indicates that the evaluation of mathematical understandings should receive heavy emphasis.

There are three principal methods of evaluation: standardized tests to measure basic understandings and skills and ability in problem-solving, teacher-prepared tests to measure mathematical understandings and judgment, and informal observation to appraise functional competence in numbers. Many schools have not gone beyond the first level, and only a few are operating with all three.

63. Teaching Multisensory Arithmetic *

STANLEY MCKEE

M OST ARITHMETIC TEACHERS agree that children must be able to understand and to use the number system in order to assume their responsibilities in a democratic society.

Multisensory aids and group projects long have been accepted methods of teaching arithmetic. These techniques encourage the child to express himself and to gain confidence in the use of numbers.

The techniques, however, require pupils to move from a concrete use of numbers to the abstract and back again. As Harry Grove Wheat has suggested, it is precisely while making these transitions that the child most needs help and guidance. If guidance is not available, the child's concepts are likely to remain nebulous. Utilization of multisensory aids helps the child to understand what he is doing.

To help solve this problem, arithmetic teachers in the Highland Park (District 108), Illinois, schools have developed a program which emphasizes the social importance of arithmetic and includes many multisensory projects, including the unit type of problem.

The program varies from year to year as refinements are added. Essentially, however, our attempt to make the language of number more mean-

* From Stanley McKee, "Teaching Multisensory Arithmetic," *Grade Teacher,* Special Section to Help You Teach Arithmetic (April, 1956), pp. 37, 85–86. Reprinted by permission of the author and *Grade Teacher.*

ingful involves the following special projects for grades from one through five:

First grade. Many of our first grade children encounter fund-raising activities for the first time. Teachers take special care to explain the purposes of charitable causes in order to give the pupils an understanding of why people give—and the importance of such giving.

Two community-wide campaigns have been authorized in the schools, the Red Cross and the March of Dimes. Individual teachers are given responsibility for the drives, and various rooms distribute information about the campaigns. Often the first grade children distribute the information and handle all details of the program under their own teachers.

When this is done each first grade child is given an opportunity to make the transition from the abstract to the concrete by counting the money, as one of a team. The coins first are sorted and then arranged in groups of ten. The process of counting, comparing and analyzing is repeated until every member of the class has participated. Committees then are appointed to make reports.

To children who previously have used buttons and similar materials, this first group contact with money is a rewarding challenge. In particular, it gives the children an understanding of the values of different size coins, especially if they previously have worked with buttons which are all the same size.

The shifting of groups of coins which takes place is an important help in the establishment of a vocabulary of arithmetic. For example, using piles of coins, the teacher is able to demonstrate the idea of putting together and taking away. There is nothing which helps establish the proper understanding of zero as a place holder quite so impressively as to work with groups of coins.

Each child is given responsibility for Christmas decorations in the halls of the school. This activity is under the supervision of the Student Council, and involves preplanning the decorations, getting estimates of cost, judging the relationship of cost to value, collecting contributions (never more than a nickel per pupil), making purchases, reporting on expenses and actually putting the plans for holiday decorations into effect for the enjoyment of all teachers, pupils, and parents.

This concept of budgeting is carried over to time. Pupils know the hours they spend in school and are encouraged to keep track of how the time is spent, in order to get maximum value out of each day.

Second grade. Second grade pupils in the Lincoln School have operated a school store as one of their projects. Arrangements are made with local merchants to obtain a few basic materials such as paper and notebooks at a 20 per cent discount. In setting up the store the teachers explain the meaning of discount, the concept of cost and the idea of profit. Without delving too deeply into the idea of percentage, student storekeepers are encouraged to understand that each sale involves a certain margin of profit.

The project is launched when students make estimates of the quantities of the various materials that will be needed (the variety of items carried by the school store is purposely limited).

When the list is complete, it is compared to previous lists, then taken to the local merchant who offers the material on a consignment basis. Each second grade pupil is given an opportunity to handle sales. Each child also is given an opportunity to take inventory as part of an inventory team.

Carrying the project to its logical conclusion, all second grade children calculate the profits from the store and are given a voice in the use of the funds.

Third grade. Teachers in the third grade have used field trips as one technique in developing appreciation of the social significance of number.

These trips give the teachers an opportunity to correlate previous experience in budgeting money with the budgeting of time. The pupils plan the trips (under supervision, of course) with the objective of getting the most out of the time invested.

At the same time costs of each trip are calculated in advance—buses, milk, refreshments, cookies and other items. Each child performs the calculations. Because the sums involved are relatively large, each child has an opportunity to explore the idea of ten and how tens are added, subtracted, multiplied and divided, using the idea of positional value, with the help of zero, to keep things straight.

Important, too, is the fact that using arithmetic to budget time *and* money helps establish the concept of arithmetic as a unity of related ideas. The pupils, thus, have another opportunity to discover meanings for themselves, using concrete material—the resources of the community.

In budgeting money, the actual amounts are counted and recounted in the classroom—again using as many senses as possible to establish the meaning of number.

Fourth grade. Just as fourth grade classroom activities in arithmetic are devoted largely to extending the ideas which have been taught in the previous grades (adding and multiplying in tens and powers of ten, carrying remainders and "carrying back" in subtracting and dividing), so outside activities are a review and extension.

Occasionally, for example, a fourth grade room will supervise the Red

Cross collection. Or fourth graders will be given an assignment in the office which involves determining the stamps required for mail or parcel post.

Wherever practicable, attention is given to the development of the unit type problem in arithmetic. An interesting example of this type of problem originated with a gift of venison to one of our fourth grade groups. A generous father felt that the venison might be appropriate because the students were about to terminate a project relating to pioneer life.

The children and their teacher decided to have a pioneer luncheon of venison stew. The meat first was weighed to determine the number of pounds. A committee of children was elected to go to the village to find out the cost of vegetables. Upon the committee's return, the class added up the total bill and determined how much change the clerk would give them from a five dollar bill. The committee then made the purchase.

It was unanimously decided that dessert should consist of gingerbread. This led to a discussion of cups, pints and quarts. Utensils were brought to school to do the work. Each member of the class figured out how many cakes would be needed in order to get eight pieces from one cake and twenty-four people to serve.

Finally, the students figured how much milk they would have to order if they could get four glasses from one quart. Similarly, they determined the cost of six quarts of milk. All of these expenditures then were lumped, and the students figured how to prorate the expense among the group.

The activity served as a most satisfying arithmetic experience, and the meal proved to be highly satisfactory.

Fifth grade. While the second graders handle most school supplies in their "store," the Student Council sells pencils and carries on other activities to raise revenue for the improvement of the school.

Fifth grade students begin to play an important role in the Council. For example, in order to sell pencils, they first negotiate a loan from the school fund (no interest is charged), purchase the pencils, add a small profit margin and resell the pencils in school.

In spending the money for school improvements, the Council goes through all essential steps. Under supervision, they discuss various projects and decide which one is most desirable. Last year, for example, they decided to plant two small evergreens on the front lawn. The steps involved visiting several nurserymen to price stock, setting up the budget, selecting the trees and planting them.

The Council also sponsors one movie a year. In this case, the pupils review film catalogs and (under supervision) select a movie, sell tickets, prepare announcement cards, handle the performance, and run the machine.

A popcorn committee is on hand during the movie to dispense the corn and to give token assistance in housekeeping by picking up empty popcorn cartons. In addition, Council members set up a budget for the film and make a financial report after the play is over. Teachers encourage Council members to plan fund-raising efforts and expenditures for improvements at the same time.

To the fifth grade children also falls the responsibility of drawing up simple financial reports on many school activities. About a year ago, Highland Park schools began experimenting with vertical line charts.

It was felt that, since many fifth and sixth grade pupils need horizontal lines to write on, they should not be denied a vertical line for their arithmetic work. Experience to date indicates that such lines do tend to improve coordination and to facilitate the carry-over of ten.

Each year, fifth grade pupils conduct a bicycle "clinic" which helps emphasize the social significance of number. They volunteer to check all bicycles, testing horns, pedals, lights, reflectors and brakes and to make estimates of what it will cost to make necessary repairs.

Intermediate grades. The arithmetic program in the Highland Park intermediate grades (grades six through eight) re-emphasizes the multisensory approach and continues the activities which are initiated in the primary school. They are, for example, given assignments which require them to bring practical problems of everyday living to the classroom for discussion.

The real value of the multisensory approach to arithmetic is the fact that the pupils actually see (and, in some cases, actually feel) what they are doing, and it makes sense to them. If it doesn't make sense, the teacher can spot the problem quickly and give whatever special attention is required.

As part of their preparation for the teaching of arithmetic, Highland Park teachers spend a great deal of time each year in in-service training programs. The approach is this: in starting a learning activity it is necessary to (a) decide what one is going to do with the children, (b) decide how it is going to be done, and (c) evaluate how well the job has been done.

With these objectives in mind, a number of specific projects have been adopted as part of the in-service training. These include:

1. Use of score cards to evaluate texts and to select them
2. Committee analysis of films and other supplementary materials
3. Committee analysis of professional guidance materials
4. Manufacture (in the school shop) of such arithmetic teaching materials as pegboards, counting boards and ringtoss boards.

5. Seminars on various approaches to the problem of teaching arithmetic, with authorities in the field as guest moderators

In short, we believe we have developed a type of living arithmetic which can be employed in any school system to prove that arithmetic can be fun.

64. *Addition, Subtraction, and the Number Base* *

CLIFFORD BELL

WHEN THE TEN one-digit numbers are added two at a time in all possible ways, we obtain the 100 addition facts as shown in the following table.

A great number of teachers will point out early in the teaching of these addition facts that a fact and its reverse gives the same sum. Thus $3 + 4 = 7$ and $4 + 3 = 7$. Hence all the facts in the table below the broken double line can be considered the same as their reverses which are all found above the double broken line. Thus, the omission of these reverses leaves only fifty-five facts to memorize. The zero addition facts in the first row will entail no memory work since teachers usually can convince a child that the sum of any number and zero is the number. Hence the top row of facts, above the single line, may be deleted, leaving forty-five facts, or possibly forty-six if we count the statement about adding zero as one fact. These are the addition facts that the children usually are required to memorize.

Many teachers have divided the afore-mentioned forty-five facts into easy, average, and hard groups in accordance with the results of experimentation with children. None of the twenty-five facts whose sums are ten or less are classified in the hard group. (These are bounded in the table by the broken double line to the left, the broken single line to the right, and by the single line at the top.) It is my belief that these facts should be taught first followed by the remaining twenty facts whose sums are greater than 10.

Since present-day elementary teachers make a great deal of use of the

* From Clifford Bell, "Addition, Subtraction, and the Number Base," *The Arithmetic Teacher* (April, 1955), pp. 57–59. Reprinted by permission of the author and the National Council of Teachers of Mathematics.

PRIMARY ADDITION FACTS

0	1	2	3	4	5	6	7	8	9
0	0	0	0	0	0	0	0	0	0
0	1	2	3	4	5	6	7	8	9

0	1	2	3	4	5	6	7	8	9
1	1	1	1	1	1	1	1	1	1
1	2	3	4	5	6	7	8	9	10

0	1	2	3	4	5	6	7	8	9
2	2	2	2	2	2	2	2	2	2
2	3	4	5	6	7	8	9	10	11

0	1	2	3	4	5	6	7	8	9
3	3	3	3	3	3	3	3	3	3
3	4	5	6	7	8	9	10	11	12

0	1	2	3	4	5	6	7	8	9
4	4	4	4	4	4	4	4	4	4
4	5	6	7	8	9	10	11	12	13

0	1	2	3	4	5	6	7	8	9
5	5	5	5	5	5	5	5	5	5
5	6	7	8	9	10	11	12	13	14

0	1	2	3	4	5	6	7	8	9
6	6	6	6	6	6	6	6	6	6
6	7	8	9	10	11	12	13	14	15

0	1	2	3	4	5	6	7	8	9
7	7	7	7	7	7	7	7	7	7
7	8	9	10	11	12	13	14	15	16

0	1	2	3	4	5	6	7	8	9
8	8	8	8	8	8	8	8	8	8
8	9	10	11	12	13	14	15	16	17

0	1	2	3	4	5	6	7	8	9
9	9	9	9	9	9	9	9	9	9
9	10	11	12	13	14	15	16	17	18

idea of grouping objects into units, tens, hundreds, etc., they will find this an excellent approach to the teaching of these last twenty addition facts. For example, take the fact $7 + 5 = 12$. The 7 may be represented by 7 sticks and the 5 by 5 sticks. These can be regrouped into two groups such that one of the groups contains 10 sticks. We need to know how many sticks must be added to 7 sticks to give us a group of 10 sticks. From amongst the first twenty-five addition facts, we find the answer to this question for $7 + 3 = 10$. Now we have one group of 10 sticks and a second group of only 2 sticks. Making use of our number base 10 and the place system of notation, we can write the sum as one ten and two ones or simply 12, the required sum. This method has been tried in the classroom,[1] and many teachers are now using this procedure to teach addition.

This method of learning the primary addition facts with sums greater than ten, puts a great deal of emphasis on the facts $9 + 1 = 10, 8 + 2 = 10$, $7 + 3 = 10, 6 + 4 = 10, 5 + 5 = 10$. Two numbers whose sum is 10 are said to be complementary and each number is said to be the complement of the other. Thus, 7 is the complement of 3 and 3 is the complement of 7. Some teachers may object to defining this term since it may confuse the pupil. However, it may have just the opposite effect, since the definition tends to set these facts apart and thus their learning may become easier.

As is well known, from each addition fact for which the addends are different, two subtraction facts are obtained. For example, $5 + 2 = 7$ gives the subtraction facts $7 - 2 = 5$ and $7 - 5 = 2$. For addition facts with the same addends only one subtraction fact is obtained. Thus $4 + 4 = 8$ gives only $8 - 4 = 4$. Hence the twenty-five addition facts whose sums are 10 or less give rise to forty-five subtraction facts, since there are twenty with different addends and five with the same addends. These are the subtraction facts which should be memorized.

Developing Subtraction

Actually in the regrouping method of addition, the ideas of subtraction are easily introduced. Thus, in the example $7 + 5 = 12$, when the child regroups to form a group of 10, he is discovering what he must add to 7 to make 10. This is the additive method of performing the subtraction $10 - 7 = 3$. Now when he takes the 3 from the other group, he will find how many are left at first by counting. Nevertheless he is performing the

[1] At the Seattle Meeting of the National Council of Teachers of Mathematics, Miss Dora Brosius, Lakewood Schools, Lakewood, Oregon, gave an interesting report on her success with the use of this method.

subtraction example of 5 take away 3, which is commonly called the take-away method of subtraction. Thus by the time the child has mastered his addition facts, he has actually learned the meaning of subtraction. With a little well-directed help from the teacher, memorization of the forty-five simple subtraction facts will be easy for the child.

The remaining primary subtraction facts are those which are obtained from the addition facts in the table bounded below by the broken double line and above by the broken single line. The reader may readily verify the statement that there are thirty-six such subtraction facts, and these are the ones that usually cause trouble. Again by the proper utilization of the number base, these can be made easy. Let us consider $15 - 7 = 8$. In teaching this fact, the 15 may be regrouped into the number base group of 10 objects and the group of 5 objects. The teacher should now point out to the child that if he wishes to take 7 objects away, it would be best to take them from the larger group of objects. The child then thinks of his problem as 10 take away 7. This fact has already been learned, since it occurred amongst the easy subtraction facts. If the teacher has used the term "complement," the answer to $10 - 7$ is the complement of 7, which is 3. Since these 3 objects together with the other group of 5 objects gives 8 objects, the fact $15 - 7 = 8$ is established. All of these thirty-six harder subtraction facts may be obtained in a similar manner and when presented this way most children grasp these facts very easily. Actually this method eliminates the tedious memory work for these harder subtraction facts.

This method, in which the number base plays an important role, may be used to advantage in other subtraction examples such as $54 - 18 = ?$ Writing this in vertical form and supplying the necessary crutches for the benefit of the reader, we have

$$\begin{array}{r} \overset{4}{}\overset{10}{} \\ \not5\ 4 \\ -1\ 8 \\ \hline 3\ 6 \end{array}$$

Since 8 cannot be taken from 4, we must regroup the five tens indicated by the 5 in the left-hand column into four tens and one ten. This is indicated by the small 4 over the 5 in the left column and the small 10 over the 4 in the right column. Now the procedure is to say, "10 take away 8 is 2 (which is the complement of 8); 2 and 4 are 6." In the next column we simply have 4 take away 1 which is 3. Of course, the crutches would be abandoned after understanding of the method is established.

This method is not new, but the method of presentation may be. It is known as the complementary method of subtraction and was used in more or less rule form extensively during colonial days in this country. As was customary in those days, no attempt was made to give understanding to the method presented. Gradually through the years, as it became apparent that better results were obtained when understanding of the operations of arithmetic accompanied the learning of facts, new methods of performing operations were introduced which seemed to give better understanding. The old complementary method of subtraction was abandoned and forgotten. Yet with our present-day teaching aids and emphasis on the number base, this method can be taught with as much, or even more, understanding than those in common use. It is hoped that the above discussion may encourage more teachers to try the methods of addition and subtraction indicated in this discussion.

65. *How to Use the Arithmetic Textbook* *

FOSTER E. GROSSNICKLE

A TEXTBOOK has been defined as "an assistant teacher in print." Certainly the textbook in arithmetic, when properly used, is a most effective instructional aid in that subject, especially for pupils beyond the second grade.

One of the functions of an arithmetic teacher is to provide adequately for the role the textbook should play. Many pupils use it chiefly as a source of practice material. But this limited usage destroys the textbook's chief function—to help the pupil in learning arithmetic.

The modern textbook in arithmetic provides three types of subject matter, which may be classified as *developmental, practice,* and *social applications.* The developmental work deals with the meaning of the four arithmetic processes and ways of operating with them. The practice work, or drill, consists of examples to be solved by application of the processes. The social applications provide problems arising in daily activities which may be solved by the arithmetic process.

* From Foster E. Grossnickle, "How to Use the Arithmetic Textbook," *NEA Journal* (January, 1958), pp. 41–42. Reprinted by permission of the author and the *NEA Journal.*

The greatest misuse of the textbook may occur in dealing either with developmental work or with problems based on social applications of number.

The textbook usually gives a concise explanation of an arithmetic process. However, pupils need background to interpret the quantitative statements.

Since many pupils lack this background, they should acquire it before reading the textbook. This can be done if the teacher first demonstrates the process and then has the pupils work out for themselves the steps in the development of the process by using manipulative and audio-visual materials.

Suppose we consider the development of the steps in compound subtraction that are needed to subtract in this example: $42 - 18 = ?$

The development in the textbook will show that it is necessary to change the four tens and two ones to three tens and twelve ones. This explanation is mere verbalism to pupils who do not understand the decimal structure of our number system and how it is possible to regroup a number. To be sure that pupils understand what it means to regroup a number, the teacher should demonstrate with manipulative materials how to express 42 as three tens and twelve ones.

He could use rectangular strips to represent the numbers given in the example above. A strip marked into 10 equal squares would represent one ten, and four such strips would represent the four tens in 42. Two squares cut from another strip would represent two ones.

The pupils would see that it is impossible to take eight ones from two ones and that, therefore, it is necessary to take one of the four tens and convert it into ten ones, thus making twelve ones. Now the eight ones can be subtracted.

The teacher can place 2″ x 3″ cards, splints, or other markers in the pockets of a place-value chart to show the steps in subtraction, or he can give a visual representation at the chalkboard as shown in the accompanying chart.

A marker in ten's place has a value of ten markers in one's place. The teacher has the class explain each step in the representation. Chart A shows four tens and two ones; Chart B shows the number regrouped as three tens and twelve ones; Chart C shows one ten and eight ones subtracted from three tens and twelve ones.

By watching teacher demonstrations and using manipulative and visual materials such as rectangular strips, squares, discs, and other homemade devices, pupils can discover the meaning of number and number operations. Once this has been accomplished, the textbook becomes a valuable source book which they can use to refresh their understanding as they do their arithmetic problems or when they review a process at a later date.

The second classification of subject matter in the arithmetic textbook includes examples for practice or drill. The need for drill is as great as the need for each of the other two classifications.

This phase of the program usually receives ample treatment in arithmetic classes. It is important to remember that practice or drill should come *after* a pupil understands a process. Drill does not help enrich or build concepts.

The third major classification of subject matter deals with social applications of number. Here the pupil encounters verbal problems. Some of these textbook problems have social significance, and some are verbal quantitative statements having no social application. (Social applications need not be limited to textbook verbal problems. Better ones come from the child's everyday experiences.) Verbal problems often prove to be frustrating to the pupil who lacks background because they do not convey meaning to him.

To read verbal problems with understanding, a pupil must be able to identify the problem question and the factors on which it depends. Then he is able to attempt a rational solution to the problem.

The vocabulary or the concepts used in a problem may be unfamiliar to the pupil. He may not understand the quantitative relationships among the various numbers. These and other factors may affect his ability to solve verbal problems. In the final analysis, the difficulty in problem-solving results from a lack of background in interpreting the printed page.

In order to help the pupils profit most from experiences in dealing with verbal textbook problems, the teacher should follow the five procedures given below.

1. If the problems deal with a unit theme, a picture, or a chart, discuss the unifying idea before assigning the problems on the page. Be sure the pupils understand the concepts introduced.

2. Emphasize quality of solutions rather than the number of problems to be solved. Challenge the superior pupils to give more than one way of arriving at a solution to a problem.

3. Have the slow learners skip the problems and exercises which will not

be meaningful to them. But be sure the pages skipped do not break up the continuity of the developmental program.

4. Encourage the pupil to read a problem slowly. Have him think, "What is the problem question to be answered?"

5. Use the unit themes in the textbook as a basis of further investigation to enrich the program in arithmetic.

For an effective arithmetic program, classroom materials should include (1) supplementary aids to help pupils objectify a process before they read about it and (2) a list of suitable library books for reference and research to enrich the presentation of topics in the textbook. When a classroom is so equipped, the textbook can truly become an assistant teacher in print.

66. *The Decimal Is More Than a Dot* *

FRANK C. ARNOLD

M ISSOURI must be the birthplace of all teachers since the constant cry of each is "Show me." We in Districts 45 and 46 under the aegis of Assistant Superintendent Max Gewirtz attempted to do just this in our training program for newly appointed teachers. (Districts 45 and 46 are part of the New York City school system. There are thirty-seven elementary and junior high schools with approximately 25,000 pupils and 1,100 teachers.) The demonstration teacher in each case was helped by the Elementary Mathematics Coordinators. The following is an account of one of the mathematics lessons which the neophytes of the fifth and sixth grades viewed.

Parenthetically the weakness of this viewing process, so prized by teachers, is that the new teacher does not have enough background to be able to know the graded steps that precede and follow the lessons she views. For this reason, in our demonstrations the viewer received a "Before-and-After" outline which was discussed at the briefing and follow-up periods. The outline of the lesson which we are describing will be found at the end of the article.

* From Frank C. Arnold, "The Decimal Is More Than a Dot," *The Arithmetic Teacher* (October, 1955), pp. 80–82. Reprinted by permission of the author and the National Council of Teachers of Mathematics.

A Lesson on Decimals

The lesson chosen for demonstration in this instance was concerned with the early development of decimals. The reason for this selection was that decimals are so deceptively "easy."

Now to the development of the lesson—

Actually preparation for this lesson in decimals began "many grades ago" with the emphasis on place value and on fractions. However, not to burden the reader with the sequential development through the years, we shall go back only a short time before the lesson itself.

During this preparatory period the class explored instruments which record measures in tenths. The teacher took the class to visit the neighboring gasoline stations to examine the calcometers and to observe how they record the amount of gasoline sold and its cost. Those children whose parents own cars were asked to observe the workings of the odometer. To be sure that each child had such opportunity, the teacher took the children in small groups on short rides. During the ride he directed their attention to the way the odometer recorded the distance traveled. One morning a pupil whose father has an auto supply store brought in an odometer. By using a small motor the children learned how mileage is recorded. Another pupil demonstrated the use of the cyclometer on his bicycle. Clinical thermometers were examined. Large scale models of an odometer and a clinical thermometer were constructed. Movable strips were used so that the children could "work" the odometer model. Of course, in addition to the preparation outlined above, the place value of whole numbers and the ratios involved in place value were stressed throughout the term.

The lesson itself began with the recall of the visits to the gas station, the manipulation of the odometer, etc.

The children discussed the various ways in which quantities smaller than one whole had been recorded on the various instruments they had observed, i.e., as a common fraction on the calcometer; as a differently colored number to the right of the whole numbers on the odometer, etc. They demonstrated on the model of the odometer how tenths of a mile are recorded; how ten tenths "automatically" become one more mile.

The teacher then showed whole miles on the odometer and asked such questions as, "What kind of numbers are these?" "Whole numbers." The teacher showed parts of a mile on the odometer and asked the children to identify this type of number. Some of the responses were—"smaller than a whole number," "smaller than a mile," "a fraction." On the blackboard the children recorded in fraction form (1/10, 2/10, etc.) what was shown on the odometer.

Then the teacher asked the children to represent one mile by a line on the blackboard. He directed them to represent one tenth of a mile on this line. They discussed the ratio between 1/10 of a mile and one whole mile. Two tenths were shown on the line. The child was asked to show 2/10 of a mile on the odometer. At this point the teacher went back to review the meaning of the place value of whole numbers. The teacher showed the units on the abacus. "If you were at the gas station getting gas, what would this mean?" "One gallon of gas." "If you were riding in a car what would this mean?" "One mile." A child was asked to represent on a chart the unit seen on the abacus. After discussion children were asked to show ten miles and 100 miles on the abacus. The numbers were also written on the chart. Now using the chart below the children made the following comparisons and generalizations.

Tens	Units	Tenths
1	1	1

The 1 in the tens place has ten times the value of the 1 in the units place; the 1 in the hundreds place has ten times the value of the 1 in the tens place, etc.

The children then compared the value of the 1 in the tens place with that of the 1 in the hundreds place; the 1 in the units place with the 1 in the tens place and made the following generalizations. The 1 in the tens place has one tenth the value of the 1 in the hundreds place: the 1 in the units place has one tenth the value of the 1 in the tens place.

Once more attention was drawn to the odometer. The teacher asked a child to show one tenth of a mile on the odometer. "Can we show this on our abacus?" was the teacher's question. After some discussion as to the position, the number of beads needed, etc., two children added the needed column of beads to the right of the units column. It is interesting to note that the children had no difficulty in labelling this column tenths. If children do not have an understanding of the ratios involved in place value, the usual label given to this column is halves.

"We have shown one tenth on the odometer, on the line diagram, on the abacus. Now let us show it on the chart." Here, too, the children found little difficulty in writing and labelling the column to the right of the units place on the chart.

When this was done the teacher continued, "When we write numbers, do we always label them? Suppose we did not have the labels, how would we know how to read this mileage?" The teacher now wrote 11 without labels. "What mileage does this say?" "Eleven miles." "Look at the odometer. What do we want it to say?" "One and one tenth miles." "How shall we write this so we can recognize it as one and one tenth miles?"

This was the $64 question that "stumped" the class. The teacher returned to the odometer. "How was 1/10 of a mile shown on the odometer in the car?" "It was shown by a different color." Stimulated by this reminder, the children went on to give suggestions such as, "Put in a box around the number," "Make the number smaller in size," "Make the number another color" etc. Some of these were ruled out as not practicable or clumsy. Finally a child suggested, "When you have cents, which are less than a dollar you use a dot." The teacher affirmed this child's suggestion but brought out that this form was not universal. The form $\dfrac{\text{units.tenths}}{1 \ . \ 1}$ was written on the board, and after discussion, the columns were labelled.

The children showed one tenth in a variety of ways including the decimal form.

Then the teacher gave practice in showing one tenth, two tenths, etc., in all forms—on the odometer, on the abacus, on the chart, as the common fraction, as a decimal fraction.

As a homework assignment one group was asked to find out how tenths are written in different countries other than the United States. The other groups were asked to find instances in which tenths are written in decimal form in newspapers, in social studies books, in railroad schedules etc.

We feel that after this lesson the young teachers realized that there was more to teaching decimals than the dot.

Outline for the Lesson

PRELEARNINGS

Understanding of place value of whole numbers

Understanding of common fractions

Understanding of relationships between and among common fractions and whole numbers

Special emphasis upon the tenth as a common fraction

Understanding of and generalizations concerning ratio of tens to units, hundreds to tens, etc., and vice versa

AIM OF THE LESSON

To develop the concept of a decimal fraction (initial development)

THE LESSON CONTINUED

Further emphasis on developing the concept of the tenth as a decimal fraction

Representing, reading and writing tenths as decimal fractions

Introducing terms *decimal fraction* and *common fraction*

Emphasizing common fraction equivalents for decimal fractions and vice versa

Adding and subtracting tenths (decimals and mixed decimals involving tenths)

Developing concept of cents as part of a dollar

Developing the meaning of hundredths as decimal fractions

Emphasizing relationships among hundredths and the whole, hundredths and tenths, etc. (place value)

Adding and subtracting hundredths (decimals and mixed decimals involving hundredths)

Adding and subtracting tenths and hundredths (decimals and mixed decimals)

Generalizations concerning the denominators of common and decimal fractions

Multiplying and dividing decimal fractions by whole numbers

Similar procedure with thousandths (for more mature children)

67. *Levels of Difficulty in Division* *

ARDEN K. RUDDELL

DIVISION of whole numbers is a relatively complicated computational process. It is complicated because it involves each of the other processes: addition, multiplication, and subtraction, and also includes principles unique to division alone. Thorough understanding of division is

* From Arden K. Ruddell, "Levels of Difficulty in Division," *The Arithmetic Teacher* (March, 1959), pp. 97–98. Reprinted by permission of the author and the National Council of Teachers of Mathematics.

dependent upon knowledge and understanding of the interrelationships between the four processes—addition, subtraction, multiplication, and division. Following are the understandings commonly made explicit.

"Understandings" in Division

Division is a special case of subtraction. This relationship is most basic in understanding division. For many years leading writers have mentioned this relationship, but teaching procedures which utilize the idea have been limited.

Division is the reverse of multiplication. The combinations involved in each of these processes are the same. However, multiplication consists of combining groups equal in size into one large group while division involves separating a group into smaller parts equal in size. An understanding of these relationships is essential for a complete understanding of the division process.

An understanding of the Hindu-Arabic decimal system of notation and the place value of numbers is essential to understanding the division of whole numbers. Placement of quotient figures and regrouping of integers within the dividend can be most effectively learned when based upon an understanding of value in our decimal system of notation.

Divisor-Dividend-Quotient relationships holds generalizations essential for complete understanding of the division process. As an individual grows in understanding the division process, generalizations should emerge with respect to the relationships between the divisor, dividend, and quotient. Estimating an answer or knowing whether the solution to a division problem is reasonable rests upon an understanding of these relationships. These relationships will be defined more fully in the next section.

Addition-Subtraction-Multiplication within the division process must be understood. A knowledge and understanding of addition, subtraction, and multiplication should be developed before approaching division. As the complexity of the division process increases, addition, subtraction, and multiplication are used more extensively and become more important to the process.

UNDERSTANDINGS OF DIVISION BEHAVIORALLY DEFINED

A careful analysis of the division process and all that it involves in working with whole numbers brings to light the afore-mentioned understandings, concepts, and generalizations. If an individual can quickly and accurately solve a division example it does not necessarily follow that the individual possesses even one of the basic understandings listed above. These understandings probably can best be discovered through careful scrutiny of an individual's written work coupled with a discussion or structured interview.

Listed below are examples of behavior typical of children who possess an understanding of division.[1]

Children's Explanations Show Understanding

1. *Division is a special case of subtraction.*
   a. I know there are three twos in six. If I had six blocks, I could take two blocks away at a time until they were all gone and I would take two blocks away three times.
   b. I can show you there are four threes in twelve by subtracting.

$$
\begin{array}{r}
3\overline{)12} \\
-\ 3 \\
\hline
9 \\
-\ 3 \\
\hline
6 \\
-\ 3 \\
\hline
3 \\
-\ 3 \\
\hline
\end{array}
$$

   I subtracted three four times.
   c. I have learned there are eight threes in twenty-four. So I subtract all eight threes at once.

$$
\begin{array}{r}
8 \\
3\overline{)24} \\
-24 \\
\hline
\end{array}
$$ ————8 threes

   d. I can find out how many sixes there are in forty-two by subtracting. I know there are three sixes in eighteen, so I subtract three sixes all at once. I subtract three sixes again from twenty-four. Then I subtract one six. So I find there are seven sixes in forty-two.

$$
\begin{array}{r}
6\overline{)42} \\
-18 \\
\hline
24 \\
-18 \\
\hline
6 \\
-\ 6 \\
\hline
\end{array}
$$
————3 sixes
————3 sixes
————1 six
7 sixes

---

[1] Identified as a result of a structured interview of 358 children.

2. *Division is the reverse of multiplication.*

    a. There are nine twos in eighteen because nine times two is eighteen. So I subtract all the twos at the same time.

$$2)\overline{18}$$
$$\underline{-18}$$

    b. If I used counting discs I could add three discs four times and get twelve. Or I could start with twelve discs and take away three at a time, four times. So three times four is twelve; there are four threes in twelve and I can subtract them all at once.

$$3)\overline{12}$$
$$\underline{-12}$$

3. *The place value of numbers.*

    a. Why does the 1 in the answer go above the 5?

$$\begin{array}{r} 1 \\ 3)\overline{57} \end{array}$$

      1) First, you are finding how many threes there are in five tens or fifty.

      2) Because the 5 is in the tens place and the 1 tells how many threes go in the tens place.

    b. What does the 2 mean or stand for?

$$\begin{array}{r} 1 \\ 3)\overline{57} \\ \underline{-3} \\ 2 \end{array}$$

      1) You subtracted three tens from fifty-seven and the 2 means that there are two tens left over.

    c. Why do we put the 7 beside the 2?

      1) Because you are really subtracting three tens or thirty from fifty-seven, so you have two tens and seven ones left over.

$$\begin{array}{r} 1 \\ 3)\overline{57} \\ \underline{-3} \\ 27 \end{array}$$

d. Why do we put the 9 in the answer above the 7?

$$3\overline{)57}\begin{array}{r}19\\-3\\\hline 27\\-27\\\hline\end{array}$$

1) Well, you have to change the two tens to twenty ones so that you have twenty-seven ones to divide. So the 9 goes in the ones place. Then you subtract all twenty-seven ones at once.

4. *Divisor-Dividend-Quotient relationships.* At the introductory stages, few children grasp these relationships. However, these examples indicate that some understanding is being developed.

a. I know the answer to this problem can't be forty-one because the answer must be smaller than fifteen.

$$3\overline{)15}\quad{}^{41}$$

b. Two fourth-grade children out of 358 responded to this question: How many sixes are there in forty-two?

$$6\overline{)42}$$

I can figure there are fourteen threes in forty-two. When the divisor is twice as big, the quotient is half as big. So there must be seven sixes in forty-two.

68. *Unifying Ideas in Arithmetic* *

HARRY G. WHEAT

IN OUR DISCUSSION of unifying ideas in arithmetic, it makes a difference whether we consider the first word of our topic as a qualifying adjective or as the participial form of a verb of action—that is, whether we determine that our subject is ideas, or instead human individuals who may sometimes

* From Harry G. Wheat, "Unifying Ideas in Arithmetic," *The Arithmetic Teacher* (December, 1954), pp. 1–8. Reprinted by permission of the author and the National Council of Teachers of Mathematics.

have ideas and do things with them. In the one case, we tempt ourselves to treat ideas as though they stand alone and, under proper circumstances, unite themselves; in the other, we keep away from the futile effort to abstract ideas from the human minds that conceive them. I choose the latter alternative. I prefer to think of the pupil as an active organized personality who can operate under his own power in bringing his ideas into patterns of unity. I shall not thereby neglect the characteristic unifying qualities which ideas in arithmetic possess.

Making a Start

The pupil may start unifying his ideas in arithmetic at the beginning of his schoolwork. If his teacher inquires, "How many books are on the table?" he counts to find out. He then tells his answer: *three,* let us say. At the same time, he may write the figure 3, as a way to tell his answer, with pencil or chalk. Though he has some difficulty writing the figure, he has none with the idea of its use. Writing the figure, as another way to tell his idea of the group, is none the less simpler than writing the word *George,* as another way to tell his name. It is never a mystery, except as the teacher keeps it hidden and makes it so.

A bit later, the beginning pupil may bring into a unity of thought and action the idea of a question to answer, and the writing of the expression that tells the answer. Thus he may look at the figures 2 and 3 in a column, $\frac{2}{3}$, as the question, "Two and three are how many?" When he finds the answer, he is ready to tell it, either orally or by completing or producing the column of 2 and 3, with 5 underneath, $\frac{2}{3}$, $\frac{}{5}$. His written statement, $\frac{2}{3}$, $\frac{}{5}$, tells his answer equally as well as his oral statement, "Two and three are five." In this procedure, he may move with certain confidence; for he goes forward in his thinking, directly from a question that calls for an answer, to the answer he finds and has in mind to tell. The procedure is not the usual memoriter learning of the teacher's statement, or the book's statement, of a fact—in this case a so-called "addition fact." The procedure here, though outwardly much the same, is a different one. Instead of a "fact" to learn, the pupil has a question to answer. Instead of a statement to copy, the pupil gets an idea of something to seek and find. The succeeding writing is simply the coincidence of telling what he knows when he knows it.

Contradictions in Practice

Our two illustrations of the way the pupil, at the very beginning of his work in arithmetic, may go about unifying his ideas has abundant contradiction in the common outcomes of the usual arithmetic program in the primary grades. Thousands of pupils seldom get a chance to write the numerals as expressions of ideas until they have been in school one or two years; and often then only in roundabout relation to ideas, through the words and sentences which originally have had the exclusive agency of expression. Many pupils, during the whole of their lives, at least of their school lives, never quite succeed in making numerical expressions do more than record the results of their thinking, after they somehow have done it. They never quite get around to the idea of using their numerical expressions to facilitate the combining of ideas and to aid their thinking. In the case of some, the simple notation of the nine numerals and zero in a few familiar forms is always a mysterious rite.

Yet the contradictions the large numbers of our pupils provide are only apparent contradictions. Of course there appears before many pupils, between the ideas they think and say and the expressions they must write, an impenetrable wall. But it is we, their teachers, who have built the wall. We cultivate the illusion of what we call "concrete arithmetic," which we think our pupils should understand; and then we distinguish it from an imaginary "abstract arithmetic," which, we can be sure, no one can understand. Thereby we deprive our beginning pupils of the aid to their thinking which its written expression could give; and then we remove the written expression so far from the original thinking of our pupils as to make it difficult in the extreme for them ever to bring it back to reality. For one thing, we delay our beginners, who are ready and eager to move ahead, with a lot of "readiness" activity they do not need; and, for another, we delay, often for a year or more, the writing of what little they do manage to think. The inevitable consequence is that the beginning pupils, who do manage to unify their ideas in arithmetic, are few and far between. The thing of wonder is that so many are able to gain any ideas at all. The contradictions of the possibility of unifying ideas are the contradictions which, through our procrastinating, we take pains to create.

Proper Timing

Yet not all our timing of the pupil's progress in arithmetic is thus so bad. In illustration, we may consider the practice of many teachers of delaying the introduction of terms, until the pupil has at least the essence of the ideas the terms are useful in designating. Thus, when the pupil has found answers over and over to such questions as "Two and three are how many?"
2
3 and, through repeated demonstration, has become conscious of the way to find answers, his teacher supplies the name "addition" for his activity. How to explain the term, in such case, is not a problem; for the pupil already has supplied his own explanation. The teacher has merely to provide the name for what the pupil is sure he knows. Though his knowledge of addition has just begun, he can expand his new term as he enlarges his idea. Moreover, his new term adds, or gives new emphasis, to his enlarging idea.

The whole procedure in its proper timing relieves the teacher of a great, and somewhat uncertain, responsibility. Of late, teachers have been hearing a lot about "meaningful arithmetic," including suggestions on how they should make arithmetic "meaningful" for their pupils. They have had to contemplate discussions of what the meaning actually is, which they are called upon to transmit. Since all such definitions of the meaning of meaning require further definitions of the defining terms, teachers who try to pursue them become lost in the maze of philosophic erudition, or just plain verbalism. Their only relief is a return to the basic fact that the only meaning in arithmetic, that means anything to the pupil, is the meaning he provides himself through the activity of his own thinking. In illustration, we may consider how the pupil may build his idea of *division,* for example, and bring it into use as a means of unifying other ideas he gains as he moves along.

Let us see what the pupil may make his dividing mean.

Dividing as Illustration

We may seek in the usual way an answer to the kind of question we usually raise, namely, "How does the pupil acquire the *meaning* of *division?*" But that is not the question we should ask. Such a question suggests that division is one thing the pupil learns; its *meaning,* something more. The question we should ask is rather: "What does the pupil make his dividing—the dividing that *he* does—mean to him?" If we look for an answer to a question like this, we find that dividing means to the pupil just what *he* does and thinks as he divides, no more and no less.

We find something else, if we pursue a question like the latter, that is a cardinal advantage. We find that we can maintain control of the pupil's work and thinking as he does his dividing, that we can guide the pupil's attention as he works and thinks.

The pupil divides to answer a question: "How many twos are in eight?" $2\overline{)8}$. We raise the question and we make the question clear. We see that the pupil pays attention to three things: (1) the total, (2) the equal groups, (3) the number of the equal groups. The pupil does three things, giving each careful attention: (1) He counts out eight and checks for certainty. (2) He counts out a two, then another, and another, and another, and checks to be sure that each is a two. (3) He counts the twos, and counts again to make sure. Now the pupil has his answer—*his* because *he* has found it—and he tells and writes it, "Four twos are eight," $2\overline{)8}.$

$$\begin{array}{r} 4 \\ 2\overline{)8} \\ \underline{8} \end{array}$$

Somewhat similarly, the pupil gives attention to three things when he answers the question, "How much is one half of eight?" (1) He pays attention to the total original amount. (2) He makes sure of the equality of the parts. (3) He finds the number in one of the equal parts.

Steps in Dividing

The pupil's activity of paying attention to the division question and the three things he thinks and does when he divides, with its succeeding and expanding repetitions, is the *first* step in his learning about dividing. The question for which he seeks an answer, the kind of answer he should seek, the dividing he does, and the objects of his attention throughout, are all in the simplest possible setting. Such a setting has its concrete, or objective, features reduced to the necessary minimum.

The pupil may now move to a *second* and a *third* step in dividing. In taking each of these, he continues to give attention as he did in taking the first: to the original whole amount; to the equality of the groups, or parts; to the number of equal groups, or the number of each equal part. Thus, basically, there is no difference in the three steps; the only existing difference is in their outward appearance, or in the manner in which the pupil's division question is made to appear. In the first step, the question appears, as it were, in a state of nature, unclothed in any garment that diverts the attention; and in the second and third steps, the question comes clothed in the dress of a practical situation: the familiar everyday clothes, in the one; and the somewhat unfamiliar Sunday's best, in the other. To illustrate,

Second step. The pupil deals with "problems" that familiar situations provide: "Helen earned seventy-five cents baby-sitting. She saved one third of what she earned. How much did Helen save?"

Third step. The pupil deals with "problems" requiring study of new and somewhat unfamiliar situations: "Jack and Don had a lemonade stand. Jack furnished one third of the materials. The profit, after they had paid all expenses, was ninety cents. How much was Jack's share?" In this "problem," the matters of "profit, after expenses" and proper "wages" to the two boys, complicate the division question, and must be studied and cleared to make the question clear.

Dividing as a Unifying Idea

The pupil can make his idea of dividing into equal parts a unifying idea that runs through and clarifies much of his later studies, such as fractions, measures, and decimals. He may note and recognize the common features of his working and thinking when he divides a whole into its equal parts, when he divides a measure into its equal smaller measures, when he divides into tenths and tenths of tenths, and when he deals with decimal divisions as measures.

Similarly, the pupil can make his idea of dividing into equal groups a unifying and clarifying idea as he seeks to learn the later and more complex processes, such as dividing by a two-place number. His earlier attention to total original amount, equality of the separated groups, and number in each, helps him to keep clear what the question is and what the answer should be that he must seek. Similarly also, the same clear question, and clear idea of answer to seek, bring the difficult idea of dividing by fractions out into the open, where it too can be clear. Any pupil who recognizes the example, $4 \div \frac{1}{2} =$, as the question, "How many halves are in four?" recognizes no difficulty in the task he must perform.

The pupil's meaning of dividing, as being what he thinks and does as he divides, is but an illustration of the meaning he may make of all the thinking processes he learns to perform, whether those of adding, or subtracting, or multiplying, or computing the average, or finding per cent. If he works, from the outset, toward the simpler answers his simpler questions suggest, he may gain an idea of procedure which may carry him along, when both questions and answers become complicated in newer requirements and usages. And if he attends closely to his idea, he may recognize it as a common thread running through many phases of his later work, and uniting them into a single pattern.

Our major concern is that the pupil must give his continued attention to the central, or characteristic, feature of an arithmetical process as he learns to put it into operation; or, conversely, that we must do nothing to distract his attention and draw it away from the central, or characteristic, feature.

Distractions We Make

As teachers, we seem always to go out of our way to distract the attention of pupils from the main business in which they should engage in learning arithmetic.

We no sooner introduce the pupil to the way he should work and think, as he starts learning a process, like dividing, than we begin to overwhelm him with all sorts of personal and social situations, such as divisions of his time and money, of his friends into groups for work and games, and of his property into shares; and with objects of all kinds, and shapes, and colors, in all sorts of designs, that both attract and distract. We call this the pupil's "concrete arithmetic." We properly recognize that, to begin his studies of grouping, the pupil at the outset must have objects to group; but we tend to forget that it is the *grouping* he must study, not the qualities of his objects. The paraphernalia of present-day primary arithmetic is out of all proportion to any possible arithmetical usage pupils can make of it.

That isn't all. Not content with distracting the pupil's attention from the characteristic features of the grouping he should study and learn to diverting situations and interesting concrete materials, we go further and set apart in isolation, as something "meaningless" and "abstract," such computational result as the pupil may incidentally gain. Of course it is "meaningless." There is no meaning for the pupil except that which he creates. Of course it is "abstract." It stands so far apart from everything that makes sense for the pupil that he seldom can connect it sensibly with anything. Computation and problem-solving have always been widely separated activities in the arithmetic of the school. We do very little in present-day teaching to get our pupils able to recognize them as a single thinking procedure in different dresses.

Yet when we return to our illustration of the pupil creating his meaning of dividing, for example, by paying attention to what his division question asks, and to the kind of answer he should seek, we can see how the meaning he thus creates is a common characteristic in all three stages of the dividing he must learn to perform. Thus, in the first stage, the pupil meets his question and its suggestion as to the kind of answer, unadorned and void of distracting surroundings. In the second and third stages, he may recognize and attend to the same question, and suggested kind of answer, when they are concealed in practical situations, familiar and to be learned, respectively. He thus may make his idea of question and suggested answer an idea that unifies his computations and his problem exercises.

Two Ways of Unifying Ideas

To this point we have considered the matter of the pupil unifying his ideas in arithmetic in two ways. The two ways are not sharply distinguishable, for in both the pupil must first gain ideas to be able to unify them, and the pupil is the unifying agent.

In one of the two ways, we have seen the pupil unifying ideas that normally belong together, except as someone works to keep them apart. Thus, in our illustrations, we have seen how the pupil may unify his idea of a quantity with his act of writing the proper figure to tell what it is, and, in similar manner, how he may unify his idea of a number-question and its answer with the act of writing the figures in proper form as a means of expression. We have seen, further, how the pupil may unite a process, when he has learned it, with its proper name; and how he may unify his computation and his problem-solving into a single requirement of practice in thinking.

In the other of the two ways, we have seen how the pupil may use an idea, such as that of dividing into equal parts, as a means of unifying into a common pattern of work and thinking the otherwise diverse studies of fractions, of divisions of measures, of divisions into tenths and tenths of tenths, and of decimals as measures.

In further illustration, we may consider briefly how the pupil may make his idea of "dealing with tens" as he "deals with ones" a clarifying as well as unifying idea.

Here again, whether the pupil gains the unifying idea, and uses it in unifying, depends upon the way he thinks as he works. Here again, it is a case of the thinking making the working worth while.

Ten as a Unifying Idea

Everyone must deal with tens, and multiples of ten, as he deals with ones. There is no other way to deal with them. But whether he is conscious of the fact is the point of difference.

When the child first can count to two or three, or four or five, he counts everything in the range of his senses: chairs in the room, pictures on the wall, plates on the table, trees in the yard. Later, as a pupil, he counts rows and bunches and piles and bundles of things the way he counts ungrouped objects. So, when he provides himself a few groups of tens, he can, and does, count them as he counts ones. And he counts separated groups together as he counts separated objects, and thus he demonstrates, usually without knowing it, that he adds tens the way he adds ones. It is at this point, if not also long before, that the teacher can become a guiding light, making the pupil conscious of what he does.

Thus, having learned to add 2 and 3, the pupil finally faces the task of adding 20 and 30, two tens and three tens. Yet, as a task, the new learning is of less difficulty, provided that the pupil knows and recognizes that he now has *tens* to add. This he can do, and does, in the degree that his earlier attention to the special positional value for writing tens, and his teacher's present question about how he should add tens, make him conscious of the special thinking he must do.

As the pupil moves ahead, let us say that his teacher continues to call his attention to the way he deals with *tens:* How do we subtract tens? How do we multiply tens? How do we divide tens? How do we multiply by tens? How do we divide by tens? In each case, the question comes as a constantly older, and more familiar, question that always calls for a common answer that gets easier and easier to sense. This is the reason why arithmetic can become less difficult as it becomes outwardly and apparently more complex.

The pupil not merely gains a growing mastery of his unifying idea, but also becomes increasingly conscious of the possibility of putting it to use. He looks into the new things set forth for him to learn, to discover where his idea may fit as means of rounding out the new things and making them sensible. In some such manner, especially if his teacher guides his attention by asking appropriate questions, he sees, as he undertakes the operations with decimals, how he may deal with tenths, hundredths, and thousandths as he has become accustomed to deal with ones and tens and powers of ten.

Other Illustrations

The pupil's work and thinking in learning arithmetic gives many other illustrations of unifying ideas which he may create and use, provided that his teacher guides his attention to the proper landmarks along the route of his learning. Following are a few such illustrations.

1. *Teens and Tens.* When the beginning pupil gives special attention to the single group of ten, both when it stands alone and when it stands with other smaller groups as the base of the teens, he gains the useful unifying idea that the teens have a common characteristic which makes them much alike. He may now learn, with his teacher's guidance, to look upon the thirty-six so-called "harder" additions—those having sums of 11 to 18—as the single operation of reconversion into a ten, and to attack them all with this common method of work and thinking. Similarly, he may learn to consider the thirty-six corresponding subtractions—those having minuends of 11 to 18—as the single operation of subtracting from a ten. In either case, the pupil gains an idea of procedure that he can use independently and confidently to determine his answers to what otherwise would appear as thirty-six different questions.

The pupil may extend the use of his idea of ten to the unifying of the simple multiplications which are usually a source of trouble to beginners. Thus the multiplications, "four fives" to "nine nines"—$\begin{array}{r}5\\\times 4\end{array}$, $\begin{array}{r}9\\\times 9\end{array}$—convert into the common question, "How many tens?" This common question supplies an idea of procedure the pupil can use independently and confidently to provide his answers, however much or little he learns to use other methods to supplement.

Several of my students have experimented to determine whether beginning pupils can learn and use independently methods of work and thinking, such as those just indicated, to determine answers to simple additions, subtractions, multiplications, and divisions. They have found, without regard to social background or learning speed of the pupils concerned, that all could give special attention to the idea of ten and thereby learn to use it to find their own answers independently to the questions in arithmetic put before them. Their studies merely confirmed what good teachers have long observed. Whenever the teacher makes his assignment clear, or makes his question clear, his pupils surprise him much more with successful performance than they do with evidences of inability.

Yet there are persons concerned with the teaching of arithmetic who do not take kindly to the suggestion that pupils may learn to produce their own answers independently. They say that such methods of learning are slow and roundabout, and conform not at all to the speedy and direct responses later usage requires. These persons are they who have not learned the basic pedagogical principle that methods of learning and methods of use cannot possibly be one and the same.

2. *The Three Kinds of Problems.* When the pupil learns to multiply and

divide by fractions, he soon meets the questions which we commonly classify as the "three kinds of problems," namely:

a. Finding the part of a number
b. Finding the part one number is of another
c. Finding the number when a specified part of it is known

These problems confuse with their similarities, yet they have differences which the pupil can learn to distinguish. I have observed pupils in the fifth grade looking for, and frequently observing, the distinguishing features of the "three kinds of problems" in their pursuit of answers to the questions: Does the problem mention numbers only, or a part and a number? What number (in the case of the former) does the problem ask about? Is the part (in the case of the latter) of a number that *is* given, or of a number that *is not* given?

The pupil who thus learns the distinctions between the "three kinds of problems" gains a method of attack which serves to unite the three different problems somewhat as the three sides of a triangular situation. He is prepared to carry this method of attack to the later and more commonly used statements of the "three kinds of problems" as he meets them in his study of per cents. And if he continues, or has the opportunity to continue, to keep in clear consciousness the "three kinds of problems," he may find all the varied applications of percentage he must study and learn resolving themselves into the familiar three categories.

3. *Procedure in Measuring.* When the pupil looks behind the scenes of the usages of the common measures of his earlier arithmetic, he may learn to notice the two steps of thinking and practice in the determination of the sizes and amounts of things. These steps are, first, determining or choosing a suitable measure, and second, using the measure. Though the measures he uses have long since been determined for him, he may now gain an idea of the relation between a given measure and its special usefulness. The idea, of course, is no substitute for the practice the pupil should have in the uses of the measure, and it is not a needed item for the practice; yet the idea does become a valuable one when the pupil carries it to the studies of measures which to him are uncommon. He may use the idea to unify all his measuring into a somewhat similar procedure, and thus to develop the steps of the rules of measuring that have a practical use.

4. *Asking Questions of Problems.* The pupil who learns to attack the simple one-step problems of his beginning arithmetic by raising and answering the questions (1) "What does the problem tell?" (2) "What does the problem ask?" gains thereby the means of attacking problems of more than one step as he comes to them. He has no trouble, in the case of the latter

more complex problems, in moving along to the succeeding essential question, "What else must I know to find the answer?" He may not always arrive at the desired answer, but he is on his way.

The Teacher as Guide

We do not need through further illustration to labor our discussion of the pupil at work unifying his ideas in arithmetic. In every illustration we have seen the pupil as the active agent in determining what and how he learns. Yet every illustration has suggested the guiding hand of a teacher who manages the pupil's learning. Though it must be the pupil who works out the unifying that he learns and uses, it nevertheless is his teacher who provides the sequences of his work that make it possible for him to bring it all into a pattern of unity. For example, in a certain classroom, the pupils one day were responding as follows:

Said one: "I can find seven sevens; I know four sevens are twenty-eight and three sevens are twenty-one. I add twenty-eight and twenty-one; so seven sevens are forty-nine."

Said another: "I can find nine sevens; I know three sevens are twenty-one, and nine sevens are three times as much. So I multiply, and I know that nine sevens are sixty-three."

With their oral responses, the pupils wrote:

$$\frac{\begin{array}{r} 7 \\ \times 7 \end{array}}{}, \quad \frac{\begin{array}{r} 7 \\ \times 4 \end{array}}{28}, \quad \frac{\begin{array}{r} 7 \\ \times 3 \end{array}}{21}, \quad \frac{\begin{array}{r} 28 \\ 21 \end{array}}{49}, \quad \frac{\begin{array}{r} 7 \\ \times 7 \end{array}}{49};$$

$$\frac{\begin{array}{r} 7 \\ \times 9 \end{array}}{}, \quad \frac{\begin{array}{r} 7 \\ \times 3 \end{array}}{21}, \quad \frac{\begin{array}{r} 21 \\ \times 3 \end{array}}{63}, \quad \frac{\begin{array}{r} 7 \\ \times 9 \end{array}}{63}$$

It is merely rhetorical to ask who was the person in charge of this classroom, and who made it possible for the pupils to unify otherwise separate and diverse multiplications into a single idea of procedure.

In the proper conduct of the pupil's learning in arithmetic, the teacher need not worry about how best to provide meanings and get them unified. All the teacher needs to do is ask the right questions at the right time. The pupil creates his meanings, and does his own unifying.

CHAPTER X TEACHING
SCIENCE

69. *Teaching Science in the Elementary School* *

WALTER MURRAY
AND LESTER D. CROW

CHILDREN are eager to learn about the world around them. They want to know the "why" of their experiences. It is imperative, therefore, that all children begin the study of science early in the elementary school. In order to do this effectively, teachers need to (1) train children to use the scientific method as they attempt to find answers to questions about their environment, (2) utilize the interest and activity of the learner, and (3) integrate science learning with other curriculum areas.

Basic Principles

As the teacher evolves basic teaching goals, he plans and uses various means to achieve them. Successful learning occurs in teaching-learning situations in which the child is actively involved. His learning is effective to the extent that he comes to appreciate the relationships that exist between his goals and the activities in which he participates to attain these goals. The teacher provides situations in which the child utilizes a self-inquiring approach to discover the *what, why,* and *how* of the elements inherent in his environment.

The teacher can help the child learn to use the scientific method of exploring his environment. He should not expect the child to discover new

* From Walter Murray and Lester D. Crow, "Teaching Science in the Elementary School," *Education* (March, 1960), pp. 416–20. Reprinted by permission of The Bobbs-Merrill Co., Inc., Indianapolis, Indiana.

scientific facts, but rather to discover facts already known. To accomplish this result, he must use discretion in answering the child's questions. In other words, he attempts to help a child discover facts for himself rather than to supply ready-made answers to his questions. The teacher, however, may supply the answers to selected questions asked during a science experience. For example, a child may need to have his concept of a phenomenon clarified in order to continue his study.

In general, the scientific method involves the following sequential steps:

1. Recognition of a problem
2. Definition of the problem situation
3. Study of the situation to discover all facts and clues that have a bearing on the problem
4. Development of tentative explanations or hypotheses
5. Selection of the best hypothesis
6. Utilization of experiments or other means to test the hypothesis
7. Tentative acceptance or rejection of the hypothesis and the testing of other possible hypotheses
8. Formulation of an appropriate conclusion

The classroom teacher plays a vital role in children's learning of science. Before the teacher selects his method of presentation, he attempts to discover something about the curiosity children exhibit concerning the phenomena in their surroundings. He also utilizes those principles which have proven useful in the teaching of elementary science. A few of these principles are:

1. Instruction begins at the learning level of the children.
2. Motivation emerges from within the content of science.
3. Observation is a helpful means to interpretation.
4. Problems and topics are kept within the limits of learner ability.
5. Planning is a cooperative venture between the children and the teacher.

Methods and Techniques

Teaching and learning are closely interrelated. The motivation of learner activity is a primary teacher responsibility. Approaches to the teaching of science include experimentation, demonstration, individual or group projects, reading and discussion, and field trips. A brief treatment of each of these media is presented below.

The most fruitful procedure for teaching science is to have children do things or *experiment*. The good teacher provides children with opportunities to solve problems by handling materials and by manipulating and arranging them. He makes certain that simple, inexpensive materials are used to perform experiments. Science textbooks are valuable sources of suggestions.

It is important to have the children themselves plan and perform simple experiments. Experiments can be utilized to help children to obtain answers to questions or to discover cause-and-effect relationships. A let-us-find-out attitude prevails. Even first grade children can gain an understanding of natural phenomena similar to the following by means of the experimental approach.

1. Snow and ice are made of water. They melt into water when they are warmed. Bring snow into the room in jars. Let it melt and observe the resulting water; notice the dirt in the water.

2. Water dries into the air. Children use water to paint on the chalkboard. What happened to the water we used on the chalkboard? What happens to the water in the clothes on the clothesline?

In these experiments the teacher attempts to help the children (1) discover the facts brought out by the experiment; (2) understand what was done in the experiment; and (3) formulate conclusions. Similarly, the display of objects or specimens and appropriate demonstrations of scientific activity, conducted by the teacher or selected pupils, are used to (1) solve problems; (2) verify facts, principles and generalizations, and (3) explain methods of procedure.

A demonstration can be valuable if the teacher utilizes procedures such as (1) performing it before he attempts it in class; (2) defining its purpose clearly; (3) performing it in such a way that everyone can see it; (4) using simple apparatus; (5) making it meaningful to the learner; (6) proceeding slowly with each step in order that the main ideas are understood; and (7) explaining the techniques utilized.

A *project* consists of several activities which are designed to solve problems. Special projects are utilized with both bright and slow learners. Participation in a project gives children the opportunity to develop self-reliance, initiative, and special manipulatory skills. Projects also can afford pupils opportunities to solve problems by means of lifelike situations.

A few examples of appropriate projects for elementary-school children are: soap carving of dinosaurs; papier-mâché model of housefly; clay models of rodents; construction of a fire engine; model of a house; and models of early land transportation.

One purpose of the teaching of science in the elementary school is to provide children with opportunities *to observe* the different phenomena of plant and animal life, and mineral matter, as well as the effect of the forces of nature on the materials in their environment. By helping children develop skill in observation, the teacher contributes to the expansion of interest in science, which will enable his pupils to learn more about the physical world in which they live.

When the teacher helps children develop observational skills, he encourages them to (1) note the kinds of answers given to their questions; (2) become aware of the techniques used in the discovery of facts; (3) identify and select the important or relevant details of the phenomena observed; (4) coordinate observation with other means of science learning; and (5) evaluate the results of observation critically in order to select pertinent ideas.

Through *reading and discussion* children can acquire a great deal of information about science and its applications. These are means of providing children with vicarious experiences. Hence, children need to be taught to consult textbooks and other sources of information to solve problems. If children are to derive meaning and understanding from the reading of science materials, they must be taught the unique skills required to locate appropriate information. They need to have developed the ability to (1) recognize a problem; (2) know and use general sources of reading materials, e.g., atlases, encyclopedias, and dictionaries; (3) consult a book's table of contents and index; (4) interpret charts, maps, and tables correctly; (5) skim reading material rapidly to locate scientific information; and (6) become adept in the use of library facilities.

Field trips provide children with opportunities for firsthand experiences. Trips can be so planned and organized that children derive significant learning from them as well as improve their skill in observation. Before starting a trip, the teacher alerts the children to the purpose of the trip and what might be observed. Routine procedures are kept simple. Children may assume some responsibilities in planning and carrying out the plans for trips; the teacher assumes leadership responsibility, however. After the field trip has been completed, the teacher and the class evaluate the experience in follow-up discussions.

Audio-visual Aids

Audio-visual materials are valuable aids in a program of science teaching. In fact, all materials and equipment used in science are regarded as audio-visual aids. Their purpose is to make more meaningful the child's environment and his relationship to it. Such aids provide data which might be difficult if not impossible to obtain through firsthand experiences.

Ideally, learning in science would consist of firsthand experiences with natural phenomena. Since this is impossible, teachers utilize devices which give meaning to concepts that then become the bases for new learnings. Audio-visual aids are valuable in science teaching and learning because they help to (1) clarify concepts, principles, and phenomena; (2) supply appropriate vicarious experiences; (3) make symbolic language more meaningful; and (4) motivate children toward an interest in the world of science.

Average and slow learners especially should be provided with many concrete illustrative materials to insure their understanding of abstract relationships. Audio-visual aids can be used effectively if the teacher (1) sets up definite purposes for their use; (2) utilizes appropriate aids in his plans; (3) makes preparation for their use in advance; (4) prepares the class for the particular type of aid used; (5) relates the learning material to the experiential background of the learner; and (6) provides follow-up activities to insure the achievement of the purposes for which they are used.

Lesson Planning

In science, as in other curriculum areas, there is no one best method of teaching. There are many variables in a teaching-learning situation, the utilization of which determines the outcomes of the process. Generally, there are three frames of reference currently employed in the teaching of science in the elementary school:

1. The experiences of children are utilized as a basis of learning. New learning is based on the quality and quantity of old learnings.
2. A systematic body of scientific concepts, information, and facts serves as the basis of teaching.
3. Children's previous experiences and science content are basic to the teacher's presentation of any unit of science.

Plans for directing classroom learnings include a variety of activities which are adapted to the needs of a particular class group. A lesson plan usually consists of six parts: (1) aims or purposes; (2) content of lesson outline; (3) pupil activities; (4) teaching techniques to be used; (5) specific materials to be included; and (6) evaluation of the procedures followed. A specimen lesson plan which has been used by a student teacher under the supervision of one of the authors is presented here.

AIR OCCUPIES SPACE AND EXERTS PRESSURE
(GRADE FOUR)

I. Purposes
   1. To help children learn that:
      a. Air occupies space
      b. Air exerts pressure
      c. Air is all around us
      d. Fresh air has no color, taste, or odor
      e. Air is used in breathing
      f. Air can be seen through
   2. To help children acquire an understanding of their relationship to the air around them
   3. To help children broaden their interests and gain an appreciation of science
   4. To help children grow in the ability to think clearly and logically by having them experiment, observe, etc.
   5. To help children learn to share responsibilities while working in a group.
   6. To provide children with "fun" while learning

II. Materials
   1. Several straws, tumblers, handkerchiefs, cans, balloons, cardboards, rectangles, towels, watering cans, and soup ladles

III. Time Schedule
   1. Setting up of pupil committees—30 minutes
   2. Instruction for use of material—15 minutes
   3. Class activities—40 to 60 minutes
   4. Evaluation of procedure—10 minutes

IV. Procedure
   1. Introduce topic by using well-known class game: "I am thinking of something in this room that starts with 'A'." Answer, "Air." Where do we find air? We can tell air is all around us because we feel it as wind and we breathe it. Worms and fish also breathe air from soil and water. We need air to breathe. Fresh air has no taste, color, or odor, and we can see through it. How do we know that it is real?
   2. Air takes up space. Have some child crumple a handkerchief in the bottom of a tumbler. Invert the tumbler and immerse it in a can of water. Remove the tumbler. Handkerchief is dry. Air in glass kept the water out. Repeat.

3. Air exerts pressure.
   a. Place a piece of chalk on balloon. Inflate quickly. Chalk jumps. Air pressure forced it upward.
   b. Fill tumbler with water. Slide cover of cardboard over it. Invert tumbler. Air pressure holds card and water in place.
4. Air takes up space and exerts pressure. Have a child hold one finger over the end of a straw. Immerse it in water. Water does not rise. Release finger. Water rises. Replace finger and remove straw from can of water. Water remains in straw.

V. Evaluation
   1. Discuss experiments.
   2. Have each child submit drawings and reports on the experiments.
   3. Make toys by using the principles learned, e.g., toy parachutes.

The success of this lesson depends on the teacher's ability to motivate his pupils to perform the experiments and to understand the principles involved. Adequate instructional materials also are needed if successful learning is to be achieved. Fortunately, there are available various simple materials that can be used by the resourceful teacher. Finally, careful planning by the teacher insures more effective learning on the part of the pupils.

70. Science *

EVERY DAY the results of complicated scientific discoveries are used and taken for granted. The science program aims to give children an understanding of the influence of science on modern living. Science is both a content area and a method of learning. Its content is to be found in the everyday environment of the child. There is a science content that is appropriate even for the youngest child. The method of teaching science requires investigation through manipulation, construction, reading, questioning, observation, and experimentation. Children explore problems arising from

* From *Curriculum Development in the Elementary Schools,* Curriculum Bulletin, No. 1, 1955–56 Series (New York: The Board of Education of the City of New York), pp. 22–25. Reprinted by permission.

their experiences in the classroom, home and community. Because it is the nature of the child to wonder, and since he is eager to touch, taste, smell, look, and listen, explorations in science begin at the earliest years. The elementary science program is designed to help children:

1. Acquire a functional understanding of the nature of their relationships with their environment
2. Grow in the ability to think clearly and logically, i.e., scientifically, and in the ability to distinguish fact from fancy, superstition from proven principle
3. Solve problems and discover new facts by using the methods of science
4. Gain experience, develop skills, and acquire confidence in the use of the various methods of finding out. Experimenting, observing, reading, going on planned field trips, asking questions, and consulting authorities, all help to round out and double check their finds.
5. Broaden their interest in the world about them and to foster an appreciation of the rhythm and orderliness of natural phenomena
6. Gain an appreciation of the potentialities of science for the improvement of human welfare and the dangers to civilization of its misuse.
7. Grow in those moral and spiritual values which exalt and refine the life of the individual and society
8. Develop an abiding interest in science and scientific pursuits

PREMISES

The course of study in science is built around the following basic premises adopted by the Curriculum Council (with modifications explained in footnotes):

A. The philosophy underlying the entire science program should be in harmony with the objectives of the total program of education.
B. The selection of science experiences and science learning should be governed by the degree to which they help pupils participate effectively in personal and social living.
C. The approach to science education should be experimental and should stem from pupil experiences. These should be both the natural, spontaneous kind and the planned or controlled kind; thus being related to the needs and interests of the child and of society.
D. A resource-unit approach, wherein first small and then large problems of direct interest to children offer purpose and direction in learning, will assist in providing a basic integrated program and philosophy.
E. Beyond the common basic core of science experiences, provisions for

adaptations to differences in classes, schools, communities, vocational interests, and capacities of pupils should be made.[1]

F. Science experiences and learning should also take into account other curriculum areas such as social studies, health, home economics, conservation of resources, gardening, art, mathematics, music.[2]

G. Requisite materials of instruction and equipment for good science teaching should be available at all stages of development and implementation of the science program.

H. In-service training of teachers and supervisors should proceed in connection with both the developmental and the implementation stages of any new science program.

I. Since both development and implementation of a science program will proceed on local and divisional levels as well as on a central level, adequate in-service training facilities and personnel are essential.

J. Close cooperation of colleges, science agencies, central and local pre-service and in-service training in connection with the science program should be specifically planned.

K. Appropriate course requirements in science for teaching and supervisory licenses should be instituted to enhance the teaching of science.

L. A framework for evaluation should be set up at the very outset of the science curriculum development program. Its scope might well include the objectives themselves, materials and equipment, teacher training, and pupil progress.

M. Science curriculum development and evaluation should be a continuous matter with immediate and long-time needs in view. Well designed and evaluated pilot situations should precede large-scale operations.

N. Promising evaluative techniques for measuring less tangible but equally important outcomes should be studied and used.

Scope

In the elementary science program, the child is encouraged to find the answers to questions that arise in relation to everyday living. Children's interests in science are almost as broad as the subject matter itself. Science experiences are most commonly developed in relation to a unit as a result of a problem or situation that arises in the environment.

[1] "Vocational interests" are not listed because they are not essential goals at this level.
[2] "Conservation of resources and gardening" are integral parts of the elementary science course of study.

The content for the science program in kindergarten and grades one and two is suggested for the three-year period rather than by grades. This permits the teacher to arrange the sequence that fits the needs of her children within a particular school situation. In grades three and four, although there is no differentiation in content, topics suitable for each of these grades are suggested. The teacher may rearrange the order to suit the needs of her class as well as to take advantage of current happenings. In grades five and six, topics are indicated for each grade.

KINDERGARTEN–GRADE 2

In the kindergarten, first and second grades, rich science content may be found in the everyday environment of the children. Science experiences at this level should be closely related to the child's world—his home, his school and his immediate neighborhood. During these years a basis for science activities at later years is built. The broad topics for these grades are:

The Weather Affects Where and How We Live
 dress, play, food

Plants and Animals Require Care
 growth and change of plants and animals

The World Is Made Up of Many Things
 experiences with various materials such as water, stone, clay

Rolling Along
 wheels and other things that roll

Off We Go
 airplanes, trains, boats

Sounds Around Us
 different things make different sounds

GRADES 3–4

In the third and fourth grades, the science aspects of the community are explored more closely. Children find out how people make use of science in everyday living. At this level, children are ready for science experiences, through which they discover the broader relationships that exist. The starred topics are suggested for grade three:

*The Weather Changes Daily and from Season to Season
 need for weather forecasting in daily living—different kinds of weather phenomena—protection from weather

*Living Things Need Other Living Things
   interrelationships of living things—how and why of preserving food—
   how plants and animals protect themselves

The Earth Is Always Changing
   changes made by water, wind, and heat—man's use of the earth's
   resources—experimentation with various materials

Our Earth Is Part of the Solar System
   causes of day and night—relation of earth to stars, sun, and moon

*Machines Help Us Travel
   how things move on land, on water, and in the air

Messages Travel and Are Recorded
   sounds are produced by vibrating objects—sounds are carried by air
   and other substances—sounds can be recorded

GRADE 5

As children grow older, their interests reach out beyond the immediate
community and science experiences are planned around these widened
interests. The broad topics for this grade are:

One Nation: Many Kinds of Weather
   use of weather map to compare temperature and rainfall in various
   sections of the United States

Plants and Animals Travel with Man
   influence of man on plant and animal life—where some of our plants
   and animals come from

The Earth: A Great Storehouse
   natural resources—coal, oil, natural gas—use of rocks for building—
   importance of forests—conservation of natural resources

The Moon: Our Nearest Neighbor in Space
   relation of the moon to the earth—shape, movement, visibility of
   the moon

Electricity in Everyday Life
   use of the dry cell to light a bulb, ring a bell, operate a toy—the
   switch—the electromagnet

Getting There and Back
   methods of transportation on land and sea—transportation of food
   and other goods

Our Nation Is Knit Together by Communication
>   means of communication—electricity as a message carrier—signaling
>   systems

GRADE 6

In the sixth grade, the same general topics as in the fifth grade serve as the basis for the science program. However, in the sixth grade, the science experiences are wider in scope and the problems studied are more complex.

Around the World with Weather
>   weather in the United States depends on weather that comes from
>   different parts of the world—air movements on a weather map

Plants and Animals Also Travel
>   how seeds of plants travel—animals travel to breed and to feed—
>   migration of birds

Our Changing Earth
>   the earth in a constant state of change—how soil is formed, wasted,
>   conserved—why rivers must be controlled

Farther Off in Space
>   beyond the solar system—how stars are different from planets—why
>   winter stars are different from summer stars—problems of space travel

From Powerhouse to Home
>   how electricity is brought from powerhouse to where it is used—right
>   ways to connect and disconnect electrical appliances—protection
>   against electrical dangers

The World Gets Smaller
>   general principles of airplane—why the helicopter is able to move
>   straight up and down—how a jet plane differs from a propeller air-
>   plane—how a rocket ship differs from a jet plane

Seeing More, Seeing Better
>   ways of seeing things that are far away—ways of seeing things that
>   are very tiny—recording for the future through photography

Outcomes

By the time a child has completed the sixth year, it is expected that he will have developed some fundamental, broad concepts, desirable attitudes, and basic science knowledge and skills.

CONCEPTS

Our knowledge of the world around us is the result of many centuries of exploration and thought by men and women of all lands. All plants and animals come from similar plants and animals and depend upon one another for survival. Our earth is only a small planet in a vast universe. The more we know about the world, the better we realize how slowly the fund of human knowledge grows and how much there is still to be learned. We are unceasingly engaged in efforts to use the forces of nature to our advantage and to protect ourselves from their destructive effects. The basic natural processes occur in cycles such as growth and decline, night and day, the water cycle.

ATTITUDES

A questioning attitude, a seeking for explanations based on reliable resources, an attitude of confidence in the scientific methods in the approach to problems, an exploring attitude resulting in the continuing eagerness to learn more about the world; a reverent attitude—an appreciation of the vastness, age, and complexity of the universe; a social attitude—a realization of the function of every individual in the great scheme of things; a moral-ethical attitude—directed toward the use of science and scientific advances for the common good, and toward moral and ethical goals.

KNOWLEDGE

The body, its functions and how to keep it in good condition; where food comes from, how it is protected; how homes are supplied with water, gas, electricity, light, heat, fresh air, drainage pipes; how the community is protected by traffic lights, fire alarm boxes, etc.; source and use of clothing; role of air and water in daily life; how tools and machines work; how toys work; the earth, its family, movements, outward features, buried treasures; how animals look, where they live, how they try to survive, how they can be helpful, how they can cause harm; what plants look like, how they grow, how they can be helpful, how they can cause harm; where forms of energy come from and how they are used; where materials come from and how they are used; travel on land, on water, in the air; how ideas are passed on to others by sound, light, radio, and television and preserved by printing, photographing, and recording; great scientists; conservation of animal, plant, and mineral resources; effect of the sun; travel to other planets.

SKILLS

Read thermometer; measure weight, length, time; use electrical appliances safely; wire a simple electrical circuit, using a dry cell; devise elementary science projects; set up and use simple machines; keep records of science measurements and discoveries; grow and care for plants; care for animal pets; determine north and other directions; recognize a prominent constellation and the North Star; recognize common materials by their characteristics; identify a variety of animal forms; identify neighborhood plants; identify common rocks and minerals; make a meaningful collection; interpret a simple weather map.

71. Fascinating Experiments in Elementary Science *

ALEXANDER JOSEPH

THE MAGNET is a familiar and intriguing object to most children. The principles of the magnet can be readily developed in the classroom by means of amusing and instructive pupil experiments. Other than the magnet itself, no special scientific apparatus is required. Each of the experiments also teaches an application of the magnet.

1. The Mysterious Man

First cut out a very small paper man as indicated in Figure 1. Fold over some of the paper below the feet to act as a stand. Place a small paper clip on the fold. Stand the "man" on a sheet of plastic, glass or on a dinner plate. Move a magnet under the man. The man will follow the magnet.

A small stage can be set up by the pupils with actors cut from paper with clips attached. Several magnets can then be used to cause the actors to move on the stage in any direction as they act out their parts as arranged by the pupils.

* From Alexander Joseph, "Fun with Magnets: Fascinating Experiments in Elementary Science," *Grade Teacher* (December, 1949), pp. 54–55. Reprinted by permission of the author and *Grade Teacher*.

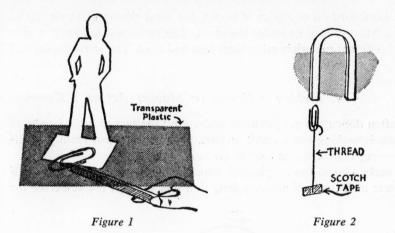

Figure 1   Figure 2

2. The Mysterious Paper Clip

For this experiment, the children hold or fasten a magnet in a vertical position. They then attach a thin black silk thread to a paper clip. Then they adjust the length of the thread so that it just does not reach the magnet. The free end of the thread is fastened to the table by means of a small piece of scotch tape.

Adjust the height of the magnet so that the clip remains suspended in mid-air under the magnet without touching it. (See Fig. 2.)

If this experiment is prepared by the teacher before the class enters the room and it is held against wet blackboards as a background, the thread will not be visible. This provides excellent motivation and challenge for a repetition by the individual pupils. It also serves to point out the fact that every apparently mysterious natural phenomenon has a scientific cause-and-effect relationship.

3. The Mysterious Tacks

The purpose of this mystery is to show that magnets will act through all substances except iron and steel. As indicated in Figure 3, set a sheet of

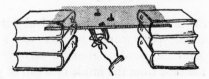

Figure 3

glass or cardboard on two piles of books. Set some thumb tacks on top of the sheet. Move a magnet under the sheet. The tacks will follow. Try thin sheets of different materials other than iron and steel. The same results will occur.

4. Making a Horseshoe Magnet Act as a Compass

It is often difficult to get pupils to understand the fact that the needle of a compass is nothing but a small magnet. This idea is most readily developed by using a horseshoe magnet to act as a compass.

First make a stand from a piece of wood four inches square and one-half inch to one inch thick. Hammer a long thin nail through the center of the

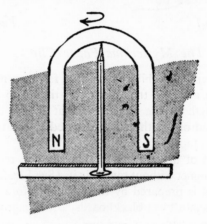

Figure 4

block as shown in Figure 4. Now file a fine point on the nail. Place the horseshoe magnet on the point of the nail so that it balances.

The magnet will turn until one pole points North and the other South. Paste a small N label on the end that points North and a small S label on the end that points South.

5. Making Magnets

Children get a real thrill in watching a steel object such as a nail file or a knife blade become permanently magnetized. Take some insulated copper wire of any kind and wind it around a narrow cardboard tube. An old mailing tube or the tube from the inside of a roll of paper towels will do nicely.

Wind about one hundred closely wound turns of the wire around the cardboard tube. Bell wire sold in the five-and-ten cent store or hardware store is excellent. Ten to twenty cents' worth is sufficient. To energize the coil, connect to a dry cell battery or a flashlight battery as shown in Figure 5.

Place the steel object to be magnetized inside the cardboard tube. Touch the two end wires to the battery for only a second. Test the magnetized object on some thumb tacks. If the object magnetized is of a hardened steel it will remain a permanent magnet.

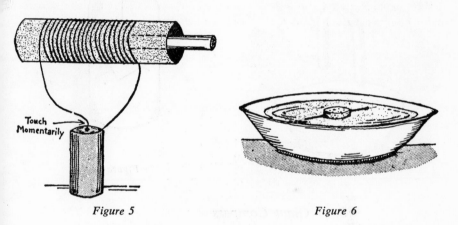

Figure 5   Figure 6

6. A Simple Floating Compass of the Kind Columbus Used to Discover America

Magnetize a large sewing needle by placing it inside a magnetizing coil or by stroking it with a strong magnet. Place the needle in a cork as shown in Figure 6. Place the cork on the surface of some water in a glass dish. Each child can do this experiment. The needle will point North and South.

The author has read the original manuscript of Columbus' order for six such magnetized needles to use on his famous voyage.

7. How Magnets Make Electric Motors Spin

Suspend a horseshoe magnet by means of a thin string. Place the suspended magnet over the floating compass needle previously made in Figure 6. Twist the string by rotating the magnet. Release the twisted string. As the magnet spins the compass needle will spin below it.

A regular pocket compass can be used in place of the homemade floating needle. This phenomenon is that employed in alternating current (a.c.) motors.

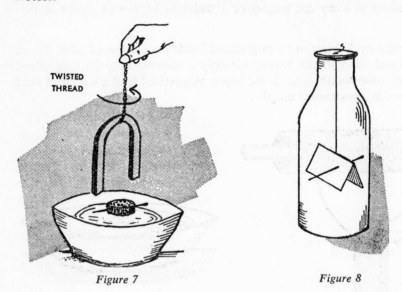

TWISTED THREAD

Figure 7   *Figure 8*

8. A Giant Compass

The compass thus far described may be too small to use in classroom demonstrations. A long steel knitting needle or an old hacksaw blade are large enough to make a compass needle that is visible to everyone in the room.

Magnetize the blade or knitting needle by placing it in the magnetizing coil. Now suspend the blade or needle by tying a string to it using a stirrup sling. Be sure to suspend it from some point in the room from which it cannot fall on any child.

9. Milk Bottle Compass

If the teacher wishes each child to make a working compass without the possibility of spilling water on the desks or floor, simple dry compasses can be made inside a milk bottle. The milk bottle cap is also required.

First fold a small piece of thin cardboad into the inverted "V" shape shown in Figure 8. Now magnetize a sewing needle and pass it through the cardboard V. Suspend the V from a thin silk thread that is attached to the milk bottle cap. The magnetized needle will turn until it points North and South.

10. Mysterious Needles

Magnetize three similar needles all held in the same position. Now pass each through a thin cork. Make a thin cork section by slicing a cork into cylindrical sections. If the needles are placed with the eyes all facing down, they will all repel each other as indicated by their rapid movement away from each other (Fig. 9).

If one needle is reversed it will be attracted to the other needles. This experiment points out the basic law of magnets, i.e., similar poles repel and opposite poles attract.

Figure 9

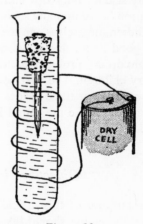

Figure 10

11. Diving Nail

Take the magnetizing coil from No. 5 and insert a test tube of water into the cardboard tube, or wind a coil around the test tube as shown in Figure 10 (but use many more turns than are shown in the illustration). Place an iron nail into a small cork. Connect the coil wires to the battery. The cork and nail will dive into the water because the coil of wire acts as an electro-magnet.

72. *What to Teach in Science* *

ALEXANDER JOSEPH

TEACHING SCIENCE in the primary grades is considered by many primary teachers to be one of their most difficult curriculum problems. Some school systems have a definite course of study in science for these grades. This is true however only in a minority of elementary schools. In schools that do have a primary science curriculum, the course is usually the traditional nature study. Although nature study has its place in primary grade science, it should not be the only kind of science instruction.

Some primary teachers solve their science problems by using some of the primary grade science texts or readers. In addition there are a few excellent primary science filmstrips and films. However, the cost of class sets makes them prohibitive in many schools. The books become most useful only after the children themselves can read them with comprehension.

As good as all these aids may be, they are only vicarious experiences. The important problem is to provide firsthand science experiences for primary children. The best source and the psychologically correct type of science study for these grades is a study of local surroundings and natural phenomena. These are found in the home, school, and neighborhood generally.

Objectives in Primary Science

The purpose of this article is to point out the direction such primary science instruction should take. All of the activities and projects described have been tried successfully by many primary teachers. It is important here to remember that the number of possible areas or units of study are greater than can usually be covered in the primary grades. It is the special function of the teacher to select the areas or units that best provide the firsthand experiences for her own pupils.

At this level children do not easily differentiate between work and play. The toys of young children therefore provide an endless source of science teaching equipment.

The principal areas in which these children appear to be interested are:

* From Alexander Joseph, "What to Teach in Science," *Grade Teacher* (November, 1949), pp. 40, 66. Reprinted by permission of the author and *Grade Teacher*.

(1) the experiences of daily living; (2) changes in the surroundings produced by the changing seasons; (3) the earth's materials and natural phenomena and how man works.

Providing Real Experiences

Teaching science at any grade level achieves greatest efficiency only when real experiences are provided. The teacher must take her cue from her children's interests and their surroundings for her choice of teaching material. Every primary grade classroom should have a science corner or table where children can place their carefully labeled contributions. The materials should be changed frequently and should be used as a part of the actual instruction. Living things under proper care are an important part of the science corner which should be carried on by a class committee under the teacher's direction.

Some Science Activities

Let us now see what some of the possible science activities are which carry out the above purposes. In the immediate area surrounding the school there may be trees, plants, animals, insects, factories, industries, transportation, telephone and power wires, utilities, etc. These are all part of an area science study.

A class observation trip in this area provides the necessary experiences.

In the classroom, a class project on a table or on a large plywood or bristol board can be used to reproduce the area. Children's small toys will help to represent the different activities and buildings. Obviously handicrafts and drawing have a definite part to play in such a project.

A study of a farm, when such a visit is possible, provides an opportunity to study farm animals and plants. The various machines of the farm suggest much valuable classwork. As an outcome project, let the children reconstruct the farm, using toys to replace the items seen on the farm.

A study of man's work as it occurs in the neighborhood is another source for a project. The trades that men work at can be worked out with the aid of small dolls. Ways of preserving food in the home is an excellent unit for firsthand science experiences. Let the children bring in examples of frozen food, canned food, pickled food, foods preserved with sugar, smoked food, dried foods, spiced food, salted foods, etc. How to prevent food spoilage is an obvious part of this project.

A good unit may be developed around the subject "How We Keep Our

Homes Warm." Shoe boxes can be used to represent houses. In each house may be shown a different type of heating, such as fireplace, stove, hot air, steam, hot water, radiant heating, and electric heating. In each case the advantage or disadvantage of each method may be discussed by the pupils. A trip to the school's heating system should be part of the work.

If there is a park or wooded area near the school, a study of the plants, animals, and rocks can be made and then built up into a model in the classroom by the use of modeling clay.

Transportation and Movement

Transportation and movement always fascinate primary grade pupils. To show the development and principle of the wheel, take a wooden box or carton and fill it with books. Have the children try to pull it along the classroom floor. Now place the box on some broomsticks or dowel rods

Figure 1

(see Fig. 1). Have the children try again. This time it will be easy to push. Next, place the box of books in a child's express wagon and have the pupils see how easily the wheels make the box move. The roller and the wheel offer an opportunity for children to study their own wheeled toys. Following these experiences, toys can be brought in or obtained at the dime stores to depict man's different modes of transportation.

Studying the Weather

As Mark Twain said, "Everyone talks about the weather but no one does anything about it." Even at the primary grade level, weather and its changes are vitally interesting phenomena. Children can keep a daily record of the thermometer if it is mounted outside the window. A definite place should be provided on the blackboard to note the daily weather data. A simple aneroid barometer can be made from a small evaporated milk can and a broomstraw or thin stick of balsa wood.

First warm the empty can. Then close the punched holes with sealing wax. With sealing wax attach one end of the broomstraw to the center of the can as illustrated in Figure 2. A paper scale is used to watch the up-and-down movement of the straw. Have the pupils listen to the radio weather reports to see if the barometer is rising or falling.

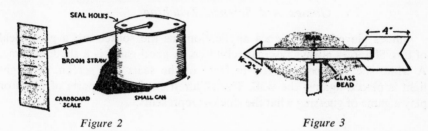

Figure 2   Figure 3

A weather vane is easily made by pivoting a stick with a metal point and tail as shown in Figure 3. The horizontal stick is 12″ x 1″ x ½″. The weather committee should note the wind direction every morning and noon. To find out how much rain fell at any given time all that is needed is an empty tin can and a ruler standing in it, as shown in Figure 4.

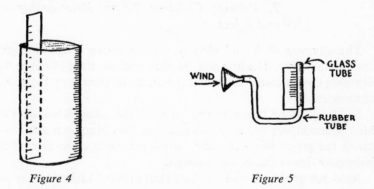

Figure 4   Figure 5

A small kitchen funnel, a short glass tube and a rubber tube make a wind-speed gage. Insert the funnel into one end of the rubber tube. Place the glass tube into the other end of the rubber tube and attach to a piece of cardboard. (See Fig. 5.) Fill the tube to the halfway mark with water. Hold the funnel into the wind. The water will rise as the wind speed increases.

A beautiful cloud chart can be obtained for ten cents from the United States Weather Bureau. These can be used to teach the names of the clouds that the children see daily. The readings of all the instruments and the kind of clouds should be recorded on the special blackboard space.

When it snows use magnifying glasses to examine the snow crystals. Inexpensive glasses can usually be obtained at the dime stores. It is best to catch the snowflakes on black cloth.

Games Aid Science Teaching

Games played with science applications as the source are a great deal of fun. Shadows always fascinate children. A good game is a shadow game. A white sheet draped directly in front of the seats is a screen. A bright light is placed against the wall. The children can act out parts of plays or play a game of guessing what the shadow represents.

73.   Developing Science Skills *

1. Primary Children Learn Relationship of Cause and Effect

The day was dark and gloomy. In the distance lightning glowed and thunder muttered. The first graders were restless. Rain began to fall and the lightning flashes came closer and closer, accompanied by the roll and crash of thunder.

Suddenly Mary began to cry. "I'm afraid, Miss Schmahl. I'm afraid." Miss Schmahl saw in many widened eyes that Mary was not alone. So she called the group to sit in their story-hour circle close around her. Proximity gave them security and comfort.

Miss Schmahl had read the Compton article "Lightning" as part of her science preparation for the year. It give her just what she needed to tell the children about thunder and lightning, perhaps to allay their fears, and certainly to teach a lesson on cause and effect.

She asked the group to tell her which came first, the lightning or the

* From "Compton's at Work in the Classroom" (Chicago: F. E. Compton and Co., 1956), pp. 6–10. Reprinted by permission.

thunder. They observed this correctly. Then she told them that the lightning caused the thunder, which was only a noise in the sky and could do no harm. She described lightning as a great spark of electricity which heated up the air to make the noise. As she and the children talked quietly together in the comfort of each other's presence they faced the facts of the situation.

"Fear does not die in one easy lesson," says Miss Schmahl, "but I have started the process of substituting facts for fears. The children learned that thunder is not a fact all by itself but only the effect of a cause which they could see. This situation gave me an opportunity to deal with one of the main purposes of all science—to peel away the mysterious from natural phenomena of all kinds."

2. Distinguishing between Fact and Fancy

Miss Smith, the fourth grade teacher, knows that as children grow older they need to emerge from the world of mixed fact and fancy in which they have lived since they were little tots. She realizes they must be helped to make this change without losing the ability to imagine and to dream. They must learn that Jack Frost, fairies, elves, and similar creatures are not real, yet they need to retain the symbols for their value in our poetic lives. *They need to keep the values of mythology without mistaking myths for facts.*

Miss Smith uses an activity on Constellations to help her children understand one of the areas where fact and fancy blend. The colored charts in the Compton article "Stars" help her show how the real stars are arranged in geometric patterns in the sky. She points out their scientific value for locating celestial objects and their use as areas of the sky, much as states and countries are areas on the earth.

Using the four-color charts showing the stars of the different seasons, she shows the progression of constellations across the sky during the year. This is all good sound fact.

Then she turns to the color pages showing mythological figures. In these pictures the geometric star patterns from the charts are outlined with the fanciful figures of mythology. She points out that these are, as the encyclopedia says, "strange creatures of myth and legend," which have nothing to do with the gaseous orbs we call stars.

In her presentation she explains how the constellation figures originated, tells some of the stories about them, and carefully distinguishes between mythology and factual astronomy.

This experience motivates her class to become familiar with the real sky. At the same time it satisfies their love of fantasy.

3. Learning to Locate Information on a Problem

The intermediate teachers were discussing the problem of helping children acquire skill in finding information from a variety of sources and in obtaining it in more than superficial form.

Mr. Davis, a fifth grade teacher, reminded the group that the modern idea of cooperatively developed units, based on problems and concerns real to the learner, requires a variety of resources rather than the single-book approach. "Yet," he added, "most of our children attempt to find all the answers in one book."

In discussing the encyclopedia as one resource, Miss Murray, a sixth grade teacher, made special mention of the Fact-Index of Compton's. "The Index helps the child locate information easily," she said, "and it enables him to find all the facts in the set that pertain to his subject. *I use the encyclopedia to help my classes discover the value of using more than one book for fact finding.*"

As an example, Miss Murray selected the topic Birds. She turned to the Fact-Index and showed that references to information about birds lead the learner to practically every volume of the encyclopedia. She pointed out that a pupil studying about birds can find information on every major topic pertaining to birds, but to do a full job of fact finding he will have to consult more than one volume.

"Look at these references on the economic value of birds!" exclaimed Miss Burns, the fourth grade teacher. "This section alone refers the child to at least twelve of the fifteen volumes."

"The list under the subhead 'Migration' calls for almost as many," added Mr. Davis.

Miss Bryan's sixth graders were studying the sun so she turned to the Index section of *Volume S*. "My youngsters will get plenty of practice using different books this week," she told the group. "These entries on the Sun send us to almost every volume in our set."

4. Helping Children Make Accurate Observations

Miss Little, a fourth grade teacher, uses the encyclopedia to help her children learn to make accurate observations. She knows this skill is best developed by studying real objects in the world around us, but the encyclopedia contains hundreds of pictures and illustrations of natural phenomena that do not occur in most communities or are difficult to observe. These pictures make it possible for her pupils to have many experiences which would otherwise be denied them.

She used the color pictures in the article "Protective Coloration" for a double purpose: *to point up the need for careful observation and as a source of basic information about nature's marvelous way of hiding its creatures.* She used them first in the opaque projector and later for individual study with small discussion groups.

The children were fascinated to see how the weed fish, the stick caterpillar or measuring worm, and the tree hoppers are so skillfully camouflaged that they are nearly invisible.

Miss Little used also the pictures of birds, birds' eggs, butterflies and moths, insects, flowers, fruits, and shells to develop the science skill of identifying, as well as the skill of accurately observing. She asked the youngsters to study the pictures, to make their observations and identifications, and then to check these with the legends and the text in the encyclopedia.

The pupils observed that the color picture of the meadow lark in the article "Birds" is another example of protective coloration. They observed that the barn swallow's nest, on the same page, is made of mud and straw.

Most of the children were familiar with the eggs of the robin, the cardinal, and the house sparrow which are shown in color in the "Egg" article. Several members of the class looked up pictures of all the birds whose eggs are included on that page.

5. Suspending Judgment until All Facts Are In

Mr. Blake's sixth grade pupils tend to jump to conclusions, often with very little evidence. He thinks this is partly due to too much reliance on the printed page for information. These children are inclined to assume that everything in print must be true and can be accepted without documentation.

To counteract this tendency, he assigns experiments that require his pupils to wait until the very end before drawing their conclusions. For this week's assignment he selected experiments described in the article "Plant Life" in the classroom encyclopedia. He asked the class: "What conditions are necessary for the growth of seeds, roots, and stems?"

Mr. Blake made out cards that gave directions for doing the experiments but contained no indication as to how they should turn out. For example:

What is the best temperature to grow seeds?
Plant bean seeds in three small flower pots.

Water each.

Place one in the refrigerator, another over a hot radiator, the third in a room at an even 70° temperature.

Record what happens to each every day.

After two weeks answer the question.

Some of the pupils felt they knew the answer without doing the experiment, but after they had completed it many of them found the results were not what they expected. Some discovered that their ideas had not been correct. A few found they had not followed directions accurately. In both cases Mr. Blake observed that the children had begun to appreciate the need to suspend judgment until the facts are in.

6. Using a Microscope for Observing and Recording Data

Miss Carpenter came into the classroom with a microscope under her arm. The children were immediately interested and curious. She set up the instrument and gave each child an opportunity to look through it at a variety of objects.

After several "looking" sessions a small committee of children, with specialized interests and abilities in science, planned a group of activities on the use of the microscope. They were to record their findings and eventually to report to the class.

One boy was intrigued by the picture he found in the encyclopedia of a cross section of a microscope, because it showed parts he could not see by just looking at the real microscope. He decided to make a large drawing of this picture and to make his report on the microscope itself.

The page of diatoms pictures, in the "Microscope" article, prompted another child to make a special study of these "tiny plants of exquisite design." Another member of the committee became interested in the *color pictures showing artistic patterns in objects observed through the microscope*. He made several semiabstract paintings based on his own observations of objects through the microscope.

Miss Carpenter gave the group a test tube filled with pond water, which contained a variety of protozoa. They looked at these through the microscope and drew pictures of them. The encyclopedia article "Protozoa" provided valuable information about one-celled creatures for their report. The drawing of a paramecium prompted the group to make further observations through the microscope and to fill in more details in their drawings.

Miss Carpenter reported that this activity, which involved skills in using an instrument and reference books, resulted in a committee report full of visual recording and accurate facts.

7. Learning to Think Critically and to Evaluate Data

The seventh grade was noisy as Mr. Keller walked in. Some of the boys were in animated conversation. They were surrounded by most of their classmates.

As Mr. Keller appeared the small group rushed to him, all talking at once: "Gee! Have you seen the show at the Varsity? It is all about rockets and space travel. Wow! Is it good!" "They had the neatest rockets! But I didn't catch on to what makes them go." "What kind of fuel do they use?" "How big would they have to be?" "How can they run out in space where there is no air?" "How fast would they have to go?" "What's a space station?" "How could they build on one in space?" "What keeps it up?" "Could people really live out in space?"

Mr. Keller brought the entire group to order and after they were seated he guided the questions and comments into an orderly discussion. The questions were listed and many others added. Some dealt with ideas gained from TV fiction programs about space travel; others came from science fiction books, movies, or comics.

It was evident to Mr. Keller that he had a real opportunity to help the group sift fact from fiction in the field of rockets and space travel. He decided that now was the time to help this group evaluate data and do some critical thinking.

To get started, Mr. Keller reached for the *S* volume of their new encyclopedia. He found a full-scale article on "Space Travel," expertly illustrated with some of the famous Bonestell pictures. Mr. Keller read the article to the group and asked them to take notes on all the data which had a bearing on the questions they had listed. The discussion which followed was lively and satisfyingly factual. The group discovered that they needed to go more deeply into the topic. They turned to the bibliography on Rockets, Guided Missiles, and Space Travel at the end of the "Space Travel" article. Groups were organized to look for these books and to begin further committee work with them.

Mr. Keller referred one committee to the article "Rockets" in *Volume QR* of the encyclopedia and to "Guided Missiles" in the *GH* volume. Here they found detailed information about the construction and operation of rockets and much other pertinent information.

One committee decided to make a large model of a three-stage rocket. The full-page drawing in the "Space Travel" article, showing a three-stage rocket in cross section, gave them the help they needed.

Under Mr. Keller's wise guidance the question of space travel, which had been brought into the classroom from the "outside," was studied in such a way that facts were separated from fiction. Pupils were led to see that confusing fiction with fact has caused many persons to try to discredit the explorations and the sober scientific progress which are being made in this field.

8. *Being Open-minded—Willing to Change Ideas*

Miss Brogan wants her children to realize that not all science ideas are proved facts. They need to learn that some ideas are not easily tested in the laboratory and that there is a clear difference between theories and facts.

To provide such a lesson she asks, "Where did the earth come from?" and "Where did the first man come from?"

The children find several theories about the earth's origin in their encyclopedia. The article "Earth" tells about the progression from the *nebular hypothesis* to the *planetesimal theory;* also the *gaseous-tidal theory* and the current *dust cloud hypothesis*. The children discover that a final answer to the first question simply is not available.

In the article "Man" they learn that conjectures about early man are based on scanty evidence. *Miss Brogan calls attention to the careful wording and the qualifying statements.* She points out such phrases as "is supposed to have lived," "is commonly estimated," "is believed to be," which indicate uncertainty.

Then for contrast she suggests that they look up a subject for which proved facts are available. She asks what air is made of. The children find in the encyclopedia article a graph showing the composition of air. Miss Brogan copies it on the board. There are no qualifications here. These are known facts.

In additional lessons to bring out the difference between proved facts and theories and to show that there are large areas for which there are not even good theories, Miss Brogan asks these questions:

How were the craters on the *moon* formed?
Where does *rain* come from?
What caused the *ice age?*
When did *horses* first appear in America?

What causes the *Gulf Stream?*
Why are many *mountain ranges* near the borders of continents?

The children look up the questions in the encyclopedia. In each instance they write brief statements of the information found and indicate whether this is fact or theory. Reports are discussed and checked in class.

Miss Brogan encourages her pupils to watch for examples of positive statements and qualified statements in all their reading. She helps them phrase their own comments so that they accurately express facts or qualify statements when uncertainty exists.

9. Learning from Demonstrations and Experiments

Miss Shaw, a new teacher, knows that elementary science depends in large measure upon visual demonstrations and actual experiments to put ideas across. But lack of time often prevents her using actual experiments for everything.

"Wouldn't it be wonderful if one could sometimes get the value of a demonstration without actually doing it?" she said in the library one day. Miss Jacobs, the librarian, asked, "Have you tried using the illustrations in your encyclopedia? Some of the teachers tell me the children often get the idea as easily from the pictured demonstration as they do from actually performing the experiment."

Miss Jacobs turned to the Compton article "Sound" and showed Miss Shaw the illustration of the jet airplane and its relation to the sound of its jets. *"This puts the point across as well or better than actually watching a real jet outside,"* said Miss Shaw. "And this illustration of the gong producing compression and rarefaction waves shows that phenomenon better than a real gong could, since the waves are invisible. What else is there?"

She turned to the diagram of the Doppler effect and the graph on speed of sound. "These are just what I need," she told Miss Jacobs. "They give visual explanations which are not observable when the actual phenomena occur."

10. Helping Pupils Define Their Problems

The seventh grade curriculum calls for a unit on Electricity. Miss Collins, the teacher, makes a practice of involving the children in planning their work so that they will have a personal interest in the study. In the planning session for this unit, she asked the pupils to indicate what they considered important in the study of electricity.

The first discussion produced weak results because it was based on the children's rather superficial thinking. Miss Collins suggested that the class search out some books that might give them ideas of what should be included in the unit and might help them locate and define the problems to be studied.

After examining books in the classroom and during the library period, the children decided their classroom encyclopedia would give them the help they needed. In the Fact-Index of *Volume DE* they found more than one-half column of subtopics under "Electricity" and on the same and adjoining pages *a long list of topics related to electricity.*

Each pupil wrote on a piece of paper the topics he felt were important. In the class discussion which followed, one of the pupils suggested that they should find out first of all what electricity is. The others agreed. "Then I think we ought to find out what makes electric current," said another.

In this way and with Miss Collins' help an outline emerged which was based on an authoritative list of topics. These topics, in addition, carried references to information in the different volumes of the encyclopedia and to books which would help answer the questions and solve the problems the class had set up.

11. Learning to Collect, Organize, Classify, and Identify

Each year Mr. Smith, the eighth grade science teacher, assigns projects which give his pupils firsthand contacts with nature and provide opportunities to develop skill in collecting, organizing, classifying, and identifying objects from nature. This year his assignment was on insects and leaves.

The children kept their encyclopedia in constant use. Those who chose insects for their topic used the two pages of directions and illustrations on "Insect Collecting and Mounting as a Hobby" as their "guide book." The four pages of reproductions of color paintings of common insects helped this group identify their collections. These pictures also stimulated many of the children to make drawings to accompany the collections. The long list of subheads under Insects in the Fact-Index gave further aid in identification by leading the child to such sections as the illustrated articles on "Butterflies" and "Beetles" in the *B* volume.

The children were fascinated with the encyclopedia drawings showing different parts of an insect—mouth parts, different kinds of legs and antennae, and metamorphosis. This and the other information in the nineteen pages on "Insects" made this project a *rich start for a comprehensive understanding of insects and their role in the life on earth.*

The article "Leaves" provided helpful suggestions for the pupils who decided to collect leaves. From the pictures "How nature plays with leaves" these children learned how leaves are classified. The reference to the article "Trees" led them to a full page of pictures which aided in leaf identification. From both articles they obtained interesting facts about leaves and trees for the papers which Mr. Smith had asked them to prepare to accompany their collections.

12. Using Common Scientific Instruments

Mr. Cook, the science teacher, uses one period a week for individual laboratory work of each child's own choosing. He discovered that during these periods his pupils were using the encyclopedia as much as any book in the room.

Since an encyclopedia is not ordinarily thought of as a means of teaching skill with instruments, Mr. Cook investigated to see what was happening.

Some of the pupils were doing the experiments with air illustrated in *Volume A,* which call for skills in using glass tubing, test tubes, beakers, flasks, glasses, spools, and paper. Two boys had borrowed another *A* volume from one of the other rooms and were busily engaged with model-making skills, measurement, drawing, cutting, assembling, and trial-and-error tryouts. Their guide was the section on "Building and Flying Model Airplanes."

The colorful illustrations in the "Winds" article had stimulated other pupils to make diagrams of their own, using ruler, compass, and drawing skills. Three were constructing a windlass, based on the drawing in the "Mechanics" article. In previous periods they had measured, sawed, and, with the help of the science supervisor, bored holes for the arm crank and work arm. Today they were fitting the frame together.

Mr. Cook found other children using magnet, wire, and galvanometer to make an electric current as illustrated in *Volume DE.* In another part of the laboratory *Volume S* lay opened at the illustration labeled "No sound in a vacuum." The children in this group were working with bell jar, buzzer, battery, and switch to "document" that statement.

Mr. Cook's investigation disclosed that every volume of the encyclopedia led the children to activities using equipment. Their encyclopedia was a stimulus for activity as well as a repository of facts.

74. *Creative Arts and the Child* *

ERNEST ZIEGFELD

AMONG THOSE who are concerned with education as preparation for full participation in a democratic society it seems generally agreed that a crucial test of the success of our educational system is the extent to which the young people coming out of our schools are capable of creative living. We sometimes fall into the error of believing, however, that a creative approach to living is something which is "taught" to young people in much the same way that the rules of grammar or the facts of history are taught. Actually it would seem to be closer to the truth to state that creative activity is a natural and essential part of human growth and development and that it is the difficult task of education to preserve and foster the irrepressible drive to creative action which we find in young children.

The methods by which very young children discover their world and establish relationships with it are essentially creative. The child's life is a constant succession of new experiences: the myriad sensations of a single day, the pronouncements from the adult world, the expanding relationships with other human beings, the child's own reactions to everything that he is doing and undergoing—all these constitute a continuous chain of events which are new in his life. These experiences carry no labels which the child can read and which will tell him how they relate to him as an individual and to his known world. This he must discover for himself, and the nature of his discoveries is essentially creative.

These discoveries come about through constant trial and experiment. A

* From Ernest Ziegfeld, "Creative Arts and the Child," *Educational Leadership* (January, 1954), pp. 233–36. Reprinted by permission of the author and *Educational Leadership*.

fork, the first time it is introduced to a child, is something to eat with only because his mother says so. For him it may have a hundred possible uses, each one to be tried. And though the social amenities demand that he abandon most of his hypotheses, the day that he accepts a fork as something to eat with and nothing more is, in a sense, a very sad day. Out of his trials and experiments emerge relationships which the child accepts or rejects depending upon how well they fit into the constantly expanding concept of world and self which he is creating.

As a larger and larger percentage of the child's experiences become familiar through repetition and as the pressure toward conformity to routinized standards of adult behavior increases, the range of outlets for the child's creative drive is narrowed, and the arts begin to assume a more important place in his activities. It frequently appears to be a tacit assumption of those who are primarily concerned with the teaching of the arts that they have a corner on creativity, that only through the arts does the child—or the adult, for that matter—have any opportunity for creative activity. This is most unfortunate for, in the first place, it is a claim which is obviously false and, in the second place, it tends to obscure the truly unique contributions which the arts can make to the development of the individual. While it is true that the arts are essentially creative in nature, it is also true that every area of the curriculum presents opportunities for creative learning; the arts are not unique in this respect. Therefore to propose that the arts should have an important place in the curriculum because they are creative is to present only a part of the case.

A Personal Mode of Action

The unique quality of the arts is to be found in the fact that they are rooted in and develop out of the emotional and intuitive life of the child. Too often in the past we have tended to think of education as being concerned exclusively with the training of the intellect and to ignore the child's whole world of emotion and feeling as being either ineducable or inappropriate to the classroom. The idea that the emotions may be educated and that this education may best be achieved through experience in the arts is only beginning to be understood. Because the essence of creative activity in the arts is the individual and the personal, it is related to the experience of the child in such a way as to distinguish it from creative activity in any other area of human endeavor.

The uniqueness of this relationship has two aspects. First, because of the emotional and highly personal nature of art activity, it provides the child a means for dealing with aspects of his experience which defy adequate expression in any other type of activity. Each of us, even to the most thoroughgoing extrovert, has a private world of intense concerns and absorbing interests. These interests and concerns which form the core of the individual personality demand to be acted upon, and because they are personal and individual, they demand a personal mode of action—a mode of action which is the realm of the arts. It is true of children and adults alike that many of their feelings cannot be verbalized. This may be because the feelings are of such nature that they defy adequate verbal expression and can be stated more completely and more precisely in a nonverbal form of communication. Again, what the child feels about some experiences may not be clearly enough defined to be dealt with at the verbal level. Here the arts provide a means for further exploration and clarification of such feelings to the end that the child himself will better understand how he feels about such experiences. Or the child's feelings may be such that the rules of social conduct forbid him to act upon them directly. Some of his most intense feelings of revolt and aggression may be channeled into creative activities in the arts. While it is necessary that we recognize the importance of such motivation for art activities, it is also necessary to recognize that the field of art therapy is a very special field and that both diagnosis and treatment must be left to the specialist.

We have then, on the one hand, the private world of the child which, by its very nature, can be most adequately dealt with in the medium of the arts. This by itself might appear to make of art activity an almost morbidly introspective affair. But there is, on the other hand, the fact that through art activities the child can most adequately relate himself to many aspects of his more public world. Whatever concept or experience the child may be concerned with in his art activity, he can deal with it in his own terms and in his own way. The validity of his activity is verifiable not in terms of some outside criterion but only in terms of his own experience. He is not concerned with the statement of facts which are true in the experience of everyone, but rather with the statement of his feelings about those facts— feelings which are true in his own experience. Through art activities he has a means for integrating his understandings and his attitudes and establishing a pattern of values which is consistent with his own experience of the world.

New Areas of Experience

If the foregoing paragraphs can be considered as a general statement of the unique and indispensable function of art activities in the learning of the child—and therefore an indispensable part of the curriculum—then it may be possible to draw some conclusions as to the nature of art activities in the classroom and the kind of environment which is most conducive to creative development. The actual content of the art curriculum in the school is the experience of the child. It is recognized today, of course, by leaders in education that this is true of the total curriculum, but the concept seems to be of particular importance in the arts, first, because of their highly personal nature and, second, because art activity is essentially a means whereby the child brings his experiences together into unified patterns, lives himself into them, and makes them a part of himself. What the child learns from an art experience is not what the teacher has dictated or suggested but what he has been able to feel and express and clarify for himself. To achieve such expression he may often need the help and guidance of the teacher, but if he is to maintain his integrity as an individual what he accepts or rejects must be his own decision based upon his own purpose.

If this appears to relegate the teacher to the position of an almost helpless bystander, it must be pointed out that one of the most important functions of the teacher is to motivate children to explore new areas of experience. The child is not born with a full and complete set of purposes and motivations. These result from the impact of the environment upon his particular psychobiological make-up. Nor can creative activity proceed from a vacuum. It is rooted in direct experience, and the full range of human experience provides material for artistic creation. At the same time, the particular aspects of experience which provide motivation for creative expression vary widely from one individual to another. What is of intense interest to one child may be a matter of complete indifference to many of his classmates. It is important therefore that the school environment should be rich in direct experiences with as wide a range as possible, and that children should have opportunities to engage in art activities which are related to all areas of their experience. It is equally important that the teacher should take full cognizance of the diversity of interests to be found in any group of children, not only making allowances for it but actively fostering it to the extent that it is consistent with desirable social growth. Lest it appear that this is placing too great an emphasis upon the individual, it should be stated that many of the richest experiences are those which children are able to share with one another. The crucial factor is not whether the child is operating *alone* as an individual, but whether he has the freedom and the opportunity to operate as an individual either alone or in the pursuit of a shared goal.

In his art activities the child is giving of himself more completely and more deeply than in almost any other kind of activity. Many times also he is exploring unfamiliar territory, attempting to find his way through a web of uncertainties. In such situations, his greatest need is an atmosphere of security and understanding with the assurance that he is respected as an individual and that his creative efforts will be equally respected.

The skills which the child learns must be understood as having a place of secondary importance. They are a means whereby he is able to increase the range and adequacy of his expression. This does not mean that the introduction of new materials or techniques must always await the expressed need of the child. On the contrary, the experience of new materials and modes of expression may often stimulate the child to explore new areas of experience or to deal with previously explored experiences in new ways. In fact, it is important that the school should provide as wide a range of materials as possible, but the use of materials and the learning of skills and techniques must always be understood as being instrumental to the basic purpose of art activities and should never become ends in themselves. For if we ask ourselves, "What shall we teach?" the answer must be that we shall teach the child to become alive to his world, to feel it as well as to understand it, to experience it deeply and, through such experience, to develop a sense of selfhood.

75. *Art for Children: What It Is and What It Does* *

JOHN O. GOODMAN

ART FOR CHILDREN is little different from art for adults except perhaps that young children are more courageous and free in their attempts to express their ideas, their feelings, and their reactions. They are less concerned with standards imposed upon their efforts by others. As they mature, children seem to become more and more conscious of critical attitudes, imagined or real, to which their creative efforts in graphic or glyptic art

* From John O. Goodman, "Art for Children: What It Is and What It Does," *Education* (February, 1955), pp. 361–65. Reprinted by permission of the author and The Bobbs-Merrill Co., Inc., Indianapolis, Ind.

may be subjected. This factor of limitation in creative effort is also apparent in the other arts such as music, drama, poetry, story writing, and crafts.

It is, of course, true that some children do continue to grow in their ability to express themselves in an original way. A few, and it is far too few, are able to disregard the subtle, and sometimes not so subtle, impositions of archaic and adult standards which teachers and parents try to force upon them. The number is indeed so small, that by the time they reach high school, such children are the deviates.

Art for Children: What It Is

In trying to determine what art for children means, this difference can be disregarded. Art for children should carry every bit of meaning that it does for all people with the addition of a ready means of expression available to a young mind that has not yet developed its full capacity for verbal expression and communication.

So very many attempts have been made to define art by professional artists, philosophers and art critics that one hesitates to add to the confusion. However, clarity may be brought to the subject of this paper by a definition of art *per se* that is practical in terms of its functions.

Declaring that "art is life and life is art," while it may be profound and inclusive, is actually no definition at all. It is certainly circuitous enough to be without end and leaves no dangling bits by which one may grasp its meaning.

First of all, it seems that art is a way of expressing oneself. This implies originality. The expression may be for purposes of communication or simply for release. It may express knowledge gained, a fact, a reaction to an experience, a feeling, an emotion, or an interpretation of a sensory experience. It is axiomatic that before an artistic expression takes place the artist must have something to express and that something must be his very own. Certainly this need for expression and the source of expression originates with experience. Expression in art form requires, very often, a vivid and moving experience.

Secondly, art is a sharp awareness of things around one, the environment in which the artist moves. A true function of art is to enable one to see clearly, to hear accurately, and to feel keenly. To the young child and to the artist the sky is not always blue, the grass green, and the ground brown. This is a clarity of vision in art so precious and necessary to the full life that teachers and parents ought never to dare to supplant it with the "brown-gravy" world of preconceived prejudice wherein the things around us are seen not as they are, but as we are taught to believe they are.

One of the most satisfying experiences in art that the writer has enjoyed is that reawakening of a sharp awareness of the environment in adult students who were beginning to paint for the first time in many years. There comes a day after only a little sketching in color from nature when their faces light up with a new recognition. "Why, I had no idea," they say, "that there were so many colors or that a tree trunk or a field could have one harmony of colors on one day and another on a different day or even for different times of the day." They actually begin to see again, or perhaps more accurately stated, they begin to see as they were able to see when they were very young.

This sharp awareness is most certainly a true factor in the meaning of art, not separate, of course, from the expression in art and certainly a requisite attribute of the artist, be he young or old. It should be the legacy of every child who enjoys the privilege of attending our elementary schools.

Thirdly, art is an appreciation of harmony and order in nature, of skill and strength in artistic expressions. To be a true factor in the meaning of art, this too must be free of imposed standards, of prejudice, and of pseudo attitudes and stylized reactions put on to impress the initiated. The appreciation must be a real and not an imagined source of enjoyment, a contributing element of a fuller life.

Art then is a way of expression that is original, a sharp awareness of the environment, and an appreciation of harmony, order, skill, and strength.

The reader will no doubt think that beauty is forgotten in this definition. Beauty has not been forgotten but it has been left out because it is apparent that the child artist does not always deal with beauty in his expression, and that he is aware of and appreciates the ugly and the commonplace as well as what his adult associates might define as beauty. What one classifies as the beautiful is so often the object he has been taught ought to be called beautiful. Beauty is not a quality inherent in the object of art or the element of the environment.

Art expression for children, at least for young children, is an expression of high intensity originating from extreme sensitivity, conveying their appreciation of experiences, their insight and immediate feelings. It probably needs to be nothing more than this. Realistic reproduction, picture making according to what teacher thinks it should be, and meticulous handicraft or "coloring within the lines" has nothing to do with art. These may be concerned with skill in manipulation and may or may not be desired activities but they cannot properly be called art.

The art work of the child, if it is to contribute to his growth as a well-adjusted individual, must be the art of a person on good terms with life. It must be an expression of his awareness, of what he himself sees and feels. Furthermore, it must be an activity from which he draws satisfaction and pleasure. Art work as an imposed task hedged about by standards does nothing for the development of art as an expression, an awareness, or an appreciation.

Art for children, then, is their own expression as they want it to be, the development of their own sensitivity, and the appreciation of the pictures and the elements of their surroundings as they are able to appreciate as children; that is, they paint as children, they see as children, they enjoy as children, with their hands, through their eyes, and by their own reactions.

The art work of the child approaches truth for him in direct proportion to the degree in which the work is really his own. As teacher or parent imposes upon his work adult standards, the work increases in falsity. Children recognize this deviation from the truth, but are inclined to seek to perform in the manner required of them.

In a very real sense, the picture painted by the child is an ideogram of his experience, of some inner part of him and meaning caught from the reality of his visible world.

An experience with a group of kindergarten children will serve to illustrate this point.

A group of children from a city kindergarten were taken on a short excursion to see a cow. As they were inspecting the patient bovine, Mrs. Harris, their teacher, pointed out the place where the milk came from. This, of course, was the most interesting part of the creature because of the association with the children's experience with milk. The next day many easel pictures of the cow appeared and the udder was hung on most any place from "stem to stern," but it was plainly an udder and it was big. These pictures were ideograms of the children's experience on the excursion and as such were entirely true regardless of the lack of realism of anatomic correctness. They were not meant to be pictures of a cow but simply an expression of a personal reaction to an experience. They should be, and were, left as such.

The child's art is an art of personal feeling. When things are going well with them in their world of art they are apt to dash off picture after picture without an attempt to contemplate or correct. This method of working is far more conducive to the development of art as a way of expression, a sharp awareness, and a growing appreciation than the "start-stop-criticize" method of the dominating teacher.

The child's art should be allowed to become an avenue for continually enlarging his own personality rather than trying to ape an adult way of expression and profess an adult's appreciation.

Children's art is a personal experience, it is an intimate thing, not like reading, writing, and arithmetic. If it is to be an element of an ever growing personality, the personal quality must be retained. Skill will come as the child realizes the need of it. If the demand for skill is made too early or as unessential to the type of expression he is seeking, the freedom of expression, so essential to personal growth through art, will be supplanted by fear. Nothing will be gained. Even though he may acquire some manipulative skill or dexterity, without the impulse to express himself through art forms the skills will never be put to use. On the other hand, if the child has been encouraged to work creatively, he can easily acquire the desired dexterity in the use of materials and tools because his motivations will remain strong.

Art for Children: What It Does

The elementary schools are not charged with the responsibility of training professional artists, nor are they in any manner equipped to perform such a function.

Art in the elementary school must be considered in the light of what it can do for children, all children, at each child's stage of intellectual development. To think of art for young children in any other way is most apt to destroy a strong potential for personal and individual development. Of all the areas of the elementary-school curriculum, art has the greatest potential for encouraging growth in individual differences. This principle is far too often violated through a penchant for regimentation.

If art is to be useful for children, they must be encouraged to make use of it for their own ends in their own way.

The role of the teacher becomes that of encourager, stimulator, and helper, encouragement through acceptance of work as it is, through recognition of the original, the new, and the exciting, through use of art as a legitimate means of expression, stimulation through enriched experiences, discussion, and shared appreciations, help through providing suitable work areas and materials, through guidance in skills when there is a need for new skills.

Children need a facile way of expressing ideas, feelings, and reactions. Art in the elementary school is especially suited to supply this need. Young children have not yet developed great facility in verbal expression, but they can get their story told in art forms. This way of expression is a valuable asset to children. Teachers should learn to encourage children to make better and better use of it and to avoid setting up barriers of fear.

Children have a right to expect the fullest possible opportunity for self-growth which comes only through self-expression. Self-development through art can be encouraged if children are given an understanding of the many forms of expression and freedom to use the forms best adapted to their immediate needs.

All children have the right to be participating, contributing members of their classroom group. The less academic child can oftentimes make valuable contributions to his group through some graphic or glyptic expression when he would be unable to do so verbally. To give him these opportunities will, through his better acceptance in the group and his improved adjustment to the school situation, improve his development in other areas. The teacher needs to be alert for opportunities for these children to contribute to group projects through pictures, models, and crafts.

Some use should be made of all children's art work. A simple mounting will do wonders for most any picture and not only will the young artist appreciate his own work more because of the mounting but his classmates will appreciate him more because the teacher took time to do it for him. A museum or a display shelf, tastefully decorated and arranged, will enhance the glyptics and children will value their carvings and clay models because they have been displayed.

Art work will seem to be a greater contribution to the work of the group when it is a part of the regular daily activity. Art is an expression, a way of sharpening awareness, and as an appreciation is a valuable part of the activities of any area of the curriculum. Activities in art can be used to increase the effectiveness of teaching and learning in all of the curriculum of the elementary school. The best art is undoubtedly taught outside the specialized art period and by the classroom teacher because it is art with a purpose which supplies a need and utilizes the child's best method of expression.

Children need new experiences; they are, by nature, adventuresome and enjoy exploring the new and different.

Art performs an important function here if the teacher provides a variety of materials and plans new experiences with children attended by some form of art activity. An art corner, well stocked with common materials which children can bring from home as well as prepared materials and tools, will prove to be an exciting place for many children. Children will also enjoy the delegated responsibility for keeping it in order.

Children need to have many opportunities to appreciate the artistic, the beautiful, the good, the different around them. The first element of the environment over which the school has any control is the classroom. By all means this should be attractive and decorative. The impact of this element of children's environment will be enhanced if children have a real part in planning it.

Picture study can very well be replaced by picture enjoyment. A good way to get started right is to bring a picture suited to the children's level of interest and appreciation to the classroom and with a minimum of talk and information put it up in a good spot where it can be seen easily by the children. A question or two at an appropriate time will bring it to their attention, "Did you notice our new picture? How do you like it?" will be sufficient to start a conversation about it. Care should be taken to avoid wearing out the interest by exhaustive study and facts concerning the picture. Oftentimes a picture will furnish a good motif for room decoration.

Appreciation is a pleasant experience. If it is not enjoyed by children the instruction has failed to approach its purpose.

Appreciation is increased when the tools of appreciation are developed. As children are given experiences with art and with an enlarged environment, they acquire the vocabulary and the sensitivity to enable them to discuss their experiences and to react more completely to the artistic.

Summary

Art for the purposes of this paper has been defined as a way of expression, a sharp awareness of one's surroundings, and an appreciation of order, harmony, skill, and strength.

Each factor of the meaning of art is a personal, individual element and the practice of art in the elementary-school curriculum will be consistent with this principle.

There can be no truly artistic expression by children unless they are encouraged and helped to acquire vivid and moving experiences and unless they are encouraged to see clearly, hear accurately, and to feel keenly.

Art as a way of expression is especially helpful to children because their verbal ability to express themselves is not fully developed.

76. Art Education in the Portland Elementary School *

RUTH ELISE HALVORSEN

"Art must be seen in relation to the stuff of day by day living if it is to serve everyone."

—HOLLIS CASWELL

O F COURSE we can teach art! The success of teaching art depends upon our attitude toward it, for teaching art is doing anything in the most beautiful way possible. We, who are teachers, are spending the best part of the day in the classroom. Each day as we open the door to our classrooms, our thoughts are, how attractive can we make this environment? It is the responsibility of each of us to help provide the atmosphere conducive to good work for all children. A well-organized room where the thought for care of materials and putting things in their place at the end of work is a part of art. Such laboratory planning is not only important to art education but to all other areas of learning as well. It doesn't matter what the physical aspects of the room are, it is what we can do with what we have, that is important.

Children are wonderful workers when they group themselves into committees to care for the classroom, making arrangements for bulletin boards, dish gardens, browsing corners, cupboards, chair groupings, and varied displays. The teacher sparks this program in group planning, which brings about group action.

We, in art education, recognize that children's reactions to everyday experiences reveal much of their character. Good work habits are dependent upon good working relations. These are, "understanding the other fellow," and assuming responsibilities. This calls for good social action, and when we offer our children opportunities to develop good social relations, we have helped them to establish the atmosphere for good art work. We have a flexible art program,—a program that has art problems so arranged as to enrich the general curriculum, and again, other art problems for the aesthetic pleasure that it will give our children. Varied learning ways have been provided through charts and organized file materials of painting,

* From Ruth Elise Halvorsen, "Art Education in the Portland Elementary School," *Education* (February, 1955), pp. 383–85. Reprinted by permission of the author and The Bobbs-Merrill Co., Inc., Indianapolis, Ind.

sculpture, and architecture. Films, filmstrips, and slides are on hand. This is valuable material when properly used. However, discretion must be used to show enough but not too much. We provide for models, nature specimens, and illustrative material. The placing of this material in the room is very important. A room should never be overcrowded with displays. Quiet wall areas are essential so as to give proper emphasis to material displayed.

Our communities with their varied industries, businesses, and art centers, are made available to the students. Our communities are proud of our schools, and have become a part of the schools. Our children will soon be homemakers, interested in city planning, and engaged in various enterprises. Therefore, the schoolroom is the place to build appreciation of home and community.

We want our children to read well, and to write well; therefore, the printed page and advertisement play an important role in our economic age. Good lettering and appreciation for the written page displaying children's work is stressed. However, these displays should be changed frequently. Many years have gone into developing skills and appreciation of the three R's, and in addition our program provides progressive learning in the appreciations and skills of art in order that students will have pride in their achievement.

Since we endeavor to set the stage for organized work, creative experiences are provided all pupils. Children show evidence of wanting to draw at an early age, therefore this inner urge to draw and paint must be fostered daily. We give the child the big tools in the primary grades, and as his skill progresses we expect him to be able to satisfactorily handle the finer tools. As Plato said, ". . . we must make art the basis of education because it can operate in childhood, during the sleep of reason; and when reason does come, art will have prepared a path for her . . ." We want the child to think creatively about his painting and drawing. This requires the stimuli and understanding of the good teacher. We are fully aware that the attention span for creative work is very limited in the primary grades but increases as the child grows. It is interesting to watch these children develop a quality of patience so necessary to live in this highly accelerated age.

Use of Various Media

Nearly all children like to work with clay. The modeling and sculpturing program, which begins in the kindergarten, continues through all the grades. The children begin with simple problems of rolling, squeezing, and patting the clay into symbolic forms, typical of their ages. The technical minded child wants to model automobiles, planes, and such. Later, carving in soap and lightweight woods, also provides interesting problems.

Then, too, we work with textiles. The art of printing, stenciling, and weaving are essential crafts for all. A wide assortment of spools, dowels, sponges, and kitchen utensils are satisfactory tools for printing on paper and fabrics. Here we have an opportunity to know the child's ability to organize his material. We observe the child's interest to use specific materials. Weaving is a program that begins with simple paper strips. These are cut into different widths, and a color assortment, typical of what children like to use, is left for them to choose. It is important to watch the children's color selections, for again their choice of colors reveals innate interests. Since 90 per cent of us are stirred by color, weaving offers an excellent outlet for developing color appreciation. Paper weaving continues all through the grades. However, the problems become more and more involved as the child progresses. Again, the success of the weaving problem is dependent upon the challenge of the teacher. Later, we stress cardboard weaving, box weaving, Austrian weaving, and table loom weaving. Class discussions are then held regarding the use of scrap yarn, reeds, and grasses in the production of attractive and artistic items for the home.

In all groups of children there are those who like to construct. These children are likely to become engineers, machinists, or city planners. Scraps of wood from shops, scrap wire, cardboard, corrugated board, orange crates, and newspapers handled as papier-mâché offer an unbounded amount of material for possible creative work.

We all like to engage in play acting, costuming, and stage setting. In the primary grades, there are grocery and post office constructions. Later, as skills develop, children like to build models such as a lumber mill, the farm, and terrains of countries, near and far. The social study units become more meaningful when revealed in this constructive way. Many children enjoy dramatizing through puppetry. There are stick puppets for young children; there are sock puppets, and marionettes for older children. The children plan where they want the dramatic scenes to take place in their room. This acting area requires but a small space and can add to the decorative beauty of the room.

Appreciation and Evaluation

With all of these problems in drawing and painting, sculpturing, modeling, textiles, and constructions, we must also think of the appreciations and evaluations of work well done. We realize that the process is more important than the product. Nevertheless, the product should represent the best effort of the child. In all classrooms we find children with genuine interest and talent. Each child shows a specific interest, therefore, a classroom provides adequate and varied materials in order that exploration and experimentation can be carried on. Leather, metal, plaster of paris, raffia, soap, yarns, and wood, are always at hand. Discarded ice-cream cartons are excellent for the care of material.

We always think that all areas of learning must be considered, for each fulfils a related need. We like to know our children's individual potentialities; some abilities are revealed in one way, and some in other ways. For instance, there are children who like to work independently with certain kinds of materials and tools, and others who contribute much in committee groups.

We think about our time allotment for art work as a minimum of time per week so that these activities may be related either to the curriculum or to a specific kind of aesthetic interest for the child.

A culmination of many of our projects calls for developing understandings of these by parents and the community. Parents are invited to come to the school and share in culminating activities; thereby, the parents understand more of the child's interests and abilities to express himself. A culture is revealed in its artistic expression, and the art program is basic for cultural growth. Therefore, we endeavor to give our children a beautiful environment and adequate materials and tools so that their social wellbeing, as carried on in the schoolroom, continues in their community living. These opportunities afford the best in enriched living with good decorations, fine dramatic play, and appreciation of art in advertising, industry, and architecture. Most important of all, the value of art education is the change the child makes in the use of materials which reveal improvements in his attitudes and ways of living. We believe the varied opportunities for creative expression help the child to develop a healthy personality with continued intellectual, social, and aesthetic growth.

77. *Rural Schools Go for Modern Art* *

RICHARD H. HUEBNER

Y<small>OU'RE</small> not cut out for a job like that."

"Rural schools and modern art just do not mix!"

These are but two of many comments thrown my way when I accepted a job as county art supervisor for Tuscarawas County, Ohio, in July of 1947. My previous teaching experiences had been in high schools located in fairly large cities. And although I was certificated to be an art supervisor for all grades, I had never worked with small children except at a summer day camp.

On my new job, an automobile was an absolute necessity, since I would have to travel from school to school throughout the county. Fortunately, I was able to pick up a good secondhand one, although cars were scarce in those postwar days.

I wasn't quite so lucky, however, when it came to learning to drive! Finally I managed to pass the driving test. Then I spent a few days practicing maneuvers on Tuscarawas' hilly roads.

As I rambled around the countryside, I found out that the residents of the county are proud of their rich historical heritage. Romantic names dot the maps of our area—Fort Laurens, Schoenbrunn, Gnadenhutten, Tuscarawas, Zoar, and many others.

Religion plays a prominent part in the lives of the inhabitants, a number of whom are Amish. The beautiful rolling hills remind them of God's nearness.

I was told about a first grader who visited the town of Schoenbrunn and then illustrated his impressions of the trip. He first drew a large number of Indians in ceremonial attire and then colored the whole area green. This, he explained to the class, indicated the grass covering the graves of Indians buried in "God's acre."

His sky, a lovely blue, had a large white open space, through which peered a very happy face. It was the face of God, the child said, "as He goes with us and watches us wherever we go."

I had little more than this rough idea of the community and its children when I nervously entered my first school on opening day. At the start, I

---

* From Richard H. Huebner, "Rural Schools Go for Modern Art," *NEA Journal* (March, 1955), pp. 165–66. Reprinted by permission of the author and the *NEA Journal*.

found the pupils in the lower grades quite unresponsive until it suddenly dawned on me that I was talking over their heads. Once I corrected my mistake, the youngsters were eager to work and really welcomed me each time I arrived to spend the day with them. The teachers in this school were helpful and cooperative, and everything came out beautifully there.

Things didn't turn out so well in the other schools, where the teachers thought of art as just "pretty pictures"—the more realistic, the better. The many and varied art experiences that I wanted each child to have meant little to the teachers. Consequently, a great wall was being built between the teachers and me.

It was obvious that before real progress could be made we would have to discuss the art program with the teachers. The county superintendent, the elementary supervisor, and I decided that the best approach was in-service education. The subsequent workshop for teachers went a long way toward easing the situation.

In all my daily classroom teaching I stressed with youngsters the importance of design as the basis for art work, for I believe that without a good basic design, the finished product is not very exciting.

My first request for work in design immediately brought forth a chorus of "I can't's." This problem was solved by having students draw simple straight lines—and crooked ones too—in pleasing arrangements. Another technique that built up their self-confidence was "scribble art." This involved drawing large loops with black crayon or pencil, making sure that the loops overlapped and crossed each other. The spaces between loops were then colored in solid.

Three of their favorite colors were chosen by the children and applied so that identical colors were not used in adjacent spaces.

I used a more elaborate variation in the upper grades. Again three colors were chosen, but instead of making all solid spaces, the children used polka dots and lines also. Regardless of the color, no solid color was to be used next to a solid color, nor could a color be used in either polka dots or lines right next to the same color. The youngsters' satisfaction with their colorful designs gave them new confidence.

My main purpose in wanting the boys and girls in Tuscarawas County, from the first grade through high school, to have all possible art experiences was not to make artists of them. Instead I wanted to give them the experience of making attractive things inexpensively so that some day, when they have homes of their own, they can make various articles to add color and beauty to their surroundings.

This was my underlying thought three years ago when a group of our teachers, our county superintendent, and Geneva College in Beaver Falls, Pennsylvania, asked me to teach an extension course in art education. Some of the teachers needed extra credit; others did not, but felt that they would like some additional work. Naturally, I was pleased, and I decided to try this new experience, which has turned out to be a delightful one for me.

These teachers, I presumed, did not want a class in theory, but rather a course which would enable them to make articles they could take back to their classrooms. Since the enrolees had to furnish their own materials— and I wanted them to carry their work over to their own jobs—I decided to use only low-priced materials.

At the first meeting, after outlining the aims of the course, I urged the teachers to hand in written requests if there were any things they felt they particularly needed. This resulted in a deluge of requests.

Since the demand was greatest for practice in the mixing, blending, and use of color, we started on this basic need in art. We worked with color itself—just plain mixing—and explored the unlimited possibilities of color.

We painted in various colors. We made articles of different shades. We established moods with color. With a free brush technique, we painted colorful impressions of music played from a record player. We made scrapbooks of color. Before we were through, quite a few of the teachers were painting the odd chairs, tables, desks, and even the piano in their own classrooms!

"Just why can't you use blue and green together?" someone asked during a color discussion one day.

"Don't blue flowers look all right with green stems and leaves?" I asked. This seemed to turn the trick, and now blue and green are used without any qualms whenever necessary.

Among other units we have taken up in the extension class are: printing (speedball, potato, eraser, scrap, and silk screen); puppetry (hand, string, and shadow); use of crayons, water colors, tempera, ink, oils, charcoal, chalk, pastels (singly and in combination); papier-mâché; paper sculpture; decorative art (textiles, glass, wood, plastics, ceramics, leather, plaster, and many, many others); murals, bulletin boards; and art history and appreciation.

This is my seventh year as art supervisor for the county. I am currently teaching my sixth class for the college, and we have had two in-service art workshops. Teaching from the first grade through to college level has been no sinecure, but the county has really become art conscious. And I've become a devotee of country living.

78. *Paper Sculpture: How to Do It* *

MARY GRACE JOHNSTON

WHY NOT TRY paper sculpture the next time you and your students want to decorate a hall, a show-case, or a bulletin board? As an attention-getter, paper sculpture has no equal! And as a class art project, paper sculpture is excellent.

As you no doubt know, the art consists principally in cutting, scoring, folding, and manipulating heavy paper into shapes and forms that show depth. Here are some directions for performing those and other necessary operations.

The larger the worktable the better. Of course, it should be at a comfortable height. Protect the working surface with chip board, which can be replaced when it becomes gouged and nicked.

The necessary tools are few: scissors, several industrial razor blades, a sharp knife and a long dull knife, metal-edged ruler, compass, pencil, small stapler, cellophane tape or masking tape and household cement—and plenty of good strong paper.

Choose a paper that has some weight, is fine-textured, but tough and pliable. Avoid stiff paper that cracks when folded.

Construction paper is recommended for classroom work. It is inexpensive, has the required resiliency, comes in a beautiful range of colors, and is available already cut in sizes 12 x 18 and 18 x 24 inches. White detail paper, by the roll 36 inches wide and 24 feet long, is excellent for large designs. Larger sheets and wider rolled paper become unwieldy when used in class.

A special paper which is used by professional window decorators may be purchased by the yard. It is on sale at display supply stores and comes in varied widths up to 12 feet. It is useful in building large displays and decorations.

Clean-cutting instruments are essential in doing paper sculpture. A sharp pair of scissors held open will slice through a length of paper with ease. A single-edged commercial razor blade will cut a free-flowing edge if the paper rests on a flat protected surface.

Ragged edges mar the purity of line so important in any design, so

* From Mary Grace Johnston, "Paper Sculpture," *NEA Journal* (May, 1954), pp. 290–91. Reprinted by permission of the author and the *NEA Journal*.

scissor cutting must be slow and deliberate. Straight edges are best made by cutting against a metal strip or metal-edged ruler.

Always keep the free hand back of the knife or razor blade and cut away from it. Cut with a free, swinging motion toward your body.

For practice, begin by cutting familiar geometric shapes—squares, rectangles, triangles, ovals, and disks. Try cutting them with the scissors; then try it with a sharp knife or razor blade. The next step is to cut out other designs from within these shapes. For instance, a square inside a circular piece, a circular opening within a rectangle, a triangular cut inside a semicircle, and so on until you gain confidence in your ability to cut any given shape.

Scoring the paper is necessary to get a sharp fold or crease. Use the corner of a dull razor blade, the tip of a dull kitchen knife, a crochet hook, or even the back of a scissor blade—anything that will press or cut into the paper without breaking it.

Practice scoring and folding on the shapes you have already cut out. Score and fold on one side, turn, score and fold on the other. Score and fold in parallel lines, in lines radiating from a point, in concentric circular lines, and in curved lines converging to a given point. Press each fold into place and observe the resulting shadow.

The most difficult fold to make is one that will look like a wrinkle in a sleeve or a trouser leg. Score lightly from within the space to the edge, reverse the paper and score from the identical point to the edge again. Keep these folds short and shallow and press gently into place. The fold may be made on either straight or curved lines.

To get the paper to take the desired position, coax and humor it into place. Avoid lines curved in opposition to each other. Keep all folds going the same way.

Paper has a tendency to curl, especially when it comes in a roll. Take advantage of this fact. To curl a strip of paper even more, use a long dull table knife. Hold the knife against the back of the paper, and pull the strip between the knife and your thumb. Practice will teach you just how much pressure to exert with your thumb.

If you wish a tighter curl, wind the strip tightly into a roll between your fingers. If you need many tight curls, dampen the end of each strip and wind the strips around a pencil or knitting needle. The moisture will hold the strips tight until the curls are set.

It may be necessary to use several pieces of paper sculpture to complete a design. This entails fastening one part to another. If the point of contact is to be concealed or covered, use a small desk stapler, needle and thread, rubber cement, household cement, cellophane tape, or masking tape—anything that will hold two pieces of paper together.

If, on the other hand, the point of joining will show, then a tab or several tabs must be left on one piece and slits made in the other piece to receive the tabs. After they have passed through the slits, these tabs should be fastened down with cellophane tape on the wrong side of the design.

I hope that these few directions on paper sculpture will start you on your way. If you're really interested in the possibilities of paper sculpture for school decoration or as another art form for teaching your students, there are some good books on the subject.

Choose to do something simple as a start, such as flowers, garlands, birds, or trees. Anything that can be carved out of a solid block or built up of clay can be done in paper sculpture. And paper sculpture can have quality of line, diversity of form, and excitement of color, that make it an art in itself.

79. Yes, You Can Teach Creative Music *

MARJORIE MALONE

QUITE UNNECESSARILY, the term *creative* frightens many teachers. Creating does not mean making up something out of nothing, and in music it does not necessarily mean *composing* a song. I like to think of *creative* as being an approach to learning—an open-minded, all-inclusive, experimental attitude which seeks above all to bring a gleam to the eyes and a smile to the lips of children.

Success or popularity of any activity depends upon the atmosphere which permeates that activity and its participants. Music is no exception. If musical activities are pursued as a part of the child's interest pattern, they will be more likely to be within the range of his understanding, imagination, and enjoyment.

Experiences in music should, therefore, be integrated with other classroom activities. Then singing, dramatizing, listening, playing instruments, creating movements to music, and expressing the swing in music can serve a dual purpose. They can teach music and also provide a means of self-expression, emotional release, spiritual satisfaction, and intellectual stimulation when small bodies become restless.

Too often, we seem to be thinking of children as little problem-solvers rather than little dynamic, growing, reacting people. They need to express their feelings about living in addition to reciting correct answers to stereotyped questions.

The classroom teacher has the definite advantage over the visiting music

* From Marjorie Malone, "Yes, You *Can* Teach Creative Music," *NEA Journal* (November, 1951), pp. 536–37. Reprinted by permission of the author and the *NEA Journal*.

teacher of knowing her children better, and she alone can sense which tendencies toward creative digression from the regular program are most likely to be of value to her pupils. This suggests one way in which a regular teacher can help the visiting music teacher.

The Musical Frog

One day we were studying about the frog. Harriet said, "Let's sing 'Frog Went A-Courtin'." So, we sang it right then because everyone was ready for it.

We had felt that the science lesson was rather drab that day, and the singing gave us a lift. When we finished the song, Henry further suggested that we make up new words to tell what we had learned about the frog. Someone said, "We could do that instead of taking a test," and we followed his suggestion, also. This is the poem we composed together:

The Frog

Mrs. Frog lays her eggs in a water hole, h'm, h'm, (repeat)
And then they hatch to little tadpoles, h'm, h'm.
So, now, they've grown their little hind legs, h'm, h'm,
They've grown out of the tadpole stage, h'm, h'm.
The front legs now have begun to appear, h'm, h'm,
The long tail now will disappear, h'm, h'm.
The frog has a music all his own, h'm, h'm,
He sings in a very deep, deep tone, h'm, h'm.
The frog rolls over with his four legs up, h'm, h'm,
He plays like he's a big, dead duck, h'm h,'m.
The frog can breathe, but he doesn't have a lung, h'm, h'm,
He swallows the air and it goes chur-rung, h'm, h'm.
He uses his tongue to catch his prey, h'm, h'm,
He catches the bugs that come his way, h'm, h'm.
Mr. Frog has big round eyes, h'm, h'm,
He pulls them in when we go by, h'm, h'm.
Now, winter comes as sure as fate, h'm, h'm,
Mr. Frog crawls in to hibernate, h'm, h'm.

We liked our song so well that we made up a little play about it. Part of the class sang the song while others acted out the words. Since everyone wanted a copy of the song he helped to write, we copied it from the board for a writing lesson and drew pictures of Mr. Frog to illustrate our poem. We made a frieze of all the pictures to decorate our classroom bulletin board.

Meeting Children's Needs

Through her daily show of respect for and enjoyment of such creative outbursts as the above, which tend to integrate music with other classroom activities, the classroom teacher is able to nurture creative effort and to encourage child development of a highly coordinated and integrated type. With this approach to learning she will be serving not only the child's intellectual but his emotional needs as well.

Proficiency in music is wonderful, and, for a music specialist, it is a "must." For the classroom teacher, however, technical proficiency in music is not as important as ability to improvise ways of using various situations for the development of child potentiality through music.

All teachers recognize the necessity for creative improvisation in all teaching in order to meet the needs of individual children, to overcome unanticipated occurrences, and to create a pleasant atmosphere for work in spite of lack of needed materials. Let's allow ourselves as teachers, and the children under our guidance, to practice being creative in our approach to music in the classroom where we are living and learning together.

The Dancing Pompons

When one third grade group of children became tired of being fairies, animals, and brownies to music, their teacher decided to integrate art, music, rhythm, and drama with other studies in this way:

She and the children cut various colors of crepe paper into pairs of pompons. Then, interspersed with their lessons and other music activities, several children at a time were allowed to go to the table and choose pompons (their favorite colors or ones that matched their clothing).

After listening to the phonograph music to be dramatized, they would use the pompons as extensions of their arms and wave and dance to their hearts' delight. Other children decided what they were reminded of on seeing the dancers or what they would like to have the dancers do.

The teacher discovered that often the dramatizations reflected ideas and feelings about learning activities which had been a part of the child's day. It was clear that the children were using music and drama as a means of expressing what they felt about many things.

Some Creative Ideas

Possibly you do not feel capable of conducting a music lesson. All right, then, don't consider music an activity confined to any particular period of the day. When you sense a need for emotional relaxation, yours or theirs, let music serve as a medium of mental regeneration. Here are some ideas to try, even if you do not sing, play an instrument, or feel like skipping around the room:

1. Allow children to sing together songs that they know.
2. Realize together that everything we do in the classroom goes easier if we put swing into it. Sing with swing; draw with swing; count with swing; read with swing. Swing is our inherent feeling for rhythm, and by swinging into things we get more of ourselves mixed up into the meaning of our activities. Just about everything we do can be thought of as either a march, a waltz, or a fox trot.
3. Encourage every form of creation during music experiences: poetry, making tunes, drawing, storytelling, collecting pictures and mounting them, dancing, dramatizing the story in music, decorating the room, making toy instruments, and the like.
4. Encourage integrated thinking concerning music and other classroom activities. If they see a relationship between music and history, be happy, not annoyed.

   Allow children to listen to music in various ways—quietly, or creatively and dramatically. Permit them to make up ideas about the music and develop movements to the music.
5. Use phonographs, films, pictures, and other audio-visual materials as often as possible to develop a love for music and to show music's relation to other interests of your children.
6. Learn something about musical instruments—their relation to modern life, their rich history, and their relation to the history of man. Know the contributions to music of the cave man, the Hebrews, the Egyptians, the Greeks, the Romans, the medieval man (in church and everyday life), the early scientists, the early court and church musicians.
7. Have an attractive bulletin board to which the children contribute regularly. They will be urged to creative acts and thoughts through its power of suggestion.
8. Encourage individual choices and leadership through the medium of music. Find something to praise in every child if only his choice of a song.
9. Plan cooperatively for music to be used on holidays and in programs; projects to raise money for purchasing music materials; contributions from home of music, phonograph records, pictures, magazines, family talent, community talent.

You Can Do It

Notice that singing to the children or teaching them to read music has not been mentioned. If you can do these things, well and good. However, much can be done without the teacher's being an accomplished singer or player. If she will encourage the children to relate music in as many ways as possible to the classroom activities, and encourage them in *their* singing and playing, she will be guiding them to develop their talents and tastes, and will be a better than average teacher.

Music can be so handy in the classroom throughout the day. It does not take a specialist to play a phonograph or radio, or to allow children to play musical games, sing things they already know, or express what they feel in the music they hear. Nor does it take a specialist to see relationships between music and other subjects, to see when children need emotional release.

Children's feelings, their exuberance, and their tensions are going to spill over if some medium of release is not provided, of that we may be assured. Let us provide a handy and acceptable medium through which children may be creative and expressive at the moment they feel that way.

Why not explore music with your children and see if it is not one of the most potent means of clinching ideas, relaxing tense nerves, and creating a happy, wholesome, cooperative atmosphere in your own classroom?

80. *Music-reading Skills in the Elementary Grades* *

JOSEPH C. HARTLEY

DOES MUSIC READING have a place in the elementary-school curriculum? Should *all* children learn to read music, or is this an activity for the few who have special training or aptitude?

I believe that even in a class with a wide range of individual differences

* From Joseph C. Hartley, "Music-reading Skills in the Elementary Grades," *NEA Journal* (October, 1954), pp. 404–5. Reprinted by permission of the author and the *NEA Journal.*

music reading deserves a place in the modern program along with rhythms, dramatizations, and other creative experiences designed to develop enjoyment and appreciation of music.

It should be recognized at the outset that elementary music is in many cases a teacher-centered activity. And, of course, children are more demanding of the teacher after they have progressed through the early intermediate grades.

Some teachers have had difficulties with classroom control at this point because they taught one activity at a time for *all* of the class. This meant that some of the pupils were vitally interested, and some were passively interested, while others were definitely bored. If many of the class were in the last two groups, a distressing situation arose.

For this reason some means should be devised for working with small groups within a class. A few suggestions will be made later about how to handle this problem.

Students often want more instruction in notation.

In an experimental seventh grade class at Peninsula School, Portland, Oregon, twenty-seven pupils were asked what they would like to do in a general music class. When questioned about reading and singing, twenty-two replied they would like to learn more about notes and how to use them. Twenty wanted to know how to produce a better singing tone. Of the others, five felt they were having an adequate music experience and were quite satisfied with their own performance. Only two "just didn't care."

After five months of instruction, the questions were asked again. Seven of the twenty-two students who had wanted to know about notation stated they had learned how to read music. The teacher noted their increased interest and participation.

The teacher also observed that the other fifteen showed various degrees of growth. Nine of the twenty students who wished to produce a better singing tone stated they had improved and enjoyed singing more than they did previously.

These replies seem to indicate that children of this age sincerely demand more refinement of instruction and deeper understanding of the musical offerings of the curriculum.

It should be realized that background for music reading begins in the primary grades when the child first takes part in a musical activity. As he grows in musical understanding, he shows many signs of readiness for reading that the teacher should observe. Some of them are:

1. An interest in wanting to learn new songs.
2. An awareness of similar tonal and rhythm patterns.

3. An awareness of tones—loud and soft tones, high and low, long and short—and varying tempos.
4. Taking part in rhythmic activities such as dancing, marching, and creative rhythms.
5. Active participation in singing.
6. A desire to know about instruments—their tones and mechanical manipulation.
7. A desire to play an instrument.
8. A desire to learn to read music.

Obviously the first experiences in music should be of a broad nature to develop readiness for music reading. At the intermediate grade level the teacher must carefully observe the reading readiness of each child. And, of course, in order to grasp fully the child's musical needs, the teacher should understand the program of music instruction that has taken place in the primary years.

Once the teacher has decided which children are ready to read music, he must work out a satisfactory plan to teach them within the organization of the regular classroom. Here are a few tips:

1. Group together those children who are to be introduced to music reading. Give the rest of the children in the class something else to do.
2. However, tell these children that they may listen and even take part if they wish. No child should feel left out of any kind of music class experience.
3. Make the music class an enjoyable time rather than a monotonous drill type of activity.
4. If the school is large enough, it may be possible to include in the group children from other rooms or grades who show music-reading readiness. Those who are not a part of the group might go to another teacher's room.

In the past, some teachers have thought that teaching music meant teaching information about key signatures and other abstract facts. Knowledge of this kind does not lead to reading skill, though it may help the student understand musical notation better after he can perform independently.

Music reading is the coordination of the ear and eye to transfer the symbol to music production. Each child must discover how to make his voice or instrument do what the symbol says. He may use a combination of "so-fa" syllables along with a number system, or he may read by position alone.

Regardless of what system he uses, it must be discovered and used as his very own. For this reason, teachers should recognize the factor of individual differences and make all their plans with that constantly in mind.

It would be futile to try to get all children of an age group to perform equally well. There is no one way to teach music reading, and so each teacher must develop different techniques to fit different groups of children.

It is also important to guide music-reading activities into as many channels of musical expression as possible. Therefore, it is imperative that a variety of approaches be made to meet the problem of individual differences.

Above all, music-reading experiences must be kept sufficiently simple and understandable to provide success. Children love to succeed and need to see progress in their own development. This factor is very influential in sustaining pupil interest.

The teacher is the focal point of any music program. Therefore, his attitude about music and about the musical problems that children bring to the classroom will have much to do with the success of his teaching. The teacher who is sincere and willing to learn with the children can give youngsters worth-while experiences with music even though he doesn't have too much musical background.

Now as to the actual teaching of music reading, here are a few suggestions:

1. Begin by making very simple tonal patterns. These might contain only four quarter notes arranged in a 1-3-2-1 pattern. These tonal patterns might be taken from songs the class has learned.

   Write them in notation on the blackboard or staff card *without words*. The class should sing them with some easy syllable since words have a tendency to distract the eye from the musical symbol.

2. Copy from familiar songs the repeated last phrases for comparison. This technique can be varied by discovering likenesses and differences.

3. Give opportunity for the children to read at sight many unfamiliar songs. If possible, use an old set of books and obliterate or cover up the words.

4. Attempt many reading songs with words after tonal and rhythmic patterns have been established, making sure that no problem arises that has not been studied previously and understood by the children in the group.

5. Make the school chorus a very select group for the skilful and talented. Emphasize quality rather than quantity. In this small group

musical weaknesses can be readily discerned and corrected so that the quality of the group performance can be constantly raised. This group can be used as a motivator for music reading.

6. Give the students opportunity to be creative by letting them compose their own simple melodies. This gives them a chance to become familiar with some of the mechanics of music reading.
7. Sing many songs in unison before attempting part singing.
8. Establish a room quartet or ensemble from the reading group which shows rapid progress.
9. Give opportunity for the reading group to perform at special programs. This will help sustain interest.

Instruction in music reading will naturally have uneven results. Some children have the ability to become excellent independent readers. It is important that they be given opportunities to realize fully their capabilities. Other children have the ability to become partially independent readers, and still others will never be able to read music confidently. However, all children can develop a minimum ability to follow the printed score.

While music reading is only a small part of the total musical experience a child should receive, it is an important part. When children are exposed to music-reading activities as a part of a gradual process throughout the grades, participation in singing becomes a real joy, and many new avenues of musical experience are opened.

81. *Greatness in Music Teaching* *

ROBERT PACE

W HAT ARE the qualities of a "great" teacher? Probably each of us has some very strong opinions pertaining to this subject. Is a great teacher demanding or permissive, domineering or sympathetic, sarcastic or understanding? Is he a teacher who can develop intelligent listeners and performers with the practical skills of sight reading, harmonizing, and improvising? Is he the teacher who can salvage a child with a poor musical

* From Robert Pace, "Greatness in Music Teaching," *Music Journal* (March, 1959), pp. 32, 81. Reprinted by permission of the author and the publisher.

beginning and transform him into a self-reliant young musical enthusiast? Or is he the teacher who devotes his energies to a select group of gifted students that have promise of becoming outstanding performers?

There are those who maintain that, as teachers, we are judged by the performing ability of our students. A teacher, they say, can be only as successful as his students' quality (or talent) will permit. Some teachers feel that their success is hampered by the fact that there are so few "talented" students in their vicinity. This may be true to a degree but it depends largely upon one's definitions of *success* and *failure*. What are the teacher's musical aims and objectives? What skills and understandings does he expect to develop in his students?

It would be a grave error to judge a teacher's greatness merely upon the ability of his students to win awards. Most of us will agree that the majority of the students studying music will never pursue it as a career. Surely the teacher who can develop his students' abilities to the extent that music plays a vital and rewarding role throughout life must be considered not only successful, but great. How different must be his approach to teaching from the person who merely assigns "pieces."

A really good teacher will make certain that all of his students can sight-read, improvise, harmonize, and transpose, as well as *perform* good piano repertoire.

The pupil of the teacher who merely assigns pieces would be completely bewildered if he was asked to do any of these things. Such inadequacies are usually justified by the teacher on the basis that "Johnny just isn't talented." In this case, it is the teacher who lacks the talent.

The mention of this unfortunate student leads us to the recognition of another type of "great teaching." Have you encountered the frustrated, yet still hopeful parent whose child has "used up" two or three teachers, and who now pins his last hope on you? To turn this child's defeat into any degree of musical success takes great skill. This student may accomplish very little by professional performance standards, yet if his musical experience can somehow become a personal asset rather than a liability, his teacher has turned the tide from negative to positive.

What about the gifted students—the one in a thousand? Undoubtedly, many of them are so perceptive that their results would be superior despite inferior teaching. As a matter of fact, their results would be superior only in comparison with average ability, and not in terms of their own potential.

Great musical acumen is required to develop gifted students' unusual musical talent to the fullest. Rarely do these students attain anything approaching their possible artistic level of achievement. They may develop dazzling technical facility and gradually learn to imitate their teachers to perfection. However, it will not be personal nor sensitive playing because it will only be imitative. It takes genuine musical understanding on the part of both the teacher and the student to develop the highest level of musical integrity, individuality, and sensitivity.

An outstanding example of this inspired type of teacher is Mme. Rosina Lhevinne, who has produced so many versatile and excellent pianists during her years of teaching. Together with her late husband, Josef, she exemplifies, in the minds of many, the highest order of musical integrity.

I recall with great satisfaction my own experiences as a pupil of the Lhevinnes. In their studio one would have found, at any time, students of varying backgrounds and performing abilities. Each student was treated as a distinct musical individual. The demands made upon him were related not only to past training, but also to his future possibilities. One soon found that he must accept certain responsibilities in the preparation of lessons. Every lesson was a challenge where pupil and teacher were both dedicated to the proposition that the greatest satisfaction comes only from a job well done. There was no lavish or false praise. Rather, after the "storm" was over, there was an honest evaluation, a word of encouragement, and the feeling that progress had been made.

Another recollection of that eventful period of study is the air of exploration and experimentation which pervaded the studio. Whether it was a new edition, a new treatise on ornamentation or a new composition, different ideas were always welcomed into that musical circle.

Just recently Mme. Lhevinne, with the enthusiasm of a college freshman, told me about the new concerti, chamber works, etc., which she is presently learning. This attitude typifies the expression that "It isn't *what* you play, but *how* you play it."

Finally, I recall the way in which these two artists prepared each student for his own individual career. With amazing speed and accuracy, Mme. Lhevinne could spot a student's weaknesses, and, with equal skill, prescribe a remedy. This ability to verbalize and be articulate *about music* (many teachers are articulate as performers, but are quite hazy *about music*) enabled her to bring out the individual qualities of each student. The obvious joy this famous team obtained from their teaching probably influenced many of their students in choosing the career of "performer-teacher."

We have discussed several aspects of great teaching. From this we can draw certain conclusions. First of all, a great teacher meets the student at his level and deals with him in terms of his specific musical needs. He gains the student's confidence and never allows him to be defeated by criticism.

The great teacher develops the basis for a broad musical understanding. His student learns that composers have expressed themselves musically in many different ways, and that he must be conversant with each composer's musical vocabulary.

Third, a great teacher shows his student the open road to greater musical accomplishment and that nothing, however perfect it may seem, is ever *finished*. He instills in his student the desire for musical exploration, expansion and achievement throughout his life.

In conclusion, the truly great teacher treats his student as an eventual peer—not a subordinate. It is his desire to make each pupil musically independent and his fondest dream is to see his musical offspring go beyond his own limitations. In the broadest sense, as this pupil searches for new materials and better ways to perform, he will retain the vitality and inquisitive characteristics of his student days, yet will mature into the sensitive musician which only experience and his own personal "self" can bring.

So it is that *great teaching* encourages by personal example the utmost in the learner as it strives to produce the most artistic results.

82. *An Approach to Elementary Music Education* *

DORIS T. SCHMIDT

A CREATIVE SCHOOL is a happy school. It is a live school. It is a school where things are happening that stimulate the interest of all the students—and the teachers. In this kind of school creativity permeates the music program. This means that every individual, child and adult, approaches all music activities with the idea he has something to contribute from his background of experience, from his own individuality and his own thinking; that while he is learning he is also using all that is within himself to give to the venture at hand.

This does not mean that he is thinking of himself alone; in fact, he

* From Doris T. Schmidt, "An Approach to Elementary Music Education," *Music Educators Journal* (January, 1955), pp. 23–25. Reprinted by permission of the author and the *Music Educators Journal*.

forgets himself completely by submerging everything of himself in the activity of the moment. It consumes him entirely. This approach leaves no room for artificiality or dilettantism; there is no question of that. It helps the child to use initiative and imagination toward growth in self-expression and onward toward growth in musical insight.

We still have far to go in helping our children to work and think together and to build a music program on this basis. But we are getting away from the tradition of letting adult standards and planning prevail, for we have found that children who were trained to accept these adult plans frequently did not understand them and therefore learned little from them and enjoyed them less. We are attempting to stimulate the imagination of students and to provide incentive for creative thinking. It may be true they cannot find their own way in the learning process; elementary children need much guidance, and it is the task of the classroom teacher and the music consultant to lead the way.

Music educators now are thinking beyond the idea that music learning means the ability to read fluently with syllables. That aim, born with the "singing schools," has been superseded by one more comprehensive. We know a person learns mathematics by doing much more than memorizing and reciting the multiplication tables; and he learns reading by understanding the meaning of sentences and paragraphs rather than learning to pronounce words. So we know that music comprehension comes with the opening up of meanings in the music itself. And these meanings are taught through the revelation of what music does to individuals who use it creatively.

Building Musical Insight

Musical insight for the elementary child appears to be built on many activities and experiences of a simple nature, all of which point to an understanding of the music itself and to its uses. In the performance of music the child works from his background of experience and understanding toward a vital and artistic interpretation which he and his group have chosen. After evaluation of an initial trial performance he may elect to use another interpretation. He evaluates and tries again until he is satisfied that he has achieved his best production. He has given to it ideas and feeling tones which are peculiarly his own.

Cooperative evaluation and interpretation are a fairly common occurrence in the elementary classroom. Individual thinking is stimulated whenever the teacher enlists the help of her students in working out an interpretation with the anticipation of using their ideas toward a more effective performance. "How can we show the other boys and girls that Molly is a ghost in the last verse of 'Cockles and Mussels'?" "By singing it slowly and softly and sadly," was the reply. "And by saying the word *ghost* mysteriously," added a boy.

Again from these backgrounds of understanding the child absorbs the meaning of musical symbols. He observes in the musical score what he has already learned to sing. The contour of a melody looks as it sounds. Time values of notes take on performance meaning through continuous use. The half note conveys a feeling of two beats both in singing and in playing.

The child learns how to obtain effects that he anticipates by using his voice or playing his instrument. Through different approaches he finally achieves results satisfying to him, and thus learns to understand and to use the most effective approach.

He plans activities and programs and, in the process, learns the use of music to enlarge and enrich his school life. When he listens to music he brings his previous experience and employs it to further his understanding. He composes, the highest type of musical creativity.

He learns to understand the various kinds of tonalities and tonal tendencies that have developed as man experimented with music through the ages. These he learns through the use of music, through the observance of its characteristics, and through experimentation in composing his own music. With such songs as the Chinese folk tune "The Bamboo Flute," the Scotch "Loch Lomond," old Irish music, and songs from our American Indian, he learns the five-tone scale. He gets the feeling of the quarter-tone system of India by actually observing samples; he experiences the feeling of the whole-tone system from such compositions as "The Little Shepherd" from the *Children's Corner Suite* by Debussy. These he compares with our modes and tonalities and finds their similarities and differences. And through this study he gains the concept of man's endeavor to make his own kind of music express emotions that all mankind has in common.

Corollaries of Creative Program

In a well-conducted creative program certain corollaries obtain.

1. *There must be boundaries within which children work*. They have neither the experience nor the breadth of understanding to be allowed absolute freedom. This would be license which has no place in the program since it lacks organization toward any goal. The teacher helps the children set up goals which they can understand, goals toward which they decide to work.

With elementary children these goals are tangible and immediate: they want to learn a song, they desire to play a composition or dramatize a ballad. The teacher's goals for the children add an understanding of the way in which music can express feeling, of the satisfaction in its use, of an increasing knowledge of tonality and form in music, and a growing understanding of the universality of emotion which spreads itself over the entire world.

The teacher wants the children to know that music can express widely varied emotions: the love of all mothers for their children, the delight in dancing, a belief in a deity, the wonder about the mysteries of our universe. These the teacher sees as ultimate goals for her children. She provides the opportunity for initiative, for a guided freedom of choice within a certain situation.

Such a situation may arise when a group wishes to select songs for use in a play. The teacher has in mind a list of music from which the children make their choices. During the process they investigate much music, incidentally becoming acquainted with considerable material in the songbooks and in the library. They are observing ways in which music can display feeling; and they are absorbing the structure of the music.

In a fifth grade room guided freedom was exhibited in preparation for a play about a city. Songs of a city provided the incentive for dramatization of a day in a metropolis: the skyscrapers, a gas station, the newsboys, a subway, the groceryman, etc. The children realized their goals in learning and dramatizing the songs. The teacher's goals added a growing insight into music and its uses, and an introduction to city life. The songs set up the structure within which the children created their dramatization.

2. *The teacher is the focal point in a creative program and in establishing a creative viewpoint.* It is she who provides the framework within which the children can operate creatively. She helps them realize that they have freedom in planning their activities and, with the acceptance of freedom for initiative, they accept also the responsibility for results. She must have well in mind an organization which will foster the development of some specific understandings. She stimulates their imagination and helps them to make full use of their abilities. A teacher whose group worked together rather poorly suggested that they plan a program for an assembly. The students' aims were accomplished in the program; the teacher's aims were achieved through the students' cooperative planning and management.

The teacher helps children to organize into small groups to carry out special plans. And she advises children who have difficulty in adjusting to others.

3. *The creative act must be a genuine expression of each individual and of the group as a whole.* Children need little incentive for genuine expression; it is natural to them. But a teacher needs to consider carefully her own plans to be sure that they foster experiences which are real for her children. It is easy to become too ambitious or to set up false standards or standards beyond the children's level of maturity. Many are the performances which adults praise for their "cuteness" in imitating adult ways or for their "well-disciplined" execution. A teacher will do well to question their educative value and to help parents to question them also. For frequently parents provide incentive with their approval and with the publicizing of such events: a sophisticated dramatization in which the teacher writes lines beyond the comprehension of the speakers; the familiar rhythm band performance with children dressed in beautiful uniforms and trained to respond automatically like robots in a well-practiced orchestration. This is not to say that rhythm band is ineffective for music education; it has a number of values and it provides a powerful teaching force if approached wisely and with understanding.

In a real creative experience the children must experiment with their own ideas and, from their experimentation, select values which they can understand. They may have chosen to sing "Jacob's Ladder" for an assembly. They try various interpretations, using a solo for one verse, alto on another. They compose a descant and try an instrumental accompaniment and an introduction. They sing one verse very softly and crescendo on the next. In the process of evaluation they have become well acquainted with the music itself, they have observed the effects of various interpretations, and they have set up their own standards for performance, standards which are challenging to them and yet are not beyond their maturity level.

In actual composition the teacher has the splendid opportunity to encourage originality. She allows the children to experiment freely with any combination of tones. And she accepts with pleasure and appreciation any composition which contains genuine feeling of tone or mood, no matter how unfinished it may sound to her ears. She does not need to have the rules of harmony on her lips; what she does need is an understanding heart and the capacity for enjoyment of honest, emotional expression. . . .

4. *Creativity encourages more creativity.* As a child experiments with sound and finds melodies and tone combinations which please him, he becomes intrigued with the act of composition and completely forgets himself in it. He may spend an hour at the keyboard with intense concentration and with no conception of the passing of time. But time is of no consideration in composition. Sometimes the germ of a musical idea appears immediately

and the entire development consumes but a few moments. Again the composer works off and on for several weeks before satisfying himself with the results. Or perhaps he eventually discards the idea as worthless.

Each composition should be accepted as of genuine worth in the process of creative growth. But creative efforts of children should not be exploited beyond their value. It is natural for many children to compose music and a few compositions do not indicate genius. Excessive praise and publication have a tendency to atrophy further efforts or to set a pattern for composition which "jells" at its present stage and grows no more.

The creative attitude toward music activities other than composition, such as orchestra and chorus, becomes a game in which each individual strives to perfect his own performance and to make it more ably express the composer's intent and message with each performance.

5. *Creativity provides a method of approach which is a stimulant to growth of personality and character.* A creative atmosphere frees the person to become himself and to use his native ability. Frequently first attempts at being creative produce a negative result or one that is imitative of the creative work of others. But with repeated effort and friendly encouragement, individuality asserts itself and results become truly creative. At the first realization of this power within himself the creator is delighted that he possesses good judgment, good insight, good ideas; with eagerness he grasps his newly acquired self-confidence. Small children gain this confidence and this approach much sooner than their elders who have suffered from years of criticism of any efforts toward individuality.

A creative attitude and approach encourage the individual to think for himself, to come to his own conclusions, and to act upon them, and to make his own unique contribution to the group of which he is a part. With freedom to act for himself and with the sort of guidance which assists him to recognize desirable values and stimulates him to consider the results of his previous decisions and actions, he tends to raise his standards and to strive progressively for higher goals in his personal life.

6. *Creativity can start in any part of the school program and can include many activities.* In a third grade the study of grasshoppers made the children observant of songs about these insects. One of the children wrote a rhyme about a grasshopper; the group composed a melody for the rhyme. A short dramatization of grasshopper life developed from this activity. The children gave their play for other groups of children, using the songs they had learned from their songbooks and their own composition.

For the spring festival each year one school chooses a theme around which each group builds its own activity for performance. Mexico, Scandinavia, cowboy life, Indian customs, and the westward movement in the United States all have furnished themes at various times. The children help to choose their activities, selecting some from materials which the teachers present, and creating others as they grow in knowledge and understanding.

7. *Materials for creativity are not sought in unusual places. They are found in the folk songs and folk ways that we have known always.* They are the songs in the school songbooks. They are the ballads which our grandparents sang to us. They are the simple instruments which children make and the tunes which they hum in their work and play. Furthermore, they are the children themselves with their honest, refreshing expression of growing thought. And they are the teachers whose resourcefulness serves as a freshet to encourage new, complete living in each new, promising day.

Briefly then, the creative approach involves initiative and freedom of choice. Each person and each group must be allowed the opportunity for this choice. They must follow through by using the choice actively, noting the results, drawing conclusions from these results, and then finally acting upon the conclusions. The process is continuous. Skills in using materials and the knowledge of fundamentals build upon those already acquired and become increasingly mature. In using these expanding skills the child realizes their values and therefore desires to make them a part of his equipment. This desire determines learning and true assimilation. It is in this process that growth materializes—growth in the understanding of music and in its social values. As Hughes Mearns has said, "Experience, in fact, is the only verity that anyone ever knows. So we make it the sole material of self-expression. And we get results instantly." [1]

83. *Music throughout the Day* *

O. M. HARTSELL

IS THE MUSIC PROGRAM in your elementary classroom planned and operated on the "faucet system"? Is music turned on for twenty minutes and then turned off and no use made of it otherwise throughout the day?

The elementary classroom is a place for living and learning, and music

[1] Hughes Mearns, *The Creative Adult: Self Education in the Art of Living* (New York: Doubleday & Co., 1940), p. 91.

* From O. M. Hartsell, "Music throughout the Day," *NEA Journal* (February, 1956), pp. 78–79. Reprinted by permission of the author and the *NEA Journal*.

when used appropriately throughout the day is a way of enriching that living and making the environment for learning more effective. It is generally agreed that the elementary-school program should provide opportunities for each child to develop to his fullest capacity—physically, mentally, emotionally, socially, and spiritually. Music can contribute directly to all these phases of the child's growth and development.

Who Should Teach Music?

If music is going to be a living part of the daily life of both children and teacher, then any idea of a music period coming once or twice a week and being taught by the music supervisor is untenable. The music specialist— whether called supervisor, consultant, or helping teacher—can be an invaluable resource person for the classroom teacher, but he ought not to be the person who provides all the musical experiences for children in any given classroom.

Each elementary classroom teacher can and should be responsible for carrying on a varied, interesting, and worth-while program of musical activities in his own classroom. In the ideal cooperative situation, the classroom teacher feels perfectly free to call upon the consultant for all kinds of assistance.

In the thousands of elementary classroom units where the services of a music consultant are not available, classroom teachers must be encouraged to take the initiative in planning and carrying on the best possible program of musical activities in their own classrooms.

Daily Uses of Music

All classroom teachers can use music at different times throughout the day in a number of ways and for valid educational reasons. The "sitability span" of children is rather brief, and musical activities offer a pleasant nonfatiguing way to vary the daily routine of classroom work. Good for this purpose are finger-play songs, action songs, singing games, dramatizations of songs or instrumental selections, playing instruments, or other activities involving expressive bodily movement.

Excess energy also can be channeled constructively into similar things-to-do-to-music, and the observant teacher frequently can prevent discipline problems by anticipating them and making use of the child's natural vitality in educational ways involving music.

Group singing can be used before or after those classroom activities which largely involve individual work and response. Singing together at any time during the day is a way of getting group focus and easily and quickly obtaining group unity.

Music is essentially a social art. One makes it *for* other people. One makes it *with* other people. When children sing a song, for example, each child can give a part of himself to the group endeavor with the result that cooperating and sharing can become realistic parts of his classroom experiences.

Children's moods often change as a result of inclement weather, playground happenings, or other classroom circumstances. A carefully selected song or other musical activity usually helps to counteract periods of moodiness or restlessness.

Some children complete assignments before the group as a whole has finished. Where facilities permit, such youngsters might listen to their favorite recordings in an adjacent room until time for the next classroom activity. Children who find special delight in listening to music will often work harder to complete a more routine but equally important assignment in another subject area in order to enjoy this particular privilege.

Leading a section of the class in a part song or rhythmic activity can help to develop self-confidence and leadership in individual boys and girls. This type of experience may also stimulate the child's awareness that he may lead at one time and be a member of the group at other times.

Perhaps most important of all, the frequent use of music in the classroom takes into consideration two basic human needs—belonging to a group and expressing one's self in as many ways as possible. Music can help every child to develop a sense of belonging to his group in school, regardless of his social background or financial status. It can likewise be a satisfying means of expressing his feelings and releasing his emotional tensions.

Helping children to discover music as a worthy leisure-time activity might well be a fine by-product of any music-throughout-the-day plan.

Consequently, the ways of using music throughout the day in the elementary classroom are limited only by the teacher's point of view, his imagination, his understanding of how children grow and develop and respond to music, and his sensitivity to their moods, feelings, and general well-being.

More Effective Pre-service Preparation Needed

In most instances, college preparation in music for prospective elementary classroom teachers needs to be different in character and higher in quality from what has existed in the past. What is generally overlooked at the college level is that improving the musical experiences of prospective teachers involves bringing about changes in them.

It means increasing their desire to make music a part of the daily classroom living of every boy and girl, strengthening their belief that with adequate preparation they can teach their own music, demonstrating to them that music can and should be an enjoyable experience for both teacher and student, extending their knowledge about children and about music, and helping them gain the necessary skill to bring music to children.

There is no longer a place in the few preparatory courses offered in music at the college level for the traditional beginning course erroneously called "fundamentals of music." A knowledge of the rudiments of music is definitely essential and important, but the rudiments should be presented and learned *not by isolated drill* but as *an integral part of all the musical activities* which the prospective teacher will later be expected to use in bringing music to children.

More attention might well be given at the college level not to the "fundamentals" but to the fundamental things about which elementary teachers must know.

This includes such things as singing many different kinds of songs, listening to a variety of recorded vocal and instrumental music, participating in rhythmic activities suitable for different grade levels, playing instruments, including the autoharp and piano, relevantly associating music with other subject areas, and, whenever appropriate in all these activities, introducing and dealing specifically with the rudiments of music as a means of helping children develop some degree of skill, understanding, and enjoyment in using musical notation.

There are many ways of experiencing music, and the classroom teacher must be able to provide a variety of musical experiences through which every child can have the opportunity to discover his particular musical interests as well as to develop his inherent musical potentialities.

In-service Education Important

We all know many elementary classroom teachers who are enthusiastic about teaching their own music and who are doing effective work in this respect. However, there will always be some teachers who will need the help of a carefully planned program of in-service education in music. Such a program can be a practical means of solving the problem of inadequate preparation for teaching music in the self-contained classroom.

Leadership for initiating in-service education in music can and should be taken by state departments of education in cooperation with colleges and local school systems. States where this has been done report excellent response from school administrators, classroom teachers, and parents.

Such educational help in music takes many forms: preschool conferences in which all new teachers participate in groups with the local music consultant or a special guest music educator, area conferences conducted by the state music supervisor or county music consultants, three-day county-wide music workshops or institutes, extension courses in music, and summer courses on college campuses.

Some local school systems are also adding an experienced music consultant to their staffs. This is the most direct and often the most desirable means of assuring the in-service growth and continued musical development of classroom teachers in any elementary-school situation.

In-service education projects can enable all participating individuals to examine and try out new classroom materials and equipment. Teachers can also become familiar with and learn how to use special resources such as the recordings and detailed guides which accompany each book in the series of music texts now available for use in elementary schools.

Coda

The idea of doing things with music at different times throughout the day is for those elementary classroom teachers who are sensitive to the daily needs of boys and girls and who want to use music as one of the most inviting avenues through which children may grow and develop—physically, mentally, emotionally, socially, and spiritually. It is never too late to begin to live better with music.

84. Health Education and the Classroom Teacher *

CARL E. WILLGOOSE

"While health itself is not the finest flower of life—it is the soil from which the finest flowers grow."

—DUNCAN SPAETH

HEALTH EDUCATION includes every educational influence that helps to improve the health of the school child. It is a process of changing health behavior in such a way that boys and girls will not only be able to learn better, but will have the necessary wherewithal to live a rich and full life.

There is no person in the school system better fitted to make a significant contribution to the health of school children than the classroom teacher in the elementary school. She alone occupies the key position for improving child health. With her interest, enthusiasm, and understanding the school health program moves ahead. Without her support, however, the health education program never really gets started.

The Role of the Classroom Teacher

The role of the classroom teacher is unique; no other person sees the child as she does. She can readily compare his appearance and actions today with what they were yesterday or a month ago. Or she can compare

* From Carl E. Willgoose, "Health Education and the Classroom Teacher," *Education* (April, 1958), pp. 451–55. Reprinted by permission of the author and The Bobbs-Merrill Co., Inc., Indianapolis, Ind.

him to the other thirty children in the classroom who are about the same age. This provides the alert teacher with a vantage point that neither the parents or family physician can match. Thus, every classroom teacher holds a potentially powerful job for building sound health. The extent to which she does this will depend upon many things. She will need a warm personality and feeling for children, and she will need to use her powers of observation carefully.

How the Classroom Teacher Promotes Health

Specifically, the classroom teacher promotes health as follows:

1. *By cooperating with the school health service personnel.* Children are properly prepared for a visit to the school physician or nurse for periodic physical examinations. Teachers take a positive approach to the examinations by saying to their pupils, "The doctor is coming to see how many healthy boys and girls we have." Teachers help in the screening of children for defective vision and hearing. Learning to visit medical personnel and come away happy is an education in itself. Any experience that is satisfying or "feels good" to the child is effective in terms of his future behavior. The nurse, the doctor, and the dental hygienist should be their friends.

2. *By detecting health abnormalities and referring them to proper authorities for appropriate follow-up and correction.* The teacher who uses her "eyes to see" can observe a variety of items related to the onset of poor health. The child with frequent colds and sore throats who is continually snuffing in class may have any one of a number of difficulties involving the upper respiratory area. Likewise, the child that squints his eyes to see or turns his head to hear simple questions may be in need of medical aid right away. The child who often exhibits signs of emotional upset may be missed entirely by the parents, but spotted by the teacher as one who behaves differently than the group and needs individual attention. It should be remembered that the younger a person, the easier they respond to a distracting stimulus. Where an adult can in effect say to a stomach-ache or pain, "get thee behind me," the small child simply cannot ignore it. His ability to learn, therefore, is directly impaired. The same thing is true with the child who scores well on a test of learning aptitude, yet produces work in class that is hardly better than average. He is the kind of pupil that bears watching.

3. *By making the school environment pleasant and desirable for the*

pupils. The school, to be at all effective, must be the kind of place a child wants to go to. The classroom is made comfortable by the teacher. She regulates such physical items as temperature, ventilation, lighting, and seating. Her own attitude toward the students has much to do with the health and happiness of the class. There are numerous children who dislike school and show this by coming down with "morning sickness"—a disease that fails to appear on Saturdays Sundays and holidays.

4. *By providing health instruction in the classroom.* Teaching is done both informally and formally. The teacher seldom misses an opportunity to refer to the child's health and welfare. Health as a topic is also correlated with other materials. It is taught with the aim of changing habits and attitudes. Health knowledge as such must lead to the kind of understanding that results in changed behavior.

Following Up Deviations from Normal Health

There are great numbers of children who come from homes in this country who do not have adequate preparation for school. They lack the sleep, food, or emotional climate that makes for satisfactory school work. Poverty, ignorance, and parental indifference are behind this. In the classroom the child falls short of what is expected of him. He may appear listless or lazy, easily discouraged, and show low scholarship. The alert teacher may be able to notice his dry hair and scalp, sallow skin, poor posture, lack of energy in physical activities, restlessness, and general irritability. It is important that something be done quickly. This situation is no different than one where a child is in need of glasses because he cannot see the blackboard. Expert medical judgment is needed. Follow-up to see that something is done is vital. Here, parents and teachers cooperate, but it is the teacher who is in a position of *control.* She actually controls the situation from the classroom where she has a day-by-day check on the pupil concerned. Nevertheless, pupils still appear year after year with the same defects or difficulties despite the efforts of school personnel.

The following case report from a teacher in Florida represents a practical approach to a problem of malnutrition. It is more difficult than most cases, but is the type of case that is present in almost every community. It clearly demonstrates the role of the classroom teacher as a *prime mover* in following up basic health abnormalities. The classroom teacher speaks:

Melvin was 10½ years old and in my third grade. There were three younger children in his family. He repeated the second grade where he was considered to be a slow student. He was thin and small for his age and showed other signs which made me suspect that he was malnourished. He was very pale and his skin had a sallow look; his hair was dry, stringy and dull looking; he had dark circles under his eyes; and had a pinched look on his face.

Melvin came to school all year barefooted and his skin was so dirty it looked rusty in spots. He looked as if no one had ever seen that he had a bath. He was absent from school quite often. Sometimes his excuse was that he had a cold or didn't feel good or that he had to stay home and look after his baby brothers. Often he complained of being tired or sleepy.

I talked to Mrs. Irvin, our school nurse, and she told me to bring him around so that she could see him. She examined the mucous membranes of his eyes. She looked at his teeth and found several small cavities. She talked to him for some time and found that quite often he came to school without breakfast. His mother's health was bad and he would get up too late to fix breakfast for himself and his other little brother who was in the second grade. He said he never drank milk at home because it was needed for the babies.

Mrs. Irvin had both the boys checked for hookworm and when that came back negative she decided to visit Melvin's home. From this visit she found out that Melvin's father made fair wages but was a heavy drinker and often used the grocery money for buying whisky, leaving barely enough for food. She said that many times Melvin sat up rather late at night to keep his mother company when the father was out. Mrs. Irvin impressed upon the mother how important it was for the children to get the proper amount of rest. The mother needed medical attention but could not afford it so Mrs. Irvin made an appointment for her and the children to see the county health physician. She consulted the Welfare Department regarding the family situation.

After her visit we talked to the school principal and the lunchroom supervisor. We made arrangements for Melvin and his brother to have milk each morning when they arrived at school. The children had been going home for lunch so we arranged for them to be put on free lunches.

Within two months' time Melvin improved considerably, both in his contacts with fellow pupils and in his scholastic achievement. He was simply a different boy.

Parents and Teachers

The average schoolteacher and the average parent have little difficulty getting together to discuss the status of the child—the welfare of which is their mutual concern. There are cases, however, where the child suffers because the teacher is unobserving or is "too busy" to consider the pupil individually and follow up suspected weaknesses. There are also many occasions when the parent fails to do his share of cooperating. For one thing, children sometimes never seem as much in need of attention to the parent as they do to the school authorities. All too often the child in need of eyeglasses doesn't get them right away because the father or mother knows he can see. It is obvious to them that he can see because he doesn't walk into the side of the barn. In most communities parents understand quite well the purposes of the school. Others are indifferent. To illustrate this point the story is told of the school nurse who called at the farm home of the mother of Mary to tell her about the girl's long-standing case of head lice. After the nurse took some time to explain the girl's situation, the mother simply shrugged her shoulders, looked out across the cornfield, and said, "Well, everybody has a few."

The classroom teacher's effectiveness with parents can be greater during the primary grade years than at any other time. This is the period when parents willingly visit the schools and lean heavily on the teacher for all kinds of information regarding their offspring. It is also the time when children listen and believe about everything the teachers say. With parental help and encouragement, therefore, most children will profit considerably from the health instruction given at school. In a dental health unit, for example, the parents can be most helpful. Children who are keeping a record at home of their toothbrushing habits can be encouraged, not only in terms of brushing them, but using an effective method. In one community the parents got together and supplied the teacher with toothpaste and brushes so that the children, under the teacher's supervision, could brush their teeth following the midday lunch. This is the kind of health education that does more than impart knowledge. It satisfies immediate and long-term needs of boys and girls because the parents and teachers are working together.

Health Teaching

Health is successfully taught on an informal basis in the primary grades. Instruction becomes a little more formal on the intermediate level. Such an informal basis for teaching permits the teacher to engage the class in a wide variety of activities, both in the school and the community. Health and safety instruction can be quite "down to earth." Learning experiences, in which various instructional methods are used, are commonplace today. Teachers employ audio-visual aids, library materials, panel discussions, etc., to motivate children. In some areas students work on their own health and safety committees. They take field trips into the community. They put on school health assembly programs, provide health news for student publications, carry on community health surveys, etc. In one Georgia community the elementary-school sixth grades studied mosquito control, formed classroom committees, and began in a small way to spread oil on stagnant waters. Their project caught the interest of the townsfolk and other organizations in the community joined in the effort to control mosquitoes. The whole thing was immensely successful and the amount of first-rate learning that occurred was impressive.

Other student activities of a practical nature that have proved to be commendable health education activities are as follows:

—Radio and television broadcasts of health programs prepared and presented by pupils over the local radio or television station.

—Participation in community cleanup campaigns as a part of health instruction program.

—Upper graders conducting a survey of the number and kind of eating places in the community.

—Pupils assisting teachers in classroom duties, such as control of lighting, heating and ventilation in the room.

—Students assuming responsibility for the selection of their own chairs and desks.

—Class members taking part in the planning of school lunches and the operation of the school lunchroom.

—Pupils having the opportunity to practice safety procedures with respect to fire drills, and passing to and from classes.

It may be seen from what has been written that health education is broad in its scope, and includes health services, healthful school environment and health instruction. Yet, without the enthusiastic help of the classroom teacher, only a limited effort can be made to improve the health of boys and girls.

85. *Changing Growth Patterns of the American Child* *

CREIGHTON J. HALE

ACCUMULATED documentary evidence suggests that the rate of physical and mental maturation of the American youth has been accelerated. Children of today are taller, heavier, healthier, possess greater mental capabilities and demonstrate advanced physical skills which in many in-

* From Creighton J. Hale, "Changing Growth Patterns of the American Child," *Education* (April, 1958), pp. 467–70. Reprinted by permission of the author and The Bobbs-Merrill Co., Inc., Indianapolis, Ind.

stances surpass the best achievements of older age groups of previous years.

The evidence of earlier maturity is of great import to education. Our American system has frequently been criticized because of the "lock-step" pattern by which children must advance from grade to grade at the same pace regardless of ability. Based upon the present developmental acceleration it appears that our children may be moving forward not only in "lock step" but also in the wrong "platoon" since for the same chronological age, children today are biologically older than in previous years.

Today's Children Are Taller, Heavier, More Mature

For the past few years extensive research has been conducted on boys participating in Little League Baseball. The size, skill and maturity of the boys playing on tournament teams was particularly impressive. These young players, although only 11 and 12 years of age, were as tall and as heavy as the average fourteen- and fifteen-year-old of today and as tall and as heavy as the average sixteen- and seventeen-year-old of twenty-five years ago. The majority of these preteen-agers, as established by Crampton's pubic-hair index, were physiologically 15 years old, hence adolescent and not preadolescent as their chronological age would indicate.

It has been found that children who excel in sports are usually one to two years advanced in maturity. However the recent studies on boys in Little League reveal an advance in maturation rate of three or four years.

But what about the average child? Has his growth pattern changed as those who possess athletic prowess? Although research on physiological growth over an extended period of time is not available, anthropometric data show dramatic changes.

Since 1880, a period of only seventy-five years, the average fourteen-year-old boy has gained five inches in height and twenty-four pounds in weight. In weight alone this represents a 25 per cent increase. In the same period, the average ten-year-old girl has gained four inches in height and fourteen pounds in weight. In the last twenty-five years the average twelve-year-old boy and girl has gained three inches in height and fifteen pounds in weight, and the average fourteen-year-old boy of today has grown to the size of the sixteen-year-old.

Numerous reports show that the average height and weight of our entire population has increased. However, the greatest change is to be found in children at the age of pubescence or just preceding pubescence thus indicating an advancement in the rate of maturation.

Earlier Maturation of Sports' Skills

One of the most impressive indications of earlier maturation of American youth is the outstanding athletic performances of youthful participants. Unusual achievements are being recorded each year by younger athletes.

In Little League eleven- and twelve-year-old boys have been found to run as fast as average fifteen- and sixteen-year-old boys. Pitchers in this program throw baseballs as fast as seventy miles an hour which is equivalent to some college pitching and certainly remarkably fast for preteen-age youngsters when compared to the speed of the professional pitchers in the major leagues most of whom throw fast-balls at speeds of 90 miles an hour.

Also extraordinary and almost incredible is the 100-mile-an-hour speed at which some players in Little League can swing a bat. Mickey Mantle, celebrated and exceptionally strong center fielder of the New York Yankees and winner of the triple batting crown in 1956, swings his bat at 115 miles an hour which is only 15 miles an hour faster.

In individual sports such as track and field and swimming there is unmistakable evidence that teen-agers are fast approaching world record performances and have already surpassed world record achievements of earlier years.

In the 100 yard dash there is but 1/10 of a second difference between the record time run by a high school student and the fastest time this distance has ever been covered by man. In the 220 yard dash the difference between the record performance by a high school student and the world record is a slight 7/10 of a second. Only 9/10 of a second separates the high school record and the world record for the 440 yard run.

The world record in the high jump was established in 1956 at the Herculean height of 7 ft. ½ in., yet this is less than three inches better than the high school record of 6 ft. 9¾ in. This high school record surpassed every Olympic high jump performance until 1956 when Charles Dumas established the standard of 6 ft. 11¼ in. The pole vault also provides an interesting comparison. In 1957 a high school track star vaulted 15 ft. ⅛ in., a height which, many years ago, most believed could never be achieved by anyone. This teen-age record performance actually exceeds the Olympic record for this event. The most rigorous and the best test for all-around ability in track and field is the decathlon. To capture the gold medal in this event the champion must demonstrate advanced maturity in skills, physique, and physiological processes. In the 1948 Olympics in London the decathlon was won, with a record performance, by a teen-ager, Bob Mathias, who was 17 years of age.

Many will recall or have read about the golden era of athletics in the years just preceding the First World War. This was the period of spectacular Jim Thorpe. Yet, of the twelve world records in track of Jim Thorpe's era, nine now have been surpassed by teen-age athletes.

Some people will debate that this sensational improvement in track and field performances is the result of better athletic equipment and more favorable conditions of track and field. Such may be true; however, swimming performances reveal a similar trend and certainly water has always been water and recent record times cannot be attributed to any particular modification of the bathing suit.

The 1957 AAU swimming championship in Houston, Texas, serves as an excellent example of exceptional achievements by youthful performers. Seventeen-year-old Carin Coke set a record in the 110 yard backstroke, seventeen-year-old Nancy Raney surpassed the record in the 110 yard butterfly, fifteen-year-old Carolyn Murray set a new standard in the mile free style, fifteen-year-old Sylvia Ruuska set two records but most impressive was thirteen-year-old Chris Von Saltza who shattered no less than three marks.

It is obvious that the modern record performances are achieved, in most instances, by athletes who are much younger than in previous years. Such accomplishments have been made possible because of accelerated maturation.

Academic Ability of Today's Children

Changes in mental capabilities are difficult to identify but there are evidences which strongly suggest that modern students are academically more competent than students of earlier years.

It has been found repeatedly that early physical maturation favors good scholarship and late physical maturation poor scholarship. Since children are maturing physically earlier today it can be concluded that mental maturation has also been accelerated.

Within the past few months a report "They Went to College Early" was released by The Fund for the Advancement of Education which gives illuminating evidences that outstanding junior and senior high school students are capable of completing college academic requirements. Twelve institutions of higher learning throughout the United States in this five-year research program all found that the students selected to attend college at an early age were capable of satisfactory conduct and achievements. In many instances the "Early Admission" students were more successful than their comparison students who had graduated from high school before enrolling in college. Some efforts have been made to remedy this situation but this program has been limited in scope. It is apparent that entire school curricula should be evaluated in light of present data which indicate an accelerated mental maturation of American youth.

In Conclusion

Several evidences indicating that the rate of maturation of American children has accelerated have been presented. Although it is not possible to establish the exact cause or causes of this quickened growth pattern the outstanding advances in medicine, our increased knowledge of nutrition and the control of our environment must be considered primary factors. Antibiotics and vaccines have eliminated or lessened many childhood diseases. The diphtheria, smallpox, whooping cough, malaria, typhoid fever and scarlet fever that were often part of the histories of their grandfathers and great grandfathers are largely unknown to present-day youths. The vitamin-fortified and balanced diets which are now within the financial means of almost everyone provide for more optimum growth.

Certainly as education strives to keep students informed of the prodigious technological progress of this modern era, it must not overlook the fact that these great advances may have effected a change in its own product and the country's most valuable resource, the American child.

86. The Emotionally Disturbed *

FRITZ REDL
AND STANLEY JACOBSON

IT ISN'T EASY to become *an emotionally disturbed child*. We don't mean that it isn't easy to have an emotional disturbance—that's the easiest and most natural thing in the world. All of us have to meet the frustrations and

---

* From Fritz Redl and Stanley Jacobson, "The Emotionally Disturbed," *NEA Journal* (December, 1958), pp. 609–11. Reprinted by permission of the authors and the *NEA Journal*.

disappointments that are standard procedure in living, and all of us react with more or less disturbance.

We feel hurt or angry or anxious or depressed or some subtle variation of some unnamed emotion. We behave in ways we wouldn't approve of—hopefully not for long and with minimum damage to ourselves or others. Then we get over the disturbance, and maybe we even learn from it so that the next time we face the frustration we aren't thrown quite so fast or far.

For children, especially, this process is as regular as meals, only more frequent. And with good reason. Children are still busy learning to recognize feelings and urges that are an old story to us. To learn to cope with those emotions is one important job of the growing child, and to make it doubly hard, he can't do it alone. He has to depend on us to help him. We expect the process to be punctuated by an occasional "disturbance," just as we expect a healthy child to suffer an occasional cold.

Because school is a natural focus for so much of the growing, school is also bound to be the scene of some of the disturbances. We learn to recognize the symptoms—a sudden change from typical behavior, more fighting or more crying or more absence or less concentration. Six-year-old Johnny suddenly refuses to come to school. Twelve-year-old Bobby cries when he sees the C in math on his report card. Teen-age Sally, an A student, suddenly stops trying.

As we probe behind this behavior with parent, child, or school counselor, we find there is a reason:

"Ever since the baby came, Johnny hangs around me all the time."

"My father said he'd buy me a bike if I got an A, and now he won't buy it."

"If I can't go away to college, I'm not going to do anything."

Then we apply the first aid that is usually all that is required. Johnny and his mother get some counseling about the meaning of the new baby. Bobby's father begins to look at his son's ability realistically. Sally learns the economic facts of life, and her parents learn about adolescent independency striving. And all is fixed.

But to become *an emotionally disturbed child* is another matter. For one thing, transient disturbances like the ones we mentioned above must have been repeatedly ignored, misjudged, or badly handled earlier in the game, before the child reached school age as well as afterward, so that anger or distrust or despair, a feeling of badness or wrongness in himself or in the world, has already begun to look like a permanent fixture in the personality.

By then, no one-sided, one-step remedy will work. By then, it isn't *simply* the chemistry of the glands or the focus of the eyes or the level of the IQ or what Papa said just before Johnny left for school this morning. By then, warmth and caring are not enough.

What is an emotionally disturbed child like? First of all, the term itself is much too broad. It covers illnesses as simple as measles and as serious as cancer, as different as tonsillitis and a broken arm.

For example, if little Johnny's screaming and vomiting and refusal to come to school continue even after ample demonstration that he is loved and appreciated as fully as the newly arrived infant, chances are that the baby is not the source of the problem, but only the last straw.

Johnny and his mother may need guidance deeper in focus and longer in duration. Mother may need to take an unsettling new look at her child-rearing attitudes, and Johnny may have to let off considerable steam in the safety of a therapist's office before he can take the risk of growing up.

There may be another Johnny in the same first grade class who comes to school obediently day after day and goes robot-like through his classroom paces; but his teacher notices a masklike quality about him, a pseudo understanding. He's in another world.

Now it *may* be that this Johnny is by inheritance an especially slow child, as yet unequipped for the rigors of first grade life. Or perhaps he is one of those unfortunate children so badly hurt by early experiences that his thinking is twisted, and he really *cannot* understand the world as we do. Both are certainly disturbed, but they are as different from each other as they are from our first Johnny.

As a fourth variety of disturbance, take the kind of child we have been studying at the National Institute of Mental Health. In the first grade, this Johnny would probably have the teacher threatening to resign, for he's the boy whose hand is quicker than his head, who wants but cannot share, who acts as if yesterday never happened and tomorrow's an eternity away. He's the acting-out boy, long on aggression and short on self-control.

All these children, and many more varieties, are emotionally disturbed. We could have added at least a fifth child—the wonderfully cooperative one whose private life is an anxious striving to meet self-imposed, perfectionistic goals—but we are not trying to list all the kinds of disturbance. That would be impossible in any case. Our point is that the term *emotionally disturbed* is too broad to have any practical meaning.

To say a child is emotionally disturbed is like saying that he has a fever: Both statements merely point out that something is wrong without indicating the nature of the illness, how serious it is, or what remedies are indicated to effect a cure.

Notice too, that there is a difference between *disturbed* and *disturbing*. The child who causes us most trouble may happen to be the most deeply troubled child in the room; but sometimes he is a normal child engaged in a temporary campaign—perhaps to overcome immigrant status in a new community or to prove he's "somebody" to the girl across the room. The opposite child, the quiet oasis of calm in a too easily distracted group, often needs our attention more, even though he does nothing to force it.

It is no doubt clear by now that emotional disturbances defy generalization. On the face of it, symptoms know no logic. Every situation requires its own analysis, every illness its own cure.

This means that general prescriptions for handling disturbed children in the classroom will have limited relevance for individual cases. It does not mean, however, that there are no guides for thinking about what to do. These there are, and many of them are already familiar to you. Here are only a few we would like to suggest:

A teacher is to teach. Children bring their emotional problems to the classroom, and the teacher has to find ways of helping them to cope with the problems while they are in school. When the emotional disturbances become entangled with classroom and learning situations, it is the teacher's job to try to disentangle them for the duration. It is not the classroom teacher's job to solve the child's difficulties for good and all.

Disturbances are real. It may be true that a particular child "could" do the work if he "wanted" to, but this doesn't mean he isn't really disturbed. It only means that the trouble lies in the motivational machinery instead of in the cognitive machinery. We may call him stubborn, negative, resistant, or withholding; but whatever we call him, chances are the condition is beyond his control and as real a disturbance in its way as faulty vision.

This is also true of the child who promises but can't deliver, the one who has to keep his eye on everything but his assignment, and many others who try our patience day after day.

It isn't personal. Not only are disturbances real; they also run deeper than the events of the day, as we have tried to indicate. The boy who continues his nasty disruptions in spite of your efforts to contain him probably has nothing against you personally, nor have you created the problem by failing to smile his way in the morning. You may symbolize all the adults who "do nothing but boss me around all the time," or you may be an innocent casualty in a battle to win prestige in the gang.

The exceptional child is an exception. Although many disturbed children can be helped in a regular classroom, the fact remains that the disturbed child is exceptional, and the techniques that provide stimulating learning experiences for most normal children may only stimulate the disturbed child's pathology.

If a promising activities program leads to chaos in the classroom, the trouble may lie in one or two children with faulty control systems and not in the technique itself. Even in a very small class, with more than one teacher, some children cannot manage a program which depends on inner controls and self-maintained task-centeredness. On the other hand, one can see the very same activities producing significant learning in large classes of relatively normal children.

Is the answer to assign disturbed children to separate groups? Perhaps, but not for all of them. Some disturbed children need special classes or special schools and some cannot manage school at all, but the majority need the presence of a normal group in order to develop an image of constructive social behavior.

For these children, the answer lies in the kind of flexible planning that many schools are finding easier to achieve than they had imagined. Children are going to school part time, moving to different rooms and grades as their needs require it, staying home on bad days—and the schools are seeing the programs bear fruit.

What is right for any disturbed child still depends on an analysis of that case alone, but there are plenty of alternatives if a school is willing to be imaginative.

You can't go it alone. What we have just said is not meant to imply that a teacher has to find a way to teach every child on the class roster. In the first place, some *disturbing* children are unmanageable (and therefore unteachable) even if they are not seriously *disturbed*. Others who might be reached are all too frequently lost because of special school conditions.

When the teacher is hamstrung by a rigid curriculum, a dearth of special facilities, ragged equipment, and short supplies, he can only choose the path of sanity and admit his limitations. Too many teachers still stand like martyrs, alone and unprovided with necessary tools, struggling to accomplish a task which requires artistry even under the best of circumstances.

Refer it. Tell somebody. The guidance counselor, the principal, the pupil personnel worker, the school social worker, the school psychologist—tell whichever person in your school has the job of knowing the resources for the troubled child and how to get child and resource together. And if the child you refer is lucky enough to arrive at the source of help, remember, specialists in helping troubled people can't go it alone either.

To be a specialist means to have special knowledge and skill in a specific area. It also means having less knowledge and skill in other areas. Psychiatrists, psychologists, and social workers may know as little about the classroom as teachers may know about the clinic. The helping specialist will depend on information from you to help him understand the case and plan the treatment *outside* the school.

As for the classroom program, that remains your area of specialty, and it will be up to you to translate findings about the child's personality and needs into classroom action. Education has perhaps done too little to develop specific educational techniques for the emotionally disturbed child, but that gap is being filled by a growing catalog of literature and course work on the subject, and we urge you to take advantage of it.

Speak up. Disturbed children need special services, not only in the school but in the recreation, health, and welfare fields as well. For too many years, teachers have tried to provide services beyond their scope because those services were not available elsewhere in the community. It is time the teachers shoved back—not to get even, but because it is hard enough to be what classroom teachers are trained to be without also trying to be social workers, psychologists, and psychiatrists. Only if we speak up can the community understand the need and begin to meet it.

87. Health Instruction
[in Kindergarten through Grade 6] *

HEALTH INSTRUCTION in the elementary school should provide the type of program that meets the physical, social, intellectual, and emotional needs of the individual child. Instruction is carried on in connection with the teacher's health observations, through discussions, through experiments, and by many other activities.

1. HEALTH LEARNINGS: GRADES K-2

Health learnings at this level are achieved largely by guidance of children in the following experiences:

Daily health observation
Planned health teaching

* From "Curriculum Research Report, A Memorandum of Courses of Study in Health Education, Grades K–6 and Grades 7–12 for Boys and Girls" (New York: The Board of Education of the City of New York), pp. 7–14. Reprinted by permission.

Work periods
Play periods
Recess periods
Snacks, lunches, and school parties
Directed physical activities
Dismissals and drills
Trips about the school and neighborhood

The teacher relates such topics as the following to the foregoing experiences:
Cleanliness of the body
Cleanliness of clothing
Exercise and play
Sleep and rest
Healthful food and good eating habits
Care of teeth, eyes, and ears
Health workers: the doctor, the school nurse, dentists, and others
Safety at work and at play
Good toilet habits

2. HEALTH LEARNINGS: GRADES 3-6

As the child matures, it is necessary that he become self-reliant in recognizing and in solving his health problems. In addition, it is important that the child realizes his responsibility in regard to the health of others.

The following topics will suggest ways of developing the health instruction program in grades 3-6. The list of topics is flexible and should be adapted to fit the needs of the school and the maturation level of the children involved. For example, health learnings started in one grade may be expanded in the grade that follows. It must be remembered that health teaching is an integral part of the total school program.

The aim of the health learnings program in these grades is to give children increased knowledge of good health practices and to encourage them to apply this knowledge for their own good and for the good of the community.

Physical environment

Need for circulating fresh air indoors
Importance of a well-lighted room
Proper lighting for viewing television, for reading, and for doing close work
Desirable room temperature
Proper ways to store outdoor clothing and classroom materials

Importance of a neat, attractive environment, classroom, lunchroom, lavatories, home, and community

Cleanliness and health protection

Use and care of handkerchief, towel, washcloth, comb, toothbrush, and other personal articles

Need for frequent baths and clean clothing

Need for washing hands before handling food and after toileting

Reasons for washing raw fruits and vegetables before eating

Need for remaining at home when ill; keeping away from others who have colds or other infectious diseases

Using public facilities—pools, beaches, toilets, drinking fountains

Avoiding sunburn, frostbite, chapped hands and infection from poisonous plants

Cooperating with community agencies concerned with health protection

Foods and eating practices

Washing hands before eating or handling food

Importance of eating a good breakfast

What constitutes a desirable lunch

Limited use of sweets and sweetened carbonated drinks

Desirable between-meal snacks

Amount of milk needed by growing children

Good table manners

Relation between appetite and attractiveness of food

Relation of good nutrition to growth and health

Basic groups of food and daily food requirements; planning balanced meals

Distinguishing food facts from fads and fancies

Interpreting labels on food

Body structure and function

Reasons for reporting to an adult any signs of improper functioning or unusual symptoms

Differences in height and weight among normal boys and girls of same age

Importance of periodic physical examinations and correction of remedial physical defects

Factors that contribute to good posture—proper diet, adequate sleep and rest, properly fitted shoes and clothing, exercise and fresh air, happy feelings

Importance of regular elimination

Ways of building strong bones and muscles

Dental health

Relation between good nutrition and dental health

Visits to dentist; purpose, frequency, importance

Proper and regular brushing of teeth; rinsing mouth after eating whenever possible

Care of first set of teeth

Causes of toothache; need for immediate treatment

Criteria for evaluating advertised dentifrices

Value of good teeth as an aid to personal attractiveness

Care of the eyes

Importance of adequate light for reading; of holding book properly; of using reading materials that are clearly printed

Importance of correcting vision defects; of wearing glasses when needed; of keeping glasses clean

Recognizing eyestrain and the need for having eyes examined

Desirable practices for viewing television

Ways of protecting the eyes at home, in school, at play, and while traveling

Need for having foreign bodies carefully removed from the eye by a qualified person

Simple first-aid procedures

Care of the ears and hearing

Ways to protect ears in cold weather

Ways to protect ears when swimming or diving

Reasons and safe methods for cleaning ears, safe ways to blow the nose

Common safety precautions for prevention of accidents to the ears

Value of periodic hearing tests

Importance of immediate care for earache or ear discharge

Care of ears after colds or other respiratory infections

Importance of wearing hearing aid if needed

Value of lip reading instruction

Cooperating with those who have impaired hearing

Sleep and rest

Sleep requirements of children

How to get adequate rest and sleep

Importance of fresh air while sleeping

Avoiding overfatigue; relation of sufficient rest to enjoyment of work and play

Effect of tea and coffee on sleep

Effect of noise on nervous system

Effects of exciting television and radio programs, and movies on sleep

Importance of maintaining proper balance between active and nonactive types of recreation

Value of relaxation and rest after meals
Safety and first aid
Reasons for using "Safe Route" to and from school
Importance of cooperation during all types of school emergency drills
Safety procedures on stairs, in corridors, lunchroom, play areas, street, and
    public conveyances
Safety at play
Safety with pets and other animals
Recognition of poisonous plants and berries
Fire safety precautions; reporting a fire; escaping from a burning building;
    extinguishing a fire on clothing; first aid for burns
Common causes of home and school accidents
Simple first-aid procedures for accidents
Stimulants and narcotics [1]
Harmful effects of tea, coffee, and alcoholic beverages on the diet
Dangers of accepting food, candy, or invitations from strangers
Use of narcotic drugs in medicine to relieve pain
Dangers of self-medication
Effect of alcohol, tobacco, and other narcotic drugs on general health
Economic and social effects of alcohol, tobacco, and narcotic drugs

Directed Physical Activities

The directed physical activities program for children in the grades K-6
should be planned and organized to provide a variety of activities that will
help to meet the needs for growth and development of all children. When
weather and facilities permit, the program should be enjoyed out of doors.
The safety of children in any activity should be emphasized.

Physical Activities for Elementary Schools (Curriculum Bulletin No. 1,
1948–49 Series) contains materials from which the teacher may select
activities to meet the New York State requirement of 150 minutes each
week of physical activities for all classes. The activities are graded to provide continuity and balance. Illustrations from the bulletin (including page
references) giving various types of activities follow:

1. CREATIVE ACTIVITIES

Experiences of children, both in and out of school, provide opportunities
for creative expression through body movements. In the development of a
"story" of these experiences, every opportunity should be given to the chil-

[1] In compliance with State Education Law, Section 804.

dren for contributions which will help them express their individuality. Pages 18–21 present a series of suitable stories; "A Visit to the Seashore," "The Circus," and "Snow Play." The stories may serve as guides to the development of original stories.

2. RHYTHMS

Rhythms are fundamental for acquiring graceful body movements. They are important also as a basis for the dance program in that they offer opportunities for creative expression in response to music. Rhythms may be classified as fundamental, imitative, or interpretive. Pages 22–39 include a variety of these rhythms to fit many needs and interests. For example, skipping is a fundamental rhythm; "high stepping horses" is imitative; and "falling leaves" is interpretive.

3. SONG PLAYS

Song plays include singing games, play-party games, dramatizations of nursery rhymes, and stories set to music. They enrich rhythmic and dramatic impulses, especially for children in kindergarten and the primary grades. Pages 40–77 contain numerous song plays. Illustrations from each category are: "Gay Musician," a singing game; "Paw Paw Patch," a play-party game; "Sing a Song of Sixpence," a nursery rhyme; and "Sleeping Princess," a story set to music.

4. FOLK DANCES

Dancing provides enjoyment and helps to develop muscular coordination and flexibility of movement, it also helps to develop an understanding of, and appreciation for, our American culture and the culture of other peoples. Folk dances are representative of various cultures. A few illustrations are·

United States	*The East*
Prayer for Rain	Feast of Lanterns
Circassian Circle	Tscherkessia
Life on the Ocean Wave	Hora
Europe	*Latin America*
Swedish Schottische	La Cucaracha
Puttjenter	Fado Blanquita
Cumberland Square	Tamborito
Sicilian Tarantella	

5. ORGANIZATION ACTIVITIES

Group activities are valuable in getting large numbers of children to move quickly and safely in response to commands. Devices that may be used include commands and practice in taking floor places, marching, and changing direction. A minimum amount of time should be spent on these activities.

6. SELF-TESTING ACTIVITIES

Self-testing activities are suitable for children of varying ages and abilities. By fostering achievement and success, these activities stimulate children to practice and to develop better skills and techniques. One illustration from each category of activity follows: Animals and Birds, "Bird Hop"; Toys, "The Top"; Nature, "Crossing the Brook"; Jumping and Hopping, "Ankle Grasp Jump"; Miscellaneous, "High Kick"; Activities Using Mattresses, "The Scissors."

7. ATHLETIC ACTIVITIES

Athletic activities provide opportunities for exercise, social contact, mental stimulation, and personal satisfaction. Appropriate dashes, relays, and squad activities are suggested.

8. GAMES

For younger age groups, activities such as running, chasing, and ball games are suggested; for older age groups, lead-up games introductory to baseball, volleyball, and basketball are described.

9. PUBLIC SCHOOL ATHLETIC LEAGUE ACTIVITIES

P.S.A.L. activities provide additional opportunities for children to participate in many recreational activities such as tournaments, field days, athletic tests (park fetes, and intramural games). In addition, boys may participate in approved invitation games.[2]

Evaluation

The growth and progress of children toward the objectives of health education may be evaluated in the following ways.

Study. Analysis of the results of tests concerning health knowledge may reveal growth in basic health information. A study of children's achieve-

[2] For details see New York State Education Law, Article 18, Section 159, Item 14.

ments in the self-testing activities suggested in *Physical Activities for Elementary Schools* (pages 205–209) may reveal children's growth in skill and coordination. A study of records of absence for a period of years due to significant illnesses, and a study of information recorded on the health cards may reflect the effectiveness of the school's health education program. An analysis of accident reports filed over a period of years may measure the value of the safety teaching.

Observation. Observance of the health habits and practices among children, such as covering the mouth and nose when coughing and washing hands before eating, may help to evaluate growth in good health practices. The manner in which children assume responsibility for the health and safety of others may indicate progress in the direction of the desired objectives.

88. *The Promotion Policy Dilemma* *

HAROLD G. SHANE

AMERICANS have faced a good many problems in the past century or two. With a happy mixture of imagination and applied common-sense they have dulled—or removed—the horns of many a dilemma.

In the field of education, as in every phase of American life, there have been problems and dilemmas aplenty. Invariably over the years, vision and the courage to experiment sanely and persistently have helped the teaching profession to create better educational policies and a better school environment for children and youth.

At present, in our elementary schools, there is a long-standing need to act more constructively with regard to the problem of how best to help children progress through the grades. Some applied common-sense and a good-sized dash of imagination are in order if we are to resolve the promotion policy dilemma.

It is ironic that the controversy over what constitutes sound promotion policies smoulders around the question of *means* rather than *ends*. There is practically no disagreement that as one of its *ends* a body of good promotion policies should insure that children leaving the elementary school are literate in a broad sense of the term; that they are intellectually alert, well-informed, equipped with a good set of personal values, and emotionally well-balanced.

Disagreement occurs with regard to whether or not children should be held up to grade standards. Some maintain that if a child hasn't mastered

* From Harold G. Shane, "The Promotion Policy Dilemma," *NEA Journal* (October, 1953), pp. 411–12. Reprinted by permission of the author and the *NEA Journal.*

certain subject matter he must repeat a grade. Others argue that promotion systems based on arbitrary standards of achievement are inconsistent with the fact that each child is unique and that all children in a class cannot, therefore, be expected to progress at a similar rate.

Fortunately, creative imagination is at work in some of our schools, and educationally desirable values are being applied to promotion policies in ways which promise to resolve the question of what can be done to help insure the desired end product of well-educated, well-balanced elementary-school graduates. By such graduates we mean neither children who have lived in an intellectual vacuum "where it didn't matter what they learned as long as they were happy," nor children who have spent six years in grades which harmed personalities by unreasonable or premature pressure for academic achievement.

Last year I had the privilege of studying several dozen good school systems. The paragraphs which follow present, in narrative form, what seems to be an intelligent policy of "continuous progress" in some of these elementary schools. The narrative describes no one school exactly, but is a composite of fresh approaches to the promotion dilemma from several districts in which creative leadership in educational thinking is in action. Let us trace in this composite school what happens to a young lady named Sue.

When she is four, Sue is admitted to kindergarten. Kindergarten isn't a one-year experience; it is an experience of indeterminate length. Perhaps Sue will spend two years in the junior (four-year-old) and senior (five-year-old) groups—most children in her school do.

But if she is one of the youngest fours in the group and immature for her years, she may spend up to three years growing physically, maturing socially, and developing readiness for successful school living when she arrives in grade one.

Bear in mind that the extra year does not mean that our Sue has "flunked kindergarten"! She has merely had one more year in which to become ready for successful achieving.

During the years in kindergarten (let's assume there were but two) Sue's teachers came to know her very well. Each teacher had a mixed group of fours and fives. However, most fours tended to be in the morning group so that they could nap in the afternoon.

Toward the spring of her second year, Sue and her classmates were discussed carefully by the kindergarten directors, the principal, and the school psychologist. Professional judgment and various records suggested that

Sue was ready to move into the ungraded primary years. The next decision was into whose group she would go for the next several years.

Everything pertaining to education involves human personality. Which of the several ungraded primary teachers would be the best for Sue to work with? Each was good, but each was different.

Miss A was a whiz at stimulating children, but she overstimulated some. Miss B was quiet and relaxing—a first-rate person for the tense or immature child. Mrs. C was particularly gifted in the art of challenging the mature and academically inclined child but sometimes a bit impatient with children who learned slowly. It seemedly likely that Sue could progress steadily if she went into Miss A's group.

As in kindergarten, there was no predetermined span of time Sue would work with Miss A. And if it seemed "right"—educationally appropriate, that is—she might spend part of the coming years with either Miss B or Mrs. C. Some children spent two years in the ungraded primary, others spent four. Like most, Sue spent three years therein: two years with Miss A and the last year with Mrs. C.

Work was planned by the teachers and children, and the things they did together varied each year as did the membership of each class. Tom, who entered the ungraded primary a year before Sue did, never "repeated" work, but it took him an additional year to do what Sue did, and they moved along together into the ungraded intermediate years.

During the intermediate period Sue worked with a new teacher, Miss D, who taught children who were nine, ten, and eleven, plus a few who became twelve during the year. The group was similar to a combined fourth-fifth grade; but whether they were the younger or the older members of the group, the children did much of their work together.

They shared in planning social studies activities, wrote and produced assembly programs, and enjoyed the same science projects. The more mature children read the more difficult books, and (in arithmetic, for example) they were likely to be using different materials, of course.

Each child did as much as he could, as his experience and native endowment permitted. Most of them spent two years in the ungraded intermediate classroom. An occasional child moved ahead in one year; a few were with Miss D (or were transferred to Mrs. E, who had a similar age group) for a third year.

At the end of eight years, two of which were spent in kindergarten, Sue finished the sixth grade. Tom went on to the junior high at the same time but had spent an extra year in the process.

At times Sue had been "above grade" on standardized tests, once or twice a bit below. Her sometimes uneven but generally steady progress was similar to that of many of the boys and girls who had entered school with her. Tom had been somewhat more leisurely in his progress toward maturity, but he, too, had moved along continuously.

There was no "flunking," no repeating of a particular grade. Both Sue and Tom moved on to new experiences as the beneficiaries of the best guidance and individualized teaching that a group of professionally minded, sincere teachers could devise.

There may be those who will feel that Sue's story is idealistic rubbish—if they read this far! But the idea of a smooth, continuous transition through the elementary years is no flight of fancy. As circumstances permit, the concept of ungraded primary and intermediate levels—the concept of flexible grouping—might well be introduced into more schools.

Some of the educationally sound principles which support a flexible interpretation of *promotion identified with continuous progress* may serve to clarify why some of our educationally interesting school districts are erasing rigid grade lines. These principles may be considered fundamental to good promotion policies as many educational leaders are beginning to interpret them:

1. The decision as to whether a child is to progress at the same rate as his age mate should be made only after careful study of the child's total development. One slow learner who is socially and physically immature may profit from being shifted to a younger group, while another with an equally indifferent record who is socially and physically mature may very much need to remain with his classmates.
2. Insofar as they can be detected, the *causes* of his difficulties rather than the mere *fact* that he is not faring well in academic work should be the basis for deciding his rate of progress.
3. The academic progress that a child makes in any *one* year is insufficient *in itself* for reaching a decision as to whether he is to spend additional time in the elementary school. The *trend* of a child's growth—intellectually, socially, physically, and emotionally—should be studied over a period of several years.
4. With due consideration for the total development of the child who falls within the broad range of "normal," it is reasonable to expect that he will acquire a significant amount of information and basic skills in elementary school. If he does not progress at a rate which is deemed satisfactory in the staff's professional judgment, he may need to spend more than six years completing the first six grades.

5. If it is necessary for a child to be transferred to a group of younger children, that is, to remain longer at the same level, great care needs to be exercised to insure that he is not merely re-exposed to experiences which meant too little to him before.

These five points are a reflection of the belief that sound promotion practices are closely allied to the school's study of children. Appropriate policies are not arbitrary and related to whether the child "comes up to grade." They consist of applying professional intelligence to the analysis of what is most likely to help the individual child.

89. *What Research Says about Test Anxiety in Elementary-School Children* *

SEYMOUR B. SARASON

WE LIVE in a test-conscious and test-giving culture in which the lives of people are in part determined by their test performance.

In light of this emphasis on tests (in the educational process in particular), it has long surprised me that there are no systematic studies of the attitudes of children toward tests and the effects of their attitudes on test performance.

To the clinical psychologist, who usually operates in the face-to-face, diagnostic testing situation, it is obvious that individuals vary tremendously not only in their reactions to the process of testing but also in the ways in which their reactions affect performance.

In fact, one of the reasons the clinical psychologist is hesitant to report test scores to the nonpsychologist is his awareness that scores can be misleading if interpreted without intimate knowledge of the reactions elicited in the individual by the testing situation.

For the past six years, a research team at Yale has studied the reactions of elementary-school pupils to the testing situation. We have focused on two groups of children: those who react anxiously and those who react nonanxiously to testing and testlike situations.

* From Seymour B. Sarason, "What Research Says about Test Anxiety in Elementary-School Children," *NEA Journal* (November, 1959), pp. 26–27. Reprinted by permission of the author and the *NEA Journal*. A full report on this topic is contained in a book by S. B. Sarason, K. S. Davidson, F. Lighthall, R. Waite, and B. Ruebush, entitled *Anxiety in Elementary School Children: A Report of Research* (New York: John Wiley and Sons, 1960).

To determine these reactions, we used a group-administered series of questions (*A Test Anxiety Scale for Children*). Pupils were asked to circle "yes" or "no" on their answer sheets in answer to questions such as:

When the teacher says she is going to find out how much you have learned, does your heart begin to beat faster?

When the teacher asks you to write on the blackboard in front of the class, do you sometimes feel that the hand you write with shakes a little?

Do you worry a lot *before* you take a test?

Do you worry a lot *while* you are taking a test?

After you have taken a test, do you worry because you think you did not do well?

When the teacher says she is going to give the class a test, do you get a nervous (or funny) feeling?

While you are taking a test, do you usually think you are not doing well?

We have conducted studies with children in grades one through six in several different school systems. It is impossible to present these findings in detail in this article, but here are some of the major ones in abbreviated form:

1. Test anxiety is by no means an infrequent occurrence among elementary-school children. The level of test anxiety tends to increase with grade.

2. The higher the test anxiety, the lower are the scores on conventional group measures of intelligence. This negative correlation between anxiety and intelligence-test score is significantly reduced when the intelligence test employed is more "gamelike" than "testlike."

3. When pairs of children are matched for grade, sex, and IQ, but one of the pair is high-anxious while the other is low-anxious, the problem-solving performance of the high-anxious children tends to be significantly inferior to that of the low-anxious children.

4. Test-anxious children are at the greatest disadvantage when they are not sure what is expected of them and when they are expected to function independently. When the problem-solving situation partially satisfies pupils' needs for direction and dependence, there is little difference in the performance of high- and low-anxious children; in fact, the high-anxious children tend to do better than low-anxious children.

5. The test-anxious child is one who tends to be anxious about many things, has a derogatory self-picture, and has a predominant tendency to blame himself for failure. There are differences in the parent-child relationships between high- and low-anxious children. The mother

of the high-anxious child is one who is much concerned with what is right and wrong and with what other people think of herself and her child. She discourages the expression of aggression in her child and tends to keep the child in a dependent relationship.

6. It has been assumed by many that test anxiety is affected by social class; that is, that as one goes up the social classes there is increasing emphasis on school performance and intellectual achievement, with a corresponding increase in the number of children who experience anxiety about tests. Our findings cast much doubt on such an assumption. Test anxiety seems to occur with equal frequency in different social classes.

7. Sex differences are significant in anxiety. Girls admit to more anxiety than do boys. Despite this, however, the predicted differences between high- and low-anxious children are found more consistently among boys and girls.

Our explanation of this is that in our culture it is far more difficult for a boy to admit to anxiety than for a girl to do so. A girl's admission of anxiety is not viewed by her or others as a derogation of her femininity, whereas such an admission in boys is viewed as a derogation of their masculinity. A boy who admits to anxiety, therefore, is experiencing more disturbance than a girl who makes a similar admission.

An important implication of our findings is that the potentialities of the high-anxious child are not likely to be discerned by conventional testing procedures. This is because the performance of the high-anxious child in such procedures reflects the interfering effects of anxiety.

These effects are perhaps least apparent when one tests the *bright but anxious* child whose absolute level of performance may be more than adequate (for example, his school grades and achievement-test scores may be well above average). When this child is compared to the bright but non-anxious child, we see more clearly the interfering effects of anxiety.

Up to now have testing programs paid enough attention to children's attitudes toward the process of testing? Research provides abundant evidence that performance and behavior in a situation in part depend on attitudes held toward that situation.

When one considers the importance attached to test performance, and the current tendency to use more tests more of the time, our lack of knowledge about children's reactions to test procedures and about the effects of such procedures on children can no longer be tolerated.

It should be stressed that many children do not experience undue anxiety about tests and are not adversely affected by such procedures. There can be little doubt, however, that a large number of children approach the testing situation with a degree of trepidation which interferes with problem-solving efficiency.

Many aspects of test anxiety still need to be studied: the role of the school and family in eliciting and reinforcing test anxiety, the effects of anxiety on motivation for achievement, the relation between anxiety and creative use of knowledge and ability, and the long-range effects of anxiety over academic and vocational choices and on personal adjustment.

In light of our finding that the test-anxious child is one who is anxious in many situations and one who already shows evidence of personality disturbance at the elementary-school level, follow-up studies of such children seem particularly important.

In conclusion, I would like to suggest that educators would do well to re-examine their dependence on tests and their practices with them. Is it not true that the primary use of tests in our schools is to determine what children know and at what level they perform? Is it not also true, however, that how productively a child can utilize what he knows will depend, at least in part, on how he views himself in relation to the learning process?

If this is true, and I hardly think it debatable, one must conclude that testing programs have failed to focus on these reactions which can help illuminate the psychological significances of objective but ambiguous indices of knowledge and performance.

90. The ABC's of Test Contruction *

JULIAN C. STANLEY

CONSTRUCTING a good test is one of the teacher's most difficult duties. Good tests do not just happen. Actual test construction, therefore, requires much thought and careful planning.

Planning the Test

A well-planned test will provide the means for evaluating progress toward the expected outcomes of instruction, as expressed in the educational

* From Julian C. Stanley, "The ABC's of Test Construction," *NEA Journal* (April, 1958), pp. 224–26. Reprinted by permission of the author and the *NEA Journal*.

philosophy of the particular school and as defined in the objectives of the particular course.

If the school hopes to produce "good citizens" with "integrated personalities," for example, tests must measure the development of good social attitudes and a widening range of significant interests.

For any given course, instructional objectives must be expressed in terms of the specific changes in pupil behavior or growth which the teacher hopes to bring about.

A teacher, for instance, should be conscious that such an objective as the development of an appreciation of literature may express itself in various forms of student reaction. He sets out then to phrase test questions which will determine whether a particular piece of writing gave individual students a sense of satisfaction and enthusiasm, made them want to read more by the same author, stimulated their own creative expression.

The well-planned test will reflect the relative amount of emphasis each objective has received in the actual teaching of the course. The same test might not be equally valid for two teachers of general science if one has emphasized the memorizing of isolated facts, while the other was more concerned with the interrelation of facts. Each teacher would be helped by drawing up in outline form a kind of table of specifications to indicate not only the objectives of the course, but also the relative amount of time spent on each.

The content of the test should show a similar proportion in regard to the *number* of items to be included but not the *type,* for the type of item depends upon the nature of the objective to be measured.

The well-planned test must be designed to accomplish the purpose it is to serve. If the purpose is to give the basis for school marks or classification, it will attempt to rank the pupils in order of their total achievement. But if the purpose is diagnosis, its value will depend upon its ability to reveal specific weaknesses in the achievement of individual pupils.

Diagnostic tests would cover a limited scope, but in much greater detail than a test of general achievement, and would be arranged to give scores on the separate parts. The range of difficulty of items is relatively less important, also, in diagnostic tests. This is true, too, of mastery tests administered at the end of a teaching unit to see whether minimum essentials have been achieved.

The well-planned test will also fit the conditions under which it is to be administered, such as the time available for testing, facilities for duplicating the test copies, and cost of materials, as well as the age and experience of the pupils being tested.

Preparing the Test

In actual construction of a test, these suggestions have helped:

1. Prepare a rough draft of the test as soon as possible. Many teachers jot down items day by day for possible inclusion to help ensure that no important points will be omitted, particularly those appearing in supplementary material that might be overlooked if the textbook itself is the chief basis of the test.

2. Do not make the test items too easy. Many teacher-constructed tests fail to make the items difficult enough. This, no doubt, is due in part to the influence of the "70 per cent should be the passing grade" tradition. However, the test that is too easy is not an efficient instrument for measuring pupil progress.

3. Include more items in the first draft than will be needed in the final form. This will permit cutting out of weak items and those not needed to produce proper balance.

4. Subject the test to critical revision some time after it is drafted by checking items against the table of specifications to see if they show the desired emphasis on various topics. If tests are submitted for criticism to other teachers of the subject, points of doubtful importance can be weeded out and ambiguous wording corrected.

5. Include more than one type of item in the test. A variety of test types is more interesting to students. The test situation may also require that three or four forms of objective items be used, or that these be combined with discussion or essay questions.

6. Place all items of one kind together in the test. Sometimes completion, true-false, and multiple-choice questions are thrown together in random order. This arrangement is rarely, if ever, desirable. When like items are grouped, the pupil can take full advantage of the mind-set imposed by a particular form, and the teacher will find scoring and interpretation of scores easier.

7. Arrange test items in an ascending order of difficulty. The placing of very difficult items at the beginning is likely to produce needless discouragement for the average or below-average student.

8. Avoid a regular sequence in the pattern of responses. If items are arranged alternately true and false or two true and two false, pupils are likely to catch on and answer correctly without considering the content of the item at all.

9. Make directions to the pupil clear, concise, and complete. Instructions

should be so clear that the weakest pupil knows what he is expected to do, though he may be unable to do it.

It is better to tell young children to "draw a line under" than to "underline." In lower grades, teachers find it helpful to read instructions aloud while the class follows silently the written instructions. If the form of the test is unfamiliar or complicated, a generous use of samples correctly marked, or practice tests, is recommended.

Regardless of how carefully a test is planned and edited, it is impossible to know solely by inspection exactly how good it is, or which are the weak items. If possible, therefore, the test should be given some advance tryout which will approximate the conditions under which the real test will be given, show the actual length of time it will require, and indicate what scoring difficulties may result.

Because various studies have shown that a majority of teachers, especially at the high school level, use a combination of essay and objective questions, the uses and limitations of both will be briefly examined here.

The Essay Test

The essay test has both unique advantages and serious disadvantages. Some authorities claim that it calls forth less than half the knowledge the average pupil possesses on a subject, compared with results from an objective test, and takes twice the time to do it; that it overrates the importance of knowing how to say a thing and underrates the importance of having something to say; and that the score resulting from an essay test depends more upon *who* reads it and *when* than upon the student who wrote it.

Offsetting the serious scoring difficulties connected with essay tests and their frequently low degrees of validity, reliability, and usability, there is much to indicate that such tests have a legitimate place in the modern school.

Specifically, they are useful for measuring functional information, certain aspects of thinking, study skill and work habits, and an active social philosophy. These are educational objectives which emphasize the *functioning* of knowledge rather than its mere possession.

Such tests are especially valuable in courses in English composition and journalism, where the student's ability to express himself is a major instructional objective, and in advanced courses in other subjects where critical evaluation and the ability to assimilate and organize large amounts of material are important.

Essay tests have at least one other general merit: When pupils expect the test to be of that type, in whole or in part, they seem more likely to employ such desirable study techniques as outlining and summarizing, and to make a greater effort to recognize trends and relationships.

Despite popular opinion to the contrary, a high-quality essay test is more difficult to construct than is a good objective test. These three rules, however, should be helpful in improving the construction and use of essay tests:

1. Restrict such a test to those functions for which it is best adapted.
2. Increase the number of questions asked and decrease the amount of discussion required for each.
3. Make definite provisions for teaching pupils how to take such examinations.

Types of Objective Tests

The simple *recall test* item employs a direct question, a stimulus word or phrase, or a specific direction to elicit from the pupil a response based on his previous experience. The typical response is short—hence its other name, the short-answer question.

The main problem is to phrase these test items so that they will call forth responses from a higher level than mere memory, and so that they can be readily scored.

Example: Eight is what per cent of sixty-four?

The *completion test* consists of a series of sentences in which certain important words or phrases have been replaced by blanks to be filled in by the students. This test has wide applicability, but unless very carefully prepared, it is likely to measure rote memory rather than real understanding, or to measure general intelligence or linguistic aptitude rather than school achievement.

Scoring is also more subjective, and complicated by the fact that the missing words are written in blanks scattered all over the page, rather than in a column. This difficulty can be avoided by a form such as this:

1. The man who headed the first expedition to circumnavigate the globe was —————————.
2. The Articles of Confederation were in force from 1781 to ————.

An *alternative-response test* is made of items each of which permits only two possible responses. The usual form is the familiar true-false item and its cousins, the right-wrong, yes-no, same-opposite, and multiple-choice questions.

While the true-false type of question is popularly considered easy to prepare, experienced test makers point out that this type of test requires great skill, and care must be taken in wording so that the *content* rather than the *form* of the statement will determine the response. The following suggestions may be useful in constructing such tests.

1. Avoid specific determiners, that is, strongly worded statements containing words such as "always," "all," or "none," which may indicate to pupils that the statement is likely to be false.

2. Avoid using the exact language of the textbook, with only minor changes to give the true-false pattern, because this puts too great a premium on rote memory.

3. Avoid trick statements which appear to be true but which are really false because of some inconspicuous word or phrase, such as "The Battle of Hastings was fought in 1066 B.C."

4. Avoid "double-headed" statements, especially if partly true and partly false, as in this sentence: "Poe wrote *The Gold Bug* and *The Scarlet Letter*."

5. Avoid double negatives lest pupils versed in grammar conclude that two negatives equal an affirmative, while others think such statements are emphatic negatives.

6. Avoid unfamiliar, figurative, or literary language and long statements with complex sentence structure—for reasons which should be obvious.

7. Avoid words that may have different meanings for different students. "Often" may mean once a week to one child; three times a year to another.

A *multiple-choice test* is composed of items which require the student to select a correct or definitely better response from two or more alternatives (at least four whenever possible). This is one of the most useful test forms. It may be used to ascertain the ability to give definitions, identify purposes and causes, similarities and differences, or to ask many other varieties of questions.

In phrasing multiple-choice questions, it is essential to avoid giving irrelevant or superficial clues, and to assure that the question measures more than memory. The diagnostic value of this type of item depends as much on the skillful wording of the incorrect choices presented as upon correct statement of the right choice.

Scoring may be facilitated by arranging the items in groups, putting together all items with the same number of choices, and requiring the simplest possible method of recording the response.

Other useful rules are:

1. Make all responses grammatically consistent. For example, if the verb is singular, avoid plural responses.
2. Use direct questions rather than incomplete statements whenever possible. This helps eliminate irrelevant clues.
3. Arrange the responses so that the correct choice occurs about equally in all positions, and do not consistently make the correct answer longer or shorter than the others.
4. Make all the responses plausible, and when testing at higher levels, increase the similarity in the choices under each item in order to test the powers of discrimination better.

A *matching test* involves the association of two things in the mind of the learner by requiring him to pair the items in two columns: events and dates, events and persons, terms and definitions, laws and illustrations, and the like. Matching exercises are well adapted to testing in *who, what, where,* and *when* areas but not to measuring understanding as distinguished from mere memory.

Since most of the tests used in classrooms are teacher-made, it is highly important that teachers develop proficiency in the building of tests by discriminating use of what is now known, by keeping themselves informed on new studies of testing techniques and methods, and by careful evaluation of their own testing, day by day.

91. *Ten Essential Steps in a Testing Program* *

ARTHUR E. TRAXLER

STANDARDIZED tests have been used in our schools for about fifty years. Many schools have long carried on testing programs and are well acquainted with the uses and limitations of these instruments. Other schools have recently introduced tests on a regular basis or are about to do so. It is for these schools that it seems desirable to set down as clearly and

* From Arthur E. Traxler, "Ten Essential Steps in a Testing Program," *Education* (February, 1959), pp. 357–61. Reprinted by permission of the author and The Bobbs-Merrill Co., Inc., Indianapolis, Ind.

definitely as possible the minimum essentials of planning and carrying on a program of objective testing.

The use of tests is increasing rapidly at the present time. According to a survey by the American Textbook Publishers Institute, about 100,000,000 standardized tests were used in the schools and colleges of the United States in 1956. A year later, in 1957, the number had increased to approximately 108,000,000. This is more than two tests for every pupil enrolled in the schools of this country. There is urgent need to do everything possible to make sure that these millions of tests are administered correctly, interpreted wisely, and used effectively.

The first step in a testing program is to ask the question WHAT. What do we want to find out? What do we want to measure?

Generally, it is best to start with measurement in two broad areas—scholastic aptitude, which is sometimes called intelligence, and achievement in basic skills and content fields.

In order to decide what to measure in the field of achievement, a school should study its objectives and its curriculum. These are the clues to what should be measured in any school. Some schools may want to emphasize the measurement of basic skills and knowledge, while others may choose to stress evaluation of general educational development.

Interests, character, and personality are of prime importance too, but, in the beginning, a school will be well advised to concentrate upon scholastic aptitude and achievement. These are the hard core of any testing program. Measures of interests and personality tend to be less dependable, and greater test sophistication is required in the interpretation of their results.

There is another *what* question—what specific test shall be given—but this question comes considerably later.

A second step is to ask the question WHY. Why is the school developing a testing program? For what purpose? For administrative and supervisory uses? To help teachers do a better instructional job? For use in guidance? For admission and placement? For purpose of public relations?

The answer will determine to some extent the nature of the testing program and the kinds of tests given, although it is well to remember that most tests have multiple uses.

Generally speaking, by far the most important purposes of testing are to improve instruction and guidance. Probably at least 90,000,000 of the 108,000,000 tests administered annually in the schools of the United States are given for these purposes.

A third step is to ask the question WHEN. When should the tests be given? At what time of year? This is a more important question than at first it seems to be. It is related to the applicability of test norms and to the uses that are to be made of the test results.

Tests are usually administered in the early fall or in the spring, and most tests are normed for one or both of these periods. Very few tests are accompanied by midyear norms.

Generally, fall testing is to be preferred for scholastic aptitude tests, tests of basic skills, and tests of broad fields, such as general achievement in science. If the tests are given about the second week of the fall term, after the pupils have settled down, and if the scoring is done without delay, the results will be available early enough in the school year for the scores to be used effectively by instructors, counselors, and remedial teachers.

Spring testing is advisable when tests of achievement in specific courses, such as algebra, biology, or world history, are employed. These tests should be given several weeks before the close of the term so that there will be time to score the tests and report the results to the teachers before the school year ends.

A fourth step is to ask the question WHERE. Where in the pupil's school course should tests be given? At what grade levels?

The ideal practice is to give tests of scholastic aptitude and achievement every year and to keep cumulative records of the results. But many schools must, for budgetary reasons, be satisfied with a testing program less than ideal. Where tests in only certain grades are possible, preference should be given to those points where major decisions are made about a pupil's school placement and his educational and vocational plans. These are: at the time of school entrance; in grade three when all pupils should have learned to do independent silent reading; near the end of grade seven or the beginning of grade eight when choice of high school course is being considered; and again near the end of grade eleven or the beginning of grade twelve when decisions about college going and vocational choices are uppermost.

A fifth step is to ask the question HOW. How should the testing program be carried on and the results organized for effective use? How may the most valid tests be selected, administered, and used so as to assure maximum value in scores? This question leads to a series of other steps. The next five steps are all concerned with various aspects of the question *how*.

A sixth step is to choose the tests to be used in each testing program. This is a complicated procedure. There are about twenty test publishers, of which at least seven may be regarded as major publishers with numerous test offerings. More than 5,000 different objective tests have been published, and at least 1,000 of these are on the active lists of the publishers.

How may a school decide which tests are preferable for its needs? This kind of decision ought not to be attempted by one person, such as the principal, or the director of research, or the head counselor. If the school participates in a state-wide or national testing program, its job of selection is somewhat simplified by the fact that a selected list of tests is recommended for use by participating schools. For example, in connection with the annual fall and spring testing programs of the Educational Records Bureau, a committee of representatives of the member schools meets with the Bureau staff twice each year to decide what tests are to be recommended. The Bureau then issues an announcement to member schools listing and describing the tests chosen for use in the next program, together with price lists and order forms. All member schools are free, however, to use as much or as little of the program as they desire, or in fact, to reject all of it and to plan a testing program of their own for which the Bureau will render scoring and reporting services just as it does for the program tests.

Regardless of whether a school participates in an organized testing program or plans its own program, it should have a committee on tests consisting of representatives of all departments of the school. Some one person, presumably the director of testing, should take responsibility for screening the available tests and for bringing the more promising ones before the committee for consideration. Certain reference works will be found useful in screening the tests and in reaching decisions about those which are the most reliable and valid and those which best fit the school's objectives and curriculum.

The choice of tests may depend partly upon the types of norms that are needed for evaluation. In some instances, representative national public-school norms will be desired, while in other cases norms for college-bound pupils will be preferred.

In choosing tests, it should be kept in mind that no one publisher has a clear advantage over another test publisher. For some purposes, the tests of one publisher are preferable, while for a different purpose or in a different field, the tests of another publisher will do the better job. If a school undertakes a thoroughly comprehensive testing program, at least three different test publishers, and perhaps more, are likely to be represented in its test choices.

A seventh step is to make sure that the tests are carefully administered, with meticulous attention to the directions. It is difficult to impress upon some staff members the necessity for faithful adherence to the manual of directions; yet, it is imperative that this be done, for the results of poorly administered tests may not only be useless, they may be a menace.

Staff members who are to cooperate in the administration of the tests should be carefully chosen and thoroughly briefed in advance. They should have an opportunity to practice by taking the tests themselves and to go through a "dry run" in giving them. This means that it is necessary to let the teachers who are to serve as examiners have copies of the tests in advance. This in itself involves a certain hazard in instances where teachers are to administer achievement tests to their own pupils. The temptation to give the pupils a bit of coaching on the test items may be considerable, particularly where teachers feel insecure over the outcome. A safeguard against this tendency is obtained when the administration of the school adopts a policy of using tests for purposes other than evaluation of teachers and consistently adheres to it.

What to do about absentees is a troublesome question in connection with test administration. This is especially true when tests are administered to younger children, particularly in the spring when respiratory illnesses may be prevalent. It is imperative that absentees be required to take the tests, and this should be done as soon as possible after they return to school. This is a necessary procedure, even though it is very time-consuming, for otherwise there will be numerous gaps in the cumulative tests information about many of the pupils.

An eighth step is to provide for rapid and accurate scoring of the tests and statistical treatment of the results. The scoring process should not be turned over to individual teachers without supervision. Many good teachers make poor scorers; in fact, an imaginative and creative teacher may, for that very reason, be ineffective in routine clerical work, such as the scoring of objective tests.

Ideally, teachers should not be required to score standardized tests at all. School administrators sometimes say that teachers can learn a great deal about their pupils by scoring their objective tests. This is a pleasant fiction which has little factual basis. Efficient objective scoring is a rapid clerical task in which the scorer simply compares answers with a key. It is incompatible with analysis of the strengths and weaknesses of the individual whose paper is being scored. Of course, a teacher may stop intermittently during the scoring procedure and study the student's paper, but this is diagnosis, and it should not be intermingled with scoring to the detriment of both processes.

However, if teachers are required to do the scoring in spite of the limitations involved, the scoring work should be carefully organized, with the teachers working as a team. The teachers who have had the more scoring experience should check the work of the others for errors. A number of the teachers should not score papers but should be trained to prepare distributions of the scores of class groups and to compute medians and quartiles (or means and standard deviations) and percentiles.

Local scoring can be carried on more effectively and at less actual cost by a specially trained clerical staff, and this procedure has the advantage of freeing teacher time for more creative activities.

Numerous schools have found that the most effective and economical plan of all is to use the services of an outside organization whose special function is test scoring. Among the agencies that specialize in the scoring and reporting of test results to schools in organized fashion are the Measurement Research Center at the State University of Iowa, Testscor in Minneapolis, the central offices of the various state testing programs, and the Educational Records Bureau in New York City.

A ninth step is to organize the test results for use by teachers, counselors, principals, and other school functionaries who have access to the scores. For use as quickly as possible after the testing program, the results should be arranged in distributions, with medians and quartiles or means and standard deviations, shown at the bottom of the sheets, and on class lists where the pupils are listed alphabetically and the scores and corresponding percentile ratings are given. As soon as time can be found for the clerical work involved, the scores should be transferred to individual cumulative record cards which show the pupil's growth from year to year in measured aptitude and achievements, as well as in classwork, personal qualities, extra-class activities, work experience, plans for the future, and other aspects. Organizations such as the American Council on Education and the Educational Records Bureau publish cumulative record cards which may be used either in their entirety or as samples from which ideas may be drawn for the preparation of the school's own cumulative record form.

The tenth step in a testing program is to inform and train the faculty in the nature and purposes of tests and testing and the use of test results. This step is mentioned last, but it should be started as soon as a school begins planning for a testing program, and it should be carried on continuously. Without teacher understanding of tests, little can be accomplished even with the best tests ever devised. But with teacher understanding and acceptance of tests and competence in the use of test results, the education and guidance of all pupils may be greatly improved, notwithstanding the lack of complete reliability and validity which is characteristic of all tests.

Some of the main ways of educating the faculty in the fundamentals of testing are (1) to have the testing program undertaken by the school explained fully and frankly by the school head; (2) to invite a test specialist who is not too technical to speak to the faculty and answer their questions;

(3) to carry on a series of "workshop" meetings centered around examination of specific tests and study of the practical problems of testing; (4) to send faculty members who are to have main responsibility for the testing program to do summer study in measurement and statistics; (5) to carry on case conferences with faculty members about individual students and to use test scores as one of the main kinds of data about the individual; and (6) to make available and to use as bases of discussion books and articles written especially to help schools do a better measurement job.

92. *The Parent-Teacher Conference Can Be an Effective Means of Reporting* *

LOUIS ROMANO

THE PARENT-TEACHER CONFERENCE is becoming more and more an important part of school reporting procedures. How are these conferences arranged? How many are needed a year? Where does the teacher find time for conferences? How can parents who live far from school be reached?

To answer these and other questions about this important type of reporting, the *Journal* asked teachers and supervisors in four different school systems to tell about their parent-teacher conference programs. Here are their stories:

An Established Program

For the past thirty-five years the Shorewood (Wisconsin) Schools have enjoyed the benefits of parent-teacher conferences. In the elementary schools, two conferences are held with the parents of each child yearly; in the secondary school, one conference is scheduled, although additional meetings are often held.

Conferences are considered an integral part of the school program, not just another appendage to the already full school day. On eighteen days each year, elementary children are excused from school at half past two so

* From Louis Romano, "The Parent-Teacher Conference Can Be an Effective Means of Reporting," *NEA Journal* (December, 1959), pp. 21–22. Reprinted by permission of the author and the *NEA Journal*.

that the staff can hold conferences with parents. At the secondary level, ten such conference days are planned for teachers and parents.

Pupils, as well as parents and teachers, often participate in these conferences. They are included at the elementary level when the teacher sees a need for this, and in the junior and senior high schools they are regularly present during all conferences.

The conference is not intended merely as a session of reporting or lecturing by the teachers; it is an attempt to discuss the concerns of each participant and to plan mutually for improvement of the individual child. A majority of the secondary conferences are held in the evenings so that the fathers may participate.

Our teachers have found that planning before conferences helps to ensure effective results. This preparation includes:

Assembling a file of pertinent samples of the pupil's work

Reviewing the anecdotal record of significant observations

Reviewing data in the pupil's cumulative folder

Evaluating recent test results in light of the pupil's performance

Contacting other teachers for their observations of the pupil

Considering the value of interviewing the pupil before the conference if he is not to be present

Parents too have a responsibility to plan prior to attending the conference. A group of parents who studied our reporting system designed a *Parent Conference Guide,* which explains the purposes of the conferences. It also urges parents to discuss children's growth and development in advance of the conference, and to prepare a list of observations or questions concerning their children. The guide includes space for writing down this list as well as for recording the plans mutually formed at the conference to help children's development and achievement.

The guide is a timesaver. Not only is discussion planned ahead of time, but questions and comments written in the guide by parents help focus the conference on important concerns. The guide serves an additional purpose if only one parent can attend the conference: The parent who does take part can later refer to notes made in the guide during the conference and thus be in a better position to discuss the meeting with the spouse who could not attend.

Although the parent-teacher conference is excellent in its purpose and potential, it can do more harm than good unless it is handled skillfully by the classroom teacher. These simple guidelines have helped teachers in our school to conduct conferences:

1. Establish a friendly atmosphere free from interruptions.

2. Be positive—begin and end the conference by enumerating favorable points.
3. Be truthful, yet tactful.
4. Be constructive in all suggestions to pupils and parents.
5. Help parents to achieve better understanding of their child as an individual.
6. Respect parents' and children's information as confidential.
7. Remain poised throughout the conference.
8. Be a good listener; let parents talk.
9. Observe professional ethics at all times.
10. Help parents find their own solutions to a problem.
11. Keep vocabulary simple; explain new terminology.
12. If you take notes during the conference, review them with parents.
13. Invite parents to visit and participate in school functions.
14. Base your judgments on all available facts and on actual situations.
15. Offer more than one possible solution to a problem.

93. *Grading, Marking, and Reporting in the Modern Elementary School* *

JOHN A. JONES

SOME OF THE TERMS in this title have such widely varying meanings as to make definition desirable. The term *grading,* as here used, refers to grade placement to indicate the level of attainment in the educational ladder. *Marking* refers to the symbols used to indicate the quality or degree of achievement on a particular test or for a definite period of time. *Reporting* is limited in meaning to the systematic method or procedure used to inform parents as to the progress their children are making toward the attainment of the objectives of the school. *Modern elementary school* is used to characterize the present-day elementary school that places emphasis upon the social, emotional, and physical development of the child as well as upon his intellectual development. It is a school which bases its program of instruction upon the widely varying interests, purposes, and needs of the children

* From John A. Jones, "Grading, Marking, and Reporting in the Modern Elementary School," *The Educational Forum* (November, 1954), pp. 45–54. Reprinted by permission of the author and the publisher.

who attend it. It is one that attempts to provide an environment in which each child may live as efficiently as possible as a member of the groups with which he is associated and at the same time acquires those abilities, skills, understandings, attitudes, and appreciations which will enable him to continue to function as a good member of a democratic group. It stands in contrast with the traditional school in which the task of the teacher was academic instruction and that of the pupil, memorizing and reciting.

Grading, marking, and reporting are administrative measures invented and developed as instruments to aid in bringing about the desired education of children in our schools. They are interrelated problems with which American educators have been struggling for a century or more. Vast amounts of time and energy have been expended in efforts to deal with them successfully; yet they are still among the most troublesome problems with which teachers have to deal today. The frequency with which they appear as items in educational literature and on the agenda of faculty meetings, and educational conventions, and conferences, is ample proof of this statement, if any proof were needed. Most of the time and energy has been spent in trying to find better ways of using them, but some of it has been devoted to efforts to eliminate them. An examination of some of the problems involved may help us to understand the reason why these efforts have not been successful.

Perhaps the chief reason lies in the nature of the objectives of education and of the teaching and learning processes. Many of the objectives of education can be attained more economically through group instruction than through individual instruction; some of the most important ones, those pertaining to social and emotional development, cannot be attained otherwise. Children learn to cooperate, to be good leaders or good followers, to respect the rights of others, to be good losers as well as good winners by living as members of groups.

Group instruction is a fundamental feature of our educational system, and grading, or the graded school, is one of its products. Marking and reporting are products of the graded school. When pupils are classified according to grades, the term *grade* implying level of attainment, it becomes necessary that teachers give attention to the progress that each child is making and to make some kind of record of his progress. Marks of various kinds are resorted to as a means of doing this. Along with progress in attainment, with its accompanying features of promotion and failure, comes an increased interest on the part of the parents in knowing what progress their children are making. Report cards and reporting then become one of the fundamental features of each school.

These interrelationships of grading, marking, and reporting with group instruction make it difficult, if not impossible, to eliminate them without eliminating group instruction. It seems that herein lies the reason why efforts to eliminate grading, marking, and reporting as we have had them for approximately a century have not yet been successful.

However, each of the three, grading, marking, and reporting, has about it certain basic features that make it difficult to use satisfactorily, even though these interrelationships did not exist. An examination of some of these features will help to show why our efforts to use them have not been satisfactory.

What Are Some of the Problems Basic to Grading?

Grading carries with it the idea of progression from grade to grade and in this we have the problem of promotion and failure—one with which we have been struggling since grades were invented. Much time and energy have been expended by each generation of teachers in studying it. Policies have been established only to be modified or abolished because theories upon which they were established have been proved impractical or false. Use of the so-called normal or probability curve has been, and doubtless still is, frequently applied to elementary-school classes to determine the distribution of marks and eventually the number of promotions and nonpromotions or failures. The fallacy of such a procedure is too well known to require further comment. Studies by Caswell, Cook, Otto, and others show that the reasons once given to justify a high percentage of nonpromotions, such as maintaining high standards of achievement, have been proved to be unsound; and this has led to a new policy, often referred to as "one-hundred-per-cent promotions." With this policy the term *grade* implies a year in school and not a level of attainment.

Perhaps the greatest reason why the use of grades as an administrative device in our educational program has been and continues to be difficult to use satisfactorily lies in the fact that children differ. They differ so greatly and in so many ways as to make the term *grade,* as it is used to refer to levels of attainment in school, a misnomer. It is common knowledge that when the best available measuring device, the standardized test, is applied to any grade the results show great variation in levels of attainment. A standardized test in arithmetic given to a fifth grade class selected at random will usually show that there are pupils in that class who rate third grade or even second grade and others who rate seventh grade or higher. Since such results are almost always obtained regardless of the grade or subject, is it not logical to conclude that the term *grade* does not indicate level of attainment, or that we as teachers have not yet learned to measure the product of our instruction? There is, of course, some justification for either conclusion, but the weight of evidence seems to favor the former. The term *grade* is meaningless when used in the sense of indicating the amount of progress a group or an individual has made in school. A fifth grade is not a fifth grade. It is more probably a group of pupils ranging in achievement in the various school subjects from the third grade to the seventh grade or higher, the variations being due as much to differences in traits within each individual as to differences among the individuals of the group. Since individuals differ by reason of widely varying heredity and environment, factors over which teachers have little or no control, the term *grade,* or level in the school system, can never be made to indicate with any degree of accuracy the level of educational attainment of any group of children or even any individual child.

Let us now examine the extent to which the conclusion is justified that teachers have not yet learned to measure adequately the results of instruction. This conclusion seems especially valid in the field of activities that distinguishes the modern elementary school from the traditional one. We have not yet developed any instrument or method for measuring adequately the results of our efforts to aid our pupils in developing desirable attitudes, ideals, appreciations, and other such personality factors which educators today believe to be a vital part of the education. Until such time as we learn to measure the progress pupils are making toward the attainment of the objectives of our educational programs, the term *grade* will continue to be a troublesome factor in our educational machinery.

Our inability to measure accurately or adequately the progress which our pupils make toward the attainment of our educational objectives combined with the fact that groups of children always vary greatly in their levels of attainment serves to make the term *grade* meaningless and creates administrative problems. These problems are perpetuated because group instruction is essential to our educational program, and for this some sort of grading seems essential.

What Are Some of the Problems Basic to Marking?

The problems involved in marking are so closely related to those in grading and reporting that it is impossible to separate them. Reference has been made to the point that we have not yet learned to measure adequately the product, or results, of our teaching. Further illustration of this point will help to show why we find it so difficult to deal satisfactorily with marks. We are all familiar with the study reported by Starch and Elliot in which 116 mathematics teachers were asked to assign marks to a geometry paper, and the marks ranged from 28 per cent to 92 per cent with not more than six teachers assigning the same mark. Later studies have yielded similar results, and our own experiences tell us that such results are not unusual. They are the rule rather than the exception. It may be argued that this is evidence that we do not know how to evaluate the results of our testing and not of our teaching. However, the results are the same. The marks assigned by one teacher do not have the same meaning for the child, his parents, another teacher, or anyone else that they had for the person who assigned them. Further, there is good reason to believe that the teacher who assigned the marks, if given the same evidence at a different time under different circumstances, would assign different ones. Wrinkle refers to this failure to convey accurately or adequately the meaning intended as being the Number 1 fallacy in the use of the single A-B-C-D-F mark. He also presents evidence to show that certain other opinions commonly held concerning such marks are fallacious.

The fact is, a mark of any kind, whether it be a number or a letter, is only a symbol, and the degree to which the reader of the symbol gets the meaning intended by the writer is determined by the extent to which the two individuals are exactly alike, especially as to experiential background. Casual reflection upon the improbables involved is sufficient to indicate clearly why our traditional marking systems are unsatisfactory.

What Are Some of the Problems Basic to Written Reports to Parents?

Perhaps the greatest problem teachers have to face in attempting to report to parents in the modern elementary school results from the fact that the teacher is concerned with the total growth of the child and not only the amount of information he has acquired. The symbols (per cents) that we first used as well as those which replaced them (letters) were developed when the teacher's primary concern was to indicate to the parent the progress the child was making in his efforts to acquire information, to read, to write, and to use numbers. She felt little or no responsibility for giving the parent information concerning the social and emotional growth of the child.

Broadening of the goals of education, as the modern elementary school does, has brought with it a host of new problems in grading, marking, and reporting. Among the more important questions raised are these: Should the progress which a child has made in his social and emotional development be given consideration in determining his grade placement? Should parents be informed as to the progress the child is making in the broader aspect of education as well as in the more limited aspects, such as in reading and arithmetic?

Teachers in the modern elementary school answered these questions affirmatively, and so complicated the problem of marking and reporting. Marks are given to indicate progress, or attainment, which in turn indicates that some measurement has been made. Valid and reliable measurement has not been achieved and, for many teachers, has not been attempted. This condition alone precludes effective marking or satisfactory reporting. However, since a modern elementary school is much concerned with attainment in the traditional school subjects, and since, as previously stated, we have not yet learned to make accurate measurements of attainment in them, the problem of satisfactory reporting is more difficult than the newer objectives make it.

We have examined some of the basic problems connected with grading, marking, and reporting. Let us now review the steps that have been taken and are now being taken to solve them.

What Progress Have We Made in Our Efforts to Solve the Problem of Grading?

The trend toward one-hundred-per-cent promotions is only one of the several steps that have been taken to solve the problem of grading. The main advantages claimed for a policy of no failures is that children are kept with their own age groups, thus avoiding the social problem created by overageness or, in the case of double promotions, underageness; and the harm done by "branding" a child as a failure is eliminated. While there is much truth in both of these contentions, there is also some room for doubt. Having a child remain with his age group does not always prevent social problems, as children vary in the rate at which they develop. Girls usually develop faster than boys and enter the adolescent stage about two years younger. Also, the experiences of the writer in trying out the theory, indicate that behavior problems still arise. As a pupil who is able to make little or no progress academically is permitted to advance from grade to grade, he may become aware of his lack of attainment and be very unhappy about it. Unless the teacher is unusually understanding and resourceful his unhappiness may lead to undesirable behavior. Perhaps the theory of one-hundred-per-cent promotion cannot and should not be rigidly followed. Exceptions should be made whenever and wherever the welfare of the pupil indicates they should be. This is getting close to the original idea that pupils should be retained when the evidence indicates that they cannot do the work of the next grade; that is, they will do better work by repeating a grade, which theory has been proved largely unsound.

Our inability to solve the problems inherent in any kind of system of grading has led to procedures for supplementing the systems that we have.

The two procedures which have been most widely used are homogeneous grouping and ability grouping. Homogeneous grouping came in the wake of intelligence testing, but efforts to form homogeneous groups soon disclosed the fact that all that was achieved was some reduction in heterogeneity below that which was achieved when some pupils were placed in an elementary school and others in a high school, and again when in each school each pupil was placed in a particular grade. However, homogeneous grouping could not even be attempted in large numbers of schools, because the number of pupils enrolled in each grade was not sufficiently large to divide the grade into classes. The result has been that a shift to ability grouping has been made.

This is another controversial subject in education. There is no definite or widespread agreement as to what the term means or as to its relative advantages and disadvantages. It seems that some "ability" groups have been formed on the basis of less heterogeneity as determined by intelligence tests, while others have been formed on the basis of ability to achieve in a single subject. In either case such groups must have varied so greatly in other respects as still to leave the teacher with a great task of providing for individual differences and needs.

A recognition of the fact that grouping according to any specific ability, which reduces heterogeneity for that ability, may not reduce at all the heterogeneity of the group with reference to other abilities has led to the most recent development in grouping, flexible or temporary grouping within the class. With this procedure the personnel of the various groups are different for different kinds of work and may change from day to day. It is a compromise between common instruction for the whole group and individualized instruction. Space does not permit discussion of its relative values or the prevalence of its use, but it seems to lack some of the weaknesses of homogeneous grouping or ability grouping. It is a procedure that has perhaps not had sufficient trial to provide a true measure of its worth.

One other aspect of the problem of grading deserves consideration. Many elementary schools have established what Caswell calls a "primary-unit plan." The idea behind this procedure is to eliminate formal progress measures during that period of time. While there is some variation in the way the plan is set up and operated in different schools, it usually results in a flexible type of grouping to meet individual needs better and eliminates the usual practice of promotion and nonpromotion. School systems which have tried the plan vary in their estimates of its worth, but the weight of evidence seems to favor it. The flexible curriculum which it makes possible appears to be one of its most desirable features. It may be that this step in the primary grades will lead us to a more satisfactory method of dealing with the problem of grading at all levels of the elementary school.

What Progress Have We Made in Our Efforts to Solve the Problem of Marking?

When Starch and Elliot made their famous report in 1912 on the unreliability of teachers' marks, they started a movement in marking to which Wrinkle has referred as "manipulating the symbols." The change from the 100-point system to the five-point letter system was followed by numerous other such manipulations, the ultimate in simplification being the S (satisfactory) and U (unsatisfactory).

Practices of this kind have been so numerous and varied as to include almost all the letters of the alphabet, yet none appears to have been satisfactory. However, there are other reasons why our traditional approach to the problem of marking has not met the need. These are related to our changing philosophy of education.

The force which brought to our attention the inadequacies of our traditional marking practices was the same as that which brought into being the modern elementary school. It was a realization that education is something more than acquiring information. When we brought into the realm of our educational objectives the social and emotional aspects of a child's development, we came face to face with a need for a change in marking practices. This called for more than a manipulation of symbols. It required that we identify the various factors that indicate social and emotional growth and evaluate the progress which pupils were making toward the attainment of these objectives as well as those of the traditional subjects.

Visible results of our first efforts to deal with this problem appear in the form of traditional symbols or marks assigned to such terms as "conduct" or "deportment." This has in it the same weakness as does the assigning of a mark to a term so broad or general as "social studies" or "arithmetic." Such marks do little to fulfill either of the major functions of marks, which

Ross lists as "administrative" and "instructional." A realization of this weakness resulted in efforts to separate the major items of both the newer and the older objectives into their lesser components. Instead of trying to evaluate the pupil's achievement in arithmetic and assigning a single mark for that subject, teachers began to think about some of the specific abilities and skills in arithmetic, such as, "knows number combinations," "solves problems suited to his grade level," "shows skill in the fundamental processes," and "works accurately." The child's personal development was thought of in terms of behavior or his way of working and playing in such ways as the following: "works to his ability," "follows directions carefully," "is courteous in manner and speech," "respects the rights and property of others," "shows good sportsmanship," and "tries to keep himself neat and clean."

Another factor which entered into the thinking of teachers which increased still further the problem of marking, as well as reporting, was that of deciding the base upon which the system of marking was to rest. Was it upon prescribed standards for each grade and the mark assigned used as indication of the progress which the child had made toward the attainment of these standards? Or, was the mark assigned to be indicative of the child's achievement in relation to his ability? Some schools favored the former, some the latter; some both.

No great amount of insight is necessary to see how complex the problem of marking had become. The number of items for consideration in the assigning of marks became almost limitless. As the number increased, overlappings in meanings increased, creating confusion in the thinking of the one who was assigning the marks and the one who was trying to interpret them. It became evident that marks could fail to fulfill their functions by having too many as well as too few. Efforts then were centered upon the problem of trying to determine the most appropriate number of items to use and what these items should be. That is where we stand today. We are, of course, aware that what may be appropriate for one school may not be for another. For that reason the quest for an answer to the problem continues at a fast tempo and in a multitude of places, which is as it should be.

What Progress Have We Made in Our Efforts to Solve the Problem of Reporting to Parents?

Since one of the functions of marks is to indicate achievement, or progress toward the attainment of the objectives of education, and since that was the purpose of the traditional report to parents, the problems of the two are somewhat the same. However, reporting to parents presents some problems over and above those connected with marking. Parents do not interpret the marks in the same way that the teachers who assign them do. They have never done so, but the difference in interpretation has become far greater since so many new factors have been put into the report that were not there when it contained but few marks. Parents, and teachers, too, have become more conscious of the differences. Differences have always existed, but we were not so conscious of them until we began trying to improve our marking and reporting systems.

Efforts to improve reports to parents have brought us face to face with an entirely new problem, a very important and difficult one. The traditional report card was used so long and our parents were so well educated or indoctrinated in its use that they have resisted our efforts to change it. Thus we have been faced with the problem of educating, or re-educating, parents in the use of a new type of report or system. When five letters or symbols have been reduced to two, many parents have been puzzled, disturbed, even resentful, even though special efforts have been made to explain why the change was made and how the new marks were to be interpreted.

Manipulating the symbols has not by any means created the problems that changing the base for the symbols or greatly increasing the number of items created. As teachers attempted to change the base from "attainment in proportion to set standards" to "attainment in proportion to the ability of the individual to attain," a great majority of the parents became puzzled and many of them dissatisfied. A parent who was accustomed to looking at B on a report card and thinking "my child is above the average of the class in his efforts to attain the objectives of the class" felt that he had evidence that was very definite in meaning. That he was almost always in error in his interpretation made no difference, since he was not aware of the error. Usually he was satisfied because the mark was a B, even though the child had not done as well as he was capable of doing. When such a parent was confronted with a B which mean that, in the teacher's judgment, the child was a little better than the average in attainment, in proportion to his ability to attain, he was a most unusual parent if he did not feel that he had not been told enough. Having been educated in a system of grades, with promotions and failures at regular intervals, it was only natural that he wanted evidence that would tell him whether or not his child was passing or failing. What he saw did not do that, and he was not satisfied. The problem involved is much greater than that of marks and reporting. It is nothing less than a whole philosophy of education, which is not always easy to explain to a puzzled parent.

Reference has been made to the problem created by increasing the number of items to be marked. Further analysis is in order, since it carries over into the field of reporting. As teachers and administrators sought to increase the number of items to cover all aspects of a child's education in their report in a more detailed and meaningful report, they soon came to have so many items in the reports for each of the thirty or forty pupils to make the task burdensome. Many teachers in trying to use such reports became discouraged and soon ceased to fill them out carefully. The more conscientious, who sought diligently to fill them out correctly, discovered that the number of items was so large as to cause them to become rather mechanical— follow a pattern in their markings. A report prepared according to either of these patterns did not do what it was intended to do. Parents were not given the evidence which the markers of the report wanted them to have. The evidence that was presented confronted the parents with such a multitude of details that many were as puzzled and dissatisfied as they had been with the change of base for the marks. Others were not satisfied because of the time factor in giving attention to so many details. This dissatisfaction among both teachers and parents resulted in a reduction of the number of items.

Another means which has been developed for dealing with the problem of having too many items and marks has been the arrangement of the items on the report so that only those of concern to the particular child for whom the report is being made need be checked. This may greatly reduce the number of marks which the teacher has to make and the parent to observe. The weakness of such a report is that it invites the teacher to keep the number to a minimum and she too often does not use enough marks.

The discussion of marks has, thus far, dealt with the developments in connection with reports that use symbols. Since symbols have the inherent weakness of not being interpreted in the same way by any two people, many schools and school systems have resorted to other means of reporting, either to supplement or to replace the report which uses symbols. The two procedures most commonly used are informal letters and parent-teacher conferences. Both of these appear to be used more to supplement than to replace.

The use of the informal letter has certain advantages over the formal report, but it has the disadvantage of being very time-consuming. Unless the teacher writes the letter at regular intervals as the need arises, she is likely to find herself following a rather stereotyped set of statements which are relatively meaningless. If the teacher uses such letters as a means of supplementing the formal report she is likely to avoid this danger, because she will write them about the specific problem of some particular child. What she writes will probably be more meaningful to the parent than the symbols she made on the formal report. However, as McKee points out, words are only symbols, and often do not mean the same to the reader as they did to the writer. For that reason parent-teacher conferences constitute the most satisfactory type of report. Lack of proper understanding can usually be detected and rectified. But parent-teacher conferences are the most time-consuming and most difficult to provide of all the reporting devices or measures. They are so important, however, that some school systems are providing substitute teachers to relieve regular teachers, in order that they may have conferences with their parents under as favorable circumstances as possible. The extra money spent for such purposes appears to be a good investment. The trend is toward more such plans.

It seems appropriate to close this discussion with a quotation from Wrinkle's book, *Improving Marking and Reporting Practices*. He presents a summary of the work which he and his colleagues have done over a period of about twenty years in attempting to develop a more effective system. He says:

> In Chapter One, I said, "You shouldn't expect to turn back to the last chapter of this book and find the perfect report form. It won't be there. I have never seen one and I am sure you haven't. I doubt if there is one. What might be good in one school might not be good in another. Each school has to work out its own forms and practices on the basis of its own objectives, its own philosophy, and its own staff."

What Wrinkle said about reporting may also be said about grading and marking. We have not yet found a perfect plan for either, and may never find it, but we can always have the stimulation, pleasure, and profit of trying. As the poet has said:

> Ah, But a man's reach should exceed his grasp
> Or what's a heaven for?

94. On Telling Parents about Test Results *

JAMES H. RICKS, JR.

LIKE ANY OTHER ORGANIZATION dealing with people, a school has many confidences to keep. School administrators, teachers, and especially guidance workers inevitably come to know items of private information. A gossip who carelessly passes such information around abuses his position and his relationship with his students. It is both right and important that some kinds of information be kept in confidence.

What about test results? Do they belong in the category of secrets, to be seen only by professional eyes and mentioned only in whispers? Or is their proper function best served when they become common knowledge in the school and its community? (In some towns, names and scores have been listed in the local newspaper, much like the results of an athletic contest.)

We think neither extreme is a good rule. Sometimes there is reason to make group data—figures such as the average and the range from high to low—generally public. Seldom should individual results be published except for the happy announcement of a prize won, a scholarship awarded, and the like. But short of general publication, school guidance workers face a particularly important question: Should parents be told their children's test results?

Hard questions, often, are hard because they deal with genuinely complicated problems. Simple "solutions" to such questions are likely to be a trap rather than an aid if their effect is to divert our attention from the difficulties we truly face. Simple rules or principles, on the other hand, can be of real help as one tackles complex problems and situations. This article will present some rules that we have found useful in facing questions such as—

"What should I say when a mother wants to know her son's IQ?" "Should we send aptitude test profiles home with the children?" "We feel that parents in our school ought to know the results of the achievement tests we give, but then it's hard to explain the discrepancies between these and the teachers' grades."

No single procedure, obviously, can be appropriate for every kind of test. Nor for every kind of parent. To Mr. Jones, a well-adjusted and well-educated father, a report of his daughter's test scores may enhance his under-

* From James H. Ricks, Jr., "On Telling Parents about Test Results," *Test Service Bulletin,* No. 54 (December, 1959), pp. 1–4. Reprinted by permission of The Psychological Corporation.

standing of her capacities and of what the school has been giving her. To Mr. Green, a somewhat insecure and less knowledgeable man, the identical information may spark an explosion damaging to both child and school. And the counselor or teacher often has no sure way of knowing which kind of person he will be reporting to.

Two principles and one verbal technique seem to us to provide a sound basis for communicating the information obtained from testing. The two "commandments" are absolutely interdependent—without the second the first is empty, and without the first the second is pointless.

The first: *Parents have the right to know whatever the school knows about the abilities, the performance, and the problems of their children.*

The second: *The school has the obligation to see that it communicates understandable and usable knowledge.* Whether by written report or by individual conference, the school must make sure it is giving *real* information—not just the illusion of information that bare numbers or canned interpretations often afford. And the information must be in terms that parents can absorb and use.

Few educators will dispute the first principle. It is in parents that the final responsibility for the upbringing and education of the children must lie. This responsibility requires access to all available information bearing on educational and vocational decisions to be made for and by the child. The school is the agent to which parents have delegated part of the educational process—but the responsibility has been delegated, not abdicated. Thoughtful parents do not take these responsibilities and rights lightly.

The parents' right to know, then, we regard as indisputable. But, to know what?

Suppose that, as a result of judicious testings, the school knows that Sally has mastered social studies and general science better than many in her ninth grade class, but that few do as poorly as she in math. In English usage she stands about in the middle, but her reading level is barely up to the lower border of the students who successfully complete college preparatory work in her high school. The best prediction that can be made of her probable scores on the College Boards three years hence is that they will fall in the range which makes her eligible for the two-year community college, but not for the university. She grasps mechanical concepts better than most boys, far better than most girls. Looking over the test results and her records, her experienced teacher recognizes that good habits and neatness of work have earned Sally grades somewhat better than would be expected from her test scores.

All of these are things Sally's parents should know. Will they know them if they are given the numbers—Sally's IQ score, percentiles for two reading scores, percentiles on another set of norms for several aptitude tests, and grade-placement figures on an achievement battery? [1]

Telling someone something he does not understand does not increase his knowledge (at least not his correct and usable knowledge—we are reminded of the guide's observation about the tenderfoot, "It ain't so much what he don't know, it's what he knows that ain't so that gits him in trouble"). Transmitting genuine knowledge requires attention to content, language, and audience. We have already referred to some of the characteristics of parents as an audience. Let's look at the other two elements.

Content means that to begin with *we* must ourselves know what we are trying to get across.

We need to know just what evidence there is to show that the test results deserve any consideration at all. We need equally to know the margins and probabilities of error in predictions based on tests. If we don't know *both* what the scores mean *and* how much confidence may properly be placed in them, we are in trouble at the start—neither our own use of the information nor our transmission of it to others will be very good.

Content—what we are going to say—and *language*—how we are going to put it—are inseparable when we undertake to tell somebody something. In giving information about test results, we need to think about the general content and language we shall use and also about the specific terms we shall use.

To illustrate the general content-and-language planning: a guidance director may decide that he wants first to get across a sense of both the values and the weaknesses of test scores. One excellent device for his purpose would be an expectancy table or chart. Such a chart can make it clear to persons without training in statistics that test results are useful predictors *and* that the predictions will not always be precise. Local studies in one's own school or community are of greatest interest. But the guidance director who lacks local data may still find illustrative tables from other places helpful in preparing parents and students to use test results in a sensible way.

Specific terms used in expressing test results vary considerably in the problems they pose. Consider, for example, the different kinds of numbers in which test results may be reported.

IQ's are regarded as numbers that should rarely if ever be reported as such to students or to their parents. The reason is that an IQ is likely to be

---

[1] The implied "No" answer to this question does not, of course, refer to those few parents trained in psychometrics—perhaps even to a point beyond the training of the school staff. Parents include all kinds of people.

seen as a fixed characteristic of the person tested, as somehow something more than the test score it really represents. The effect, too often, is that of a final conclusion about the individual rather than that of a piece of information useful in further thinking and planning. Few things interfere more effectively with real understanding than indiscriminate reporting of IQ scores to parents.

Grade-placement scores or *standard scores* of various kinds are less likely to cause trouble than IQ scores are. Still, they may substitute an illusion of communication for real communication. Standard scores have no more meaning to most parents than raw scores unless there is opportunity for extensive explanations. Grade placements *seem* so simple and straightforward that serious misunderstandings may result from their use. As noted in a very helpful pamphlet,[2] a sixth grade pupil with grade-placement scores of 10.0 for reading and 8.5 for arithmetic does not necessarily rank higher in reading than he does in arithmetic when compared to the other sixth graders. (Both scores may be at the 95th percentile for his class—arithmetic progress much more than reading progress tends to be dependent on what has been taught, and thus to spread over a narrower range at any one grade.)

Percentiles probably are the safest and most informative numbers to use PROVIDED their two essential characteristics are made clear: (1) that they refer not to per cent of questions answered correctly but to per cent of people whose performance the student has equalled or surpassed, and (2) that they refer to who, specifically, are the people with whom the student is being compared. The second point—a definite description of the comparison or "norm" group—is especially important in making the meaning of test results clear.

Much more can be said about the kinds of numbers used to convey test score information. Good discussions can be found in a number of textbooks.[3] But a more fundamental question remains—*are any numbers necessary?*

We intend nothing so foolish as suggesting a ban on the use of numbers in reporting test results. But we have been struck repeatedly by the fact that some of the very best counselors and many of the best written reports present numerical data only incidentally or not at all.

[2] M. R. Katz, *Selecting an Achievement Test*, E. & A. Series No. 3 (1958), p. 26. Available free from Educational Testing Service, Princeton, New Jersey.

[3] See, for example, Robert Ladd Thorndike and E. P. Hagen, *Measurement and Evaluation in Psychology and Education* (New York: John Wiley and Sons, 1955), chapters 17 and 18, or Donald Edwin Super, *Appraising Vocational Fitness* (New York: Harper and Bros., 1949), pp. 556–63 and 584–88.

Along with the two "commandments" at the beginning of this article, we mentioned a verbal technique. Generally, we dislike formulas for writing or speaking. This one, however, seems to have advantages that outweigh the risks attending its suggestion. It's just a few words:

"YOU SCORE LIKE PEOPLE WHO . . ." Or, to a parent, "Your son (or daughter) scores like students who . . ."

The sentence, of course, requires completion. The completion depends on the test or other instrument, the reason for testing, and the person to whom the report is being given. Some sample completions:

". . . people who are pretty good at office work, fast and accurate enough to hold a job and do it well."

". . . people who don't find selling insurance a very satisfactory choice. Three out of four who score as you do and become insurance salesmen leave the job for something else in less than a year."

". . . students who find getting into liberal arts college and getting a B.A. degree something they can attain only with extra hard work. On the other hand, they find a year or two of technical school interesting and they probably do well in the jobs to which that leads."

". . . students who are disappointed later if they don't begin a language in the ninth grade and plan to take some more math and science. It's easier to head toward business later if you still want to than to go from the commercial course into a good college."

". . . students who don't often—only about one out of four—manage to earn a C average their freshman year at State."

". . . students who have more than average difficulty passing in arithmetic— you [*or, to a parent,* he] may need some extra help on this in the next few years."

Many more samples will come readily to mind. The most important thing to note is that a satisfactory report combines two kinds of information: (1) the test results of the individual person, and (2) something known about the test or battery and its relationship to the subsequent performance of others who have taken it. Also, a satisfactory completion puts the school or the counselor out on a limb, at least a little. Some variant of "That's not so!" or, more politely, "How do you know?" will be the reaction in some cases, probably less frequently voiced than it is felt.

Well, let's face it. The decision to use a test at all is a step out on a limb. Some limbs are broad and solid and the climber need feel little or no anxiety. Some are so frail that they offer only hazard, with the bait of an improbable reward. We climb out on some limbs of medium safety because there is evidence of a real chance that they will help us, and those whom we we test, toward a worth-while goal.

The words of the formula need not actually be used in each case. Sometimes percentiles, grade-placement scores, or a profile may be what the parents should receive. But it is well to try first mentally stating the meaning of the results in the language suggested above. If this proves difficult or discomforting, a warning signal is on—reporting the numbers is likely not to be constructive in the case at hand!

The audience of parents to which our test-based information is to be transmitted includes an enormous range and variety of minds and emotions. Some are ready and able to absorb what we have to say. Reaching others may be as hopeless as reaching TV watchers with an AM radio broadcast. Still others may hear what we say, but clothe the message with their own special needs, ideas, and predilections.

The habit of using the formula, and of thinking a bit about what answer to give if the response is a challenging or doubting one, puts the interpreter of test scores in the strongest position he can occupy. In the case of achievement tests, it requires him to understand why and how the particular test or battery was chosen as appropriate for his school and his purpose. In the case of aptitude (including scholastic aptitude or intelligence) tests, it requires him to examine the evidence offered in the test manual and research studies to back up the test's claim to usefulness. And it reminds him always that it is in the end *his* thinking, *his* weighing of the evidence, *his* soundness and helpfulness as an educator or counselor that is exposed for judgment— not the sometimes wistful ideas of the test author or publisher.

The school—or the counselor—*is* exposed for judgment when telling parents about the abilities and performances of their children. The parents have the right to know. And knowledge in terms they can understand and absorb is what the school must give.

Index

Index